Studying Hinduism

Studying Hinduism is an indispensable resource for students and researchers wishing to develop a deeper understanding of one of the world's oldest and most multi-faceted religious traditions. Sushil Mittal and Gene Thursby, leading scholars in the field, have brought together a rich variety of perspectives which reflects the current lively state of the field. *Studying Hinduism* is the result of cooperative work by accomplished specialists in several fields which include anthropology, art, comparative literature, history, philosophy, religious studies, and sociology. Through these complementary and exciting approaches, students will gain a greater understanding of India's culture and traditions, to which Hinduism is integral. The book uses key critical terms and topics as points of entry into the subject; these include:

Art • Body • Cinema • Cognitive Science • Colonialism • Diaspora • Ecology • Ethnography • Ethnosociology • Exchange • Experience • Fiction • Gender • Intellect • Kinship • Law • Memory • Myth • Nationalism • Orientalism • Postcolonialism • Psychoanalysis • Ritual • Romanticism • Sacred • Stratification • Structuralism • Subaltern

Studying Hinduism reveals that although Hinduism can be interpreted in sharply contrasting ways and set in widely varying contexts, it is endlessly fascinating and intriguing.

Sushil Mittal is an Associate Professor and the Director of the Mahatma Gandhi Center for Global Nonviolence at James Madison University in Virginia. **Gene Thursby** is an Associate Professor at the University of Florida. Together they have co-edited *Religions of South Asia* (2006) and *The Hindu World* (2004), also published by Routledge.

Studying Hinduism

Key Concepts and Methods

Edited by

Sushil Mittal

and

Gene Thursby

Routledge
Taylor & Francis Group
LONDON AND NEW YORK

First published in the USA and Canada 2008
by Routledge
270 Madison Ave, New York, NY 10016

Simultaneously published in the UK
by Routledge
2 Park Square, Milton Park, Abingdon, Oxon OX14 4RN

Routledge is an imprint of the Taylor & Francis Group, an informa business

Typeset in Sabon by
HWA Text and Data Management, Tunbridge Wells
Printed and bound in Great Britain by
Antony Rowe Ltd, Chippenham, Wiltshire

British Library Cataloguing in Publication Data
A catalogue record for this book is available from the British Library

Library of Congress Cataloging-in-Publication Data
A catalog record for this book has been requested

ISBN: 978–0–415–30125–1 (hbk)
ISBN: 978–0–415–30126–8 (pbk)
ISBN: 978–0–203–93973–4 (ebk)

To
T.N. Madan
and
McKim Marriott

in appreciation for their exemplary service to scholars, scholarship, and the subcontinent

Contents

Contributors ix

Introduction **1**
Sushil Mittal and Gene Thursby

1 **Art** **3**
Heather Elgood

2 **Body** **19**
Barbara A. Holdrege

3 **Cinema** **41**
Philip Lutgendorf

4 **Cognitive Science** **59**
Ellen Goldberg

5 **Colonialism** **73**
Sharada Sugirtharajah

6 **Diaspora** **86**
Maya Warrier

7 **Ecology** **97**
Lance E. Nelson

8 **Ethnography** **112**
Mathew N. Schmalz

9 **Ethnosociology** **125**
Richard H. Davis

10 **Exchange** **139**
Diane P. Mines

11 **Experience** **155**
June McDaniel

12 **Fiction** **167**
Amardeep Singh

13 Gender **178**
Ann Grodzins Gold

14 Intellect **194**
Douglas L. Berger

15 Kinship **207**
Maya Unnithan-Kumar

16 Law **218**
Donald R. Davis, Jr.

17 Memory **230**
Christian Lee Novetzke

18 Myth **251**
Herman Tull

19 Nationalism **265**
Peter Heehs

20 Orientalism **278**
Carl Olson

21 Postcolonialism **289**
Saurabh Dube

22 Psychoanalysis **303**
Paul B. Courtright

23 Ritual **314**
Kathryn McClymond

24 Romanticism **327**
Dorothy Figueira

25 Sacred **339**
Ramdas Lamb

26 Stratification **354**
Joseph W. Elder

27 Structuralism **366**
Carl Olson

28 Subaltern **378**
Christian Lee Novetzke and Laurie Patton

Index 400

Contributors

Editors

Sushil Mittal is associate professor of Hinduism and director of the Mahatma Gandhi Center for Global Nonviolence at James Madison University, Harrisonburg, Virginia.

Gene Thursby is associate professor of religion at the University of Florida, Gainesville.

They have previously co-edited *The Hindu World* and *Religions of South Asia*, also published by Routledge.

Contributors

Douglas L. Berger is assistant professor of philosophy at Southern Illinois University, Carbondale.

Paul B. Courtright is professor of religion in South Asia at Emory University, Atlanta.

Donald R. Davis, Jr. is assistant professor of languages and cultures of Asia at the University of Wisconsin-Madison.

Richard H. Davis is professor of religion and Asian studies at Bard College, Annandale.

Saurabh Dube is professor of history at El Colegio de México, Mexico.

Joseph W. Elder is professor of sociology at the University of Wisconsin-Madison.

Heather Elgood is course director in Asian art at the British Museum, United Kingdom.

Dorothy Figueira is professor of comparative literature at the University of Georgia, Athens.

Ann Grodzins Gold is professor of religion and anthropology and director of the South Asia Center at Syracuse University.

Ellen Goldberg is associate professor of religious studies at Queen's University, Canada.

Peter Heehs is associated with the Sri Aurobindo Ashram Archives and Research Library, Pondicherry, India.

Barbara A. Holdrege is associate professor of religious studies and chair of the South Asian Studies Committee at the University of California, Santa Barbara.

Ramdas Lamb is associate professor of religion at the University of Hawaii, Honolulu.

Philip Lutgendorf is professor of Hindi and modern Indian studies at the University of Iowa.

Kathryn McClymond is associate professor of religious studies at Georgia State University, Atlanta.

June McDaniel is professor of religious studies at the College of Charleston.

Diane P. Mines is associate professor of anthropology at Appalachian State University, Boone.

Lance E. Nelson is professor of religious studies at the University of San Diego and chair of the Department of Theology and Religious Studies.

Christian Lee Novetzke is assistant professor of South Asia studies and religious studies at the University of Pennsylvania.

Carl Olson is professor of religious studies at Allegheny College, Meadville.

Laurie Patton is professor of early Indian religions and chair of the Department of Religion at Emory University, Atlanta.

Mathew N. Schmalz is associate professor of religious studies at the College of the Holy Cross, Worcester.

Amardeep Singh is assistant professor of English at Lehigh University, Bethlehem.

Sharada Sugirtharajah is senior lecturer in Hindu Studies at the University of Birmingham, United Kingdom.

Herman Tull is an independent scholar residing in Princeton, New Jersey.

Maya Unnithan-Kumar is reader in anthropology at the University of Sussex, United Kingdom.

Maya Warrier is lecturer in Indian religion at the University of Wales Lampeter, United Kingdom.

Introduction

Sushil Mittal and Gene Thursby

With admirable brevity and clarity, the poet Wallace Stevens (1879–1955) memorably evoked "Thirteen Ways of Looking at a Blackbird." No two were alike, but several overlapped and were mutually enriched by others. In some of the thirteen, the blackbird's presence seemed incidental or surprising. Here in your hands is a book that offers twenty-eight ways of looking at Hinduism. For scholars who contribute to this book, as the blackbird for Wallace Stevens, Hinduism is not a simple thing that could be apprehended by means of any single approach. It can be interpreted in sharply contrasting ways and can be set in widely varying contexts. Once evoked, however, one finds it endlessly interesting and intriguing. Evidently there is no skeleton key to unlock a ready-made understanding of Hinduism or a single exclusive and rationally demonstrable logic of Hinduism, but efforts can be made toward articulating a poetics of Hinduism.

Each chapter is a newly written proposal to the reader by a contemporary working scholar and can be regarded as a contribution toward such a poetics. Each of the twenty-eight chapters offers a point of entry into the study of Hinduism and a vantage point from which it can be interpreted. Chapters are arranged in alphabetical sequence so that each reader will be free to think about how the chapters could be differently ordered according to whatever theme or method may seem most appropriate or useful for the individual reader's own projects and purposes.

The approaches to the study of Hinduism that are offered here are exemplary and illustrative but neither definitive nor exhaustive. Their presence is justified by previous influence on the academic study of Hinduism, and we are grateful that several accomplished scholars were willing to share this project with us by writing on these topics and themes. What you have here is not a handbook—that is, a succinct summary of a highly codified field of study. Instead, you have a set of overlapping approaches that are potentially useful and mutually enriching for use in the study of Hinduism as a comprehensive tradition that continues to be integral to a great civilization.

Inevitably there are lacunae in this single volume; that is, there are gaps, fissures, and topics or references that are missing. For instance, scholarly discussion of Hinduism for more than a decade has been stuck at the definitional level. The reader would do well to search out scattered publications by Julius J. Lipner, David Lorenzen, and Will Sweetman, each of whom writes discerningly on problems involved in attempting to reduce things Hindu to a brief definition. A more convenient point of entry into the definitional discussion is J. E. Llewellyn, ed., *Defining Hinduism: A Reader* (New York: Routledge, 2005). Among other missing pieces is music. We offer a chapter on art and one on cinema but none on music. Again, some topics are of such signal importance that a chapter (or a book-length study) could not be adequate to them. Ethnography is a noteworthy instance, and a partial remedy is available in the expanded edition of *The Camphor Flame: Popular Hinduism and Society in India* (Princeton: Princeton University Press, 2004) by C. J. Fuller.

In addition, we acknowledge with appreciation that our friend and colleague, Carl Olson, took up two thankless tasks: the first was to write on the increasingly threadbare topic of Orientalism on which he had prepared a longer chapter for our *Religions of South Asia* book, and the second was to write on structuralism in relation to deconstruction. Each has had a significant influence on academic study of Hinduism and, like ethnography, is impossible to treat adequately in a single brief chapter. Among scholars whose work is not mentioned in the structuralism chapter—but merits acknowledgment—is Hans H. Penner, who has been a sophisticated advocate of semiotic and structuralist approaches to study of Hinduism.

Finally, as with our earlier effort to introduce *The Hindu World* (2004) and to set the *Religions of South Asia* (2006) into a shared context, we are grateful to the editorial and production staff and particularly to the wise and discerning Lesley Riddle at Routledge for making it possible to transform a set of conversations into a more lasting form of communication that can serve the English-reading public around the planet in a period in which mutual respect and understanding are so urgently needed. We also thank the anonymous prepublication readers who generously reviewed the individual chapters and the book as a whole. And, as a reader of the published version, you are invited to send your comments to the coeditors after you have had an opportunity to work with the book, too. Please let us know how it serves you while you are engaged in studying Hinduism.

1

Art

Heather Elgood

Problems of Definition
Icons in Worship
Affinities Between Sound, Forms, and Ideas
Material Embodiment of the Divine
Hinduism through Study of Hindu Art

Exploring India's religious imagery provides an alternative to textual interpretation as a basis for understanding Hinduism. As Diana Eck rightly stated:

> *Hermeneutics* has been used to describe the task of understanding and interpreting ideas and texts. In a similar way, we need to set for ourselves the task of developing a hermeneutic of the visible, addressing the problem of how we understand and interpret what we see, not only in the classical images and art forms created by the various religious traditions, but in the ordinary images of people's traditions, rites, and daily activities.
>
> (1985: 14; emphasis in original)

From this point of departure, the chapter considers Hindu sacred art, the factors that gave rise to the use of icons, and affinities among sound, form, and philosophical concepts in Hinduism.

Problems of Definition

Any definition of Hindu art might appear to require a definition of Hinduism, but the desire to codify a religion and to identify its unique features is a Western preoccupation. Julius Lipner (1994) compares Hinduism to "an ancient banyan tree" which "unlike the botanical model...is not uniform to look at. Rather, it is a network of variety, one distinctive arboreal complex shading into another, the whole forming a marvelous unity-in-diversity" (1994: 5–6). Lipner also characterizes Hinduism as "both a way of life and a highly organized social and religious system, quite free from any dogmatic affirmations concerning the nature of God" (Lipner 1994: 2, citing Zaehner 1966: 2). He is seeking to correct distorted perspectives that have persisted in two hundred years of Indological scholarship owing to overreliance on ancient Brāhmaṇical texts for interpreting Hinduism. The study of Hindu religious art can make a contribution to an appropriately broader view of Indian religious development.

Can one define Hindu art? Scholars have argued that one cannot distinguish between Hindu, Buddhist, and Jain imagery and iconography in the formative period of Hindu art from the second century BCE to the third century CE (Chandra 1983: 22). The earliest known depiction of the Hindu goddess Gajalakṣmī is found on a second-century Buddhist *stūpa* at Bharhut (Elgood 2004: 333–36). As late as the ninth century, Jain temple sculpture at Osian is barely distinguishable from that at the roughly contemporary Hindu temple of Jagat. However, Doris Srinivasan (1997: 4, plate 1.1a; 6) argues that certain concepts such as multiplicity are inherently Vedic and by extension Hindu; consequently, multiple heads and arms on some Hindu sculpture distinguish it from Jain and Buddhist imagery.

Hindu art consists of a range of anthropomorphic, aniconic, and ritual objects. According to Michael Meister:

> Images that designate divinity clothe the absolute, specify a path for meditation, give form to devotion, even specify a sociology for kingship or society; they "contain" divinity called down by human ritual, embody the potency of patronage, the "beauty" of their craftsmen's inner vision, the "subtle body" that is "real" form. This is their function and their history.
>
> (1984: xxiii)

Anthropomorphic icons express mood and movement by posture and gesture but, beyond this, the figures and their animal vehicles reveal a complex iconography in which multiple heads and arms bear significant emblems. However, Hindus also recognize the deity in aniconic forms and do not inevitably require figurative art. Śiva, for example, may be represented as a sculpted *liṅga* or in the naturally occurring stones called *svayambhū liṅga*, and Viṣṇu is sometimes personified as an ammonite called *śālagrāma*. Many other objects can be perceived as spirit vessels. Hindu art is both functional and artistic, and it seeks to express the universal rather than the individual. Hindu interest in the inner spiritual over the mundane outer form is seen in ritual practices, such as the worship of icons that are blackened with smoke or concealed by cloth, by respect for such impermanent sacred art as *kōlam* or *rangoli* designs at domestic thresholds, and in the discarding of images at the completion of some rituals.

Hindu sacred art nonetheless has a highly developed aesthetic. Alfred Gell (1998) argues that the separation of the functional from the aesthetic is a Western distinction and is meaningless in a Hindu context wherein strict adherence to a fixed iconography serves as a stimulus for the worshipper. Ancient prescriptive texts support his argument and link ritual efficacy with the appropriate form and method of preparation of sacred images. The deity's attraction to the beauty of the icon and its recognition of itself is ritually enacted by the practice of holding a mirror in front of a newly crafted image during its consecration ritual. Ralph Hallman argues that the viewer's response to an art object consists of two parts—"that which is *immediately* present in perception, and that which is *mediately* present through suggestion"—and claims that the retinal image is not identical to the intellectual image (1954: 493; emphasis in original). His argument becomes obvious when one considers that most icons in a Hindu worship setting are barely visible to the devotee owing to their covering by layers of garlands and clothing. In other words, the devotee contemplates the icon while visualizing the living deity.

According to the *Śilpaśāstra*s, the craftsman (*śilpī*) should undergo ritual purification and conduct rites that include due respect for the wood, stone, paint, and his tools before starting work. The texts also stress the need for the artist to be guided by inner vision and revelation, conceptualizing the appearance of the work during this mental state of openness and receptivity. Traditional sculptors see themselves not as creators or innovators but as attempting to express an order that already exists and acting as a vehicle to represent it to the world (Coomaraswamy 1956: 153). According to Jitendra Banerjea (1974: 13–14), the status of traditional artists was based on their claim to spiritual connection with the lineage of the Vedic Sapta Ṛṣis and mythic figures like Viśvakarma and Māyā, which established the artist's pivotal role as a bridge between the mundane and the supramundane. In sum, the role of the artist as a spiritual vehicle is central to understanding his significance and his faithfulness to a common aesthetic and iconographic language.

Alongside prescribed form and measurement was a sophisticated aesthetic theory, known as *rasa* (literally, "taste") that was codified by about the fourth to fifth century CE. *Rasa* theory developed as a part of Hindu dramaturgy and emphasized the importance of taste received by the recipient or *rāsika*. The *Viṣṇudharmotarra Purāṇa* revealed precise guidelines for the depiction of pure (*satya*) deities that included facial details, such as eyes like lotuses and a head like an egg. The text advises that an image should be seen from the front and should not be bent or crooked; it should be given a beautiful countenance, the cheeks well formed; the face should have a pleasant expression; good arms, hands, and a full chest. The eyes of the figures, their expressions, limbs, and hands have to be treated as in dance. The deities should be depicted in an idealized form, one that is youthful and immortal (with the exception of some of the more terrifying, or *ghora*, aspects) and at the peak of their energy. Deities are heroic or voluptuous, sensuous, and perpetually beautiful. In the epics and devotional Tamil poetry, divinity and beauty tend to be synonymous (Shulman 1980). Early inscriptions also provide evidence of the importance given to aesthetics or beauty. Whereas icons within a temple might be largely invisible, the temple exterior is visible and was expected to attract devotees and deity toward the interior.

The purpose of Hindu images, icons, or sacred objects can best be understood by the term "*vigraha*" ("something to hold onto"), a tool for grasping God. The image provides a focus in the ritual exchange of offerings in return for the acquisition of spiritual merit and divine union. Though the spiritual essence within the icon has paramount importance, the correct outer form is essential to remind the devotee and to support the deity's recognition of itself. The purpose of the image

> is to represent some fundamental aspect of the universe which is not perceptible to our senses, and to act as a metaphor to enable the religious devotee to more easily recognize that truth. Essentially the image is intended to reveal divinity to man and to help manifest divinity in man, in other words, to represent and participate in this process. The image is also intended to assist the concentration of the worshipper by providing a focus for his devotions.
>
> (Elgood 1999: 27)

Icons in Worship

There are examples of sculpture and figurative seals from the Harappa or Indus Valley culture (*ca.* 2800–1500 BCE) that continue to stimulate scholarly discussion and controversy. However, there is widespread consensus that the absence of sculpture and icons in wood or stone during the Vedic period (*ca.* 1500–200 BCE) indicates a lack of interest in this imagery. Ananda K. Coomaraswamy describes Vedism "at least in orthodox and official circles, as to constitute by itself a complete artistic vocabulary and an iconography without icons" (1927: 290–93). Images of Vedic deities apparently were held in the collective mind and described in hymns but not represented in tangible form. Perhaps heightened or altered consciousness due to drinking *soma* may have contributed to intense visions of Vedic and later Hindu gods with multiple heads and arms. Despite the absence of stone sculptures, a large number of terracotta figurines have been excavated and assigned to

2000–300 BCE. These have been interpreted as votive offerings destined for Goddess shrines or as offerings to non-Vedic cult shrines (Ahuja 2001: 67, 172–78; Jayakar 1953–54). It has been suggested that Hindu goddesses with distinctive functions who came into prominence later may have developed from a more amorphous generic female deity (Elgood 2004: 337), and evidence of the close interaction of Vedic and non-Vedic society is provided by archaeological excavation. Himanshu Ray posits multilayered societies, particularly at Nagarjunakonda. "Almost every sacred spot was associated with more than one religion....Practices such as that of pilgrimage provided wider connectivity through movements of groups and communities, thereby linking several spots across the religious landscape" (2004: 357). Such interaction, according to Srinivasan (1997: 190), may be seen in the burial of non-Vedic male and female clay pots in the foundation of the Vedic altar. The early form of the goddess Lajjā Gaurī, imaged in the shape of a filled vessel, is also associated with non-Vedic fertility rites (Elgood 2004: 216).

The earliest surviving Indian stone sculpture[1] is Mauryan and dates from 300 BCE in the region of Sarnath. Many stone images dating from 200 BCE and the third century CE have been found in the Mathura district of Uttar Pradesh. Mathura was a wealthy mercantile community where lay donors made gifts to priests and local monasteries. The city was situated at the junction of major trade routes and was noted for its diverse religions and its artisans. Surviving sculptures dating from the first century BCE to the first century CE show a developed iconography. Scholars have taken the view that image worship arose from the use of votive images and aniconic shrines in non-Vedic cults. This is reinforced by the fact that the earliest sculpture dates from the second to the first century BCE with excavations revealing goddesses, *yakṣa*s, *yakṣī*s, *nāga*s, and *nāginī*s among the stone and terracotta images of early historical Mathura. One of the earliest freestanding *yakṣa* images in the Mathura region represents Maṇibhadra, who was a tutelary deity of merchants and travelers and was worshipped in important trading centers (Singh 2004: 383–84). Under the name Jakheiya, it is still worshipped in modern Mathura. This demonstrates mercantile investment in the propitiation of deities associated with wealth, access to whom was not controlled by Brāhmaṇas. The massive size of the third-century BCE *yakṣa* images suggests the importance of this religious following, and the fully formed character of the images suggests that their development predates this period. Serpent deities were also popular in Mathura and associated with water and fertility. Apsidal temples at Sonkh near Mathura have a *mātṛkā* plaque, *nāga* and *nāginī* terracotta figurines, inscriptions, and the top half of a stone *nāga* image demonstrating that these images were worshipped in structural temples (Singh 2004: 391–92). Other inscriptions reveal urban wealthy patrons, for example, the gift of *nāga* and *nāginī* figures from

Girdharpur Tila, northwest of Mathura, from a cloak maker (Singh 2004: 386–87). Another factor in the rise of icons associated with Hinduism and the development of image worship may have been growing popularity of Buddhist and Jain anthropomorphic imagery.

Despite the coexistence of a variety of religious cults, Mathura was the stronghold of Brāhmaṇical culture and therefore of a strong Sanskritic cultural milieu. Recent scholarship has begun to refute the claim for lower caste initiative in the creation of sculptural icons. Evidence of the patronage of high-ranking officials and foreign influence for these early images is provided by inscriptions. One example is the inscription that reveals the foreign patron Heliodorus on the pillar at Besnagar,[2] whereas the other suggests the patronage of wealthy urban classes, referring to the installation of images of the five heroes by a woman named Toṣā in the late first century BCE at Mora (Lüders 1937–38: 194).[3] Gilles Tarabout (2004: 70) points to the popular use of stone or tree markers but not precise figuration and notes that the old notion that images developed from the uneducated classes has been discarded by scholars of Buddhism and now should be set aside for Hinduism. This is consistent with the views of Gregory Schopen who argued that the initiative for the creation of Buddhist monumental sculpture arose not from the lower classes but from the need for a visual language by the monks themselves. The use by Buddhists and Hindus of common imagery makes it likely that there were some shared ritual practices in the use of images (Schopen 1989: 153–68). The earliest Hindu imagery is found in Mathura. This reinforces Tarabout's view that the priests themselves may have devised complex anthropomorphic representation. During the Kṣatrapa and Kuṣāṇa periods, the warrior and trader classes gave offerings to Brāhmaṇas, the former to seek legitimacy and the latter for material well-being and useful astrological predictions. Trade also brought foreigners, new ideas, and cultural diversity.

Fully formed iconography that included reference to distinctly Vedic concepts, such as multiplicity, also strongly suggests the involvement of Brāhmaṇical prescriptions in establishing the form of these early Hindu images. Examples of this ready-made iconography can be seen as early as the second century BCE. One example is an aniconic stone *liṅga* image of Śiva with five heads from Bhita in Uttar Pradesh and assigned to the second century CE (Srinivasan 1997: plate 14.3). Another early anthropomorphic image is on a *liṅga* at Gudimallam, a two-armed Śiva holding an axe and a deer, supported by a dwarf (Apasmura), assigned for stylistic reasons to the second to first century BCE (Srinivasan 1997: plate 17.9). The earliest dated Vaiṣṇava image has multiple arms and is from first-century BCE Malhar in Madhya Pradesh. It is a four-armed Vāsudeva-Viṣṇu carrying the mace or *gadā* and *cakra* or discus in the upper hands and a *śaṅkha* or conch in the lower hand (Srinivasan 1997: plate 14.1). Scholars suggest that the four arms express the extension of divine sovereign power to all four quarters of the universe symbolized by the lotus and by the discus, conch, and mace (Srinivasan 1997: 22). A small Kuṣāṇa relief shows Kubera, Gajalakṣmī, and Śiva in androgynous form, each with two arms, whereas Vāsudeva-Kṛṣṇa is shown with four (Srinivasan 1997: 19, plate 1.3). This reveals that from the beginning of Hindu iconography, multiple arms were limited to Vāsudeva and suggests that the Brāhmaṇical elite were themselves involved in commissioning these sculptures. From the first century BCE, there was an increase in the number and variety of Vaiṣṇava images in Mathura, which appears to have become a center for this art. Most frequent are the depictions of Vāsudeva-Kṛṣṇa, four-armed Viṣṇu on Garuḍa, and Viṣṇu in his boar form.

The Kṣatrapa dynasty from the late first century BCE and their successors—the Kuṣāṇas from the first quarter of the first century CE—were responsible for many of the earliest Hindu sculptures. The Kuṣāṇas were an immigrant tribe, free of Brāhmaṇical constraint, and brought with them new concepts of power, divine kingship, and portraiture, yet inscriptions reveal Kṣatrapa and Kuṣāṇas seeking legitimacy through material offerings to the priests (Singh 2004: 393–95). The Kuṣāṇas brought with them Indo-Greek, Scythian, and Zoroastrian influences. They did not discriminate between faiths and invested in Buddhist, Jain, and Hindu monuments. During this period, Śiva, Vāsudeva, and Lakṣmī appear on the coinage of local kings, and the goddess Durgā is depicted for the first time (Cribb 1997). Purāṇic deities, such as Śiva, Viṣṇu, and Sūrya, and goddesses Durgā and Lakṣmī began to supplant the *yakṣa*s, *nāga*s, and goddesses, such as Hārītī and Vasudhara (who was associated with wealth and prosperity) that were found in the Śūṅga period of 200 BCE (Singh 2004: 387). By the third century CE, under the Gupta Empire, there was a virtual displacement of non-Vedic cults and the eventual triumph and iconographic codification of the Brāhmaṇical tradition.

With the proliferation of Hindu stone sculpture, the housing of images in freestanding temples became popular from the fourth to fifth century CE. Sophisticated sculptures from such fifth-century Gupta temples as Nachna or Deogarh were based on an established iconographic formula. With the growth of *bhakti* or devotional Hinduism, the pantheon of deities grew to include the elephant-headed god Gaṇeśa, Viṣṇu in his boar incarnation, and the goddess Durgā in her manifestations as destroyer of the buffalo-demon and river goddess. There is a notable rise in royal investment (*pūrtadharma*) in temples and in sacred art for the acquisition of spiritual merit or to fulfill a pledge made in return for a successful military campaign. Gifts of temples, frieze sculpture, and ornamentation became signs of the king's power and legitimacy in which he was empowered by the Brāhmaṇas who benefited from his munificence. Brāhmaṇical literature from this time shows a departure from rituals requiring live sacrifice to the vegetal offerings that became associated with devotional and temple Hinduism (Inden 1982).

There are two possible lines of development regarding the formulation of early Indian images. On the one hand, textual evidence and early monumental stone images, in particular from the Mathura region in the second century BCE, strongly indicate the popular nature of non-Vedic cults and their impact on the development of later Hindu image worship. *Yakṣa*, *yakṣiṇī*, *nāga*, hero cults, and cults of the goddess were associated with mercantile and other activities. These have been shown through textual and archaeological evidence to have been worshipped in shrines and on a domestic level with terracotta offerings. From the first century BCE, we find not only non-Vedic cult icons, such as *nāga*s placed in covered shrines, but ritually housed portraits of the king, now seen as divine—part of the legacy of the Kuṣāṇa kings. From the first century CE, Graeco-Roman sculptural influence is evident in northwest India and greatly influences the developing forms of Buddhist, Jain, and Hindu imagery. Tarabout's proposal that Brāhmaṇa priests were responsible for the development of religious images fails to take sufficient account of the early Sanskrit texts that record Brāhmaṇical disdain for images and the prolific number of the non-Vedic sculptures that predate Hindu icons. Furthermore, he does not cite inscriptional evidence that refers to wealthy urban patrons of religious imagery from the second century BCE to the first century CE. He also does not take sufficient account of the significance of popular practices, such as women's concerns seen in ritual propitiation of the goddess. The rise in economic prosperity is reflected in early inscriptional evidence that refers to women making gifts, a practice which still continues in the form of women's ritual vow-making (*vrata*) in return for family protection and prosperity.

On the other hand, there is evidence of priestly initiative in the development of the complex iconography of Hindu sculpture, first in inscriptional evidence from the first century CE, suggesting that interdependence developed between immigrant Kuṣāṇa kings and Brāhmaṇas, which enhanced the former's royal legitimacy and the latter's authority and prosperity. Second, evidence of priestly pragmatism can be seen by the adoption of certain non-Vedic rituals, such as burial of a filled vessel in the *yajña* ritual and the later reshaping of domestic ritual to supplant the cosmo-regal sacrifice. This does not rule out the role of the priests or monks in seizing the initiative from local cult practices or imported hero cults and reinterpreting their own complex symbolic identities during the rise of temple Hinduism. In my opinion, the Brāhmaṇas reconstructed some non-Vedic rituals and images in a strictly Brāhmaṇical form that corresponded to the inherited inner vision of the gods. This may be compared with Buddhist incorporation of protective cult spirits on monumental *stūpa*s from the second century BCE.

The rise of Buddhism as a state religion from the Mauryan dynasty in the third century BCE would have diminished the prevalence of live sacrifice and with it Brāhmaṇical authority. The Brāhmaṇas appear to have reshaped their rituals and attitudes toward images, recognizing the benefits of image use and temples as sources of revenue. Tarabout argues that images were available for all to see, and this gave rise to a culture in which the public made investments and established a temple economy that contributed to Brāhmaṇical prosperity. The economic and social development of urban centers and a need for Brāhmaṇas to establish religious and economic control were factors that encouraged the rise of temple Hinduism. Mathura itself might serve as an example of craftsmen undertaking diverse commissions from Buddhist and Jain monks, Brāhmaṇa priests, and wealthy secular cult worshippers. The initial rise in permanent temple structures seems to have coincided with the rise of political unity under the Gupta Empire and increased prosperity at that time. Once images had become popular with the priestly caste, it has been suggested by such scholars as Tarabout, it was politically and economically expedient to give these images public airing and for the priesthood to provide themselves permanent structures for worship and offerings.

Affinities Between Sound, Forms, and Ideas

"Homology,...a form of realising or experiencing a...*real* correspondence between an aspect of the individual (the microcosm) and a feature of external reality (the macrocosm)" was the foundation for religious action in the Vedic period (Lipner 1994: 33–34; emphasis in original). Vedic ritual was a tool for control of the forces of nature by communication with gods of the elements. Success of the ritual and realization of its objectives of wealth, health, victory, and immortality depended on the correct utterance of sacred words. Spells were believed to resonate with power and to release the inner force of anything at which they were directed. Sound and efficacy have remained paramount in the training and daily practice of priests within temple Hinduism as has the preeminence of oral over written tradition. Underlying sacred practice in Vedic and Hindu ritual is the power of the *mantra*. Brāhmaṇism evoked the deities through the correct vibration of sound and therefore saw no ritual need for icons. However, domestic issues, such as health, fertility, and protection from the spirit world, may have been factors that encouraged the lower castes to use talismanic terracotta votive figurines (Ahuja 2001: 67). A large number of second-century BCE erotic plaques have been interpreted as indicators of a desire for protection or fertility. In certain contemporary rural shrines, there is still found a belief in the link between flesh and earth or clay (Elgood 1999: 203; Jayakar 1953–54); for example, to heal a wounded arm, a clay substitute is offered to the deity. Many of these rural cult centers focus on goddess worship.

A major distinction between Vedic and non-Vedic worship concerns ethereal visualized forms associated with the elemental deities in the former and rooted, localized, more tangible gods, goddesses, and tree or *nāga* spirits of the latter—and the differing means of communicating with them. Associated with the ethereal is the Vedic notion of *dhī*, meaning insight, vision, or seeing rather than thought. Early reference to the concept of multiplicity together with a preoccupation with sound, visualization, and imagination can be seen in the conception of Viśvarūpa and Rudra in the *Ṛg Veda* and in the *Mahābhārata* (Srinivasan 1997: 133). Vedic gods, such as Soma, Agni, Varuṇa, Sūrya, and Vāyu, are envisaged as powerful elemental forces of transformation in the form of a vision-inducing drink, fire, water, sun, and wind, respectively. A complex symbolism develops, drawing on Vedic and non-Vedic beliefs expressing the power of the divine elements; for example the lotus symbolizes the earth or the cosmos, the snake is linked to water, the discus to the sun, and the conch to the primeval sound. These and other attributes and vehicles are associated with an evolving formula intended to define the appearance of the deities of emerging devotional Hinduism. From the third century BCE, these visions acquire concrete form and contribute to the rise of temple Hinduism. This reaches its ultimate expression in the paradigm of the temple as the body of man himself.

Associated with the complex symbolism is the idea of correct measurement. An image corresponds to the deity it represents not only because it resembles it but because it conforms to prescribed measurements. The *Śilpaśāstra*s recommend appropriate materials, measurements,[4] proportion, details of decoration, and symbolism. Such religious texts as the *Bhagavad Gītā* popularized identities and attributes that solidified the final forms of divine iconography. Explanation for the metaphysical significance of each stage of manufacture and the prescription of specific *mantra*s to sanctify the process and to invoke the power of the deity into the image are also found in the liturgical handbooks known as the Āgamas and Tantras. What do these rules tell us about Hinduism? They suggest the belief that not only do precise forms and measurement trigger the expectation of priests and devotees but they fulfill divine criteria acceptable to the deity itself. Does this suggest that the deity shows an element of choice in his or her willingness to enter into the icon? If so, then one would need to entreat the deity appropriately and offer regular devotion to ensure its permanent presence.

Material Embodiment of the Divine

> These forms can be iconic, that is, with a resemblance to human form; or aniconic, in other words, in an abstract symbolic form such as a pile of stones or a linga. Organic and inorganic matter is perceived as a potential residence for a deity or spirit, particularly the sacred images produced for veneration in a temple or domestic shrine. The image is generally required to be beautiful to encourage the deity to enter it, and the material from which it was made must be unblemished.
>
> (Elgood 1999: 14)

How widespread among Hindu priests and devotees was the belief in spiritual embodiment?

As already mentioned, third- to second-century BCE male and female tree spirits in stone are the earliest known freestanding Indian sculptures. Jain and Buddhist oral traditions, subsequently written in texts, also provide evidence of these statues (Coomaraswamy 1971). The possession ritual, which forms a part of the *yakṣa* cult, suggests a belief in spirit transference. Similar ideas appear in modern rituals involving tribal and Brāhmaṇa priests. The *Viṣṇudharmottara Purāṇa* (*ca.* 400 CE) devotes a chapter to procuring wood that, perhaps owing to the cult of tree worship and the availability and ease of working, was the most popular material for temple and image making. The fifth-century CE *Bṛhatsaṃhitā* (58.10–11) contains a *mantra* to be uttered by a craftsman before felling a tree to make an image:

> Oh thou tree, salutation to thee, thou art selected for being fashioned into the icon of this particular deity; please accept this offering according to rules; may they pardon me today (for disturbing them); salutation to them.
>
> (Banerjea 1974: 206)

Evidently society believed the tree spirits capable of transmigration. This principle is apparent in the consecration of wooden shrines in the Himalayas (Berti 2004) and in the image-renewal ceremony of the Puri temple in Orissa. The images in the Puri temple are regularly renewed and reconsecrated by the Daitas (ex-tribals) who alone know how to create this image. They keep even from the Brāhmaṇa priests the secret of the actual nature of the "life-substance" (*brahmapadārtha*) of the image. The crucial material is found in a casket in the belly of the old image that the Daita remove in the dead of night. Brāhmaṇas believe it is a sacred stone, possibly a river pebble from the Himalayas, containing fossilized ammonites. In essence, the vitality of the image is both in the internal casket and second in the complex stages of the preparation by Kāyasthas and Brāhmaṇas, who wrap, dress, paint, and anoint the images, offering life-endowing *mantra*s and the final stroke of paint to the pupils of the eyes of the images (Eschmann, Kulke, and Tripathi 1978: 262–64). In the Himalayan and the Orissan ceremonies, the tribal group is responsible for the empowering material while Brāhmaṇas breathe life-giving *mantra*s in the consecration of the prescribed form.[5]

What are the ritual components in the consecration of orthodox Hindu icons? Within the context of temple Hinduism, the objective is *prāṇa pratiṣṭhā*, which literally means "to endow the image with divine power" (*śakti*). Still today consecration consists of meditation, sound, and water. These elements are held to be essential. For example, it is essential for the officiating Brāhmaṇa to be mentally prepared and purified before the ceremony while vivifying sound in the form of *mantra*s is directed toward a vessel filled with water which will subsequently be poured over the image to suffuse it with power (Davis 1991: 8). The fact that the power of the image can be transferred temporarily into other containers, such as a jar of water or a diagram of the sun, suggests that despite the ritual concern with dimension and form the essence is paradoxically shapeless.

Are images such as these efficacious because ceremonies of consecration have spiritually charged them, or is it because they are linked by the power of mimesis to the deities they represent (Freedberg 1989: 95)? The issue is contentious. Hans-Georg Gadamer (1989) assigns primacy to representation, arguing that images work because they have intrinsic signifying functions that can be separated from the kind of efficacy possessed by religious objects, such as relics that have not been shaped and formed by art into the semblance of persons, deities, and so on. On the one hand, the concept of life in divine images would appear to be dependent on *pūjā*, or devotional worship, yet on the other hand, it relies on the mechanical building of power by strictly following the prescribed construction, as is also believed to happen in the construction of *yantra*s and temples. Both processes appear to be empowering, but, from the manner in which redundant icons are treated or disposed of, it is clear that the physical form can lose its spiritual content.

Integral to temple Hinduism is a belief in *darśana*, an act of positive visual and mental engagement with the god or seeing and being in its presence (Eck 1985: 20). "The key to the process of animation seems, initially at least, to depend on the logic of looking and being seen" (Gell 1998: 118). Gell refers to a kind of optical oscillation in which idol's and devotee's perspectives shift back and forth, interpersonal boundaries are effaced, and union is achieved. As Jan Gonda (1963: 22, 1969: 5) has demonstrated, the association of seeing with the acquisition of transcendental knowledge has ancient roots in Vedic tradition. He refers to the ancient Indian understanding of the eye as an agent actively involved in the process of seeing through its illumination of its object. He suggests that the seeing of a powerful object imparts to the seer some share in the object's potency.

The attitude of Hindu priests toward imagery and whether icons embody life and power is inconsistent. Gérard Colas (2004: 165) provides evidence from the study of three, fourth- to eleventh-century texts that, despite initial Brāhmaṇical disapproval, there was a shift from disdain toward icons to a positive acceptance of sacred forms in the later texts. He suggests that these texts indicate that it was not a positioning of the deity in the image but an act of consciousness on the part of the deity toward the image that defined the relationship between the spirit and the mundane. The maintenance of this volatile presence provided a clear reason for lay support of the temple structure and the priesthood itself.

A belief in a transient spirit world inhabiting natural forms seems to lie in an ancient non-Vedic culture. Archaeological evidence of the use of male and female terracotta vessels at Vedic ritual sites and contemporary Himalayan and Orissan images wherein tribal practitioners have the responsibility for transfer of the spiritual essence to the interior of the icons supports this theory. However, the importance of sound, vision, and such concepts as multiplicity seem all to lie in the earliest Brāhmaṇical imagination, which is Vedic in origin. The authority of temple priests in the later consecration and iconography of Hindu sacred images became paramount. The persistence of image worship and the wealth of investment in temple Hinduism suggest widespread Hindu belief in both icon and temple as living embodiments of the divine. Despite the fact that the belief in the embodied image is pivotal in temple ritual, still today there are Brāhmaṇas who give priority to visualization rather than to the material form of the deity.

Hinduism through Study of Hindu Art

What has this study of Hindu art taught us about Hinduism? First, that Hindu art cannot be understood without acknowledging its link with religious action and devotion. Vedic ceremonial was concerned with sound-vibration. This was thought to be the source of primeval creation and to have the power to transmute the mundane into the sacred. For centuries, Vedic ritual hymns that envisioned elemental deities were memorized and transmitted aloud, generation after generation. These practices and other ritual beliefs link Brāhmaṇism with modern Hinduism. Meanwhile, the excluded lower castes developed their own relationship with spirits in trees, snakes, and other natural forms. The roots of Hindu anthropomorphism lie in the Brāhmaṇical vision and in non-Vedic beliefs and rituals. Hindu art covers a wide range of objects, including images of deities, monumental architecture adorned with figural decoration, pots, rosary beads, swords, trees, or simple unmarked stones. It expresses a reverence for a formless deity that is encouraged to permeate form.

Hindu art has a complex aesthetic, with the craftsmen's inspired vision expressed within the boundaries of prescribed iconographic convention. The Hindu artist portrays the deity in a human form that is characterized by a rhythmic beauty, idealized immortality, and identifiable emblems and attributes. The icon's beauty acts as a trigger to attract and ensure the deity's recognition of itself, whereas the devotee responds not to the sensory perception of the object but to his or her individual preconception of the divine. The early icons tell us more about early religion than do the texts because they ingenuously and directly express the spiritual feelings of a broader spectrum of society, predating the written texts in some cases. Despite the fact that some Brāhmaṇa priests even today may regard Hindu icons as superfluous, elaborate and beautiful figural imagery adorns temple walls, and icons still act as recipients for offerings in exchange for material prosperity or spiritual merit. Hinduism's worldview is flexible and syncretic, encompassing animistic beliefs, a sense of the miraculous, and a highly sophisticated correspondence of forms and ideas.

Notes

1 The Mauryan dynasty introduced the use of stone, seen in the Aśokan pillars. These show clear Achaemenid influence particularly in the addorsed lion of the Sarnath pillar. Mauryan sculpture is distinctive by virtue of its precision and high polish. A monumental female image interpreted as a *yakṣī* also dates from this period.

2 The earliest evidence of the worship of the five heroes (Pañcavīra Vṛṣṇis) outside northwestern India is the inscribed pillar in Besnagar. Recent excavations reveal the former existence of four neighboring pillars with capitals. The inscription records the worship of Vāsudeva from the second–first century BCE (Srinivasan 1997: 213–16).

3 Singh (2004: 388–89) cites other inscriptions suggesting that Mora was an important religious center and record the king's wife, Yaśamātā, making donations to a temple to Vāsudeva.

4 The craftsman was given dimensions linked to the length of his own finger joint.

5 Gell (1998: 148–49, citing Gombrich 1966) describes the consecration of a Buddha image in Sri Lanka (cf. the discussion in Freedberg 1989: 84–87, 95). Minute relics of the Buddha are placed inside to render the image efficacious. Unlike Puri, where the Daita puts the life-substance inside and the priest paints the eyes, in Sri Lanka the roles are reversed, and it is the monk who places the relic and the lay craftsman who paints in its eyes.

References Cited

Ahuja, Naman Parmeshwar. 2001. "Early Indian Moulded Terracottas: The Emergence of an Iconography and Variations in Style, circa Second Century BC–First Century AD." PhD dissertation. London: School of Oriental and African Studies Library.

Banerjea, Jitendra Nath. 1974 [1941]. *The Development of Hindu Iconography.* Calcutta: University of Calcutta.

Berti, Daniela. 2004. "Of Metal and Cloths: The Location of Distinctive Features in Divine Iconography (Indian Himalayas)." *In* Phyllis Granoff and Koichi Shinohara, eds., *Images in Asian Religions: Texts and Contexts*, 85–116. Vancouver: University of British Columbia Press.

Chandra, Pramod. 1983. *On the Study of Indian Art.* Cambridge: Harvard University Press.

Colas, Gérard. 2004. "The Competing Hermeneutics of Image worship in Hinduism (Fifth to Eleventh Century AD)." *In* Phyllis Granoff and Koichi Shinohara, eds., *Images in Asian Religions: Texts and Contexts*, 149–79. Vancouver: University of British Columbia Press.

Coomaraswamy Ananda K. 1927. "The Origin of the Buddha Image." *The Art Bulletin* 9: 287–328.

Coomaraswamy Ananda K. 1956 [1934]. *The Transformation of Nature in Art.* New York: Dover.

Coomaraswamy, Ananda K. 1971 [1928 and 1931]. *Yaksas.* New Delhi: Munshiram Manoharlal.

Cribb Joe. 1997. "Shiva Images on Kushan and Kushano-Sasanian Coins." *In* Tanabe Katsumi, Joe Cribb, and Helen Wang, eds., *Studies in Silk Road Coins and Culture: Papers in Honour of Ikuo Hirayama on his 65th Birthday*, 11–66. Kamakara: The Institute of Silk Road Studies

Davis, Richard H. 1991. *Ritual in an Oscillating Universe: Worshipping Śiva in Medieval India.* Princeton: Princeton University Press.

Eck, Diana L. 1985 [1981]. *Darśan: Seeing the Divine Image in India.* Chambersburg: Anima.

Elgood, Heather. 1999. *Hinduism and the Religious Arts.* London: Cassell.

Elgood, Heather. 2004. "Exploring the Roots of Village Hinduism in South Asia." *World Archaeology* 36, 3: 326–42.

Eschmann, Anncharlott, Hermann Kulke, and Gaya Charan Tripathi, eds. 1978. *The Cult of Jagannath and the Regional Tradition of Orissa.* New Delhi: Manohar.

Freedberg, David. 1989. *The Power of Images: Studies in the History and Theory of Response.* Chicago: University of Chicago Press.

Gadamer, Hans-Georg. 1989 [1960]. *Truth and Method* (trans. Joel Weinsheimer and Donald G. Marshall). New York: Crossroad.

Gell, Alfred. 1998. *Art and Agency: An Anthropological Theory.* Oxford: Clarendon.

Gombrich Richard. 1966. "The Consecration of a Buddhist Image." *The Journal of Asian Studies* 26, 1: 23–36.

Gonda J. 1963. *The Vision of the Vedic Poets.* The Hague: Mouton.

Gonda J. 1969. *Eye and the Gaze in the Veda*. Amsterdam: North Holland.

Hallman, Ralph J. 1954. “The Art Object in Hindu Aesthetics.” *The Journal of Aesthetics and Art Criticism* 12, 4: 493–98.

Inden, Ronald. 1982 [1978]. “The Ceremony of the Great Gift (Mahadana): Structure and Historical Context in Indian Ritual and Society.” *Colloques Internationaux de Centre National de la Recherche Scientifique*, 582: 131–36. Paris: Éditions du Centre de la Recherche Scientifique.

Jayakar, Pupul. 1953–54. “Some Terracotta Figurines from Tribal Gujarat.” *Mārg* 7, 1: 27–32.

Lipner, Julius J. 1994. *Hindus: Their Religious Beliefs and Practices*. London: Routledge.

Lüders, H. 1937–38. “Seven Brahmi Inscriptions from Mathura and the Vicinity.” *Epigraphica Indica* 24: 194–200.

Meister Michael W. 1984. “Introduction.” *In* Michael W. Meister, ed., *Discourses on Śiva: Proceedings of a Symposium on the Nature of Religious Imagery*, xvii–xxiv. Philadelphia: University of Philadelphia Press.

Ray, Himanshu Prabha. 2004. “The Apsidal Shrine in Early Hinduism: Origins, Cultic Affiliation, Patronage.” *World Archaeology* 36, 3: 343–59.

Schopen, Gregory. 1989. *Bones, Stones, and Buddhist Monks: Collected Papers on the Archaeology, Epigraphy, and Texts of Monastic Buddhism in India*. Honolulu: University of Hawaii Press.

Shulman, David Dean. 1980. *Tamil Temple Myths: Sacrifice and Divine Marriage in the South Indian Śaiva Tradition*. Princeton: Princeton University Press.

Singh, Upinder. 2004. “Cults and Shrines in Early Historical Mathura (c. 200 BC–AD 200).” *World Archaeology* 36, 3: 378–99.

Srinivasan, Doris Meth. 1997. *Many Heads, Arms and Eyes: Origin, Meaning and Form of Multiplicity in Indian Art*. Leiden: E.J. Brill

Tarabout, Gilles. 2004. “Theology as History: Divine Images, Imagination, and Rituals in India.” *In* Phyllis Granoff and Koichi Shinohara, eds., *Images in Asian Religions: Texts and Contexts*, 56–84. Vancouver: University of British Columbia Press.

Zaehner, R. C. 1966 [1962]. *Hinduism*. Oxford: Oxford University Press.

2

Body

Barbara A. Holdrege

The Ritual Body
The Ascetic Body
The Purity Body
The Devotional Body
Concluding Reflections

In the last decade, there has been an explosion of interest in the "body" as an analytical category in the social sciences and humanities, particularly within the context of cultural studies. In recent years, a number of scholars of religion have begun to reflect critically on the notion of embodiment and to examine discourses of the body in particular religious traditions. Many of these studies are concerned with categories of the body that have been theorized by scholars in philosophy, the social sciences, or feminist and gender studies: the lived body, the mindful body, the social body, the body politic, the sexual body, the alimentary body, the medical body, the gendered body, and so on. Although scholarship on the body in religion has made significant advances in recent years, the dominant trends of analysis are problematic in that scholars of religion have tended to adopt the categories theorized by scholars in other disciplines and have consequently not given sufficient attention to generating analytical categories and models that are grounded in the distinctive idioms of religious traditions.[1]

Hindu traditions provide extensive, elaborate, and multiform discourses of the body, and a sustained investigation of these discourses can contribute in significant ways to scholarship on the body in the history of religions and in the human sciences generally. The body has been represented, disciplined, regulated, and cultivated from a variety of perspectives in Hindu ritual traditions, ascetic movements, medical traditions, legal codes, philosophical systems, *bhakti* (devotional) movements, Tantric traditions, the science of erotics, martial arts, drama, dance, music, and the visual arts.

An analysis of Hindu discourses of the body brings to light a variety of different models. The structural dimension of these models comprises a multileveled hierarchy of structurally correlated bodies corresponding to different orders of reality, which I term "integral bodies": the divine body, the cosmos body, the social body, and the human body. The transactional dimension of the models comprises various modalities of the human body, which I term "processual bodies,"[2] that mediate transactions among the integral bodies in distinctive ways: the ritual body, the ascetic body, the purity body, the devotional body, the Tantric body, and so on (see Figure 1).[3] While the Tantric body has been treated extensively in a number of studies (see, for example, Silburn 1988; White 1996; Flood 2006), the following analysis will focus on four processual bodies—the ritual body, the ascetic body, the purity body, and the devotional body—that have received less scholarly attention but are of critical importance to our understanding of Hindu notions of embodiment. We will briefly examine how these four processual bodies are represented, respectively, in four distinct discourses of the body: the discourse of sacrifice (*yajña*) in the Vedic Saṃhitās and Brāhmaṇas, the discourse of knowledge (*jñāna*) in the Upaniṣads, the discourse of *dharma* in the Dharmaśāstras, and the discourse of devotion (*bhakti*) in the Gauḍīya Vaiṣṇava tradition.[4]

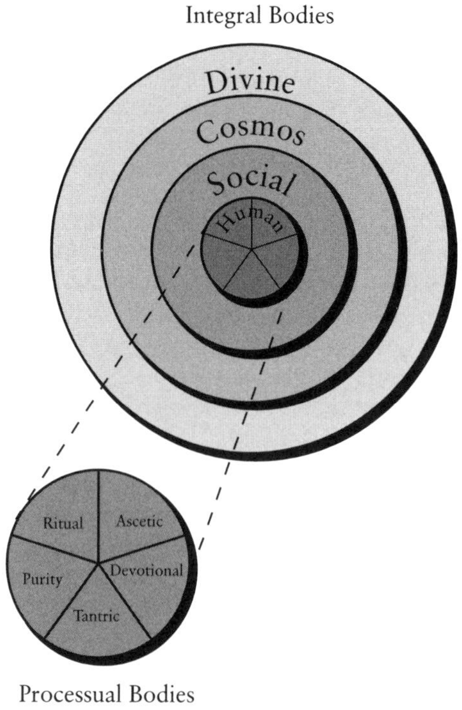

Figure 1 Integral Bodies and Processual Bodies

The Ritual Body

Vedic sacrificial traditions, as represented in the Vedic Saṃhitās (*ca.* 1500–800 BCE) and the Brāhmaṇas (*ca.* 900–650 BCE), ascribe central importance to the ritual body as the processual body that mediates the connections among the fourfold hierarchy of integral bodies. The earliest formulation of this quadripartite model is found in the *Ṛg Veda Saṃhitā* (*ca.* 1500–1200 BCE) in the Puruṣa-Sūkta (10.90), which is the *locus classicus* that is frequently invoked in later Vedic and post-Vedic discourses of the body.

The Puruṣa-Sūkta celebrates the ritual and cosmogonic functions of the divine body, which is identified in the hymn as the body of Puruṣa, the cosmic Man, who is the unitary source and basis of all existence. The divine body of Puruṣa is represented as the primordial totality that encompasses and interconnects the cosmos body, the social body, and the human body. The hymn depicts the primordial sacrifice (*yajña*) by means of which the wholeness of Puruṣa's body is differentiated, the different parts of the divine anthropos giving rise to the different parts of the universe.

> When they divided Puruṣa, into how many parts did they apportion him? What was his mouth? What were his arms? What were his thighs and feet declared to be? His mouth became the Brāhmaṇa; his arms were made the Kṣatriya; his thighs became the Vaiśya; from his feet the Śūdra was born. The moon was born from his mind; from his eye Sūrya, the sun, was born; from his mouth came Indra and Agni, fire; from his breath Vāyu, wind, was born. From his navel arose the midregions; from his head the heaven originated; from his feet came the earth; from his ear, the cardinal directions. Thus they fashioned the worlds.[5]
>
> (*Ṛg Veda* 10.90.11–14)

In these verses the divine body is portrayed as coextensive with the cosmos body. The three principal sections of Puruṣa's body (head, navel, and feet) are correlated with the three worlds (heaven, midregions, and earth), whereas specific parts of his psychophysiology (mouth, breath, eye, ear, and mind) are correlated with specific components of the natural order (fire, wind, sun, cardinal directions, and moon), together with their presiding deities (Agni, Vāyu, and Sūrya). The hymn also depicts the body of Puruṣa as encompassing the social body, establishing homologies between particular parts of his corporeal form—mouth, arms, thighs, and feet—and particular social classes (*varṇa*s)—Brāhmaṇas (priests), Kṣatriyas (royalty and warriors), Vaiśyas (merchants, agriculturalists, and artisans), and Śūdras (servants and manual laborers). The Brāhmaṇical social order is re-presented as part of the natural order of things, inherent in the structure of the divine body since primordial times.

The body of the cosmic Man is thus depicted in the Puruṣa-Sūkta as the primordial totality, the microcosmic counterpart of which is the human body—more specifically, the male body. However, the transcosmic divine body of Puruṣa extends beyond the limits of both the microcosmic human body and the macrocosmic cosmos body, for Puruṣa is portrayed as simultaneously immanent and transcendent. On the one hand, as the immanent principle that manifests as the universe, the body of Puruṣa *is* the body of the cosmos and is represented in the form of a cosmic Man with circumscribed boundaries, possessing a head, two eyes, two arms, two feet, and so on. On the other hand, as the transcendent reality that is beyond the cosmos, Puruṣa cannot be contained within boundaries and is represented as a limitless form, possessing "a thousand heads, a thousand eyes, a thousand feet." The hymn asserts that only one-quarter of Puruṣa is manifested here as all beings, while the other three-quarters are immortal (*Ṛg Veda* 10.90.1–5).

Although the Puruṣa-Sūkta makes reference to the different body parts of the divine anthropos, it does not describe any emblematic characteristics of the physical appearance of Puruṣa that might serve to distinguish his corporeal form from other divine bodies—apart from his thousand heads, thousand eyes, and thousand feet, which are at times invoked as a distinctive feature of Puruṣa's form in later Vedic and post-Vedic texts. This lack of concrete specificity in portraying the divine body is characteristic of Vedic texts, which tend to make formulaic allusions to the bodies of the gods while eschewing individualized descriptions of their corporeal forms. This tendency is consonant with the aniconic orientation of the Vedic tradition, which is characterized by an absence of iconic representations of deities and of temples or other permanent shrines.[6] As we shall see, it is only with the advent of *bhakti* traditions in post-Vedic "Hinduism" that we find a shift to iconic forms of worship, with temples and *pūjā* ceremonies centered on images of the gods.

The divine body of Puruṣa is celebrated not for its distinctive appearance but for its ritual and cosmogonic functions. Puruṣa, as the sacrificial victim, is identified with the sacrifice itself, and it is this primordial sacrifice that provides the prototype for all future sacrifices: "With the sacrifice (*yajña*) the gods sacrificed (root *yaj*) the sacrifice (*yajña*). These were the first rites (*dharma*s)" (*Ṛg Veda* 10.90.16, cf. 10.90.6–7). The divine body of Puruṣa is thus represented as the paradigmatic ritual body, the body of the sacrifice itself, which serves as the means of manifesting the cosmos body, the social body, and the human body.

The Brāhmaṇas, sacrificial manuals attached to the Saṃhitās, foster a discourse of sacrifice (*yajña*) that is founded upon the speculations of the Puruṣa-Sūkta and that ascribes primacy of place to the ritual body as the processual body that mediates the connections among the divine body and its multiple manifestations. In this context, the sacrificial discourse of the Brāhmaṇas evidences three principal concerns: to establish the identity of Puruṣa with Prajāpati, who is celebrated as the supreme god and creator in the Brāhmaṇas; to establish the cosmic import of the sacrifice as the counterpart of the Puruṣa Prajāpati; and to delineate the theurgic efficacy of the sacrificial order (*adhiyajña*) as the instrument for enlivening the inherent connections (*bandhus*) among the human order (*adhyātma*), the natural order (*adhibhūta*), and the divine order (*adhidaiva*).[7]

The sacrifice is represented in the Brāhmaṇas not only as the means of mediating the connections among the divine body and its corporeal counterparts but also as the means of *constituting* these multiple bodies. First, the sacrifice is celebrated as the *cosmogonic* instrument through which the creator Prajāpati generates the cosmos body, setting in motion the entire universe (*Pañcaviṃśa Brāhmaṇa* 25.6.2, 25.17.2) and bringing forth all beings (*Aitareya Brāhmaṇa* 4.23; *Kauṣītaki Brāhmaṇa* 6.15, 5.3; *Śatapatha Brāhmaṇa* 2.5.1.17, 2.5.2.1, 2.5.2.7, 2.6.3.4; *Pañcaviṃśa Brāhmaṇa* 6.1.1–2, 8.5.6, 4.1.4, 22.9.2; *Jaiminīya Brāhmaṇa* 1.67). The initial generative act of Prajāpati is generally represented in the Brāhmaṇas as resulting in a chaotic creation rather than an ordered cosmos. The sacrifice therefore serves not only as the instrument of creation but also as the instrument of rectification by means of which Prajāpati structures an ordered cosmos. Second, the sacrifice is represented as the *theogonic* instrument through which the divine body of Prajāpati himself, which is disintegrated and dissipated by his creative efforts, is reconstituted and restored to a state of wholeness.[8] Third, the sacrifice is portrayed as the *anthropogonic* instrument through which the defective human being produced through biological reproduction is born anew out of the ritual womb and reconstituted through ritual labor. The Brāhmaṇas emphasize in particular the role of the sacrifice in perfecting the embodied self (*ātman*) of the *yajamāna*—the patron of the sacrifice, who is the human counterpart of Prajāpati—and in ritually constructing for him a divine self (*daiva ātman*) through which he may ascend to the world of heaven (*svarga loka*).[9] Finally, the sacrifice serves as the *sociogonic* instrument that constructs and maintains the social body as a hierarchy of bodies differentiated according to social class (*varṇa*) and gender.[10] The ritual body, as the body that is constituted through the sacrificial ritual, thus has multiple significations in the Brāhmaṇas' discourse of sacrifice, encompassing the divine body that is revitalized, the cosmos body that is renovated, the human body-self that is reconstituted, and the social body that is constructed through the sacrifice.[11]

The Ascetic Body

In the metaphysical speculations of the Upaniṣads (*ca.* 800 BCE–200 CE), the epistemological framework shifts from the discourse of sacrifice, the *karma-kāṇḍa*, to the discourse of knowledge, the *jñāna-kāṇḍa*. In contrast to the priestly exponents of the Brāhmaṇas' concern with ritual action (*karman*) as a means of regenerating the realm of embodied forms, the forest-dwelling sages of the Upaniṣads give priority to knowledge (*jñāna*)—in the sense of both intellectual understanding and direct experience—of ultimate reality as a means of achieving liberation (*mokṣa*) from the bondage of *saṃsāra* and its endless cycles of embodiment. The body assumes new valences within the context of the Upaniṣads' ontological and epistemological concerns regarding ultimate reality. Thus, whereas discussions of the body in the Brāhmaṇas center on the paradigmatic body of the creator Prajāpati, the primordial sacrificer, the Upaniṣads reframe the discussion in terms of the relation of the body–mind complex to the ultimate reality—generally designated as Brahman or Ātmaṇ—that is the source not only of the phenomenal world but of the creator himself. In its discursive reshaping of the body, the Upaniṣadic discourse of knowledge interjects two new emphases. First, the divine body is recast in relation to Brahman-Ātman—either directly, through references to the body of Brahman or the body of Ātman (*Kauṣītaki Upaniṣad* 1.7; *Bṛhadāraṇyaka Upaniṣad* 3.7.3–23), or indirectly, through references to the body of Puruṣa, who is generally identified as an aspect of Brahman-Ātman.[12] Second, the ascetic body displaces the ritual body as the processual body of central significance, which is to be cultivated through minimizing transactions with the cosmos body and the social body in order to attain realization of Brahman-Ātman.

The Upaniṣads emphasize Puruṣa's role not only as the all-pervading reality whose divine body is coextensive with the cosmos body but, more important, as the inner Self (*antar-ātman*) that resides within the cosmos body. This dual role of Puruṣa—as the divine body *qua* cosmos body and as the inner Self of the cosmos body—is celebrated in the *Śvetāśvatara Upaniṣad*:

> He who is the face, the head, and the neck of all, who abides in the heart of all beings, and who is all-pervading—he is the Lord.... Puruṣa, the measure of a thumb, is the inner Self (*antar-ātman*), ever seated in the heart of living beings.... With a hand and foot on every side, with an eye, head, and face on every side, with an ear on every side, it stands

> encompassing everything in the world....He is swift, and he grasps yet has no foot or hand; he sees yet has no eye; he hears yet has no ear....They call him the great primordial Puruṣa. Subtler than the subtlest, greater than the greatest is the Self (Ātman) that is established here in the heart of a living being.
>
> (3.11–20)

On the one hand, invoking the language and imagery of the Puruṣa-Sūkta, the passage celebrates the thousand-headed Puruṣa who is "greater than the greatest" and whose body *is* the body of the cosmos. On the other hand, the passage depicts Puruṣa as the inner Self that is "subtler than the subtlest" and that abides in the hearts of all embodied beings. Puruṣa's relationship to the body is thus portrayed in the passage as multileveled. First, his divine body, with its omnipresent heads, eyes, ears, hands, and feet, is represented as encompassing the cosmos body in its totality on the macrocosmic plane and the bodies of all beings on the microcosmic plane. Second, he is depicted as the Self, Ātman, that is hidden in the hearts of these embodied beings. Finally, Puruṣa is portrayed as without form—without eyes, ears, hands, and feet—and hence as ultimately the transcosmic reality that is beyond all embodiment. The last two points are connected, for, according to Upaniṣadic metaphysical speculations, the Self, Ātman, that is hidden within the body is itself bodiless, formless. The Self is subtler than the subtlest, beyond the gross and subtle realms of the cosmos body and beyond the gross and subtle manifestations of the human body.

The Upaniṣadic sages locate the source of bondage in the embodied self's attachment to the body–mind complex and consequent failure to recognize its true identity as Brahman-Ātman, which in its essential nature is unmanifest, nonchanging, unbounded, and formless. In this context, the human body is often ascribed negative valences in the Upaniṣadic discourse of knowledge, becoming associated with ignorance, attachment, desire, impurity, vices, disease, suffering, and death. The *Maitri Upaniṣad* asserts:

> In this foul-smelling, unsubstantial body, which is an aggregate of bone, skin, muscle, marrow, flesh, semen, blood, mucus, tears, rheum, feces, urine, wind, bile, and phlegm, what good is the enjoyment of desires? In this body, which is afflicted with desire, anger, greed, delusion, fear, despondency, envy, separation from what is desired, union with what is not desired, hunger, thirst, old age, death, disease, sorrow, and so on, what good is the enjoyment of desires?
>
> (1.3, cf. 3.4)

In contrast to the ritual body—which is constituted as a means of enlivening the connections among the divine body, the cosmos body, the social body, and the human body—the ascetic body, as described in the Upaniṣads and in later post-Vedic ascetic traditions, is constituted as a means of overcoming attachment to all forms of embodiment. The cultivation of the ascetic body involves minimizing transactions with the cosmos body, which is renounced as the field of *saṃsāra* and hence the domain of bondage. The construction of the ascetic body also involves the "deconstruction" of the social body, as Patrick Olivelle (1995) has emphasized. The ascetic body is defined in direct opposition to the social body constituted by Brāhmaṇical norms, for the realm of social norms is viewed as inextricably linked to saṃsāric existence. The world-renouncing ideologies and practices of ascetic traditions are antithetical to the world-maintaining ideologies and practices promulgated by Brāhmaṇical authorities to regulate the human body and perpetuate a social hierarchy of bodies ranked according to class and gender. The renunciant ideal is predicated on the abandonment of the prescribed rituals and social duties of *varṇāśrama-dharma* that regulate the four social classes (*varṇa*s) and stages of life (*āśrama*s). Brāhmaṇical householder traditions concerning marriage and sexuality, which are concerned with regulating the transactions of the sexual body as the instrument of procreation, are countered by ascetic practices that renounce householder life, marriage, and procreation altogether and seek instead to restrain the sexual impulse through the observance of celibacy. Brāhmaṇical food practices and norms, which are concerned with regulating the alimentary body through a complex system of food transactions and dietary laws, are countered by ascetic disciplines that are aimed at minimizing food production and consumption through such practices as begging and fasting. Brāhmaṇical constructions of the social body—together with the concomitant constructions of the ritual body, sexual body, and alimentary body—are thus negated and supplanted by renunciant constructions of the ascetic body.[13]

Having abandoned the accoutrements of worldly *dharma*—home, family, sexuality, food production, ritual practices, and social duties—the ascetic adopts a regimen of practices, including meditation, breathing exercises, and physical austerities, which is designed to discipline and transform the mind, senses, and bodily appetites and overcome the fetters of the body-mind complex. The encompassing term that is at times used for this regimen of ascetic practices is *tapas* (literally, "heat"), which refers to the spiritual "heat" that is generated through such practices and that burns up ignorance and attachments, leading to the ultimate goal of the ascetic path: realization of Brahman-Ātman.[14]

The Purity Body

In the Dharmaśāstras (*ca.* first to eighth centuries CE), Brāhmaṇical legal codes, the body is re-figured in accordance with the epistemological framework of the discourse of *dharma* and, more specifically, *varṇāśrama-dharma*. The Dharmaśāstras' discursive reshaping of the inherited model of integral bodies results in two new emphases. First, the ideological representations of the Dharmaśāstras give priority to the social body and attempt to provide transcendent legitimation for the Brāhmaṇical system of social stratification by invoking the imagery of the Puruṣa-Sūkta, in which the body of the divine anthropos is portrayed as the ultimate source of the hierarchically differentiated social body consisting of four *varṇa*s. Second, the processual body that is of central significance to the Dharmaśāstras is the purity body, which must be continually reconstituted through highly selective transactions with the cosmos body and the social body. The ideology of purity serves in particular to legitimate the Brāhmaṇical system of *varṇāśrama-dharma*, and therefore the purity body's relation to the social body is of paramount significance. Louis Dumont, in his classic study of the caste system, *Homo Hierarchicus* (1970, 1980), maintains that the opposition between the pure and the impure constitutes *the* fundamental ideological principle that undergirds the social hierarchy.[15] Although, as Dumont's critics have argued, the pure/impure opposition alone is not sufficient to account for the *historical actualities* of the caste system,[16] issues of purity and pollution are nevertheless a central preoccupation in the Dharmaśāstras' *ideological representations* of the social hierarchy.

The *Manusmṛti* (*ca.* first to second centuries CE) mentions the divine body a number of times in its cosmogonic narrative in the first book. In accordance with its focus on the discourse of *dharma*, the *Manusmṛti* is primarily concerned with connecting the divine body to the social body, and therefore it is only in the text's accounts of the emergence of the four *varṇa*s that we find references to specific parts of the divine anthropos. Invoking the imagery of the Puruṣa-Sūkta, the *Manusmṛti* declares: "For the sake of the welfare of the worlds, he [the creator] brought forth from his mouth, arms, thighs, and feet the Brāhmaṇa, the Kṣatriya, the Vaiśya, and the Śūdra" (1.31). The text interjects the same image again at the conclusion of its creation narrative in order to provide a transition to the discourse of *dharma* that is its primary concern (*Manusmṛti* 1.87). After describing the duties of the four *varṇa*s, the creation narrative concludes with extended praise of the Brāhmaṇa class, which is born from the purest part of the divine body—the mouth—and hence is deemed to be preeminent among the social classes (*Manusmṛti* 1.88–101). The image of the four *varṇa*s emerging from the divine body is also invoked elsewhere in the *Manusmṛti*, where it is used to define the non-Āryans as "all those peoples in the world who are outside [the community of] those born from the mouth, arms, thighs, and feet [of the divine body]" (10.45).

The image of the divine body is thus used in the *Manusmṛti* to legitimate the Brāhmaṇical system of social stratification and to establish a hierarchy of purity based on a series of successive dichotomies. First, the Āryans, as the four *varṇa*s born from the divine body, are distinguished from the non-Āryans, who are excluded from the claim to divine origins. Second, among Āryans, the twice-born Brāhmaṇas, Kṣatriyas, and Vaiśyas are distinguished from the once-born Śūdras, who are born from the most impure part of the divine body, the feet. Third, among the twice-born classes, the Brāhmaṇas, as the first-born who emerge from the purest part of the divine body, the mouth, are distinguished from the Kṣatriyas and Vaiśyas, who are born from less pure portions, the arms and thighs, respectively. The Brāhmaṇas, as the quintessential embodiments of purity and of *dharma*, thus claim for themselves the status of the lords of creation.

In the purity codes of the *Manusmṛti* and other Dharmaśāstras, the hierarchy of purity is extended beyond the social body to include the cosmos body that is the differentiated manifestation of the divine body. Through the taxonomic enterprise the cosmos body is divided into a variety of distinct categories of bodies—gods, humans, animals, plants, minerals, and so on—and each of these categories is further subdivided into a series of classes ranked according to a scale of purity and impurity. For example, certain animals, such as the cow, are ascribed a high degree of purity, whereas other animals, such as the dog, pig, and cock, are held to be impure (see, for example, *Manusmṛti* 5.133, 3.239).

The human body, as a component of the organic world, is also associated with impurities. Natural bodily processes and functions, such as eating, sleeping, urinating, defecating, sexual intercourse, and menstruation, are considered polluting (see, for example, *Manusmṛti* 5.138, 5.145). The bodily secretions associated with such processes, including urine, feces, semen, menses, saliva, phlegm, and sweat, are similarly classified as inherent impurities of the human body. The *Manusmṛti* declares: "Oily secretions, semen, blood, fatty brain substance, urine, feces, nasal mucus, ear-wax, phlegm, tears, rheum, and sweat are the twelve impurities of human [bodies]" (5.135, cf. 5.123).

Because the human body is itself the locus of certain polluting substances, the purity body is not a given but rather an ideal to be approximated. The purity body, its boundaries constantly threatened by the inflow and outflow of impurities, must be continually reconstituted through an elaborate system of regulations and practices. In contrast to the cultivation of the ascetic body, which involves renouncing the cosmos body and the social body in order to obtain liberation from *saṃsāra*, the structuring of the purity body involves highly selective transactions with the cosmos body and the social body in order to maintain the smooth functioning of the social and cosmic orders. The male members of the twice-born *varṇa*s, in upholding the ritual and social duties of *varṇāśrama-dharma*, are enjoined in the Dharmaśāstras to minimize contact with impure persons and substances, to maximize contact with pure persons and substances, and to undertake a regular program of purificatory procedures to mitigate the polluting effects of embodied existence.

The Dharmaśāstras are particularly concerned with the purity body's relation to the social body, as we have seen. The social body includes not only the four *varṇa*s but the numerous *jāti*s, or castes, which the Dharmaśāstras claim were generated through the intermixing of the *varṇa*s (*varṇa-saṃkara*). In this extended pyramidal hierarchy of purity, the Brāhmaṇas maintain their place at the apex, as the paradigmatic representatives of the purity body, whereas the large number of "debased" castes generated through illicit (*pratiloma*) marriage unions are deemed to be of impure origin and relegated to the bottom of the social hierarchy.[17]

Thus, although all human bodies—even Brāhmaṇa bodies—are to a certain extent tainted by the impurities of organic life, different degrees of natural defilement are ascribed to different human bodies by virtue of their birth in a particular caste with its associated occupation. However, the purity status of a caste and of its individual members is not fixed but may be modified through interactions with other castes—more specifically, through a complex network of transactions involving the exchange of women (in marriage), food, and services. The regulations and procedures delineated in the Dharmaśāstras for structuring the purity body thus include both laws of connubiality to regulate the transactions of the sexual body and laws of commensality to regulate the transactions of the alimentary body. The laws of connubiality delineate the effects of various types of marriage transactions—in particular, endogamous, hypergamous, and hypogamous unions—on a caste's purity status (see *Manusmṛti* 10.5–72, 3.12–19). The laws of commensality circumscribe food transactions among castes, determining who may receive food and water from whom, and thereby serve to strengthen the hierarchical gradations of purity that both separate and connect castes (see, for example, *Manusmṛti* 4.205–23, 11.176, 11.181).[18]

The Devotional Body

With the emergence of *bhakti* movements in the post-Vedic period, the body is re-figured to accord with the epistemological framework of the discourse of devotion (*bhakti*). The historical shift from Vedic traditions to post-Vedic *bhakti* traditions is accompanied by a shift from abstract, translocal notions of divinity to particularized, localized notions of divinity and a corresponding shift from aniconic to iconic traditions and from temporary sacrificial arenas to temples. I would suggest that the various aspects of this historical shift can best be understood in terms of newly emerging conceptions of divine embodiment in *bhakti* traditions (see Holdrege n.d.a, n.d.b; Ramanujan 1993: 135–36; Waghorne and Cutler 1985), which interject two new emphases in their discursive reframing of the body. First, the divine body is given precedence as the most important in the hierarchy of integral bodies and is represented in a standardized repertoire of particularized forms of the deity who is revered as the object of devotion—whether Viṣṇu, Kṛṣṇa, Śiva, or Devī (the Goddess). Second, the devotional body emerges as the processual body of central significance, which is to be cultivated as a means of appropriating, engaging, experiencing, and embodying the deity.

The Gauḍīya Vaiṣṇava tradition, an influential *bhakti* movement inspired by the Bengali leader Caitanya (1486–1533 CE), provides a striking example of the multileveled models of divine embodiment that are developed by certain *bhakti* traditions. The Gauḍīyas' theology of embodiment, as articulated by the six Gosvāmins and their disciple Kṛṣṇadāsa Kavirāja, celebrates the deity Kṛṣṇa as Puruṣottama, the supreme Puruṣa, who is Anantarūpa (literally, "having endless forms"), his limitless forms encompassing and interweaving the transcosmic, macrocosmic, microcosmic, and mesocosmic planes of existence. The Gauḍīyas invoke *Bhāgavata Purāṇa* 1.2.11 in order to provide a scriptural basis for their hierarchical assessment of the three aspects of the supreme Godhead: Brahman, Paramātman, and Bhagavān. Brahman, the lowest aspect of the Godhead, is the impersonal, attributeless, formless, and undifferentiated ground of existence that is beyond the material realm of *prakṛti* and is the radiant effulgence of the absolute body of Bhagavān. Paramātman, the intermediary aspect of the Godhead, is the indwelling Self that on the macrocosmic level animates the cosmos body and on the microcosmic level resides in the hearts of all embodied beings. Bhagavān, the highest aspect of the Godhead, is transcosmic—beyond both the macrocosm and the microcosm—and is personal, endowed with innumerable qualities, and possessed of a nonmaterial, unmanifest absolute body (*vigraha*). In allotting the highest place in their ontology to the personal Godhead, Bhagavān, the Gauḍīyas assert the supremacy of *bhakti* as the highest path (*mārga*) to realization. They maintain that although those who follow the *jñāna mārga* may realize their identity with the impersonal Brahman of the Upaniṣads, and those who follow the *yoga mārga* may experience Paramātman, neither the *jñānin* nor the *yogin* realize Bhagavān, who is attained through the *bhakti mārga* alone.[19]

The Gauḍīyas' theology of embodiment emphasizes that the absolute body of Bhagavān, like his essential nature (*svarūpa*), consists of existence (*sat*), consciousness (*cit*), and bliss (*ānanda*). Paradoxically, the Gauḍīyas assert that the essential form of Bhagavān's absolute body is the two-armed form that he manifests on earth as Gopāla Kṛṣṇa, the cowherd (*gopa*) of Vṛndāvana, whose *līlā* (play) is extolled in the *Bhāgavata Purāṇa*. It is the beautiful adolescent form of the cowherd Kṛṣṇa—with its distinctive color, dress, ornaments, and emblems—that is celebrated as the absolute body of Bhagavān on the transcosmic level (see, for example, *Bhaktirasāmṛtasindhu* 2.1.22–23).[20]

Although the absolute body of Kṛṣṇa, in his supreme status as Bhagavān, remains one on the transcosmic level, he has the capacity to assume simultaneously innumerable forms and shapes on the macrocosmic, microcosmic, and mesocosmic planes of existence. The Gauḍīyas invoke the *Bhāgavata Purāṇa*'s declaration that "Kṛṣṇa is Bhagavān himself (*bhagavān svayam*)" (1.3.28) in order to establish that Kṛṣṇa is *pūrṇa bhagavān*, the full and complete Godhead, and as such he is the *avatārin* who is the source of all *avatāra*s and who descends to earth periodically and assumes a series of manifest forms in different cosmic cycles (see, for example, *Caitanya Caritāmṛta* 1.5.3).[21]

On the mesocosmic level, the Gauḍīyas describe Kṛṣṇa as becoming embodied in a number of intermediate structures that mediate between the transcosmic absolute body and the microcosmic human body by serving as vehicles through which human beings can access and engage the supreme Godhead. Kṛṣṇa is revered as becoming instantiated in five mesocosmic modes of divine embodiment that are not unique to the Gauḍīya tradition but are also found in other *bhakti* traditions: embodiment in *śāstra*, scripture; embodiment in *līlā*, play; embodiment in *dhāman,* place; embodiment in *mūrti,* image; and embodiment in *nāman*, name.[22]

Kṛṣṇa is celebrated as becoming embodied in *śāstra*, scripture, in the *Bhāgavata Purāṇa*, which is extolled as *bhagavad-rūpa*, the form of Bhagavān, and as Kārṣṇa-Veda, the Veda that is identical with Kṛṣṇa. The *Bhāgavata Purāṇa* is the "representative embodiment of Kṛṣṇa" that Kṛṣṇa leaves behind when, at the onset of Kali Yuga, he departs the earth and returns to his transcendent abode (*Tattva Sandarbha* 26, citing *Bhāgavata Purāṇa* 1.3.45). The concrete book in both its oral-aural and written forms is thus revered as a "text-incarnation" of Kṛṣṇa, which is to be worshiped accordingly.[23]

Kṛṣṇa is also extolled as becoming embodied in *līlā*, play, which is the spontaneous expression of the *hlādinī-śakti*, the bliss that is intrinsic to Bhagavān's nature. The Gauḍīyas maintain that Kṛṣṇa's *līlā*, which is recorded in narrative form in the tenth book of the *Bhāgavata Purāṇa*, occurs simultaneously on the unmanifest (*aprakaṭa*) and manifest (*prakaṭa*) levels. Kṛṣṇa's unmanifest *līlā* goes on eternally as a self-referral play within Bhagavān in the transcendent sphere of Goloka, the eternal Vraja, beyond the material world of *prakṛti* and beyond Brahman. In this perspective, the various associates of Kṛṣṇa that are described in the *Bhāgavata Purāṇa*—for example, his attendants, cowherd friends (*gopa*s), adoptive parents Nanda and Yaśodā, and cowmaiden lovers (*gopī*s)—are eternal expressions of Kṛṣṇa's blissful nature, his *hlādinī-śakti*. At a particular time and place in history, in approximately 3000 BCE, Kṛṣṇa descends with his eternal associates to the earthly domain of Vraja in North India, where he discloses himself in his manifest *līlā*.[24]

The corollary of Kṛṣṇa's embodiment in *līlā* is his embodiment in *dhāman*, place, and more specifically in Vraja-*dhāman*. Vraja is represented in the Gauḍīya tradition both as a transcendent space—which is the nonmaterial abode of Kṛṣṇa's absolute body and the site of the unmanifest *līlā*—and as a geographic place—which is the material abode of his manifest form and the site of the manifest *līlā* during his sojourn on earth. Moreover, the earthly Vraja-*dhāman* is held to be the manifest counterpart of the unmanifest Vraja-*dhāman*, which is simultaneously immanent and transcendent, and therefore from this perspective Kṛṣṇa does not cease to dwell in the terrestrial Vraja even after he departs from the earth (see *Bhagavat Sandarbha* 60–78; *Kṛṣṇa Sandarbha* 105–7).[25]

Kṛṣṇa's embodiment in place is not limited to the sacred geography of Vraja. He is also celebrated as assuming localized forms in temples and shrines throughout the Indian subcontinent. The Gauḍīyas emphasize that Kṛṣṇa, out of his grace, descends and dwells in consecrated *mūrti*s, or images. Moreover, they assert that these "image-incarnations" (*arcāvatāra*s) are nondifferent from Kṛṣṇa and that those adepts who are advanced in the practice of *bhakti* have the ability to perceive the living presence of Bhagavān within the *mūrti* (see, for example, *Bhakti Sandarbha* 286).[26]

The Gauḍīyas maintain that Kṛṣṇa also incarnates in his *nāman*s, divine names, which are revered as *varṇāvatāra*s of Kṛṣṇa in the form of sound. The name is held to be a concentrated form of *sat-cit-ānanda* and thus is identical with Kṛṣṇa's essential nature (*svarūpa*) and his absolute body (*vigraha*): "The name, the *vigraha*, and the *svarūpa*, these three are one *rūpa*; there is no division among the three; the three are the *cidānanda svarūpa*. There is no division in Kṛṣṇa between the body and the possessor of the body, nor between the name and the possessor of the name" (*Caitanya Caritāmṛta* 2.17.127–28; Dimock 1999: 588–89).[27]

The ultimate goal of life, according to the Gauḍīyas, is to attain that sublime state of realization in which the *jīva*, the individual human soul, awakens to the reality of Kṛṣṇa as *svayaṃ bhagavān*, the supreme personal Godhead beyond Brahman, and realizes its true identity as a part of Bhagavān and as an eternal participant in the unmanifest *līlā* that goes on perpetually as the self-referral play within the Godhead. The path to the goal involves the construction of a devotional body by means of an elaborate system of embodied practices termed *sādhana bhakti*, which comprises two main phases: *vaidhī bhakti* and *rāgānugā bhakti* (see *Bhakti Sandarbha* 235–340; *Bhaktirasāmṛtasindhu* 1.2–1.4; *Caitanya Caritāmṛta* 2.22.55–96).

Vaidhī bhakti entails engaging in devotional practices that are derived from scriptural injunctions (*vidhi*s), centering on sixty-four practices. Among these practices, five are singled out as most important for cultivating *prema bhakti*, the highest stage of selfless love (*prema*) for Kṛṣṇa: association with holy persons; singing the names of Kṛṣṇa; listening to the *Bhāgavata Purāṇa*, which extols the glories of Kṛṣṇa's *līlā*; dwelling at Mathurā in the area of Vraja; and worship of Kṛṣṇa's image.[28] Four of the five fundamental practices of *vaidhī bhakti* thus involve engaging the mesocosmic forms of Kṛṣṇa discussed earlier: *śāstra*, *līlā*, *dhāman*, *mūrti*, and *nāman*. Through these practices the *bhakta* focuses all aspects of the psychophysical organism on Bhagavān, including the mind, the sense organs—ears, sense of touch, eyes, tongue, and nose—and the organs of action—mouth (speech), hands, feet, and so on. The Gauḍīyas invoke the *Bhāgavata Purāṇa*'s description of the embodied practices of the paradigmatic *bhakta*:

> He engaged his mind on the lotus-feet of Kṛṣṇa, his words in recounting the virtues of Vaikuṇṭha, his hands in cleaning the temple of Hari, his ears in hearing glorious stories about Acyuta, his eyes in seeing the images and temples of Mukunda, his sense of touch in touching the bodies of his servants, his nose in smelling the fragrance of the *tulasī* placed at his lotus-feet, his tongue in tasting the food that had been offered to him, his feet in traveling by foot to the holy places of Hari, his head in bowing to the feet of Hṛṣīkeśa, and his desire in serving him.[29]
>
> (9.4.18–20)

In *rāgānugā bhakti*, the advanced phase of *sādhana bhakti*, the *bhakta* enters into a more intimate relationship with Kṛṣṇa characterized by passionate love (*rāga*). This stage of *bhakti* is achieved through emulating the eternal associates who reside with Kṛṣṇa in the transcendent Vraja-*dhāman* and who are called *rāgātmika*s because their very essence (*ātmika*) is spontaneously absorbed in passionate, all-consuming love (*rāga*) for Kṛṣṇa (see *Bhaktirasāmṛtasindhu* 1.2.270). The process of emulation involves cultivating one of the four principal models of relationship (*bhāva*s) with Kṛṣṇa—whether that of servant, friend, parent, or lover—that are exemplified by the paradigmatic *rāgātmika*s. The *bhakta* seeks to actualize the *bhāva*, first, by emulating the chosen *rāgātmika* through performing practices with the external body, the *sādhaka rūpa*, that engage Kṛṣṇa's mesocosmic forms, and, second, by cultivating a state of inner absorption through meditative practices, which culminates in the construction of an eternal body, *siddha rūpa*. Having constructed an eternal body, *siddha rūpa*, the *bhakta* realizes his or her essential nature, *siddha svarūpa*, and enters into Kṛṣṇa's transcendent *dhāman* as a participant in the unmanifest *līlā* in eternal relationship with Bhagavān.[30]

Concluding Reflections

Hindu traditions thus provide a variety of discourses of the body that can contribute in significant ways to our ongoing investigations of the body in the history of religions, and in the human sciences generally, by bringing to light new categories and models that are grounded in the idioms of religious traditions themselves. Certain categories that have been theorized by scholars, such as the sexual body and the alimentary body, are ascribed entirely different valences when they are incorporated in the more encompassing modalities delineated by Hindu discursive representations and practices, such as the ascetic body, the purity body, and the devotional body. These processual bodies themselves assume distinctive valences when they are incorporated in the even more encompassing interpretive framework of integral bodies. Hindu discourses of the body thus provide a variety of models and categories of embodiment that may prove fruitful in illuminating comparable constructions in other religious traditions.

Notes

1 For a discussion of recent scholarship on the body in the social sciences and humanities, and more specifically in religious studies, see Holdrege (1998: 341–46, n.d.b).

2 The term "processual body" reflects the Hindu notion that the human body is not "individual" but is rather "dividual"—to use McKim Marriott's (1976a) term—that is, a constellation of substances and processes that is connected to other bodies through a complex network of transactions.

3 Figure 1 provides a schematic representation of the integral bodies and processual bodies. The specific configuration of the integral bodies in the figure reflects early Vedic constructions of the ritual body, in which the divine body is the encompassing totality within which the cosmos body, social body, and human body are subsumed. A separate figure could be generated for each of the other processual bodies, in which the integral bodies would be reconfigured to highlight the relative importance of, and changing relationships among, the four bodies.

4 For extended analyses of Hindu discourses of the body, see Holdrege (1998, n.d.b).

5 The translations of all Sanskrit passages are my own.

6 Malamoud (1996) has emphasized the links between Vedic aniconism and the perspectives on divine corporeality propounded in Vedic texts.

7 As Smith has emphasized, this system of *bandhus* is founded on the Vedic principle of "hierarchical resemblance," which as a "central principle of Vedism" (1989: 78) encapsulates the "ancient Indian notion that the universe was composed of mutually resembling and interconnected, but also hierarchically distinguished and ranked, components" (1994: vii).

8 For a discussion of the role of the sacrifice in constructing an orderly cosmos and reconstituting the creator Prajāpati, see Smith (1989: 50–81).

9 For a discussion of the anthropogonic function of the sacrifice, see Smith (1989: 82–119).

10 For an extended analysis of the ways in which the discourse of sacrifice in the Brāhmaṇas serves to perpetuate and legitimate the *varṇa* system, see Smith (1994).

11 The theurgic efficacy of the sacrifice as the instrument that constitutes and interconnects the divine body and its corporeal counterparts is particularly evident in the *Śatapatha Brāhmaṇa*'s discussion of the construction of the bird-shaped fire altar in the *agnicayana* ceremony (see Holdrege 1998: 357; Malamoud 1996; Tull 1989: 72–102).

12 In *Bṛhadāraṇyaka Upaniṣad* 1.4.1, for example, Ātman is said to exist alone in the beginning in the form of Puruṣa. However, the Upaniṣads at times appear to distinguish Ātman and Puruṣa, as, for example, in *Aitareya Upaniṣad* 1.1.1–4.

13 For an illuminating discussion of ascetic modes of deconstructing the social body, see Olivelle (1995). See also Dumont's (1960) seminal analysis of the dialectical relationship between the ideal types of the "renouncer" and the "man-in-the-world."

14 For a discussion of the role of "meditative *tapas*" in the Upaniṣads and later ascetic traditions, see Kaelber (1989).

15 The importance of the categories of purity and impurity in the caste system has also been emphasized by Srinivas (1952), Stevenson (1954), Orenstein (1965, 1968, 1970), and Tambiah (1973).

16 Among the numerous critiques of Dumont's (1970, 1980) work, see Marriott (1969, 1976b); Marriott and Inden (1977); Marglin (1977). See also the edited collection by Carman and Marglin (1985), which examines the relationship between the pure/impure dichotomy and the auspicious/inauspicious dichotomy in Indian society.

17 For a discussion of the mixed castes that result from permissible (*anuloma*) and illicit (*pratiloma*) marriage unions, see *Manusmṛti* 10.5–72, 3.12–19. See also Tambiah's (1973) incisive analysis of the generative rules that govern the production and ranking of mixed castes in the *Manusmṛti*'s account.

18 My analysis here concurs with Tambiah's "transactional theory of purity and pollution" (1973: 217), which emphasizes not only the boundaries that separate

(Douglas 1966) but also the interactions that connect castes. Such an approach provides a mediating position between Dumont's (1970, 1980) structural model of a fixed caste hierarchy based on the pure/impure opposition and Marriott's (1968, 1976a) transactional model of a dynamic system of caste interactions involving the exchange of food, women, and services.

19 The *Bhagavat Sandarbha* begins, in Anucchedas 1–9, with a discussion of the three aspects of Kṛṣṇa—Brahman, Paramātman, and Bhagavān—and then continues with an extended analysis of the nature of Bhagavān. See also the discussion of the three aspects of Kṛṣṇa in *Caitanya Caritāmṛta* 1.2.2–18, 2.24.57–60.

20 The absolute body (*vigraha*) of Bhagavān is discussed in *Bhagavat Sandarbha* 26–59; *Kṛṣṇa Sandarbha* 105.

21 For discussions of the Gauḍīya *avatāra* system, see De (1960); Dimock (1999: 142–43).

22 For an extended study of these mesocosmic modes of divine embodiment, see Holdrege (n.d.b).

23 For an analysis of the strategies used by the *Bhāgavata Purāṇa* to establish its transcendent authority as Kārṣṇa-Veda and *bhagavad-rūpa*, see Holdrege (2006).

24 For extended analyses of the category of *līlā* in the Gauḍīya tradition, see Haberman (1988); Wulff (1984). For more general treatments of *līlā*, see Kinsley (1979); Sax (1995).

25 For extended studies of Vraja (Hindi, Braj), see Entwistle (1987); Haberman (1994); Corcoran (1995).

26 Among recent studies of image worship in the Gauḍīya tradition, see Valpey (1998, 2006).

27 The identity between Kṛṣṇa and his name is also emphasized in *Bhaktirasāmṛtasindhu* 1.2.233–34, with Jīva Gosvāmin's commentary. See also Hein's (1976) discussion of the theology of the name that undergirds the central Gauḍīya practice of *nāma-kīrtana*, chanting of the divine names.

28 This enumeration of the five practices follows *Caitanya Caritāmṛta* 2.22.74–75, which invokes *Bhaktirasāmṛtasindhu* 1.2.90–3. See also the discussion of the five practices in *Bhaktirasāmṛtasindhu* 1.2.225–44.

29 See *Bhaktirasāmṛtasindhu* 1.2.266–68; *Caitanya Caritāmṛta* 2.22.78, which both cite this passage from the *Bhāgavata Purāṇa* (9.4.18–20).

30 For an overview of the progression from *rāgānugā bhakti* to *prema bhakti*, see *Bhaktirasāmṛtasindhu* 1.2.270–1.4.21. See also the discussion of *rāgānugā bhakti* in *Bhakti Sandarbha* 310–40. For an extended analysis of *rāgānugā bhakti*, see Haberman (1988).

References Cited

Aitareya Brāhmaṇa. 1895–1906. *The Aitareya Brāhmaṇa of the Ṛg Veda* (ed. Satyavrata Samasrami). 4 volumes. Calcutta: Asiatic Society of Bengal.

Aitareya Upaniṣad. 1958. *Aitareya Upaniṣad. In* V. P. Limaye and R. D. Vadekar, eds, *Eighteen Principal Upaniṣads*, 62–67. Poona: Vaidika Samsodhana Mandala.

Bhagavat Sandarbha (of Jīva Gosvāmin). 1951. *Śrīśrībhagavatsandarbhaḥ* (ed. Puridasa Mahasaya). Vrindavan: Haridasa Sarma.

Bhagavat Sandarbha (of Jīva Gosvāmin). 1983. *Śrībhagavatsandarbhaḥ* (ed. Haridasasastri). Vrindavan: Srigadadharagaurahari Press.

Bhāgavata Purāṇa. 1983. *Bhāgavata Purāṇa of Kṛṣṇa Dvaipāyana Vyāsa* (ed. J. L. Shastri). Delhi: Motilal Banarsidass.

Bhaktirasāmṛtasindhu (of Rūpa Gosvāmin). 1946. *Bhaktirasāmṛtasindhu* (ed. Puridasa Mahasaya). Vrindavan: Haridasa Sarma.

Bhakti Sandarbha (of Jīva Gosvāmin). 1951. *Śrīśrībhaktisandarbhaḥ* (ed. Puridasa Mahasaya). Vrindavan: Haridasa Sarma.

Bhakti Sandarbha (of Jīva Gosvāmin). 1985. *Śrībhaktisandarbhaḥ* (ed. Haridasasastri). Vrindavan: Srigadadharagaurahari Press.

Bṛhadāraṇyaka Upaniṣad. 1958. *Bṛhadāraṇyaka Upaniṣad. In* V. P. Limaye and R. D. Vadekar, eds, *Eighteen Principal Upaniṣads*, 174–282. Poona: Vaidika Samsodhana Mandala.

Caitanya Caritāmṛta (of Kṛṣṇadāsa Kavirāja). 1948–52. *Caitanya Caritāmṛta* (ed. Radhagovinda Natha). 6 volumes. Calcutta: Sadhana Prakasani.

Carman, John B. and Frédérique Apffel Marglin, eds. 1985. *Purity and Auspiciousness in Indian Society*. Leiden: E. J. Brill.

Corcoran, Maura. 1995. *Vṛndāvana in Vaiṣṇava Literature: History, Mythology, Symbolism*. Vrindavan: Vrindaban Research Institute.

De, Sushil Kumar. 1960. "The Doctrine of Avatāra (Incarnation) in Bengal Vaiṣṇavism." *In* Sushil Kumar De, *Bengal's Contribution to Sanskrit Literature and Studies in Bengal Vaisnavism*, 143–53. Calcutta: K. L. Mukhopadhyaya.

Dimock, Edward C., Jr., trans. 1999. *Caitanya Caritāmṛta of Kṛṣṇadāsa Kavirāja* (ed. Tony K. Stewart). Cambridge: Department of Sanskrit and Indian Studies, Harvard University.

Douglas, Mary. 1966. *Purity and Danger: An Analysis of Concepts of Pollution and Taboo*. London: Routledge.

Dumont, Louis. 1960. "World Renunciation in Indian Religions." *Contributions to Indian Sociology* 4: 33–62.

Dumont, Louis. 1970 [1966]. *Homo Hierarchicus: An Essay on the Caste System* (trans. Mark Sainsbury). Chicago: University of Chicago Press.

Dumont, Louis. 1980 [1970]. *Homo Hierarchicus: The Caste System and Its Implications* (trans. Mark Sainsbury, Louis Dumont, and Basia Gulati). Chicago: University of Chicago Press.

Entwistle, A. W. 1987. *Braj: Centre of Krishna Pilgrimage*. Groningen: Egbert Forsten.

Flood, Gavin D. 2006. *The Tantric Body: The Secret Tradition of Hindu Religion*. London: I. B. Tauris.

Haberman, David L. 1988. *Acting as a Way of Salvation: A Study of Rāgānugā Bhakti Sādhana*. New York: Oxford University Press.

Haberman, David L. 1994. *Journey through the Twelve Forests: An Encounter with Krishna*. New York: Oxford University Press.

Haberman, David L., trans. 2003. *The Bhaktirasāmṛtasindhu of Rūpa Gosvāmin.* Delhi: Motilal Banarsidass.

Hein, Norvin J. 1976. "Caitanya's Ecstasies and the Theology of the Name." *In* Bardwell L. Smith, ed., *Hinduism: New Essays in the History of Religions*, 15–32. Leiden: E. J. Brill.

Holdrege, Barbara A. 1998. "Body Connections: Hindu Discourses of the Body and the Study of Religion." *International Journal of Hindu Studies* 2, 3: 341–86.

Holdrege, Barbara A. 2006. "From Purāṇa-Veda to Kārṣṇa-Veda: The Bhāgavata Purāṇa as Consummate Smṛti and Śruti Incarnate." *Journal of Vaishnava Studies* 15, 1: 31–70.

Holdrege, Barbara A. n.d.a. "Interrogating *Bhakti.*" *International Journal of Hindu Studies* 11.

Holdrege, Barbara A. n.d.b. *Bhakti and Embodiment: At Play with Kṛṣṇa's Limitless Forms.*

Jaiminīya Brāhmaṇa. 1986 [1954]. *Jaiminīya Brāhmaṇa of the Sāmaveda* (eds Raghu Vira and Lokesh Chandra). Delhi: Motilal Banarsidass.

Kaelber, Walter O. 1989. *Tapta Mārga: Asceticism and Initiation in Vedic India.* Albany: State University of New York Press.

Kauṣītaki Brāhmaṇa (Śāṅkhāyana Brāhmaṇa). 1970. *Śāṅkhāyana-Brāhmaṇaṃ* (ed. Harinarayan Bhattacharya). Calcutta: Sanskrit College.

Kauṣītaki Upaniṣad. 1958. *Kauṣītaki Upaniṣad. In* V. P. Limaye and R. D. Vadekar, eds, *Eighteen Principal Upaniṣads*, 301–24. Poona: Vaidika Samsodhana Mandala.

Kinsley, David R. 1979. *The Divine Player (A Study of Kṛṣṇa Līlā).* Delhi: Motilal Banarsidass.

Kṛṣṇa Sandarbha (of Jīva Gosvāmin). 1951. *Śrīśrīkṛṣṇasandarbhaḥ* (ed. Puridasa Mahasaya). Vrindavan: Haridasa Sarma.

Kṛṣṇa Sandarbha (of Jīva Gosvāmin). 1983. *Śrīkṛṣṇasandarbhaḥ* (ed. Haridasasastri). Vrindavan: Srigadadharagaurahari Press.

Maitri Upaniṣad. 1958. *Maitri Upaniṣad. In* V. P. Limaye and R. D. Vadekar, eds, *Eighteen Principal Upaniṣads*, 325–57. Poona: Vaidika Samsodhana Mandala.

Malamoud, Charles. 1996 [1989]. "Bricks and Words: Observations on the Bodies of the Gods in Vedic India." *In* Charles Malamoud, *Cooking the World: Ritual and Thought in Ancient India* (trans. David White), 207–25. Delhi: Oxford University Press.

Manusmṛti. 1972–85. *Manu-Smṛti* (ed. Jayantakrishna Harikrishna Dave). 6 volumes. Bombay: Bharatiya Vidya Bhavan.

Marglin, Frédérique Apffel. 1977. "Power, Purity and Pollution: Aspects of the Caste System Reconsidered." *Contributions to Indian Sociology* (*n.s.*) 2, 2: 245–70.

Marriott, McKim. 1968. "Caste Ranking and Food Transactions: A Matrix Analysis." *In* Milton Singer and Bernard S. Cohn, eds, *Structure and Change in Indian Society*, 133–71. Chicago: Aldine.

Marriott, McKim. 1969. Review of *Homo hierarchicus: Essai sur le système des castes*, by Louis Dumont. *American Anthropologist* 71, 6: 1166–75.

Marriott, McKim. 1976a. "Hindu Transactions: Diversity without Dualism." *In* Bruce Kapferer, ed., *Transaction and Meaning: Directions in the Anthropology of*

Exchange and Symbolic Behavior, 109–42. Philadelphia: Institute for the Study of Human Issues.

Marriott, McKim. 1976b. "Interpreting Indian Society: A Monistic Alternative to Dumont's Dualism." *Journal of Asian Studies* 36, 1: 189–95.

Marriott, McKim and Ronald B. Inden. 1977. "Toward an Ethnosociology of South Asian Caste Systems." *In* Kenneth David, ed., *The New Wind: Changing Identities in South Asia*, 227–38. The Hague: Mouton.

Olivelle, Patrick. 1995. "Deconstruction of the Body in Indian Asceticism." *In* Vincent L. Wimbush and Richard Valantasis, eds, *Asceticism*, 188–210. New York: Oxford University Press.

Orenstein, Henry. 1965. "The Structure of Hindu Caste Values: A Preliminary Study of Hierarchy and Ritual Defilement." *Ethnology* 4, 1: 1–15.

Orenstein, Henry. 1968. "Toward a Grammar of Defilement in Hindu Sacred Law." *In* Milton Singer and Bernard S. Cohn, eds, *Structure and Change in Indian Society*, 115–31. Chicago: Aldine.

Orenstein, Henry. 1970. "Logical Congruence in Hindu Sacred Law: Another Interpretation." *Contributions to Indian Sociology* (*n.s.*) 4: 22–35.

Pañcaviṃśa Brāhmaṇa (Tāṇḍya Brāhmaṇa). 1870–74. *Tāṇḍya Mahābrāhmaṇa* (ed. Anandachandra Vedantavagisa). 2 volumes. Calcutta: Asiatic Society of Bengal.

Ramanujan, A. K., trans. 1993 [1981]. *Hymns for the Drowning: Poems for Viṣṇu by Nammāḻvār*. New Delhi: Penguin.

Ṛg Veda Saṃhitā. 1890–92 [1849–74]. *Rig-Veda-Saṃhitā* (ed. F. Max Müller). London: Oxford University Press.

Śatapatha Brāhmaṇa. 1964 [1855]. *The Śatapatha-Brāhmaṇa* (ed. Albrecht Weber). Varanasi: Chowkhamba Sanskrit Series Office.

Sax, William S., ed. 1995. *The Gods at Play: Līlā in South Asia*. New York: Oxford University Press.

Silburn, Lilian. 1988 [1983]. *Kuṇḍalinī: The Energy of the Depths. A Comprehensive Study Based on the Scriptures of Nondualistic Kaśmir Śaivism* (trans. Jacques Gontier). Albany: State University of New York Press.

Smith, Brian K. 1989. *Reflections on Resemblance, Ritual, and Religion*. New York: Oxford University Press.

Smith, Brian K. 1994. *Classifying the Universe: The Ancient Indian Varṇa System and the Origins of Caste*. New York: Oxford University Press.

Srinivas, M. N. 1952. *Religion and Society among the Coorgs of South India*. Oxford: Clarendon Press.

Stevenson, H. N. C. 1954. "Status Evaluation in the Hindu Caste System." *Journal of the Royal Anthropological Institute of Great Britain and Ireland* 84, 1–2: 45–65.

Śvetāśvatara Upaniṣad. 1958. *Śvetāśvatara Upaniṣad. In* V. P. Limaye and R. D. Vadekar, eds, *Eighteen Principal Upaniṣads*, 283–300. Poona: Vaidika Samsodhana Mandala.

Tambiah, S. J. 1973. "From *Varṇa* to Caste through Mixed Unions." *In* Jack Goody, ed., *The Character of Kinship*, 191–229. Cambridge: Cambridge University Press.

Tattva Sandarbha (of Jīva Gosvāmin). 1954 [1951]. *Śrīśrītattvasandarbhaḥ* (ed. Puridasa Mahasaya). Vrindavan: Haridasa Sarma.

Tattva Sandarbha (of Jīva Gosvāmin). 1982. *Śrī Tattvasandarbhaḥ* (ed. Haridasasastri). Vrindavan: Srigadadharagaurahari Press.

Tull, Herman W. 1989. *The Vedic Origins of Karma: Cosmos as Man in Ancient Indian Myth and Ritual*. Albany: State University of New York Press.

Valpey, Kenneth R. 1998. "Kṛṣṇa-Sevā: Theology of Image Worship in Gauḍīya-Vaiṣṇavism." M.A. thesis. Berkeley: Graduate Theological Union Library.

Valpey, Kenneth Russell. 2006. *Attending Kṛṣṇa's Image: Caitanya Vaiṣṇava Mūrti-Sevā as Devotional Truth*. New York: Routledge.

Waghorne, Joanne Punzo and Norman Cutler, in association with Vasudha Narayanan, eds. 1985. *Gods of Flesh/Gods of Stone: The Embodiment of Divinity in India*. Chambersburg: Anima.

White, David Gordon. 1996. *The Alchemical Body: Siddha Traditions in Medieval India*. Chicago: University of Chicago Press.

Wulff, Donna M. 1984. *Drama as a Mode of Religious Realization: The Vidagdhamādhava of Rūpa Gosvāmī*. Chico: Scholars Press.

3

Cinema

Philip Lutgendorf

Seeing
Hearing
Tasting
Telling
Concluding Reflections

Indian popular films have a definite "flavor." This is generally recognized (and one indigenous descriptor of them is indeed as *masālā* or "spicy"), even by Anglo-Americans who encounter them while surfing cable TV channels—and not simply because the actors happen to be Indian. The films look, sound, and feel different in important ways, and a kind of cinematic culture shock may accompany a first prolonged exposure. An American film scholar, after viewing his first "*masālā* blockbuster," remarked to me that the various cinemas he had studied—American, French, Japanese, African—all seemed to play by a similar set of aesthetic rules, "but this is a different universe." Experienced viewers are familiar with the sometimes negative responses of neophyte visitors to this universe: The complaint that its films "all look the same," are mind-numbingly long, have incoherent plots and raucous music, belong to no known genre but appear to be a mish-mash of several, and are naive and crude imitations of "real" (i.e., Hollywood) movies, and so on—all, by the way, complaints that are regularly voiced by some Indians as well, particularly by critics writing in English. They also know that millions of people, including vast audiences outside the Indian subcontinent, apparently understand and love the "difference" of these films.

In film studies, a long-reigning Copernican discourse on "cinema" in general (i.e., American and, to a lesser extent, European) occasionally digressed to consider "national cinemas" as represented by a few auteurs. India was associated with the Bengali "art films" of Satyajit Ray, with an occasional bemused reference to "the lip-synched Bollywood musical" (Pramaggiore and Wallis 2005: 341; cf. Corrigan and White 2004: 375)—a designation that dismisses (by conservative estimate) more than 30,000 feature films produced since the advent of sound in 1931. That this enormous and influential body of popular art is now beginning to receive scholarly notice suggests the need for, at least, systemic realignment (as when a big new planet swims into our ken); a more audacious suggestion is that its "different universe" might make possible an Einsteinian paradigm shift by introducing new ways of thinking about the space-time of cinematic narrative.

That is, of course, if the universe is truly "different." Assertions of the distinctive "Indianness" of Indian popular cinema—or its lack—have emerged from a variety of scholarly approaches,[1] namely:

1 Cultural-historical: This approach traces the distinct features of Indian cinema to older styles of oral and theatrical performance, some of which survive into modern times. A fairly standard genealogy cites the ancient epics *Rāmāyaṇa* and *Mahābhārata*, classical Sanskrit drama, regional folk theaters of the medieval-to-modern period, and the Parsi theater of the late nineteenth and early twentieth centuries (e.g., Dissanayake and Sahai 1992: 9–17; Lutze 1985; Mishra 1985, 2002: 4–15, 39–45).
2 Technological: Here the distinctive features of Indian cinema are traced to the advent of technologies of image reproduction during the second half of the nineteenth century, resulting in the rapid evolution and dissemination of a common visual code for theatrical staging, poster art, cinema, comic books, advertising, and so on (Jain 2007; Pinney 1999; Rajadhyaksha 1987; Ramaswamy 2003). A related approach, confined to cinema itself, analyzes camerawork and sound, noting Indian filmmakers' rejection of the "invisible style" and "centering" principle of classic Hollywood in favor of an esthetic of "frontality" (especially in early "mythologicals"), "flashy" camerawork, and a consciously artificial style, further heightened by the use of non-synch sound and "playback" singing (e.g., Dissanayake and Sahai 1992: 19–20; Manuel 1993: 37–59; Vasudevan 2000b: 105).
3 Psychological-mythic: This approach reads popular films as "contemporary myths which, through the vehicle of fantasy and the process of identification, temporarily heal for their audience the principal stresses arising out of Indian family relationships" (Kakar 1983: 97). The favored approach is psychoanalytic (e.g., Kakar 1989: 25–41), although there has been one ambitious attempt to use a "mythological" film to modify a basic Freudian paradigm with respect to Indian culture (Kurtz 1992).
4 Political-economic: The political-economic approach, drawing on the Marxist-influenced critical social theory of the Frankfurt school, attributes the distinctive features of Indian popular cinema to the material and sociopolitical conditions of twentieth-century India and of the film industry itself and argues that the films encode an ideology that "subsumes" a modernist agenda of egalitarianism, individualism, and radical social change within a feudal and nonegalitarian status quo (e.g.,

Kazmi 1999; Prasad 1998). Other similarly ambitious surveys see popular films as essentially allegorizing the political history of the nation-state (e.g., S. Chakravarty 1993; Virdi 2003).

These approaches are neither exhaustive nor incompatible; many scholars combine two or more. It is fairly common to invoke the first by way of sketching a cultural background and then to proceed to one or more of the others, perhaps analyzing a single film in their terms (e.g., Dissanayake and Sahai 1992). At times, however, there is an element of antagonism between proponents of the first and fourth approaches. On the one hand, one encounters grandiose claims that the classical tradition—and especially the two Sanskrit epics—constitute "the great code" of popular filmmaking and that "any theoretical critique of Bombay Cinema must begin with a systematic analysis of the grand Indian metatext and 'founder of (Indian) discursivity,' namely the…[*Mahābhārata/Rāmāyaṇa*]" (Mishra 1985: 145). This is a claim that is sometimes made by filmmakers themselves, as when Mumbai director Dharmesh Darshan tells an interviewer, "In India, our stories depend on the *Ramayan*—all our stories are somewhere connected to this holy book" (Kabir 2001: 93; see also Thomas 1995: 182n35). On the other hand, a Marxist scholar criticizes "anthropologists and Indologists or others employing the tools of these disciplines" for their tendency "to read popular cinema as evidence of the unbroken continuity of Indian culture and its tenacity in the face of the assault of modernity" (Prasad 1998: 15). He warns that such "eternalist proclamations…while claiming to reveal the truth about Indian cinema, actually contribute to the maintenance of an Indological myth: the myth of the mythically minded Indian" (Prasad 1998: 17).

In what follows, I use my training as a folklorist and student of oral performance and popular narrative traditions to revisit the first approach cited above, but I do so mindful of the criticisms just offered. I have no wish to contribute to what Fareed Kazmi calls "the fetishisation of tradition" (1999: 62), to suggest that there is an unchanging "essence" of Indian performance, or to imply that some genetic inheritance predisposes South Asians to relish three-hour spectacles of music, dance, and high emotion. Such tastes reflect nurture, not nature. They are influenced by diverse forces that change over time, as are the films that cater to them. The claim that popular films are all based on epic archetypes is demonstrably groundless, as is the hyperbolic (and insulting) generalization that they reflect folk traditions "that impinge on the Indian's psyche and never allow him to escape from the psychological parameters of being an Indian villager" (Saari 1985: 16)—an assessment that reduces a population of more than one billion (increasing numbers of whom now live in urban areas) to (male) embodiments of an inescapably rustic "Indian psyche." But the Marxist reduction is scarcely more satisfying: M.

Madhava Prasad's argument (1998: 64–72) for the decades-long dominance of a single ideological master narrative hinges on a few roughly sketched plot outlines, omits questions of reception, and ignores the films' poetic and musical component altogether.

The practices and conventions that I discuss are observably pervasive of the Indian cultural environment, alluded to in verbal idioms, body language, and ubiquitous iconography. Hence, they can be relearned by successive generations, though their precise forms at a given moment are of course subject to historical contingency and outside influence. Indeed, the "hybridity" of Indian popular cinema is another of its proverbial features: its pastiche and parody of foreign forms and practices and its frequent borrowing of camera shots, plot ideas, and musical styles. Although every cinema borrows, the specific forms that borrowing assumes in the postcolonial South Asian context and the economic and cultural forces that influence it are indeed deserving of study. Here I only propose that the visual and musical hybridity of this cinema has itself become, like other ingredients in its overall *masālā* mix, one of its distinctively "Indian" features—identifying it as, in Anil Saari's words, "an eclectic, assimilative, imitative, and plagiaristic creature that is constantly rebelling against its influences" (1985: 16).

Rosie Thomas has observed that "films are in no sense a simple reflection of the wider society, but are produced by an apparatus that has its own momentum and logic" (1995: 179). She thus underscores the power of cinematic conventions, whatever their genealogy, to rapidly become self-perpetuating, serving to educate both audiences and producers in the expectation of what a film ought to be. Because the makers of commercial films constantly strive to fulfill audience expectations, it may well be true that the single biggest influence on Indian popular cinema has long been Indian popular cinema. Yet it is equally clear that the distinctive conventions of this art form, which have tenaciously resisted the influence of Western cinemas, did not arise in a cultural vacuum.

The aim of this chapter, first of all, is to give novice students of Indian popular cinema an acquaintance with some of the terms, texts, and narrative genres that are regularly cited in studies of its cultural origins, along with references to relevant primary and secondary sources. In addition, I seek to correct certain imbalances and omissions in the standard genealogical narrative, as outlined earlier, by presenting material (e.g., on the Indo-Islamic romance tradition) that has been omitted by other scholars. Finally, I aim to suggest ways in which selected resources drawn from the Indian cultural heritage might be applied not only to the study of Indian cinema (as an exotic "other" to Western cinemas) but more broadly to the study of cinema in general.

Seeing

Academic scholarship took more than half a century to begin to look at cinematic "looking" and indeed at cinema itself as a subject of serious inquiry. The delay may have reflected not merely the inertia of disciplines but a more ingrained prejudice toward text over image traceable at least to the Reformation and Enlightenment. The subsequent proliferation of ever more sophisticated technologies for the reproduction of images was experienced by some scholars as a worrisome onslaught on the cerebral realm of verbal discourse, which may explain why film studies as a discipline initially arose as an offshoot of literary criticism, accommodating film as another form of "text." As Prasad points out, the development of critical vocabulary for analyzing the visual aspect of film (such as the concepts of "male gaze" and "scopophilia"; e.g., Mulvey 1975) has tended to assume an essentially "realist" cinema whose spectator "occupies an isolated, individualized position of voyeurism coupled with an anchoring identification with a figure in the narrative" (Prasad 1998: 74)—an assumption that is problematic when applied to Indian commercial films. A yet more holistic appreciation of the cinematic experience remains a challenging agenda, and sound and music continue to be relatively neglected in scholarship. As I note shortly, this intellectual genealogy may be contrasted to an Indian synaesthetic discourse, dating back some fifteen centuries, which is based squarely on visual and aural performance.

Vision and sound already interact in the hymns of the *Ṛg Veda*, attributed to poets who were known both as "singers" (*kavi*) and "seers" (*ṛṣi*) and were credited with the ability to "see" the gods and the "sound-formulas" (*mantra*) of the hymns, suggesting a blurring of the senses in mystical experience. *Ṛṣi*, conventionally translated "sage," comes from the Sanskrit verb root *dṛś*, which has a double meaning also found in comparable verbs used in modern Indian languages (e.g., the Hindi verb *dekhnā*): it means both "to see" and "to look at." Indeed, "seeing" was (and continues to be) understood as a tangible encounter in which sight reaches out to "touch" objects and "take" them back into the seer (hence *dekhnā* is normally compounded with *lenā*, "to take," also used for verbs of ingestion). Likewise derived from *dṛś* is the noun *darśana*, "seeing, looking at," a term that assumed great importance after the decline of the Vedic sacrificial cult and the rise, during the first millennium of the Common Era, of the worship of gods embodied in tangible images.

The iconic prolixity of Hinduism is a commonplace. There are said to be "three hundred thirty million gods," and their representations typically bristle with supernumerary heads, arms, and weapons. A shared and striking feature of the deities is their eyes, often huge and elongated, which gaze directly at the viewer. The theo-visual spectacle of the Hindu pantheon was, however, "hard to see" for most European observers prior to the twentieth century, and they dismissed it either as "demonic" or as a distorted simulacrum of the "realist" aesthetic of Greco-Roman civilization (Mitter 1977)—the latter assessment prefiguring one common Western response to the visual code of Indian popular films. When Hindu images are crafted, their painted or inlaid eyes are customarily added last and then ritually "opened," establishing the deity within the icon and making him or her available for the primary act of worship, which is "seeing-looking" (*darśana*; Hindi *darśan*). In Indian English, people go to temples "to take *darśan*"; Hindi favors "to do *darśan*" (*darśan karnā*)—both idioms imply a willful and tangible act. "Darśanic" contact invites the exchange of substance through the eyes, which are not simply "windows of the soul" but portals to a self that is conceived as relatively less autonomous and bounded and more psychically permeable than in Western understandings (F. Smith 2006). *Darśan* may also refer to the auspicious sight of powerful places and persons; holy people and kings (and politicians and filmstars) "give *darśan*" to those who approach them.

The derivatives of Sanskrit *dṛś* do not exhaust the vocabulary of seeing in South Asia. The word "*nazar*" ("look" or "glance"), imported from Arabic and Persian, has similar connotations of tangible exchange and is common both in everyday speech (where it figures in a large number of idioms) and in Indo-Islamic religious discourse. It is applied to the eye contact of lovers, especially the first sight that arouses passion, and also to the benign gaze of Ṣūfī masters, which watches over and protects their disciples. A similar range of meanings is conveyed by idioms using the Persian-derived *nigāh*, which translates as "look" or "glance," yet connotes a more potent contact than these English words. It also connotes, in the context of a culture that idealized (and sometimes practiced) the veiling of respectable women, an illicit glimpse that can give rise to intense "love at first sight" that is disruptive of social and familial hierarchy. Another potentially dangerous side of sight—when negative feelings or forces exit or enter through the eyes—is also invoked through idioms of a "black" or "evil" gaze (*kālī nazar, burī nazar*) from which one seeks protection. Such looks are associated with powerful and proscribed desires—especially lust, envy, or covetousness.

Long overlooked even by scholars of Hindu religious traditions, the everyday concept of *darśan* (for which the key text is Diana Eck's 1981 study) has recently come to be invoked in scholarship on Indian cinema (Prasad 1998: 74–78; Vasudevan 2000a: 139–47, 2000b: 119–20n52). The ideology and practice of *darśan*/*nazar* has contributed to a cinematic aesthetic of "frontality," especially in early mythological films that recapitulated the conventions of poster illustration: The deity-actor, often centrally framed within a static tableau, was positioned to invite sustained eye contact with the viewer (A. Kapur 1993: 92; G. Kapur 1987: 80). It likewise contributes to the more ubiquitous fetish, across all cinematic genres and periods, for eyes and glances, especially in scenes between lovers (Taylor 2002), and the great emphasis (also notable in Indian dance, folk theater, and miniature painting) on the eyes as communicators of emotion (e.g., the popular 1970s and 1980s technique of repeated facial zoom shots, locking on the eyes, during moments of high emotion). But there is more to cinematic "seeing" than this, because *darśan* is a "gaze" that is *returned*. In a crowded Hindu temple, one can observe worshipers positioning themselves so that their eyes have a clear line of contact with those of the god. Their explanations emphasize that they do not merely want to *see* the deity, but to *be seen by him or her* so that the deity's powerful and unwavering gaze may *enter into* them. I have sometimes translated *darśan* as "visual communion," but "visual dialog" or "visual intercourse" might be better, if one tones down the latter phrase's sexual vibe—without removing it entirely. But whereas a deity's act of seeing is normally only vicariously sensed by his or her observer, the invention of the motion picture camera and of the shot-reverse shot technique enabled the film viewer for the first time to assume, so to speak, *both* positions in the darśanic act. This is evident in surviving footage from pioneer filmmaker D. G. Phalke's *Kaliya Mardan* (The Slaying of Serpent Kaliya, 1919), in which a poster-like frontal tableau of the child Kṛṣṇa (played by Phalke's daughter Mandakini) dancing on a subdued serpent yields to a Kṛṣṇa-eye-view of the assembled crowd of worshipers, gazing at "him" in reverent awe. This technique became a commonplace in mythological films (for a sustained example, see the first song sequence in *Jai Santoshi Maa*, 1975), but its ubiquity should not obscure its religious significance. The camera's invitation to gaze through the deity's (or star's) eyes heightens the experience of the reciprocity of *darśan*, closing an experiential loop to evoke (in a characteristically Hindu move) an underlying unity (Lutgendorf 2002: 28).

Sensitivity to the interactive nature of *darśan* might provide a different way of thinking about the visual experience of film. If cinematic "realism" offers an essentially voyeuristic peep into, in Christian Metz's (1986) words, "a world that is seen without giving itself to be seen" (cited in Prasad 1998: 72), the self-conscious style of the Indian popular film provides what Prasad rightly calls "a representation that gives itself to be seen" (1998: 73). This indeed parallels what Hindu deities do on the stages of their shrine-theaters, but their viewers' response is neither stupefied nor mute. Unlike the "gaze" of Western film theory, *darśan* is a two-way street: a visual interaction between players who, though not equal, are certainly both in the same theater of activity and capable of influencing each other, especially in the vital realm of emotion.

Hearing

Discussions of the conventions of Indian popular cinema in terms of those of premodern performance genres often invoke ancient Sanskrit drama and its authoritative treatise, the *Nāṭya Śāstra*, yet they seldom offer detailed information about this text. A treatise in thirty-six chapters, the *Nāṭya Śāstra* purports to describe the origin and development of drama and to treat virtually every aspect of the composition and staging of plays.[2] Although the text at one point concedes the possibility of a theatrical style based on naturalistic imitation of human behavior (which it terms *lokadharmī* or "according to the way of the world"—that is, "realistic"), it disposes of this in a mere two verses (*Nāṭya Śāstra* 14.62–63; Rangacharya 1996: 115) and instead devotes itself to what it terms the "theatrical" or "artificial" style (*nāṭyadharmī*), though *nāṭya* (literally, "to be danced") should not be translated generically as "theater." Rather, it refers to an operatic dance-drama characterized by an alternation between spoken and sung passages and in which "speech is artificial and exaggerated, actions unusually emotional, gestures graceful" (*Nāṭya Śāstra* 14.64–65; Rangacharya 1996: 115).

The fact that drama itself is sometimes defined synaesthetically in the *Nāṭya Śāstra* as "visible poetry" (*dṛśya kāvya*; Rangacharya 1996: 356) suggests the aptness of the standard Indian-English word for the visuals in a modern filmsong sequence, which are identified as the "picturization" of the music and lyrics. This format of alternately spoken and sung performance, which gave great emphasis to poetic and musical expression of emotion, survived the demise of Sanskrit drama toward the end of the first millennium CE and became characteristic of a range of regional folk dramatic forms using vernacular languages; it was transferred to the urban proscenium stage by the (mainly Hindi-Urdu language) "Parsi theatre" troupes of the nineteenth century. It also became, after the introduction of film sound to India in 1931, the standard format for commercial cinema. Just as, in Sanskrit and most regional languages, there was no word for "play" that did not imply "music-and-dance drama," so Indian-English "film" normally means one incorporating songs and dances, and there has never been a separate genre category of "musical" in the Hollywood sense.

The rhetorical and musical dimensions of Indian popular cinema, like those of older genres of performance, present a challenge to English-language viewers. Although the hybrid melodies, instrumentation, and rhythms of film songs may be appreciated as music, the poetry of their lyrics is lost—even when (as is unfortunately not always the case) song sequences are subtitled on commercial DVD releases. Dialog subtitles too mostly fail to convey the clever colloquial patois, dramatic innuendo, wordplay, double entendre, and intertextual referencing that abounds in these films and that makes "*filmī* dialog" a performance genre unto itself—an artificial but admired speech register that is jokingly referred to in such Hindi expressions as "*filmī ḍāylog mārnā*" (to speak in an exaggeratedly emotional manner). To a far greater extent than is the case in America, the remembered language of popular films—phrases from dialog and lyrics of songs—circulate in everyday speech together with other bodies of oral tradition (such as aphoristic couplets from such medieval poet-saints as Kabīr and Mīrābāī) and contribute to a range of casual "performances"—as when one speaker cites part of a line of film dialog and another completes it.

In successful Indian films, substantial artistic weight is carried by dialogs structured as rhetorical set-pieces and by songs that are sometimes penned by renowned poets. Given their importance to audiences, the rhetorical and musical aspects of popular films have been grossly neglected in scholarly analysis—dismissed as insignificant relics of earlier performance genres (Prasad 1998: 111, 136) or as mere "spectacle" randomly inserted into the cinematic narrative (Dissanayake and Sahai 1992: 18). Other scholars, however, have proposed that the "message" of an Indian film is hardly confined to its plotline (especially given the characteristically "loose" form of the latter, to be discussed shortly) and that the work of song, dance, and dialog is at times precisely to fissure the surface ideology of a film, by allowing the expression of suppressed desires and subjectivities (Booth 2000: 126; Mishra 2002: 161–65; Vasudevan 2000b: 117).

Tasting

One of the most influential and intriguing components of the *Nāṭya Śāstra* is its aesthetic theory, elucidated mainly in chapters six and seven. These serve as locus classicus for the concepts of *bhāva* ("emotion, mood") and *rasa* ("juice, flavor, essence"), which were further developed by later writers on drama and poetry and indeed by theologians and metaphysicians—for aesthetic pleasure came to be regarded as on a continuum with or as a means to transcendent bliss (*ānanda*). The seeds of this understanding are already present in the *Nāṭya Śāstra*'s own frame story that identifies theater as a "fifth Veda" synthesizing and in a sense superceding the traditional four bodies of revealed knowledge.

Like the Greek philosophers, ancient Indian thinkers were interested in why people enjoy theater and in what they "get" from it; specifically, in why they derive pleasure from seeing things on stage that would not be pleasurable in everyday life. Whereas Aristotle posited *katharsis*, a purgation or cleansing, the authors of the *Nāṭya Śāstra* and their successors favored a more complex explanation. In their view, primary and individualized human emotions (*bhāva*) generated by the multifarious experiences of life are transmuted, through their representation by actors in a dramatic spectacle, into universalized emotional "flavors" (*rasa*) that may be savored by audience members at the safe remove that theater provides (Masson and Patwardhan 1970, 1: 24). The complexity of the theory arises in part from the elucidation of the primary emotions comprising love, mirth, anger, pity, heroic vigor, wonder, disgust, and terror—these eight become sixteen, as each *bhāva* induces a corresponding *rasa* that then proliferate geometrically into further subcategories (e.g., *Nāṭya Śāstra* 7.6–8; Rangacharya 1996: 65). What is most notable for my purpose is the assumption that, though a given performance will have a predominant *rasa* (thus a farce will be dominated by *hāsya rasa*, or the comic flavor, and a martial saga by *vīrya rasa*, or the heroic), it is expected to offer a range of others as well. The imagery used is somatic and in fact gustatory, locating aesthetic pleasure in the body as much as in the mind; thus, the text asserts that a drama's *rasa* may be likened to the taste produced "when various condiments and sauces and herbs and other materials are mixed" (*Nāṭya Śāstra* 6.31–33; Rangacharya 1996: 55). Further, it is understood that *rasa*s are fleeting and may be enjoyed serially; a successful performance is thus akin to a well-designed banquet or smorgasbord, serving up *rasa* after *rasa* for spectators to savor.

Although modern filmgoers seldom specialize in classical aesthetic theory, the vocabulary of *bhāva* and *rasa* remains in use in Indian vernaculars, and the broad cultural consensus is that a satisfying cinematic entertainment ought to generate a succession of sharply delineated emotional moods. Whereas Western viewers are sometimes distressed by what seem to them a mélange of genres (comedy, action-adventure, romance, and so on) and too-abrupt transitions in mood (a tragic scene yielding to a comic one, and then to a romantic song set in a fantasied landscape), Indian audiences take such shifts in stride and may even complain if a film does not deliver the anticipated range of emotions (though they also at times complain of pointlessness in film sequences if the moods evoked do not in some sense cohere into a satisfying whole). Performance theorist Richard Schechner (2001) has observed that whereas Western theater tends to be "plot-driven," Indian theater is more typically "*rasa*-driven" and has suggested that a familiarity with (what he terms) "rasaesthetics"—a more somatically based understanding of the effect of performed emotions on the spectator—could enlarge the conceptual vocabulary of Western critical theory (cf. Schechner 1985: 136–42).[3]

Telling

There is general consensus among scholars that the storytelling conventions of Indian popular cinema are significantly different than those of most other film industries. Accounts of that difference generally focus on the "complexity" and "loose structure" of the plots, their lack of a "linear" narrative, and the presence of "discontinuities" in the form of both subplots and song and dance sequences. Such understandings take the form of assessments either negative or positive. Bengali director Satyajit Ray complained, back in 1976, of the commercial cinema's "penchant for convolutions of plot and counter-plot rather than the strong, simple unidirectional narrative" (23), such as he favored in his own films. Wimal Dissanayake and Malti Sahai, conversely, offer a more appreciative and culture-specific assessment: "Although...Indian cinema was heavily influenced by Hollywood, the art of narration with its endless digressions, circularities, and plots within plots remained distinctly Indian" (1992: 10–11).

Indian filmmakers are well aware of the alternative, "tighter" narrative models of foreign cinemas, yet they consistently reject these, even as they readily appropriate specific plot elements and shot sequences. The influence of the classical epic traditions must be noted. References to the *Rāmāyaṇa* and the *Mahābhārata*—each of which should be understood not as a fixed, Sanskrit-language text but rather as a multiform and intertextual storytelling tradition existing in hundreds of literary versions as well as in oral and visual performances—abound in popular art, from ubiquitous "god posters" to comic books to television advertising. Their themes (which include the tension between social duty and personal satisfaction and between the lifestyles of renunciant and householder, the nature and transmission of authority, and the proper relationships between family members and social classes) are alluded to in everyday speech and formal discourse; images of their principal divine characters inhabit countless temples and shrines. Yet the assumption that these epics "influence" popular films must be qualified.

Though there have been scores of film versions of each epic or (more commonly, given their length and complexity) of subsidiary episodes drawn from them, the sum total of such productions still comprises only a small portion of cinematic output. Far more common are allusions, in "secular" stories, to epic motifs via character names, dialog, or visual coding. As Gregory Booth observes, epic content "usually forms a secondary or allusory subtext rather than primary text" in Hindi films (1995: 173). Such allusions presume an audience that is broadly familiar with the epics and offer it a pleasurable experience of recognition, but they coexist with many other references—to folktales, historical and current events, and indeed other films. It is the structure of the epics and of a much larger body of popular narrative rather than their specific content that presents a parallel to the way in which film stories unfold. Dissanayake and Sahai observe,

> Instead of the linear and direct narratives that conceal their narrativities, that we encounter in Hollywood films, the mainline Indian cinema presents us with a different order of diegesis that can best be comprehended in terms of the narrative discontinuities found in the *Ramayaṇa* and the *Mahabharata*.
>
> (1992: 11)

What is the nature of these "discontinuities"?

Apart from their sheer prolixity, with stories that span generations (three in the *Rāmāyaṇa*, seven in the *Mahābhārata*) and introduce scores of important characters, the pan-Indian epics share a number of structural features. They are both "emboxed" by frame narratives that identify their authors (who are themselves characters in their stories) and the circumstances of their telling and that thus recapitulate the conventions of oral performance. Yet once the "main" tale begins, unfolding as a flashback, it too may be regularly interrupted by subordinate tales, which branch off from and return to it and which it, in turn, "frames." These substories often recapitulate themes found in the larger plot, but with variations—as in a baroque fugue or (more aptly) a classical *rāga*. Though they may strike Western readers as "digressions" from the "main story," they are not regarded as such by their primary audience, which savors the slow unfolding of the tale through such detours.

Yet the *Rāmāyaṇa* and *Mahābhārata* have always shared the spotlight, and in a real sense interacted, not merely with each other but with other genres of popular storytelling that adhere to some of the same narrative conventions—favoring sprawling, epic tales—but that foreground rather different values. Regional folk epics, such as that of Pābūjī in Rajasthani (J. Smith 1991), Ḍolā in Hindi (Wadley 1989, 2004), Palnāḍu in Telugu (Roghair 1982), and the "three twins" in Tamil (Beck 1982), often celebrate the ethos of lower-status but upwardly mobile groups, linking them to pan-Indian and Sanskritic mythology but also asserting local identity and agency. Like many modern films, these complex tales may themselves make oblique reference to the pan-Indian epics, as when the popular Hindi martial cycle of Ālhā-Ūdal is interpreted as a "*Mahābhārata* of the *kali yuga*," in which the vanquished warriors of the older epic, now reincarnated, become victors (Schomer 1989; Hiltebeitel 1999: 121–23). Structural analysis of such epic storytelling—traditionally performed by bards in multisession, all-night performances—has yielded some interesting typologies, such as Stuart Blackburn and Joyce Flueckiger's (1989) division of Indian folk epics into the broad categories of martial, sacrificial, romantic, and mythic. Booth (1995: 176–79) has proposed that these categories might better serve for analyzing mainstream films than the vague and overlapping commercial "genre" divisions sometimes invoked (for example, "mythological," "social," and "historical").

The prestige of the Sanskrit epics has also tended to eclipse, at least for outsiders, the popularity of narrative traditions that, although similarly imbued with myth and fantasy, express a decidedly more worldly, sensual, and entertainment-oriented ethos. Such are the popular tales of the first millennium CE that eventually found their way into the massive Sanskrit anthology *Kathāsaritsāgara* (Ocean of Rivers of the Great Story), where they are framed as a heavenly entertainment told by Śiva to his wife, Pārvatī. These tales often feature heroes who are wily merchants, disenfranchised princes, or poor (but not especially pious) Brāhmaṇas and whose aim is less the pursuit of *dharma* than the acquisition of wealth and worldly power; they also enjoy love affairs with glamorous women along the way. To accomplish their ends, the heroes often undertake impersonations, commit thefts, and carry out adulterous seductions, and though they are occasionally assisted by supernatural forces, they just as frequently skewer both pious pomposity and folk superstition. The pace and style and the self-assertive ethos of these "action-adventure" tales, which are characterized by abrupt plot turns and mood shifts, dramatic reunions and recognitions, and lyrical interludes set in demi-divine or magical realms, are indeed suggestive of *masālā* films (see, for example, van Buitenen 1959: 111–27, 179–258). They also include a feature that is generally not foregrounded in the ancient epics (though it sometimes enters into their oral retelling): a strong current of (often irreverent) humor. Though recorded in a number of famous texts, such stories remained in oral circulation throughout the premodern period and, with the coming of typography, found their way into the flourishing Hindi-Urdu chapbook literature known as *qissā* and *kahānī* (Pritchett 1985).

There remains another confluent current of Indian popular narrative to be noted, one that is of special significance for popular cinema. I refer to a strongly Islamicate strain, which has generally been overlooked by scholars invoking the "epic" genealogy of mainstream films. I use "Islamicate" rather than "Islamic" to refer not to the impact of Muslim religion but to the influence of a cosmopolitan urbanized culture that set norms for much of western, central, and South Asia for roughly a thousand years. This culture, reflected in, for example, styles of dress, diction, architecture, and music, was embraced to a considerable extent even by polities that remained "Hindu" in their ritual practices or that even articulated an "anti-Islamic" ideology (Kesavan 1994: 245–46; Wagoner 1996). The narrative traditions of the medieval Perso-Arabic and Turkic-speaking world had themselves been influenced by ancient Indian story literature (for South Asia, or al-Hind, was famed to the West as the "land of story"), but they had also evolved their own distinctive tales, in which fairies and *jinns* took the place of the demi-divine beings of Indian lore, sorcerers replaced Tantric adepts, and the hero's love affairs were inflected with a Ṣūfī flavor, permitting readings as allegories of a divine quest. Though the pain of separated lovers had long been celebrated in Indian poetry and story, the Ṣūfī influence, together with the strict gender codes of many Islamic societies accentuated the theme of a hero's consuming infatuation for an inaccessible beloved, culminating in romantic desperation and even death ("martyrdom" in the way of love, mystically allegorized to *fanā* or the "annihilation" of self in divine unity).

The Islamicate strain in cinema is often overlooked. Although the Maharashtrian Brāhmaṇa D. G. Phalke based his early feature films on Hindu legend, the growing industry soon reached out to a broader narrative pool. With the coming of sound, Persianized Hindi-Urdu with its strong literary and romantic associations became the dominant language of Bombay cinema (Kesavan 1994), and plots were often drawn from Indo-Persian romances, as in the five remakes of the story of Lailā and Majnūn—a tale that ranks with that of *Devdas* as one of the most often filmed in Hindi cinema (Booth 1995: 179). The highly charged lyrics of Hindi filmsongs, with their Islamicate vocabulary, are not merely conventionalized inserts without "social currency" (Prasad 1998: 111); they evoke a world of romantic and refined entertainment that encodes powerful emotional ideals and a history of cultural syncretism.

Concluding Reflections

While studying the popular culture of premodern India—a society that prized the tactile act of "seeing" as a medium of communication; delighted in episodic, nonlinear tales that were elaborately and self-consciously framed; and regarded operatic dance-drama as the ultimate art form—it has often struck me that its heroes and heroines were eagerly awaiting cinematic reincarnation. Within their profuse intertextual world, premodern Indian storytellers were already fond of flashbacks, lyrical interludes, surreal landscapes, and vast and crowded Cinemascopic tableaux; their language was visually intense, almost hallucinatory: screenplays awaiting the screen. A gaze that is more sensitive to Indian contexts will be better able to take in the audiovisual epics of their cinematic heirs and to savor (and critically evaluate) the *rasa* they offer to hundreds of millions of filmgoers.

Notes

1 With a few exceptions (e.g., Dickey 1993; Pandian 1992), most English-language scholarship has focused on the widely distributed Hindi-Urdu cinema based in Bombay-Mumbai, despite the fact that this industry has always existed

in a complex and interactive relationship with cinemas in other languages. Although my own linguistic limitations oblige me to perpetuate this imbalance, I look forward to emerging scholarship that will contribute to a more nuanced picture of intra-Indian influences. It is equally important to note that I do not intend to conflate "Indian" cultural forms with exclusively "Hindu" ones. The much longer journal article from which this brief chapter is extracted makes these crucial qualifiers more evident (see *International Journal of Hindu Studies* [2006] 10).

2 The *Nāṭya Śāstra*, variously dated to between the fifth century BCE and the eight century CE, is available in two English translations, one complete (Ghosh 1961, 1967) and one abridged (Rangacharya 1996). In addition, two of its most influential chapters (six and seven, which deal with the expression and reception of emotion) appear in a full translation with commentary (Masson and Patwardhan 1970).

3 There have been fledgling attempts in this direction. Booth (1995: 175) offers a brief analysis of the *rasa* sequences of the 1958 film *Amardeep*; Sanskritist Gerow (2002) compares the *Poetics* of Aristotle to the elucidation of *rasa* aesthetics in the tenth-century Sanskrit text *Dhvanyāloka* of Ānandavardana, using brief analyses of films as diverse as Jean Renoir's *Boudu sauvé des eaux*, Terry Gilliam's *Brazil*, Akira Kurosawa's *Ran*, and Satyajit Ray's *Devi*; Joshi (2004) uses *rasa* theory to analyze what he terms the "affective realism" of the popular 1998 film *Kuch Kuch Hota Hai*.

References Cited

Beck, Brenda E. F. 1982. *The Three Twins: The Telling of a South Indian Folk Epic*. Bloomington: Indiana University Press.

Blackburn, Stuart H. and Joyce Burkhalter Flueckiger. 1989. "Introduction." *In* Stuart H. Blackburn, Peter J. Claus, Joyce B. Flueckiger, and Susan S. Wadley, eds, *Oral Epics in India*, 1–11. Berkeley: University of California Press.

Booth, Gregory D. 1995. "Traditional Content and Narrative Structure in the Hindi Commercial Cinema." *Asian Folklore Studies* 54, 2: 169–90.

Booth, Gregory D. 1995. 2000. "Religion, Gossip, Narrative Conventions and the Construction of Meaning in Hindi Film Songs." *Popular Music* 19, 2: 125–45.

van Buitenen, J. A. B., ed. and trans. 1959. *Tales of Ancient India*. Chicago: University of Chicago Press.

Chakravarty, Sumita S. 1993. *National Identity in Indian Popular Cinema, 1947–1987*. Austin: University of Texas Press.

Corrigan, Timothy and Patricia White. 2004. *The Film Experience: An Introduction*. Boston: Bedford/St. Martin's Press.

Dickey, Sara. 1993. *Cinema and the Urban Poor in South India*. Cambridge: Cambridge University Press.

Dissanayake, Wimal and Malti Sahai. 1992. *Sholay: A Cultural Reading*. New Delhi: Wiley Eastern.

Eck, Diana L. 1981. *Darśan: Seeing the Divine Image in India*. Chambersburg: Anima.

Gerow, Edwin. 2002. "Rasa and Katharsis: A Comparative Study, Aided by Several Films." *Journal of the American Oriental Society* 122, 2: 264–77.

Ghosh, Manomohan, ed. and trans. 1961, 1967. *The Nāṭyaśāstra, Ascribed to Bharata-Muni*. 2 volumes. Calcutta: The Asiatic Society and Manisha Granthalaya.

Hiltebeitel, Alf. 1999. *Rethinking India's Oral and Classical Epics: Draupadī among Rajputs, Muslims, and Dalits*. Chicago: University of Chicago Press.

Jain, Kajri. 2007. *Gods in the Bazaar: The Economies of Indian Calendar Art*. Durham: Duke University Press.

Joshi, Sam. 2004. "How to Watch a Hindi Film: The Example of *Kuch Kuch Hota Hai*." *Education About Asia* 9, 1: 22–25.

Kabir, Nasreen Munni. 2001. *Bollywood: The Indian Cinema Story*. London: Channel 4 Books.

Kakar, Sudhir. 1983. "The Cinema as Collective Fantasy." *In* Aruna Vasudev and Philippe Lenglet, eds, *Indian Cinema Superbazaar*, 89–97. New Delhi: Vikas.

Kakar, Sudhir. 1989. *Intimate Relations: Exploring Indian Sexuality*. Delhi: Viking.

Kapur, Anuradha. 1993. "The Representation of Gods and Heroes: Parsi Mythological Drama of the Early Twentieth Century." *Journal of Arts & Ideas* 23–24: 85–107.

Kapur, Geeta. 1987. "Mythic Material in Indian Cinema." *Journal of Arts & Ideas* 14–15: 79–108.

Kazmi, Fareed. 1999. *The Politics of India's Conventional Cinema: Imaging a Universe, Subverting a Multiverse*. New Delhi: Sage.

Kesavan, Mukul. 1994. "Urdu, Awadh and the Tawaif: The Islamicate Roots of Hindi Cinema." *In* Zoya Hasan, ed., *Forging Identities: Gender, Communities and the State*, 244–57. New Delhi: Kali for Women.

Kurtz, Stanley N. 1992. *All the Mothers are One: Hindu India and the Cultural Reshaping of Psychoanalysis*. New York: Colombia University Press.

Lutgendorf, Philip. 2002. "A Superhit Goddess/A Made-to-Satisfaction Goddess: *Jai Santoshi Maa* Revisited." *Manushi: A Journal About Women and Society* 131: 10–16, 24–37.

Lutgendorf, Philip. 2006. "Is There an Indian Way of Filmmaking?" International Journal of Hindu Studies 10, 3: 227–56.

Lutze, Lothar. 1985. "From Bharata to Bombay: Change and Continuity in Hindi Film Aesthetics." *In* Beatrix Pfleiderer and Lothar Lutze, eds, *The Hindi Film: Agent and Re-Agent of Cultural Change*, 3–15. New Delhi: Manohar.

Manuel, Peter L. 1993. *Cassette Culture: Popular Music and Technology in North India*. Chicago: University of Chicago Press.

Masson, J. L. and M. V. Patwardhan, trans. 1970. *Aesthetic Rapture: The Rasādhyāya of the Nāṭyaśāstra*. 2 volumes. Poona: Deccan College Research Institute.

Metz, Christian. 1986. "The Imaginary Signifier." *In* Philip Rosen, ed., *Narrative Apparatus Ideology: A Film Theory Reader*, 244–78. New York: Columbia University Press.

Mishra, Vijay. 1985. "Towards a Theoretical Critique of Bombay Cinema." *Screen* 26, 3–4: 133–46.

Mishra, Vijay. 2002. *Bollywood Cinema: Temples of Desire*. London: Routledge.
Mitter, Partha. 1977. *Much Maligned Monsters: History of European Reactions to Indian Art*. Oxford: Clarendon Press.
Mulvey, Laura. 1975. "Visual Pleasure and Narrative Cinema." *Screen* 16, 3: 6–18.
Pandian, M. S. S. 1992. *The Image Trap: M. G. Ramachandran in Film and Politics*. New Delhi: Sage.
Pinney, Christopher. 1999. "Indian Magical Realism: Notes on Popular Visual Culture." *In* Gautam Bhadra, Gyan Prakash, and Susie Tharu, eds, *Subaltern Studies X*, 201–33. Delhi: Oxford University Press.
Pramaggiore, Maria and Tom Wallis. 2005. *Film: A Critical Introduction*. London: Laurence King Publishing.
Prasad, M. Madhava. 1998. *Ideology of the Hindi Film: A Historical Construction*. Delhi: Oxford University Press.
Pritchett, Frances W. 1985. *Marvelous Encounters: Folk Romance in Urdu and Hindi*. New Delhi: Manohar.
Rajadhyaksha, Ashish. 1987. "The Phalke Era: Conflict of Traditional Form and Modern Technology." *Journal of Arts & Ideas* 14–15: 47–78.
Ramaswamy, Sumathi, ed. 2003. *Beyond Appearances? Visual Practices and Ideologies in Modern India*. New Delhi: Sage.
Rangacharya, Adya. 1996. *The Nāṭyaśāstra: English Translation with Critical Notes*. New Delhi: Munshiram Manoharlal.
Ray, Satyajit. 1976. *Our Films, Their Films*. Bombay: Orient Longman.
Roghair, Gene H. 1982. *The Epic of Palnāḍu: A Study and Translation of Palnāṭi Vīrula Katha, a Telugu Oral Tradition from Andhra Pradesh, India*. New York: Clarendon Press.
Saari, Anil. 1985. "Concepts of Aesthetics and Anti-Aesthetics in the Contemporary Hindi Film." *In* Beatrix Pfleiderer and Lothar Lutze, eds, *The Hindi Film: Agent and Re-Agent of Cultural Change*, 16–28. New Delhi: Manohar.
Schechner, Richard. 1985. *Between Theater and Anthropology*. Philadelphia: University of Pennsylvania Press.
Schechner, Richard. 2001. "Rasaesthetics." *The Drama Review* 45, 3: 27–39, 41–44, 46–50.
Schomer, Karine. 1989. "Paradigms for the Kali Yuga: The Heroes of the Ālhā Epic and Their Fate." *In* Stuart H. Blackburn, Peter J. Claus, Joyce B. Flueckiger, and Susan S. Wadley, eds, *Oral Epics in India*, 140–54. Berkeley: University of California Press.
Smith, Frederick M. 2006. *The Self Possessed: Deity and Spirit Possession in South Asian Literature*. New York: Columbia University Press.
Smith, John D. 1991. *The Epic of Pābūjī: A Study, Transcription, and Translation*. Cambridge: Cambridge University Press.
Taylor, Woodman. 2002. "Penetrating Gazes: The Poetics of Sight and Visual Display in Popular Indian Cinema." *Contributions to Indian Sociology* 36, 1–2: 297–322.

Thomas, Rosie. 1995. "Melodrama and the Negotiation of Morality in Mainstream Hindi Film." *In* Carol A. Breckenridge, ed., *Consuming Modernity: Public Culture in a South Asian World*, 157–82. Minneapolis: University of Minnesota Press.

Vasudevan, Ravi S. 2000a. "The Politics of Cultural Address in a 'Transitional' Cinema: A Case Study of Indian Popular Cinema." *In* Christine Gledhill and Linda Williams, eds, *Reinventing Film Studies*, 130–64. London: Arnold.

Vasudevan, Ravi S. 2000b [1993]. "Shifting Codes, Dissolving Identities: The Hindi Social Film of the 1950s as Popular Culture." *In* Ravi S. Vasudevan, eds, *Making Meaning in Indian Cinema*, 99–121. Delhi: Oxford University Press.

Virdi, Jyotika. 2003. *The Cinematic ImagiNation: Indian Popular Films as Social History*. New Brunswick: Rutgers University Press.

Wadley, Susan S. 1989. "Choosing a Path: Performance Strategies in a North Indian Epic." *In* Stuart H. Blackburn, Peter J. Claus, Joyce B. Flueckiger, and Susan S. Wadley, eds, *Oral Epics in India*, 75–101. Berkeley: University of California Press.

Wadley, Susan S. 2004. *Raja Nal and the Goddess: The North Indian Epic Dhola in Performance*. Bloomington: Indiana University Press.

Wagoner, Phillip B. 1996. "'Sultan among Hindu Kings': Dress, Titles, and the Islamicization of Hindu Culture at Vijayanagara." *Journal of Asian Studies* 55, 4: 851–80.

4

Cognitive Science

Ellen Goldberg

Cognitive Theories of Religion
Concluding Reflections

Cognitive science is a relatively new and diverse interdisciplinary field of knowledge. Its theoretical presuppositions can be traced to the Hixon Symposium on "Cerebral Mechanisms in Behavior" featuring Warren McCulloch, Karl Lashley, Alan Turing, John von Neumann, and Walter Pitts and held in 1948 at the California Institute of Technology. Their innovative papers challenged the prevailing dogmas in the study of human behavior and their critical insights laid out the essential tenets and defined the characteristics for future cognitive scientists. A conference held at MIT on "Information Theory" in September 1956 advanced the foundational ideas set out in 1948, elucidated the major themes and assumptions, and, according to George Miller, officially launched cognitive science as a distinct field of scientific inquiry (Baars 1986: 3; Chomsky 1997: 15; Gardner 1987: 28). Miller, along with Noam Chomsky, Alan Newell, Herbert Simon, and other leading figures, presented papers on such topics as the logic machine, experimental psychology, computational models of mind, and the linguistic structures of language acquisition on syntactic theory. Today, this broad-based project that began more than fifty years ago links six heterogeneous fields of scientific research—artificial intelligence (AI; robotics, and computer science), psychology, linguistics, neuroscience, anthropology, and philosophy—in the pursuit of an empirically based understanding of human cognition, including perception, memory, decision making, language acquisition, pattern recognition, and (most important) the nature of consciousness.

Cognitive science also brings a new and vital theoretical approach to the field of religious studies. Broadly stated, the emerging discourse in the cognitive theory of religion attempts to explain the nature of religious experience from the perspective of the neural or cognitive functioning of the human mind-brain. In other words, cognitive theorists of religion study the cognitive basis of religious behavior and phenomena, rather than simply "*sui generis*" accounts.

Social scientific theories deriving from F. Max Müller, Émile Durkheim, Clifford Geertz, and Karl Marx, among others, have explained religion primarily in terms of culture, whereas cognitive theories of religion tend to explain religion in terms of the universality of the panhuman properties of the mind-brain. However, it is important to bear in mind that there is no consensus in the cognitive sciences as to how the physical and mental infrastructures that underly our experiences and behavior are actually connected, as this is still an emerging field. Nevertheless, as Todd Tremlin recently declared, "The cognitive science of religion is already proving itself to be the most significant and fruitful approach to the subject ever undertaken" (2006: 9).

To understand the cognitive revolution in science, we need to identify, albeit briefly, three approaches that have shaped the study of cognition: (1) the computational-symbolic computer metaphor (this includes connectionism or neural network models), (2) the biological-evolutionary model, and (3) the mind-brain identity thesis. The computational-symbolic theory of mind, initially inspired by insights and developments, such as the Turing machine (Turing 1981) and the neuronal model (McCulloch and Pitts 1943), proposes a fluid analogy between the human brain and computational hardware. Basically, it is a mechanistic, rule-governed approach designed to understand the higher functions of the brain on the basis of sequential, logical, and axiomatic methods used in computers. More specifically, computational approaches are premised on seeing cognition as (nothing but) the computations of symbolic representations and the human mind-brain as a digital machine with domain-specific modules for processing information and acquiring knowledge. The computational-symbolic approach applies the metaphor of information processing, including computer programs, to human cognitive functioning to understand—and perhaps one day solve—the enigma of human consciousness (see, for example, Crick 1994; Dennett 1991; Fodor 1981; Koch 2004; Putnam 1997).

A prime example of this approach is the early work of Chomsky, who single-handedly spearheaded the cognitive revolution in linguistics. He argued rigorously against the prevailing empiricist and behavioral models of B. F. Skinner and disputed the fundamentally flawed idea of John Watson (and John Locke) that the mind is a *tabula rasa,* or blank slate, that is environmentally determined. Chomsky also inaugurated our understanding of the relationship between language and biological evolution. He claimed that the mind is genetically programmed or predisposed toward unconscious linguistic mechanisms and syntactic structures. These linguistic domains, or the language organ, as Chomsky calls it, are characterized by a universal grammar and form an innate, genetic part of the human brain's infrastructure (Chomsky 1957, 1980, 1997; Gardner 1987; Goldberg 2005). This idea of a generative or universal grammar based on information-processing rules that are then formalized by a mathematical algorithmic set of computational procedures was revolutionary insofar as it illustrated that the acquisition of language and, by extension, human behavior was not simply a product of culture but a biological and evolutionary process integral to the complex structures of the human mind-brain. Chomsky's iconoclastic method of analyzing syntax as if it were autonomous from other aspects of language (and culture, for that matter) builds on the initial insights of Turing, von Neumann (e.g., serial digital computer), Claude Shannon (e.g., development of information theory), and other early cognitivists who attempted to explain all forms of human cognition in terms of a modular and computational-symbolic approach to human anatomy. Today, among scholars interested in the cognitive and biolinguistic perspectives of language, Chomsky's ideas are embedded in a series of ongoing debates and attacks, even though current research in neuroscience is beginning to confirm the hypothesis of innate language specialization. As we see further on, Chomsky's legacy has definite implications for the cognitive study of religion.

Rather than displacing the early functionalist approaches of the computational-computer model using symbols and strings, connectionist or neural network models (also called the parallel distributed processing model or PDP) provide an alternative and oppositional modal orientation by replacing localized (serial) information processing with global or distributed (parallel) networks. Von Neumann's mathematical formulation using sequential computation created a cumbersome "bottleneck" problem that is resolved via the parallel processing of algorithms, that is, they compute simultaneously; therefore, the process is much faster. Neural network models use the term "neuron" purely as a metaphor to represent the fundamental "units of information" that are used to generate computer models and simulate artificial systems (or networks) based on human physiology. These interactive models are most often applied in neuroscience because they capture the actual cooperative properties and patterns of neuronal activity in the architecture of the brain better than the sequential or symbolic models of the computational approach and, therefore, offer more advanced explanatory theories as to how ordinary human behaviors actually work, such as the ability to control motor activity (e.g., walking, eating, standing) or the ability to adapt and organize symbols and recognize patterns (e.g., reading, memory, vision, speech, and auditory pattern recognition). One example of connectionist applications is the transference of actual genetic coding to cognitive neural network models. We also see this model applied in E. Thomas Lawson and Robert McCauley's cognitive theory of religion.

The second approach to cognitive science, namely, evolutionary-biology, presupposes the primacy of adaptation and the basic principles of the neo-Darwinian stance. That is to say, evolution as a global program of gradual modification occurs through hereditary or transgenerational reproductive strategies, and its central feature, natural selection, is based on optimizing the replication of a species efficiency, fitness, and survival along a historical network of lineages (e.g., DNA molecules, genes). Furthermore, adaptation accounts for the variation of design that we observe in nature. It is precisely this model of evolution based on claims about genealogy and natural selection that represents the received view within cognitive science.

The human brain is a product of evolution. It typically has a universal structure. Natural selection works as a homogenizing force, so not only do all humans have the same organs, they have the same cognitive or mental organs as well (Maturana and Varela 1998). Cognitive evolutionary-biologists look specifically at the structures of these determined systems. In the case of humans, this research extends to the recognition that the acquisition of knowledge (cognition) depends ultimately on the structures of cognition (mind-brain), which in turn is influenced by our evolutionary biology. As Maturana and Varela explain, knowing is rooted in the very organization and materiality of our bodies. They write, "We cannot take the world naively but must see it instead as having the mark of our own structure" (Maturana and Varela 1998: 16). The external world is not inseparable from our bodies or from language and culture. Rather, Varela claims it presents a type of chicken-and-egg model. Consequently, understanding the material basis of cognition is inseparable from and as important as understanding the dynamics of our environments. This approach has influenced current cognitive theories of religion.

The mind-brain identity thesis, although in some ways an extension of the two preceding models, also represents a radical departure. Though it is impossible to understand the mind-brain without the computational and the evolutionary-biological approaches, this theory of mind is augmented by extensive research in the neurosciences. The underlying assumption is that there is a basic, coextensive relationship between behavior (or experience) and specific brain structures. Karl Lashley, who devoted his entire professional life to studying the nervous system (i.e., the hardware) and its effects on and relationship to behavior, proposed a doctrine of "neurological equipotentiality" that maintains that psychological functions are related to brain structures. Lashley's early theories led the way for other cognitivists, such as Chomsky; Francis Crick and his "astonishing hypothesis"; Christof Koch, who is actively searching for the neural correlates of consciousness; and Miller.

To sum up, Steven Pinker explains: "The mind is a system of organs of computation designed by natural selection to solve the problems faced by our evolutionary ancestors in their foraging way of life" (1997: x). Extensive research into the physiology of the human mind-brain and the nervous system in neuroscience and neurophysiology and in artificial neural networks, using computational theories of mind and a process referred to as "reverse engineering," has contributed to our ever-increasing understanding of the intricacies and the mysteries of the human mind-brain (Pinker 1997: 21). It also has contributed to the conviction, especially among materialists, that the human brain is who we really are (Dennett 1991; Feigel 2002; Place 2002). Put another way, the mind is nothing but an epiphenomenon (or by-product) of the brain. This approach essentially equates brain states with mental states, and although it has been challenged, the biological-materialist argument remains dominant. However, even though there is an increasing wealth of data from the cognitive sciences pertaining to the architecture of the brain, what remains clear is that there is little consensus about how to interpret these findings; thus, the human brain-mind remains an enigma even to science. Furthermore, although these theories often produce some useful data, Sunny Auyung (2000) cautions against what she calls "nothing-but-ism" or positions in cognitive science that rely strongly on the untenable theory of ontological reductionism.

Cognitive Theories of Religion

As I mentioned at the outset of this chapter, the emerging discourse in cognitive studies of religion attempts to explain the nature of religious experience from the perspective of the neural or cognitive function of the human mind or, as Jensine Andresen (2001: 1) explains, "from the bottom up" rather than simply as "*sui generis.*" Generally, cognitive studies of religion rigorously test the cognitive structures of religious conceptualization and ritual enactment without explaining away the systems of belief from which these phenomena derive. This new approach argues in favor of a cognitive basis of religion while respecting the integrity and subjectivity of religious experience, behavior, and phenomena. However, we must bear in mind that cognitive theories of religion are still largely conjectural, given their basis in a science with few definitive explanations as to how the body, the mind, and the mental infrastructure that underlies our experience is actually connected.

Before we begin to look at specific areas wherein cognitive science and, by extension, cognitive theories of religion can be useful to Hindu studies, it is necessary to mention some of the major contributions in the field. Current cognitive studies of religion are introducing us to ambitious theories that move well beyond the foundational role of experience pursued in the pioneer research of psychologist William James (1842–1910). Yet, to some extent, they also reaffirm and build on his original hypothesis of the biological nature of mind and its cognitive role in religious experience.

Theories of mind as a symbolic-computational model have been stimulated by cognitive psychology, linguistics, and cultural studies in anthropology and have substantively influenced the biological-evolutionary theories of Pascal Boyer (1994, 2001); Stewart Guthrie (1980, 1993); E. Thomas Lawson and Robert McCauley (1990, 2002); and Dan Sperber (1996). Each of these theorists claims that religious activity, along with all other human activity, results from precisely one and the same cognitive system, or mind-brain.

When Guthrie proposed the first elements of a cognitive theory of religion in 1980, he based his argument on the idea of anthropomorphism. Influenced by the work of Robin Horton, and others, Guthrie claims anthropomorphism—that is, our ability to assign agency in the environment—is an innate feature of the human mind-brain (see also Guthrie 1993). Guthrie claims that this biological, cognitive propensity is part of our evolutionary adaptive survival strategy and that by looking at this aspect of cognition, we can better understand the essential features of human religiosity, such as the attribution of superhuman agency to nonhuman things or events. Guthrie's theory that religion is a form of anthropomorphism could perhaps be useful to the study of Hindu religion, though at present it seems little more than a method of classification.

Boyer's cognitive theory of religion is marked by his emphasis on "counter-intuitivity" in the cultural transmission of religious ideas. For Boyer, the mind-brain is equipped with innate and intuitive ontological categories or modules for making (common) sense of the world. When these intuitive domains are violated by counter-intuitive ideas, it enhances the likelihood of the transference and memory of religious representations. Recent studies of religion by Justin Barrett (2004) and Ilkka Pyysiäinen (2003) presuppose and build on this theory. Boyer also hypothesizes that the rise of fundamentalism is not a reaction against modernity or colonialism but rather is based on cohesive psychological mechanisms of "tribal solidarity" and "coalition behavior." By explaining fundamentalism in this way, Boyer offers theoretical insights that could well be applied to a study of Hinduism.

Sperber's theory of culture is based on an "epidemiology of belief" using cognitive causal chains and the effective, though "imperfect," propagation of memes. Lawson and McCauley (1990) draw on Sperber and the work of Chomsky, though their theoretical presuppositions do not represent an uncritical endorsement of either. Rather, they attempt to understand the principles and rule-governed structure of ritual practice, for example, the *darśapūrṇamāseṣṭi* (new and full moon sacrifices) and the *agnyādhāna* (establishing of sacred fires), as yet another type of universal (or generative) language or human cultural symbol-system. Using the principles of superhuman agency, the principle of superhuman immediacy, and the theory of high-performance frequency or extraordinary emotional stimulation, Lawson and

McCauley (2002) stress the structural and psychological integrity of ritual patterns and agency.

There also are cognitive theories of religion being generated within cognitive science itself. In fact, religion has recently become a "hot" topic (e.g., see Dennett 2006). Any cognitive approach to human behavior raises the question about the possible biological correlates of religion. Neuroscientists, such as Eugene D'Aquili and Anthony Newberg (1999), Michael Persinger (1987), and V. S. Ramachandran and Sandra Blakeslee (1999), to name just a few, have explored the neurobiological structures of religious experience, leading cognitive scientists to ask whether we are "hard-wired for religion." However, these studies suggest that even though religion is linked to circuits in the brain, it seems unlikely that religion is "genetically specified" (Ramachandran and Blakeslee 1999: 184).

Overall, recent cognitive theories of religion have had little to say on the subject of Hinduism. In fact, this is one area that has yet to be seriously examined. Here I offer only preliminary observations, speculating on two significant areas of contact between cognitive science and Hindu religion: Vedic ritual and *yoga*.

According to Victor Turner, human "brain activity gives rise to deep universals of culture" (1983: 77). Consequently, he insists that recent research in the cognitive sciences must be considered to better understand myth and ritual. Lawson and McCauley (1990) have shown that cognitive science can help scholars to develop a unified theory to explain the cognitive or pan-human aspects of ritual. Using Chomsky's cognitive approach to linguistics and connectionist models of mind, as outlined above, Lawson and McCauley examine two Vedic rituals (mentioned earlier). Frits Staal (1989), in his pioneer study of the Nambudiri Brāhmaṇas of South India, looks at the Vedic *agnicayana* ritual. Having found little theory to account for his data, he draws on the wider field of cognitive science. More recently, Jan Houben (2004) applies Richard Dawkins' theory of memes to develop a biological-evolutionary or morpho-memetic approach to Vedic ritual. What these preliminary studies show is that although Vedic ritual and *mantra* provide extraordinary examples, cognitive approaches, though fruitful, are still very much in their infancy.

Even though we have painstakingly detailed textual and anthropological materials, Staal holds that most studies of Vedic ritual are, nevertheless, primarily descriptive rather than explanatory. Or, as Laurie Patton puts it, "The study of the Vedas has been philologically rigorous yet theoretically moribund" (1994: 1). Consequently, Houben, Lawson and McCauley, and Staal look to cognitive linguistics and evolutionary biology to provide a methodology for their investigations. Perhaps one reason why the cognitive study of language, such as Chomsky's generative grammar, is suitable is because it offers a plausible rule-governed approach, similar, says Staal (1989: 55), to Pāṇinī. Clearly, a cognitive approach to the Vedas and such schools of Vedic exegesis as Pūrva-Mīmāṃsā is practical and timely, especially in light of Barbara Holdrege's repeated references to Vedic *mantra*s as "the original cognitions of the rishis" (1994: 38, 39, 41). However, a thorough cognitive theory of any Hindu *yajña* requires Vedic scholars well trained in the precise pronunciation of *mantra* (e.g., the *ṛc*s or verses, the *yajuses* or formulas, and the *sāman*s or songs), the importance of meter (*chandas*), and other oral, performative, and liturgical components. Also, it is vital that a cognitive study of Hindu ritual consider, in the words of Michael Witzel (2004), the historical worldview of the Vedas as "a *system* that includes mythology, ritual, customs and beliefs" (2004: 581; emphasis in original). This is seriously overlooked in Lawson and McCauley's ahistorical study. Future studies might also be applied to a comparative analysis of cognition and logic in the *prāṇāyāmavāda* (epistemology) of Advaita and Nyāya. Surely a study of the highly sophisticated modes of knowing (*pramāṇa*) articulated in Hindu philosophy could be instructive for cognitive science as well.

As stated earlier, cognitive scientists in the West are attempting to explain religious experiences using the most recent research in neurobiology (Ashbrook 1993; d'Aquili and Newberg 1993, 1999, 2000; Gelhorn and Kiely 1972; McNamara 2001; Persinger 1987; Andresen 2000). For example, recent studies on meditation show a correlation with specific activity in the sympathetic and the parasympathetic peripheral nervous systems.

To extract these and other findings, cognitive neuroscientists employ a variety of devices, such as electroencephalography to measure the amplitude and rhythms of brain waves during meditation. State-of-the-art imaging technologies, such as hexamethylpropyleneamine and single-photon emission computed tomography, positron emission tomography imaging, and functional magnetic resonance imaging are proving particularly useful in determining metabolic functioning and the electrical signals of the brain during these subjective meditative states, particularly in the thalamus, amygdala, and right and left frontal lobes. The idea is that the more phenomenological material is collected, the more cognitive scientists will be able not only to comprehend the mechanics of meditation but to map the physical and biological correlates of such experiences.

Given the potential plasticity of our brain and neural systems, cognitive researchers can determine the efficacy of various practices, such as *dhyāna*, *āsana*, and *prāṇāyāma*, and they can track any physical and emotional health benefits, such as the effects on the nervous and endocrine systems, immune function, attention and memory, blood pressure, asthma, anxiety, and other related issues. As stated, there are ambitious projects currently underway to study mature meditators (e.g., Tibetan Buddhists) using highly sophisticated medical technology (Davidson and Harrington 2001). However, what is perhaps less known is that since the early 1900s, the laboratory has also been a place to study Hindu *yogīs*. Early examples of distinguished research projects on *yoga*, or what Joseph Alter (2004) refers to as the "historicization of yoga as a science," have been conducted at the All India Institute of Medical Sciences in Delhi, the Banaras Hindu University in Varanasi, the Medical College in Madras, and the National Institute of Mental Health and Neurosciences in Bangalore, to name just a few institutions (Anantharaman 1996; Joshi and Cornelissen 2004). Alter also looks in some detail at the early medical research on *yoga* by Svāmī Kuvalayānanda at Lonavali and more extreme experiments, such as the closing of Ramaṇa Maharṣi in an air-tight enclosure. For a useful bibliography, Alter compiles an exhaustive amount of empirical data specific to this topic.

More relevant to our study is the concern of the cognitive neurosciences with the mind-brain, specifically the nervous and circulatory systems, and the search for the neural correlates of consciousness by neuroscientists. We see empirical evidence of a cooperative and interdependent relationship emerging between bodily systems that, according to Auyung, "underscores the inseparability of brain and body in supporting mental processes," including possible unitary states of mind (2000: 329). We also see related arguments that suggest that consciousness is an emergent property of the neuronal functions of the brain (Koch 2004).

In *yoga* and *tantra*, the inseparability that Auyung refers to is crucial. Whereas only some recent cognitive scientists seem to find this line of inquiry productive, *yogīs* and *yoginīs* have been examining the inseparability between body and mind with great rigor since ancient times. The hypothesis that mind is a product of a highly organized central nervous system also has a close connection with the logic behind various *yoga* practices. For example, we see in many schools of Hindu religion that the body of the devotee is a sacred site and that through ritual engagement and *yoga* practice matter and consciousness meet (e.g., Ardhanārīśvara; Goldberg 2002). To realize this end, *yogīs* have developed systematic strategies (*sādhana*) for cultivating introspection and self-knowledge (*ātmavidyā*). As mentioned, behavioral medicine has recently become interested in the efficacy of some of the practices that adept practitioners have known and experienced for centuries. Prolonged and intense practice of advanced *yoga* techniques, such as *ṣaṭkarmas* (six actions of purification), *prāṇāyāma* (breathing techniques), *mudrā* (advanced postures or *āsanas*), *bandha* (internal locks), *dhyāna* (meditation), and *nāda* (inner sound), enable the *yogī*/*yoginī* to control aspects of the autonomic system (Goldberg 2002, 2005). All these practices directly or indirectly affect the nervous and circulatory systems and, in more advanced states, propel the mind (*citta*) into deep states of absorption (*laya*).

Therefore, advanced states of *yoga* result in stilling not only the mind but the circulatory and nervous systems. In *haṭhayoga*, this is considered only the "gateway" to *yoga* (union) or what Auyung, d'Aquili, and Newberg refer to as "unitary consciousness experiences." Our understanding of *yoga* can be enhanced by cognitive science. Furthermore, cognitive science is empirically confirming through scientific research and technical terminology relating to the body and the brain some ideas that Hindu traditions have espoused for centuries: that mind is matter, that mind and body are not separate, that duality is a fiction, that free will does not exist, and that the mind is not a *tabula rasa*.

Finally, recent papers presented by Kelly Bulkeley, Glen Alexander Hayes, Kerry Martin Skora, and Staneshwar Timalsina at the 2006 American Academy of Religion meeting in Washington D.C. show a growing interest in the dialog between cognitive science and Hindu Tantra. Bulkeley (2006) continues his research on cognitive science, sleep, and dreaming from a Tantric point of view. Meanwhile, Hayes (2006), Skora (2006), and Timalsina (2006) each apply Gilles Fauconnier and Mark Turner's contemporary metaphor theory of "conceptual blending" to explain aspects of Mukunda-deva's seventeenth-century Vaiṣṇava Sahajiya texts, Abhinavagupta's use of bodily metaphors, and *rasa* theory in complex Tantric texts, respectively. Overall, these new approaches, reported at the 2006 AAR annual meeting, hold promise for bridging a dialog between Tantric studies and cognitive science.

Concluding Reflections

David Chalmers's (2002) theory of "panpsychism," or the idea that consciousness is everywhere, resonates broadly with Hindu thought. For Chalmers, and Hinduism, consciousness is an integral part of the evolutionary process that reaches its most complex expression (as far as we know) with the human nervous system. For many cognitive theorists, empirical evidence that consciousness is a by-product of the brain does not necessarily imply that consciousness is nothing but the brain. This argument does not deny the biological roots of mind; rather, as John Searle states, it acknowledges "the validity of higher orders of human experience as having a reality of their own" (2002: xx). By the same token, one-sided materialist theories of Hinduism would also fail to adequately capture Hindu insights into the nature of consciousness (e.g., Śiva, *puruṣa*) if "reality" is conceived in terms of matter (*śakti*, *prakṛti*) only.

Briefly, cognitive scientists propose a new way of thinking about religion. The basic premise, according to James Ashbrook, is the idea that "mind and matter meet in the brain" (1993: 4). Hindu religion with its repeated references to the brain as the "thousand petalled lotus" (*sahasrāra*), its emphasis on *yoga*, its penchant for ritual, and its stress on cognition and *citta*, to give just a few brief examples, can provide extraordinary data for a cognitive science of religion, and it can also help to redefine our cross-cultural understanding of "religion" as profoundly embodied and natural. Also, further research into the living traditions of Hindu religion would enhance empirical content that can assist in providing evidence of specialized methodologies and techniques for accessing and understanding the nature of human consciousness.

References Cited

Alter, Joseph, S. 2004. *Yoga in Modern India: The Body between Science and Philosophy*. Princeton: Princeton University Press.

Anantharaman, T. R. 1996. *Ancient Yoga and Modern Science*. Delhi: Project of History of Indian Science, Philosophy, and Culture.

Andresen, Jensine. 2000. "Meditation Meets Behavioral Medicine: The Story of Experimental Research in Medicine." *Journal of Consciousness Studies* 7, 11–12: 17–76.

Andresen, Jensine. 2001. "Introduction: Towards a Cognitive Science of Religion." *In* Jensine Andresen, ed., *Religion in Mind: Cognitive Perspectives on Religious Belief, Ritual, and Experience*, 1–44. Cambridge: Cambridge University Press.

Ashbrook, James. B. 1993. *Brain, Culture, and the Human Spirit: Essays From an Emergent Evolutionary Perspective*. Lanham: University Press of America.

Auyung, Sunny Y. 2000. *Mind in Everyday Life and Cognitive Science*. Cambridge: MIT Press.

Baars, Bernard J. 1986. *The Cognitive Revolution in Psychology*. New York: Gifford.

Barrett, Justin, L. 2004. *Why Would Anyone Believe in God?* Walnut Creek: AltaMira Press.

Boyer, Pascal. 1994. *The Naturalness of Religious Ideas: A Cognitive Theory of Religion*. Berkeley: University of California Press.

Boyer, Pascal. 2001. *Religion Explained: The Evolutionary Origins of Religious Thought*. New York: Basic Books.

Bulkeley, Kelly. 2006. "Less Than Meets The Eye: What Cognitive Science Adds to Tantric Studies." Paper presented at the 2006 American Academy of Religion Meeting, Washington, D.C., November 18–21.

Chalmers, David J. 2002. *Philosophy of Mind: Classical and Contemporary Readings*. Oxford: Oxford University Press.

Chomsky, Noam. 1957. *Syntactic Structures*. The Hague: Mouton.

Chomsky, Noam. 1980. *Rules and Representations*. New York: Columbia University Press.

Chomsky, Noam. 1997. "Language and Cognition." *In* David Martel Johnson and Christina E. Erneling, eds., *The Future of the Cognitive Revolution*, 15–32. New York: Oxford University Press.

Crick, Francis. 1994. *The Astonishing Hypothesis: The Scientific Search for the Soul*. New York: Charles Scribner's Sons.

D'Aquili, Eugene G. and Andrew B. Newberg. 1993. "Religious and Mystical States: A Neuropsychological Model." *Zygon: Journal of Religion and Science* 28, 2: 177–99.

D'Aquili, Eugene G. and Andrew B. Newberg. 1999. *The Mystical Mind: Probing the Biology of Religious Experience*. Minneapolis: Fortress.

D'Aquili, Eugene G. and Andrew B. Newberg. 2000. "The Neuropsychology of Religious and Spiritual Experience." *Journal of Consciousness Studies* 7, 11–12: 251–66.

Davidson, Richard J. and Anne Harrington. 2001. *Visions of Compassion: Western Scientists and Tibetan Buddhists Examine Human Nature*. New York: Oxford University Press.

Dennett, Daniel C. 1991. *Consciousness Explained*. New York: Little, Brown.

Dennett, Daniel C. 2006. *Breaking the Spell: Religion as a Natural Phenomenon*. New York: Viking.

Feigl, H. 2002 [1967]. "The 'Mental' and the 'Physical'." *In* David J. Chalmers, ed., *Philosophy of Mind: Classical and Contemporary Readings*, 68–72. Oxford: Oxford University Press.

Fodor, Jerry A. 1981. *RePresentations: Philosophical Essays on the Foundations of Cognitive Science*. Cambridge: MIT Press.

Gardner, Howard. 1987. *The Mind's New Science: A History of the Cognitive Revolution*. New York: Basic Books.

Gelhorn, E. and W. F. Kiely. 1972. "Mystical States of Consciousness: Neurophysiological and Clinical Aspects." *Journal of Nervous and Mental Disease* 154, 6: 399–405.

Goldberg, Ellen. 2002. *The Lord Who Is Half Woman: Ardhanārīśvara in Indian and Feminist Perspective*. Albany: The State University of New York Press.

Goldberg, Ellen. 2005. "Cognitive Science and *Hathayoga*." *Zygon: Journal of Religion and Science* 40, 3: 613–29.

Guthrie, Stewart. 1980. "A Cognitive Theory of Religion." *Current Anthropology* 21, 2: 181–203.

Guthrie, Stewart. 1993. *Faces in the Clouds: A New Theory of Religion*. New York: Oxford University Press.

Hayes, Glen Alexander. 2006. "Blended Worlds and Emergent Beings: Metaphors, Cognitive Science, and the Study of Tantra." Paper presented at the 2006 American Academy of Religion Meeting, Washington, D.C., November 18–21.

Holdrege, Barbara A. 1994. "Veda in the Brāhmaṇas: Cosmogonic Paradigms and the Delimination of Canon." *In* Laurie L. Patton, ed., *Authority, Anxiety, and Canon: Essays in Vedic Interpretation*, 35–66. Albany: State University of New York Press.

Houben, Jan E. M. 2004. "Memetics of Vedic Ritual, Morphology of the Agniṣtoma." *In* Arlo Griffiths and Jan E.M. Houben, eds., *The Vedas: Texts, Language and Ritual*, 385–416. Groningen: Egbert Forsten.

James, William. 1980 [1902]. *The Varieties of Religious Experience: A Study in Human Nature*. Middlesex: Penguin.

Joshi, Kireet and Matthijs Cornelissen. 2004. *Consciousness, Indian Psychology and Yoga*. Delhi: Centre for Studies in Civilization.

Koch, Christof. 2004. *The Quest for Consciousness: A Neurobiological Approach*. Englewood: Roberts and Company.

Lawson, E. Thomas and Robert N. McCauley. 1990. *Rethinking Religion: Connecting Cognition and Culture*. Cambridge: Cambridge University Press.

Lawson, E. Thomas and Robert N. McCauley. 2002. *Bringing Ritual to Mind: Psychological Foundations of Cultural Forms*. Cambridge: Cambridge University Press.

Maturana, Humberto and Francisco Varela. 1998. *The Tree of Knowledge: The Biological Roots of Human Understanding*. Boston: Shambala.

McCulloch, W. and W. Pitts. 1943. "A Logical Calculus of the Ideas Immanent in Nervous Activity." *Bulletin of Mathematical Biophysics* 5: 115–33.

McNamara, Patrick. 2001. "Religion and the Frontal Lobes." *In* Jensine Andresen, ed., *Religion in Mind: Cognitive Perspectives on Religious Belief, Ritual, and Experience*, 237–56. Cambridge: Cambridge University Press.

Patton, Laurie L. 1994. "Introduction." *In* Laurie L. Patton, ed., *Authority, Anxiety, and Canon: Essays in Vedic Interpretation*, 1–18. Albany: State University of New York Press.

Persinger, M. 1987. *Neurophysiological Basis of God Beliefs*. New York: Praeger.

Pinker, Steven. 1997. *How the Mind Works*. New York: W. W. Norton.

Place, U. T. 2002 [1956]. "Is Consciousness a Brain Process?" *In* David J. Chalmers, ed., *Philosophy of Mind: Classical and Contemporary Readings*, 55–59. Oxford: Oxford University Press.

Putnam, Hilary. 1997. "Functionalism: Cognitive Science of Science Fiction." *In* David Martel Johnson and Christina E. Erneling, eds, *The Future of the Cognitive Revolution*, 32–45. New York: Oxford University Press.

Pyysiäinen, Ilkka. 2003. *How Religion Works: Towards a New Cognitive Science of Religion*. Leiden: Brill.

Ramachandran, V. S. and Sandra Blakeslee. 1999. *Phantoms in the Brain: Probing the Mystery of the Human Mind*. New York: HarperCollins.

Searle, John. 2002. "Can Computers Think?" *In* David J. Chalmers, ed., *Philosophy of Mind: Classical and Contemporary Readings*, 68–72. Oxford: Oxford University Press.

Skora, Kerry Martin. 2006. "The Way Abhinavagupta Thinks: Bodily Metaphors, the Vitality of Language, and the Poetics of Intertwining." Paper presented at the 2006 American Academy of Religion Meeting, Washington, D.C., November 18–21.

Sperber, Dan. 1996. *Explaining Culture: A Naturalistic Approach*. Oxford and Cambridge: Blackwell.

Staal, Frits. 1989. *Rules Without Meaning: Ritual, Mantras and the Human Sciences*. New York: Peter Lang.

Timalsina, Staneshwar. 2006. "Fluids, Metaphor, and Self-Realization: Reading Tantra Through the Lens of Rasa." Paper presented at the 2006 American Academy of Religion Meeting, Washington, D.C., November 18–21.

Tremlin, Todd. 2006. *Minds and Gods: The Cognitive Foundations of Religion*. New York: Oxford University Press.

Turing, A. M. 1981 [1950]. "Computing Machinery and Intelligence." *In* Douglas R. Hofstadter and Daniel C. Dennett, eds., *The Mind's I: Fantasies and Reflections on Self and Soul*, 53–69. New York: Basic Books.

Turner, Victor. 1983. "Body, Brain, and Culture." *Zygon: Journal of Religion and Science* 18, 3: 221–45.

Witzel, Michael. 2004. "The Ṛgvedic Religious System and its Central Asian and Hindukush Antecedents." *In* Arlo Griffiths and Jan E. M. Houben, eds., *The Vedas: Texts, Language and Ritual*, 581–636. Groningen: Egbert Forsten.

5

Colonialism

Sharada Sugirtharajah

Privileging Textual Knowledge
Hermeneutical Presuppositions
Colonial and Missionary Perceptions of Hinduism
Hinduism as a Problematic Category

Ever since Europe's engagement with India began, Hinduism has come to be constructed in manifold ways both by Europeans and Hindus. Western perceptions of Hinduism have been diverse, complex, and ambivalent—ranging from romantic appreciation to denigration. There are both continuities and discontinuities between precolonial, colonial, and postcolonial portrayals of Hinduism. The study of religion, especially the European encounter with Hinduism, is closely linked with and informed by colonialism; by European Enlightenment notions, such as modernity, linear progress, the search for the origins, and privileging the written word; and by such theories as common origins and evolution and various Protestant theological presuppositions.

Colonialism has taken diverse forms and has had various kinds of impact on the colonized in different parts of the world. Among other things, it began as a commercial enterprise undertaken by Western nations from the late seventeenth century onward (although some attribute its origins to a much earlier date: to the fifteenth- and sixteenth-century European "voyages of discovery"). Whatever the case may be, "Colonialism was a lucrative commercial operation, bringing wealth and riches to Western nations through the economic exploitation of others" (McLeod 2000: 7). How a commercial enterprise ended up as a territorial conquest and how a territorial conquest in turn led to a civilizing mission is a complicated story. One of the Orientalists to endorse not only territorial conquest but intellectual and spiritual conquest was none other than the well-known German Orientalist F. Max Müller, who adopted England as his home. He declared in no uncertain terms in one of his letters: "After the last annexation the territorial conquest of India ceases—what follows next is the struggle in the realm of religion and of spirit, in which, of course, centres the interests of the nations. India is much riper for Christianity than Rome or Greece were at the time of St. Paul" (1902, 1: 182). In this enterprise, the study of religion and classical languages, such as Sanskrit, became an important exercise. Müller, who was involved in the translation and production of the Sacred Books of the East series, remarked: "You know that at present and for some time to come Sanskrit scholarship means discovery and conquest" (1892: vi). He also asserted that when the two volumes of the Veda were published, it would signify, among other things, the "conquest of the world by means of commerce, colonization, education, and conversion" (Müller 1902, 1: 289). As Bernard Cohn aptly remarks:

> The British conquest of India brought them into a new world which they tried to comprehend using their own forms of knowing and thinking.... Unknowingly and unwittingly they had not only invaded and conquered a territory but, through their scholarship, had invaded an epistemological space as well. The British believed that they could explore and conquer this space through translation: establishing correspondences could make the unknown and the strange knowable.
>
> (1996: 53)

Furthermore, both the colonizer and colonized saw British rule as Divine Providence, although this perception did change. The colonizer considered it a moral duty undertaken by enlightened cultures for the benefit of the unenlightened, thus justifying colonial intervention.

Privileging Textual Knowledge

One of the effects of colonialism can be seen in the textualization of India and its religions. The East India Company, which hitherto had been a private trading company, was later transformed into a colonial power. Although British rule had not been formally established in late eighteenth-century Bengal, a colonial government was being formed under the governorship of Warren Hastings who was both an administrator and a scholar. The early British scholar-administrators were engaged not only in discovering India and its ancient culture but also in producing knowledge about it that would be advantageous for the empire-in-the-making. Hastings paved the way for the production of textual knowledge about the Orient to serve both scholarly and political concerns. He was keen to govern and protect the natives according to their own laws rather than alien laws, and he assumed that an accurate knowledge of Hindu laws could be obtained from ancient Sanskrit texts and Muslim laws from the Quran. The knowledge acquired was seen as serviceable for a successful implementation of British rule in India. With the establishment of the Asiatic Society of Bengal in 1784 in Calcutta, a significant number of textual projects, ranging from editing to translation, came to be initiated and commissioned by the colonial government from the eighteenth century onward. These scholarly papers came to be published in the Society's journal, *Asiatick Researches*, thus turning the Oriental project into a corporate enterprise and paving the way for what came to be termed as "Oriental Renaissance" (Schwab 1984).

Though not all Orientalist projects can be associated with colonial intentions, nevertheless such textual projects as the English translation and publication of two treatises on Hindu law—Nathaniel Halhed's *A Code of Gentoo Laws* (1776) and William Jones's *Institutes of Hindu Law* (1794)—were not totally apolitical ventures. Other textual projects supported by the British East India Company include Charles Wilkins's English translation of the *Bhagavad Gītā* and Müller's translation and edition of the six-volume *Ṛg Veda*. Hastings used the *Gītā* for promotional purposes: to convey to the British public back at home the advanced state of the ancient culture of Hindus so as to win support for his Oriental style of government (Rocher 1994: 241). As Eric Sharpe remarks:

> The political implications of Orientalism need to be borne in mind. The reason why East India Company in London had been prepared to fund the first translation of the Gita was partly that they had allowed themselves to be persuaded that it might prove politically expedient for them to do so....Max Müller's text of the *RigVeda* was funded by the same commercial company on the same grounds.
>
> (Sharpe 1985: 45)

As pointed out a little earlier, Orientalist projects privileged Sanskrit texts and sought to represent India textually. Assuming that the locus of religion was to be found in ancient texts, Orientalists embarked on studying, translating, and reordering them. A good example of the process of textualization at work can be seen in the translation and recodification of Hindu laws by William Jones, the Welsh Orientalist and Justice at the Calcutta Court. Though Jones was keen for the British to rule the natives by indigenous laws, those laws were not considered to be adequate as they were, and native interpreters were seen as unreliable. Hindu laws were regarded as lacking not only the rationality of Western systems of judiciary but any sense of political liberty. Furthermore, Hindus were seen as politically immature, needing the guidance and protection of the British government (Jones 1799, 1: 150). Jones set about tailoring these laws to fit in with European legal categories, and, in the process, these Hindu laws were distanced from their own *śāstric* principles. Jones sought to transform diverse Sanskrit legal texts into a single, uniform, and fixed body of knowledge, thereby displacing the Sanskrit original. In making the Brāhmaṇical laws conform to European law, Jones was substituting indigenous expertise with colonial authority. The British administrators, in effect, became what J. Duncan Derrett calls "patrons of the *śāstra*" (1968: 225). The Manu *Dharmaśāstra* came to be understood as the laws of Hindus, and a legal legitimacy was accorded to social and customary practices for which pan-Indian applicability was claimed (Thapar 1993: 72). Jones not only resurrected *The Laws of Manu*, a text of marginal importance, but invested it with an authoritative status "as the premier book on Hindu law" (Rocher 1994: 229). The heterogeneous Indian society was compelled "to conform to ancient *dharmaśāstra* texts, in spite of those texts' insistence that they were overridden by local and group custom" (Rocher 1994: 242). Although both Orientalists and native *paṇḍit*s were no doubt joint collaborators in the recodification of Hindu laws, the final authority rested with the former. Native *paṇḍit*s were necessary for the production and endorsement of Oriental projects, but, at the same time, their expertise was distrusted.

What textualization has done is to strengthen the link between knowledge and power, a link that has become a key hermeneutical issue since the publication of Edward Said's *Orientalism* (1978), though it had been explored earlier by Bernard Cohn. Although Said has spoken largely with reference to the Middle East, his concept of Orientalism has become a contentious category. It is nevertheless seen as a hermeneutical tool for interrogating and uncovering hidden assumptions about the Other. Not all Oriental forms of knowledge are colonial in nature, but there has been a tendency to see the Other largely in terms of intellectual and cultural exploration, underplaying the political and economic domination of the West.

Hermeneutical Presuppositions

Orientalist constructions of Hinduism reflect varying Christian hermeneutical presuppositions. First, they worked on the notion that the ancient Sanskrit texts were pure, free from any later accretions, and that therefore it was important to recover the original purity of the text. Informed by the Enlightenment notion of lost-pure origins and subsequent decadence (which has resonances with Hindu notions of gradual decline from a pristine state), Orientalists were looking for an unsullied past in ancient Sanskrit texts. They were engaged in cleansing the text of its impurities. Jones (1799, 3: 62) found the Hindu laws riddled with meaningless superstitions, absurd customs and ceremonies, and wicked priestcraft, yet containing sublime devotion and noble thoughts about humanity. Because he found these laws lacking in clarity and uniformity, Jones set about restoring their original character by searching for an *ur*-text in the belief that there was already in existence a fixed body of pure laws established by legal experts, laws that had over the centuries become tainted by accretions, varied interpretations, and commentaries (Cohn 1996: 29).

If in the eighteenth century William Jones was trying to restore the lost purity to Hindu laws, Müller in the nineteenth century was engaged in recovering what he saw as the lost purity of the Veda and making it known to the world. Müller found in the Veda both noble and childish thoughts. He set himself the task of looking for the "precious stones" concealed in this rubbish and restoring Hinduism to what he saw as its immaculate, original glory (Müller 1868: 27). He urged Hindus to return to this flawless past and discard all superstitious beliefs and practices that had nothing to do with pure Hinduism.

Applying a modified form of nineteenth-century evolutionary hypothesis to the Veda, Müller represented it as an infantile document of great historical value for the study of the origin and evolution of religious ideas. Establishing an evolutionary link between the Veda and Immanuel Kant's *Critique of Pure Reason*—the former representing the "childhood" of humanity and the latter "the perfect manhood of the Aryan mind"—Müller fixed the place of the Veda (Müller 1901: 249). For Müller, the value and meaning of the Veda lay in its being the product of a child yet to grow into full maturity.

Second, Orientalists and missionaries regarded the written word as a mark of modernity and progress and tended to view oral forms of knowledge as unreliable and as a sign of backwardness. For Hindus, however, orality indicated a highly developed culture: The Veda was transmitted orally before it was committed to writing, and the very act of writing was considered as polluting. As already pointed out, most Western scholars adopted a heavily text-oriented approach to the study of Hinduism, and this is even reflected in some contemporary introductory material on Hinduism.

Most nineteenth-century Orientalists and missionaries imposed an idiosyncratic canonical status on Hindu texts. Some texts were privileged and others were peripheralized. Influenced by deism, Orientalists saw in the Veda and Vedānta pure religion divorced from idolatrous beliefs and practices, and Vedānta, especially Advaita Vedānta, came to be seen as representative of the entire Hindu tradition. Most Orientalists (Müller, M. Monier-Williams, and Horace Hayman Wilson) privileged the Veda and were dismissive of *smṛti* texts, such as the *Bhagavad Gītā* that the early Orientalists (Hastings, Jones, and Charles Wilkins) valued highly. Müller regarded the entire Sanskrit literature, except the Veda, as no more than "literary curiosities" (1878: 142), though later he came to regard the Vedānta highly. For J. N. Farquhar (1913: 440–41), the nineteenth-century

Scottish missionary, Hindu texts, such as the Upaniṣads and the *Bhagavad Gītā*, stood no comparison with the Christian Gospel. Nineteenth-century Baptist missionaries, such as William Ward (1817, 1: xciii, xcv), regarded the Purāṇas and *The Laws of Manu* as being defiled and defective and as having no salvific value. Both Orientalists and missionaries viewed Hinduism largely through a narrow restricted lens and subscribed literal meaning to the texts, overlooking the symbolic and various layers of meanings embedded in them. It is primarily through selective Sanskrit texts that the entire tradition was seen and represented, and textual prescriptions were taken for actual descriptions of society. Sanskritic Hinduism came to occupy a dominant position at the expense of vernacular sources.

Third, biblical monotheism provided the framework to interpret and evaluate Hinduism. Though most missionaries found no sign of monotheism in Hinduism, Orientalists (Jones, Müller, Monier-Williams, and Harold Wilson) found glimpses of monotheism in the Veda. It was either a distorted or a fragile monotheism. As a repository of natural revelation, the Veda offered a monotheism still in its infancy. In brief, European constructions of Hinduism had much to do with Protestant and biblical notions of monotheism.

Fourth, Orientalist and missionary constructions of Hinduism were undergirded by varying theories prevalent at that time. Hindu texts were domesticated by subjecting them either to a monogenetic or an evolutionary view of history. In so doing, Hinduism was represented as ahistorical—timeless and static. Some Orientalists, such as Jones, situated Hindu texts within the biblical chronological time-framework to affirm and validate the truth of biblical revelation; others adopted the nineteenth-century evolutionary perspective (Farquhar, Müller, and T. E. Slater), placing Hindu texts at the lower end of the evolutionary scale. Hindu texts were thus rendered safe—they no longer posed any serious challenges and confirmed the primacy of biblical truth. For some Protestant missionaries, however, Hindu texts were totally corrupt and far removed from the truth of Christianity (William Carey, Alexander Duff, and William Ward).

With the discovery of an Indo-European family of languages and common origins, India and Europe came to be closely linked. It led scholars to find parallels between the Graceo-Roman and the Hindu world and look for traces of their lost European childhood in Sanskrit literature. Being products of classical education, such Orientalists as Nathaniel Brassey Halhed, Hastings, Jones, and Wilkins were able to appreciate the similarities between Sanskrit and such European languages as Greek and Latin. Jones not only found Sanskrit literature more appealing than Greek literature but found validation for biblical truth in Sanskrit texts. As Hindus and Europeans shared not only a common European classical past but a common biblical ancestry, Hinduism posed no threat. For Max Müller, who initially equated linguistic affinity with racial affinity, Europe's origins were to be found in the East. The discovery of Sanskrit meant that Hindus and Europeans were not strangers but in fact belonged to the Āryan race, and the Veda was seen as Europe's "oldest inheritance" embodying the lost innocence of the European race (Müller 1902, 2: 74). The innocent Hindu past represented Europe's own childhood and therefore was useful for Europe's definition of its own lost identity. Hinduism was seen as still in its infancy and in need of the help of the progressive European culture.

Müller, among others, popularized an evolutionary approach to religions. With the publication of Charles Darwin's *Origin of Species* in the latter part of the nineteenth century, an evolutionary view of progress came to be applied to various disciplines, including religion, thus inaugurating what came to be called the "Science of Religion" or "Comparative Religion." The evolutionary theory of religion worked on the principle of a linear and progressive revelation, from natural to special—Christianity being the crowning glory. Though this approach challenged conventional missionary exclusive claims to divine truth, it at the same time reduced Hinduism and other religions to the status of natural revelation or infantile religion. The application of evolutionary hypothesis to the study of religions, which later came to be challenged, was then seen as objective and scientific. On this perspective, the question was not whether religions were true or false but lesser or more true, the lesser ones progressing from the lower to the higher. Religions were at various stages in their development and would eventually find fulfillment in Christianity, which had already reached a higher degree of ethical and moral perfection. Müller hoped that his translation of the Sacred Books of the East series would help missionaries to appreciate the value of an inclusive approach to other religions, but some missionaries with evangelical leanings were skeptical of his theory of natural revelation and nondoctrinal form of Christianity (Müller 1902, 2: 395, 455–56).

As shown, the hermeneutical exercise, among other things, involved the following: searching for the origins or the *ur*-text; locating purity in ancient texts; privileging the written word; translating, editing, classifying, and codifying texts; recovering obscure texts; collaborating with native *paṇḍit*s; imposing uniformity and constructing a fixed body of knowledge; and looking for European childhood in ancient Sanskrit texts. Textualization both domesticated and democratized ancient Sanskrit texts. It has both strengths and shortcomings. Though the text-based approach unearthed some valuable texts and made them available to a wider audience, other equally significant avenues of knowledge transmitted through dance, music, art, and folk traditions were marginalized. It is important to remember that textualization had little impact on the day-to-day religious practices of Hindus.

Colonial and Missionary Perceptions of Hinduism

The colonial project was also influenced by Christian missionary agendas. By the middle of the nineteenth century, the East India Company had firmly established its rule in most parts of the Indian subcontinent. The link between colonialism and the history of Christian missions is a complex one. Missionaries, who believed that British rule was a god-sent opportunity to civilize the benighted natives, were against the East India Company's policy of neutrality with regard to what they considered as the idolatrous practices of Hindus. The British East India Company, a trading company primarily interested in protecting its mercantile interests, was reluctant to allow missionaries into its territories for fear that missionary interference in religious matters would be a hindrance to the Company's commercial prospects. Although the 1698 charter had made provision for the instruction of "Gentoos" in the Christian faith, the Company succeeded in overturning it, and any missionary or traveler could enter India only with the Company's license. With the mounting pressure from Protestant Evangelicals, such as Charles Grant and William Wilberforce, the Company's charter was renewed in 1833, allowing missionaries to enter the Company's territories. Eventually such missionaries as William Carey came to play a significant part in the service of the empire as teachers of Oriental languages at Fort William College in Calcutta, where British civil servants were trained. Christian missionaries also came to intervene in such local customs as *satī*, putting pressure on the colonial government to abolish it.

In the nineteenth century, Orientalist formulations of an idealized Hinduism came to be undermined by Anglicists, Utilitarians, and Christian missionaries. All three devalued the Orientalist construction of an ideal Hindu past; they regarded both Hindu past and present as decadent and devoid of any enduring virtues. Such Anglicists as Thomas Macaulay, who privileged English education, were dismissive of Sanskrit learning and scholarship. Such missionaries as Alexander Duff, who shared Macaulay's vision of India as a degraded civilization, saw English education as a means of converting Hindus to Christianity, whereas other missionaries, such as Carey, sought conversion through vernacular languages. James Mill, a Benthamite Utilitarian and a product of the Scottish Enlightenment, devalued the classical past affirmed by Orientalists, and he attacked Hindu practices and also Orientalists' sympathetic view of Hinduism. For Mill, India had no sense of history and needed to be brought into history by the enlightened West. His three-volume *History of British India* became an indispensable text for those training to become colonial administrators. Mill's classification of Indian history and Hinduism, which is based on a Western linear periodization (Ancient, Medieval, and Modern India), continues to inform Western academic discourse (see King 1999: 106).

Christian missionaries and colonial administrators highlighted such issues as infanticide, child marriage, polygamy, widow remarriage, and *satī* (meaning a "good woman") to demonstrate the barbaric nature of Hinduism. These practices were presented as integral to the tradition. Two particular aspects—Hindu worship of images and *satī*—became contentious issues not only in missionary and colonial discourse but among Hindus themselves. In both cases, the central question was whether scriptures sanctioned these practices.

Most missionaries portrayed Hinduism as an effeminate religion. They associated idolatry with effeminacy, and effeminacy with all possible vices, such as lying, dishonesty, perjury, and immorality (Ward 1820, 3: 294–96). For Orientalists, by contrast, Hindu effeminacy was a mark of infancy rather than depravity. Most missionaries saw Hindu gods and goddesses as embodiments of vice, lacking in moral virtues and qualities, and thought therefore that those who worshipped them imbibed the immoral qualities of their deities (Ward 1817, 1: lxxxviii–lxxxix). The missionary concept of Hinduism as an effeminate religion formed part of the larger colonial construction of India as an effeminate nation and as lacking any sense of order, progress, rationality, or the history that characterized Protestant Christianity and Western civilization. The implication was that India and Indian women could not be protected by effeminate men but only by manly British men. Colonialists and missionaries justified their continued presence and intervention by constructing an effeminate India which was incapable of uplifting itself.

Among issues concerning women, *satī*—a minority practice—became the object of colonial and missionary gaze in nineteenth-century India. British attitudes to *satī* ranged from admiration to ambivalence to utter disdain. The high-caste Hindu woman became a convenient battleground for advocates of *satī* and for anti-*satī* campaigners, both from within and outside the tradition. In missionary writings, *satī* was sensationalized, and it was used not only to draw attention to the low status accorded to Hindu women but to justify their civilizing mission and Christian intervention.

Hindu scriptures came to play a significant part in the discourse on *satī*. Colonialists, missionaries, Hindu reformers, and pro-*satī* proponents were engaged in selective hermeneutics—privileging certain texts to argue for and against the abolition of practice of *satī* (abolished in 1829). The East India Company initially did not legislate against *satī* if it was a voluntary act undertaken by women. In seeking scriptural sanction against *satī*, missionaries who had been raised on Evangelical thinking advanced the Protestant principle of citing a text as evidence in order to challenge the practice of *satī*. The feminist historian Lata Mani has extensively discussed the nineteenth-century discourse on *satī* in her book *Contentious Traditions: The Debate on Sati in Colonial India* (1998).

Drawing on Orientalist constructions of a distant glorious Indian past, such Hindu reformers as Rammohan Roy and Dayānanda Sarasvatī were constructing a pure form of Hinduism based on ancient Sanskrit texts—a Hinduism free from idolatrous practices and beliefs. In so doing, these reformers reduced Hinduism to a rigid monotheism. They divested Hinduism of its heterogeneous features, thus homogenizing it to demonstrate that its monotheism was on a par with Christian monotheism or even superior to it in that it (their version of Hindu monotheism) rejected any notion of incarnation. This form of textualized Hinduism is rather elitist and has not had a wider appeal.

The impetus for "reform" of Hinduism has been largely seen as the result of Western modernity that came in the wake of colonialism. Such a view overlooks the fact that nineteenth-century Hindu reformers were heirs to a long-established tradition of an indigenous critique of image worship, caste, and priestly authority, even before the advent of colonialism and the missionary enterprise. The process of reformation had already been initiated and set in motion by *bhakti* poets, such as Basavaṇṇa in the south and Tukārām, Kabīr, and Mīrābāī in the north, by the Sikh *gurus*, and by Ṣūfī sects. In other words, the nineteenth-century Hindu critique of image worship and popular practices was not entirely new, although accentuated by the colonial and missionary presence. The conventional perception that modernization of Hinduism occurred in the nineteenth century and that it was entirely due to Western influence is therefore hard to sustain. Furthermore, it has come to be increasingly questioned that the nineteenth-century "Hindu Renaissance" is comparable to the European Renaissance that liberated Europe from darkness in the Middle Ages.

One of the main differences between the nineteenth-century Hindu reformers and some current proponents of Hinduism is that, though the former rejected iconic worship and saw it as a hindrance to moral, social, and economic progress, the latter have been actively involved in restoring temple Hinduism both in India and in the diaspora. What European Orientalists, missionaries, and Hindu reformers saw as degenerate Hinduism is now seen by the present advocates of Hinduism as a sign of vitality, progress, and renewal of Hindu values. Current politicized forms of Hinduism, which project Hinduism as a monolithic system and India as a unified nation with a unified vision, wittingly or unwittingly tend to replicate Western notions of modernity and nationhood. They are keen to represent a unified and sanitized Hinduism—one that transcends caste, class, and sectarian and other differences. They define *nation* in narrow and purely Hindu terms, thus creating a Hindu India that needs to be protected from the threat posed by Muslims, Christians, and secular forces (Sugirtharajah 2003: 136–37). The impact of colonialism on Islam is also equally traumatic and deserving of greater attention, but it is beyond the scope of this chapter.

Hinduism as a Problematic Category

The question whether the term "Hinduism" is a nineteenth-century Western construct has been extensively discussed by scholars of religion. The titles of recently published books, such as *Was Hinduism Invented?* (Pennington, 2005) and *Who Invented Hinduism?* (Lorenzen, 2006), indicate the nature of current academic discourse on the subject. The term "Hinduism" continues to be a problematic one. In fact, there is no consensus among scholars of religion as to whether it is a colonial invention. Though some Western scholars, such as Wendy Doniger, David Lorenzen, and Brian Pennington, dispute its Western origins, such others as Vasudha Dalmia, Robert Frykenberg, and Heinrich von Stietencron argue to the contrary. The question cannot be neatly resolved. The emergence of modern Hinduism is a complex process involving British Orientalists, missionaries, and indigenous nationalists. Both colonial and postcolonial constructs of Hinduism and India are closely linked with the concept of the nation-state introduced by the imperial rulers. The concept of the nation-state is the result of British colonialism, and the construction of Hinduism as a national religion followed.

Not all European scholars treated Hinduism as a unified system. Some were aware of the religious diversity within the tradition but saw this as a sign of weakness rather than strength. There was no doubt a perception among European scholars that Hinduism was a homogeneous system, as can be seen from their use of such phrases as "the Hindoo system" and "the Hindu religion." They also assumed that this system of religion was engineered and controlled by wicked priests. Whether Hinduism is a European construct or not, what is clear is that the notion of a unified, homogeneous Hinduism emerged in the colonial era, largely as the result of European engagement with it. This does imply that there was no identifiable religious identity or structure in precolonial Hinduism. Romila Thapar's remarks are relevant here: "Identities were, in contrast to the modern nation state, segmented identities. The notion of community was not absent but there were multiple communities identified by locality, languages, caste, occupation and sect. What appears to have been absent was the notion of a uniform, religious community readily identified as Hindu" (1993: 77).

References Cited

Cohn, Bernard S. 1996. *Colonialism and its Forms of Knowledge: The British in India*. Princeton: Princeton University Press.

Derrett, J. Duncan M. 1968. *Religion, Law and the State in India*. London: Faber and Faber.

Farquhar, J. N. 1913. *The Crown of Hinduism*. London: Oxford University Press.

Halhed, Nathaniel Brassey, trans. 1776. *A Code of Gentoo Laws, or, Ordinations of the Pundits, from a Persian Translation Made from the Original, Written in the Shanscrit Language*. London: East India Company.

Jones, William, trans. 1794. *Institutes of Hindu Law or, the Ordinances of Menu, according to the Gloss of Cullūca, Comprising the Indian System of Duties, Religious and Civil*. Calcutta: Honourable Company's Press.

Jones, William 1799. *The Works of Sir William Jones in Six Volumes* (ed. Anna Maria Jones). London: Robinson and Evans.

King, Richard. 1999. *Orientalism and Religion: Postcolonial Theory, India and "The Mystic East."* London: Routledge.

Lorenzen, David N. 2006. *Who Invented Hinduism?: Essays on Religion in History*. New Delhi: Yoda Press.

Mani, Lata. 1998. *Contentious Traditions: The Debate on Sati in Colonial India*. Berkeley: University of California Press.

McLeod, John. 2000. *Beginning Postcolonialism*. Manchester: Manchester University Press.

Müller, Max F. 1868 [1867]. *Chips from a German Workshop*. Volume 1: *Essays on the Science of Religion*. London: Longmans, Green & Co.

Müller, F. Max. 1878. *Lectures on the Origin and Growth of Religion as Illustrated by the Religions of India*. London: Longmans, Green & Co.

Müller, F. Max. 1892 [1883]. *India: What Can it Teach Us? A Course of Lectures Delivered Before the University of Cambridge*. London: Longmans, Green & Co.

Müller, F. Max. 1901. *Last Essays: Essays on Language, Folklore and Other Subjects*. First Series. London: Longmans, Green & Co.

Müller, F. Max. 1902. *The Life and Letters of the Right Honourable Friedrich Max Müller* (ed. Georgina Adelaide Max Müller). 2 volumes. London: Longmans, Green & Co.

Pennington, Brian K. 2005. *Was Hinduism Invented?: Britons, Indians, and the Colonial Construction of Religion*. New York: Oxford University Press.

Rocher, Rosane. 1994. "British Orientalism in the Eighteenth Century: The Dialectics of Knowledge and Government." *In* Carol A. Breckenridge and Peter van der Veer, eds., *Orientalism and the Postcolonial Predicament*, 215–49. Delhi: Oxford University Press.

Said, Edward. 1978. *Orientalism*. Harmondsworth: Penguin Books.

Schwab, Raymond. 1984 [1950]. *The Oriental Renaissance: Europe's Discovery of India and the East, 1680–1880*. New York: Columbia University Press.

Sharpe, Eric J. 1985. *The Universal Gītā: Western Images of the Bhagavadgītā*. London: Duckworth.

Sugirtharajah, Sharada. 2003. *Imagining Hinduism: A Postcolonial Perspective.* London: Routledge.

Thapar, Romila. 1993 [1992]. *Interpreting Early India.* Delhi: Oxford University Press.

Ward, William. 1817 [1815]. *A View of the History, Literature, and Religion of the Hindoos: Including A Minute Description of their Manners and Customs, and Translations from their Principal Works.* 2 volumes. London: Black, Parbury, and Allen.

Ward, William. 1820 [1811]. *A View of the History, Literature, and Mythology of the Hindoos: Including a Minute Description of their Manners and Customs, and Translations from their Principal Works.* 4 volumes. London: Black, Parbury, and Allen.

6

Diaspora

Maya Warrier

Patterns of Hindu Migration
Hindu Attitudes to Migration
The Perpetuation and Transmission of Culture
Hindu Identities in the Diaspora
Topics for Further Study

Migration of South Asian populations to destinations outside the Indian subcontinent is not a new phenomenon. Right from precolonial times, there have been sizeable movements of populations from the Indian subcontinent to places in Southeast Asia, the Persian Gulf, and East Africa. However, with colonialism, the scale and pace of migration changed drastically. The large-scale movement of South Asians generally, and Hindus in particular, to other parts of the British empire set in motion patterns and processes of settlement and community formation that had no ready parallel in precolonial history. The migration of Hindus to other parts of the world continues well into the postcolonial period and has been the subject of considerable discussion in academic literature right through the second half of the twentieth century to the present.

Today, Hindu populations have a noteworthy presence in places as far flung as Western Europe, North America, Africa, Australia, the Caribbean Islands, Fiji, Mauritius, the Middle East, Singapore, and Malaysia. Even though conventionally the term "diaspora" is used to describe dispersed *ethnic* groups, scholars feel justified in referring to a Hindu diaspora because they see Hinduism as more than just a "religion." According to Bhikhu Parekh (1994), Hinduism constitutes an "ethnic religion" because of its rootedness in India and its inextricable links with India's sacred geography.

The Hindu diaspora is highly heterogeneous. Beliefs and practices among diasporic Hindus reflect the diversity that marks Hinduism in the Indian subcontinent. The particular worldviews and practices of different sections of Hindus in the diaspora are determined by a number of factors. These include origins (their specific regional and linguistic, caste, sectarian, and class backgrounds), the route and pattern of their migration, and the culture and politics in the host country. Different groups in the diaspora have developed along different lines and evolved different identities that distinguish them both from one another and from Hindus in India. Scholars studying diasporic populations often use the term "creolization" to describe this phenomenon, thus referring to the adaptive effects of living in new environments and mixing with other societies and cultures (see, for instance, Korom 2002). Noting the diversity in the Hindu diaspora, Parekh thus likens it to "a group of people sharing a basic grammar and vocabulary, but possessing distinct idioms of their own and using these complex conceptual resources to say different things" (1994: 617).

Patterns of Hindu Migration

The bulk of Hindu migration has occurred in three stages. The first stage took place in precolonial times and goes back a long way to the early centuries CE. The second stage took place during the colonial period in the nineteenth and early twentieth centuries. The third phase of migration took place in the aftermath of World War II after the colonies had won their independence.

The first phase of migration in the early centuries of the Common Era saw the movement of Brāhmaṇas to Southeast Asia (present-day Cambodia, Thailand, and Bali). They were invited there by local rulers to consecrate their kingdoms (Coedes 1968). They stayed on, married locally, and introduced into the host culture such aspects of Brāhmaṇical culture as their deities and scriptures, which are in evidence even today. As Kim Knott (1998: 95) points out, for instance, we see the continuing significance of the god Brahmā in the Dheva Satarn temple in Bangkok and in Thailand's royal ceremonies. Thailand and Indonesia also have popular cultural performances of the *Rāmāyaṇa*. Additionally, Tamil Ceṭṭiyārs, a South Indian banking community, extended their business to Burma, Malaysia, Mauritius, and other parts of Southeast Asia. There have also been strong trading links between western India and East Africa for many centuries.

In the second phase of migration, under the colonial regime, the movement was mostly of laborers from India to other British colonies. Indian labor was mostly either contracted or indentured. Contract labor was the ordinary form of wage labor, and employers paid the laborers' two-way passage. This form of labor was recruited mainly for work in Burma, Malaysia, and Sri Lanka. Indentured labor was a new form of labor started by the British and replaced slavery after the Slavery Abolition Act of 1833. Labor under this scheme was recruited mainly for work in plantations in the West Indian colonies and in Fiji, Mauritius, and South Africa. According to Hugh Tinker (1974), this type of labor simply constituted a new system of slavery in place of the old. Many of the recruits were illiterate and entered into contracts they could not readily comprehend. Workers were indentured to work for an employer for a fixed period, usually five years. They were provided a basic pay, free accommodation, food rations, and a return passage to India. Indentured laborers were required to live on the plantation, work unlimited hours, and not take up any other employment during the specified period. If they transgressed the rules, they were penalized financially and physically punished. At the end of the specified period, only about one-third returned home; the rest reindentured and eventually purchased land and stayed on in their new homes. In addition to the movement of this type of labor, there was also the migration of Gujarati and Punjabi groups in the early part of the twentieth century to the growing towns that were located in Kenya, Uganda, Tanganyika (now Tanzania), and Nyasaland (now Malawi) and were administered by the British; these groups worked as small traders or seized opportunities to work on the new railroads.

The third phase of migration, after World War II, brought Hindus first to Britain, between 1956 and 1965, where they were recruited to work in the labor-hungry British industries. These skilled and semi-skilled laborers were later joined both by professionals, mainly doctors, and by businessmen. Professionals also began to migrate to the United States in the latter half of the twentieth century, most of them serving as engineers, managers, doctors, and, more recently, software personnel in the private sector. Since the 1970s there has been the movement of skilled labor from South Asia to the Arab Gulf states. There has also been the phenomenon of "twice migration," with Hindus moving from one part of the diaspora to the other (e.g., Caribbean Hindus moving to Miami, London, or New York, and Kenyan and Ugandan Hindus moving to Britain in the 1960s and early 1970s owing to nation-building policies in these countries that favored indigenous populations). A more recent phenomenon is the movement of refugees, mainly Sri Lankan Tamils, seeking political refuge abroad.

It is difficult to provide accurate counts of Hindus in different parts of the world, particularly as many countries do not collect data on religious adherence as part of their census surveys. There is moreover the question of precisely who can be defined as a Hindu, because Hinduism encompasses a diversity of traditions. Steven Vertovec (2000: 14) provides some rough estimates for Hindus around the world based on a range of sources for the mid-1990s. He suggests that outside of India there are nearly 50 million Hindus and that outside of South Asia there are more than 12 million. The highest concentrations of Hindus outside South Asia (as a percentage of the total population) are in Mauritius (nearly 50 percent), Fiji and Guyana (about one-third of the total in each), and Trinidad and Tobago (almost one-fourth). Indonesia and Malaysia have a high number of Hindus (3.4 and 3 million, respectively, in the mid-1990s according to Vertovec [2000]), but they do not make up a very high proportion (well below 10 percent) of the total population. In the United Kingdom, according to the 2001 census, there are more than 500,000 Hindus who make up 1.1 percent of the total population. In the United States, there are more than one million Hindus today, but, here too, they make up less than 1 percent of the total population.

Hindu Attitudes to Migration

Parekh (1994) notes that although Hindus have traveled abroad for centuries, they (especially high-caste Hindus) were traditionally antipathetic to migration. According to him, the traditional Hindu preoccupation with notions of purity and pollution was in large part responsible for this attitude. Whereas the Hindu classificatory system ranked everything known and familiar according to levels of relative purity and impurity, that which was unknown and completely outside this system of classification held a potential threat to the Hindu social order. Traveling overseas to unknown lands and mixing with "outsiders" was traditionally considered irretrievably polluting (Burghart 1987: 1–2).

The antipathy toward overseas travel was also inextricably linked with the Hindu understanding of the Indian sacred geography, its mythological landscape populated by gods and goddesses and marked by places of worship, holy rivers, and pilgrimage destinations. Given the sense of emotional and ritual attachment to this landscape, any travel that necessitated separation from it, and the crossing of the "seven seas," met with disapproval and was undertaken reluctantly. When Hindus did travel, therefore, it was often not in a mood of adventure or exploration but out of economic necessity. The fact that, despite all such reservations, a fair number of Hindus (especially "high-caste" individuals) did tend to migrate overseas clearly suggests that the purity–pollution considerations were either not as central to Hindu social organization as some scholars have suggested or that other considerations often came into play and tempered the effects of the former (Raheja 1988).

Attitudes toward migration have changed in modern times. Hindus in India today, particularly those who are educated and financially well off, are intensely aware of developments in other parts of the globe and are, more often than not, keen to seize educational and job opportunities overseas, particularly in the more affluent countries. Whereas Hindu migrants in the past may have been viewed in terms of their "displacement" from the homeland, many of the Hindus who migrate overseas in the present have little or no desire to return to their place of origin and do not see themselves as "displaced" in any real sense. Moreover, Hindus in the diaspora have, in myriad different ways, sought to create an often-abbreviated version of the Hindu sacred landscape in their host countries, by demarcating and sanctifying space for ritual and worship.

Hindus have by and large shown themselves to be resourceful and adaptable, capable of living, working, and creating communities and networks in a variety of different settings, though some have also experienced racial discrimination and have been victims of hate crimes. Hindus in the West have tended mostly to achieve high educational levels and good standards of living. As Biju Mathew and Vijay Prashad (2000) perceptively note, Hindus in the diaspora are often plagued by a sense of guilt about living comfortable lives in their affluent host countries while their brethren back in India struggle with poverty and other social injustices. They often seek to assuage this guilt by making financial donations to charities in India. Those who do return to India after an extended stay overseas often attempt to recreate in India the lifestyle and comforts to which they were accustomed, as immigrants, in such places as western Europe and North America.

The Perpetuation and Transmission of Culture

Modes of cultural and religious reproduction and transmission among diasporic Hindus over time and across generations is a topic that has been fairly extensively researched by scholars of Hinduism. Roger Ballard (1994) and Raymond Williams (1992) refer to these processes of perpetuating and reproducing culture in an alien context as diasporic "strategies of adaptation," thus implying that they are the result of rational and conscious choice on the part of the individuals and groups concerned. Vertovec (2000), however, argues that perhaps the element of conscious negotiation and strategizing is overplayed here. He argues that due recognition must be given to *unconscious* elements in the process of intercultural adaptation that takes place within and across generations in the diaspora.

Cultural reproduction and processes of adaptation take place both in the domestic sphere and in the public sphere. In the case of the former, particularly interesting is the role of women in perpetuating Hindu tradition (e.g., Kurien 1999). Mothers have traditionally been seen as the transmitters of cultural and religious values to their children, and women in the diaspora have sought in different ways to fulfill this expectation. Often the larger community provides resources they can use for this purpose, and cultural transmission and reproduction become activities taking place more in the public sphere than in individual homes.

Cultural reproduction in the public sphere takes place in a variety of ways. The widespread use of modern mass media and communication systems, for instance, have important implications for processes of socialization and networking in the diaspora (Mathew and Prashad 2000). Films and television serials; such journals as *Hinduism Today*, published by the Himalayan Academy in Hawaii; Hindu sites and chat rooms on the Web; children's illustrated books (notably the highly popular *Amar Chitra Katha* series) narrating Hindu mythological tales; and stories about important historical figures in Hinduism's history all play a vital role in Hindu cultural reproduction.

Caste associations and sectarian and linguistic groups, often with a transnational reach, and umbrella organizations networking between and across these also have a major role to play in this regard (Kurien 1999, 2004; Raj 2000). Similarly, the establishment of temples and of educational institutions and youth groups that are often attached to temples and the hosting of religious and cultural festivals all play a vital role in diasporic cultural reproduction (Baumann 1998; Baumann, Luchesi, and Wilke 2003; Knott 1986a; Kurien 1999, 2004; Narayanan 1992; Nye 1995; Shukla 1997; Waghorne 2004; Williams 2001: 197–231). Transnational *guru* organizations attracting Hindu (and non-Hindu) adherents from across the world too contribute to the movement of "Hindu" symbols and meanings across vast geographic spaces (Coney 1998; Knott 1986b; Nye 2001; Warrier 2005; Williams 2001). The role of these modern *gurus* in Hindu cultural reproduction in the diasporic context is a subject that remains relatively under-researched. As John Y. Fenton (1992) points out, religious studies departments in universities, which offer programs on Hinduism and attract Hindu students, also can have the unintended effect of influencing modes of cultural reproduction in the diaspora.

Hindu Identities in the Diaspora

In an immigrant situation, Hindus often find themselves forced to explicitly articulate and explain the meaning and content of their religion and culture that, in their country of origin, they might have taken for granted. This process of articulation, indeed of "reification" wherein cultural attributes are removed from their everyday contexts, fashioned into symbols, and idealized, is central to identity formation and group mobilization. Scholars have noted how this process is necessarily selective, such that some elements seen as indispensable to religious doctrine and practice are retained while others are eliminated. This self-conscious reflection on religious tradition and identity serves to ethnicize religion and is inherently a political process (van der Veer 1995: 10). Often the process of identity creation and political mobilization in diasporic Hindu communities relies on defining, reifying, and stereotyping an "other" or "others"—a group or groups in opposition to whom the Hindu "self" is then defined.

As noted earlier, the particular social and historical circumstances of immigrant Hindus in different parts of the world determine the ways in which they come to articulate their religious and cultural identity. The result is that Hinduism has come to have different ethnic meanings in different parts of the world. Vertovec (2000: 162–64), in attempting a comparative sketch of the articulation of Hinduism in different sociocultural contexts, outlines three different trends in Hinduism's manifestations in different parts of the world.

The first of these is sectarian or parochial (particularistic) Hinduism in which caste, sectarian, and linguistic differences between Hindu subgroups remain more or less intact in the diaspora, as is the case in East Africa and the United Kingdom. In this case, subgroups maintain their identity by perpetuating distinctive modes of ritual and other activity and minimizing interaction with other subgroups. This form of Hinduism, Vertovec argues, is unlikely to sustain itself because caste, linguistic, and regional markers are tending to lose their meaning and fade away for newer generations of Hindus in diasporic contexts.

The second is a form of Hinduism that is deemed to be universal. In this case, though diversity in Hindu belief and practice is welcomed, all such diverse traditions are seen as permutations of the same basic elements. This form of unitary Hinduism has been promoted by Hindu nationalist groups in India and, according to scholars researching the diaspora, holds considerable sway over Hindus across the world. A vast body of literature has emerged in the last two decades on the appeal of Hindu nationalistic ideologies and politics across the Hindu populations in the diaspora (e.g., Kurien 2004; Mathew and Prashad 2000; Raj 2000), and scholars have noted the significant financial support provided to Hindu nationalist organizations by Hindus living outside the Indian subcontinent. Support for Hindu nationalism, of course, also has important implications for the way in which Hindu groups relate to other groups of Indian origin (most notably Muslims) in a diasporic context (Kurien 2001) and often leads to interreligious tensions and conflicts.

The third trend is toward what Vertovec (2000: 162–64) describes as an ecumenical form of Hinduism in which a variety of Hinduisms are recognized and coexist, even while certain pan-Hindu umbrella organizations, activities, and celebrations occasionally bridge the differences between them. This appears to be one of the trends in the United States (Williams 1988, 1992: 238–40). Vertovec reminds us that these trends are not mutually exclusive but that instead aspects of all of these might be present in any given situation or context.

Vertovec hints at another form of Hinduism that might be emerging in the diaspora. This is a cosmopolitan form of Hinduism in which Hindus show a capacity to live in multiple environments and to possess multiple identities, such that different identities (alterities) are foregrounded depending on the context and environment in which they find themselves. This is a form of Hinduism and Hindu identity that has not been adequately studied so far.

Topics for Further Study

In the past, scholars studying the Hindu diaspora tended to treat Hinduism in the Indian subcontinent as the "authentic" version and were concerned primarily with pointing out the differences between diasporic Hinduism and the Hinduism of the Indian subcontinent. More recently, such scholars as Vertovec (2000) have urged researchers to stop seeing Hinduism in India as a yardstick for authenticity and instead to examine diasporic Hinduism on its own terms, analyzing the different ways in which Hindus outside the subcontinent seek to organize and represent themselves and recreate a Hindu community on foreign soil.

Though treating Indian Hinduism as the yardstick for "authenticity" is certainly unhelpful, a comparison of Hindu populations across different sociocultural contexts is in itself by no means undesirable. In fact, we need more studies making explicit comparison not just between Hinduism in the Indian subcontinent and in the diaspora but between different groups within the diaspora. Vertovec (2000) provides a comparison between geographically distant groups of diasporic Hindus and suggests a theoretical framework for making such comparison. Other comparative studies include those by T. S. Rukmani (1999), Knut Jacobsen and Pratap Kumar (2004), and Harold Coward, John Hinnells, and Raymond Williams (2000). Comparative studies should ideally also take into account the mutual perceptions of different groups in the diaspora. How, for instance, do new Hindu immigrants in the United States view second- and third-generation American Hindus and vice-versa? How do Trinidadian Hindus in Britain view Gujarati Hindus? How do "once migrants" view "twice migrants?" And finally, how do Hindus in India view their counterparts in other parts of the world? The answers to these questions have important implications for issues of identity construction in the Hindu diaspora.

Comparison should moreover extend further to take in the differences between different generations of diasporic Hindus. How far are values and practices upheld by first-generation immigrants shared by subsequent generations? Parekh (1994) outlines some common features of Hindu migrants in the colonial period. These include such factors as their relative lack of interest in, or curiosity about, the indigenous ways of life in the host country; clannishness and exclusiveness in their social interactions; emphasis on the importance of education for their children; preoccupation with making money; communal self-renewal through participation at social events marking birth, marriage, and death; and strong kinship and family ties. How far have these attitudes and practices been transmitted to, and absorbed by, subsequent generations? How do different generations of immigrant Hindus relate to, and perceive, each other?

An important study in this respect spanning nearly a century and a half of Hindu immigrant experience in Trinidad is that by Baumann (2004). Ballard (1994: 29–34) offers some interesting and perceptive reflections on "code switching" and "cultural navigation" on the part of second- and third-generation Hindu immigrants in the West. He suggests that these individuals participate more widely in the host culture than did their parents and move between different social arenas that are often organized around contradicting, even conflicting, values and conventions. Rather than perceive them as being "trapped between two cultures" or besieged by "culture conflict," Ballard points to the ways in which these individuals develop the competence to navigate skillfully between cultures and to switch codes as necessary with relative ease. This is not to say, however, that situations of conflict simply do not arise. When they do, Ballard notes, the cause is not merely the difference in underlying values in the different cultural arenas but the markedly negative perception each side holds of the other. To better understand the processes of cultural navigation and conflict handling and resolution, there is a need for in-depth empirical studies of intergenerational relations in the Hindu diaspora across the world, and particularly in the West.

Cosmopolitanism, as noted before, is an aspect of diasporic Hinduism that has not been adequately researched to date. There is one further strand in diasporic Hinduism that has so far simply not received the attention that it deserves. Studies of the Hindu diaspora invariably focus on communities and groups. Hindus who do not align themselves with any recognizable group tend to be absent from these studies. A shift away from clearly defined groups as the focus of study to more loosely constructed networks of individuals (who define themselves as Hindu but have no institutional affiliations) is likely to yield interesting insights into ever more ways in which Hinduism outside its place of origin comes to be conceptualized and formulated in diverse social contexts.

References Cited

Ballard, Roger. 1994. "Introduction: The Emergence of Desh Pardesh." *In* Roger Ballard, ed., *Desh Pardesh: The South Asian Presence in Britain*, 1–34. London: Hurst.

Baumann, Martin. 1998. "Sustaining 'Little Indias': The Hindu Diasporas in Europe." *In* Gerrie ter Haar, ed., *Strangers and Sojourners: Religious Communities in the Diaspora*, 95–132. Leuven: Uitgeverij Peeters.

Baumann, Martin. 2004. "Becoming a Colour of the Rainbow: The Social Integration of Indian Hindus in Trinidad, Analysed along a Phase Model of Diaspora." *In* Knut A. Jacobsen and Pratap Kumar, eds., *South Asians in the Diaspora: Histories and Religious Traditions*, 77–96. Leiden: Brill.

Baumann, Martin, Brigitte Luchesi, and Annette Wilke, eds. 2003. *Tempel und Tamilen in zweiter Heimat. Hindus aus Sri Lanka im deutschsprachigen und skandinavischen Raum*. Würzburg: Ergon.

Burghart, Richard. 1987. "Introduction: The Diffusion of Hinduism to Great Britain." *In* Richard Burghart, ed., *Hinduism in Great Britain: The Perpetuation of Religion in an Alien Cultural Milieu*, 1–14. London: Tavistock.

Coedes, George. 1968. *The Indianized States of Southeast Asia*. Hawaii: East-West Center.

Coney, Judith. 1998. *Sahaja Yoga*. London: Routledge

Coward, Harold, John R. Hinnells, and Raymond Brady Williams, eds. 2000. *The South Asian Religious Diaspora in Britain, Canada and the United States*. New York: State University of New York Press.

Fenton, John Y. 1992. "Academic Study of Religions and Asian Indian-American College Students." *In* Raymond Brady Williams, ed., *A Sacred Thread: Modern Transmission of Hindu Traditions in India and Abroad*, 258–77. New York: Columbia University Press.

Jacobsen, Knut A. and Pratap Kumar, eds. 2004. *South Asians in the Diaspora: Histories and Religious Traditions*. Leiden: Brill.

Knott, Kim. 1986a. *Hinduism in Leeds: A Study of Religious Practice in the Indian Hindu Community and in Hindu-Related Groups*. Leeds: Department of Theology and Religious Studies, University of Leeds.

Knott, Kim. 1986b. *My Sweet Lord: The Hare Krishna Movement*. Wellingborough: Aquarian.

Knott, Kim. 1998. *Hinduism: A Very Short Introduction*. Oxford: Oxford University Press.

Korom, Frank J. 2002. *Hosay Trinidad: Muharram Performances in an Indo-Caribbean Diaspora*. Pennsylvania: University of Pennsylvania Press.

Kurien, Prema. 1999. "Gendered Ethnicity: Creating a Hindu Indian Identity in the U.S." *American Behavioral Scientist* 42, 4: 648–70.

Kurien, Prema. 2001. "Religion, Ethnicity and Politics: Hindu and Muslim Indian Immigrants in the United States." *Ethnic and Racial Studies* 24, 2: 263–93.

Kurien, Prema. 2004. "Multiculturalism and Ethnic Nationalism: The Development of an American Hinduism." *Social Problems* 51, 3: 362–85.

Mathew, Biju and Vijay Prashad. 2000. "The Protean Forms of Yankee Hindutva." *Ethnic and Racial Studies* 23, 3: 516–34.

Narayanan, Vasudha. 1992. "Creating the South Indian 'Hindu' Experience in the United States." *In* Raymond Brady Williams, ed., *A Sacred Thread: Modern*

Transmission of Hindu Traditions in India and Abroad, 147–76. New York: Columbia University Press.
Nye, Malory. 1995. *A Place for Our Gods: The Construction of an Edinburgh Hindu Temple Community*. Richmond: Curzon.
Nye, Malory. 2001. *Multiculturalism and Minority Religions in Britain: Krishna Consciousness, Religious Freedom and the Politics of Location*. London: Routledge Curzon.
Parekh, Bhikhu. 1994. "Some Reflections on the Hindu Diaspora." *New Community* 20, 4: 603–20.
Raheja, Gloria Goodwin. 1988. *The Poison in the Gift: Ritual, Prestation and the Dominant Caste in a North Indian Village*. Chicago: University of Chicago Press.
Raj, Dhooleka Sarhadi. 2000. " 'Who the Hell Do You Think You Are?': Promoting Religious Identity among Young Hindus in Britain." *Ethnic and Racial Studies* 23, 3: 535–58.
Rukmani, T. S., ed. 1999. *Hindu Diaspora: Global Perspectives*. Montreal: Concordia University.
Shukla, Sandhya R. 1997. "Building Diaspora and Nation: The 1991 'Cultural festival of India.' " *Cultural Studies* 11, 2: 296–315.
Tinker, Hugh. 1974. *A New System of Slavery: The Export of Indian Labour Overseas 1830–1920*. London: Hurst.
van der Veer, Peter. 1995. "Introduction: The Diasporic Imagination." *In* Peter van der Veer, ed., *Nation and Migration: The Politics of Space in the South Asian Diaspora*, 1–16. Philadelphia: University of Pennsylvania Press.
Vertovec, Steven. 2000. *The Hindu Diaspora: Comparative Patterns*. London: Routledge.
Waghorne, Joanne P. 2004. *Diaspora of the Gods: Modern Hindu Temples in an Urban Middle Class World*. New York: Oxford University Press.
Warrier, Maya. 2005. *Hindu Selves in a Modern World: Guru Faith in the Mata Amritanandamayi Mission*. London: Routledge.
Williams, Raymond Brady. 1988. *Religions of Immigrants from India and Pakistan: New Threads in the American Tapestry*. Cambridge: Cambridge University Press.
Williams, Raymond Brady. 1992. "Sacred Threads of Several Textures." *In* Raymond Brady Williams, ed., *A Sacred Thread: Modern Transmission of Hindu Traditions in India and Abroad*, 228–57. New York: Columbia University Press.
Williams, Raymond Brady. 2001. *An Introduction to Swaminarayan Hinduism*. Cambridge: Cambridge University Press.

7

Ecology

Lance E. Nelson

Possibilities and Potential Resources
Problematics
Gandhi and Current Developments
Concluding Reflections

When examining an ancient tradition, such as Hinduism, for material that speaks to our contemporary concern for ecology and the environment, one must begin with an awareness that this concern, along with its particular conceptual construction of "the environment," is quite new, dating perhaps from the mid-twentieth century when events first triggered awareness of an impending environmental crisis. This means that, as Rosemary Ruether has pointed out, "there is no ready-made ecological spirituality and ethic in past traditions" (1992: 206). The Hindu tradition has only fairly recently begun to address the environmental question directly. So when asking, as of any of the great religions, "What does it say about ecology?," we must perforce look for indirect rather than direct evidence, for ideas and practices that can now be reinterpreted by the living tradition itself to help meet the current crisis. This chapter surveys Hindu attitudes toward the natural world and the role of human beings therein, as expressed in theology, symbol, law, and practice. Contemporary developments are considered to the extent permitted within the limits of a short article.

The attitudes to nature found in Hinduism are as multifaceted as the tradition itself. As in other traditions, the visions are sometimes in conflict. Hinduism has elements that are potentially supportive of environmental awareness and action. It also has elements that are not. As we shall see, traditional attitudes range from the reverencing of nature as a manifestation of divinity through dismissal of the world, in relation to authentic spiritual existence, as illusory (*māyā*) and insignificant (*tuccha*). Passages here and there, especially in courtly poetry and drama (*kāvya*), express appreciation for the beauty of nature and the sustenance it provides to human beings. One has to look hard, however, for hints of the late modern awareness of nature as nature, where the natural world is valued in itself for its diversity, the uniqueness and welfare of certain species, and so on. And always, the contrast between textual theory and actual practice, to be expected as a feature of all human traditions, may be so striking as to appear, or truly be, contradictory. In thinking about Hindu approaches to nature, moreover, caution must be taken to avoid reading contemporary concerns and outlooks into ancient texts, a practice that—in addition to being anachronistic—often results in a kind of inauthentic romanticism. There certainly are possibilities in the Hindu tradition when it comes to environmentally supportive material, but there are also problems. Both are explored in what follows.

Possibilities and Potential Resources

Hindus recognize the Vedic scriptures (*ca.* 1500–400 BCE) as the most ancient source of their tradition. The poetry of the Vedas was liturgical in nature, functioning largely as an element of a sometimes complex sacrificial ritual. The sacrificial milieu of Vedic religion was not without its own forms of violence—even cruelty, as Buddhists were wont to declare—involving as it did on occasion the ritual killing of animals. Nevertheless, the Vedic hymns show considerable evidence of the veneration, indeed divinization, of aspects of nature. Vedic deities include Earth (Pṛthvī), Dawn (Uṣas), Fire (Agni), Wind (Vāyu), and so on. The Pṛthvī Sūkta, "Hymn to the Earth," of the *Atharva Veda* (*ca.* 1000 BCE) addresses the earth as a goddess, Devī Vasundharā, and the poet declares, "The earth is the mother, and I the son of the earth!" (12.12). The earth "bestows wealth liberally" (12.44) on humanity, and this fact seems indeed to be the primary concern of the poet. In appropriating her gifts, however, humanity must observe limits, not exceeding that which is renewable: "What, O earth, I dig out of thee, quickly shall that grow again: may I not, O pure one, pierce thy vital spot, (and) not thy heart!" (12.35). In their daily recitations of the sacred Gāyatrī-*mantra* (*Ṛg Veda* 3.52.10), generations of Hindus have paid homage to the sun and proclaimed their connectedness with "earth, atmosphere, and heaven" (see *Bṛhadāraṇyaka Upaniṣad* 6.3.6).

The Upaniṣads (*ca.* 900–400 BCE), part of the later Vedic corpus, develop the notion—important in differentiating the Hindu vision from that of Abrahamic monotheism—of the one ultimate Being that has become the universe, rather than having created it as an external product. This idea had already been adumbrated in *Ṛg Veda* 10.90, in which the cosmos is created through the sacrificial dismembering of the body of a divine "Person" (*puruṣa*). Moving from myth to philosophical theology, the *Chāndoyga Upaniṣad* (3.14.1) proclaims, "All this is Brahman," a doctrine that has supported the variety of Hindu thought known as nondualism (*advaita*). Hindu nondualism, as formalized and elaborately articulated in several schools of theology, sees the world—and indeed the inner spiritual self of all beings (not just humans)—as inseparable from ultimate reality. It is this trend of thought in particular that has inspired the idea that Hinduism sees all of nature as sacred and worthy of reverence.

The *Bhagavad Gītā*, certainly the most well known of Hindu scriptures, echoes this notion of God embodied in nature. The *Bhagavad Gītā*'s mystically sacralized view of the world is founded on an all-encompassing view of the Divine: "Of all manifestations," Lord Kṛṣṇa declares, "I am the beginning, the end, and the middle" (10.32). The true devotee, he says, "sees Me in all things, and all things in Me" (6.30). In chapter 10, "The Yoga of Divine Manifestations (*vibhūti*)," Kṛṣṇa identifies himself with elements of the natural universe: sun, moon, stars, the ocean, the Himalayas, the wind, and the holy Ganges. Chapter 11, "The Vision of the Universal Form (*viśva-rūpa*)," provides compelling intimations of the later Vaiṣṇava doctrine of the world as the body of God. "The sun and the moon," says Arjuna in awe, "are your eyes" (11.19).

The *Bhagavad Gītā* creatively integrates this vision of world-sacrality with an ethic of ascetic restraint and selfless activity. This, of course, is the famous teaching of *karmayoga*, in which the religious seeker—instead of renouncing worldly life and action—remains at his or her station, working without egoism, selfish desire, and attachment. The motivation for such activity is declared to be *loka-saṃgraha* (3.20), literally the "holding together" or "maintenance" of the world. The sage of the *Bhagavad Gītā*, we are told, acts out of concern for the "welfare of all beings" (*sarva-bhūta-hita*; 5.25). This ideal of social engagement for world-benefit through spiritually disciplined action was the chief basis of the esteem in which the *Bhagavad Gītā* was held by nineteenth-century Hindu nationalists, such as Mohandas K. Gandhi and Balwantrao Gangadhar Tilak (Nelson 2000: 132).

In the later theistic, devotional traditions of Hinduism, the idea of world as manifestation of God recurs and is accentuated. The *Viṣṇu Purāṇa* proclaims, "Verily, this whole [world] is the body of God" (*tat sarvaṃ vai hareḥ tanuḥ*; 1.12.38). The Vaiṣṇava theology of Rāmānuja (eleventh century CE) develops this image: The world is as intimately related to God as body (*śarīra*) to the soul that is embodied (*śarīrin*). In his *Siddhāntamuktāvalī*, the Kṛṣṇaite theologian Vallabha (sixteenth century CE) teaches the "pure nonduality" (*śuddhādvaita*) of God and world through a striking analogy. No devotee of Gaṅgā Devī (Goddess Ganges), he says, would worship her only as personified deity and fail to reverence her embodiment in the holy river. Instead, the devotees of Gaṅgā Devī go on pilgrimage to the holy river, bathe in and drink her water, and, if possible, live on her sacred shores. In the same way, no one who worships the universal Deity Kṛṣṇa should devalue the world, which is nothing less than his cosmic embodiment.

Among Vaiṣṇavas, as in the Veda, the earth is divinized, now as Bhū Devī (Goddess Earth), and when she is in danger of destruction by demonic forces, Lord Viṣṇu himself descends as *avatāra* to rescue her. Devout Vaiṣṇavas ask Earth in their daily prayers to forgive the abusive touch of their feet. Expanding this kind of sensitivity, it is understood that Earth/the earth is supported by human righteousness (*Atharva Veda* 12.1) and can be offended by immorality and by physical mistreatment. Human beings should act ethically or "risk the wrath or discomfiture of the earth itself" (Kinsley 1995: 58).

The subcontinent of India—crisscrossed by pilgrimage routes that connect holy places, many associated with rivers, mountains, and other natural features—assumes in Hindu eyes a kind of sacred topography (Kinsley 1998; Van Horn 2006). The phenomenon of *śākta-pīṭha*s, sacred sites connected with the Goddess, illustrates this mode of awareness. The myth of Satī, spouse of Śiva, describes the dismemberment of the goddess' body, the parts being deposited at various locations throughout the subcontinent. At such locations, important goddess temples (*pīṭha*, literally "seats") and pilgrimage centers were established. Though the exact number of these sites is disputed—often the number fifty-two is given—the myth and the system of interrelated shrines create a unifying topographic network. As David Kinsley writes, "Taken together, the *pīṭhas* constitute or point toward a transcendent (or, perhaps better, a universally immanent) goddess whose being encompasses, underlies, infuses, and unifies the Indian subcontinent as a whole" (1998: 230). A similar geographically sacralizing effect arises from the related system of the twelve Jyotir Liṅga, shrines dedicated to the god Śiva scattered across India. A more localized example would be the system of the Aṣṭa Vināyaka, the "Eight Gaṇeśas" and their temples, which sacralize the land of Maharashtra and give identity and sense of place to Maharashtrians.

Hindu law books (*dharmaśāstra*) contain numerous edicts that might now be considered as ecofriendly, involving protection of animals, land, trees, rivers, and so on, such protection being described particularly as the responsibility of kings. Though these texts are of course not operating out of what we would call an ecological model, they "advocate conservation strategies and demonstrate awareness of the impact of human interaction with the environment" (McGee 2000: 80). Each of the great classes of Hindu society is conceived as having its particular *dharma* or sacred duty. The *dharma* of the ruler is to protect—not only people and polity but the land as well. A surprising number of synonyms for king in Sanskrit reflect the ruler's duty to protect the earth: *bhū-pāla* and *bhū-pa*, Earth-Protector; *bhū-bharaṇa* and *bhū-bhartṛ*, Earth-Maintainer. Others suggest a special spousal, and therefore similarly protective, relationship with the earth: *bhū-*

pati, Earth-Husband; *bhū-ramaṇa* and *bhū-vallabha*, Beloved of the Earth (McGee 2000: 63). Included in the scope of a king's solemn responsibility is, as we might expect, the obligation to oversee the development of the earth's resources for the benefit of human beings. But there is also a clear awareness of humankind's dependence on nature. The texts prescribe for royalty balancing duties to ensure that the use of nature's resources remains with the limits of sustainability and to punish those who violate those limits. Crop rotation, planting of trees, various provisions for the protection of animals from cruelty, trees from cutting, and water from pollution are enjoined. Such measures include fines and other sanctions. As McGee observes: "It is clear from many classical Indian texts on the duties of kings that a king had a responsibility to reap the benefits of the nature's resources for the sake of his kingdom and its citizens; yet it is also clear that the successful and ideal king had to carefully manage these resources and respect the earth" (McGee 2000: 73).

Ann Grodzins Gold has studied villagers' reports of the ecological situation in the kingdom of Sawar in what is now Rajasthan, North India, as it prevailed under Vansh Pradip Singh, the state's last pre-independence ruler. During Vansh Pradip Singh's rule of more than thirty years, from 1914 to 1947, there is ample evidence that "the jungle was dense and wild animals were prosperous" (Gold 2000: 320). The king protected the forest and wildlife, and under his protection, both increased. Vansh Pradip Singh died in 1947, the year of India's independence, with no children. In any event, the princely states were being gradually incorporated into the Indian Republic, depriving the old rulers of their power. The people of Ghatiyali, part of Vansh Pradip Singh's former kingdom, report rapid deforestation of their region in the post-independence era and recollect as intertwined realities "the former ruling kings, old growths of indigenous trees, and wild animals." As Gold reports the villagers' experience, "These three came to an end together" (2000: 321). The king's ecological record was not perfect by modern standards—he once had large numbers of lizards exterminated on flimsy grounds. Still, Gold is able to report an extraordinary proclamation, as remembered by the villagers, for which Singh was well known: "*If you cut the smallest branch of a tree it is just as if you cut my finger*" (2000: 323; emphasis in original). In this graphic image, Gold argues, the king's "responsible authority" (*zimmedārī*) for the preservation of the land was epitomized.

Problematics

In thinking about how such ideas and practices as those that have been described might function positively in terms of environmental awareness in India, one needs to avoid premature enthusiasm. The problematics of Hindu attitudes toward nature and the environment must also receive some attention.

As a starting example, the notion of the sacred river in Hinduism is illustrative of some of the potentially detrimental dimensions of symbol systems that at first sight might appear to be ecologically positive. Indeed, an examination of this phenomenon raises questions about the value for ecology of the whole concept of sacralization of nature or aspects of nature. To take the most famous example, consider the holiness of the Ganges. The Ganges is not only a river, she is—as has been mentioned—a goddess, Gaṅgā Devī, and, as such, an object of pious veneration. She is not only inherently pure but powerfully purifying. Bathing in the Ganges is spiritually cleansing: It relieves one of kārmic and other religious impurities going back lifetimes. Ganges water is a purifying substance, bottled and distributed for ritual use all over India and abroad.

A story is told of a king who happens to sleep on the banks of the holy river. Waking in the night, he sees a group of women, covered in the foulest dirt, going to bathe in the sacred waters. Having finished their bath, they emerge radiantly clean, only to vanish. Intrigued, the king comes again the next night and the next, witnessing each time the same phenomenon. Finally, his curiosity wins out and he asks the women, "Who are you?" "We are the rivers of India," they reply. "Every day, the people bathe in us, and we absorb all their sin. We come to the Ganges so that we ourselves may be purified" (Narayanan 2000: 116). Residents of Banaras, who bathe daily in the river's waters, say that, because Mother Ganges is the supreme purifier, she cannot be polluted.

But of course, the Ganges *is* polluted. Hindu awareness of a distinction between ritual-spiritual purity and physical cleanliness means that something can be ritually pure but physically dirty, and vice versa. The religious perceptions of devout pilgrims and the clerics who minister to them—actors quickly offended and put on the defensive by any suggestion that the holy Ganges could be polluted—may actually make it more difficult to mobilize action to clean up the river. The problems caused by divergences among religious, scientific, and political conceptions of the Ganges' purity/pollution have been explored by Kelly Alley (1998).

In South India, there is a parallel situation with regard to the Kāverī River, referred to as Dakṣiṇā Gaṅgā (Ganges of the South) and Kāverī Amman (Mother Kāverī) and divinized as the spouse of Lord Viṣṇu. As such, local Hindus worship her in temple icons and remember her in folklore and festival. In the monsoon season, when the river is swollen by the rains, they say she is pregnant. Vasudha Narayanan (2000: 117–18) describes how those who live along the river in Tamil Nadu celebrate the river's "pregnancy food cravings" through festival picnics along the banks of the river. Sadly, the neighboring state of Karnataka has dammed the river to the extent that the flow in Tamil Nadu often drops to a trickle, and the Kāverī is barely able to give life to the land. Politicians in both states continue to fight over the vital waters of this river, which in other contexts they might regard as a manifestation of maternal deity.

Further complexities of nature sacralization are discussed by Vijaya Nagarajan (1998), who has studied the ecological implications of the South Indian *kōlam*, ritual designs that women create on the ground in daily morning offerings to Bhū Devī, the goddess Earth. Village women understand that the beautiful and carefully laid out patterns help to cancel the human debt to Earth while being a gesture of thankfulness for her patient bearing of our lives and behavior, good and evil. The ritual designs also help to fulfill each household's duty to "feed a thousand souls every day." Feeding so many humans would be difficult, if not impossible. But, as the *kōlam* is made of rice powder, it becomes food for myriad smaller creatures (Nagarajan 1998: 275). In framing the meaning of this ritual, Nagarajan argues that human-nature interactions are embedded in complex cultural webs, so that what may appear "ecological" to the outsider may not be understood that way from within. "I was puzzled," Nagarajan writes, "by the contradiction between women's reverence for Bhū Devī and their seeming disrespect to her throughout the day, as they threw trash and garbage on the earth, the very same place that they considered to be sacred" (Nagarajan 1998: 275). She offers the notion of "intermittent sacrality" to explain this seemingly contradictory behavior. Awareness of sacrality is not, and perhaps cannot, be sustained: The sacrality of a given aspect of nature may wax and wane, the ritual relationship that recognizes that sacrality may lapse, or simple issues of survival may intervene (1998: 277–80).

It is clear that, in the Hindu context, to say that an aspect of nature is sacred is not automatically and unambiguously an ecological plus. Indeed, as Alley, Nagarajan, and others have noted, the sacralization of nature may paradoxically undermine ecological consciousness, particularly if, as is often the case with maternal goddess imagery, it portrays nature as protecting, cleansing, and forgiving—and powerfully needing no protection from humans in return. "The natural world is a divine being," Nagarajan observes, "and therefore capable of cleaning herself" (1998: 277). As she is our mother and we are her children, we can go on heedlessly, leaving her to clean up our mess. A feminist hermeneutic is obviously possible here. Narayanan discerns a parallel between the abuse of nature, especially rivers envisioned as female, and the abuse of women in India:

> The rivers, flowing through India and personified as women...have absorbed the greed and follies of human beings and the slime, sludge, and excreta of human greed and consumption. It is hard not to draw a comparison between the rivers and the plight of women who are now the target of crimes of greed and power.
>
> (2000: 118)

Even in theology, however, the sacralization of nature goes only so far. It is often claimed that Hinduism's unitary vision of world as Brahman involves the sacralization of not just particular aspects of nature but the entire cosmos. Although there is some evidence for such a conclusion, as we have seen above, it is less true than one might suppose. The prestigious Nondualist or Advaita Vedānta, in its classical formulation, achieves its monism not by divinizing the world but by eliminating it, as *māyā*, from the realm of the real. Advaita and other Hindu theologies in fact involve the same kind of hierarchical dualism of God-world, spirit-matter, soul-body that is often portrayed as a purely Western affliction. Adherents must practice "discrimination" (*viveka*) between these elements, characterized as "the eternal and the noneternal." Manuals of nondualist spirituality encourage detachment from the material world, recommending that aspirants think of it as mere straw, a dead rat, dog vomit, or crow excrement (Nelson 1998: 70–81). Although theistic Hindu theology, unlike Advaita, recognizes the reality of the world, it also displays a tendency to denigrate physical existence in favor of the more highly valued spiritual body (*siddha-deha*) and transcendent realms (*śuddha-sattva*, *goloka*, and so on).

A number of contemporary Hindu ecofeminists have attempted to reconfigure the notion of *prakṛti*—perhaps the closest concept in Sanskrit texts to the Western idea of Nature—as supportive of an Indian ecological ethic. For example, Vandana Shiva—an important environmental activist and thinker—writes: "Nature as *prakṛti* is inherently active, a powerful, productive force in the dialectic of the creation, renewal, and sustenance of all life" (1989: 48; see also Vatsyanan 1995). Any attempt, however, to revalorize *prakṛti* as a locus of ultimate concern or resource for ecofeminist thinking will not be authentic unless it begins with a recognition that the traditional Hindu understanding of *prakṛti* is embedded in the same hierarchical dualism that pervades much of Hindu religious thought. Outside its Tantric transformations, *prakṛti* is everywhere in Hindu theology regarded as unconscious matter (*jaḍa* or *acit*), devalued in relation to conscious spirit (*puruṣa*, *ātman*, *jīva*, and so on). This is, of course, true for classical Sāṃkhya thought but also for the Advaita theologian Śaṅkara and for Rāmānuja, Madhva, Nimbārka, the Gauḍīya Gosvāmins, and other Vaiṣṇava theologians (Nelson 2000: 157–58). No doubt, *prakṛti* is grammatically feminine and is symbolically construed as such by the tradition. But we have seen how the maternal imagery used for India's rivers is fraught with difficulties. So too, the construal of nature as a powerful feminine force in Hinduism comes with problematic baggage, issues that are not all that different from those that beset the symbolism of "Mother Nature" in the West.

The ultimate religious goal for most Hindus is of course *mokṣa*, defined as "liberation" of the individual from rebirth in the natural world (*saṃsāra*). This world-transcending ambition is supported by the traditional Hindu view of cosmic time, which predicts that the world for thousands of years hence will progressively and inevitably decline into increasing levels of moral, social, and environmental chaos. In this vision, the Kali Yuga, or Dark Age, in which we live is inescapably polluted and morally bankrupt, and things are only getting worse. Together, these elements further sharpen the spirit-matter dualism and—to whatever extent they are taken seriously—provide potential disincentives to ecological activism.

It is well known that Hindus believe in reincarnation. Indeed, Hinduism regards all beings—"from [the god] Brahmā down to a blade of grass," to use a frequently repeated formula—as having equal spiritual potential by virtue of their being equally endowed with *ātman*. Thus, human beings are not the only animals to possess souls. This idea—potentially fruitful in terms of ecological awareness—is among the considerations underlying the Hindu ethics of nonviolence (*ahiṃsā*) and vegetarianism, about which more could be said if space permitted (see Bryant 2006; Nelson 2006). Still, the tradition does not escape a pronounced anthropocentricism. All humans were once, in their long chain of existences, incarnated as animals and even plants. Nevertheless there is a hierarchy of births, and human birth is the highest, even superior to birth as a god, because only humans, with rare exceptions, may attain *mokṣa*. On the other hand, humans who commit evil deeds are threatened with rebirth in "lowly wombs," that is, those of animals or insects (Nelson 2006).

Gandhi and Current Developments

In the modern era, among the most interesting and well-known exponents of Hindu values—as they were then beginning to intersect with international currents—was Mohandas K. Gandhi. Living still prior to the awareness of the ecological crisis that emerged in the 1960s, Mahātmā Gandhi nevertheless has been an inspiration for ecological thought and action in India. Indeed, historian Ramchandra Guha has identified him as "the patron saint of the Indian environmental movement" (1998: 65). In his method of Satyāgraha, or "holding to the truth," Gandhi expanded the ancient Indian ethic of *ahiṃsā*, or nonharming, from a morality of noninterference and letting things be to a practice for political change. In this transformation of ancient Indic ideals, he was of course influenced by certain Western strands of thought, but he was equally supported by Hindu notions, particularly the ideal of detached action for "world-maintenance" derived from the *Bhagavad Gītā*. Gandhi's activist revisioning of the traditional nonviolence ethic renders it political without, however, stripping it of its moral sensitivity. Gandhian *ahiṃsā* includes an awareness of the multifaceted and interconnected negative ramifications of violence, an awareness that parallels ecological thinking about sensitive environmental networks and the unforeseen consequences of environmental interference. Thus, contemporary Gandhians are able to speak of ecological violence while simultaneously possessing effective tools for resistance to such violence.

Also supported by the *Bhagavad Gītā*'s vision of ascetic detachment and desire-free (*niṣkāma*) living—and by the yogic ethic of "nonpossession" (*aparigraha*)—is the Gandhian ideal of simple living, one that nowadays we would associate with notions of "low ecological footprint" and "sustainability." This side of Gandhi's vision is made plain in this stern but provocative reminder of the difference between human need and human greed: "God never creates more than what is strictly needed for the moment. Therefore whoever appropriates more than the minimum that is really necessary for him is guilty of theft" (Gandhi 1960: 5). Partly as an extension of this mode of thought, Gandhi also, to the dismay of some of his developmentalist contemporaries, propagated the vision of an India based on decentralized, self-reliant village economies. In so doing, he anticipated on one hand our contemporary concern for the dangers of globalization and on the other the "small is beautiful" economics of E. F. Schumacher. He was among the first in India to lament—in addition to the physical assault on land and health—the moral, spiritual, and aesthetic debilitation wrought by industrialization:

> This land of ours was once, we are told, the abode of the Gods. It is not possible to conceive Gods inhabiting a land which is made hideous by the smoke and the din of mill chimneys and factories and whose roadways are traversed by rushing engines, dragging numerous cars crowded with men mostly who know not what they are after.…I refer to these things because they are held to be symbolical of material progress. But they add not an atom to our happiness.
>
> (Gandhi n.d.: 354)

In thinking of resources for environmentalism in India, the question of leadership also arises: specifically, what kind of leadership is likely to be most successful in motivating India to ecological action? Here Gandhi also contributes. His beloved *Bhagavad Gītā* held up for emulation and admiration not only frugal living, but especially the iconic figure of the detached and enlightened ascetic, free from selfish ambition, which became for Hindus a cultural ideal of sainthood. Gandhi, whether consciously or unconsciously, successfully embodied this Hindu archetype for his followers, giving him marvelous effectiveness as a leader in mobilizing people for change. The Gandhian tradition has continued, most notably but by no means exclusively in the Sarvodaya (Universal Uplift) movement (Shepard 1987), galvanized by such leaders as Vinoba Bhave, Jayaprakash Narayan, Narayan Desai, and Sunderlal Bahuguna. Its concerns, originally political and social, have gradually taken on ecological dimensions as awareness of environmental issues suffused the activist community in India.

The most-cited example of a modern environmental movement with Gandhian inspiration is the Chipko *andolan*, which began as a peasant protest movement in the early 1970s in the Gharwal region of Uttaranchal (then the northernmost district of Uttar Pradesh) in the foothills of the Indian Himalaya. The name *Chipko*—from the Hindi verb *cipkānā*, "to stick, to cling, to embrace"—came from the nonviolent tactic of village women and men "hugging" trees to prevent their being felled by outside lumber companies. Whether or not it was known to these villagers and their leaders, this tactic had historical precedent in the actions of the Biṣṇoīs, a people of Rajasthan who venerated trees out of religious commitment. In the mid-eighteenth century, more than three hundred Biṣṇoīs are said to have sacrificed their lives clinging to trees to protect them from being felled by the army of a local king (Callicott 1994: 220; Gold 2000: 327–28). The modern Chipko movement began when the government—oblivious to the suffering that massive deforestation was causing the locals—gave a sporting goods company permission to log trees for tennis racquets, having just refused long-established forest access to a local Gandhian cooperative movement, the Dasoli Gram Svarajya Sangh (Dasholi District Self-rule Association). This group had sought a small amount of wood for making agricultural implements. In the face of an advancing phalanx of loggers, Chandi Prasad Bhatt, leader of the Sangh, famously proclaimed, "Let them know that we will not allow the felling of ash trees. When they aim their axes upon them, we will embrace the trees" (cited in Weber 1989: 40). The movement spread rapidly, and by 1981, its campaigns had convinced then Prime Minister Indira Gandhi to impose a fifteen-year moratorium on commercial tree-felling in the Himalayan forests (Callicott 1994: 218). Its leaders, Bhatt and Sunderlal Bahuguna, have become India's most well-known environmentalists (Gadgil and Guha 1992: 224).

Demonstrating the Gandhian dimensions of this movement, Bahuguna has sought to embody the ideal of leader as religious ascetic who, like Gandhi, has abandoned self-seeking in favor of concern for the masses. He has on a number of occasions used the hunger strike as a weapon of nonviolent protest. This happened in the Chipko campaigns both against deforestation and, more recently and in the same region, in the struggle against the construction of the massive Tehri Dam on the Bhāgīrathī River, the main tributary of the Ganges. This dam threatens devastating consequences for an area that is at once highly seismic and the home of some of the most sacred sites for Hindus. Bahuguna's fasts, which have lasted as long as seventy-four days and have led to his being arrested by the authorities, have been accompanied by ritual recitations of the *Bhagavad Gītā*.

Bahuguna has not been without controversy. Among other reasons is his recent openness to Hindu nationalist involvement in his causes, particularly the Tehri Dam campaign. This points to a disturbing aspect of the melding of environmentalism and religion in India: the potential of right-wing Hindu nationalists harnessing, or even diverting, the energies of ecological movements in service of Hindu chauvinist goals. The Tehri Dam, by its very nature and design, was intended to obstruct and manipulate the flow of the river most sacred to Hindus, the Ganges. Moreover, the enormous structure's possible failure (the region, as indicated, is prone to earthquakes) would entail catastrophic consequences for the sacred sites, religious institutions and leaders, and masses of Hindu pilgrims downstream. On this basis, the project has been played up by the Visva Hindu Pariṣad (the World Hindu Council)—not as a threat to the ecology or the villagers of the region—but rather as a threat to Hinduism and Hindutva, the essential "Hinduness" of the nation. Furthermore, the cause has been charged with anti-Muslim, communalist sentiment through comparison of the dam with the Babri Masjid, a mosque in Ayodhya branded a symbol of Muslim oppression and destroyed by Hindu militants in 1992. To this end, it has also been identified as a likely target—easy but potentially devastating—for Islamic-Pakistani terrorists seeking to destroy the heart of Hindu India. Emma Mawdsley (2005) argues that, in all this, environmental and resettlement issues, of vital importance to the people of the region and the original inspiration of the anti-dam movement, have been subordinated to the Parisad's quest for political power and its goal of Hindu nationhood. More starkly, Meera Nanda (2004) sees the Parisad's "dharmic ecology" as a "Trojan horse," part of a stealth campaign to hijack the ecological movement as a vehicle of Hindutva ideology. One is reminded here how the perhaps overly close association of Gandhi and the Congress Party with Hindu symbolism during India's independence struggle led to disaffection among non-Hindus and helped to move India toward the tragedy of Partition (see Coward 2003). At the very least, assuming that the environment of India belongs to all Indians, there are dangers in associating the environmental movement too exclusively with Hinduism.

Concluding Reflections

India today boasts perhaps the world's largest environmental movement (Peritore 1993). As Peritore reports, it is well organized and intellectually sophisticated, with rich cultural and religious resources to draw on, not the least the legacy of Gandhi. Conversely, it is hampered by governmental corruption, paralyzing bureaucratic inertia, and—more recently—the emergence of a divisive communalist politics that complicates especially any effort to harness religious symbolism to environmental causes. All of this is framed by the problem of India's relentless population growth and the environmental stress caused by, on the one hand, the country's burgeoning consumerist middle class (supposedly the largest in the world) and, on the other, its masses of rural and urban poor. Thus, Peritore concludes: "The movement, far from being a vanguard, is fighting a rearguard action for cultural and ecological survival" (1993: 818).

The word "survival" is important here. It reminds us that the concern for nature as nature and the universalizing environmental ethics and spirituality of postmodern "religiously inspired environmentalism" may not have much relevance in India or any other developing country (Tomalin 2002). Situations understood in a wider framework as ecological problems by Westerners, or indigenous Western-educated elites, are likely to be read as human-centered problems of justice and survival by villagers. As Emma Tomalin (2002: 19–26) and others have pointed out, the latter may adopt elements of religion to their "ecological" struggles more for their pragmatic utility as symbolic motivators and legitimators than out of any overarching spiritual or ecological sensibility that outsiders might impute. Indeed, it is a real question as to whether religion "is an appropriate or sufficient frame through which to tackle the massive environmental problems confronting modern India" (Mawdsley 2005: 2). Nevertheless, it is both desirable and inevitable that Hindus will continue to engage in a conscious, thoughtful, sustained, and finally pragmatic effort to reconstruct their traditions so as to address contemporary concerns, be they environmental or otherwise. And it is clear they have plenty of resources to do so.

References Cited

Alley, Kelly D. 1998. "Idioms of Degeneracy: Assessing Gaṅgā's Purity and Pollution." *In* Lance E. Nelson, ed., *Purifying the Earthly Body of God: Religion and Ecology in Hindu India*, 297–330. Albany: State University of New York Press.

Atharva Veda. 1973 [1897]. *Hymns of the Atharva Veda* (trans. Maurice Bloomfield). New Delhi: Motilal Banarsidass.

Bryant, Edwin. 2006. "Strategies of Subversion: The Emergence of Vegetarianism in Post-Vedic India." *In* Kimberley Patton and Paul Waldau, eds., *A Communion of*

Subjects: Animals in Religion, Science, and Ethics, 194–203. New York: Columbia University Press.

Callicott, J. Baird. 1994. *Earth's Insights: A Survey of Ecological Ethics from the Mediterranean Basin to the Australian Outback*. Berkeley: University of California Press.

Coward, Harold, ed. 2003. *Indian Critiques of Gandhi*. Albany: State University of New York Press.

Gadgil, Madhav and Ramachandra Guha. 1992. *This Fissured Land: An Ecological History of India*. Berkeley: University of California Press.

Gandhi, M. K. 1960. *Trusteeship* (ed. Ravindra Kelekar). Ahmedabad: Navajivan Trust.

Gandhi, M. K. n.d. [1933]. *Speeches and Writings of Mahatma Gandhi*. Madras: G. A. Natesan.

Gold, Ann Grodzins. 2000. " 'If You Cut a Branch You Cut My Finger': Court, Forest, and Environmental Ethics in Rajasthan." *In* Christopher Key Chapple and Mary Evelyn Tucker, eds., *Hinduism and Ecology: The Intersection of Earth, Sky, and Water*, 317–36. Cambridge: Harvard University Press.

Guha, Ramachandra. 1998. "Mahatma Gandhi and the Environmental Movement in India." *In* Aren Kalland and Gerard Persoon, eds., *Environmental Movements in Asia*, 65–82. Richmond: Curzon.

Kinsley, David. 1995. *Ecology and Religion: Ecological Spirituality in a Cross-Cultural Perspective*. Englewood Cliffs: Prentice Hall.

Kinsley, David. 1998. "Learning the Story of the Land: Reflections on the Liberating Power of Geography and Pilgrimage in the Hindu Tradition." *In* Lance E. Nelson, ed., *Purifying the Earthly Body of God: Religion and Ecology in Hindu India*, 225–46. Albany: State University of New York Press.

Mawdsley, Emma. 2005. "The Abuse of Religion and Ecology: The Vishva Hindu Parishad and Tehri Dam." *Worldviews: Environment, Culture, Religion* 9, 1: 1–24.

McGee, Mary. 2000. "State Responsibility for Environmental Management: Perspectives from Hindu Texts on Polity." *In* Christopher Key Chapple and Mary Evelyn Tucker, eds., *Hinduism and Ecology: The Intersection of Earth, Sky, and Water*, 59–100. Cambridge: Harvard University Press.

Nagarajan, Vijaya Rettakudi. 1998. "The Earth as Goddess Bhū Devī: Toward a Theory of 'Embedded Ecologies' in Folk Hinduism." *In* Lance E. Nelson, ed., *Purifying the Earthly Body of God: Religion and Ecology in Hindu India*, 269–95. Albany: State University of New York Press.

Nanda, Meera. 2004. "Dharmic Ecology and the Neo-Pagan International: The Dangers of Religious Environmentalism In India." Paper presented at the Eighteenth European Conference on Modern South Asian Studies, Lunds University, Sweden, July 6–9.

Narayanan, Vasudha. 2000. "'One Tree is Equal to Ten Sons': Some Hindu Responses to the Problems of Ecology, Population, and Consumerism." *In* Harold Coward and Daniel C. Maguire, eds., *Visions of a New Earth: Religious Perspectives on Population, Consumption, and Ecology*, 111–29. Albany: State University of New York Press.

Nelson, Lance E. 1998. "The Dualism of Nondualism: Advaita Vedānta and the Irrelevance of Nature." *In* Lance E. Nelson, ed., *Purifying the Earthly Body of God: Religion and Ecology in Hindu India*, 61–88. Albany: State University of New York Press.

Nelson, Lance E. 2000. "Reading the *Bhagavadgītā* from an Ecological Perspective." *In* Christopher Key Chapple and Mary Evelyn Tucker, eds., *Hinduism and Ecology: The Intersection of Earth, Sky, and Water*, 127–64. Cambridge: Harvard University Press.

Nelson, Lance E. 2006. "Cows, Elephants, Dogs, and Other Lesser Embodiments of Ātman: Reflections on Hindu Attitudes Towards Non-Human Animals." *In* Kimberley Patton and Paul Waldau, eds., *A Communion of Subjects: Animals in Religion, Science, and Ethics,* 179–93. New York: Columbia University Press.

Peritore, N. Patrick. 1993. "Environmental Attitudes of Indian Elites: Challenging Western Postmodernist Models." *Asian Survey* 33 (August): 804–18.

Ruether, Rosemary Radford. 1992. *Gaia and God: An Ecofeminist Theology of Earth Healing*. San Francisco: HarperSanFrancisco.

Shepard, Mark. 1987. *Gandhi Today: The Story of Mahatma Gandhi's Successors*. Washington, D.C.: Seven Locks Press.

Shiva, Vandana. 1989. *Staying Alive: Women, Ecology, and Development*. London: Zed Books.

Tomalin, Emma. 2002. "The Limitations of Religious Environmentalism for India." *Worldviews: Environment, Culture, Religion* 6, 1: 12–30.

Van Horn, Gavin. 2006. "Hindu Traditions and Nature: Survey Article." *Worldviews: Environment, Culture, Religion* 10, 1: 5–39.

Vatsyayan, Kapila, ed. 1995. *Prakṛti: The Integral Vision*. 5 volumes. New Delhi: Indira Gandhi National Centre for the Arts..

Weber, Thomas. 1989. *Hugging the Trees: The Story of the Chipko Movement*. New Delhi: Viking Penguin.

8

Ethnography

Mathew N. Schmalz

Encountering Hinduism
Catholic Investigations
British Approaches
Representing Hinduism
Hierarchy and Fluidity
Themes and Symbols
Pictures and Words
Experiencing Hinduism
Pilgrimage and Coming Home
Love and Longing

India and Hinduism have long held a special place in the Western imagination. Ancient Greek and Roman historians related tales of India's splendor with its exotic peoples and larger-than-life flora and fauna. In the Middle Ages, India was a source of myth and legend, sometimes associated with the king Prester John or with tales of the Christian hermit Barlaam and his successful efforts to convert the Indian royals Prince Josaphat and the cruel King Avineer. In the age of imperialism, India became fertile ground for economic and missionary endeavors. If India were to be governed by colonial powers, Hinduism needed to be understood. Hindus were different and "other," of course, but their religion appeared strangely familiar when seen against the background of the Western past. Although now India may seem closer to the West, its exotic appeal remains. In Greenwich Village, or in any other "hip" section of a large American city, one might very well see a few pedestrians and window shoppers wearing tee-shirts with Devanagri letters, sporting tattoos of such Hindu religious symbols as "Oṃ," and displaying fashionable applications of *mehndī* on their hands, possibly with a pierced nose and a well placed *bindī* on the forehead. Such Indian-inspired fashion sensibilities, along with the continuing popularity of *yoga* and *āyurveda*, testify to how India and Hinduism continue to be constructed and appropriated by and within a variety of Western imaginations.

Though ethnographers would certainly not describe themselves as pedestrians or window shoppers, ethnography does involve travel and observation, not to mention the collection of souvenirs. Whereas fieldwork is conventionally associated with social scientific observation and analysis, imagination lies at the heart of ethnographic study. The importance of imagination is particularly significant in ethnographic study of Hinduism. There the scholarly and artistic imaginations together encounter, represent, and experience Hinduism as an identifiable and distinct phenomenon. Of course, the status of Hinduism is the subject of debate, with such scholars as Richard King (1999) arguing that Hinduism is a European Orientalist creation and others, such as Julius Lipner (1994), maintaining that "Hinduism" refers to a coherent set of beliefs and practices that had a history before it was supposedly invented to serve imperialist interests. When Catholic missionaries and English civil servants encountered the religions of India, the preferred descriptive category tended to be "Brāhmaṇism." The term "Hinduism" later comes into play in earnest in the representations of Indian and Western ethnographers as they alternatively emphasize the hierarchical and interactive nature of Indian religiosity. These ethnographic constructs are templates that order and represent the Hinduism that is lived by Hindus but also is experienced by ethnographers themselves.

Encountering Hinduism

Some of the first significant writings about Indian religiosity come from two Catholic missionaries, Roberto de Nobili and Jean-Antoine Dubois. Priests that they were, De Nobili and Dubois not surprisingly placed Brāhmaṇas at the forefront of their ethnographic portrayals. British civil servants, such as Francis Buchanan and William Crooke, had more pragmatic administrative goals in mind in their ethnographic investigations. Ironically, however, for both the Catholics and the British, the encounter with Hinduism was dominated not just by a sense of "otherness" but by a sense of familiarity.

Catholic Investigations

The Italian Jesuit Roberto de Nobili (1577–1656) went to Madurai as a missionary in 1606. His *Customs of the Indian Nation*, written in 1613, was one of the first extensive treatments of Hindu practices that could properly be called "ethnographic" in its concern with observation and descriptive detail. Dressing as a Hindu renunciant himself, he wished to present Christianity as something that did not necessarily entail pollution or degradation. But to adapt Catholicism to an Indian environment, he had to make a distinction between religious and social customs. In *Customs of the Indian Nation*, De Nobili observes that "Brahmins are not managers of temples nor are they priests" (2000: 228). As a whole, the Brāhmaṇa class can be most accurately described as a collection of learned men or philosophers who remain custodians of various technologies of knowledge, such as logic and linguistics. In De Nobili's view, most Brāhmaṇical customs, such as wearing the sacred thread or sandal paste, were social in nature and emphasized the Brāhmaṇa as "the noblest of men" (2000: 73). The priests as he described them are no higher than "plebeians" and are associated with a variety of "idolatrous" sects relating to particular *kuladēvarkal* or "caste deities" (De Nobili 2000: 73). His conclusion was that as India had both idolatrous religion and important social customs, Catholic missionary work was justified, as was the appropriation of a wide range of local symbols and customs by De Nobili's Madurai mission.

Unlike De Nobili, Jean-Antoine Dubois (1765–1848) did have the category "Hindu" available to apply to the practices he observed. On the basis of his travels in the Deccan and the Madras Presidency early in the nineteenth century, Dubois centered on the institution of caste (*jāti*) as crucial to understanding the structure of Hinduism. He claimed that though Brāhmāṇas are at the apex of this social pyramid, they are not the men of wisdom that De Nobili so admired. Instead, the Brāhmāṇas employ every "trick...to excite the fervour of the worshippers" (Dubois 1992: 590). Dubois also uses the term "idolatry" to describe Indian religious practices, such as *pūjā* and *darśana* but goes a step further to speculate on their origins. In his initial view, Hinduism shares much with Greek and Roman religion in that such divine figures as Viṣṇu, Lakṣmī, and Yama can quite easily be correlated to Neptune, Juno, and Pluto. But Dubois (1992: 548) finally argues that Hindu idolatry is far "grosser" because it focuses on the material substance of the image. Hindu religiosity is finally "allegory" gone totally awry. Dubois (1992: 545) buttresses this interpretation by arguing that the "*trimūrti*" of Brahmā, Viṣṇu, and Śiva was actually based on the natural elements of Water, Earth, and Fire. The idea of transmigration or "metempsychosis" also has its parallels in classical Greek thought, but it too is an "invention" that makes the actions of the Supreme Being intelligible while sanctifying Brāhmaṇical power.

Dubois' representation of Hinduism may seem to be the relic of another age, especially his portrayal of Hinduism as idolatrous superstition. But his focus on the machinations of Brāhmaṇas would find parallels in contemporary anthropological discussions that reveal a particularly suspicious attitude toward hierarchy and caste and toward their religious legitimation. The speculations of Dubois on the origins of Hindu "idolatry" can be seen as a precursor to the search for the origins of religion found in the work of nineteenth-century scholars F. Max Müller and Andrew Lang. Unlike De

Nobili, but like those European scholars, the Abbé Dubois sought not simply to interpret Hinduism but to explain it.

British Approaches

The manuscript prepared by Dubois was purchased by the East India Company. No doubt one of its appealing features was its encyclopedic style reflected in richly detailed descriptions of Hindu religious life. In this sense, it serves as an appropriate transition from ethnography for the purpose of cultural critique and religious conversion to ethnography that serves the purposes of commerce and governance. British ethnographic writings on Hinduism are stamped with an unmistakable concern for definition, taxonomy, and enumeration that reflect both the intellectual tenor of their age and the pragmatic needs of imperial administration. Writing at the same time as Abbé Dubois, Francis Buchanan (1762–1829) conducted a survey of the Shahabad district in Bihar. He focused on caste but extended his research to enumerate the numbers and occupations of specific castes he encountered. Buchanan did not recognize any underlying theology in Hinduism but concluded that if there were a distinctively Hindu organizing principle, it would be the distinction between the pure and the impure. For example, Buchanan lists castes for whom pork is forbidden and those for whom it is permitted. His discussion of such sects as the Kaviras almost exclusively focuses on how their eating habits differ from caste Hindu practice. In Buchanan's view, Hinduism is an assemblage of customs ranging from the fire sacrifices and widow burnings of higher castes to the exorcisms and magic of lower castes. For Buchanan, Hinduism does not exist as a "religion" but instead is a collection of connections and exchanges between and among human beings and various supernatural entities. His ethnographic research is thus tailored to the local administrative requirements of dealing with multiple social groups, each with their own distinct customs and boundaries.

Though Buchanan did not speculate on questions of origins, William Crooke (1848–1923) engages such issues directly. Writing as a member of the Bengal Civil Service in the last decade of the nineteenth century, Crooke develops a taxonomy of Hindu "godlings," including "godlings of nature," "heroic godlings," and "godlings of disease." He concludes that Hindus have a primitive penchant for personifying various forces that are beyond human control. What accounts for the personifications are numerous confusions and conflations. For example, he speculates that the worship of the god Hanumān most probably combines "pagan" monkey worship with the memory of a tribal hero or other luminary of the past (Crooke 1978: 87–88). Crooke agrees with Buchanan about the significance of purity and pollution but goes into much greater detail about particular practices related to his taxonomy of Hindu "godlings." Through Crooke's eyes, Hinduism (Brāhmaṇism is the term he prefers) would appear to be a complex religious and social hierarchy. Crooke describes his motive in writing as dual—to further research and to help administrative "officers...to understand the mysterious inner life of the races with whom their lot is cast" (1978: v).

Representing Hinduism

De Nobili and Dubois refracted Hinduism through a distinctly Catholic prism. The two priests concentrated on the clerical aspects of Hinduism, not only in terms of their specific interest in the Brāhmaṇa class, but through their discussion of the more general importance of hierarchy and ritual. Buchanan and Crooke saw Hinduism through British-made spectacles. Though their initial encounters with Hinduism occurred in India, they quickly subsumed it within an unabashedly Western framework of knowing that draws on the natural sciences in its use of taxonomy and within its evolutionary presuppositions. These early ethnographies of encounter assume that Hinduism could be described in readily available terms and by means of historical parallels, without recognizing any intellectual and cultural chasm between Indians and Europeans. Of course, this begs the vexing question: What exactly is Hinduism? Ethnography attempts to answer the question from the inside out by representing how Hindus think and act. However, every effort of representation is a translation, and if ethnography tells us anything at all, it is that the language of Hinduism is not reducible to a single grammar—particularly one that is quite foreign.

Hierarchy and Fluidity

The enthnography of the village of Rampura in Karnataka by M. N. Srinivas (1916–99), based on research he began in 1948, has stood the test of time. Srivinas wrote the ethnography after his field notes had been destroyed by fire, hence the title *The Remembered Village* (1976). In his analysis of the structures of village life, Srinivas draws our attention to hierarchy and develops the term "Sanskritization" to refer to the process by which a particular caste attempts to change its status by imitating customs of castes higher in village social ranking. Sanskritization, as a sociological construct and interpretative frame, shapes Srinivas' portrayal of Hinduism as he found it in Rampura. The divine hierarchy mirrors the social hierarchy: The gods of the higher castes tend to be vegetarian, whereas the lower caste deities are meat-eating. Although the social and divine hierarchies are connected, it does not mean that Rampura's villagers blindly accept their given status.

Sanskritization itself is a way to explain how individuals and groups assert their agency in relation to one another and in relation to their gods. In one instance, the villagers confront the local god, Basava, during a drought, argue with him about failing to protect the village, and finally abandon his temple. This may bring to mind the attitude of erstwhile Catholic and British ethnographers, especially when Srinivas recalls how he himself had to control his laughter when witnessing the event. But unlike earlier Catholic priests and British civil servants, Srinivas is self-reflexive and discerningly situates himself and his work within a broader intellectual and social context. He observes that "popular Hinduism" has been ignored or disparaged almost equally by Western and by Indian commentators because of its seemingly "superstitious character." Srinivas goes against that tendency by presenting a multifaceted portrayal of Hinduism that includes blood sacrifice, the use of *karma* to explain misfortune, and a local taxonomy of gods and goddesses invoked to cure disease and ward off natural dangers. In *The Remembered Village*, Hinduism is presented as transactional, contentious, and multilayered precisely because it is embodied and acted out within the specific limits of localized human life.

Although Srinivas emphasizes hierarchy, anthropologists recently have been accused of placing too much importance on hierarchy in studies of India in general and of Hinduism in particular. Ravindra S. Khare examines the worldview of those who would seem to benefit least from Hinduism's supposed valorization of hierarchy. In *The Untouchable as Himself* (1984: xi), Khare examines how the Camārs of Lucknow find themselves caught between a religious worldview that emphasizes *dharma* and *karma* as "cosmic fair play" and the more worldly "democratic premise of free and fair play." Untouchable religious visions attempt to "contain" caste Hinduism by articulating countervailing notions of a "*homo justus*" represented by socially involved asceticism. Khare introduces us to a variety of untouchable "ideologists" who construct Hinduism as intractably hierarchical. According to this view, Hindus slavishly worship their gods in a manner that mirrors the slavishness demanded by the social hierarchy. To combat such insidious forms of religious hierarchy, the Camārs of Lucknow pragmatically combine elements from Hindu "monism" (*advaita*), public service, and Buddhist understandings of "vacuity" (Khare 1984: 79). Khare's effort to see the untouchable "as himself" means first and foremost setting aside the construct of "Hindu" in favor of the more inclusive "Indic." In this way, such concepts as *dharma* or *karma* are treated as cultural suppositions rather than as religious doctrines associated with a particular community. Untouchables thus can speak for themselves within an ethnographic framework that does not understand their religious identity or social context as monolithically Hindu.

Srinivas and Khare emphasize different themes, but their mode of representation is similar and conventional: language and the written word. Whereas Srinivas situates himself in an ethnographic narrative and Khare reproduces interviews, their ethnographic portrayals are similarly author-driven. For the anthropologist McKim Marriott, such forms of ethnographic representation are limited by their reliance on the constricted dimension of the written word and by the replication of Western categories that are poorly suited to an Indian context. Envisioning what he calls a "Hindu ethnosociology," Marriott (1989) draws on representational opportunities offered by three-dimensional modeling. He argues that such static Western categories as class or dualisms, such as nature versus culture, cannot capture the interactive fluidity of Hinduism as it is lived. Marriott's three-dimensional "constituent cubes" are thus intended to provide the building blocks for an ethnoscience derived from Hindu constructs and themes. For example, a cube representing Hindu understandings of human aims (*puruṣārtha*) would have three pairs of sides composed of a human aim and its opposite: advantage (*artha*)-disadvantage (*anartha*); attachment (*kāma*)-nonattachment (*niṣkāma*); coherence (*dharma*)-incoherence (*adharma*) (Marriott 1989: 14). Instead of plotting actions along a single axis, a cube based on the human aims allows for a more complex representation of the multiple aspects and implications of behavior. Hence, something such as bathing during a particular astrological conjunction can be understood and portrayed in relation to multiple variables. Though Marriott spent a number of years as an ethnographic fieldworker in India, his three-dimensional graphs are predominately derived from Hindu textual sources. But their ethnographic relevance lies in their ability to represent the agency of Hindus through their own indigenous categories. As Marriott (1989: 9) himself makes clear, the cubes are "metaphors" or "mnemonics" for Indian spaces. The cubes are therefore drawn as transparent to remind us of their perspectival and provisional nature.

Themes and Symbols

Marriott wants to speak of Hinduism in a way that does not reduce it to a Western epistemological dynamic. But ethnographies are written primarily for a predominately Western-trained or Western-influenced academic audience. To this extent, some sort of representational reductionism is inevitable. Taking a cue from Marriott but also remaining within conventional modes of scholarly representation, some scholars have defined Hinduism in terms of distinctive themes and symbols. In *Redemptive Encounters* (1986), Lawrence A. Babb seeks to explore "the Hindu religious imagination." Babb examines three relatively recent Hindu movements: Rādhāsoāmī, the Brahmā

Kumārīs, and the cult of Satya Sāī Bābā. Much of *Redemptive Encounters* is conventional ethnographic description: Babb explains Rādhāsoāmī's fluid vision of the world, characterizes the Brahmā Kumārīs in terms of renunciation of sexuality as an Indian feminism, and interprets Satya Sāī Bābā's miracles as a return to a "magical worldview."

But in the conclusion, Babb reflects on the Hindu religious imagination in terms of "images" or themes in a way that Marriott might find compelling. Babb directs our attention to "ingesting," "seeing," and "recognizing" as ways through which "the existence of an extraordinary, transcendental other-awareness" is made real (1986: 220). Through this lens, the reader finds at the heart of Hinduism a journey to rediscover oneself as an emanation of the Supreme Being.

Babb diagrams broad images or themes in the Hindu religious imagination. Joseph S. Alter's focus is more specific: the symbolic resonances of the human body. In *The Wrestler's Body* (1992), Alter presents the ethnography of a wrestler's *akhārā* in Banaras. He diagrams how wrestlers model their bodies on such supernatural beings as Hanumān and ingest huge quantities of "cooling" and strengthening foods, such as *ghī* and almonds. For these wrestlers, the universe is "mobius": "finite but unbounded" and "bigger inside than outside" (Alter 1992: 257). The wrestler effectively reshapes the universe by realigning the "coordinates of psychosomatic existence" (Alter 1992: 257) through diet and exercise. Alter, somewhat like Babb, focuses on the ways in which Hinduism allows the individual to reimagine his or her experience of the world. However, Alter also extends his analysis beyond the individual to the social level. Indeed, the wrestler's body is both a vehicle for individual transformation of identity and a metonym for a reinvigorated Hindu India.

Pictures and Words

Though texts can be used in a variety of creative ways, the printed word can limit the range of ethnographic representation. In recent years, cyberspace has become a representational vehicle that has been used to supplement or even take the place of the bounded medium of the academic monograph and journal. Virtual reality software, for example, can allow a perception of participation and motion. The use of pop-ups, hot-spots, and hyperlinks also allows for a more layered representational idiom. "Arampur: A Virtual Village on the Worldwide Web," developed by Peter Gottschalk and Mathew Schmalz (http://virtualvillage.wesleyan.edu/), attempts to take advantage of these possibilities. "Arampur" is a pseudonym for a real village in Bihar that was the subject of *Beyond Hindu and Muslim* (2000), an ethnography written by Peter Gottschalk. The core of the "Virtual Village" is the "Roam" feature that uses virtual reality software to allow the visitor to move through Arampur. The cursor reveals such "hot spots" as shrines, mosques, and stores that can be further explored. The virtual visitor can also meet residents, read translations of interviews with them, and listen to segments in the original Hindi-Urdu. Hyperlinks direct visitors to essays on village life, Hinduism, Islam, and the particular role of the living dead. The web site also has a section called "My Life" in which residents of Arampur have posted their own photographs along with descriptions they have written about themselves.

The interviews in the Virtual Village were composed of a series of standard and open-ended questions that avoided asking about or presuming a religious identity. One of the few residents who volunteered his religious identity quickly was Shiv Mistri. A member of a local Rāṣṭrīya Svayamsevak Saṅgh cadre, Shiv Mistri defined Hindus as those who worship "images." Though recalling the pejorative evaluations of De Nobili and Dubois, Shiv Mistri is concerned to distinguish Hinduism from Islam. Most other residents preferred the term "eternal (*sanātana*) dharma" to Hinduism, but they nonetheless evoke images of "Hinduism" corresponding to conventional representations. For example, two women explain their recitation of the Durgā *cālīsā* as a means of pleasing the goddess—an explanation that would recall Srinivas's depiction of the invocations made to deities in Rampura. The transactional model of Hinduism, embraced by Marriott and others, would find confirmation in the detailed explanations of worship at the temple of Shastri Brahm and the exchanges made by devotees to ensure healing and prosperity. The themes of "seeing" and "ingesting," given emphasis by Babb, find expression in Ajay Upadhyaya's explanation of *darśana* as a longing to be seen by the deity and *prasāda* as a "substance filled with grace." The body also has its religious significance, especially in the many discussions of the symbolism of the rice-balls, or *piṇḍ*, that represent the body in ritual and in the prevalence of offerings in the temple of Shastri Brahm, such as wooden sandals and water jugs, that are associated with the bodies of Brāhmaṇas. Hierarchy and fluidity and themes and symbols can be found in the words and images that represent Hinduism in the Virtual Village. But the underrepresentation of the village's Dalits or untouchables and the absence of interreligious tension also suggests that the virtual version online is not in fact identical to the real village on which it is based in Bihar.

Experiencing Hinduism

The Virtual Village does not conceal discontinuity and the contextual difficulties of research. In the audio files, one can hear ethnographers and informants struggling at times to make sense of each other. Even in translated transcripts, one can see quite readily the dynamic of query, evasion, and riposte that so often characterizes the ethnographic interview. The research and writing that produce ethnographic scholarship do not proceed simply from disinterested observation to the collation and transcription of data. Instead, ethnographic observation is inevitably participatory, and it is participatory nature of fieldwork that tends to attract scholars to ethnography. It should not be surprising that ethnographers who endeavor to describe the experience of Hinduism often seek to experience Hinduism themselves.

Pilgrimage and Coming Home

An element of Hinduism that lends itself to participatory ethnography is pilgrimage. To tell the story of pilgrimage, one must go along and experience it. Depicting pilgrimage easily flows into a narrative in which self-reflective mention of the ethnographer seems natural rather than intrusive or out of place. But there is something about pilgrimage that may express the hidden desires behind ethnography itself. E. Valentine Daniel, in *Fluid Signs: Being a Person the Tamil Way* (1984), writes of joining devotees making a pilgrimage to the mountain Sabari Malai in Kerala to honor Lord Ayyappan, the son of Śiva and Viṣṇu. Daniel takes a vow of celibacy with the other pilgrims and experiences the incongruity of taking a ritual bath and having afterward to comb away "night soil" caked in his hair. Daniel notes the erasure of caste and ethnic boundaries during the journey to Lord Ayyappan and uses the semiotics of Charles Pierce to represent the signs, symbols, and experiences of the pilgrimage itself. Although narrative gives way to intellectual abstraction, most intriguing is Daniel's experience in being both insider and outsider to the pilgrimage. He interviews pilgrims but finds his academic knowledge criticized; he eats with other pilgrims, but jealously guards his bottled water. Though the experience of Hinduism is there in the shared rigors and rituals of pilgrimage, Daniel the ethnographer remains inevitably separate and apart.

Like Daniel, anthropologist Ann Grodzins Gold went on pilgrimage. But her pilgrimage was preceded by deep doubts about her ability to complete her ethnographic research on the various religious "journeys" made by the Rajasthani villagers with whom she lived. Gold (1988) writes that the villagers described her as "simple" and how she once broke down in tears when the frustrations of the research became too much to endure. For those writing in the Anglo-American tradition of ethnography, such experiences of doubt and frustration are often coupled with the experience of Hinduism as a phenomenon that is simultaneously intimate and distant, welcoming and impenetrable. When Gold writes of her later experience going on pilgrimage, she seems closer to her Rajasthani companions, who go to a crossing point on the Gaṅgā River to "sink" the flowers that are understood to be "bones" carrying the souls of their departed loved ones. Gold's interviews with fellow pilgrims reveal a variety of understandings of "sinking flowers," such as paying debts, helping the spirits of the dead to find peace or release, avoiding social stigma, and continuing a village and family tradition. Experience of Hinduism thus becomes polyvalent, correlated to a variety of social contexts and personal aspirations that cannot be reduced to single analytic framework. For Rajasthani pilgrims who go to a Gaṅgā crossing point, what is most important is coming home with a sealed jar of Gaṅgā water. Of course, ethnography too can become a pilgrimage defined by coming home—with the academic monograph taking the place of sacred Gaṅgā water.

Love and Longing

Just as an ethnography about pilgrimage can become a pilgrimage itself, so can an ethnography about love become a love affair. In *Notes on Love in a Tamil Family* (1992), Margaret Trawick uses the Tamil text of the *Tirukkōvaiyār* as a frame for writing about her experiences learning from her teacher Themoziyar and living with his extended family. *Tirukkōvaiyār* is a poem that describes the love between a man and a woman as well as the exploits of the god Śiva. Trawick writes about the multiple expressions of "love" within her Tamil family and represents their relational complexity through thematic dyads, such as "mirroring/twinning," "complementation/dynamic union," and "projection/introjection." Trawick also writes about the failure of her own marriage as a relational counterpoint to the subject of her ethnography. Sarah Caldwell (1999) embarks on a much deeper form of self-disclosure in her study of the Kerala ritual-drama Muṭiyēṯṯu, in which a male actor is possessed by a form of the goddess Kāḷi. Caldwell intersperses her analysis of Muṭiyēttu with excerpts from her own diary that reveal the violence in her marriage and her romantic relationship with Abhilash, a friend and informant. But Caldwell writes of these experiences in terms of her fear and love for Kāḷi, a goddess who is the "raw expression of that power of human beings to reach to their deepest emotions and inflict harm on one another, but also to break free" (2001: 278). Caldwell's experiences of pain and breaking free thus mirrored the terrible and liberating experience of the Goddess that lies at the heart of Muṭiyēṯṯu as ritual drama.

Not all ethnographers would praise Caldwell for her confessions. After all, what matters are not the experiences of ethnographers but those of their informants. But whether ethnographers encounter Hinduism or represent it, at heart there is an experience of both love and longing. Of course, as Caldwell would remind us, love is often a painful and conflicted thing. Though British and Catholic ethnographers might seem to dismiss Hinduism as superstition, they nonetheless were drawn to it. Scholars who represent Hinduism through sociological categories, broad themes, complex diagrams, or virtual reality software, might at first glace seem removed from such emotions as love and longing. But a longing for experience and a love of intelligibility most certainly grounds the ethnographic enterprise in even its most rarefied forms of presentation.

The experience and intelligibility that ethnography claims to offer lies in its effort to engage and retrieve the worldview of "the native." However, in the case of ethnographies of Hinduism, this has always been an engagement and retrieval for a particular audience and constituency. Ethnographies of encounters were constructed for clerical or bureaucratic needs, whereas ethnographies of representation were designed to meet the concerns of the academy. Ethnographies of experience responded to the rebellious instincts of some academics who sought to challenge and deconstruct the objective pretense of scholarly work. Of course, all these ethnographic approaches relied on particularly favorable configurations of power, authority, and financial resources. With rising new constituencies in India and abroad, the framework for the ethnographic study of Hinduism will surely change and be sensitive to different issues of encounter, representation, and experience. However, what will certainly not change will be the continuing importance of the ethnographic imagination in shaping our understanding of the worlds of meaning that Hindus and Hinduism have created.

References Cited

Alter, Joseph S. 1992. *The Wrestler's Body: Identity and Ideology in North India*. Berkeley: University of California Press.

Babb, Lawrence A. 1986. *Redemptive Encounters: Three Modern Styles in the Hindu Tradition*. Berkeley: University of California Press.

Buchanan, Francis. 1986 [1934]. *An Account of the District of Shahabad in 1812–13*. New Delhi: Usha Publications.

Caldwell, Sarah. 1999. *Oh Terrifying Mother: Sexuality, Violence, and Worship of the Goddess Kāḷi*. Delhi: Oxford University Press.

Crooke, William. 1978 [1896]. *The Popular Religion and Folklore of Northern India*. Volume 1. New Delhi: Munshiram Manoharlal.

Daniel, E. Valentine. 1984. *Fluid Signs: Being a Person the Tamil Way*. Berkeley: University of California Press.

De Nobili, Roberto, S. J. 2000. *Preaching Wisdom to the Wise* (trans. Anand Amaladass, S.J. and Francis X. Clooney, S.J.). St. Louis: The Institute of Jesuit Sources.

Dubois, Abbé J. A. 1992 [1897]. *Hindu Manners, Customs and Ceremonies: The Classic First-Hand Account of India in the Early Nineteenth Century* (trans. Henry K. Beauchamp). New Delhi: Asian Educational Services.

Gold, Ann Grodzins. 1988. *Fruitful Journeys: The Ways of Rajasthani Pilgrims.* Berkeley: University of California Press.

Gottschalk, Peter. 2000. *Beyond Hindu and Muslim: Multiple Identity in Narratives from Village India.* New York: Oxford University Press.

Gottschalk, Peter and Mathew N. Schmalz. 2006. Arampur: A Virtual India Village. Available: http://virtualvillage.wesleyan.edu/.

Khare, R. S. 1984. *The Untouchable as Himself: Ideology, Identity, and Pragmatism among the Lucknow Chamars.* Cambridge: Cambridge University Press.

King, Richard. 1999. *Orientalism and Religion.* New York: Routledge.

Lipner, Julius J. 1994. *Hindus: Their Religious Beliefs and Practices.* London: Routledge.

Marriott, McKim. 1989. "Constructing an Indian Ethnosociology." *Contributions to Indian Sociology (ns)* 23, 1: 1–39.

Srinivas, M. N. 1976. *The Remembered Village.* Berkeley: University of California Press.

Trawick, Margaret. 1992. *Notes on Love in a Tamil Family.* Berkeley: University of California Press.

9

Ethnosociology

Richard H. Davis

Ethnic- and Ethno-disciplines
Ethnosociology Constructed
Critics of Ethnosociology
Ethnosociology and the Study of Hinduism

Ethnosociology emerged as an important approach to the study of Indian culture and religion in the 1970s. Articles jointly authored by McKim Marriott and Ronald Inden on "Caste Systems" (1974) and "Towards an Ethnosociology of South Asian Caste Systems" (1977) laid the foundation for this approach, and it was continued and expanded by Marriott in "Hindu Transactions: Diversity Without Dualism" (1976a) and by a number of Marriott's students at the University of Chicago and by others over the next three decades.[1] Along with other ethno-disciplines, ethnosociology offers valuable strategies for the study of Hinduism and Indic cultures more generally. In this chapter, I briefly sketch the initial development of ethnosociology as an approach to the study of India, note some of the criticisms made of it, and comment on a few of its contributions to the study of Hinduism.

As initially articulated by Marriott, Inden, and others, ethnosociology may be outlined in terms of three methodological aims: (1) to use indigenous Indic terms as much as possible in the analysis and explication of Indic social systems and cultural practices; (2) to develop from indigenous systems of knowledge more general principles that pertain to all Indic or Hindu society, throughout Indian history; and (3) to "deparochialize Western social sciences" by generating new universal or nomothetic sociological terms and concepts from Indic social discourse, thereby mitigating the Western-centric vocabulary of the current social sciences.

Ethnic- and Ethno-disciplines

The adjective "ethnic" derives from the Greek word "*ethnos*," referring to a group of people living together. By virtue of collective life, people living together in an *ethnos* may share customs, traits, and a view of life (*ethos*). In English usage, ethnic groups have been referred to as "nations," "races," "tribes," "cultures," and "subcultures." Modern lexicographers prefer a neutral definition, such as "population subgroup with a common national or cultural tradition," as in the 1998 *New Oxford English Dictionary*.

The combining form of "ethnic" is "ethno-," which first appears in English words for disciplinary forms of knowledge in the early nineteenth century. "Ethnology" and "ethnography," used in English during the first half of the nineteenth century, both refer in their early usage to the scientific study of races and peoples of the world. By the late nineteenth century, a different use of "ethno-" appears in a new field: "ethnobotany." This is a discipline that explores the traditional knowledge and customs of ethnic peoples concerning plants.

The difference between the two types of ethno-disciplines may be seen readily if we analyze the words in terms of Sanskrit grammatical categories. Both "ethnography" and "ethnobotany" would be classified as *tatpuruṣa* compounds, in which the first element is used adjectivally to modify the second element. The significant difference lies in the grammatical or case relation between the two elements. Ethnography, as the scientific study by Western scholars about other peoples, involves an accusative relationship: taking other peoples as the direct objects of scientific writing. The knowledge, in other words, is possessed by the Western writer, not by the ethnic object of inquiry. In the case of ethnobotany, by contrast, the relation is genitive: It is the study of knowledge concerning plants of, or possessed by, the ethnic group. The discipline of ethnobotany studies the local knowledge of particular ethnic communities and to some degree grants legitimacy to that local knowledge as a viable way of knowing plants.

The distinction is valuable for observing how ethnoterminology changes over time. Earlier definitions of "ethnoscience," for example, regarded this discipline to be the scientific study of peoples, in the accusative relationship. More recently, ethnoscience is defined as the study of scientific knowledge held by different cultures, in the genitive sense. The term "ethnohistory" has a similar duality: It can be defined either as the study of the history of peoples, especially non-Western ethnic groups and nations, or it can be defined as the study of historical knowledge maintained and transmitted by those peoples. It is clear that this distinction also signals a difference in attitude toward the forms of knowledge constructed by peoples outside the Western intellectual tradition. In the first, "science" and "history" are regarded as unique intellectual accomplishments of the Western tradition. It is up to the West, accordingly, to study other ethnic groups scientifically and to write the scientific history of those Others. Eric Wolf captures this split succinctly in the title of his study, *Europe and the People Without History*

(1982). In the genitive usage, "science" and "history" are understood as more universal enterprises of knowledge, pursued by different groups in a variety of distinctive "ethnic" ways. This grants intellectual validity to these enterprises and the knowledge systems they have constructed. One can generate other new ethno-disciplines along genitive lines: "ethnomedicine," "ethnomusicology," "ethnopsychology," and so on.

Clearly the new ethnodiscipline of "ethnosociology," as formulated by Marriott, Inden, and others in the 1970s, is of the second or genitive type. It aims, quite explicitly, at a "cultural analysis of caste systems, using concepts that are believed to be understood and accepted by all sorts of South Asians in discussing their own social systems" (Marriott and Inden 1977: 227). A useful knowledge of the Indic social system is already embedded in the indigenous categories and images used by South Asians in their own social discourse, and the task of the ethnosociologist is to recover and restate native or "ethnic" sociological understandings, which are considered to be the most adequate way to analyze native society. Many of these categories are in fact specifically Hindu terms. This slippage between "Indic" and "Hindu," we will see, is one point at which ethnosociology has been criticized.

In a later essay, Marriott takes the genitive view one step further. All disciplines, he observes, are ultimately ethnodisciplines. "All social sciences develop from thought about what is known to particular cultures and are thus 'cultural' or 'ethno-' social sciences in their origins. All are initially parochial in scope" (Marriott 1989: 1). In other words, such Western disciplines of knowledge as, say, sociology are in fact based on Western "ethnic" presuppositions and make a premature claim to universal applicability. For example, Marriott comments that the ambitious "general theory of action" articulated by sociologists Talcott Parsons and Edward Shils should be seen as "the highly abstract, essentialized forms of that culturally specific sociology" that may be productive for looking at American society but does not make sense of a different society, such as that of India (Marriott 1991: 296). Therefore, the ethnosociologist who articulates "a culturally related, but non-European people's thought about their own realities" may aim "to expand the world repertory of social sciences" (Marriott 1989: 1). As Marriott continues, this may assist social scientists working in a supposedly normative Western disciplinary tradition, such as sociology, to become more conscious of the premises and partialities of their disciplinary knowledge.

Ethnosociology Constructed

The fundamental approach of ethnosociology to its Indic sources, whether textual or ethnographic, is *emic*, rather than *etic*, to use a dichotomy commonly cited in the 1970s. An emic approach investigates the internal elements and their relations and interactions as a system, as *phonemics* looks at the internal sound system within a particular language. It studies a cultural phenomenon, insofar as possible, in its own terms. An etic method, by contrast, seeks to study elements of a phenomenon in terms of broader universal categories, as *phonetics* categorizes sounds of particular languages in reference to a general classification of all human speech sounds.

More directly, ethnosociology draws on the "cultural approach" to the study of kinship pioneered and advocated by David Schneider in *American Kinship: A Cultural Account* (1968). To analyze how modern Americans understand relations of kinship, Schneider chose to explore the terms and symbols that Americans use in talking and thinking about kinship rather than observing their behaviors. This would enable him to describe this dimension of American culture in its own terms, as "a coherent system of symbols and meanings" (Schneider 1968: 8). Inden and Ralph Nicholas (1977) adapted Schneider's method in their analysis of kinship in Bengal. Echoing Schneider, they "seek to understand how these symbols are connected and how Bengalis use them to define relationships" (Inden and Nicholas 1977: xiii).

In *American Kinship*, Schneider finds that Americans understand their kinship ties in terms of two distinct symbolic realms: nature and law. Natural kin ties result from natural or organic acts, says Schneider, particularly love and sexual intercourse. Law refers instead to codes for proper conduct by persons who are related as kin to one another. Inden and Nicholas find similar symbolic domains in Bengali culture. For nature, Bengalis use the organic symbols of blood and genetic substance; for law, they cite the Indic concept of *dharma* as a code for conduct. However, Inden and Nicholas also make a striking observation. When a Bengali woman marries, they observe, her body itself is considered to be transformed and so too is her inborn code of conduct. The code for conduct for a particular group or family is thought to be embedded in the bodily substance shared by persons of that group:

> Bodily substance and code for conduct are thus thought to be not fixed but malleable, and to be not separated by mutually immanent features: the coded substance moves and changes as one thing throughout the life of each person and group. Action enjoined by those embodied codes are thought of as transforming the substances in which they are embodied.
> (Marriott and Inden 1977: 228)

So the rite of marriage, transforming the female as daughter in one household into wife in another, is believed to transform the very substance of the bride and, with that material transformation, also to alter her code of conduct. Now her *dharma* will be that of wife in the new kin group of her husband.

The Bengali culture of kinship, then, is nondualist in that it does not accept a fundamental opposition between "nature" and "law." Similarly, say Inden and Nicholas, "no distinction is made between a 'material' or 'secular' order and a 'spiritual' or 'sacred' order" (1977: xiv). Moral and "spiritual" qualities are considered to be embedded within the material. The monistic and substantivist premises of this Indic cultural system constituted a striking and provocative finding.

Equally striking and provocative was their claim of remarkable consistency over time and region. Schneider based his study primarily on extensive interviews carried out in Chicago in the 1960s. The informants included a cross-section of ethnic groups within that multiethnic urban area but clearly represented an "ethnographic present." Though he did take Chicago as synecdoche for "American" culture, Schneider made no attempt to extrapolate from his findings to speak about American kinship of the colonial period or even that of the nineteenth century. Inden and Nicholas also employed interviews carried out in the Bengali present but supplemented this with textual materials of both medieval and recent vintage. Bengali kinship, then, was consistent over a long time. Marriott and Inden affirm this cultural persistence over an even longer stretch:

> We here find ourselves restating a cognitive treatment of caste systems that is continuous from the Vedas, Brahmanas, and Upanishads...through the classical books of moral and medical sciences and the late medieval moral code books of certain castes in Bengal,...and on into twentieth-century explanations of their behavior by living peoples....We combine such diverse materials not because we suppose that one determines or directly influences the other, but simply because we find that they agree on certain major ways of defining the situation.
>
> (1977: 229)

Note that here, Marriott and Inden present the Indic cultural continuity over time as an observation, drawn from many sources, not as an assumption of a unitary South Asian culture. As Marriott elsewhere points out, this seamless juxtaposition of Indology and ethnography, based on studies of both past and present, reflects the earlier efforts at the University of Chicago by Robert Redfield (1956) and Milton Singer (1964) to look at India as a cohesive "social organisation of traditions," through a combination of humanities and social scientific approaches (Marriott 1990: xi; see also R. Davis 1985).

It is no accident that ethnosociology focused initially on caste systems. Caste was a central topic in South Asian anthropology of the 1960s and 1970s. Marriott and Inden were especially concerned to distinguish their approach from that of the structural anthropologist Louis Dumont, whose *Homo Hierarchicus* (1966, 1970, 1979) was the most prominent work of South Asian anthropology of the period. Dumont's work is a grand synthesis, in the French mode. It starts from a fundamental division of humanity itself into two social modes of being: *homo aequalis* and *homo hierarchicus*. If the ethos of nineteenth-century American egalitarian individualism, especially as described by the French royalist observer Alexis de Toqueville, offers the closest approximation to the ideal type of *homo aequalis*, the pervasive Indian regime of caste society most closely approaches the *homo hierarchicus* type. For Dumont, the fundamental basis of caste society does not lie in the empirical operations of power but in a religious ideology. Caste hierarchy rests on the conception of society as an organic whole, within which social divisions are grounded and graded on a single dominant religious scale, that of purity and impurity. Dumont mobilizes classical Indological texts (mainly Brāhmaṇical ones, such as Manu's *Dharmaśāstra*), British colonial sociology, and contemporary ethnographies of rural Indian villages to create a portrait of Indian society as thoroughly imbricated with the values of hierarchy and purity.

Dumont's impressive work was extremely influential, including among its proponents such students of Hinduism as Madeleine Biardeau (1976, 1989). It was also very controversial. Many Indian observers complained about Dumont's reification of "brahmanic" values and ideological frameworks as being essentially "Indian." Some disapproved that Dumont had cast India as the "Other" to the egalitarian West. From his 1969 review of the French publication of *Homo Hierarchicus*, Marriott became perhaps Dumont's most perceptive and persistent critic within the Anglo-American anthropological profession. After a detailed summary and critique of Dumont's work, Marriott grants it a kind of heuristic virtue: "In sum, Dumont's attempt to construct a model of hierarchical society is, perhaps, most interesting as an essay in pure theory and criticism, and as an imposing specimen of intellectualist model-building. It asks and answers questions that have been little asked, yet are immensely worth asking" (1969: 1173). Marriott goes on to detail some of the questions raised by the book and concludes that "exploration of these possibilities may lead to construction of a more representational model of Indian civilization" (1969: 1174).

It is apt to see ethnosociology as Marriott's alternative construction. Ethnosociology shares Dumont's ambitious agenda of creating a unitary "model of Indian civilizations" that will encompass Indian society past and present. However, it seeks to construct this model using Indic terms rather than Dumont's allegedly Western-based ones. So ethnosociology identifies the life-enhancing values of *maṅgala*, *kalyāṇa*, and the like as more relevant to the understanding of Indian or Hindu purposeful action than is the value of purity seen as separation from "the organic aspect of human life" (Marriott 1976b: 194). It claims to bring a more comprehensive set of sources into its synthesis. Marriott's essays are always admirably filled with generous citations of the works of students and colleagues that flesh out his synthetic formulations. Most important, it aims to replace Dumont's structural penchant for binary oppositions or dualism, a supposedly Western predilection, with a nondualist or monist orientation, more closely grounded in the Indic cognitive style.

Ethnographic nondualism finds its most elegant formulation in Marriott's 1976 essay, "Hindu Transactions: Diversity Without Dualism." His task here is to show how a monist perspective can nevertheless generate "some of India's fabled diversity." Marriott begins by drawing out the implications of nondualism for a distinctive Indian notion of personhood.

> Correspondingly, persons—single actors—are not thought in South Asia to be "individual," that is, indivisible, bounded units, as they are in much of Western social and psychological theory as well as in common sense. Instead, it appears that persons are generally thought by South Asians to be "dividual" or divisible. To exist, dividual persons absorb heterogeneous material influences. They must also give out from themselves particles of their own coded substances...that may then reproduce in others something of the nature of the persons in whom they have originated.
>
> (Marriott 1976a: 111)

Here again is a pointed difference with Dumont. Whereas Dumont denies Indian persons their individuality in favor of society as an encompassing whole, Marriott more poetically asks readers to envision Indian persons as "dividual selves" in the midst of flowing substance, whose own bodily substance-codes are repeatedly transformed through material transfers and transactions. Society is the outcome of ongoing transforming interactions rather than of an overbearing ideological whole.

From this standpoint, Marriott argues that social differentiation and power rankings arise precisely through those transactions rather than on the basis of more permanent caste attributes. Or rather, actors and their transactions change together; thus, attributional rankings and interactional rankings turn out to be two aspects of the same thing (Marriott 1976a: 114; see also Marriott 1959: 106). He goes on to demonstrate how a variety of give-and-take relationships can give rise to group rankings. Most compelling here is Marriott's examination of different transactional strategies, correlated loosely to the Hindu scheme of four *varṇa*s. Some groups, he observes, engage in a maximum number and variety of transactions with others (broadly, Kṣatriyas, that is, landed, dominant, ruling groups) whereas others pursue a strategy of minimal transacting outside group boundaries (Vaiśyas, merchant groups, Jains). Brāhmaṇas exemplify an "optimal" strategy, whereas Śūdras, who must receive without giving to others ranked higher, are relegated to a "pessimal" strategy. He suggests that these four strategies can be mapped also onto the four stages of life in the classic Hindu *āśrama* scheme and many other realms of Indian social action.

If different groups within the same community practice divergent strategies with different criteria for success, one might ask, does this make caste ranking solely a matter of perspective? Dumont's reliance on purity as a universal criterion has already been rejected. But what has happened to power, that compelling force behind social dominance and subordination? Marriott would answer, consistently, that "power" must be redefined within an indigenous conception. "Transactors and transactions are oriented ultimately neither toward 'purity' nor toward 'power' as usually understood in social science but toward a unitary Indian concept of superior value—power understood as vital energy, substance-code of subtle, homogeneous quality, and high, consistent transactional status or rank" (Marriott 1976a: 137).

Though Inden largely abandoned the ethnosociological approach in the late 1970s, Marriott continued to work along the trajectory established in the 1970s moment of definition. He also advised numerous graduate students in the University of Chicago Department of Anthropology, whose work in India added ethnographic ballast to the edifice of ethnosociology (see below for select examples). Two outcomes of Marriott's subsequent work along these lines were commonly referred to in Chicago as "the game" and "the cube."

The game is "SAMSARA." The well-known Indic term *saṃsāra* designates the world as a realm of continuing fluctuations and transmigratory human life lived within that changing world. Marriott developed the game as a pedagogical device for initiating students into thinking transactionally through Hindu common sense and categories. Players are required to act and transact with one another, "while striving to continue and/or alter their house populations, their wealth, their markings of relative precedence and deference, their lifetimes, their recyclings and rebirths, and/or their releases from SAMSARA [the game, and the circle of transmigration]" (Marriott 2004a). In other words, they play "SAMSARA" according to the premises, rules, and goals of human actors within Indic or Hindu rural life, as articulated by ethnosociological study. Over the years, Marriott has supervised many playings of this game and refined it through the experiences of players, but there is not yet any published version or full description of "SAMSARA."

A good example of the "cube" model may be found in Marriott's chapter "Varṇa and Jāti" (2004b). Extending the view sketched in "Hindu

Transactions," Marriott here seeks to view Hindu society in terms of "multiplex, multidimensional models" that will recognize Indian diversity. These models, it turns out, need to be three-dimensional cubes. He incorporates still more Indian viewpoints into the synthesis: along with the Vedic, Brāhmaṇical, and ethnographic, we also find such systems as the ontologically dualist Sāṃkhya philosophy, the heterodox schools of Buddhism and Jainism, and more. Though I admire Marriott's effort here to recognize greater historical diversity within Indian social discourse, I must confess that I have never quite followed this latest step in the ethnosociological path.

Critics of Ethnosociology

As with Dumont's *Homo Hierarchicus*, the ethnosociological approach has inspired numerous critical responses, directed at it from several directions. Perhaps the first response was from a Dumontian perspective. In 1976, three American anthropologists (Barnett, Fruzzetti, and Östör 1976) took on the ethnosociological position primarily on epistemological grounds. Marriott and Inden claim a privileged access to indigenous thought: "The data themselves are directly translatable into meaning, since they are declared to be South Asian, indigenous, and ethnic" (Barnett, Fruzzetti, and Östör 1976: 632). By contrast, Dumont situates his characterization of Indian society in a dichotomy of two ideological systems and locates himself as a "knower" in dialectical relation to the Indian "known." Dumont himself took up this point in his preface to the second edition of *Homo Hierarchicus*.

> Does Marriott believe he can rid himself of this dualism [between knower and known]? If so, his monism deserves the name of mysticism and his "ethnosociology" is akin to theosophy. The claim to master the whole field of India's vast and complex literatures in the different disciplines... and the incredible levity of Marriott and his disciples towards philological knowledge...tend in this direction.
>
> (1979: xxix)

A more common criticism has pointed to the supposed partiality of ethnosociology. Though it claims to depict Indian or at least Hindu social thought as a whole, it privileges certain communities, texts, or viewpoints. One of Marriott's own criticisms of Dumont was on the same grounds. Dumont looked at such classical Brāhmaṇic works as Manu, Marriott observed, but failed to take into account the Kṣatriya perspectives reflected in such texts as the epic *Mahābhārata* (Marriott 1969: 1170). Ethnosociology may incorporate more Indian materials into its synthesis, but it is still susceptible to the challenge of exclusion. Critics fault it for failing to accommodate adequately Dalit, Islamic, or other non-Hindu categories or ways of thinking about an Indian society in which these communities also participate constructively. Too often, critics argue, it conflates "Hindu" terms with Indic, as if Indian culture is essentially Hindu in its discursive foundations. Of course there is also a political dimension to this criticism. As was the case with Dumont's work, some accuse ethnosociology of reinforcing an upper-class perspective that marginalizes others who might resist their marginality. Perhaps this is a danger for any attempt at comprehensive social description: It inevitably threatens to reify the very social conditions that allow some to dominate and subordinate others.

Along similar lines, some have criticized ethnosociology for a failure to recognize historical diversity. Inden's move away from ethnosociology was largely on these grounds. In *Imagining India* (1990), Inden criticizes the long-standing Indological notion that caste was the defining feature of Indian society throughout its history, a notion to which Marriott and Inden's "Caste Systems" had contributed. Inden observes that his own earlier work had argued for the historicity of caste in Bengal:

> There I showed that it was the collapse of Hindu kingship which led to the formation of "castes" in something resembling their modern form (albeit not as usually described). That is, the distinctive institution of Indian civilization does not appear until the thirteenth or fourteenth century, at the earliest; and castes are not the *cause* of the weakness and collapse of kingship, but the *effect* of it.
>
> (1990: 82; emphasis in original)

Here changes in authority at the level of polity bring about shifts in the basis of social relations leading to caste structure. In his subsequent work, Inden pursued the study of these broad historical shifts using the notion of "imperial formations" (1990: 2). The political construction of Indian social discourse was also characteristic of the Chicago school of ethnohistory, as defined by Bernard Cohn (1980) and Nicholas Dirks (1993, 2001). It should be noted that Cohn and Dirks treat the compound "ethnohistory" as a *dvandva* or copulative compound (that is, as a method combining ethnography and history) rather that one seeking to reconstruct India's ethnic knowledge of its own history.

Finally, some Indian critics have been uncomfortable with the "otherness" of Indian discourse that emerges within ethnosociological studies. As with Dumont's work, ethnosociology postulates a significant difference between Western and Indic social categories as its point of departure. From the perspective argued first and most forcefully by Edward Said (1978), approaches that rely on the radical distinction of Western knower and Eastern known are charged as "Orientalist." Of course this is unfair to the intentions of Marriott, Inden, and all others who have shared the ethnosociological approach. It also places ethnosociology in a paradoxical situation. Attention to indigenous categories gains interest through the juxtaposition of these categories with supposedly Western ones, but to the extent that it stresses differences between the two it falls into the Orientalist trap.

Ethnosociology and the Study of Hinduism

Ethnosociology has certainly exercised a long-term impact on the study of Indian religions. Its most profound effect resides simply in the emphasis it has always placed on close attention to "native categories." Within Indian studies, the broad agenda of ethnosociology has provided the basis for a series of important anthropological studies. A select list would include Babb 1975, Wadley 1975, M. Davis 1983, Daniel 1984, Gold 1988, Raheja 1988, Trawick 1990, Lamb 2000, Sax 2002, and Mines 2005. This agenda has also provided a direct impetus for other ethnodisciplines, such as ethnopsychology (Kakar 1978; Roland 1988) and ethnomedicine (Zimmermann 1987; Cohen 1998). These are too varied to constitute a "Chicago school," but they share an attentiveness to local categories, a sensitivity to the ways in which local understandings participate in larger pan-Indian conceptual systems, and a willingness to grant epistemological validity to indigenous social discourse. Indigenous categories are not just good to think about, but also good to think with.

Beyond the study of kinship and caste, many ethnosociological studies have contributed more directly to the study of Hinduism. Such topics as village Hindu practices, goddess worship (Babb, Mines, Wadley), pilgrimage (Gold), and religious performance (Sax) have all benefited enormously from ethnosociologically inflected studies. Conversely, the use of Hindu (singular) categories as the equivalent of Indic indigenous social discourse may at times have suggested or reinforced a notion of Hinduism as a unitary or historically monolithic religion rather than as a historically varied and contentious congregation of diverse schools of thought and practice.

Finally, the greatest value of ethnosociology to the study of Hinduism may lie in its reflexivity. The corollary to its emphasis on attentiveness to local categories is a healthy hermeneutical suspicion of the "universal" categories of Western disciplinary knowledge. Ethnosociology has promoted a willingness to subject one's own common sense understandings and disciplinary premises to critical scrutiny, through juxtaposition with Indic cognitive schemes. All students of Hinduism can profit from this effort at deparochializing one's own thinking.

Note

1 A word on my subject-position here would be appropriate. From 1978 to 1986, I was a graduate student in South Asian studies at the University of Chicago, though not in the Department of Anthropology. I was able to take classes with McKim Marriott, Ronald Inden, Ralph Nicholas, and Bernard Cohn during that time, and I followed the debates over ethnosociology with keen interest. Certainly the ethnosociological emphasis on close attention to indigenous categories had a major impact on the "internalist" approach of my dissertation, "Ritual in an Oscillating Universe" (R. Davis 1986), for which Ron Inden served as advisor. I am grateful to Marriott and Inden for recent correspondence concerning this essay. I also thank my colleague at Bard College, Sanjib Baruah, for comments on an earlier draft. Marriott writes that he is currently working on a book-length historical account of ethnosociology, so readers of this brief sketch who wish to follow up may look forward to Marriott's much more detailed treatment.

References Cited

Babb, Lawrence A. 1975. *The Divine Hierarchy: Popular Hinduism in Central India*. New York: Columbia University Press.

Barnett, Steve, Lina Fruzzetti, and Ákos Östör. 1976. "A Hierarchy Purified: Notes on Dumont and His Critics." *Journal of Asian Studies* 35, 4: 627–45.

Biardeau, Madeleine. 1976. "Le sacrifice dans l'hindouisme." *In* Madeleine Biardeau and Charles Malamoud, *Le sacrifice dans l'Inde ancienne*, 7–154. Paris: Presses Universitaires de France.

Biardeau, Madeleine. 1989 [1981]. *Hinduism: The Anthropology of a Civilization* (trans. Richard Nice). Delhi: Oxford University Press.

Cohen, Lawrence. 1998. *No Aging in India: Alzheimer's, the Bad Family, and Other Modern Things*. Berkeley: University of California Press.

Cohn, Bernard. 1980. "History and Anthropology: The State of Play." *Comparative Studies in Society and History* 22, 2: 198–221.

Daniel, E. Valentine. 1984. *Fluid Signs: Being a Person the Tamil Way*. Berkeley: University of California Press.

Davis, Marvin. 1983. *Rank and Rivalry: The Politics of Inequality in Rural West Bengal*. Cambridge: Cambridge University Press.

Davis, Richard H. 1985. *South Asia at Chicago: A History*. Chicago: Committee on Southern Asian Studies, University of Chicago.

Davis, Richard H. 1986. "Ritual in an Oscillating Universe." Ph.D. dissertation. Chicago: University of Chicago Library.

Dirks, Nicholas B. 1993. *The Hollow Crown: Ethnohistory of an Indian Kingdom*. Ann Arbor: University of Michigan Press.

Dirks, Nicholas B. 2001. *Castes of Mind: Colonialism and the Making of Modern India*. Princeton: Princeton University Press.

Dumont, Louis. 1966. *Homo hierarchicus: Essai sur le système des castes*. Paris: Gallimard.

Dumont, Louis. 1970 [1966]. *Homo Hierarchicus: An Essay on the Caste System* (trans. Mark Sainsbury). Chicago: University of Chicago Press.

Dumont, Louis. 1979 [1966]. *Homo Hierarchicus: The Caste System and Its Implications* (trans. Mark Sainsbury, Louis Dumont, and Basia Gulati). Chicago: University of Chicago Press.

Gold, Ann Grodzins. 1988. *Fruitful Journeys: The Ways of Rajasthani Pilgrims*. Religious Traditions of the World. Prospect Heights: Waveland Press.

Inden, Ronald B. 1990. *Imagining India*. Oxford: Basil Blackwell.

Inden, Ronald B. and Ralph W. Nicholas. 1977. *Kinship in Bengali Culture*. Chicago: University of Chicago Press.

Kakar, Sudhir. 1978. *Inner World: A Psycho-Analytic Study of Childhood and Society in India*. Delhi: Oxford University Press.

Lamb, Sarah. 2000. *White Saris and Sweet Mangoes: Aging, Gender, and Body in North India*. Berkeley: University of California Press.

Marriott, McKim. 1959. "Interactional and Attributional Theories of Caste Ranking." *Man in India* 39: 92–107.

Marriott, McKim. 1969. Review of *Homo hierarchicus: Essai sur le systeme des castes*, by Louis Dumont. *American Anthropologist* 71, 6: 1166–75.

Marriott, McKim. 1976a. "Hindu Transactions: Diversity without Dualism." *In* Bruce Kapferer, ed., *Transaction and Meaning: Directions in the Anthropology of Exchange and Symbolic Behavior*, 109–42. Philadelphia: Institute for the Study of Human Issues.

Marriott, McKim. 1976b. "Interpreting Indian Society: A Monistic Alternative to Dumont's Dualism." *Journal of Asian Studies* 36, 1: 189–95.

Marriott, McKim. 1989. "Constructing an Indian Ethnosociology." *Contributions to Indian Sociology (ns)* 23, 1: 1–39

Marriott, McKim. 1990. "Introduction." *In* McKim Marriott, ed., *India Through Hindu Categories*, xi–xvi. New Delhi: Sage.

Marriott, McKim. 1991. "On 'Constructing an Indian Sociology'." *Contributions to Indian Sociology (ns)* 25, 2: 295–308.

Marriott, McKim. 2004a. "A Description of SAMSARA: A Realization of Rural Hindu Life." Unpublished manuscript.

Marriott, McKim. 2004b. "Varṇa and Jāti." *In* Sushil Mittal and Gene Thursby, eds, *The Hindu World*, 357–82. London: Routledge.

Marriott, McKim and Ronald B. Inden. 1974. "Caste Systems." *In*, *Encyclopaedia Britannica*, 3 of 24: 982–91. Chicago: Encyclopaedia Britannica.

Marriott, McKim and Ronald B. Inden. 1977. "Toward an Ethnosociology of South Asian Caste Systems." *In* Kenneth A. David, ed., *The New Wind: Changing Identities in South Asia*, 227–38. The Hague: Mouton.

Mines, Diane P. 2005. *Fierce Gods: Inequality, Ritual, and the Politics of Dignity in a South Indian Village*. Bloomington: Indiana University Press.

Raheja, Gloria Goodwin. 1988. *The Poison in the Gift: Ritual, Prestation, and the Dominant Caste in a North Indian Village*. Chicago: University of Chicago Press.

Redfield, Robert. 1956. *Peasant Society and Culture: An Anthropological Approach to Civilization*. Chicago: University of Chicago Press.

Roland, Alan. 1988. *In Search of Self in India and Japan: Toward a Cross-Cultural Psychology*. Princeton: Princeton University Press.
Said, Edward W. 1978. *Orientalism*. New York: Penguin.
Sax, William Sturman. 2002. *Dancing the Self: Personhood and Performance in the Pāṇḍava Līlā of Garhwal*. Oxford: Oxford University Press.
Schneider, David M. 1968. *American Kinship: A Cultural Account*. Englewood Cliffs: Prentice-Hall.
Singer, Milton. 1964. "The Social Organization of Indian Civilization." *Diogenes* 45: 84–119.
Trawick, Margaret. 1990. *Notes on Love in a Tamil Family*. Berkeley: University of California Press.
Wadley, Susan Snow. 1975. *Shakti: Power in the Conceptual Structure of Karimpur Religion*. Chicago: University of Chicago, Department of Anthropology.
Wolf, Eric Robert. 1982. *Europe and the People Without History*. Berkeley: University of California Press.
Zimmermann, Francis. 1987 [1982]. *The Jungle and the Aroma of Meats: An Ecological Theme in Hindu Medicine*. Berkeley: University of California Press.

10

Exchange

Diane P. Mines

Reciprocity
Redistribution: Honor and Power in Hindu Worship
Disposal: Kings, Brāhmaṇas, and the Meaning of *Dāna*
Intercaste Exchanges
Self and World—Transactional Worldview
Concluding Reflections

Walk into almost any Hindu temple and you are likely to see a lot of *something*. In a village goddess temple, hundreds of glass bangles of all colors hang on long strings along one wall in front of the deity's chamber, the *garbagrāha*. At a roadside shrine hang dozens of small wooden cradles from the branches of a *pīpal* tree. An image of Śiva is strewn with ball after ball of butter thrown by worshipers. In a sacred grove, hundreds of terracotta horses line the route to a small open-air shrine to the god Aiyaṉār. Names of donors adorn the walls—whether inscribed in old stone walls or on new brass plaques. And during temple festivals, both deities and worshipers may become bodily centers of dense material adornment: In some places, children and youths vowing pots of milk to the goddess are smothered with cloth and garlands and cash gifted by affines; possessed dancers bury their ankles, arms, and necks with jewelry in silver and gold; and everywhere the gods are dressed in bright clothing, stacks of necklaces, and piles of garlands and are presented with heaps of *ghī*, grain, silk vestments, or other gifts. So, although many people associate Hinduism with a vague and ethereal "spirituality," it is in fact impossible to ignore the utter materiality of Hindu practice and meaning. Exchange lies at the heart of this material practice.

Exchange—the give and take of objects and substances—pervades human social life, from economic transactions to gifts of state to the intimate exchanges of words and bodies that make up our everyday social life. In the social sciences, at least since Marcel Mauss's classic study, *Essai sur le don* (The Gift, 1923–24), exchange is thought to underlie our sociality, our very connectedness as human beings to one another and to our world, broadly defined. This chapter introduces some of the key discussions surrounding the ways in which the Hindu world has been made and remade through exchange. As we see, it is through exchanges that Hindus not only have connected intimately to deities but have articulated polity, social order, and self.

Reciprocity

Even the simplest and most everyday forms of Hindu worship (*pūjā*) begin and end with exchanges: the giving of devotional gestures or small material gifts to the deity in return for the deity's gift of *prasāda* and the exchange of vision called *darśana*. First, *darśana*, the act of seeing and being seen by the deity, challenges our commonsense understandings of vision as a passive reception of images on the retina. Indeed, South Asian understandings of perception may more broadly inform studies on the phenomenology of perception, for Hindus see vision as a material exchange, a kind of touching (Eck 1981: 6–9; see also Babb 1981: 393; Fuller 1992: 59–61). As a result, *darśana* is a means for devotees to partake literally in the deity's qualities, especially, as C. J. Fuller argues, its power (*śakti*). Through visual exchanges devotees obtain "good fortune, well-being, grace, and spiritual merit" (Fuller 1992: 59; see also Babb 1981: 388). The deity's power emanates from the eyes of the image, and care is taken to protect devotees from dangerous and prolonged exposure to this power (see Fuller 1992: 60 for debates on whether qualities emanate *from* or *through* the image). Whereas human eyesight also transacts qualities from the gazer to that which is gazed on (Babb 1981; Trawick 1990: 93), the eyesight of deities is thought to have such great force that even the architecture of temples, city planning, the location of businesses (Parker 1989: 184–97) and houses (Daniel 1984: 139), and even such everyday human activities as choosing a place to stand or a path to take (Eck 1981: 7; see also Hanchett 1988: 157) must accommodate the deity's flow of vision. One simply cannot thrive in a place that is subject to the power of the deity's constant gaze.

Second, worshipers are unlikely to leave a temple without receiving *prasāda*, the transvalued "leftovers" of the deity or, literally, the "grace sent down" via returned offerings (Courtright 1985: 39). *Prasāda* is the return for the worshiper's acts of devotion, whether simple gestures of prayer, deferential gazes, or gifts to the deity. What could be more common than the sight of a man, woman, or child on the way to work, home, or school and bodily marked with the leftovers of their morning worship—a smear of ash or dot of vermillion, a flower tucked delicately behind the ear, the taste of sweet rice or fruit? Substances given from deity to worshiper (usually via the priest or, in domestic worship, via an elder), such as *darśana*, enable worshipers to take part in the god's material qualities of purity, light, and grace. (For rich depictions of material and devotional aspects of deity-human relations, see Babb 1975, 1986; Gold 1988; Waghorne and Cutler 1985.)

Many gifts are given to deities as vows. These gifts are considered returns for favors bestowed by deities on their devotees, such favors as healing an ill relative, helping a youth pass an important exam, ensuring a healthy delivery. Such vows may take many forms, from gifts of milk, cloth, or grain to more substantial support for the temple process (funding festivals, renovation, temple construction, electrification, a loud speaker system, and so on). Often large gifts to a temple or deity serve not only to facilitate beneficial exchanges with the deity, they build individual or community power by legitimizing one's social position via the divine sanction of the deity. For a temple community (be it a lineage, company, worker's union, caste association, or village), the exhibition of material wealth accumulated and displayed through a community's gifts converts into reputation and well-being for the community and social power for its most beneficent donors. The materiality of worship is, thus, not merely about personal transactions with and transformations by the deity; the gifts that accumulate in and move through Hindu temples signify and promote the power and reputation of the temple community and its leaders.

Redistribution: Honor and Power in Hindu Worship

Though the intimacy of personal relations with the deity is clearly manifest in material lovingly given, received, and reciprocated (cf. Mauss 1990), these exchanges contribute to a wider social story about polity, power, and caste in Hindu society. A significant set of studies articulating the relation between temple exchanges and forms of Hindu polity, particularly in South India, appeared in the 1970s through 1990s. These studies not only elucidated the Hindu political process, they pointedly refuted previous depictions of Hindu politics founded on colonial and Orientalist writings.

Colonial writers had criticized the shape of the Indian polity and understood the lavish gifting activities of kings and local luminaries as little more than bribery, a form of corruption that, of course, ultimately justified colonial intervention in political life (Dirks 1987: 4–5). To remedy this colonial reading of kingship as corruption, several scholars studied South Indian kingship to investigate what part gifts actually played in the political process. A second critical problem was the now-well-known analytical separation of religion and politics made famous by Louis Dumont's (1970) depiction of Hindu ideology as bifurcated into these two oppositional categories. Dumont argued that religious values determined the shape of the Hindu social world as a hierarchical caste structure based on the (Brāhmaṇical) distinction between pure and impure. Kingship, and political activity generally, he subordinated to a separate sphere of material and merely temporal interest encompassed ultimately by religious value. Dumont's valorization of the religious effectively made caste hierarchy the fundamental framework for understanding all social life while reducing kingship to a secondary subject and rendering the king an arbiter of merely material relations.

Others argue against these two perspectives by demonstrating (1) that gift giving was in fact a legitimate political tool for articulating political communities and expanding political influence and (2) that political practice was hardly subsumed by religious value but rather fully implicated in religious process. Nicholas Dirks, for example, explains how, beginning as early as the Pallava kingdom from 600 to 900 CE, South Indian kingship was based increasingly on a redistributive system in which resources were pooled by local chiefs and "little kings" through taxation and then redistributed from the king as "gifts of rights to land and of various honors, emblems, titles, and privileges" (1987: 130). Such gifts were granted to a range of recipients throughout the king's territory: to Brāhmaṇas, including various sectarian leaders, the temples they served or controlled, and monasteries; to soldiers or watchmen in service to the king; and to members of agrarian communities, including village headmen, officers, and servants (such as Smiths, Potters, Barbers, and so on). Kings were, through gifts and endowments, able to assert control via patronage at the most local level of the kingdom. The gift was thus not "bribery" but in fact "a principal medium of rule" (Dirks 1987: 129; see also Appadurai 1977, 1981; Breckenridge 1977). "Power was the power of allocation" writes Pamela Price; and gift-giving was *rājadharma*, the appropriate moral *cum* physical work of the king (1979: 211).

Understanding the role of kingly gift giving also led to better understandings of the symbiotic relation between religion and politics and so allowed for the deconstruction of Dumont's separation of these two spheres. In debates on this issue, the question of the relation between religion and politics is often phrased as a conundrum or puzzle concerning the relation of Brāhmaṇas to kings (see Heesterman 1985; Trautmann 1981: 285–88). As Gloria Raheja (1988a: 502) explains it, the conundrum centers on the fact that gifts from kings to Brāhmaṇas can be interpreted both as "religious" gifts to superiors and as "royal" gifts to inferior dependents. Hence the conundrum: for a Brāhmaṇa to accept any gift from the king is to accept both superiority and inferiority. Dirks, as Norbert Peabody argues, did not so much solve as dissolve the conundrum by forming a different model, one that "explicitly claims to replace the Dumontian formulation with a construction of social hierarchy centered on the king" (1991: 745). Others, however, have argued that the Brāhmaṇa–king question is to be resolved not on one side or the other but rather through understanding the Brāhmaṇa–king relation as one of mutual dependence.

Clearly, Hindu temples and monasteries were particularly important elements in the Hindu sovereignty-through-exchange described above. Through religious endowment, political rulers converted material resources (e.g., their shares of agricultural production garnered as tax) into prestige and political legitimacy. So, even as Brāhmaṇas depended on the gifts of kings, precisely because the legitimacy of a ruler lay in large part with his relationship to temple deities and monastaries, kings depended on Brāhmaṇas, too. Arjun Appadurai (1977) characterizes this king–Brāhmaṇa relation as symbiotic (see also Breckenridge 1977). His depiction of kingship in South India is instructive. He shows that from 1350 to 1700 CE, the Vijayanagar rulers were able to extend their rule through religious endowments to religious sects. These sects, headed by Brāhmaṇas, were not merely passive recipients of these endowments, however. Sectarian leaders, by accepting endowments from kings, were actively permitting kings to establish new political and economic bases locally. Thus were they able to participate in, and manipulate for their own interests, rearticulations of political alliances via temple endowments and honors. The king needed the Brāhmaṇa's cooperation in expanding territory and control, and Brāhmaṇas needed the king's help in gaining and protecting access to honors and resources that upheld their influence (for a similar example from North India, see Peabody 1991).

Securing power through exchange with deities, or deity-like figures, remains a prominent political strategy in local community power relations (see D. Mines 2005; M. Mines and Gourishankar 1990) and in contemporary Indian democratic political practices. Price (1993, 1996), for example, argues that contemporary Tamil political parties continue to draw on "precolonial antecedents" wherein—despite the egalitarian platforms of today's political parties—hierarchical distinctions within the party continue to be created through relative proximity not to a king or deity but to the party leader. These leaders are made popular and larger than life through religious symbolism that conflates them with the gods and whose kingly qualities of largesse produce their legitimacy in the eyes of constituents. As Bernard Bate (2002) has demonstrated, Jeyalalitha, who was chief minister of Tamil Nadu in the mid-1990s (as again later), appeared in local newspaper ads taken out by her devoted constituents (local party leaders) as the divine power of the Tamil people. Deified, she was poetically praised as a goddess able to give generously to the Tamil people with the power to convert lands from dry to wet, from undeveloped to developed. Local political leaders enhanced their reputations in these newspaper ads, which displayed their proximity to the leader and graphically represented her as a goddess gazing or smiling down on them. Strategies to convert gifts into political power have played, too, into Hindu nationalist operations surrounding the construction of the Ayodhya temple. Not only did L. K. Advani, then the head of the political-religious organization, the Visva Hindu Pariṣad, represent himself as the Hindu deity Rāma, complete with bow, arrow, and motorized chariot, but the temple itself, intended to be built of the bricks gifted in 1989 by devotees all over the Hindu world (not only in India), would itself represent and redistribute divine power to the Hindu people as it would also serve as the political *cum* religious center of the Hindu nation (see, for example, Gopal 1991; Mines 2005: 202–8; van der Veer 1987).

Disposal: Kings, Brāhmaṇas, and the Meaning of *Dāna*

The king–Brāhmaṇa symbiosis does not hinge solely on the practical endowment of religious institutions. The cosmos as a whole is at stake. However, the cosmological aspects of the king–Brāhmaṇa symbiosis were little understood until scholars achieved a more thorough understanding of one particular type of gift called *dāna*.

Jonathan Parry notes that most gifts given in India are to this day "governed by an explicit ethic of reciprocity" (1986: 129) as Mauss's sociology of the gift would predict. But what, Parry asks, echoing Mauss, to make of the Indian gifts whose return is textually proscribed and ought never be returned but only digested, eliminated, or otherwise passed along like a hot potato (Shulman 1985) lest both the donors and the receivers sink into hell, as this oft-quoted passage from the *Manusmṛti* warns: "When a twice-born neither engages in ascetic toil nor recites the Veda and yet loves to receive gifts, he will sink along with the donor, as a man would sink in water along with his stone float. An ignorant man, therefore, should fear any kind of gift; for by accepting even a trifling gift an ignorant man sinks like a cow in the mud" (4.190–91; Olivelle 2005: 134).

Trautmann (1981: 285–88) explains Brāhmaṇas' reluctance to accept gifts such as these, gifts of *dāna*, as a result of their reluctance to acknowledge their dependence on the king (cf. Heesterman 1985). But a closer look reveals that the problem with accepting *dāna* is not its affirmation of dependence but rather its *function* in the political-ritual renewal of the kingdom.

Parry's ethnographic study of Brāhmaṇa funeral priests in Banaras reveals that gifts of *dāna* given by mourners to Brāhmaṇa priests were explicitly intended to transfer sins or evils (*pāpa*) from the deceased to the Brāhmaṇa funeral priest. The Brāhmaṇa, ideally, ought to be able to rid himself of that evil by doing the necessary rituals that aid him in "digesting" and divesting himself of the evils contained in the gift. In reality, however, the priests take on too much and know too little of the necessary ritual formulas to rid themselves of the evils they take on. They find themselves in a "perpetual state of moral crisis," as the "cess-pits" of the cosmos (Parry 1994: 123; see also 1986, 1989), destined to die horrible deaths as the accumulated sins eat away at them (see also Mines 1997: 182). They sink "like a cow in the mud" (*Manusmṛti* 4.191; Olivelle 2005: 134). Given these facts, it appears that it was not political subordination Brāhmaṇas feared in accepting gifts from kings. It was the biomoral danger inherent in the Brāhmaṇa's own biomoral capacity to take on these sins.

The Brāhmaṇa takes on the sins of the king, even as the king takes in the sins of the entire kingdom. Through a "biomoral" transfer of evil-sin out of the kingdom and outside the moral order, king and Brāhmaṇa together preserve the ordered world and cosmos. Hence, the gift is both dangerous and necessary. This kingly power—far from merely a "temporal" power in this world, separate from the religious cosmos-making power of the Brāhmaṇa—is also a cosmos-preserving power that is made possible neither by the king alone nor by the Brāhmaṇa conferring "authority" to the king, as J. C. Heesterman (1985) had argued, but by both operating together through the king giving and Brāhmaṇa receiving (and *not* reciprocating) the biomoral gifts of *dāna*. Kingship and Brāhmaṇism are not separate spheres of existence. Both operate together in a single *ritual-political* process, as A. M. Hocart (1950) had argued earlier.

Intercaste Exchanges

This work on *dāna* implicates not only kingship but caste as well. Raheja (1988a, 1990) found that by paying attention to the movement of *dāna* and other specifically named transactions in Pahansu, a North Indian village, she was able to reinterpret (and revive Hocart's 1950 interpretation of) the workings of intercaste, *jajmānī*-type relations as replicating a kingly mode of world-preserving disposals of evil. Here, however, it is the dominant caste and not the king who resides at the center of the system. Raheja's ethnographic work on intercaste exchange in Pahansu posits an alternative to earlier studies of such exchanges that—in parallel fashion to the reduction of kingship to temporal politics—reduced *jajmānī* relations to a merely economic function.

Some of the first anthropological models of caste posited that caste was primarily a division of labor based on a form of nonmonetary, nonmarket agricultural exchange. In 1936, William Wiser first coined the term "*jajmānī* system" to describe a pattern of nonmonetary, nonmarket exchange that he found at work in Karimpur, a North Indian village. He found that the non-Brāhmaṇa landholders (as *jajmān*s, sacrificer-patrons) in this village gave shares of their grain harvest and cooked food and other goods to other occupational *jāti*s, such as Barbers, Potters, Washermen, Carpenters, and Blacksmiths, in return for long-term service. Wiser characterized these exchanges as "mutual" or "symmetrical." That is, Wiser saw the *jajmānī* system as a division of labor wherein landholding castes reciprocally exchanged grain for the services of the other *jāti*s, exchanges that apparently worked for the mutual benefit of all those involved (see also S. Dube 1955).

As Pauline Kolenda (1963) explains, other researchers influenced in part by Marxian political-economic theory, took issue with Wiser's characterization of these relations as mutual, seeing them rather to be coerced and asymmetrical, wherein services were given to the powerful landholders who then redistributed grain in return. So, though Wiser saw the landholders engaged in reciprocal, mutually beneficial relations with occupational service castes, others saw the landholders as politically and economically powerful groups who had privileged access to the food supply and controlled these exchanges using their power as the "dominant" castes (e.g., Beidelman 1959; Bronger 1975; Gould 1958; Harper 1959).

Whether they viewed *jajmānī* relations as mutual or asymmetrical, all of these researchers painted a picture of a *jajmānī* "system" that was a more or less bounded, interdependent, and self-sufficient village exchange network among permanent, hereditary occupational groups—"castes." Such accounts evoke an even earlier picture of the much-admired self-sufficient village political-economic system. But as both Fuller (1989) and Inden (1990: 143–48) show, the systematicity and "self-sufficiency" of the village was to a great extent merely imagined and idealized by nineteenth-century scholars such as Henry Maine, Robert Baden-Powell, and Karl Marx and by many British civil servants. The view that such writers offered of the self-sufficient village community has, in fact, rarely been reproduced by contemporary ethnographers, yet it remains a popular stereotype, one that even some rural Brāhmaṇas (Mines 2005: 204–5) and Indian urban dwellers (Nandy 2001) look "back on" with nostalgia.

Writing and researching in the wake of all these approaches, Raheja (1988a) developed a comprehensive model to explore some of the dimensions of meaning surrounding caste as it played out in Pahansu. Raheja brought together (and altered) many of the ideas outlined above and identified three intersecting "aspects" of intercaste relations that helped to make better sense of villagers' own multiple and contextually shifting interpretations of their actions. These three aspects she named mutuality, centrality, and hierarchy or rank. No one aspect alone expresses the realities of caste for the villagers, yet one aspect or another may be contextually foregrounded at one time (or place) or another.

"Mutuality" refers to those reciprocal exchanges identified by Wiser. Indeed, Raheja found, village residents did talk about their interrelations this way: the dominant farming families who control the lands give grain in return for services provided by families of hereditary occupational castes, such as Washermen, Barbers, and Brāhmaṇa priests. "Rank" or "hierarchy" refers to those vertical relations of relative purity, wherein persons of castes that are more "pure" rank higher, Brāhmaṇas on top, Dalits on the bottom. Concerned with maintaining their own, purer bodily natures, members of relatively high *jāti*s will regulate quite carefully whose substances they will consume in the form of cooked versus uncooked food or exchanges of bodily fluids through sharing a pipe or a sexual relationship. Because of a longstanding emphasis on hierarchy as the primary dimension of caste distinctions, there exists a great deal of ethnographic evidence illustrating how rank orders are exhibited and reproduced in temple distributions, seating arrangements at feasts, food exchanges, and even pronoun use (e.g., Beck 1972; Levinson 1982; Marriott 1968).

"Centrality" is perhaps the most complex aspect of all and the one that links us to debates outlined above about the nature of the Indian gift called *dāna*. Centrality refers to the process whereby the powerful landowners reproduce their position at the "center" of a redistribution network. But unlike the redistributive model based solely on economic value, this distribution is always also a ritual distribution whereby the dominant landowning Gujars (in the case of Pahansu) transfer their inauspiciousness (negative *karma*, faults, and evils) as *dāna* to members of other *jāti*s in the village, including Barbers, Washermen, and Brāhmaṇas, who are said to be "appropriate" recipients capable of digesting their patron's evils without endangering themselves (Raheja 1988a: 201–2). The regular movement of evil and other kinds of inauspiciousness is necessary not only to the well-being of the Gujar patrons but to the whole village of which they are seen to be the dominant residents and on whose well-being the well-being of the entire village depends (see also Wadley and Derr 1990). Data from South Indian agrarian exchanges support Raheja's argument (especially Brubaker 1979; Inglis 1985: 99; Kapadia 1995: 120–23; Mines 2005; Pfaffenberger 1982: 40; cf. Good 1982) and support Hocart's (1950) discussion of the "priesthood" of Barbers, Washermen, and such artisans as Potters.

Any student of Indian village life would do well to heed Fuller's (1989) warning about the danger of treating the village exchange nexus as a closed system of any kind. *Jajmānī*-type relations, where they existed, were always part of wider relations in political-economic systems of patronage, kingship, and trade (see also Cohn and Marriott 1958; Inden 1990: 131–60). As Saurabh Dube (1998) phrases it, local peasants have always been "entangled" with broader political-economic process (see also Ludden 1985: 81–85). What can be said with confidence, however, is that at the turn of the twenty-first century, many Indians, rural and urban, do see their lives affected by their ability to transfer sins and evils through *jajmānī*-type service relations, as well as through exchanges with deities.

Self and World—Transactional Worldview

Raheja's aspectual view of intercaste relationships was influenced in part by the work of her teacher, McKim Marriott, who a decade earlier had posited his own aspectual rendering of caste based on transactional strategies. Marriott's transactional model arose from his abiding interest in constructing for India (1990, 1998) an "ethnosociology"—an analytic framework for social analysis that relied not on Western sociological concepts but rather on Hindu ones, notably (but not exclusively) derived from Sāṃkhya philosophy. His work transformed how many anthropologists approached the concept of person in South Asia.

According to Marriott's ethnosociological model—and so according to Hindu concepts, as he would probably prefer to put it—humans are thought to differ from one another and from other kinds of creatures and things in the universe because they all have different proportions of the same set of substances. These substances include the elements (fire, water, earth, wind, and ether), the humors (bile, phlegm, and wind), and the three qualities of *sattva* (goodness and light), *rajas* (action), and *tamas* (darkness or inertia) (Marriott 1990: 6–12; see also Daniel 1984: 3–4). Marriott and Ron Inden (1977) argued furthermore that many Hindus understand themselves not as "individuals" in the post-Enlightenment European sense of bounded, integral, and atomistic wholes but rather as "dividuals," that is, as divisible persons made up of particulate substances that can flow across boundaries and thus be shared, exchanged, and transferred. Much of the energy of personal action is devoted to maintaining or altering one's own "nature" in part by not mixing with things that might alter you in a disagreeable manner and, conversely, by seeking out transactions—such as with pure and beneficent gods or humans—that might at least temporarily enhance your qualities or "polish" them (*saṃskāra*). Hence some Hindus, for example, saw their own bodily nature and actions to both affect and be affected by the soil on which they lived and from which they ate food (Daniel 1984: 84–85; Zimmerman 1980), the houses in which they lived (Moore 1990), the deities and ancestors with whom they connect (Moreno 1985; Sax 1991), their actions in the world (Mines 1997; Wadley and Derr 1990), as well as by their proximity and intimate exchanges with others (Inden and Nicholas 1977; Lamb 2000; Trawick 1990; Wadley 1994).

Marriott showed that people from different *jāti*s used different kinds of strategies to maintain their varied natures: central, landowning *jāti*s engaged in many different transactions with all sorts of different people, while being careful to avoid polluting substances; Brāhmaṇas tended to give much more than they received in an effort to maintain their high rank. They sent out their relatively pure and cooling (*sattva*-containing) substances but did not take in the substances of others. Lower *jāti*s tended to receive more than they gave, partly because the higher *jāti*s did not wish to receive from them because of their chaotic (*tāmasik*), hot (*rājasik*), and impure (non*sāttvik*) natures and partly because they required more inputs from others to survive. And some *jāti*s seemed to avoid transacting with others in any direction, setting themselves apart almost as islands in the otherwise flowing seas of inter-*jāti* transactions. Marriott (1976) called these four transactional strategies, respectively, maximal, optimal, pessimal, and minimal.

Marriott's construction of an ethnosociology thus takes exchange or transaction to be the basic ontology of Hindu life. The work humans must do is to channel and control these ubiquitous transactions to shape self, other, and world. Significantly, recognition of such a transactional ontology shifts both analytic and practical attention from structures and oppositions to processes and actions, from how human beings are positioned to how they enact and remake their world. Hinduism begins to appear as a worldview predicated on action, flux, flow, control, and intersubjective (rather than structural) relations effected through exchanges, transferals, and movements of substances.

Concluding Reflections

It is probably no accident that so much of the energy around the topic of exchange in Hinduism arose in the 1970s and 1980s. This was the period of a powerful theoretical shift in social sciences and humanities from emphasizing structure and reproduction to emphasizing practice and production. With a focus on practice came new interest in how power works in society. As this chapter illustrates, in the study of Hinduism this theoretical shift led to new attention to kingship, ritual action, and indigenous ontologies that stress action as self-, other-, and world-making activity.

Work remains to be done to understand the materiality of Hindu practice and the changes that new forms of modernity might bring to the meanings of exchange in Hinduism. Given current social and global realities affecting contemporary South Asia, will biomoral "gift" exchanges give way to an abstract commodified and individuated world? Or will Hindu exchange practices continue, as Parry has pointed out, to offer up a significant challenge to the supposed split between tradition and modernity, expressed in the study of exchange as a split between gift and commodity? Much like S. Dube, whose careful ethnohistorical research demonstrates in countless ways the "entanglements" of social life that belie any radical split between tradition and modernity, Parry, too, (although in different terms) suggests through his analysis of *dāna* that the meaning of gifts and commodities is also entangled in Hindu practice. In Banaras, even hard cash—the most alienated exchange medium—takes on the biomoral qualities of the gift when used in *dāna* prestations. It refuses to grow, for example, so cannot be used to invest but only to purchase items for quick consumption (Parry 1989: 69). Conversely, there may be others for whom any entanglement of gifts and commodities, as also the entanglement of social relations that results from ritual forms of economy and polity, would be happily disentangled. Some Indian laborers, including those now familiar agrarian service castes, hardly see the increasing commodification of their labor as a "loss of tradition." Alienated labor remunerated by cash or check from employers gives them the freedom to refuse what from the point of view of dominant agricultural communities are often still seen as self, village, and even cosmos-preserving gifts of *dāna*. There is, for some Hindus, no nobility (Parry 1994: 124–25) in this "priesthood" of exchange.

References Cited

Appadurai, Arjun. 1977. "Kings, Sects and Temples in South India 1350–1700." *Economic and Social History Review* 14, 4: 47–73.

Appadurai, Arjun. 1981. *Worship and Conflict Under Colonial Rule: A South Indian Case*. Cambridge: Cambridge University Press.

Babb, Lawrence A. 1975. *The Divine Hierarchy: Popular Hinduism in Central India*. New York: Columbia University Press.

Babb, Lawrence A. 1981. "Glancing: Visual Interaction in Hinduism." *Journal of Anthropological Research* 37, 4: 387–401.

Babb, Lawrence A. 1986. *Redemptive Encounters: Three Modern Styles in the Hindu Tradition*. Berkeley: University of California Press.

Bate, Bernard J. 2002. "Political Praise in Tamil Newspapers: The Poetry and Iconography of Democratic Power." *In* Diane P. Mines and Sarah Lamb, eds, *Everyday life in South Asia*, 308–25. Bloomington: Indiana University Press.

Beck, Brenda E. F. 1972. *Peasant Society in Konku: A Study of Right and Left Subcastes in South India*. Vancouver: University of British Columbia Press.

Beidelman, Thomas O. 1959. *A Comparative Analysis of the Jajmani System*. New York: J.J. Augustin.

Breckenridge, Carol A. 1977. "From Protector to Litigant: Changing Relations Between Hindu Temples and the Rājā of Ramnad." *The Indian Economic and Social History Review* 14, 1: 75–106.

Bronger, Dirk. 1975. "*Jajmani* System in Southern India." *Journal of the Indian Anthropological Society* 10: 1–38.

Brubaker, Richard L. 1979. "Barbers, Washermen, and Other Priests: Servants of the South Indian Village and its Goddess." *History of Religions* 19, 2: 128–52.

Cohn, Bernard S. and McKim Marriott. 1958. "Networks and Centres in the Integration of Indian Civilization." *Journal of Social Research* 1, 1: 1–9.

Courtright, Paul B. 1985. "On this Holy Day in my Humble Way: Aspects of Pūjā." *In* Joanne Punzo Waghorne and Norman Cutler, eds, with Vasudha Narayanan,

Gods of Flesh, Gods of Stone: The Embodiment of Divinity in India, 33–50. Chambersburg: Anima.

Daniel, E. Valentine. 1984. *Fluid Signs: Being a Person the Tamil Way*. Berkeley: University of California Press.

Dirks, Nicholas B. 1987. *The Hollow Crown: Ethnohistory of an Indian Kingdom*. Cambridge: Cambridge University Press.

Dube, S. C. 1955. *Indian Village*. London: Routledge and Kegan Paul.

Dube, Saurabh. 1998. *Untouchable Pasts: Religion, Identity, and Power among a Central Indian Community, 1780–1950*. Albany: State University of New York Press.

Dumont, Louis. 1970 [1966]. *Homo Hierarchicus: An Essay on the Caste System* (trans. Mark Sainsbury). Chicago: University of Chicago Press.

Eck, Diana L. 1981. *Darśan: Seeing the Divine Image in India*. Chambersburg: Anima.

Fuller, C. J. 1989. "Misconceiving the Grain Heap: A Critique of the Concept of the Indian Jajmani System." *In* Jonathon P. Parry and Maurice Bloch, eds, *Money and the Morality of Exchange*, 33–63. Cambridge: Cambridge University Press.

Fuller, C. J. 1992. *The Camphor Flame: Popular Hinduism and Society in India*. Princeton: Princeton University Press.

Gold, Ann Grodzins. 1988. *Fruitful Journeys: The Ways of Rajasthani Pilgrims*. Berkeley: University of California Press.

Good, Anthony. 1982. "The Actor and the Act: Categories of Prestation in South India." *Man* 17, 1: 23–41.

Gopal, Savarapalli, ed. 1991. *Anatomy of a Confrontation: Ayodhya and the Rise of Communal Politics in India*. London: Zed Books.

Gould, Harold. 1958. "The Hindu Jajmani System: A Case of Economic Particularism." *Southwestern Journal of Anthropology* 16, 4: 434.

Hanchett, Suzanne. 1988. *Coloured Rice: Symbolic Structure in Hindu Family Festivals*. Delhi: Hindustan Publishing.

Harper, Edward B. 1959. "Two Systems of Economic Exchange in Village India." *American Anthropologist* 61, 5: 760–78.

Heesterman, J. C. 1985. *The Inner Conflict of Tradition: Essays in Indian Ritual, Kingship, and Society*. Chicago: University of Chicago Press.

Hocart, A. M. 1950. *Caste: A Comparative Study*. London: Methuen.

Inden, Ronald B. 1990. *Imagining India*. Oxford: Basil Blackwell.

Inden, Ronald B. and Ralph W. Nicholas. 1977. *Kinship in Bengali Culture*. Chicago: University of Chicago Press.

Inglis, Stephen. 1985. "Possession and Poverty: Serving the Divine in a South Indian Community." *In* Joanne Punzo Waghorne and Norman Cutler, eds, with Vasudha Narayanan, *Gods of Flesh, Gods of Stone: The Embodiment of Divinity in India*, 89–101. Chambersburg: Anima.

Kapadia, Karin. 1995. *Siva and Her Sisters: Gender, Caste, and Class in Rural South India*. Boulder: Westview.

Kolenda, Pauline. 1963. "Toward a Model of the Hindu Jajmani System." *Human Organization* 22, 1: 11–31.

Lamb, Sarah. 2000. *White Saris and Sweet Mangoes: Aging, Gender, and Body in North India.* Berkeley: University of California Press.

Levinson, Stephen. 1982. "Caste Rank and Verbal Interaction in Western Tamilnadu." *In* Dennis B. McGilvary, ed., *Caste Ideology and Interaction*, 98–203. Cambridge: Cambridge University Press

Ludden, David. 1985. *Peasant History in South India.* Princeton: Princeton University Press.

Marriott, McKim. 1968. "Caste Ranking and Food Transactions: A Matrix Analysis." *In* Milton Singer and Bernard S. Cohn, eds, *Structure and Change in Indian Society*, 133–71. Chicago: Aldine.

Marriott, McKim. 1976. "Hindu Transactions: Diversity without Dualism." *In* Bruce Kapferer, ed., *Transaction and Meaning: Directions in the Anthropology of Exchange and Symbolic Behavior*, 109–42. Philadelphia: Institute for the Study of Human Issues.

Marriott, McKim. 1990 [1989]. "Constructing an Indian Ethnosociology." *In* McKim Marriott, ed., *India Through Hindu Categories*, 1–39. New Delhi: Sage.

Marriott, McKim. 1998. "The Female Family Core Explored Ethnosociologically." *Contributions to Indian Sociology* 32, 2: 279–304.

Marriott, McKim and Ronald B. Inden. 1977. "Toward an Ethnosociology of South Asian Caste Systems." *In* Kenneth A. David, ed., *The New Wind: Changing Identities in South Asia*, 227–38. The Hague: Mouton.

Mauss, Marcel. 1990 [1923–24]. *The Gift: The Form and Reason for Exchange in Archaic Societies* (trans. W. D. Halls). New York: Norton.

Mines, Diane P. 1997. "Making the Past Past: Objects and the Spatialization of Time in Tamilnadu." *Anthropological Quarterly* 70, 4: 173–86.

Mines, Diane P. 2005. *Fierce Gods: Ineqaulity, Ritual, and the Politics of Dignity in a South Indian Village*. Bloomington: Indiana University Press.

Mines, Mattison and Vijayalakshmi Gourishankar. 1990. "Leadership and Individuality in South Asia: The Case of the South Indian Big-Man." *The Journal of Asian Studies* 49, 4: 761–86.

Moore, Melinda A. 1990. "The Kerala House as a Hindu Cosmos." *In* McKim Marriott, ed., *India through Hindu Categories*, 169–202. New Delhi: Sage.

Moreno, Manuel. 1985. "God's Forceful Call: Possession as a Divine Strategy." *In* Joanne Punzo Waghorne and Norman Cutler, eds, with Vasudha Narayanan, *Gods of Flesh, Gods of Stone: The Embodiment of Divinity in India*, 103–20. Chambersburg: Anima.

Nandy, Ashish. 2001. *An Ambiguous Journey to the City: The Village and Other Odd Ruins of the Self in the Indian Imagination*. Delhi: Oxford University Press.

Olivelle, Patrick, ed. and trans. 2005. *Manu's Code of Law: A Critical Edition and Translation of the Mānava-Dharmaśāstra*. New York: Oxford University Press.

Parker, Samuel. 1989. "Makers of Meaning: The Production of Temples and Images in South India." Ph.D. dissertation. Chicago: University of Chicago Library.

Parry, Jonathan P. 1986. "The Gift, the Indian Gift and the 'Indian gift'." *Man* 21, 3: 453–73.

Parry, Jonathan P. 1989. "On the Moral Perils of Exchange." *In* Jonathan P. Parry and Maurice Bloch, eds, *Money and the Morality of Exchange*, 64–93. Cambridge: Cambridge University Press.

Parry, Jonathan P. 1994. *Death in Banares*. Cambridge: Cambridge University Press.

Peabody, Norbert. 1991. "In Whose Turban Does the Lord Reside?: The Objectification of Charisma and the Fetishism of Objects in the Hindu Kingdom of Kota." *Comparative Studies in Society and History* 33, 4: 726–54.

Pfaffenberger, Bryan. 1982. *Caste in Tamil Culture: The Religious Foundations of Sudra Domination in Tamil Sri Lanka*." Syracuse: Maxwell School of Citizenship and Public Affairs, Syracuse University.

Price, Pamela. 1979. "Raja-Dharma in 19th Century South India: Land, Litigation, and Largess in Ramnad Zamindari." *Contributions to Indian Sociology* 13, 2: 205–39.

Price, Pamela. 1993. "Democracy and Ethnic Conflict in India: Precolonial Legacies in Tamil Nadu." *Asian Survey* 33, 5: 493–506.

Price, Pamela. 1996. "Revolution and Rank in Tamil Nationalism." *Journal of Asian Studies* 55, 2: 359–83.

Raheja, Gloria Goodwin. 1988a. *The Poison in the Gift: Ritual, Prestation, and the Dominant Caste in a North Indian Village*. Chicago: University of Chicago Press.

Raheja, Gloria Goodwin. 1988b. "India: Caste, Kingship, and Dominance Reconsidered." *Annual Review of Anthropology* 17: 497–522.

Raheja, Gloria Goodwin. 1990 [1989]. "Centrality, Mutuality and Hierarchy: Shifting Aspects of Inter-Caste Relationships in North India." *In* McKim Marriott, ed., *India Through Hindu Categories*, 79–101. New Delhi: Sage.

Sax, William S. 1991. *Mountain Goddess: Gender and Politics in a Himalayan Pilgrimage*. New York: Oxford University Press.

Shulman, David D. 1985. "Kingship and Prestation in South Indian Myth and Epic." *Asian and African Studies* 19: 93–117.

Trautmann, Thomas R. 1981. *Dravidian Kinship*. Cambridge: Cambridge University Press.

Trawick, Margaret. 1990. *Notes on Love in a Tamil Family*. Berkeley: University of California Press.

van der Veer, Peter. 1987. "God Must be Liberated: A Hindu Liberation Movement in Ayodhya." *Modern Asian Studies* 21, 2: 283–303.

Wadley, Susan S. 1994. *Struggling with Destiny in Karimpur, 1925–1984*. Berkeley: University of California Press.

Wadley, Susan S. and Bruce W. Derr. 1990 [1989]. "Eating Sins in Karimpur." *In* McKim Marriott, ed., *India Through Hindu Categories*, 131–48. New Delhi: Sage.

Waghorne, Joanne Punzo and Norman Cutler, eds, with Vasudha Narayanan. 1985. *Gods of Flesh, Gods of Stone: The Embodiment of Divinity in India*. Chambersburg: Anima.

Wiser, William Henricks. 1958 [1936]. *The Hindu Jajmani System: A Socio-Economic System Interrelating Members of a Hindu Village Community in Services*. Lucknow: Lucknow Publishing.

Zimmerman, Francis. 1980. "*Ṛtū-sātmya*: The Seasonal Cycle and the Principle of Appropriateness." *Social Science and Medicine* 24-B: 99–106.

11

Experience

June McDaniel

Experience in the Vedas and Upaniṣads
Experience in Yoga Tradition
Experience in Tantric Tradition
Experience in Bhakti Tradition
Critiques

In Hindu tradition, the category of religious experience is difficult to specify, mainly because there are several terms that refer to specific aspects. These are ancient terms and not simply a result of colonial influences or Western invention. In addition to general terms associated with *jñāna,* such as *abhijñatā*, translated as experience or knowledge or wisdom (Biswas 1983), two terms that more closely approximate an English-language understanding of "experience" are *darśana* and *bhāva*.

Darśana refers to experience associated with perception or observation, and it is used primarily to mean religious vision, though the term also can designate philosophy and science. It may occur spontaneously, as when a statue of a god or goddess is suddenly perceived as living and the observer is said to have *darśana* of the deity. Or the person may have acquired spiritual knowledge from repeated direct perceptions (*bhūyodarśana*). Experiential knowledge of this sort is considered valuable in various types of Hinduism, especially in devotional traditions. As Diana Eck (1981) notes, the central act of Hindu worship, from the perspective of the lay person, is to stand in the presence of the deity and to see and be seen by the deity. Though *darśana* may be understood as a gift of divine grace, it may also appear as the result of religious practice in past lives.

The term "*bhāva*" is used more popularly. Though *darśana* is found within traditional philosophy, *bhāva* tends to have different uses in literature than in popular religion. Some dictionary meanings include existence, condition, mental state, emotion, mood, and ecstasy (Biswas 1983). Other dictionaries include such terms as essence, imagination, divinity, yogic powers, rapture, and possession trance (Das 1979). However, Hindu informants divide the meaning of the term "*bhāva*" into secular (*laukika*) and religious or supernatural (*alaukika* or *ādhyātmika*) definitions. Secular definitions include responses to art and beauty, emotion, passion, feelings, and ideas. Religious definitions include the experiences of holy men and women, the relationship between the soul (*jīvātman*) and the god, surrender to the goddess, intuitive thought, forgetting the material world, and absorption in the deity (McDaniel 1989). Such *bhāva*s may be experienced inwardly or acted out as when the person is said to be *bhāvaveśa* or overcome by *bhāva*. The term "*anubhāva*" refers to the physical expression of such feelings, as in tears, sighing, and wild laughter. The *sāttvika bhāva*s, which express ecstatic emotion, include trembling, quivering, goose-flesh, crying, and fainting. They are said to occur in various degrees of intensity, from smoking to blazing.

These terms represent valued states in Hinduism, ranging from the pan-Indian Sanskrit tradition to regional traditions of West Bengal. However, they are general terms, and to understand the development of the concept of experience, we must look at terms from within some major strands of Hinduism.

Experience in the Vedas and Upaniṣads

In the *Ṛg Veda*, important descriptions of religious experience come from the *ṛṣi*s or seers, who have visions of the gods and of other worlds, from the priests who take the drug *soma* and from the long-haired ascetics or *keśin*s who "ride the winds."

The Vedic seers had experiences often called "mystical" and "supranatural," a visionary "beholding" or experiencing that allowed them to write the hymns in which gods speak in the first person and the worlds of the gods or *deva*s are described. Many hymns refer to the divine light that the *ṛṣi*s have seen and quote words of the gods that they have heard. These hymns are considered revelatory (*śruti*) and are highly valued.

Religious experience involves vision of the "shining ones," of the heaven of endless light (*svarga*), and of Brahman or the source of the greatness of the gods.

The most famous description of ecstatic religious experience in the *Ṛg Veda* is probably that of the drinkers of *soma*, whose insights were respected by the community. In *Ṛg Veda* 8.48.3, a seer speaks of his experiences: "We have drunk the Soma; we have become immortal; we have gone to the light; we have found the gods. What can hatred and the malice of a mortal do to us now, O immortal one?" (O'Flaherty 1981: 134–35).

Another example is the Keśin hymn of *Ṛg Veda*, which describes the flight of the long-haired ascetics who were believed to visit other worlds and become possessed by gods. The hymn moves from third person to first person: "These ascetics, swathed in wind, put dirty red rags on. When gods enter them, they ride with the rush of the wind. 'Crazy with asceticism, we have mounted the wind. Our bodies are all you mere mortals can see'" (*Ṛg Veda* 10.136.2–3; O'Flaherty 1981: 137–38).

Though the third person is more common in the hymns, many accounts speak directly of personal experience, and seers speak the words of the gods directly.

The Vedic seers describe the light of lights, which is sweet as honey, and its overflowing sweetness that brings human beings to the land of immortality. They go to the gods, ascend into the light, and are transformed. Religious experience is important in Vedic tradition, because it confers supernatural vision and immortality on the seer.

In the Upaniṣads, there are many stories and metaphors that describe the practice and goals of contemplation. These texts contain first-person accounts of contemplative states, which in general involve blissful joy, union with the ultimate state of Brahman, and the dissolution of the individual ego. This last state is compared to a grain of salt dissolving in water and becoming one with it and with the rivers that run to the sea and enter it fully. A description comes at the end of the *Kuṇḍikā Upaniṣad* (Olivelle 1992: 127–28):

> Stirred by the wind of illusion,
> the waves of the whole universe
> Repeatedly rise and fall
> within me, the ocean of total bliss...
> Like the sky am I,
> far beyond the reach of time...
> Like the sea am I,
> without a farther shore...
> I am pure consciousness, the witness of all!
> I am free from the thought of "I" and "mine"!
> I have no lord!...
> I do not act, I do not change.
> I have no parts, I have no form.
> I am eternal, I have no thought.
> I am unique, I have no support.
> All are myself and I am all!
> I am unique and I transcend all!
> I am my own eternal bliss,
> pure undivided consciousness!

In the *Paramahaṃsa Upaniṣad* 2.49 (Olivelle 1992: 138), the state of Brahman is described more simply:

> I am indeed that calm and unchanging Being, a single mass of bliss and consciousness. That alone is my highest abode....By knowing that the highest Self and the lower self are one, the difference between them dissolves into oneness.

Brahman is also represented as a force, the actions of which are beyond the power of philosophy or ritual to determine, that grasps the individual. As the *Muṇḍaka Upaniṣad* 3.2.3 states (Olivelle 1996: 276):

> This self cannot be grasped,
> by teachings or by intelligence,
> or even by great learning.
> Only the man he chooses can grasp him,
> whose body this self chooses as his own.

Direct experience gives knowledge of this ultimate state, as the *Kena Upaniṣad* 2.4 states (Olivelle 1996: 228):

> When one awakens to know it,
> one envisions it, for then
> one gains the immortal state.
> One gains power by one's self (*ātman*).
> And by knowledge, the immortal state.

This value of this state of experience is described by the sage Yājñavalkya in the *Bṛhadāraṇyaka Upaniṣad* 4.3.32–33. As he explains to the king (Olivelle 1992: 62):

> "He becomes the one ocean, he becomes the sole seer! This, Your Majesty, is the world of *brahman*." So did Yājñavalkya instruct him. "This is his highest goal! This is his highest attainment! This is his highest world! This is his highest bliss! On just a fraction of this bliss do other creatures live."

The Upaniṣads speak of the divine eye with which people perceive Brahman, the light of lights. Union with Brahman is supreme unsurpassable bliss; indeed, there is a level of the self or *ātman* composed entirely of bliss. This union brings freedom from death and rebirth, from suffering, from ignorance, from "the knots of the heart," desire, doubt, and fear. Such experience is eternal delight and peace and unlimited freedom in all worlds. One is able to recognize truth, consciousness, and bliss (*sat, cit, ānanda*) and alternatively goodness, beauty, and truth (*śivam, sundaram, satyam*).

Though the Upaniṣads are often thought to avoid personal religious experience, if we look closely we can see that the religious claims of these texts often arise from personal religious experience. Though the writing involves paradox, as does most mystical writing, we nevertheless see writers who are trying to describe experiences that they find difficult to express in ordinary language. These writings are later interpreted through the schools of Vedānta, which include those of nonduality (Advaita), duality (Dvaita), and qualified nonduality (Viśiṣṭādvaita).

Experience in Yoga Tradition

According to the *Yoga Sūtra* of Patañjali, liberation comes through asceticism and contemplation as *citta-vṛtti-nirodha*, the silencing of the activities of consciousness. This leads to the state of perfect contemplation or *samādhi*, which in turn leads to the ultimate state of liberation or *kaivalya*. During meditation, the mind becomes like transparent crystal and is able to make direct contact with its object of perception. As meditation advances, the person may become that object of concentration, "shining with the light of the object alone." Though liberation is the ultimate goal, the *Yoga Sūtra*s detail the various supernatural experiences or *siddhi*s that may occur during meditation. These perfections or attainments may occur due to birth (and the *karma* from past lives), *mantra*s, *tapas* (asceticism and purification), and states of *samādhi* (Prasāda 1988). They allow the person to develop discrimination and to be able to differentiate between pure spirit (*puruṣa*) and the *guṇa*s or aspects of life and thought that belong to matter, and they are aids in the development of concentration. They are less valued than higher forms of experience described in *Yoga Sūtra* 1.18–19. These involve the two forms of *samādhi*: *samprajñāta*, which has four substages and is achieved by yogic effort, and *asamprajñāta*, which is a state that occurs spontaneously to humans and supernatural beings.

Other texts on *yoga* emphasize the dissolution of the intellectually created world of concepts and the revelation of the interior world of the spirit. Sense perception is suspended, and the person experiences the bliss of dissolution in the practice of *layayoga*. Svātmarāma's *Haṭhayoga-pradīpikā* describes the *yogī* as "empty within and without like an empty pot in space, and also filled within and without like a pot in the ocean." In the ultimate state, the *yogī* is empty yet full, experiencing the union of *jīvātman* (individual soul) and *paramātman* (absolute or highest Self).

Though most yogic texts are written in the form of handbooks and manuals, we do have personal accounts of *yogī*s and *yoginī*s. For instance, the Kashmiri *yoginī* Lallā Devī describes her meditation in poem 53 (Parimoo 1978: 117):

Focussing on the Praṇava and making it yield to me,
It was a process of burning myself to white-heat;
Forsaking the six cross-roads, I took to the path of Truth,
Thus I, the seeker, reached the Abode of Light!

The major value of yogic experiences during meditation is to lead to the ultimate experience, to the abode of infinite light, the experience of perfect liberation (*jīvanmukti*) in this life.

Experience in Tantric Tradition

There is a close relationship between the yogic and Tantric traditions. The origins of Tantra are usually said to be around 500 CE (though some scholars point to older precursors). Over the next thousand years it elaborated theories and practices that have influenced both philosophical and devotional traditions in Hinduism.

Whereas Hindu devotionalism describes the highest religious experience as intense love of the deity, in Tantra union with a deity is considered not only possible but the goal of human life. Tantra emphasizes the union of opposites: spirit and matter, Brahman and the physical world (*jagat*), and god and humanity. Though modern sensationalizing of Tantra has emphasized sexual union, this is only one form of union among several others that are more important to the tradition. In Kaula tradition, the highest goal is the "vision of the truth of the *kula* (*kula-tattva-artha-darśana*), which is the direct intuition of ultimate reality. One gains Śiva's perception, in which all things appear the same, divine and otherwise (*sama-darśana*). In the Śrī Vidyā tradition, the momentary ecstasies or states of *kṣaṇa samādhi* are temporary instances of the highest state of *sahaja samādhi*, a spontaneous state in which the person can perceive any world, divine or human, equally.

Many Tantric texts discuss the importance of religious experience. In some, ecstatic states verify religious claims, while in others these states are themselves the goal of the practice. The medieval *Kulārṇava Tantra* has long been an important text for both Kashmiri and Bengali Tantric traditions. It describes the state, and the value, of absorption in the god Śiva, which it calls *samādhi* (*Kulārṇava Tantra* 9.14–15, 25–26; my translation):

He [the *yogī*] does not hear, or smell, or touch, or see; he does not know pleasure and pain, he does not analyze. Like a log, he does not think, he is not aware of anything [material]. One who is thus absorbed only in Śiva is said to be in *samādhi*. Just as no differences exist when water is poured into water, and milk into milk, *ghī* into *ghī*, so there exists

> no difference between the individual self (*jīvātman*) and the highest self (*paramātman*)....In comparison to the pure and supreme state of consciousness attained by the great *yogī*, even the states of gods and other divine beings have no value. For one who has seen (*darśana*) the all-pervading, peaceful, blissful, and imperishable, nothing remains to be attained or known.

The *Kulārṇava Tantra* is a text that speaks clearly and unambiguously about the importance of experience, especially that of union with Śiva (*śivatva*).

Experience in Bhakti Tradition

Most Hinduism today involves some form of *bhakti* or loving devotion to one or more deities (Klostermaier 1994). More than ordinary respect and obedience, *bhakti* can refer to *parama prema*, the highest love that brings a person to perfection. It may begin from a passionate longing for God's presence and end in the joy that results from such longing (*premānanda*, the bliss of selfless love) as will bring both immortality and knowledge of the god. The *bhakti* tradition rejects religious limitations on the basis of caste and gender and offers access to God to people of all sorts.

Although there are many *bhakti* lineages (*sampradāyas*), most devotees worship some form of Viṣṇu, including his popular *avatāras* or incarnations Kṛṣṇa and Rāma. These are followed by dedication to Śiva and to the goddesses Śakti or Devī (especially known in her forms of Kālī, Durgā, and Pārvatī). In this section, we focus on Vaiṣṇava *bhakti*, which has the largest breadth of devotional literature.

Though *bhakti* can refer to a variety of approaches to the deity, the most intensely loving form is called by Friedhelm Hardy (1983) "emotional Kṛṣṇa *bhakti*" as distinguished from the earlier tradition of *bhakti* as loyalty and respect. Hardy writes that it grew up with the *Bhāgavata Purāṇa* and Āḻvār saints of South India from about the seventh to ninth centuries CE. Since that time, many Vaiṣṇava works have discussed the importance of religious experience. In the tenth-century CE *Bhakti Sūtras*, which are dedicated to the god Kṛṣṇa, the writer Nārada describes degrees of devotional love. One begins by glorifying and appreciating the god's greatness, then loving his beauty, worshipping him and remembering him constantly, identifying with being the god's slave, then his friend, then his parent, then loving him as a wife loves her husband. The devotee should entirely surrender to Kṛṣṇa and feel absorbed in him and yet still feel sorrow at the pain of separation from him. This feeling of union yet separation is considered to be the highest religious state by Nārada in his *sūtra* 82 (Tyāgīśānanda 1978: 23).

Such experience is not intended to be left behind when a person achieves liberation. Ideally it goes on forever.

Rāmānuja identifies the god Viṣṇu with the Brahman of the Upaniṣads, and yet he descends to Earth to give mankind salvation. The most important religious attitude is self-surrender or *prapatti*. This is a state of absolute delight, resulting from Viṣṇu's mercy, and the highest state to be attained by human beings. For Madhva, the ideal state for the devotee is reflecting God's splendor, perfectly identifying with Viṣṇu and seeing the world through his eyes. For Vallabha, God's grace leads the devotee to an eternal passionate love that makes possible participation in the god's eternal play (*nitya līlā*). The devotee attains the emotional states of *bhajānanda* (the bliss of love) and *svarūpānanda* (the bliss of perceiving the god's true form) and becomes like Kṛṣṇa's milkmaids or *gopīs* with their minds entirely focused on the god.

One of the clearest examples of the importance of religious experience in Hinduism comes in the Gauḍīya Vaiṣṇava tradition of West Bengal. Gauḍīya Vaiṣṇavism was inspired by the fifteenth-century saint or *siddha*, Caitanya Mahāprabhu, who was believed to be a joint incarnation of the god Kṛṣṇa and his consort Rādhā. Caitanya was a visionary ecstatic who was believed to be able to speak as Kṛṣṇa, as Rādhā, and as his human personality. His ecstatic experiences became the basis for the analyses of religious experience found in Gauḍīya tradition. The highest religious goal of this tradition is to experience all of the variations of intense love, the sort of passionate love experienced by Rādhā and her milkmaid friends, the *gopīs*. The legitimacy of these states of love is shown by the ecstatic experiences known as the *sāttvika bhāvas*, which include trembling, sweating, paralysis, crying, hair standing on end, changing skin color, and loss of consciousness.

Such emotional states may result from meditative practice in current or past life or occur spontaneously as a gift of Kṛṣṇa's grace. When the states of intense emotion (*bhakti bhāva*) develop, the emotion is said to become deepened and condensed and to yield a heart full of continual burning desire. The devotee goes through many stages of love until he or she reaches the highest state or *mahābhāva* in two modes: sharing the loving bliss found only in Rādhā and the *gopīs*, and sharing the state of passionate delirium found only in Rādhā herself in which she experiences all possible emotions simultaneously. Such texts as the *Bhaktirasāmṛtasindhu* and the *Ujjvalanīlamaṇi* of Rūpa Gosvāmī describe the spiritual development of the devotee, from the mild emotions that occur as a result of ritual to the passionate love that comes from true devotion (McDaniel 1989).

For some forms of Gauḍīya tradition, the ability to love Kṛṣṇa involves developing a new spiritual body, known as the *siddhadeha*. This is an eternal body in the form of a handmaiden to the *gopīs*, and it is understood as immortal. The religious emotions engendered by intense Vaiṣṇava practice are too strong for an ordinary soul to bear; one needs a spiritual self whose essence is love. This self can hold the religious passions in this life and continues to exist in the presence of Rādhā and Kṛṣṇa in their eternal paradise after death. Because the flow of Kṛṣṇa's love is like an ocean of bliss, a body of nonphysical bliss is needed to contain it.

Though this is the highest state in Gauḍīya Vaiṣṇava theology, other states are valued: appreciation of beauty and its essence (*rasa*) in which religious and aesthetic experience are related, joy that comes through chanting *mantras* and singing hymns (*kīrtana*), and appreciation that arises during visualizations of the Vaiṣṇava paradise. Though yogic traditions emphasize the importance of religious knowledge, Vaiṣṇavism values love more highly, and the true devotee is one who experiences and expresses that love.

In pan-India Vaiṣṇavism, religious experience is described in such texts as the *Mahābhārata* and *Rāmāyaṇa*. Perhaps most important is Kṛṣṇa's revelation of his universal form in the *Bhagavad Gītā*, which is both an ecstatic vision and a statement of Kṛṣṇa's power. In the *Gītā*, the vision accorded to Arjuna serves to harmonize competing or conflicting traditions within Hinduism.

Critiques

Study of religious experience has been subjected to a wide range of critiques, from the constructivist claim that religious experience is a culturally relative construct, to the psychoanalytic claim that it is unconscious projection, to the historical claim that it is an artifact of colonial influence, to the philosophical claim that the term "religious experience" is far too vague and subjective to be meaningful. Can we say that the idea of religious experience itself is so vague that it is useless? This might be the case in analytic philosophy, or for pragmatism, wherein the only worthwhile questions have very clear and unambiguous answers. However, such an approach denigrates all subjective experience, so that discussions of appreciation of music, the feelings of love and joy, and emotional involvement with drama and theater become useless, and Hinduism's *rasa* analysis of aesthetic experience values all of these. Far more than religion would be lost were we to deny the significance of all subjective experience.

If we compare understandings of religious experience in Hinduism and in the West, what is striking is their similarity. They are alike in differentiating natural and supernatural religious experiences, both include understandings of the divine as personal (a God or gods) and impersonal (an Ultimate Reality or Source), and both include types that value religious love and wisdom. Though the West may have more emphasis on conversion and faith, and

India more emphasis on mystical union and purification, there is a large area of cross-cultural and interreligious overlap between their understandings.

Is it the case that all religious experience can be dismissed because of false claims about it by individuals? In Christianity there is a long tradition of spiritual discernment, including ways to distinguish the origins of religious claims in God, Satan, or the human imagination, and this is why spiritual direction is important to religious practitioners.

In Hinduism there is "discernment of spirits" in the role of the *guru* and in the philosophy of religion. The *guru* is a person whose authority is often charismatic and based directly on those "exalted spiritual states" mentioned as irrelevant by critics of religious experience. It is these states that allow the *guru* to be understood as able to evaluate the experiences of others. *Gurus* may gain their status from lineage (there are people who are born into *guru* status and others who are named by institutions) or based on their experiences, the *bhāva*s they undergo and can transmit to others. *Guru* and saint (*siddha*) biographies abound in stories of spontaneous supernatural events, religious emotions shared by crowds in "waves of *bhāva*," *guru*s who have visions and can read the thoughts of their devotees and bless them in special ways. Many *guru*s are outside of lineages and institutions, with only an initiating figure far in the past (whose religious persuasions are often unknown) and sometimes only a call from a god or goddess in a dream or vision. Yet they are understood to be able to judge and guide the religious experiences of others and are often called on to do so. Such *guru*s are generally believed to have undergone deep personal religious experiences (and even if they do not speak of it themselves, their disciples can generally be relied on to make the claims for them).

Questions of false or illusory experience have long been of interest to Hindu philosophers. They did not make a blanket claim that all experiences were reliable but also did not dismiss all experiences because some claims were problematic. Many thinkers would allow for the existence of a "flash of intuition" (*pratibhājñāna*) about a future event. More controversial may be the status of intuition of sages (*ārṣajñāna*) and *yogī*s (*yogīpratyakṣa*). For sages, the merit that resulted from austerities was understood to create a special type of perception, knowledge that is valid but not of sensory origin. Yogic perception comes about through the removal of mental impurities and can include occult perception (*siddha-darśana*). It typically has been divided into two types: ecstatic, which gives insight into the essential nature of the universe, and nonecstatic, which gives information of subtle, hidden, and remote objects (Sinha 1969). Because *yoga* philosophy traditionally accepts that all events, past and future, exist simultaneously and that temporal order is a construction of the intellect, the *yogī* may have access to all times and all objects.

However, there is room for error. The *yogī*'s perceptions may be distorted by such qualities as illusion, egotism, and restlessness. A major problem is the identification of self and mind, which can appear identical but are different. The mind (*buddhi*) is changeable and capable of error, subject to past memories (*saṃskāra*) and their intellectual and emotional associations, whereas the deeper self is beyond these problems. There may be misidentification, distorted interpretation, or simply wrong perception. There are supernatural events that precede the state of liberation, and they can be confused with illusory ones. It is only when the sage is understood to be free of the effects of *karma* that his or her experiences become true for all devotees. Otherwise, they are judged in terms of probabilities and individual faith in the *guru* and god.

In modern academic scholarship, there is a trend that can be termed "the scholarship of erasure." Here, scholars are not interested in developing new ideas as much as in erasing or negating older ideas. This trend gained publicity in the art world when the artist Robert Rauschenberg literally erased a pencil sketch by DeKooning with the intent to "purge" himself of artistic tradition. Metaphorically it came to be continued in the field of art criticism by the erasure of beauty as sentimental and old-fashioned and of realism as primitive now that we inhabit the age of electronic reproduction. In psychology, there has been the erasure of altruism (too idealistic) and more recently of consciousness itself (too vague and subjective, not provable). Similarly in the field of religious studies, some writers have attempted to erase the value of religious experience, attributing the origins of such experience to trauma, colonialism, projection, or failure of understanding.

Most of these critiques come from non-Hindu writers, and though their approaches have met support from some Hindu scholars, there has been vocal opposition from others and even protests in the popular Indian press. The nature of religious experience is an ongoing debate, but it has been an important facet of Hindu belief and practice and cannot be dismissed easily.

References Cited

Biswas, Sailendra, comp. 1983 [1918]. *Samsad Bengali–English Dictionary*. Calcutta: Sahitya Samsad.

Das, Jnanendramohan. 1979. *Bāṅgālā Bhāsār Abhidān*. Calcutta: Sahitya Samsad.

Eck, Diana L. 1981. *Darśan: Seeing the Divine Image in India*. Chambersburg: Anima.

Hardy, Friedhelm. 1983. *Viraha-Bhakti: The Early History of Kṛṣṇa Devotion in South India*. Delhi: Oxford University Press.

Klostermaier, Klaus K. 1994 [1989]. *A Survey of Hinduism*. Albany: State University of New York Press.

McDaniel, June. 1989. *The Madness of the Saints: Ecstatic Religion in Bengal.* Chicago: University of Chicago Press.

O'Flaherty, Wendy Doniger, trans. 1981. *The Rig Veda: An Anthology of One Hundred and Eight Hymns.* New York: Penguin.

Olivelle, Patrick, trans. 1992. *Saṃnyāsa Upaniṣads: Hindu Scriptures on Asceticism and Renunciation.* New York: Oxford University Press.

Olivelle, Patrick, trans. 1996. *Upaniṣads.* Oxford: Oxford University Press.

Parimoo, B. N. 1978. *The Ascent of Self: A Re-Interpretation of the Mystical Poetry of Lalla-Ded.* Delhi: Motilal Banarsidass.

Prasāda, Rāma, trans. 1988 [1912]. *Pātanjali's Yoga Sutras, with the Commentary of Vyāsa and the Gloss of Vāchaspati Miśra.* New Delhi: Munshiram Manoharlal.

Sinha, Jadunath. 1969. *Indian Epistemology of Perception.* Calcutta: Sinha Publishing House.

Tyāgīśānanda, Swāmī, trans. 1978 [1940]. *Aphorisms on The Gospel of Divine Love, or Nārada Bhakti Sūtras, with Sanskrit Text, Word-by-Word Meaning, English Rendering of the Text and Elaborate Explanatory and Critical Notes.* Madras: Sri Ramakrishna Math.

12

Fiction

Amardeep Singh

Hinduism in Early Indian Fiction (1855–1955)
Narrative Experiments in Contemporary Literature
Concluding Reflections

The representation of Hinduism in prose fiction is a relatively recent phenomenon, one that emerged in the mid-nineteenth century with the first published novels in Bengal and spread rapidly throughout India. As it spread, the medium of fiction became an important part of the presentation and defense of Hindu beliefs and practices by Indian intellectuals during and after the colonial era. It also became a medium by which arguments have been made to reform practices thought to be backward, from the nineteenth-century ban on widow remarriage to the ongoing quandary that is posed by hereditary caste hierarchies and untouchability. While many popular fiction writers who have engaged with Hinduism have been secularizing in orientation, some have offered spirited defenses of the tradition against what they perceived as incorrect or distorted images produced by—and for consumption in—the West. Thus, the problem of the representation of Hinduism in Indian fiction has corresponded closely to the problem of Indian or Hindu nationalism itself: how to describe an ancient religious tradition that is so internally diverse and has been so much altered by waves of conquest and colonialism spanning several centuries?

For analytical purposes, fiction dealing with Hinduism can be divided into two chronological eras: the colonial era and the postcolonial era. The latter chronologically begins in 1947 but really emerges in the imagination of novelists in the 1960s and 1970s (Williams and Chrisman 1994). Fictional representations of Hinduism in the colonial era tend to be preoccupied with questions of what Hinduism should be and how Hindu tradition should be reformed to further the cause of social justice and the aims of a secular nationalist movement. In the postcolonial era, such novelists as Salman Rushdie, Ashok K. Banker, and others have adapted and reinvented elements of Hindu mythology, especially the *Rāmāyaṇa*, using the conventions of magical realism and science fiction, to place them in new contexts. Other writers, especially such feminist novelists as Githa Hariharan and Manju Kapur, have dealt with the ways in which some elements of traditional Hinduism have been reactivated with the reemergence of the militant ideology of postcolonial Hindu nationalism. The novels referred to in this chapter can be instructively read as providing a historical sketch of the evolution of Hinduism in the context of the political upheavals of the Indian subcontinent leading up to and after independence. Many of these novels also provide rich material for lay readers and those interested in learning about Hindu tradition as it is lived and felt in the everyday lives of more than 800 million Hindus in India and elsewhere.

Hinduism in Early Indian Fiction (1855–1955)

It is generally accepted that the modern novel emerged in Europe in the eighteenth century (Watt 1957), though there were certainly in Europe traditions of prose writing and elsewhere that preceded it. Before the advent of British colonial rule in the mid-eighteenth century, the overwhelming bulk of imaginative literature in India was composed in verse form and recited orally. Much of it was in some sense devotional and tied to the Hindu tradition, though there were exceptions to this rule. Modern prose fiction was made possible by the introduction of the printing press, starting in Bengal around 1800 (Sen 1960: 178–79). The first printing presses in India were used to print materials used by missionaries, including translations of the New Testament in Bengali, the first printed edition of which appeared in 1801, and editions of key Hindu scriptures, the *Rāmāyaṇa* (1801–3) and the *Mahābhārata* (1802–4). In the sense that its first function was specifically religious, the history of the printing press in India seems to mirror that of Europe—where the first book printed by Johannes Gutenberg was the Bible. However, the rapid secularization of the uses to which the press was put, and the eventual proliferation of printing presses around India, also resembled European print-culture in that it quickly became a secularizing and modernizing force in Indian cultural life.

The first modern Indian novels were written in Bengali and printed at the Serampore Press. Bhabanicharan Bandyopadhyay's *Nababābuliās* (The Babus Today, 1825) may have been the earliest Bengali novel, though most established critics have identified the first true Bengali novel as Peary Chand Mitra's *Ālāler Gharer Dulāl* (Pampered Son of a Front Rank Family, 1858). Sukumar Sen (1960: 230) summarizes it as a picaresque satire of a wealthy young man who does not appear to have had much engagement with Hinduism and who brings financial ruin on his family. It seems appropriate to accept it as the first "modern" novel because it uses vernacular Bengali and has a realistic setting, both of which seem to be important constituent features of modern fiction.

The first canonical Bengali novelist to make a major statement on the status of Hinduism is Bankimcandra Chatterji (1838–94) who was brought up in an orthodox Brāhmaṇa family. He was educated at British-run institutions, including the Presidency College in Calcutta, and by *paṇḍita*s who taught him Sanskrit and classical Hindu literature (Lipner 2005: 10–11). He was in the employ of the colonial government, but much of his writing contains veiled criticisms of colonialism. He began his career as a poet but started writing novels in the 1860s, beginning with the English-language *Rajmohan's Wife* (1864). All of his remaining works were written in Bengali. Many of Bankim's novels were domestic romances, and several had historical settings. His novel *The Poison Tree* (Biṣabṛkṣa, 1873) represents debates on widow remarriage that had been initiated by the reformer Ishwarchandra Vidyasagar, who successfully exploited emerging Bengali print-culture in the 1850s to argue that the ban on widow remarriage be lifted (Bose 1969: 29–42). Bankim takes what might be understood as a conservative position in *The Poison Tree* in imagining catastrophic results following from the remarriage of a widow who falls in love with a married man. The critic Tanika Sarkar (2001) has read this novel as, in fact, progressive with regard to women, and perhaps she has a point. Bankim *is* notable in that he gives his female characters a strong personality and will, which his contemporaries did not always do. But both this novel and *Kṛṣṇakānter Uil* (Krishnakanta's Will), written in the wake of the widow remarriage debates of the 1850s, show the harm that sexualized widows can do to established society.

Bankim's most famous novel is *Ānandamaṭh* (1882), a historical account of the Sannyāsī Rebellion of 1773. The novel is rich with references to Hinduism as a belief system that can motivate resistance to colonial authority (portrayed as primarily Muslim), and as such it has been both highly influential and controversial because some of its passages can be interpreted as "communal" in the modern usage of the word: "For a long time we've been wanting to smash the nest of these weaver-birds, to raze the city of these Muslim foreigners (*jaban*), and throw it in the river—to burn the enclosure of these swine and purify mother earth again!" (2005: 103).

The text of the song "Vande Mātaram" first appeared in *Ānandamaṭh*. It is an ode to a female goddess and became closely associated with Indian resistance to colonial rule and efforts to achieve independence. However, because of its explicitly Hindu themes and the anti-Islamic tenor of the novel that was its source, Rabindranath Tagore's "Jana Gana Mana" replaced it as a national anthem.

The deification of a feminine nationalist spirit in *Ānandamaṭh* and "Vande Mātaram" coexists comfortably with a very conservative view of the role of women. However, despite Bankim's conservative views on women's roles, a female character has one of the central roles in the novel. Shanti is the wife of a resistance fighter and receives an education in Sanskrit as part of her preparation to join a band of freedom-fighting mendicants (*santān*). In the final edition of the novel, Shanti becomes a kind of militant woman who dresses and acts as a man without losing her femininity—the embodiment of a new, fighting image of "mother India" and an emblem of the new nationalist spirit.

Gender issues are also at play in debates on Hinduism in many of Rabindranath Tagore's novels, including the two most famous, *Ghare Bāire* (The Home and the World, 1916) and *Gorā* (Fair Faced, 1910). Tagore's family was one of the pillars of the reform movement known as the Brāhmo Samāj, which was highly influential in Bengal beginning in the mid-nineteenth century (Kopf 1979). Along with its monotheistic theological framework came a strong focus on social reform, including the eradication of rigid caste boundaries, emancipation of women, and modern education in the British style.

By the time *Gorā* was published, the Brāhmo Samāj had perhaps passed its prime. It had also experienced significant internal division and had evolved to some extent into a kind of Brāhmaṇical subcaste of its own. Gora is a young man in a devout Brāhmaṇa family and becomes involved with a young woman from the Brāhmo Samāj community, but he balks at the thought of breaking caste by marrying her. "Gora" is of course only a nickname, which can be translated from Bengali (and Hindi) as "fair faced." In common speech, "Gora" can also be translated pejoratively as something akin to "whitey." He is referred to in this way by his friends and members of his family, none of whom know the secret of his birth—that he is adopted from an Irishman who had died in the uprising of 1857. Until the moment he discovers the secret, the nickname "Gora" signifies a harmless physical difference, without indicating outsider status. Until then, Gora is "white" in the sense that his physical complexion is fair, but he is not White in the sense of being outcaste or *mleccha*.

Gorā is a novel intensely preoccupied with caste. In contrast to Bankim's *Ānandamaṭh*, at the denouement of the novel the overcoming of narrow traditionalism enables the advent of a new nationalism. Once he realizes he is by his foreign birth necessarily a *mleccha*, or outcaste, Gora is freed to marry the young woman he loves and is free to embrace *Indian* (and not only Hindu) nationalism.

Caste is as important in Mulk Raj Anand's early novels, especially *Untouchable* (1935) and *Coolie* (1936). He aims to show the myriad ways in which caste presides over everyday life. The outcaste status of the novel's main character, Bakha, bars him from participation in Hindu rituals in his local village temple, limits his access to sources of water and food, and restricts him to life as a sweeper. Anand's early works promote Gandhian ideals, and *Untouchable* has a famous scene in which Mohandas K. Gandhi makes a speech deriding untouchability. Bakha struggles to live with dignity but is repeatedly stymied, including when he enters a Hindu temple and watches the beginning of a *pūjā* only to be greeted by protests from the *paṇḍita*s, who forcefully eject him. Strikingly, at the same moment, Bakha discovers that his sister has been sexually assaulted by one of the *paṇḍita*s at the temple. For Bakha merely to enter the temple causes pollution, yet the Brāhmaṇa men in the novel do not admit pollution if it interferes with their ability to exploit women of lower castes.

Unlike more recent fiction focusing on untouchability—especially from the school of Dalit writers who have emerged since the 1970s—Anand clearly aims to reform caste, not necessarily revolutionize it. His concerns echo Gandhi's concern with the right to temple entry. Anand quotes Gandhi to this effect:

> I am an orthodox Hindu and I know that the Hindus are not sinful by nature....They are sunk in ignorance. All public wells, temples, roads, schools, sanatoriums, must be declared open to the Untouchables....Two of the strongest desires that keep me in the flesh are the emancipation of the Untouchables and the protection of the cow. When these two desires are fulfilled there is *swaraj*, and therein lies my soul's deliverance.
>
> (1935: 149)

Sexual relations between a Brāhmaṇa man and a low-caste woman also form the core of U. R. Anantha Murthy's 1965 Kannada novel *Samskāra* that is set in a village that has seen few incursions of modernity. It therefore seems somewhat appropriate to consider it alongside such novels as *Untouchable*, *Gorā*, and *Ānandamaṭh*. The village is an exclusively Brāhmaṇa stronghold called *agrahāra*. Within the village, transgressions by one member are seen to pollute the entire community and to require ritual purifications. A resident named Naranappa has significantly exceeded all caste taboos by discarding his Brāhmaṇa wife for a low-caste prostitute, fishing in the temple water tank with Muslim friends, and consuming both meat and alcohol. Mainly because they feared the loss of status that would come with publicly acknowledging Naranappa's fall from grace, his peers never excommunicated him from the *agrahāra* during his life. When he dies suddenly, however, they are forced to reckon with the gravity of his transgressions. To cremate him in the manner of a proper Brāhmaṇa might destroy their status, but not to cremate him seems unthinkable. The task of deciding the fate of his corpse is left to the unimpeachable Praneshacharya, who has dedicated his life to Sanskritic learning. Over the course of making this difficult decision, Praneshacharya himself sleeps with Naranappa's former mistress and begins to transgress his status in other ways as well.

Perhaps in contrast to Anand's *Untouchable* or Tagore's *Gorā*, Anantha Murthy's *Samskāra* gives emphasis to the positive and constituting features of caste alongside its negative, exclusionary aspects. For the characters in *Samskāra*, to give up caste entirely is akin to a kind of total dissolution of the self—a kind of suicide. Praneshacharya cannot quite conceive of what his life would be like if he renounced his caste identity entirely, to become a fully "secular" individual. The way out for Praneshacharya is not as easy as it is for Tagore's Gora. Disavowal of hereditary status would not only lead to loss of privileges, it would lead to complete loss of self, a kind of "ghostliness" that he could scarcely imagine. Alongside the more abstract considerations of reform-oriented writers, such as Tagore and Anand, the intimate experience of orthodox, caste-identified Hinduism in Anantha Murthy's novel is an important representation of Hinduism in Indian fiction.

Though much early Indian fiction written in Bengali, Marathi, Hindi, and other Indian languages was concerned with presenting aspects of Hinduism to Indians, such writers as Mulk Raj Anand, Raja Rao, and R. K. Narayan wrote in English and had a sizeable impact on perceptions of Hinduism abroad. Of course, their influence was dwarfed by the influence of such writers as E. M. Forster, whose rather derogatory representation of Hinduism in *A Passage to India* (1924) has had a surprising resiliency owing to other strengths of Forster's elegantly constructed novel. Hinduism is embodied for Forster primarily in the maddeningly metaphysical character Godbole, whose nondualistic thinking is seen as distasteful to the rationalist liberal Fielding. Godbole represents to Fielding and by implication to early non-Indian readers of the novel, the "muddle" of trying to make sense of the vast range and complexity of traditional Hindu beliefs and practices. The muddle seems to attach itself to Chandrapore, the town where the novel is set and a place at which the Ganges ("which happens not to be holy here") is described as slow and muddy as well. In contrast, references to Islamic theology and architecture in the novel evoke the play of light and dark and a space of erotic and intellectual ferment. Hinduism, for Forster, is not only the paradigmatic "Oriental" religion but a foil to what he imagined as a more charming and comprehensible Islam.

Many Indian writers after 1924 found themselves questioning Forster's version of Hinduism in *A Passage to India*. Among them is Nirad Chaudhuri's "Passage To and From India" (1954). Chaudhuri strongly reprimands Forster for writing a jaundiced and insulting account of Hindus and of India. A more oblique, humorous defense of Hinduism against patronizing attitudes of British colonialists can be found in Narayan's *Swami and Friends* (1935) featuring Mr. Ebenezer, a European teacher at the local English-medium school in the fictional town of Malgudi; he spends each class ranting against the irrationality of the Hindu tradition: " 'Oh, wretched idiots!' the teacher said, clenching his fists. 'Why do you worship dirty, lifeless, wooden idols and stone images? Can they talk? No. Can they see? No. Can they bless you? No. Can they take you to heaven? No. Why? Because they have no life' " (Narayan 1994: 3).

After Swami's father writes a note to the headmaster, Mr. Ebenezer is chastened and is forced to moderate his tone. Narayan's comedic spirit dominates the incident, but he is responding to a long tradition of derogatory colonial images of Hinduism, many of which were derived from early missionaries who strove to depict Hinduism as an idol-ridden, corrupt, and irrational faith. With remarkable efficiency in just a few pages in a book that could easily be understood by children, Narayan makes that particular component of the colonial project in India seem utterly absurd.

Narrative Experiments in Contemporary Literature

Fiction that presents "Hinduism" or "caste" as generalities has been displaced more recently by more localized narratives. Given the earlier emphasis on reform and critique of Hinduism, it may be more surprising that some of the most striking novels and visual media that have appeared after 1960 have attempted to resituate Hinduism—some of them in contemporary or futuristic settings using such devices as magical realism or science fiction. Rather than locate Hinduism in a conservative social and historical framework, such works as Salman Rushdie's *Midnight's Children* (1980) and Ashok K. Banker's *Prince of Ayodhya* (2003), the first in a multivolume retelling of the *Rāmāyaṇa*, attempt to rethink and reanimate stories and myths from Hindu tradition. In striking ways, recent Indian fiction has moved to reimagine many aspects of Hindu tradition, including ancient source texts themselves.

Popular and creative redeployments of Hindu myth are of course nothing new in Indian culture. The *Rāmāyaṇa* has been immensely popular, both as a serialized television broadcast and as an *Amar Chitra Katha* comic book. What is perhaps new is the way in which narrative elements from the *Rāmāyaṇa* are used by Rushdie and Banker in the context of narratives that are otherwise set in the present or the future. Rushdie's appropriation of the *Rāmāyaṇa* and of other resources from Hindu mythology is diffused throughout his novel. Several characters bear the names of Hindu deities, including Śiva and Pārvatī. There is also a gang called Ravana, and the protuberant nose of the novel's fictional narrator, Saleem Sinai, along with the nose of his grandfather is compared to Gaṇeśa's trunk. The allusions to Hindu tradition are in a sense inessential to the primary plot of the novel, but they add depth and richness to the text when understood with reference to their original referents. The epic quest of Saleem can be read as an echo of Rāma's exile and return in triumph to Ayodhyā. Parvati-the-witch is a sort of Sītā, and the sinister totalitarian leader known as the Widow (and who resembles real-life Prime Minister Indira Gandhi) may be understood as similar to Rāvaṇa.

Rushdie plays with Hinduism in ways that some readers may suppose is too irreverent, mocking, and culturally compromised, but his intent seems to be to reflect the "hybridity" of postcolonial India's cultural tapestry, which juxtaposes and intermixes elements both from multiple cultures around the planet and from traditional Hindu sources. Rushdie's writing ties together seemingly disconnected strands of narrative, religious tradition, and politics, often with sharp humor. In one chapter of *Midnight's Children*, the narrator acknowledges the humility required to retell the history of post-independent India in light of Hinduism's vast concepts of time, only to be rebuked by an illiterate peasant woman, Padma:

> Think of this: history, in my version, entered a new phase on August 15, 1947—but in another version, that inescapable date is no more than one fleeting instant in the Age of Darkness, Kali-Yuga, in which the cow of morality has been reduced to standing, teeteringly, on a single leg! Kali-Yuga...began on Friday, February 18th, 3102 B.C.; and will last a mere 432,000 years!...A little humility at this point...does not, I feel, come amiss.
>
> Padma shifts her weight, embarrassed. "What are you talking?" she asks, reddening a little. "That is brahmin's talk; what's it to do with me?"
>
> (1980: 223)

The narrator is in awe of the large scale of the Hindu concept of cyclical time. The small slice of time after independence, though rich with events, seems minuscule in comparison to the massive scale of even one *yuga*. And yet Padma swiftly deflates the thought with a strikingly direct social comment: "That is brahmin's talk." Extended discourse on the meaning of ancient Hindu scriptures is very much a caste-identified activity—and, needless to say, a gendered one, too.

The debunking comedy of the dialogs between Padma and the narrator Saleem are reminiscent of comic dialogs in an important but sometimes overlooked novel by G. V. Desani, *All About H. Hatterr* (1948). Published at the turning point between colonial fiction and the postcolonial experimentation of Rushdie—and though it is worlds away from the earnest philosophical contemplations of Raja Rao or the reformist sincerity of

Mulk Raj Anand or his precursor, Premchand—Desani's *Hatterr* delights in rhetorical disavowals and rhetorical sleights of hand, in linguistic word-play, and in mockery of the role of the colonial writer and the English-language reading public.

Desani's novel is deeply irreligious and yet is obsessed with the *guru–śiṣya* (teacher–student) model of ascetic Hinduism. All of its *gurus* turn out to be charlatans of one sort or another. Most are angling for cash, and some are sexual predators. Even so, there are quite moving passages of religious reflection in the text. Desani himself is unique among the authors treated in this chapter in that he endeavored to become a traditional Hindu, having devoted himself to living an ascetic lifestyle from about 1952 to 1964, during which period he rejected as many of the "reformed" aspects of Hinduism as he could and instead attempted to model his life on difficult and esoteric *śāstric* texts. Many of the stories he began to publish after he emerged from that period of silence seem imbued with a strong mystical Hindu sensibility, though at some point in the late 1960s, an irrepressible wordplay began to reappear in such stories as "The Second Mrs. Was Wed in a Nightingale" and "Since a Nation Must Export, Smithers!"

Prince of Ayodhya (2003) is the first installation of Banker's multivolume English-language adaptation of the *Rāmāyaṇa.* It is an adventurous and entertaining science fiction rendition that adheres closely to the story of the original Sanskrit text and might be described roughly as *The Lord of the Rings* in the context of Hindu mythology. The six-part series details the major events of the *Rāmāyaṇa*, with changes of emphasis and in the sequence and style of narration to make it accessible for contemporary readers, but Banker also makes ideas from the Hindu tradition into full-blown discourses. Yogic breathing and movement is here not just a simple physical exercise. Instead, it is an effective ritual by which warriors master the movements of the body. Some features are added to the traditional text, which may be unsettling for readers familiar with the Vālmīki version: Rāvaṇa becomes a major arch-villain rather than simply a chapter in a longer epic narrative, Mantharā becomes a servant of Rāvaṇa rather than simply a mother who wanted her child, and perhaps more unsettling is that Bharata rather than Rāma is to be crowned the next king of Ayodhyā. Banker is committed to recontextualizing and reworking details of the *Rāmāyaṇa* to make them come alive in a new way for today's readers.

Of course, the idea of "versioning" such stories as the *Rāmāyaṇa* cannot be said to be new. Paula Richman (1991, 2001) has documented the longstanding diversity of the story in different regions of India. In some versions, for instance, Rāvaṇa kidnapped an apparent rather than actual Sītā, and in others Sītā commits suicide rather than to be reunited with Rāma after he had seemed to doubt her. In one form or another, traditional narratives, such as the *Rāmāyaṇa*, continue to be incorporated into the fabric of modern fiction and continue to be among the most vital and contested elements in Hindu popular culture.

Finally, a number of major novelists have responded to the rise of Hindu nationalism in post-independence politics. Rushdie did so in *The Moor's Last Sigh* (1995), and communal violence plays a role in the works of such writers as Amitav Ghosh, Taslima Nasreen, and Vikram Seth, among others. For the most part, detailed engagement with ritual and textual aspects of Hindu tradition are absent from these representations. They focus more on *Hindus* as a social group in the contemporary context rather than on Hindu*ism*. However, some recent novelists have seriously engaged the tradition in detail in their novels. One example is Githa Hariharan. Her *In Times of Siege* (2004) explores the politicization of history and the representation of Hinduism on India's college campuses through the ordeal of Shiv Murthy, a professor of medieval Indian history at a correspondence university in New Delhi. Emotionally stunted in childhood by the disappearance of his father, who was a frustrated Indian freedom fighter, Shiv finds himself in hot water when politicized Hindus pick up on a series of lessons he has written on the twelfth-century reformer, Basava (or Basavaṇṇa). Basava was a critic of religious orthodoxies in his day but also a kind of religious prophet himself and a precursor to *bhakti* poets. He is credited with having started the Vīraśaiva (Warriors of Śiva) tradition and is held by some Indian secularists as an early example of a critic of Brāhmaṇical authority and restrictive religious dogma. Even to contemporary politicized Hindus, he can be seen as a religious hero and an image of a kind of militancy they seek to propagate.

The Itihas Suraksa Manc, or History Protection Platform, demands that Shiv make a public apology, revise his history lessons, and offer a more balanced syllabus to his students. His department chair and dean are frightened by national media attention, and they attempt to convince Shiv to revise the lessons and sign the apology. Shiv refuses to sign. This jeopardizes his career but makes him the personification of heroic secularism among progressive students at his university. The novel is a portrait of the censoriousness that is prevalent in public life (and prevalent on the Left as much as on the Right), but it also is informative about problems of historiography that arise in any effort to represent Hindu tradition, whether they involve interpretive issues related to caste, to early reformers, or to contested historical sites.

Concluding Reflections

Evidently, there is no one approach to Hinduism in the world of Indian fiction. Colonial and postcolonial authors have taken on approaches suitable to their historical eras and have used the novel as a means of addressing some of the most pressing ideological and philosophical questions raised by the Hindu tradition. In the colonial era, the first novels published in India focused on defining Hinduism in light of the presence of British colonialism and the early reform movements. In the postcolonial era, novelists' interests have been more heterogeneous, though many of the best known writers of postcolonial Indian fiction have aimed to contextualize Hinduism as a hybrid and evolving phenomenon that is as much "culture" as "religion." As such, postcolonial Indian fiction has shown that Hinduism is at once a product of India's composite culture and its primary source.

References Cited

Anand, Mulk Raj. 1990 [1935]. *Untouchable*. New York: Penguin Books.

Bose, S. K.1969. *Ishwar Chandra Vidyasagar*. Delhi: National Book Trust.

Kopf, David. 1979. *The Brahmo Samaj and the Shaping of the Modern Indian Mind.* Princeton: Princeton University Press.

Lipner, Julius J., trans. 2005. *Ānandamaṭh, or The Sacred Brotherhood, [by] Bankimcandra Chatterji*. Oxford: Oxford University Press.

Narayan, R. K. 1994 [1935]. *Swami and Friends*. Chicago: University of Chicago Press.

Richman, Paula, ed. 1991. *Many Rāmāyaṇas: The Diversity of a Narrative Tradition in South Asia*. Berkeley: University of California Press.

Richman, Paula. 2001. *Questioning Ramayanas: A South Asian Tradition*. Berkeley: University of California Press.

Rushdie, Salman. 1980. *Midnight's Children*. New York: Knopf.

Sarkar, Tanika. 2001. *Hindu Wife, Hindu Nation: Community, Religion, and Cultural Nationalism*. Bloomington: Indiana University Press.

Sen, Sukumar. 1960. *History of Bengali Literature*. Delhi: Sahitya Akademi.

Watt, Ian. 1957. *The Rise of the Novel: Studies in Defoe, Richardson and Fielding*. Berkeley: University of California Press.

Williams, Patrick and Laura Chrisman, eds. 1994. *Colonial Discourse and Post-Colonial Theory: A Reader*. New York: Columbia University Press.

13

Gender

Ann Grodzins Gold

Gendered Power
Śakti, Prakṛti, and Māyā
Devī: Her Multiforms and Singularity
Gendered Practice
Domestic Rituals and the Everyday
Outside Domesticity: Saints, Sannyāsinīs, and Gurus
Gender Beyond Male and Female
Gendered Politics

Gender both as a subject of inquiry and as a concept informing research and interpretation emerged as significant within the study of Hinduism during the second half of the twentieth century, as feminist scholarship gradually permeated the humanities and social sciences. Research processes often fueled by activist motivations developed the concept of gender not only to redress previous ignorance and imbalance but to generate fundamentally new questions about—among other things—culture, bodies, and knowledge itself. Attention to contested discourses and discrimination was central to these projects. Hence, the aims of gender studies have been transformative, aspiring to affect not only the world of scholarship but the domains of domestic, national, and global politics. Elaine Showalter helpfully summarized these contours of the field, emphasizing that "gender is not only a question of *difference*, which assumes that the sexes are separate and equal; but of *power*, as in looking at the history of gender relations, we find sexual asymmetry, inequality, and male dominance in every known society" (1989: 4; emphasis in original). As key essays confirm, the concept of gender "developed to contest the naturalization of sexual difference in multiple arenas of struggle" (Haraway 1991: 131) and as a "primary way of signifying relationships of power" (Scott 1996: 167).[1]

This chapter attempts to engage directly some ways that attention to gender, keeping in mind its crucial orientations to power hierarchies, has influenced the study of Hinduism. I also highlight some of the ways that the study of Hinduism—and more broadly of South Asia—has contributed distinctive and influential perspectives helping to shape the study of gender. Vasudha Narayanan has noted that Hindu sources yield plural understandings of gender matching various competing approaches in the field, including essentialist, constructivist, and transcendent (2003: 569). She observes of Hindu views that if, at the philosophical level, "one is urged to go beyond all dichotomies, including gender for the soul and for the deity," at the human level, "devotees happily distinguish between various gender roles but keep the boundaries permeable and fluid" (Narayanan 2003: 586). My own approach is considerably indebted to Narayanan's nuanced explications of Hinduism's fluid visions (see also Narayanan 1999).[2]

The distinctive context of Hinduism fostered signal explorations and discoveries for gender studies in two major arenas: cosmology and society. The links or gulfs between these two realms become perhaps the most vital crux of debate (Hiltebeitel and Erndl 2000). At least a quarter-century ago, a number of scholars in various disciplines highlighted the apparent paradox of divine female power versus women's everyday subordination and devaluation in Hindu contexts (e.g., Nandy 1980; Wadley 1977). This tension emerges equally in literature and the arts, as poignantly revealed in Mrinal Pande's short story, "Girls." A rebellious daughter, resisting her role as living incarnation of "the divine feminine principle" on a festival day, cries out to her mother and grandmother, "When you people don't love girls, why do you pretend to worship them?" (Pande 1991: 56). Pande's protagonist ironically questions the negative evaluation of mortal females in the context of goddess worship. Similarly paradoxical questions arise around agency: if female power animates the universe, how is it that women so often appear to be disempowered in their everyday actions? A scaled down approach more helpfully seeks to locate those arenas wherein women's actual powers manifest and to ask how, if at all, such capacities might be related to cosmic female power.

Though studies of cosmology initially tended to draw on Sanskrit texts, studies of gender roles in Hindu society were more often rooted in ethnographic fieldwork and vernacular literatures. A crucial exception to this generalization would be the *Laws of Manu*, a Dharmaśāstra text composed at least two thousand years ago and which countless writings on the roles and treatment of Hindu women have cited selectively as a scriptural charter for everyday female subordination. When anthropologists and other feminist scholars began to document and better apprehend the "unspoken worlds" of domestic ritual and women's expressive traditions—as Nancy Falk and Rita Gross's path-breaking anthology (1980) named them—many gender truisms were turned upside down, and new tapestries of alternative meanings unfolded (for a few examples, see Das 1988; Flueckiger 1996; Franco, Macwan, and Ramanathan 2000; Mukta 1994; Narayan and Sood

1997; Raheja and Gold 1994). In actuality, women's views were loudly sung or articulated in oral narratives; it is not that they were unspoken but rather unheard or unnoted. The quest for female viewpoints has flourished through explorations of incredibly rich and diverse materials in regional oral traditions. As A. K. Ramanujan put it in a brilliantly synoptic statement that continues to command contemplation, "Genders are genres. The world of women is not the world of men" (1991: 53).

In general, an association of studies of divine female power with Sanskrit texts and of women's lives with vernacular sources represents a gendered variant on major dualisms haunting scholars of South Asia over the past half-century: Sanskrit/vernaculars; great (classical) traditions/little (folk) traditions; pan-Hindu/regional; precept/practice; Indology/anthropology; writing/orality. Sometimes it appears that male/female almost lines up with these, although it would be more accurately configured as: male twice-born/everyone else. Such conceptual binaries as these are acknowledged and exemplified only to be perpetually confounded by observations that reveal ways in which the terms separated in alluring schematic polarizations perpetually interpenetrate and are mutually influential.[3] The only practical way to organize my observations in this essay was to move from cosmos to society, from classical concepts to popular counterpoints. However, throughout what follows I reveal ongoing mutual constructions of these intertwined aspects of Hindu worlds.

Part One explores strong testimonies to a pervasive power that is fundamentally female in Hindu cosmology. This is described as abstract energy (*śakti*), creation or nature (*prakṛti*), and illusion (*māyā*). Female power also is personified in the many forms of the goddess, *devī*, who is multiply embodied and ever singular and transcendent. Part Two, the larger segment, treats everyday gendered practices in Hindu religiosity and gender roles in Hindu society. Beyond domestic realms are more public spaces wherein female saints, poets, and *guru*s are seen, heard, and sometimes worshipped as *avatāra*s or incarnations. I note briefly the intersections of Hinduism with the possibilities of religiously conceived third genders or absolute genderless beings.[4] Finally, I touch equally briefly on the ways in which gender is at play in social movements and politics within Hindu society. This last turn brings us neatly back to *śakti*, or power, as female and various goddesses whose images have been politically mobilized by men and women for highly divergent purposes—including Kālī, Durgā, and the nation as Bhārat Mātā. However, as Sumathi Ramaswamy (2002) argues persuasively, a cartographic embodiment of the goddess as Mother India represents not continuity but a significant departure from meanings inherent in ancient divine females.

Gendered Power

Śakti, Prakṛti, and Māyā

All animating power is female in Hindu cosmology. The word for power is *śakti*, and it can be used to refer to energy or strength; it is also a name of the goddess. A primary text for the culminating or consolidating expression of female power in Hinduism is the Sanskrit *Devī Māhātmya* (Greatness of the Goddess), a portion of the *Mārkaṇḍeya Purāṇa*, composed between approximately 300 and 700 CE. This text, also known as the "Seven Hundred Verses to Durgā," narrates the *devī*'s mythological battles against demons but equally lays the ontological groundwork of her universal supremacy. Besides *śakti*, two other terms offering key understandings of fundamental Hindu concepts of female being are *prakṛti* (nature) and *māyā* (illusion). Along with *śakti*, these have significance in the *Devī Māhātmya* but may be traced back into the earliest Hindu scriptures, the Vedas (Coburn 1984; Erndl 2004; Pintchman 1994).[5]

Though many religions elaborate on an asymmetrical complementarity of genders, distinctive configurations emerge in each. In Hinduism, as a Sanskrit pun has it, without *śakti*, Śiva—one of the supreme male Hindu deities—is a corpse (*śava*). Cosmological pairings of male and female in Hindu understandings may be as biologically vivid as the "half-woman lord" (*ardhanārīśvara*) image of Śiva and his consort Pārvatī sharing a single body with one breast and half a mustache, or as abstract as the union of undifferentiated, singular, inactive male *puruṣa* and vital proliferating female *prakṛti*. *Prakṛti* comes to mean all of creation.

Māyā, equally female, is the power that enables a deity to display or embody himself or herself and therefore to act. *Māyā* pervades and underlies the actual world in which people live, imbuing all creatures with the will to prosper and multiply, but *māyā* is also the cause of ignorance and delusion. Thus creative grace, binding attachments, and delusive skills are all encompassed in the concept of *māyā*, identified with the supreme goddess, as Mahāmāyā or Great Māyā.

The concepts of *śakti*, *prakṛti*, and *māyā*, elaborated in Sanskrit scriptures, also pervade everyday Hindu worlds. A pioneering ethnographic exploration of *śakti* was Susan Wadley's (1975) ethnography of women's rituals in a North Indian village, where Wadley showed how female power unfolds at the domestic level, in the context of women's ritual work for the well-being of their families. Vandana Shiva (1988), along with other ecofeminist activists, celebrated the concept of *prakṛti* as testifying to close associations between women and the environment in the Hindu world view. Shiva also observed these associations at the level of practice: rural Indian women were more aware than men of the importance of conserving natural resources because women were the ones who had gendered daily duties to supply their families with fuel wood, fodder, and water. The latter point, based on livelihood rather than an essentialized affinity between women and *prakṛti*, remains critical for environmental scholars who have little patience for romanticized views of women and nature (Agarwal 1991).

Interestingly, in several South Asian vernacular tongues, including notably Bengali and Nepali, *māyā* is used casually to refer to the sweet and compelling familial attachments engendered in domestic life. Sometimes *māyā* means wealth and property; it is also used to name a particular goddess associated with material prosperity. Sarah Lamb's recent ethnography of gender and aging in rural Bengal (2000) shows the ways in which *māyā* is conceived of as a deep emotional pull that must be acknowledged even if it is ultimately understood as the essence of ties that bind.

Devī: Her Multiforms and Singularity

Treating the profusion of goddess images in women's ritual art, Pulpul Jayakar writes, "With every painting the goddess is born anew. She springs to life, energy-charged, filling the earth and the sky in a hundred forms" (1989: 102). Though the forms and identities of divine females are so multiple as to defy characterization or categorization, scholars of Hinduism frequently try hard to fix them into groups, usually by opposing two contradictory manifestations of female gender. These attempts have included breast mothers and tooth mothers (e.g., O'Flaherty 1980), or consorts and independent goddesses often characterized, respectively, as benevolent and destructive goddesses (Babb 1975; Hawley and Wulff 1996). Although such groupings help outsiders to make sense of what can seem a bewildering multiplicity, devotees often insist on divine unity or revel in the poetic and religious truths realized through seemingly mind-boggling contradictions. For example, Bengali poems to Kālī often focus on the mingling of her terrifying aspects and her compassionate qualities; her ugliness and beauty; her death-dealing and life-giving capacities: "This woman plays on the battlefield, Her left hands holding a sword and a head, and Her right signaling 'fear not!' and boons" (McDermott 2001: 21–22).

What if anything do goddesses and women have in common? This question, as noted earlier, becomes a central issue for the study of gender in Hinduism. Cynthia Humes (2000) interviewed pilgrims to a goddess temple in North India and found that the majority of them, both men and women, disassociated such powerful, martial goddesses as Durgā from ordinary women. Yet, as Madhu Kishwar observed, "playing Durga" is one option that can work for women subjected to sexual harassment in urban office contexts (1999: 171). Indeed in the *Devī Māhātmya*, beauteous Durgā is stalked and propositioned by her demon enemy, fool that he is, and her victory is all the sweeter.

Although women may indeed identify with warrior goddesses, still more pervasive are cultural continuities posed between women and those goddesses, such as Sītā, Lakṣmī, or Pārvatī, who do not bear weapons but manifest as helpmate partners of male gods. Women's songs commonly attribute to spouse goddesses yearnings for gifts, adornment, and attention; romantic jealousies; even the pain of childbirth—emotions that resonate with their own experiences and desires (e.g., Narayana Rao 1991). Some feminist rhetoric roundly rejected epic heroine Sītā as a hopelessly passive husband-worshiper (*pativratā*), but others find Sītā a more complex and self-motivated figure (e.g., Hess 1999; Kishwar 1999: 234–49).

The mythologies and iconographies of Hindu goddesses have long compelled scholarly and popular fascinations in Europe and America not only as religiohistorical phenomena unique to South Asia (Kinsley 1987) but as resources for empowerment that might be legitimately appropriated by Western women seeking a cosmos more harmonious with their desires. Pioneering feminist historian of religions Rita Gross (1983) argued that Asian goddesses offered important resources given the abysmal lack of role models for female power in the Abrahamic monotheisms. A recent plethora of publications makes Indian goddesses more accessible to non-Hindu and nonacademic readers through art (Dehejia 1999) and stories (Sharma 2003). Considerable research has also been explicitly focused on Western responses to Hindu goddesses, which may be seen as a quest for alternative balances of gender and power (see McDermott and Kripal 2003).

Devī has so many forms: temple statuary portrays her as idealized anthropomorphic beauty while village women worship her as a string with knots, a growing tree, or a temporary pile of pebbles. It is easy to imagine shape-shifting multiplicity as her very nature. However, in Tantric cosmology, we find a surpassing unity. Tantra has been defined as a tradition in which the Goddess is supreme. Douglas Brooks speaks of an "all inclusive *śakti* who in one form or another stands apart from and superior to all other aspects of divinity" (1990: 73). In the context of Tantra, Madhu Khanna (2002) finds a "goddess-woman equation" and Rita DasGupta Sherma (2000) holds that one may indeed declare, "I am she."

Gendered Practice

Domestic Rituals and the Everyday

Many anthropologists of Hindu societies have observed complex constructions of gender roles and rules in the minutiae of everyday life, including hygiene, dress, adornment, posture, sexuality, childbirth, relations with kin, work, speech, and much else (e.g., Bagwe 1995; Hancock 1999; Kapadia 1996; Lamb 2000). As an influential essay by Leela Dube (1986) first highlighted, a culturally pervasive understanding of reproductive roles, closely meshed with gender hierarchy, views male seed as superior to female field. The gendering of space itself, and the spatial aspects of gender roles, are of pervasive significance. Seemanthini Niranjana observes: "A substantial part of the social construction of gender...hinges on how female bodies negotiate everyday spaces" (2001: 116). The intersections of caste, class, and gender with religious orientations reveal complexities far beyond this chapter's scope (see Kapadia 1996 for one fine example). What follows is therefore radically simplified and lamentably decontextualized. A vast literature has grown up around a few historically notorious aspects of women's social disadvantages within Hindu societies, including *satī* (Mani 1998), widowhood (Chakravarti and Gill 2001), dowry (Oldenburg 2002), and inheritance of property (Agarwal 1995)—fraught issues that I star as critical to the field of gender and Hinduism without attempting to condense here.

Priests in temples and other public spaces are predominantly, although not exclusively, male. However, a large portion of domestic Hindu rituals lies in the hands and hearts of women. Women worship deities at permanent and temporary domestic shrines without benefit of male priestcraft. They are the chief ritual experts at many calendrical festivals and conduct important segments of weddings and other lifecycle celebrations, even while male priests are simultaneously reciting Sanskrit verses. Women's rituals offer a wealth of gendered commentary on both the everyday and the festival and sacralized spheres of life, revealing how closely the two are intertwined.

Vijaya Nagarajan's writings on Tamil women's daily creation of threshold designs—called *kōlam*—offers an exemplary window on this intertwining. The *kōlam* is a transient sacred space and work of art that Tamil women traditionally create each morning to host the goddess Lakṣmī. According to Nagarajan (1998), through creating *kōlam*, women forge and sustain an intimate relationship with the goddess of prosperity and well-being.

Women more frequently than men undertake personal vows (*vrata*)—individually or collectively—to ensure the well-being of their families (Gupta 2000; McDaniel 2003; Pearson 1996; Tewari 1991; Wadley 1975, 1983). The elements of a *vrata* usually include a partial fast, a simple worship in a domestic space temporarily purified for this purpose, and often one or more stories honoring the deities and exemplifying the rewards of the ritual or its origins. Women's ritually performed stories, sometimes published in vernacular pamphlets but sometimes only orally transmitted, frequently feature heroines who may be devotees of the deity being honored, daughters of female devotees, or persons ignorant of that particular deity who then learn about its power and blessings in the course of severe tribulations. Notably, the heroines of women's devotional stories exemplify moral virtues, ritual knowledge, devotional fervor, and transformative agency. Often, especially in oral traditions, they are bossy and stubborn.

By definition, the power women accumulate through their ritual actions should never be used exclusively for their own well-being. Selflessness is a very important virtue, exemplified by the capacity for fasting. Yet women's tales acknowledge women's hunger and desires, and often the clever heroines end up not only pleasing the gods but well fed, housed, and clothed. Moreover, because women's well-being is lodged in familial well-being, women see their own rituals as productive of better circumstances for themselves together with their loved ones. Women's stories also offer views of men and male authority that may be subtly subversive; they tend to value auspiciousness over purity, wit over obedience, and occasionally conjugal passion over patriarchal priorities (Gold 2002).

Whether and to what purpose Hindu women's ritual powers extend in any way beyond ritual spheres has been much debated in gender studies. Tracy Pintchman's fieldwork on women's rituals in Varanasi affirms the least radical of positive interpretations: "Women may derive a sense of empowerment through religious practice even when that power has nothing to do with resistance to patriarchal structures or women's economic, social, or political advancement in the public sphere" (2005: 184). Manasi Dasgupta and Mandakranta Bose (2000) analyze a Bengali ritual conducted by women—the worship of Manasā together with its accompanying narrative—that reveals, the authors argue, an interplay between "the forces that determine women's lives" and an acknowledgment of "the mystic power of the feminine over life and death." At the least, women's oral performances offer female commentaries on gender that, as they conclude, view the feminine "in its multiple, often oppositional qualities, [as] an idea that commands wonder" (2000: 158).

Outside Domesticity: Saints, Sannyāsinīs, and Gurus

Recent studies of female *guru*s and renouncers (*sannyāsinīs*), added to earlier work on women saints in North and South India, alter our visions of gendered Hindu practices by revealing alternative configurations in realms other than domestic (Khandelwal 2004).[6] To pursue lives of spiritual practice, social service, and religious leadership, some women break away from domesticity to varying degrees. How might such divergent paths and distinctive teachings contribute to understanding gender roles and female power? As Sondra Hausner and Meena Khandelwal (2006) put it, introducing a collection of new ethnographies of female renunciation across religious traditions in South Asia, by looking at such women, we may learn, "something about how women live in South Asia, through the lens of renunciation—that is, not always as wives and mothers." Moreover, they continue, female renouncers' lives "show us something about how renouncers live, through the lens of gender—that is, with particular constraints and opportunities, because they are women" (Hausner and Khandelwal 2006: 27).

In the same collection are two Hindu case studies featuring a radiantly benign, decorous, and loving *guru* presiding over a large *āśrama* and an independent, eccentric, and unkempt *sannyāsinī* camping on a sacred riverbank. These two might appear to have nothing in common except that they are renouncers with female bodies. But it seems significant that each of them in a different way brings what are stereotypically women's roles into her renouncer's life—the first by dedicated kitchen work with its larger symbolism of nourishment and care, the latter by adopting a child and raising her. Both these women have distinctly, definitively, and self-consciously separated themselves from common paths of Hindu householder women; yet their saintly identities remain gendered in a fashion that, as the ethnographers portray it, could be deliberately ironic (Khandelwal, Hausner, and Gold 2006).

Researching ideas about gender among the followers of a popular female *guru*, Lisa Hallstrom (2004) encounters devotees who insist that their spiritual teacher is not female at all but a divine being beyond gender. Hallstrom suggests that male–female difference may be less marked "in the realm of extraordinary people, such as saints, gurus, and renunciants." She speculates that "the gender of a Hindu saint, guru, or sannyasin or sannyasini" may be seen as "a kind of third gender" (Hallstrom 2004: 106). Karen Pechilis (2004a: 222–23) offers a similar but stronger "third gender" identification for another female *guru*. In these cases, it is important to realize that rather than implying alternative sexualities, "third gender" pushes toward an ultimacy without gender—performed, as Pechilis puts it, through the *guru*'s *līlā* or "divine play" (2004a: 223).

Gender Beyond Male and Female

As both cosmology and the role of female *gurus* indicate, Hindu imaginations are not confined to rigid gender dualisms. India's *hijrās*—defined by Gayatri

Reddy as "phenotypic men who wear female clothing and, ideally, renounce sexual desire and practice by undergoing a sacrificial emasculation" (2005: 2)—have attracted considerable attention from scholars of cross-cultural third-gender possibilities. The religious uses of castration can be unfortunately sensationalized, but fine-grained ethnography, such as Reddy's, reveals in *hijrā* communities some illuminating angles on sex, gender, and religion intersections. Lawrence Cohen argued in an essay on varieties of third-gender identity in India that any theory of gender must be rooted in a "corporeality of lived experience or must misrepresent it" (1995: 279). Reddy's study of *hijrā*s in Hyderabad gives very close attention to what she calls corporeal practice and to "sacred legitimization."

Reddy (2005) usefully and comprehensively tracks the existence of third-gender potentialities in Hindu traditions (see also Vanita 2002). Although these cannot be directly linked to *hijrā* practices, they open up the conceptual space for them—for example, *hijrā* identification with Śiva in his half-man–half-woman form. She helps us to comprehend the religious dimensions of a transgendered life in India at the level of everyday practice as well. *Hijrā*s of Hyderabad worship a particular goddess who sees to the healing of their sex-change surgeries. Reddy documents *hijrā* bodily experiences with sensitivity, showing how much these may be more about gender than sex, such as *hijrā*s' extensive concern with removing unwanted facial hair and growing and beautifying the hair on their heads.

Hinduism, as I noted earlier, following Narayanan, can see ultimately beyond gender altogether. A religious apprehension is that all distinctions may be dissolved or transcended. An oft-cited poem by the Vīraśaiva saint Dāsimayya, as translated by Ramanujan (1973: 110) from the Kannada language, expresses this with acute simplicity:

> If they see
> breasts and long hair coming
> they call it woman,
>
> if beard and whiskers
> they call it man:
>
> But, look, the self that hovers
> in between
> is neither man nor woman
>
> O Rāmanātha.

Gendered Politics

The multiple intersections of gender, religion, activism, and politics in the context of Hinduism bristle with complexities and contradictions. India's first—and for many years—premier feminist publishing operation was named "Kali for Women" by its founders, Ritu Menon and Urvashi Butalia. Madhu Kishwar, founder of *Manushi*, an enduring and influential feminist journal, has increasingly given attention to expansive possibilities for women in Hindu traditions and rituals. Most recently, in conjunction with her activist work to better the lives of street vendors and improve neighborhood cleanliness, she established a "secular goddess" named Svaccha Nārāyaṇī or "Cleanliness Lady" whose eight arms hold some unusual weapons, including a clock, a broom, and a video camera (Kishwar 2005). We see in these and in many other social movement contexts *śakti*'s potential energizing of progressive action (Harish and Harishankar 2003). On a global scale, some of India's transnationally popular women *gurus* have been able to institute effective philanthropic endeavors, efforts connected in part to their female gendered roles (Pechilis 2004b; Warrier 2005).

Conservative political trends in Hinduism also claim or coopt female power, and some of the most virulent anti-Muslim rhetoric has come from the mouths of women renouncers affiliated with Hindu nationalist parties (Sarkar 2001). The image of the Indian subcontinent personified as "Bhārat Mātā" or Mother India appears to engage a history of goddess worship millennia-deep (McKean 1996). However, Sumathi Ramaswamy argues against a facile view of continuity between "Puranic conceptions of land as sacred and female" and the "cartographic embodiment of Bharat Mata." She writes, ". . . Bharat Mata bodyscapes insert the image of an apparently familiar mother-goddess into the impersonal colonial map, radically and irrevocably altering the latter" (Ramaswamy 2002: 174). In other words, this is stark manipulation of gendered religious imagery to an alien purpose.

Sherry Ortner has characterized gender as "one of the central games of life in most cultures," but equally admonishes that it is never "the only game in town" (1996: 19). Ortner's sensible observations are germane to the study of gender in Hinduism as this chapter has attempted to characterize it: linked, on the one hand, to philosophical speculations on the nature of reality and, on the other, to countless aspects, emotional and political, of everyday lives. Like the *devī*, gender energizes, proliferates, and deludes; its meanings are multiple and fluid, its consequences pervasive.

Notes

1 Many thanks to Daniel Gold, Meena Khandelwal, Gene Thursby, and an astute anonymous reviewer for helpful critiques and suggestions.
2 For another recent and illuminating essay focused on the Hinduism-gender intersection, see Kannabiran (2004). Falk (1994) offers a comprehensive bibliographic survey through 1992. In this chapter, regretfully and apologetically but without further notice, I leave unexamined a great many significant contributions and cases.
3 An early watershed was Singer's (1969) edited volume on Kṛṣṇa.
4 Another relevant area of recent gender scholarship in South Asia that I am unable to consider here (owing to space constraints) is "masculinities," which intersects significantly with the study of Hinduism in various contexts, including pilgrimage (Osella and Osella 2003) and politics both colonial and postcolonial (Banerjee 2005; Nandy 1983).
5 These concepts have complex and divergent elaborations and evaluations in Hinduism's several philosophical systems that cannot be addressed here.
6 See Narayanan (1999) for many female poet-saints; Mukta (1994) for the most famous of these, Mīrābāī.

References Cited

Agarwal, Bina. 1991. *Engendering the Environment Debate: Lessons from the Indian Subcontinent*. East Lansing: Center for Advanced Study of International Development, Michigan State University.

Agarwal, Bina. 1995. *A Field of One's Own: Gender and Land Rights in South Asia*. Cambridge: Cambridge University Press.

Babb, Lawrence A. 1975. *The Divine Hierarchy: Popular Hinduism in Central India*. New York: Columbia University Press.

Bagwe, Anjali. 1995. *Of Woman Caste: The Experience of Gender in Rural India*. London: Zed Books.

Banerjee, Sikata. 2005. *Make me a Man! Masculinity, Hinduism, and Nationalism in India*. Albany: State University of New York Press.

Brooks, Douglas Renfrew. 1990. *The Secret of the Three Cities: An Introduction to Hindu Śākta Tantrism*. Chicago: University of Chicago Press.

Chakravarti, Uma and Preeti Gill, eds. 2001. *Shadow Lives: Writings on Widowhood*. Delhi: Kali for Women

Coburn, Thomas. 1984. *Devī-Māhātmya: The Crystallization of the Goddess Tradition*. Delhi: Motilal Banarsidass.

Cohen, Lawrence. 1995. "The Pleasures of Castration: The Postoperative Status of Hijras, Jankhas and Academics." *In* Paul R. Abramson and Steven D. Pinkerton, eds, *Sexual Nature/Sexual Culture*, 276–304. Chicago: University of Chicago Press.

Das, Veena. 1988. "Femininity and the Orientation to the Body." *In* Karuna Chanana, ed., *Socialisation, Education and Women: Explorations in Gender Identity*, 193–207. New Delhi: Orient Longman.

Dasgupta, Manasi and Mandakranta Bose. 2000. "The Goddess-Woman Nexus in Popular Religious Practice: The Cult of Manasā." *In* Mandakranta Bose, ed., *Faces of the Feminine in Ancient, Medieval, and Modern India*, 148–61. New York: Oxford University Press.

Dehejia, Vidya, ed. 1999. *Devī the Great Goddess: Female Divinity in South Asian Art*. Washington, D.C.: Smithsonian.

Dube, Leela. 1986. "Seed and Earth: The Symbolism of Biological Reproduction and Sexual Relations of Production." *In* Leela Dube, Eleanor B. Leacock, and Shirley Ardener, eds, *Visibility and Power: Essays on Women in Society and Development*, 22–53. Delhi: Oxford University Press.

Erndl, Kathleen M. 2004. "Śākta." *In* Sushil Mittal and Gene Thursby, eds, *The Hindu World*, 140–61. New York: Routledge.

Falk, Nancy Auer. 1994. *Women and Religion in India: An Annotated Bibliography of Sources in English 1975–92*. Kalamazoo: New Issues Press.

Falk, Nandy Auer and Rita M. Gross, eds. 1980. *Unspoken Worlds: Women's Religious Lives in Non-Western Cultures*. San Francisco: Harper and Row.

Flueckiger, Joyce Burkhalter. 1996. *Gender and Genre in the Folklore of Middle India*. Ithaca: Cornell University Press.

Franco, Fernando, Jyotsna Macwan, Suguna Ramanathan. 2000. *The Silken Swing: The Cultural Universe of Dalit Women*. Calcutta: Stree.

Gold, Ann Grodzins. 2002. "Counterpoint Authority in Women's Ritual Expressions: A View from the Village." *In* Laurie L. Patton, ed., *Jewels of Authority: Women and Textual Tradition in Hindu India*, 177–201. New York: Oxford University Press.

Gross, Rita M. 1983. "Hindu Female Deities as a Resource for the Contemporary Rediscovery of the Goddess." *In* Carl Olson, ed., *The Book of the Goddess*, 217–30. New York: Crossroad.

Gupta, Samjukta Gombrich. 2000. "The Goddess, Women, and their Rituals in Hinduism." *In* Madakranta Bose, ed., *Faces of the Feminine in Ancient, Medieval, and Modern India*, 87–106. New York: Oxford University Press.

Hallstrom, Lisa Lassell. 2004. "Anandamayi Ma, the Bliss-Filled Divine Mother." *In* Karen Pechilis, ed., *The Graceful Guru: Hindu Female Gurus in India and the United States*, 84–118. New York: Oxford University Press.

Hancock, Mary Elizabeth. 1999. *Womanhood in the Making: Domestic Ritual and Public Culture in Urban South India*. Boulder: Westview Press.

Haraway, Donna J. 1991. *Simians, Cyborgs, and Women: The Reinvention of Nature*. New York: Routledge.

Harish, Ranjana and V. Bharathi Harishankar. 2003. *Shakti: Multidisciplinary Perspectives on Women's Empowerment in India*. Jaipur: Rawat.

Hausner, Sondra L. and Meena Khandelwal. 2006. "Introduction: Women on their Own." *In* Meena Khandelwal, Sondra L. Hausner, and Ann Grodzins Gold, eds, *Women's Renunciation in South Asia: Nuns, Yoginis, Saints, and Singers*, 1–36. New York: Palgrave Macmillan.

Hawley, John Stratton and Donna Marie Wulff, eds. 1996. *Devī: Goddesses of India*. Berkeley: University of California Press.

Hess, Linda. 1999. "Rejecting Sita: Indian Responses to the Ideal Man's Cruel Treatment of His Ideal Wife." *Journal of the American Academy of Religion* 67, 1: 1–32.

Hiltebeitel, Alf and Kathleen M. Erndl, eds. 2000. *Is the Goddess a Feminist?: The Politics of South Asian Goddesses*. New York: New York University Press.

Humes, Cynthia. 2000. "Is the Devi Mahatmya a Feminist Scripture?" *In* Alf Hiltebeitel and Kathleen Erndl, eds, *Is the Goddess a Feminist?: The Politics of South Asian Goddesses*, 123–50. New York: New York University Press.

Jayakar, Pupul. 1989 [1980]. *The Earth Mother*. New Delhi: Penguin Books.

Kannabiran, Kalpana. 2004. "Voices of Dissent: Gender and Changing Social Values in Hinduism." *In* Robin Rinehart, ed., *Contemporary Hinduism: Ritual, Culture, and Practice*, 273–308. Santa Barbara: ABC Clio.

Kapadia, Karin. 1996. *Siva and her Sisters: Gender, Caste, and Class in Rural South India*. Delhi: Oxford University Press.

Khandelwal, Meena. 2004. *Women in Ochre Robes: Gendering Hindu Renunciation*. Albany: State University of New York Press.

Khandelwal, Meena, Sondra L. Hausner, and Ann Grodzins Gold, eds. 2006. *Women's Renunciation in South Asia: Nuns, Yoginis, Saints, and Singers*. New York: Palgrave Macmillan.

Khanna, Madhu. 2002. "The Goddess-Woman Equation in Śākta Tantras." *In* D. S. Ahmed, ed., *Gendering the Spirit: Women, Religion and the Post-Colonial Response*, 35–59. London: Zed Books.

Kinsley, David. 1987. *Hindu Goddesses: Visions of the Divine Feminine in the Hindu Religious Tradition*. Delhi: Motilal Banarsidass.

Kishwar, Madhu. 1999. *Off the Beaten Track: Rethinking Gender Justice for Indian Women*. Delhi: Oxford University Press.

Kishwar, Madhu Purnima. 2005. "Emergency Avatār of a Secular Goddess! Manushi Swachha Narayani Descends to Protect Street Vendors." *Manushi* 147: 4–15.

Lamb, Sarah. 2000. *White Saris and Sweet Mangoes: Aging, Gender, and Body in North India*. Berkeley: University of California Press.

Mani, Lata. 1998. *Contentious Traditions: The Debate on Sati in Colonial India*. Berkeley: University of California Press.

McDaniel, June. 2003. *Making Virtuous Daughters and Wives: An Introduction to Women's Brata Rituals in Bengali Folk Religion*. Albany: State University of New York Press.

McDermott, Rachel Fell. 2001. *Singing to the Goddess: Poems to Kālī and Umā from Bengal*. New York: Oxford University Press.

McDermott, Rachel Fell and Jeffrey J. Kripal, eds. 2003. *Encountering Kālī in the Margins, at the Center, in the West*. Berkeley: University of California Press.

McKean, Lise. 1996. "Bhārat Mātā: Mother India and Her Militant Matriots." *In* John S. Hawley and Donna M. Wulff, eds, *Devī: Goddesses of India*, 250–80. Berkeley: University of California Press.

Mukta, Parita. 1994. *Upholding the Common Life: The Community of Mirabai*. Delhi: Oxford University Press.

Nagarajan, Vijaya. 1998. "The Earth as Goddess Bhū Devī: Toward a Theory of 'Embedded Ecologies' in Folk Hinduism." *In* Lance Nelson, ed., *Purifying the Earthly Body of God: Religion and Ecology in Hindu India*, 269–95. Albany: State University of New York Press.

Nandy, Ashis. 1980. *At the Edge of Psychology: Essays in Politics and Culture*. Delhi: Oxford University Press.

Nandy, Ashis. 1983. *The Intimate Enemy: Loss and Recovery of Self Under Colonialism*. Delhi: Oxford University Press.

Narayan, Kirin and Urmila Devi Sood. 1997. *Mondays on the Dark Night of the Moon*. New York: Oxford University Press.

Narayana Rao, Velcheru. 1991. "A *Rāmāyaṇa* of One's Own: Women's Oral Tradition in Telugu." *In* Paula Richman, ed., *Many Rāmāyaṇas: The Diversity of a Narrative Tradition in South Asia*, 114–36. Berkeley: University of California Press.

Narayanan, Vasudha. 1999. "Brimming with Bhakti, Embodiments of Śakti: Devotees, Deities, Performers, Reformers, and Other Women of Power in the Hindu Tradition." *In* Arvind Sharma and Katherine K. Young, eds, *Feminism and World Religions*, 25–77. Albany: State University of New York Press.

Narayanan, Vasudha. 2003. "Gender in a Devotional Universe." *In* Gavin Flood, ed., *The Blackwell Companion to Hinduism*, 569–87. Oxford: Blackwell.

Niranjana, Seemanthini. 2001. *Gender and Space: Femininity, Sexualization and the Female Body*. New Delhi: Sage Publications.

O'Flaherty, Wendy Doniger. 1980. *Women, Androgynes, and Other Mythical Beasts*. Chicago: University of Chicago Press.

Oldenburg, Veena Talwar. 2002. *Dowry Murder: The Imperial Origins of a Cultural Crime*. New York: Oxford University Press.

Ortner, Sherry B. 1996. *Making Gender: The Politics and Erotics of Culture*. Boston: Beacon Press.

Osella, Filippo and Caroline Osella. 2003. " 'Ayyappan Saranam': Masculinity and the Sabarimala Pilgrimage in Kerala." *Journal of the Royal Anthropological Institute (n.s.)* 9: 729–54.

Pande, Mrinal. 1991. "Girls." *In* Lakshmi Holmstrom, ed., *The Inner Courtyard: Stories by Indian Women*, 57–64. New Delhi: Rupa.

Pearson, Anne Mackenzie. 1996. *"Because it Gives me Peace of Mind": Ritual Fasts in the Religious Lives of Hindu Women*. Albany: State University of New York Press.

Pechilis, Karen. 2004a. "Gurumayi, the Play of Shakti and Guru." *In* Karen Pechilis, ed., *The Graceful Guru: Hindu Female Gurus in India and the United States*, 219–43. New York: Oxford University Press.

Pechilis, Karen, ed. 2004b. *The Graceful Guru: Hindu Female Gurus in India and the United States*. New York: Oxford University Press.

Pintchman, Tracy. 1994. *The Rise of the Goddess in the Hindu Tradition*. Albany: State University of New York Press.

Pintchman, Tracy. 2005. *Guests at God's Wedding: Celebrating Kartik among the Women of Benares*. Albany: State University of New York Press.

Raheja, Gloria G. and Ann Grodzins Gold. 1994. *Listen to the Heron's Words: Reimagining Gender and Kinship in North India*. Berkeley: University of California Press.

Ramanujan, A. K. 1973. *Speaking of Śiva*. Baltimore: Penguin Books.

Ramanujan, A. K. 1991. "Toward a Counter-System: Women's Tales." *In* Arjun Appadurai, Frank Korom, and Margaret Mills, eds, *Gender, Genre, and Power in South Asian Expressive Traditions*, 33–55. Philadelphia: University of Pennsylvania Press.

Ramaswamy, Sumathi. 2002. "Visualising India's Geo-body: Globes, Maps, Bodyscapes." *Contributions to Indian Sociology (n.s.)* 36, 1–2: 151–89.

Reddy, Gayatri. 2005. *With Respect to Sex: Negotiating Hijra Identity in South India*. Chicago: University of Chicago Press.

Sarkar, Tanika. 2001. *Hindu Wife, Hindu Nation: Community, Religion, and Cultural Nationalism*. Bloomington: Indiana University Press.

Scott, Joan Wallach. 1996. "Gender: A Useful Category of Historical Analysis." *In* Joan Wallach Scott, ed., *Feminism and History*, 152–80. New York: Oxford University Press.

Sharma, Bulbul. 2003 [2001]. *The Book of Devī*. New York: Penguin.

Sherma, Rita DasGupta. 2000. " 'Sa Ham–I Am She': Woman as Goddess." *In* Alf Hiltebeitel and Kathleen M. Erndl, eds, *Is the Goddess a Feminist?: The Politics of South Asian Goddesses*, 24–51. New York: New York University Press.

Shiva, Vandana. 1988. *Staying Alive: Women, Ecology and Development*. London: Zed Books.

Showalter, Elaine. 1989. "Introduction: The Rise of Gender." *In* Elaine Showalter, ed., *Speaking of Gender*, 1–16. New York: Routledge.

Singer, Milton, ed. 1969. *Krishna: Myths, Rites and Attitudes*. Chicago: University of Chicago Press.

Tewari, Laxmi G. 1991. *A Splendor of Worship: Women's Fasts, Rituals, Stories and Art*. New Delhi: Manohar.

Vanita, Ruth, ed. 2002. *Queering India: Same-Sex Love and Eroticism in Indian Culture and Society*. New York: Routledge.

Wadley, Susan S. 1975. *Śakti: Power in the Conceptual Structure of Karimpur Religion*. Chicago: Department of Anthropology, University of Chicago.

Wadley, Susan S. 1977. "Women and the Hindu Tradition." *In* Doranne Jacobson and Susan S. Wadley, eds, *Women in India: Two Perspectives*, 113–39. Columbus: South Asia Books.

Wadley, Susan S. 1983. "Vrats: Transformers of Destiny." *In* Charles F. Keyes and E. Valentine Daniel, eds, *Karma: An Anthropological Inquiry*, 147–62. Berkeley: University of California Press.

Warrier, Maya. 2005. *Hindu Selves in a Modern World*. London: RoutledgeCurzon.

14

Intellect

Douglas L. Berger

Sāṃkhya and Yoga
Vaiśeṣika and Nyāya
Mīmāṃsā
Vedānta
Concluding Reflections

Philosophers in the Brāhmaṇical culture of classical India developed extraordinarily sophisticated conceptions of the human intellect, the mechanisms through which it functions, the nature of its awareness, and its metaphysical status. The various views of intellect in India first arose out of ancient sources of cosmological and psychical speculation in the Upaniṣads and in general systems of metaphysics such as Sāṃkhya. These early depictions of the human intellect were later forged and refined through continuous debate among the "worldviews" or "scholastic systems" (*darśana*) of Indian thought, both Vedic, such as the later Sāṃkhya, Yoga, Mīmāṃsā, Vedānta, Nyāya-Vaiśeṣika, and the non-Vedic, within the multifarious forms of Buddhism, Jainism, and Cārvāka.

It is important to state at the outset that theories of "intellect" or "mind" in classical Hindu thought did not arise out of the same philosophical vocabulary nor were they conducted in an altogether comparable conceptual environment as those of the Western tradition. In the midst of their ongoing confrontations with the Sophists, Socrates and Plato felt the need to distinguish between the awareness of the senses (*horaton*) and that of the mind (*noeton*), the latter of which was capable of both discursive demonstration (*logos*, *episteme*) and insight (*eidos*) of universal ideas as opposed to the merely particular, sensuous, and fleeting concrete nature of perceptual awareness (Plato 1987: 512–16). Though there were many revisions to this basic formulation in the unfolding centuries of the Western tradition, the salient point here is that the concepts of mind and intellect were theorized in response to a perceived need to differentiate between particular, concrete, and universal abstract knowledge, a need that demanded that the latter be invested in a mind that is not reducible to the physical body. Classical

Hindu conceptions of "mind" (*manas*), intellect (*buddhi*), or the "inner agent" (*antaḥkaraṇa*) arose within a significantly different context and were invoked to fulfill markedly different philosophical requirements. In Hindu systems, the mind is generally agreed to be a subtle physical organ (*indriya*) that, though it enables the data of external sense organs to be cognized, is itself a sense organ insofar as its objects may also be internal states, such as pleasure or pain, and insofar as it mechanically gathers, as it were, bodily sensations of all kinds. Therefore, the "mind," "intellect," or "inner agent" of classical Hindu philosophies does not separate or abstract "ideal" or "universal" mental content from "physical" and "particular" content, as in Western thought, but rather serves as a kind of repository of external and internal data for—or as an "attending" function of—consciousness (*cit*, *caitanya*), which in Vedic systems is, in one way or another, the essence of primordial and true personhood. In this sense, if the Western philosophical tradition found itself bedeviled by a mind–body problem, the Brāhmaṇical tradition of India struggled with a soul–body problem that made the mind an organ of the body but a servant of the soul. The various representations of intellect in classical Hindu thought were thus dedicated to making sense of the unique problems that arose from these convictions.

In what follows, we look at the perspectives of each of the major schools of classical Hindu thought in three pivotal issues that will help us understand their respective philosophies of "intellect": (1) How did the school theorize the functioning of the "intellect," and what does it by itself contribute to awareness? (2) How did the school theorize how the contents of outer and inner perception were illuminated or brought to awareness by consciousness? (3) What is the ontological status of the intellect, and what is its value for both the practical and the spiritual goals of human existence?

Sāṃkhya and Yoga

In all likelihood, the first philosophically systematic depiction of how the mind was structured so as to be capable of producing cognition, reflection, and introspection was provided by the "Enumeration" school of metaphysics in the *Sāṃkhyakārikā* of Īśvarakṛṣṇa (fifth century CE). What we are here calling, for lack of a better locution, the intellect (*buddhi*) is responsible for "objective discernment" (*adhyavaśaya*), but it works in concert with two other mechanisms: "ego-generation" (*ahaṃkāra*), the activity of which is "introspection" (*abhimāna*), and "thought" (*manas*), the activity of which is "ideation" (*saṃkalpaka*) to produce cognitions (*Sāṃkhyakārikā* 23–24, 27). The intellect's job then is to produce a general state of object-directed awareness, while ego-generation relates such awareness to a sense of selfhood, and thought synthesizes the objects of awareness into an intelligible recognizable whole. The harmonious functioning of these mechanisms is referred to as the work of the "inner agent" (*antaḥkaraṇa*). Although it can certainly become infected with harmful dispositions, the internal agent predominates in the quality of *sattva*, or brilliance, which is what enables it to illuminate the mostly *tamas* or heavy bodies of merely gross objects. In the Sāṃkhya view, the inner agent as a whole evolves from the dynamic energies of matter (*prakṛti*), and so it is organically related to the body and all of its psychic, affective, and physical states (29, 32). Sāṃkhya even posits that the inner agent as a whole, along with its sense capacities, makes up a "subtle body" (*liṅga*) that transmigrates from one gross body to another in the continuum of rebirth (38–41). Among all the mechanisms that constitute the inner agent, however, the intellect (*buddhi*) is thought to be primary, for it is only with the given-ness of a general sense of awareness provided by the *buddhi* that ego-generation, thought, and bodily engagement in the world can have any meaning. For this reason, the intellect is labeled by Sāṃkhya *mahat* or "the great one" (22).

The whole process of the intellect considered on its own is believed by Sāṃkhya to be entirely unconscious precisely because the intellect and the bodies it serves are merely evolutes or emanations of material nature (*prakṛti*), and the latter, though it does exist in all times in close proximity with what can properly be called consciousness, does not contain or produce consciousness. Consciousness for Sāṃkhya is the essence of personhood, the primordial person (*puruṣa*), and this person is the ultimate witness (*śākṣin*) of all that the merely mechanical intellect offers up to it (*Sāṃkhyakārikā* 36–37). The material intellect requires the illuminating presence of consciousness to function, for no genuine awareness is said to take place unless the various modifications of the *antaḥkaraṇa* that the intellect holds are literally seen by *puruṣa*. It is, however, this very passive witnessing that is the key, for Sāṃkhya, to a kind of redemptive knowledge of the ultimate, unqualified freedom and eternal indestructibility of the innermost personhood of all beings. For when the *puruṣa*, the authentic consciousness and selfhood of each person, witnesses the activities of the finite, suffering body and its fluctuating intellect, a distinction (*viveka*) between them can be made and is the key to wisdom, for this distinction motivates the isolation (*kaivalya*) of the *puruṣa* from the world and motivates the sense of detachment that is necessary to disentangle the kārmic bonds that tie the ultimate person to rebirth (42–45). The intellect is thus in Sāṃkhya enormously significant, for within it lies the key to both worldly existence and the inspiration to pursue ultimate liberation through the highest forms of abstract metaphysical knowledge.

Patañjali's *Yogasūtra* appropriates much of the Sāṃkhya model of the inner agent and its mechanisms and its depiction of ultimate personhood, though it adds many fascinating details about both the process of intellection and a technique for liberation. Intellection (*antaḥkaraṇavṛtti*) in the Yoga system is conceived in terms of specific occurrences or events that modify (*vṛtti*) the inner agent. When the senses come into contact with objective forms, the *buddhi* takes on the form (*ākāra*) of the object in a very literal way, so that the awareness produced is in the form of the particular color, sound, or feeling. As in Sāṃkhya, the contents and fluctuations of the intellect may only rise to the level of conscious awareness through the illumination of the *puruṣa*, but in such objective cognitive states, *puruṣa*, because of its conjunction with the intellect, also takes on the intellect's form (*Yogasūtra* 1.7). Because the *puruṣa* is the witness of the intellect, Yoga philosophers maintain that the resulting knowledge belongs to the transcendent person and not to the intellect. Still, commentators on the system, such as Vyāsa (*ca.* fourth century CE), Vācaspati Miśra (tenth century), and Vijñānabhikṣu (sixteenth century), debated vigorously about whether *puruṣa* was ever objectified within the intellect in any way like other objects (Rukmani 1988: 370–74). Such constant object-formations adopted by the intellect are in any event the primary causes of ignorance, egoism, passion, revulsion, and attachment to life (*Yogasūtra* 2.3), for they obscure the pristine appearance of the true *puruṣa* and chain the sense of selfhood to the fleeting and painful material world. In addition, through the many events of our interactions in the world, pursuing certain objects and states and hating others, we develop residual psychic impressions or traces (*vāsanā*) that form intentions, habits, and dispositions further increasing human enmeshment in the world (4.8–11). The depth of such psychic traces and the habituated behaviors they cause cannot, contra Sāṃkhya, be simply uprooted by abstract metaphysical analysis but must be exorcised through meditative praxis.

The Yoga system thus understands successful meditation to be the "quelling of the modifications of the mind" (*yogaḥ cittavṛtti nirodaḥ*) (*Yogasūtra* 1, 2). All of *yoga*'s techniques, the fixation of the bodily posture, the restraint of breath, the restraint of the senses, one-pointed concentration, and so forth are aimed at calming and eventually stopping entirely the agitations, confusions, desires, excitations, and attachments of the *antaḥkarṇa* by controlling the sensory and motor organs that occasion all varieties of the intellect's modifications or *vṛtti*. Indeed, because the intellect is a bodily organ connected to all of the body's sensing and thinking capacities, *yoga* must be a bodily technique. This stilling of the mind's modifications will make it impossible, according to Patañjali, for the mind to mistake itself for consciousness, for all its machinations having been stilled through meditation, the self-luminous *puruṣa* will shine forth unobstructed by merely intellectual fluctuations and activities. We can see then that Yoga has a stronger sense than does Sāṃkhya that the intellect is far more an impediment to, rather than a catalyst of, the ultimate knowledge of the transcendent personhood, because for such liberating knowledge to be brought about, the intellect's mechanic activities must be eliminated through arduous, long-term practice.

Vaiśeṣika and Nyāya

The schools of "Particularist" metaphysics (Vaiśeṣika) and Logic (Nyāya) eventually grew into very close allies in the Brāhmaṇical tradition, as the former develops a thoroughgoing ontology that the latter defends through its epistemological doctrines. Their shared depiction of the intellect differs in marked respects from the models of Sāṃkhya and Yoga. In the *Vaiśeṣikasūtra* of Kaṇāda, it is argued that such internal states as pleasure, pain, the vital functions, and the nonsimultaneous cognition of objects by the mind (*manas*) prove the existence of a unique self (*ātman*) within each organism, but the activities of the mind should not be mistaken as those of the self (*Vaiśeṣikasūtra* 3.2–18). Cognitions, however, are only possible when there is contact between the sense organs, the mind, and the self (3.1). The illustrious fifth-century Vaiśeṣika commentator, Praśastapāda, asserts that consciousness proper must be a quality of *ātman* because the mind, being physical like the other sense organs, is merely an instrumental cause (*karaṇa*) of cognitions and cannot be considered a cognizer itself (*Padārthadharmasaṃgraha* 5.44). Praśastapāda further argues that the mind (*manas*) or inner sense (*antaḥkaraṇa*)—the two terms here being considered synonymous—is an atomic substance that moves rapidly throughout the body to attend to its sensations, not all at once but in a sequential manner (5.45). The conclusion that the mind is an atomic (*aṇutva*) substance is very significant, for it implies that, like other atoms, the mind is partless and so does not have any internal structure or form (*nirākara*) of its own. There is thus no internal partition of mental functions or structures in this view as there is in the Sāṃkhya-Yoga systems, whose model of the mind represents it as having its own internal structure (*sākara*). This principle also makes the Vaiśeṣika much more of a direct realist, for the mind is not believed here to take on the forms of the objects it perceives but merely passes those forms on to the self, for the self to dispense with as it pleases.

The fourth-century Nyāya commentator, Vātsyāyana, lends in support of this picture of the mind sharp arguments that are overtly directed against the Sāṃkhya position, but significantly, these arguments demand that the mind, and the conscious awareness that it enables, be understood in a strictly physicalist sense (Ram-Prasad 2001: 381–85). Vātsyāyana accuses the Sāṃkhya model of surrendering the materiality of the intellect by claiming that the mind is formed in the shape of its objects, since, if this were the case, there would be no reason not to consider the mind the agent (*kartā*) of the awareness of cognitions and not just an unconscious instrument (*karaṇa*) (*Nyāyasūtrabhāṣya* 3, 2.3). Furthermore, if the Sāṃkhya model maintains that the form of the perceived object becomes "seated in the faculty of awareness" (*buddhyārūḍha*) and that the internal organ "pervades" or enjoins (*vyāpnuvat*) the object's form, then we would be warranted in assuming that the *antaḥkaraṇa* takes and holds on to all these forms and, in any given state of awareness, we ought to be able to be conscious of all the contents of the mind, sensations, perceptions, willings, rememberings, emotive states, and somatic states all at once (3, 2.4). Vātsyāyana insists that this cannot be the case, for we are not inundated with all the past and present contents of our consciousness at every given moment but rather have sequenced experiences, which proves that the mind is a mobile physical object that performs its activities, like all other physical entities, in time. Finally, in contrast to Sāṃkhya's belief that the *antaḥkaraṇa* helps to constitute a subtle body (*liṅga*) that attaches to the *puruṣa* from one life to the next, Nyāya argues that because cognitions require the connection between the self, mind, and sense organs, we may infer that when the body and its mind dies, the self is no longer conscious (Chakrabarti 1999: 184). If then Nyāya defends a staunch form of soul–body dualism, the mind or intellect serves the needs of *ātman* only insofar as *ātman* has embodied pragmatic needs and aspirations. Knowledge may of course be acquired in the pursuit of ultimate liberation for Nyāya, too, but like all other forms of pragmatic pursuits, even saving knowledge should be counted as merely instrumental.

Having been the premier epistemologists of the Vedic tradition, the Naiyāyikas also found themselves in the center of an important, long-conducted debate on how the mind becomes possessed by self-awareness. This was not a problem for Sāṃkhya or Yoga philosophers, who held that ego-generation or a sense of selfhood (*ahaṃkāra*) accompanied every cognition as an indelible function of the inner agent (*antaḥkaraṇa*). Given the atomic picture of mind along with the momentary theory of cognition in the Nyāya school, the issue of self-awareness had to be addressed. Their answer to this question is the concept of apperception or *anuvyavasāya*. As very cognition is thought to reveal only one object at a time, a perception, for instance, of seeing an object must be followed by another cognition that has the initial perception as its object for the cognition "I am seeing this object" to arise. This idea became known as the extrinsic illumination theory (*paraprakāśaka*), for every cognition, having only one object, must be revealed by another cognition for self-awareness to arise. This notion was attacked by the schools of Mīmāṃsā and Vedānta, who held in various ways that cognitions are always self-revealing and claimed that the Nyāya model of apperception would lead to an infinite regress of apprehensions that would be needed to illuminate the initial cognition. Nyāya thinkers consistently responded to this charge by claiming that no such regress actually ever takes place for, in most cases, we take some action prompted merely by an initial cognition of an object, and should we doubt the veracity of the initial cognition, normally only a few confirmatory cognitions are required to clear up the matter (Matilal 1986: 98–100). The issue of how cognitive events are illuminated so as to rise to the level of self-awareness was to be a central issue in Brāhmaṇical scholastic debates on the nature of the intellect and consciousness.

Mīmāṃsā

The major schools of Early Vedic Exegesis (Pūrva-Mīmāṃsā) are in substantial agreement with the Vaiśeṣika and Nyāya philosophers regarding the nature and functions of the *manas*. They agree, for instance, that the mind or intellect (these terms for Mīmāṃsā once again are synonymous) is an internal sense organ; that it is atomic in size; that cognitions occur to the mind one at a time; that the mind must be in contact with the *ātman* and the external sense organs or objects of the inner sense for cognitions to take place; and that the mind falls away on the death of the person, leaving the disembodied *ātman* entirely unconscious (Cennakesavan 1980: 22). The innovations that the most influential schools of Mīmāṃsā made with regard to the theory of intellect were on the topic of how cognitions arose to self-awareness not through the phenomenon of apperception held by the Naiyāyikas but rather through the self-revealing or self-luminous (*svayaṃprakāśa*) nature of cognitions.

The Bhāṭṭa school of Mīmāṃsā, named after its forerunning advocate, Kumārila Bhāṭṭa (seventh century CE), embraces a position on self-awareness that makes it the result of an inference. Perceptual cognitions by their very nature, for Kumārila, present their objects faithfully; they do not themselves misrepresent objective forms but rather take on the forms that their objects present (*Ślokavārtika* 2.80). Such perceptions, through their character as productions of the intellect (*bhodakatva*), confer on their objects a new property, that of "known-ness" (*jñānatā*), and it is this property that raises the initial cognition to the level of self-awareness for any subsequent cognition that reflects on it. Kumārila therefore insists that any cognition that is a genuine perception carries a sense of indubitable truth, and if an error is made, it is thought to be because of some defect (*doṣa*) that impeded the perception or the mistake of a memory for a perception (2.53). The Bhāṭṭa school as a whole tried to marry a heightened sense of certainty in the perceptual process to the model of a transparent and unstructured intellect.

The other major school of Mīmāṃsā was named after Prabhākara, who was Kumārila's contemporary. The Prabhākaras carried the realist notion of the self-awareness of cognitions much farther than their sister school. It appears that the position of this school on cognitive self-awareness developed from the initial view held by Prabhākara into the generally cited view of his commentator Sālikanātha (Chatterjea 2002: 1–8). According to Prabhākara, when we speak of *jñāna*, or cognitions, we mean that an immediate awareness (*samvit*) of an object has taken place, but because that immediate awareness can never itself be known as the perceptual object of another cognition, it is known only through an inference and that inference is what we cognize (*Bṛhatītikāśabarabhāṣya* 63). The intellect then is always self-aware, but a second-order awareness of this self-awareness can only be attained through reflection. The reason that Prabhākara adopted this complex principle was his conviction that when we recall an experience, for instance, we recall at first only the objective content of that experience, and while it is certainly the case that the experience was perceived by us on its occurrence, an extra act of reflection is required for us to report the latter fact (68). The commentator Sālikanātha dramatically revises this position in what becomes the school's doctrinal view. For Sālikanātha, this self-awareness is directly presented in each cognition and need not be inferred. This is owing to the fact that every cognition of the *manas* when it comes into contact with *ātman* reveals three things (*triputi-bhāna*), the object, the illuminating cognition, and self-awareness. Sālikanātha uses this notion to vindicate the trustworthiness of immediate awareness and links error to faulty memory or faulty practice (*Prakaraṇapañcikā* 32).

The self-luminous intellect of the Mīmāṃsā school is an invaluable servant of the person insofar as it enables him or her to follow *dharma* or the religious and social obligations enjoined by the Vedic scriptures. The *ātman*'s desire for *svarga*, or "heaven," makes Vedic learning and practice necessary, and the Vedas must be trusted and stringently followed for this ultimate goal of life to be realized. The Mīmāṃsā depiction of the self-luminous intellect amplified their theory of the intrinsic validity of certain cognitions that conferred knowledge (*svattaḥprāmāṇyavāda*), and as both perceptual cognitions and Vedic injunction fell into this category, the Mīmāṃsikas took it on themselves to offer a staunch defense of the reliability of cognitions and of the intellect that was their mediator.

Vedānta

The school of Later Vedic Exegesis (Uttara-Mīmāṃsā or Vedānta) is represented by the views of three major subschools: the Nondualist (Advaita), the Qualified Nondualist (Viśiṣṭadvaita), and the Dualist (Dvaita). These alternative views pertain to the issue of the relationship of the self (*ātman*) to the ultimate reality (*brahman*) of all things, with the Advaitins articulating a complete identity between the two, the Viśiṣṭadvaitins positing that each individuated self emanates from the ultimate reality, and the Dvaitins holding that self and ultimate reality are distinct, with the latter created by the former. The bearing that each of these metaphysical positions has on the assessments of the intellect is significant and compels the respective schools to make unique and far-reaching contributions toward its explanation.

The Advaita Vedānta so adroitly articulated by Śaṅkarācarya (eighth century) lays out a theory of the relation between intellect and transcendent selfhood and a depiction of the human intellect that are reminiscent of Sāṃkhya. There are fascinating and important departures, however. For one thing, in Śaṅkara, the sense capacities, impelled by their own desires, direct (*bahirmukha*) the senses toward their preferred objects, a suggestion that later Advaitins took to mean that the sense capacities actually left the body and latched on to their objects (Mayeda 1992: 35). It seems that Śaṅkara was unclear as to whether he would actually classify the intellect as a sense organ (*indriya*) as the other scholastic systems did, and this ambiguity led two commentarial traditions of Advaita, the Bhāmati and the Vivarṇa, to take contrary views on the issue (Cennakesavan 1980: 40–44). Śaṅkara claims in any case that the designations *manas*, *buddhi*, *ahaṃkāra*, and *vijñāna* merely refer to different functions of the inner agent (*antaḥkaraṇa*), with *manas* being a coordinator of the external sense organs and an internal sensor, the *buddhi* being the receptor of perceptual content, ego-generation being the *buddhi*'s mistaking itself as the agent of cognition, and *vijñāna* or knowing cognitions being specific modifications (*vṛtti*) of the intellect (*Brahmasūtrabhāṣya* 2, 3.32). Other assertions Śaṅkara makes about the inner agent are common to other systems, namely, that it can be considered a minute, subtle substance that transmigrates from life to life and that it is merely an instrumental cause (*karaṇa*) of cognitions and not their agent (*kartā*). It is on the issue of self-awareness where Śaṅkara's system stands out, for he asserts the ultimate and all-pervasive reality of a unitary and transcendent self (*ātman*), and this self is consciousness (*cit*). The nature of consciousness is self-luminosity (*svayaṃprakāśatva*), and it is this light that shines on the intellect and illuminates the cognitive forms (*pratyaya*) that are found there. No complex explanation, such as those found in Mīmāṃsā, is required to account for cognitive self-awareness; for the self, contrary to realist teachings, is conscious, and its own luminous nature allows it to play the role of a "witness" or subject (*sākṣin*) of all cognitive events (Gupta 2003: 113). It is, however, the sense of ego-identity that results from this process that leads human beings astray. A sense of individuated selfhood (*jīva*) that is identified with the body and its acts is produced when the reflection (*ābhāsa*) of the luminous self falls on the *buddhi*, and the *buddhi* responds by manufacturing a conceit of identity (*ahaṃpratyaya*).

This sense of ego is nonetheless a logical mistake (*adhyāsa*), a fundamental ignorance (*mūlāvidyā*) that obscures our innermost nature from us and entices us with the illusion that we are embodied individuals (*Brahmasūtrabhāṣya* 1). Śaṅkara's system insists, therefore, on a distinction between two levels of awareness: the pure, self-luminous and essential awareness of *ātman* (*svarūpa jñāna*) and awareness conditioned by empirical factors (*vṛtti jñāna*), but it is incumbent on us to know that it is the former kind of awareness that stands as the foundation for the latter, though it is at the same time entirely separable from it (Gupta 2003: 106–7). For Śaṅkara, then, the intellect has both a positive and a negative function; on the one hand, its cognitive activity enables us to navigate our way in the empirical world; on the other, it is the seat of the great illusion that imprisons human beings in transmigratory existence.

Numerous and important Advaita commentators attempted to defend, refine, and systematize Śaṅkara's philosophy of consciousness, as his conception of consciousness was in many respects uniquely provocative and drew critique from so many quarters, especially from Naiyāyikas and rival Vedāntins. The Advaita dialectician Śrīharṣa (twelfth century) undertook a profoundly sophisticated logical attempt to refute the Nyāya view that awareness was extrinsically, rather than intrinsically, illuminated by demonstrating that the former thesis is incoherent. Cognitions, for Nyāya, reveal relations between qualities and substances that are physically distinct (*bheda*). Śrīharṣa rejects this representation on the ground that if the quality and its locus require a relational tie to be brought together, we would need a further term that would tie this first quality-locus relation to itself. The only other explanation of a relation between properties and their substances for Śrīharṣa is that they are nondistinct (*abheda*, *advaita*) (*Khaṇḍanakhaṇḍakhādya* 1.110), and this demonstrates that consciousness supplies this relational tie by itself, making objective awareness self-illuminating (4.13, 63). Madhusūdana Sarasvatī (sixteenth century) brings further argumentative resources to the Advaita critique of Nyāya realism in defense of the self-luminosity thesis. He attacks a New Nyāya definition of knowledge as "a cognition of a qualified thing as the thing it is" by retorting that, because such a qualification-relation is just as true of erroneous cognitions as it is of true ones, we can assume that it is consciousness that relates all these objects and their qualities and not the things in themselves (*Advaitaratnarakṣaṇam* 30–32). In the seventeenth century, a more detailed and systematic treatment of the interaction of consciousness and the intellect was given by Dharmarāja. In Dharmarāja's extensive treatment, the intellect, both in its extension to external objects through the senses and through its modification, reveals with the light of pure consciousness worldly objects from an ignorance in which they had hitherto been hidden, and the pure consciousness of *ātman* that shines its light on the object presented by the intellect becomes limited or contingently conditioned by the particular mental mode and its specific cognition (*Vedāntaparibhāṣā* 25–26). This was Dharmarāja's explanation for how consciousness served as the illuminator of all cognitions and of the nature of self-luminosity as the nondistinction between consciousness and the contents of the intellect. The contribution of these and many other Advaita commentators was to translate the basic doctrines of Śaṅkara into the theory of knowledge and show how Śaṅkara's notion of pure, self-luminous consciousness was a better model of our understanding of objective experience than such realist models as the Nyāya or Mīmāṃsā, which posit far different theories of an essentially unconscious self and thus of subjective experience in general.

The other schools of Vedānta sharply rejected the Advaita view, however. The major purveyor of Viśiṣtadvaita, Rāmānuja (thirteenth century), agrees with the Advaitin that consciousness is self-luminous and that consciousness is the essence of the self, but the self in question here is an individuated self that is both emergent and distinct from (*bhedābeda*) Brahman or Ultimate Reality. This means for Rāmānuja that the indivduated *ātman* that, in each and every mental awareness, apprehends itself as its knower (*jñātṛ*) is no illusion, no mistaken appearance of a more transcendent reality as in Advaita, but represents the genuine, innermost identity (*Śrībhāya* I.i.41). It is not the case, then, according to Rāmānuja, that a false sense of identity appears in the *ahaṃkāra* function of the intellect, for this would amount to claiming that the material intellect had the capacity to be self-conscious. However, because we know that *ahaṃkāra* is material and unconscious, we can know that its nature is ignorance (*avidyā*) (I.i.45). Instead, Rāmānuja asserts, the empirical limiting conditions and characteristics of the embodied individual (*jīva*), which includes the *ahaṃkāra* and the intellect as a whole, along with all the transformations these extrinsically undergo, both within one lifetime and from life to life, are objects of the knowing self (I.i.40, 43). Therefore, two different levels of awareness can be spoken of in Rāmānuja's thought: the direct self-awareness of *ātman* and such self-awareness as is qualified by the bodily intellect and the objective circumstances of the empirical person; but it is the *ātman* and not the intellect that is the owner of both strata of awareness (Lipner 1986: 59). The intellect is nonetheless the means that can be used by the individual *jīva* to engage in meritorious works, study of the scriptures, practicing *yoga*, and, in its highest state of discipline, calling ever to mind the image of Brahman in contemplative devotion, all of which further the project of final liberation (Lipner 1986: 111–15). The Dvaita Vedānta view, represented by its major commentator Madhva (fourteenth century) takes a thoroughly dualist stance, formulating a strict distinctness between Brahman as God, individuated selves differentiated from one another, and material nature. All of these essences, the supreme being, selves, and material nature, are coeternal but are not of equally perfect subtlety. Therefore, for Madhva, selves are genuinely conscious knowers and agents, and they employ materially constituted bodies and their attendant subtle intellects in both empirical life and the life of devotion.

Concluding Reflections

The classical Hindu philosophical tradition produced robust, powerful, and sophisticated theories of the intellect, the role it plays in human life and knowledge, and its variously interpreted relationship to consciousness. Despite the numerous and profound differences between the scholastic views of the intellect, the commonly held assumptions about its physicality, integrative powers, and unconsciousness stand out. The intellect or mind is itself a bodily organ of great subtlety: It regulates the vital "breaths" or bodily energies; it synthesizes perceptual, somatic, affective, and conceptual data; and it manufactures a sense of bodily individuality. The intellect, however, accomplishes all of this mechanically and unconsciously. That is to say that, whereas the Brāhmaṇical assumption that the intellect is a physical phenomenon accords in some respects quite well with contemporary Western perspectives, the Brāhmaṇical philosophical tradition sharply dissents from the contemporary supposition that consciousness is an emergent property of the brain. For the classical Brāhmaṇical schools, the situation is in many ways reversed; consciousness can, under various construals, arise only through the contact between the unconscious mind and the spiritual self. It is this latter conviction that in its own turn was hotly debated for more than a millennium between the Vedic schools who upheld it and the multifarious schools of Buddhism and Cārvāka, which defended models of a physical intellect that both mechanically operates and produces consciousness of its own accord.

References Cited

Cennakesavan, Sarasvati. 1980. *Concept of Mind in Indian Philosophy*. Bombay: Asia Publishing House.

Chakrabarti, Kisor Kumar. 1999. *Classical Indian Philosophy of Mind: The Nyāya Dualist Tradition*. Albany: State University of New York Press.

Chatterjea, Tara. 2002. *Knowledge and Freedom in Indian Philosophy*. London: Lexington Books.

Gupta, Bina. 2003. *Cit: Consciousness*. Delhi: Oxford University Press.

Lipner, Julius. 1986. *The Face of Truth: A Study of Meaning and Metaphysics in the Vedāntic Theology of Rāmānuja*. Albany: State University of New York Press.

Matilal, Bimal Krishna. 1986. *Perception: An Essay on Classical Indian Theories of Knowledge*. Oxford: Clarendon Press.
Mayeda, Sengaku. 1992. *A Thousand Teachings: The Upadeśasāhasrī of Śaṅkara*. Albany: State University of New York Press.
Plato. 1987. *The Republic* (trans. Desmond Lee). London: Penguin Books.
Ram-Prasad, Chakravarthi. 2001. "Saving the Self? Classical Hindu Theories of Consciousness and Contemporary Physicalism." *Philosophy East and West* 51, 3: 378–92.
Rukmani, T. S. 1988. "Vijñānabhikṣu's Double-Reflection Theory of Knowledge in the Yoga System." *Journal of Indian Philosophy* 16, 4: 367–76.

15

Kinship

Maya Unnithan-Kumar

Divine and Human Social Organization
Marriage and Social Hierarchy
Gender and Ritual Authority
Divine and Human Reproduction and Sexuality
Renunciation, Devotion, and Attachment
Death and Social Regeneration
Concluding Reflections

Hindu iconography, mythology, and rituals provide a key insight into the nature of human relatedness in India. Ideas and practices to do with fertility, sexuality, birth, siblingship, marriage, selfhood, parenthood, and death are intertwined with and mutually shaped by conceptions of the Hindu divine order and its pantheon of celestial beings. The connections between Hinduism and the ways in which people in India regard themselves as related is most clearly manifest at the level of a Hinduism that is practiced, performed, and experienced in ordinary people's lives: a "popular" Hinduism rather than in a scriptural sense alone. Popular Hinduism, as C. J. Fuller (1992: 6) suggests, is significantly informed by the sacred texts of Hinduism and yet may not in everyday practice emphasize themes that may be central to the scriptures. One of the best ways to understand how such localized processes of religion and kinship work is to draw on the everyday accounts of Indian society by anthropologists, sociologists, and cultural psychologists.

Divine and Human Social Organization

A central feature of Hinduism, important for understanding kinship practices, is the absence of an absolute distinction between divine and human beings. Conceptualized as male or female, gods (*devtā*)—such as Viṣṇu, Śiva and Brahmā—and goddesses (*devī*)—such as Lakṣmī, Pārvatī, Durgā, and Kālī—descend to earth, as divine incarnations or in the shape of various living forms, to take part in human affairs. Humans and divine beings are mutually constitutive of the Universe where the latter are thought of as encompassing the former. Humans attain god-like status during certain rituals, as groom and bride during marriage or during illness in which the body itself becomes a "host" for the deity or supernatural being. During ritual, but also in everyday practice, gods and goddesses are treated as venerated members of a family, both feared and respected, to be provided hospitality, entreated, and placated. Gods and goddesses are also seen to embody particular kinds of human roles and activities, such as of kingship (Viṣṇu), asceticism (Śiva), and motherhood (*mātā/śakti*), and like humans display such emotion as empathy or scorn. Hindu deities are variously regarded as benevolent, beneficent, protective, malevolent, and harmful. A consequence of the fluid boundaries across divine and human is that, "Hindu ideas and practices provide a means through which the...practice of human kinship can be debated" (Good 2000: 328).

Another distinctive feature of Hinduism, copresent in the social order, is the encompassing relationship of a supreme being to its various manifestations. In rituals, texts, and ordinary conversations wherein multiple goddesses are referred to, overall these goddesses represent the different aspects of the same unified Goddess (Kurtz 1992). Bhairu, a deity associated with Śiva (variously as his son, as protector of his wife), appears as a powerful male protective force in different regional manifestations in western India and in South India (Fuller 1992; Gold 1988; Kothari 1982). The idea that one deity can be worshiped in many different guises and manifestations, and in turn that many local forms can become one deity, is a principle that is seen to order caste society as well. Thus we find that people of a single caste can be divided into numerous social groups regarded as subcastes, subsubcastes, and so on. At one level, in relation to other castes, they are all regarded as members of one caste and of a similar social status. At another level, within the caste group, its members are all regarded as divided into different social groupings and of different social status in relation to one another, of importance especially when it comes to arranging marriages within the caste group (referred to as endogamy; see below).

The relationship of the different parts to the whole in caste society and in the divine order is defined by the principle of hierarchical inequality (Dumont 1980). In both contexts, divine and human, social distinction is maintained through collectively acknowledged, albeit contested, notions of ritually based superiority and inferiority. The hierarchy between endogamous units of kins-people (castes) is maintained and legitimated through ideas and practices of ritual purity and pollution. Pollution in this context is seen to inhere in products and processes that are connected to but removed from organic life (such as saliva, nail clippings, excreta, dead flesh, menstrual blood, birth, and bodily fluids). People and groups are associated with pollution either through their contact (e.g., occupational) with polluting substances or through immoral acts that involve a transaction of such substances.

Marriage and Social Hierarchy

The principle of hierarchical inequality as constituted through notions of pollution are clearly discernible, especially in North Indian kinship patterns in the institution of marriage wherein the husband and his family (wife-takers) are regarded as socially and ritually superior (pure) as compared to the bride and her family (wife-givers). The elaborate rules and rituals involved in the processes surrounding marriage ensure that the appropriate social distance between the exogamous intermarrying caste groups is maintained, and the pollution of inappropriate alliances and related family shame and dishonor is avoided. The central position of the discourse of purity and pollution in the formation of marital alliances can be seen through two interrelated, religiously endorsed practices: the practice of hypergamy or marriage of the bride "upwards" (*anuloma*) which is regarded as socially appropriate (superior) as compared to hypogamous alliances (marrying "down" in the social hierarchy; *pratiloma*). Hypergamous marriage also enables the father of the bride to ritually conclude his obligations in protecting her from (sexual) impurity and dishonor. Moreover, through gifting his daughter without any thought of the return (symbolized by the *kanyādān* ceremony), he in turn gains merit (*puṇya*) for his actions. From my own anthropological work among a poor farming community in Rajasthan, Northwestern India (Unnithan-Kumar 1997), I have found that though such notions do indeed underlie marriage practices across the caste spectrum, there is a wide variation in the interpretation of impure practices, making for a more negotiated social order. Both among the Rājpūts and those who claim genealogical, ritual, or symbolic kinship with them, these practices point to the existence of more equal (isogamous) marriages (Parry 1979).

Isogamous marriages are a distinguishing feature of South Indian kinship practices wherein marriages are preferred to take place between cross-cousins (that is, of women with their mother's brother's son [MBS] or with their father's sister's son [FZS]). Even here, however, subtle hierarchies exist between upper-caste and elite Brāhmaṇical groups and the non-Brāhmaṇical castes. The former, for example, exhibit a preference for the FZS type of marriage, whereas the latter tend to marry their MBS (Kapadia 1995). These hierarchies become manifest in the practice of distinctive ritual practices, such as those to do with birth, where patrilineality among affines is more emphasized (among Brāhmaṇical groups) as opposed to the focus on premarital rituals of puberty, held at the onset of menstruation, among the non-Brāhmaṇical castes (Kapadia 1995).

Gender and Ritual Authority

Marriage, across caste and class are moments of particular social anxiety because it is only through an appropriate alliance that men are initiated into the highly valued role of householder: the only means by which ordinary humans are able to perform virtuous actions and meet the dhārmic striving for worldly goals (Madan 1987). The home, as Madan points out, is the prime location for ordered social conduct relating to life-cycle rituals and, I suggest, the means by which social relatedness and identity is conferred and experienced. For, "it is here that the three fires of domestic life burn:...the fire in the hearth, the fire lit periodically to perform rituals,...and the fire in one's body" (Madan 1987: 34). As individuals, men attain full ritual status before marriage (in the thread ceremony among the upper castes) that is activated at the time of their marriage when they become householders. For women, marriage is essential as it is only through marriage that they gain full ritual status, and it is through pregnancy and birth that their ritual status is confirmed.

In religious and caste (especially Brāhmaṇical) ideology and practice, male authority, sexuality, and related patrilineal descent are regarded as primary and celebrated. Yet, male divine authority is never regarded as complete without the complementary presence of a female principle. In fact, male authority is seen to derive from female power (*śakti*) and thus, while being regarded as supreme, cannot stand alone from it. The cosignificance of the male and female principles is also manifest in temples and shrines where icons of male deities are present alongside female deities or are corepresented as a composite icon, as in the case of the Snake deity worshipped by Tamil non-Brāhmaṇs (Kapadia 1995). In Rajasthan, male and female deities "sit" alongside each other, as do the priests who serve them at public shrines (here the *mātā* and *bāosi* are regarded as sister and brother). The same is seen in household shrines where the *kuldevī* (literally, clan mother) and *bāosi* (male deity, often *bhairu*) coexist to protect the interests of the family and lineage (Gold 1988; Kakar 1981; Kothari 1982; Unnithan-Kumar 1997). In certain cases, the copresence and conjugality of the celestial couples is a central theme of daily ritual (e.g., in Śaivite temples in Tamil Nadu and Kerala; Fuller 1992; Good 2000) pointing toward the significance of regular sexual and ritual relationships between them as a means of preservation of the cosmos and by extension of the social order.

Divine and Human Reproduction and Sexuality

The dependant and yet unequal relationship between male and female divine beings is reproduced among humans. Wives are regarded as subordinate to their husbands (whom they must worship as gods), and yet without them, their husband is not regarded as socially complete. A man's social status in society is derived from his ability to procreate, have sons (to continue his lineage), and offer hospitality, for all of which he is dependant on his wife. For women, their devotion to their husbands, their sexual fidelity, and their reproductive prowess gain them status in the household and society, all essential to their sense of self-worth. Women, whether in North or South India are, unlike men, morally and ritually circumscribed by the more "visible" physical role they play in reproductive processes. This is made clear in the birth-related rituals in the North (Patel 1994) and in the public celebration of puberty and birth in southern India (Kapadia 1995; Van Hollen 2003). They thus never attain a ritual or social status equal to that of the men they are so closely connected to and toward whose importance they contribute so vitally.

The female principle in Hinduism is accredited with both an autonomous and a destructive aspect that signals the power of mature women to act alone, at the same time as pointing to the dangerous potential of such action. Unmarried goddesses are also depicted as more violent and destructive than married goddesses. In human society, this has been conceptualized in terms of the dangers surrounding the rampant sexuality of single, mature women stemming from a societal inability to harness their sexuality in the appropriate manner (in becoming mothers and contributing to the continuation of their husband's patrilineage). In caste society, unlike the celestial order, it is mainly through motherhood, when women have successfully borne their husband's children, that they attain the highest and most auspicious social positions. This division between sexuality and fertility resulting in a split female image is seen to be reproduced in the contrasting kinship positions of daughter–sister, on the one hand, and wife, on the other, and thought to be reconciled through motherhood (Bennett 1983; Carstairs 1967; Gold 1988; Kakar 1981; Kurtz 1992).

The view of Hindu women's identities and related moralities as shaped by the tension between sexuality and reproduction is not universally accepted by all observers of Indian society. As Gloria Raheja and Ann Gold (1994) demonstrate through an examination of rural women's songs in northern India, erotic sexuality may be compatible with rather than opposed to procreation and motherhood. They suggest that women may consciously bridge such splits in the ways in which they manage their kinship relations. Gold (1994) found, for example, that in their recourse to oral traditions, Rajasthani women were able to create a self-image that was simultaneously sexy and motherly. Raheja and Gold's work highlights some of the pitfalls of viewing social relationships through the (predominantly male) lens of Hindu mythology and scriptures. Irawati Karve, in her classic work on kinship organization in India, makes a similar observation when she suggests that women's songs handed down through the oral traditions represent a special type of "little tradition" (popular, local practice) presenting aspects of kinship not found in the literature of the classic scriptures of the "great traditions" (1968: 21). These are also examples that serve to complicate the assumption that the Hindu pantheon can be used as a template to understand the entirety of kin-based relatedness in India.

Renunciation, Devotion, and Attachment

Renunciation and sacrifice are other Hindu themes that are relevant to human life in this world and are experienced through kinship relations in the household. The institution of *bhakti*, or deep devotion to the divinity, as Madan reminds us, "does not require one to abandon one's family and become a renouncer....*Bhakti* requires that the love of one's kith and kin should be encompassed by and not independent of the love of God" (1987: 38). The concept of devotion may also supersede the primacy of ritual purity in ordering human–divine and human-human relationships, as noted by Margaret Trawick (1990) and Karin Kapadia in their work in Tamil Nadu. Among the lower-caste Pallars, for example, it is believed that possession, where the deity descends to the human world, occurs only to those who are devoted rather than ritually pure (Kapadia 1995). Notions of devotion and duty also inform the obligations and reciprocations of parent–child relationships. The bond between mother and child is conceptualized as an enduring tie beyond the material realm, a debt (*mātr-ṛṇa*), which cannot be repaid by the child. The father–child relationship by contrast, is more circumscribed by the legal and economic realm of life (Madan 1987: 26). The irrevocable maternal bond is connected to the idea of women as primary nourishers (through their blood and milk) of the child both in its fetal state and after birth. A mother's involvement with the child is seen as one of sustenance and the related intimacy as resulting from her nurturing the child through her own bodily fluids.

The Hindu mother–child relationship has been the object of detailed psychosocial analysis and variously portrayed as bordering on the emotionally pathological by psychologists who regard it as an overly intimate and thereby unhealthy attachment between child (especially a son) and mother (Carstairs 1967; Kakar 1981). This is compared to the West, where such relationships are regarded as less emotionally invested and more individually orientated. Contrary to this view, Stanley Kurtz (1992) proposes that the notion of group nurturing, as a feature of caste society and divine kinship, decreases the significance of the mother figure and contributes to a less traumatic weaning experience of the Hindu child as compared to the Western child.

For Kurtz, the Western child experiences an involuntary renunciation of the mother's breast (the pleasure principle in Western psychoanalysis) forced on it by the mother's decisive action to withdraw breastfeeding. This is in contrast to the voluntary renunciation that the Hindu child experiences through the more ambivalent actions of its mother, who simultaneously indicates her constant availability to breastfeed and her disapproval of such breast-seeking behavior. Kurtz suggests that Hindu mothers thus subtly lead their children toward an outcome (the sacrifice of the breast) that the child feels it has voluntarily accomplished. The wider kin and caste group plays an important role in enabling this transformation. Older siblings of the child, the siblings of the parents, older women relatives, children of these older women, especially their older girls, can be conceptualized as a group of "mothers" all providing attention and care to the child. Such ministrations serve to make the child aware of its membership in the group, its own rights to impose on them, and in turn the rights of group members to impose themselves on the child. Children's sense of relatedness and identity are thus crucially shaped by the attitudes and practices of the kin group. Kurtz finds childhood attitudes toward the group to also be the bases of human attitudes toward Hindu goddesses. Through their experiences of "multiple mothering," children learn that all mothers, whether divine or human, are part of a unified group (Kurtz 1992: 108).

The role of women as wives and mothers is also ideologically connected to the notion of self-sacrifice or altruism, best understood through Hindu ideas of the *phala*, or "fruit" (positive outcome), of worthy actions. The fruits of successful and worthy actions are most respected if they are sacrificed and surrendered to others. Deities are usually the recipients of such fruits. The rewards for worthy deeds should, however, not be the primary motivation for engaging in these activities. Still, the restrained pursuit through worship and self-denial is considered virtuous (Gold 1988). These Hindu ideas play a major role in shaping women's roles, actions, and relationships within the family. As wives, women in Rajasthan, Uttar Pradesh, and elsewhere in northern India renounce food when they undertake fasts, such as the *karvā-cauth*, for the welfare of their husband and his family through which they gain merit (*puṇya*). At a more everyday level, women as mothers gain merit through feeding their husband and children before partaking of food themselves.

Death and Social Regeneration

A major set of household and family rituals are related to the worship of ancestors. Ancestors are important as they protect and look after the interests of their descendants. Ancestors, as opposed to the Gods, are associated with supernatural beings of nondivine ancestry who have to be appeased, as they cause harm if not regularly propitiated. Some ancestors, especially those who have died before their time through heroic or tragic deaths, come back as ghosts to haunt their descendants. Their presence is often manifest in the form of misfortune, including illness that befalls their descendants. They are appeased through rituals of sacrifice and healing. Death is associated with both ancestors (*pitṛ*) and ghosts (*preta*). However, unlike *preta, pitṛ* are closely associated with the welfare of their descendants. This is symbolized in the reciprocity between householders and their ancestors, which is a major theme in the rites to the ancestors (Das 1991: 163). Kinship ties between the living and the dead are thus maintained through a set of rituals that are distinct from those of divine worship. They are distinct in that they take place at separate times in the Hindu calendar (regulated by the moon), in separate sacred spaces, and often invoke a symbolism reverse from that of divine worship (see Das 1991, for example, on the right–left symbolism in the ritual categorization of space, wherein the right side is related to the Gods and the left side is associated with the ancestors).

It is through a combination of the worship of the deities and of one's ancestors that the meaning of kinship relatedness is most clearly experienced. Kinship is manifest through religious rituals and informs subsequent kinship practice. Divine and ancestral worship complement each other, reflecting at one and the same time the transcendent nature and the fallibility of human existence. Both these sets of relationships with the divine and ancestral also provide a template for creating kinship relations that are beyond those of descent, such as those based on siblingship, friendship, loyalty, and spirituality. So, for example, the annual occasion of *rākhī* that celebrates the bonds between sister and brother is also an occasion in Rajasthan for forging ties of *dharam bhāī* and *dharam bahn* (literally, religious brother and sister), a sibling type of relationship between those who are not related in the conventional (descent or marriage) sense. In both North and South India, as indeed in other parts of the country, the special (reciprocal, sacred, protective) relationship between brothers and sisters is ritually marked (Beck 1974; Trawick 1990; Wadley 1975). Similarly, ties of kinship that cut across those of ritual purity are formed through devotional worship (as experienced among members of various religious traditions, such as the Kabīr Panthī, and followers of Svāmī Nārāyaṇa, to take two examples). The central idea in devotional religious practice (*bhakti*) is that the love of god enables believers to transcend the hierarchic boundaries of caste and class.

Concluding Reflections

It is important to point out that the language of ritual purity, hierarchy, and caste is but one, albeit dominant, means of ordering kinship relations in India (Quigley 1993; Searle-Chatterjee and Sharma 1994). There are other, equally important ideological frameworks that run counter to the elite, Brāhmaṇical understandings of ritual and divine hierarchies, such as historically presented by landownership, conquest, and military prowess of royal lineages and by the more marginalized lower-caste and tribal communities that have shaped, and continue to shape, the meaning of relatedness in India. In Rajasthan, it has been the dominance of the martial Rājpūt clans and their preoccupation with war and conquest, and in turn an association with death and blood or impure substances, that have shaped the social hierarchy and discourse of kinship (Unnithan-Kumar 1997). Similarly in Pahansu in Uttar Pradesh, it is the Gujar ownership of land affording them a ritual preeminence in gifting relationships that has determined the local social hierarchy (Raheja 1988). Raheja's work follows in the footsteps of such scholars as McKim Marriott (1976) and Arthur Maurice Hocart (see Quigley 1993) for whom it was not purity and pollution but the maintenance of subordination through transactions of bodily substance that was the key to caste hierarchy. The focus on substance has enabled a new perspective on relatedness to emerge, one that emphasizes processual (as opposed to structural or functional) understandings of kinship (Carsten 2004). Such lived understandings of kinship draw on—but can equally be at variance with—the religiously prescribed norms that govern kinship behavior and practices in India, as this chapter has sought to demonstrate.

The processes of modernity, economic progress, and democratic politics have further shaped people's experiences of both religion and kinship. In some instances, an increase in modern forms of capital, material, and technological consumption has seen a parallel increase in the intensity of ritual practices (a point Van Hollen [2003] notes, for example, with regard to the Tamil pregnancy ritual *cīmantam*). In other cases, the increasing level of material demands, such as those borne by women at the time of marriage, have led to a strengthening of patriarchal tendencies across different kinship systems (Kapadia 1995; Unnithan-Kumar 1997, 2004). Such modernizing processes have involved an essentializing of caste (where being Hindu is rigidly defined by the scriptures) ignoring the local, oral, popular "little traditions" that have been so instrumental in shaping the experience and daily practice of kinship in India. Given these macro-forces of change and the micro-processes through which such change is acted on by people in their daily lives, any general analysis of the relationship between Hinduism and kinship remains very complex indeed.

References Cited

Beck, E. F. Beck. 1974. *The Kin Nucleus in Tamil Folklore*. Ann Arbor: University of Michigan.

Bennett, Lynn. 1983. *Dangerous Wives and Scared Sisters: Social and Symbolic Roles of High Caste Women in Nepal.* New York: Colombia University Press.

Carstairs, G. Morris. 1967 [1957]. *The Twice-Born: A Study of a Community of High-Caste Hindus.* Bloomington: Indian University Press.

Carsten, Janet. 2004. *After Kinship*. Cambridge: Cambridge University Press.

Das, Veena. 1991. "Concepts of Space in Ritual." *In* T. N. Madan, ed., *Religion in India*, 156–73. Oxford: Oxford University Press.

Dumont, Louis. 1980 [1966]. *Homo Hierarchicus: The Caste System and Its Implications* (trans. Mark Sainsbury, Louis Dumont, and Basia Gulati). Chicago: University of Chicago Press.

Fuller, C. J. 1992. *The Camphor Flame: Popular Hinduism and Society in India.* Princeton: Princeton University Press.

Gold, Ann Grodzins. 1988. *Fruitful Journeys: The Ways of Rajasthani Pilgrims.* Berkeley: University of California Press.

Gold, Ann Grodzins. 1994. "Sexuality, Fertility and Erotic Imagination in Rajasthani Women's Songs." *In* Gloria Goodwin Raheja and Ann Grodzins Gold, eds, *Listen to the Heron's Words: Reimagining Gender and Kinship in North India*, 30–72. Berkeley: University of California Press.

Good, Anthony. 2000. "Power and Fertility: Divine Kinship in South India." *In* Monika Bock and Aparna Rao, eds, *Culture, Creation and Procreation: Concepts of Kinship in South Asian Practice*, 323–53. Oxford: Berghahn Books

Kakar, Sudhir. 1981. *The Inner World: A Psychoanalytic Study of Childhood and Society in India.* Delhi: Oxford University Press.

Kapadia, Karin. 1995. *Siva and Her Sisters: Gender, Caste and Class in Rural South India.* Boulder: Westview Press

Karve, Irawati K. 1968 [1953]. *Kinship Organisation in India.* New York: Asia Publishing House

Kothari, Komal. 1982. "The Shrine: An Expression of Social Needs." *In* Julia Elliott and David Elliott, eds, *Gods of the Byways: Wayside Shrines of Rajasthan*, 5–32. Oxford: Museum of Modern Art.

Kurtz, Stanley N. 1992. *All the Mothers are One: Hindu India and the Cultural Reshaping of Psychoanalysis.* New York: Columbia University Press.

Madan, T. N. 1987. *Non-Renunciation: Themes and Interpretations of Hindu Culture.* Delhi: Oxford University Press.

Marriott, McKim. 1976. "Hindu Transactions: Diversity without Dualism." *In* Bruce Kapferer, ed., *Transaction and Meaning: Directions in the Anthropology of Exchange and Symbolic Behavior*, 109–42. Philadelphia: Institute for the Study of Human Issues.

Parry, Jonathan P. 1979. *Caste and Kinship in Kangra.* London: Routledge & Kegan Paul.

Patel, Tulsi. 1994. *Fertility Behaviour: Population and Society in a Rajasthan Village.* Delhi: Oxford University Press

Quigley, Declan. 1993. *The Interpretation of Caste*. Oxford: Clarendon Press.
Raheja, Gloria Goodwin. 1988. *The Poison in the Gift: Ritual, Prestation and the Dominant Caste in a North Indian Village*. Chicago: Chicago University Press.
Raheja, Gloria Goodwin and Ann Grodzins Gold, eds. 1994. *Listen to the Heron's Words: Reimagining Gender and Kinship in North India*. Berkeley: University of California Press.
Searle-Chatterjee, Mary and Ursula Sharma. 1994. *Contextualising Caste: Post-Dumontian Perspectives*. Oxford: Blackwell.
Trawick, Margaret. 1990. *Notes on Love in a Tamil Family*. Berkeley: California University Press.
Unnithan-Kumar, Maya. 1997. *Identity, Gender and Poverty: New Perspectives on Caste and Tribe in Rajasthan*. Oxford: Berghahn Books.
Unnithan-Kumar, Maya, ed. 2004. *Reproductive Agency, Medicine and the State: Cultural Transformations in Childbearing*. Oxford: Berghahn Books.
Van Hollen, Cecilia. 2003. *Birth on the Threshold: Childbirth and Modernity in South India*. Berkeley: University of California Press.
Wadley, Susan Snow. 1975. *Shakti: Power in the Conceptual Structure of Karimpur Religion*. Chicago: University of Chicago, Department of Anthropology.

16

Law

Donald R. Davis, Jr.

Law as an Instrument of Hindu Ethical Formation
Law as Command in the Hindu Religious Imagination
Law as an Affirmation of the Ordinary in Hinduism
Hindu Law as a System

Law is not usually associated with Hinduism. When it is, one typically hears either of the supposedly inviolable law of action and consequence, *karma*, or of law as a part of duty, *dharma*. It is unfortunate that the idea or category of law has not been as widely used in Hindu Studies as it has in the study of Judaism, Christianity, or Islam, because the same sort of balance brought by law to the study of these religions is helpful in understanding Hinduism as well. By balance, I mean moving beyond a view of South Asian religion rooted in colonialism and Orientalism and that focuses exclusively on ultimate spirituality or mystical experience, to a view that also recognizes the day-to-day importance of religious rituals, institutions, and goals in the structuring of everyday human life. In this chapter, I concentrate on three ways in which law advances our understanding of Hinduism: (1) by thinking of the central textual category of *śāstra* as a legalistic tool of discipline that creates a moral self in Hindu thought; (2) by interpreting law as a metaphor for a significant part of the Hindu religious imagination that places the idea of rule or command at the heart of theology; and (3) by using law as a category that reminds us of the this-worldly side of Hinduism, a religious or theological discourse of ordinary things. I also consider (4) the Hindu law tradition and its nature as a legal system more strictly defined. In each area, I use a quotation from the well-known Hindu text, the *Laws of Manu* (see Olivelle 2005, all quotes are taken from this translation) as a point of departure for discussing these four aspects of law in Hinduism.[1]

Law as an Instrument of Hindu Ethical Formation

> When a Brahmin who keeps to his vows studies this treatise, he is never sullied by faults arising from mental, verbal, or physical activities; he

> purifies those alongside whom he eats, as also seven generations of his lineage before him and seven after him....This treatise is the best good-luck incantation; it expands the intellect; it procures everlasting fame; and it is the ultimate bliss.
>
> (*Laws of Manu* 1.104–6)

Among the many Indic textual forms, the scholarly treatise, or *śāstra*, is viewed as both the systematic distillation of ancient wisdom on a host of subjects ranging from ritual to architecture to dance and the foundation for contemporary reflections on old problems. In general, a *śāstra* is "a verbal codification of rules, whether of divine or human provenance, for the positive and negative regulation of particular cultural practices" (Pollock 1989: 18). Treatises, or at least the ideas or rules behind treatises, are often held in Indic thought to impel and compel practices that conform to particular standards (Olivelle 2005: 62–65). Even if we do not accept the historical or chronological claim that a dance text preceded and prompted the first dance, we may still assent to the claim that treatises can shape the formation of people's character. Not all scholarly treatises deal with religious topics, nor are all Hindu, but Hindu traditions have almost always expressed themselves to some extent through *śāstra*, and perhaps all make reference to the paradigmatic *śāstra* of Hinduism, the Veda (see Halbfass 1991; Smith 1989).

Of equal interest to the form of *śāstra* as a codification of rules are the tremendous benefits said to derive from the study of *śāstra*s. It is hardly an exaggeration to say that the recitation and internalization of scholarly treatises, especially those of a religious nature, are viewed as an essential, perhaps the essential, element in the training of the *ideal* person in Hindu thought. Becoming good and achieving religious liberation must be preceded by training in the treatises that serve as the source of morality and character. Following the passage from Manu, we see that studying Manu's treatise creates a barrier against sins, generates a kind of radiating substance that purifies all around, and leads to prized goals of human life (see Hacker 2006). The image presented is clearly idealized but, as with all religious articulations of human perfection or perfectibility, nevertheless describes a believed religious horizon, an asymptote of what is possible. Thus, progressive discipline achieved through a knowledge of the scholarly treatises creates a person who is invulnerable to error, who radiates purity, and who finds religious salvation both in this world and beyond.

The combined image of a code of rules and the ideal religious person links law to ethical formation in Hinduism. Law is characteristically expressed in the form of a codification of injunctions and prohibitions and often presupposes a normal or ideal legal subject.[2] Whatever the historical unlikelihoods may be, the Hindu theological view of *śāstras* as creating and sustaining the cultural practices they describe is best understood by comparison with legal treatises that similarly operate under the very useful fiction that they actually control behavior rather than simply acting as standards in court for violations of their provisions after the fact. To view *śāstra* as appealing to a governing legal fiction, a conventional and pragmatic truth that exists only for the purposes of law, helps us to understand the effect that law had on the functional role of texts in Hinduism. The inevitable gap between rule and practice was acknowledged, even as the sanctity of the rules or laws was preserved and transmitted.

Śāstra is the tool or instrument of the progressive discipline at the heart of moral education and character formation in Hindu thought, a key process of religious life signaled linguistically by the use of several related words also derived from the Sanskrit root *śās*.[3] The educator's toolbox thus consists primarily of a set of scholarly treatises that set forth the laws of a particular field of study. Mastery of the laws yields not only a personal protection, a kind of religious forcefield, against sins and misdeeds but produces the capacity to transform people and things and even to declare new laws for new situations. Contemporary references to *śāstras* maintain both their unassailable authority and their open-endedness (Prasad 2006). More importantly, the symbolic power of *śāstra* as a category enables a tremendous practical openness in which even nonstandard or unorthodox ideas and practices are labeled and accepted as "*śāstra*." It would be a mistake to equate *śāstras* as legalistic treatises with modern acts of legislation or scholarly works on law, but the category of law, imperfect as it is, reveals the importance of both actual and imagined codifications of rules in Hindu ethical formation as it appeals to the foundational legal fiction that law in fact governs human behavior.

Law as Command in the Hindu Religious Imagination

> One should understand that acts prescribed by the Veda are always a more effective means of securing the highest good both here and in the hereafter....Acts prescribed by the Veda are of two kinds: advancing, which procures the enhancement of happiness; and arresting, which procures the supreme good....By engaging in advancing acts, a man attains equality with the gods; by engaging in arresting acts, on the other hand, he transcends the five elements.
>
> (*Laws of Manu* 12.86, 88, 90)

The formal centrality of rules in both *śāstra* and law is difficult to deny. An early text of Hindu orthodoxy defines the totality of duties incumbent on human beings, *dharma*, as a realm characterized by injunctions or commands, that is, a realm of rules or laws.[4] This simple statement actually implies something remarkable and often forgotten in Hindu Studies: the presence, even centrality, of a train of religious thought in Hinduism that views command or injunction (*vidhi*) as the centerpiece of human existence. In this view, commands create debts or obligations (*ṛṇa*) that are methodically discharged over the course of a person's life (Malamoud 1996: 92–108). Adherence to these commands constitutes *dharma*, and *dharma* produces both worldly and transcendent benefits.

In spite of modern efforts to redefine and expand it, *dharma* is still associated with orthodoxy in Hinduism, especially a Brāhmaṇized, elite, exclusive, and caste-ridden Hinduism. From a theological perspective, there is a certain truth in this characterization. But the theology of *dharma* also incorporates the ritual side of Hinduism more explicitly than does any other major Hindu theology by imposing scriptural commands that create a law that is equally a model of, fulfillment of, and effect of *dharma* (Hacker 2006). "Law" (*dharma*) is both the cause and the effect of "ritual" (*karma*). The famous division of religious paths in the *Bhagavad Gītā* into *karma-yoga*, *jñāna-yoga*, and *bhakti-yoga*—ritual, knowledge, and devotion, respectively—suggests that ordinary householder ritual—what Manu means by "advancing acts" (*pravṛttaṃ karma*) above—has somehow been superceded in favor of knowledge pursued through renunciation, an "arresting act" (*nivṛttaṃ karma*), or devotion, which combines both advancing and arresting elements. The fact is, however, that all these acts are part of "ritual" (i.e., they are called *karma*, the idea that human actions generally can be seen as a form of ritual and, like ritual, have effects or consequences on their performer).

Key to the Hindu conception of ritual is the idea that humans are impelled or commanded to perform rites of various kinds. The theological centrality of ritual, *karma* in its narrow sense, goes back to the Vedic tradition and persists until today, even though our knowledge of the number and types of Hindu rituals practiced has gone well beyond just Vedic rites. One influential Hindu tradition, the Pūrva-Mīmāṃsā, proclaims that the primary constituents of Hindu scriptures, especially the Vedas, are the commands and prohibitions, one could say the laws, they contain. Mīmāṃsā also postulates that the words of the Veda are eternal, that those words have no human or divine author, and that the commands of the Veda automatically compel people to follow them. Vedic commands are thought to have an inherent word-force (*śābdībhāvanā*) that parallels the force of a human authority but on a cosmic scale.[5]

Even outside the orthodox tradition of Hinduism, rituals retain a central place. Renunciation, for instance, does not mean rejection of all ritual but rather ceasing to perform householder rituals in favor of ascetic rites (Olivelle 1995). Likewise, Bhakti and Tantra traditions are both replete with ritual but with rites that sometimes differ from the orthodox. In the process, originally unorthodox rituals have sometimes been accepted into mainstream Hindu communities. Thus, what gets maintained in Hinduism is the idea of ritual itself as a necessary obligation of religious life incumbent on persons because of a cosmic or, later, a divine command. The passage from Manu in this section focuses on *karma*s prescribed by the Veda and leading to two different religious ends. Common to both is *karma*, acts, and all *karma*s are theologically, if not historically, enjoined by the Veda. The early Hindu idea that religious life is premised on cosmic commands is later overlaid with ideas about gnosis, mystic union, and divine grace. In each overlay, however, commands and the actions commanded remain a significant part of the articulation of newer forms or theologies of Hinduism.

The importance of commands or injunctions is further enhanced if connected to the category of law because commands are mere words if not backed by an authority or a sanction (or both). The most common modern notion of law, John Austin's "command of the sovereign," parallels this description precisely. Even if we do not accept this modern definition of law as correct or helpful in every case, we nevertheless learn something about Hindu conceptualizations of where religion comes from and why one should pursue it, by viewing it in legal terms. Religion, in this particular Hindu theological tradition, originates from a primordial set of commands and related explanations known as the Veda. The authority of the Veda derives from the Pūrva-Mīmāṃsā view of language as eternal, without any beginning. According to this belief, words and their meanings exist outside of time and, therefore, authorize themselves as expressions of universal truths. Humans obey the Vedic commands both because the Veda promises benefits in this world and beyond and because failure to obey leads to chaos, misery, and discord.

Imagining religious life in these terms takes law as a metaphor for the structure of human existence by placing authoritative commands at the center of a theology that builds itself around the correct adherence to and elaboration of those injunctions. This legal metaphor continues in later extensions of Hindu thought both symbolically, in the sense that the Veda retains its status as the foundation of all knowledge, even if the actual texts that fall into that category do not, and practically, in the sense that adherence to *dharma*, the model for and act of good *karma*, constantly serves as a baseline for theological, ritual, mythological, and sociological speculation and practice in Hinduism.

What is essential in this form of Hinduism is not grace, knowledge, devotion, ecstasy, union, or perfect solitude. It is law. It is perfect and true commands that exist in and give structure to the very fabric of the cosmos. To deviate from these commands is to deny reality and the inherent burden that such commands place on all beings. Obviously, the theological and practical implications of such a view need to be, and have been, worked out in great detail, but the basic point is best seen at a macro level, namely, that the important Vedic tradition of Hinduism, by which I mean not just the Vedas themselves but the whole tradition that claims a direct link to them, rests on an imagination of religious life that is best described in terms of law with its constituent connotations of command, act, order, sanction, and authority.

Law as an Affirmation of the Ordinary in Hinduism

> Student, householder, forest hermit, and ascetic; these four distinct orders have their origin in the householder....Among all of them, however, according to the dictates of vedic scripture, the householder is said to be best, for he supports the other three.
>
> (*Laws of Manu* 6.87, 89)

The idea that injunction or command is the wellspring of religious life is found most prominently in the realm of the family and the household. The relevance of law to Hinduism is clearest in texts and practices of the householder, the ideal family man. To fully appreciate the religiousness of the householder life in Hinduism, one must reject commonplace notions of what counts as transcendence. Religion need not reject this world to hold fast to an idea of transcendence. In householder Hinduism, ordinary life is sacred. In fact, it is the most sacred duty of the ideal person. Adherence to the injunctions of *dharma* is thought to produce an invisible, transcendent effect (*apūrva*) that creates a reward or benefit to the performer. Once again, the ritual is at the center and is often superior in its power to gods or *guru*s. Manu bases his praise of the householder life as the best on the fact that householders support and maintain others. The idea expressed here in the restricted context of the standard four orders of life (*āśrama*) also applies in a broader sense to Hinduism.

Religion in South Asia, as everywhere, is generally first learned in the home, and the religious practices of a family are often determining influences on the trajectory of an individual's religious life. Yet, it is possible to read widely about Hinduism and hear next to nothing about either the theory or the reality of householder religion. The theory of householder religion is found in Hindu texts called Dharmaśāstra, the treatises on religious and legal duty, such as the *Laws of Manu*. Descriptions of the reality of householder religion may be found in the many ethnographies of Hindu communities, in folklore, in literature, and, to a lesser extent, in other evidence from earlier periods of Indian history. The gap between theory and practice is wide, but that expectable gap neither vitiates the theory nor condemns the practice. Instead, we must grant that the ideal person imagined in Hindu texts on *dharma* may never have existed perfectly in reality but that the ideal remained important nevertheless as a symbol of Hindu aspirations. The ideal dhārmic householder has to some extent lost its hold on the contemporary Hindu religious imagination, especially due to the influence of colonialism and the elite articulations of Hinduism by prominent modern Hindus. The result has been the promulgation of an idea of Hinduism that is universal, tolerant, and inclusive but one that is also emptied of much of its earlier theological rigor.

A search for law in the Hindu tradition leads first to this householder religion, most conveniently summarized in the texts on *dharma*, and cuts through the contemporary fascinations with Vedānta, Yoga, Tantra, and world renunciation. As interesting and important as these traditions are, they all make reference to and derive their initial formulations from the householder tradition.[6] The point here is simply an extension of normal patterns of identity formation. A person's initial identity is usually closely associated with his or her family and its locality. It is on this foundation that more unique, individualized, and "higher" pursuits and interests forge a person's distinctive identity. Extrapolating from a person to a tradition, we see that each of the subtraditions for which Hinduism is justly famous is predicated on a foundation in the household, more specifically on the world-ordering *dharma*s of ordinary life—sacramentary rites of birth, marriage, and death; worship of ancestors and family deities; purifications of the body; and so forth. The observance of these *dharma*s progressively "refines" (*saṃskāra*) persons through a constant reconfiguration and renegotiation of the substances, both physical and spiritual, that form them as human beings (Marriott 1976). From this ordinary life, or after the debts of this ordinary life are paid, we find the numerous Hindu speculations about the union of personal and cosmic self, the realization of perfect solitude, the awakening of the Kuṇḍalinī, or the attainment of pure consciousness.

The big idea of the householder tradition in Hinduism, by contrast, is the positive valuation it places on ordinary human life. Other Hindu traditions view it as a way-station, a holding pattern, something to be experienced on the way to ultimate transcendence. The householder tradition itself, however, promotes its own view of the ultimate. Again, it is law. It is in law, in *dharma*, that one discovers what is most beneficial (*śreyas*). The obligations created by law motivate the acts, especially the ritual acts, that characterize daily Hindu life. Law and religion are connected to each other, despite efforts to separate them in modern governments. In fact, law may be seen as a form or type of religion that makes the mundane world sacred and also makes human beings cosmically creative, active participants in the religious structuring of the universe. To view law as a mere instrument of social control misses completely the spiritual value of the law as an institution that enables worldly life to function at all. Saying something is "against the law" means much more than that some police officer might arrest you for it; it means also that it is wrong, destructive, bad for you and for others.

Hindu Law as a System

> He who knows the Law should examine the Laws of castes, regions, guilds, and families, and only then settle the Law specific to each.... When he is conducting a judicial proceeding, he should pay close attention to the truth, the object of the suit, himself, the witnesses, the place, the time, and the appearance.
>
> (*Laws of Manu* 8.41, 45)

The household is but one of several institutional locations of a notion of law in Hinduism. In this final section, I consider the more specific tradition known as Hindu law and describe how best to understand it in comparison with other legal systems in the more familiar sense of law as rules and institutions that enforce legal standards.

Classical Hindu law was a variegated grouping of local legal systems that had different rules and procedures of law but that were united by a common jurisprudence or legal theory represented by Dharmaśāstra. In premodern India, the practical legal systems of any two given Hindu communities may have operated quite differently, but they were both likely to respect the "spirit" of Dharmaśāstra and incorporate it into their legal rules, processes, and institutions. The degree of correspondence between Dharmaśāstra and practical law made a system more or less Hindu.

One notable feature of classical Hindu law was its weak connection to state and government. Hindu kings did not usually make legislative pronouncements, and the lawmaking authorities were instead corporate groups of various kinds (Lingat 1973). Manu lists "castes, regions, guilds, and families" as the societal levels in which practical law was formed. Other texts expanded the list to include such groups as monastic orders, military groups, merchant cooperatives, pastoralists, and farmers. The most fertile source of substantive law in the premodern period were these sociologically intermediate groups, neither exclusively local nor transregional, neither devoid of political power nor dominant politically (Davis 2005). Individuals probably belonged to several such groups at the same time, and the laws of each group were conveyed both formally and informally. Violations of the law were tried within such groups unless the conflict necessitated either the objectivity or the authority of an outside power, especially a political ruler of some sort.

To assess the "spirit" of Dharmaśāstra that united Hindu legal systems to some extent, we may look at Manu's highly realistic description of a judicial proceeding. Essentially, Manu advocates that a judge consider multiple factors in making a legal decision, starting with the true facts of the case but including the motivations of the litigants and the circumstances of the incident. Though Dharmaśāstra texts describe the procedures of courts in great detail and give numerous substantive rules of law, the "spirit" of the system promotes realism and truth over formalism and a mechanical application of the rules (Davis 2006). In practice, then, Dharmaśāstra functioned more as a source of training or education about the law and how to judge legal issues than as a direct source of law.

The advent of colonialism in India brought significant changes to the Hindu law tradition because the British mistakenly accepted Dharmaśāstra as a code of law to be applied to all Hindus throughout India in the same way (Lariviere 1989). Failing to appreciate the true nature of the texts and the preexisting law, the British used their own translations of Dharmaśāstra to judge the cases brought to their courts by Hindus. Initially, they employed court *paṇḍita*s, Hindu men learned in Dharmaśāstra, to assist British judges in the determination of the "Hindu law" on a given point. However, the system was cumbersome, and judges frequently complained about their inability to fully understand Hindu legal logic, not least because almost none of them knew Sanskrit, and about what they perceived to be a lack of fixity in Hindu law. The British also introduced to India the case-law system whereby the decisions of early British courts were increasingly used as more authoritative guides to judging present cases than were the "original" sources of Hindu law. Over time, particularly by 1864, the accumulated body of case-law and additional British legislations replaced Dharmaśāstra and the court *paṇḍita*s as the practical reference points for Anglo-Hindu law.

Even in independent India, a basically British system of Hindu law has been preserved in that modern Hindu law is now a personal law system, codified in a series of parliamentary acts in the 1950s known as the Hindu Code Bills, that covers such legal matters as marriage, divorce, inheritance, adoption, and maintenance (see Williams 2006). In other words, the comprehensiveness of classical Hindu law has been reduced to a subsystem under the Constitution of India and deals only with personal, meaning family-related, legal issues. A parallel personal law system exists for Islamic law, as well for Christians and Parsis, in modern India. It is worth noting that Hindus did not resist these major changes in the legal system of India and that a common legal system, though as much British as Indian in origin, is one of the unifying factors of modern India (Galanter 1989).

The connection of law and Hinduism is explicit and obvious in the case of modern Hindu law, restricted as it is, but there are other significant areas of Hindu life that have been changed by modern legislative and judicial actions. Though Articles 25 to 28 of the Constitution of India guarantee a "right to freedom of religion," the precise interpretation of the constitutional guarantee has, as one would expect, been controversial and the subject of several important cases. "Interventionist" policies and judicial decisions have, for example, created a system of reservations (see Galanter 1984) in education and government for lower castes, almost always legally Hindus, and have forced Hindu temples to allow lower castes to enter and worship, even as caste itself, and particularly Untouchability, was constitutionally abolished by Articles 15 and 17. Hindu temples also became subject to a series of laws that regulated, or reformed, their governance and financial structures by creating regulatory bureaucracies and requiring that temples have boards of management or trustees (Mansfield 2001). Other questions about secularism, conversion, and gender as they pertain to Hinduism are still hotly debated in legislative and judicial contexts. Thus, the explicit connections of law in contemporary India and Hinduism extend beyond the personal law system known as modern Hindu law.

By way of conclusion, I want to explore the relationship between the broad sense of law used earlier and the narrow sense of law used to describe Hindu law and law in modern India. In general, the two are manifestations of the same idea in different contexts or at different scales. Viewed at the level of a particular dispute in a definite locality, an understanding of law and Hinduism requires the same kind of historical contextualization necessary for understanding any particular event. The instrumental idea of law, of law as social control, presupposes a need for this particularity. Viewed at the level of tradition and reflection, by contrast, law and Hinduism can be seen as linked in many other ways. The fact that the guiding quotes of this chapter are all from the same two-thousand-year-old text indicates the lack of distinction between a view of law as a practically applicable set of rules and institutions and a view that links law to the textual genre of *śāstra*, the theology of commands, or an affirmation of the religion of ordinary life. Law in Hinduism is much more than just colonial and modern Hindu law, and restricting the category to the more familiar and narrow idea of law, rather than seeing its interplay with a broader range of religious life, perpetuates an overly mystical, spiritual, and mythological view of Hinduism and obscures the important realm of householder religion. Making use of law as category for studying Hinduism brings a fresh perspective to our understandings of Hindu life and aspirations that ironically is among the oldest in Hinduism itself.

Notes

1 I thank Charles Hallisey and two anonymous reviewers of this essay for their very helpful comments and suggestions.

2 The ideal legal subject is rarely presented explicitly in the law but can be seen by contrast with the way law treats "nonnormal" or "less than ideal" persons. Think, for example, of slaves in early American law or of illegal immigrants, gay people, or even women.

3 Consider the following common forms: *śāstrin*, teacher; *śiṣṭa*, expert; *śiṣya*, student; *śāsana*, instruction. Each of these derives from a grammatical modification of the basic root *śās*, to discipline or instruct.

4 The *Pūrva-Mīmāṃsā-Sūtra*s of Jaimini 1.1.2 state: *codanālakṣaṇo 'rtho dharmaḥ*, "*dharma* (duty, good action) is an *artha* (purpose, thing, referent) whose *lakṣaṇa* (definition, mark, characteristic) is *codanā* (injunction, command)." Rendering this dense aphorism precisely in English is difficult without considerable explanation. I have merely given a paraphrase in the main text. For a thoughtful explanation of Pūrva-Mīmāṃsā and its connections with law and religion, see Clooney (1990).

5 Mīmāṃsā philosophy discusses the intrinsic effect of Vedic commands and the optative grammatical ending to force people to act. In the mundane world, hearing the command form in a language signals to a listener that he or she should act and that action will in fact occur depending on the authority of the person who gave the command. In the cosmic frame, the eternal commands of the Veda are held to be self-authorizing and, therefore, to prompt action automatically.

6 The householder tradition is sometimes called Brāhmaṇism, the religion of Brāhmaṇas, and this label has merit from the textual perspective but loses its purchase in practice. I do not limit my claim here to Brāhmaṇical religion but include the myriad varieties of householder religion in Hindu communities. The only systematic theory or theology of the householder, however, does come from this Brāhmaṇical tradition, and we must acknowledge the limitations of making large claims that it represents all householders.

References Cited

Clooney, Francis X. 1990. *Thinking Ritually: Rediscovering the Pūrvamīmāṃsā of Jaimini*. Vienna: De Nobili Research Library.

Davis, Jr. Donald R. 2005. "Intermediate Realms of Law: Corporate Groups and Rulers in Medieval India." *Journal of the Economic and Social History of the Orient* 48, 1: 92–117.

Davis, Jr. Donald R. 2006. "A Realist View of Hindu Law." *Ratio Juris: An International Journal of Jurisprudence and Philosophy of Law* 19, 3: 287–313.

Galanter, Marc. 1984. *Competing Equalities: Law and the Backward Classes in India*. Berkeley: University of California Press.

Galanter, Marc. 1989. *Law and Society in Modern India*. Delhi: Oxford University Press.

Hacker, Paul. 2006 [1965]. "Dharma in Hinduism." *Journal of Indian Philosophy* 34, 5: 475–96.

Halbfass, Wilhelm. 1991. *Tradition and Reflection: Explorations in Indian Thought*. Albany: State University of New York Press.

Lariviere, Richard W. 1989. "Justice and Paṇḍitas: Some Ironies in Contemporary Readings of the Hindu Legal Past." *Journal of Asian Studies* 48, 4: 757–69.

Lingat, Robert. 1973 [1967]. *The Classical Law of India* (trans. J. Duncan M. Derrett). Berkeley: University of California Press.

Malamoud, Charles. 1996 [1989]. *Cooking the World: Ritual and Thought in Ancient India* (trans. David White). Delhi: Oxford University Press.

Mansfield, John. 2001. "Religious and Charitable Endowments and a Uniform Civil Code." *In* Gerald James Larson, ed., *Religion and Personal Law in Secular India: A Call to Judgment*, 69–103. Bloomington: University of Indiana Press.

Marriott, McKim. 1976. "Hindu Transactions: Diversity without Dualism." *In* Bruce Kapferer, ed., *Transaction and Meaning: Directions in the Anthropology of Exchange and Symbolic Behavior*, 109–42. Philadelphia: Institute for the Study of Human Issues.

Olivelle, Patrick, ed. and trans. 1995. *Rules and Regulations of Brahmanical Asceticism: Yatidharmasamuccaya of Yādava Prakāśa*. Albany: State University of New York Press.

Olivelle, Patrick, ed. and trans. 2005. *Manu's Code of Law: A Critical Edition and Translation of the Mānava-Dharmaśāstra*. New York: Oxford University Press.

Pollock, Sheldon. 1989. "The Idea of Śāstra in Traditional India." *In* A. L. Dallapiccola, ed., *Shastric Traditions in Indian Arts*, 17–26. Wiesbaden: Steiner.

Prasad, Leela. 2006. "Text, Tradition and Imagination: Evoking the Normative in Everyday Hindu Life." *Numen* 53, 1: 1–47.

Smith, Brian K. 1989. *Reflections on Resemblance, Ritual, and Religion*. New York: Oxford University Press.

Williams, Rina Verma. 2006. *Postcolonial Politics and Personal Laws: Colonial Legal Legacies and the Indian State*. New York: Oxford University Press.

17

Memory

Christian Lee Novetzke

Modern Memory Theory
Memory Studies and Hinduism

The social and cultural study of memory, like human memory itself, is vast and amorphous. Since the early twentieth century, memory has appeared as a key concept used by anthropologists, sociologists, literary critics, folklorists, and religionists, and in all cases one finds a heterogeneity of opinion and use. Particularly since the 1980s, memory has enjoyed a bonanza of appearances in theoretical and critical scholarship, most notably as part of the postmodern critique of modern meta-theories, especially of nineteenth-century trends in professional historiography tied to the nation-state and in scientific reasoning about adjudicating past events. Understandably, historians have an ambivalent relationship to the notion of memory, many seeing it more as an enemy at the gates than a guest at the table. Scholars across disciplines outfitted their studies of memory with different adjectival designations that added to the complex character of the general field of memory research. Thus we have "collective memory" (Halbwachs 1992); "cultural memory" (Assmann 2006; Sturkin 1997); "social memory" (for Warburg 1927 see Ramply 2000; Fentress and Wickham 1992; Rampley 2000); "community memory" (Bellah et al 1985); and "popular memory" (Johnson et al 1982) in addition to "mimetic memory," "material memory," "connective memory," and "communicative memory" (Assmann 2006), all terms suggesting that memory is essentially a social phenomenon. The social situation of memory follows the seminal work of the Durkheimian sociologist, Maurice Halbwachs, who first proposed that memory is always a social and collective endeavor. Halbwachs made this proposal in a way that set his understanding of memory against the two views: one, of Sigmund Freud and others, that memory is an individual, psychological affair, and two, against the idea of memory as an "art" to buttress rhetoric or a "science of mnemonics" to aid education.[1] Contained in this social critique of memory is the inherent assumption that in modernity, memory comes into sometimes contentious relationship with other social forms, especially coercive and hegemonic ones, such as the nation-state and its official memories. This particular deployment of memory describes the work that surrounds "counter-memory" (Foucault 1977; Davis and Starn 1989) and the opposition between memory and history (Collingwood 1994; de Certeau 1988; Le Goff 1992; Nora 1989).

Despite the broad diffusion of memory studies across disciplines, the study of Hinduism fell largely outside the scope of these debates. In part this is because memory studies have tended to focus on Western religious traditions (Judaism and Christianity) and engaged specifically modern, Western historiographic issues, such as the impact of the Holocaust in Europe on teleologies of Western social progress. Yet the study of memory has in other ways always been a part of the study of Hinduism. From early understandings of religious genres of literature to contemporary ethnographies of how small communities recall the past, memory remains important to the study of Hindu life worlds and to the practice of Hinduism. Scholars have thus approached memory in several forms: as mnemonic devices used in the oral preservation of texts, particularly the Vedas; as a literary genre of sacred composition (*smṛti*) that is "derived" rather than directly revealed (*śruti*); as a part of a system of traditional education; and as a motif in secular and religious literature (as in Kālidāsa's *Śakuntalā* or in the memories of the beloved in *viraha bhakti*).

These sites for the investigation of memory in Hindu studies do not usually draw on Western social and cultural theory about memory, but the two nonetheless might profitably be brought together. For example, in arguments about the presence of historiography among Indians in precolonial India, the positive invocation of a "historical sense" within this vast period is reminiscent of the language of memory in other contexts, as we will observe (Sharma 2003; Thapar 1990). Thus, the question of what constitutes "history" in premodern South Asia is similar to the set of questions that ask about differences between memory and history as modes of recollection. Similarly, memory studies are deeply invested in considering the way in which culture preserves recollections of the past through nonliterate means. Many of the issues surrounding memory in the study of Hinduism also involve questions of orality and literacy, such as the traditional transmission of the Vedas or, in the contemporary period, the palpable memories of the Partition, which are also memories of religious communal violence. In this vein, we also note how Western memory studies often undertake the subject of trauma and suffering—with the Holocaust as the quintessential "limit event" in Western historical memory—and how similarities with the ways in which South Asians remember the Partition and independence in 1947 now offer a meeting place for these two discursive worlds, of Western memory theory and South Asian practices of memory.

Given the immense field of memory and the prodigious scope of memory within Hinduism, I restrict this chapter to those salient aspects of the two fields of study that bear a particular relationship to how memory as a critical concept is—or might be—used in the study of Hinduism. These particularly pertinent areas include (1) understanding the link drawn between memory and religion, (2) observing the relationship established between memory and suffering or trauma, (3) uncovering the connection that scholars make between memory and orality, and (4) questioning the distinction between memory and history. In the first half of the chapter, I pinpoint theories and thinkers operating within one or more of these four areas in Western critical thought. In the second portion of the chapter, I note how memory has been studied in Hinduism in particular, correlating these studies with the four key rubrics above and suggesting avenues of theoretical and practical interest. I trace what I consider the most relevant and profitable aspects of memory studies in relation to the study of Hinduism, and I can only encourage the interested reader to pursue more deeply the few iceberg tips that rise above water in this chapter.

Modern Memory Theory

Memory in Western theory is almost always construed as social, collective, and related to "identity" formations of many sorts. Memories are regularly considered localized and tied to specific places, particularly situated within the physical spaces of civic and public culture. Memory and history are often dialectically discussed, wherein memory has served the critiques of history mounted by cultural anthropologists and contained within the various forms of historical anthropology (or ethnohistory). History, conversely, tends to receive its power from the ubiquitous locales of the state and is often the domain of the archive, the repository of historical memory. Many scholars who engage in this large-scale debate about modernity's hegemonic forms come to see memory as inherently tied to modern ideas, such as the nation (Anderson 1991; Duara 1995; Hobsbawm and Ranger 1983), and the modern configuration of religion (Castelli 2004; de Certeau 1988; Herview-Leger 2000; Nora 1989); still other scholars see memory mediate between the nation and religion (Hayes 1960; Smith 1986). Given the expansive range of memory as a field of study, one finds excellent historical investigations of memory as a practice and an idea (Carruthers 1990; Coleman 1992; Hutton 1993; Matsuda 1996; Nora 1984-93; Terdiman 1993). Such "histories of memory" go a long way to explain what differentiates memory from history and for what phenomena memory remains a sign.

Modern memory studies began with Maurice Halbwachs (1877–1945) and hence are grounded in both sociology and the political climate of Europe in the years between the World Wars, in which memory and memorials to the death, suffering, victories, and defeats of the first war perhaps summoned the subject of memory more fully into the field of sociology. Halbwachs argued that memory is a collective endeavor in which "[social] frameworks are...the instruments used by the collective memory to reconstruct an image of the past which is in accord, in each epoch, with the predominant thoughts of the society" (1992: 40). In other words, almost all memories depend on a social environment to exist, an idea contravening the person-centered theories of memory espoused by Freud. As a student of Durkheim, one also sees in Halbwachs a preoccupation with religion.[2] He wrote about Catholicism, Christianity, Judaism, Buddhism, and Greek religion, granting "religious collective memory" a rubric all its own alongside "social classes," family, and locations. He chose as his first subject for the application of his ideas about collective memory the early Christian religion and the ways in which memory, and especially what he called its "localization," provided crucial social coherence. Halbwachs argued that early pilgrims and other Christian travelers set in collective memory the locales of the Gospels, wedding memory and place in a shared remembrance of the sacred geography attached to the life of Jesus.[3] Halbwachs does not argue that religion is the exclusive domain of memory, nor that memory is the only mode of recalling the past available to religion (indeed, he makes the point that formalized rational adjudication of events and ideas has always been part of Christian thought), but his choice of subjects presages the deep connections between memory and religion that would be a standard feature in the theoretical work of the 1980s and later.

While sociologists, particularly in the genealogy of Durkheim, continued their work on the social character of memory, historians became increasingly interested in memory as a subset of inquiry within the larger context of the challenges of postmodernism and the linguistic turn of the 1980s. Pierre Nora is emblematic of this renegotiation of Halbwachs' legacy between historiography and the challenge to metanarratives.[4] As such, Nora investigates one of the greatest of the modern metanarratives, the nation, through an expansive study of what he called "sites of memory" (*lieux de mémoire*) throughout France, which he defined as "any significant entity, whether material or nonmaterial in nature, which by dint of human will or the work of time has become a symbolic element of the memorial heritage of any community" (1996: xvii). Nora had in mind obvious sites, such as memorials, archives, and museums, but also ritual moments of commemoration, linguistic formulae of recollection (mottos, for example, and clichés), and visual cultural artifacts, such as books, logos, motifs, and so on. Even archives, the exemplary source of history, are sites of memory for Nora because of their symbolic power as the inchoate repository of historical memory.

In theorizing his ideas about *lieux de mémoire*, Nora observes a deep fissure between historical and memorial recollection characterized by religious sentiment: "History, because it is an intellectual and secular production, calls for analysis and criticism. Memory installs remembrance within the sacred; history, always prosaic, releases it again" (1989: 9). Nora (1989: 13–14) seems to brood over the contradictions of a society that obsessively, even "religiously," documents itself through archives and technologies of data storage, yet transforms this information into the historiography that lays waste to practices of memory. Nora's (1989: 7) sympathies for "traditional memory" are apparent and contain a kind of postmodern nostalgia for the thought worlds of the premodern. He refers to "peasant culture" as "that quintessential repository of collective memory" and clearly understands this cultural field—itself preserved as a feature of public memory and consumption—to be deeply marked by religious sentiment woven through collective memory. This dichotomy of the modern and its antithesis, set along a dialectic between history as modern and memory as nonmodern, is discussed below.

Religion is most explicitly present in discussions about trauma and in particular about the nightmare of the Holocaust and its challenge to modern historiographic teleologies of humanistic, democratic advancement. This has also occasioned special attention to Judaism as an exemplar of "liturgical memory," the way in which religious traditions bring the past into the present through ritual and recital, reenactment through invocation, often as a means of healing social suffering (Caruth 1991, 1996; Friedlander 1993; LaCapra 1998; Spiegel 2002; Yerushalmi 1982). The unification of the memory of the Holocaust and religious ritual serves the purpose of displaying the effect of unimaginable trauma on ways of recalling the past. In this case, Judaism's liturgical practices of memory are extrapolated to the collective process of maintaining memories of trauma that modern historiography, because it must seek explanatory adjudication as its ultimate mandate, must fail to represent. In the shadow of the Holocaust, history is inadequate as a tool of comprehension, and what stands as the most reliable, enduring mode of fixing the truth of this event in consciousness is human testimony, human memory. This challenge to history is also, therefore, a challenge to the nation-state, to its memory, and to its teleologies of advancement. A good deal of memory study involves, in one way or another, the nation, and here it is both aligned with historiography more generally (of which the preeminent subject is the nation-state) and in contention with professional history.

Implicit in this critique is the preserved nonmodern character of religions —Western or non-Western—and hence both their intimate connection to memory and their distrust or disavowal of history as a way of recalling the past. One aspect of this disavowal is the explicit connection made between orality and memory (Assmann 2006; Butler 1989; Connerton 1989; Fentress and Wickham 1992; *History and Anthropology* 1986, 2.2).[5] In these studies, memory tends to be aligned with orality and history with literacy.[6] Yet because these studies are also sympathetic to, or within, the larger postmodern critic of meta-theories, we often find the oral and mnemonic valorized as essential to understanding the meaning of literate phenomena—an argument that echoes Jacques Derrida's (1998) expansion of the idea that all verbal communication, whether written or oral, depends on the dynamics of orality or rather the uncertainties of language use generally. Scholars in this mode argue that writing, and historiography, distance the past from the present, whereas memory, and orality, make the present and the past coexist. Memory is, furthermore, the universal and public mode of recollection, whereas history is restricted to highly literate societies and is the preserve of the elite. Though such reasoning may drastically overemphasize the nonliterate mode of memory—think, for example, of the literate memoir or the engraving on statues, memorials, or other edifices of memory—their goal is often less a matter of documenting traces of memory than theorizing critiques of history and the supremacy of literacy.[7] Yet the central idea that history requires literacy whereas memory does not is both reasonable and self-evident to most historians whose craft of historiography, like an ethnography to an anthropologist, is both the means and the ultimate end of their endeavors.

Thus, the dialectic of memory and history, as it appears in the three categories above, remains the most basic point of contention in Western memory theory. Though late eighteenth- and nineteenth-century philosophers of history did not systematically use the term "memory" in an oppositional or conditional way with regard to "history," we can see as early as Georg W. F. Hegel the silhouette of this later debate. In *The Philosophy of History*, Hegel is broadly concerned with the alignment of the progress of reason and of "Spirit" in the course of human self-awareness and in those areas of the world (i.e., *most* areas of the world in Hegel's opinion, and especially India) that have not progressed; though they possess a past and a recollection of that past, their intelligence is only "half-awakened," preserved in "legends, Ballad-stories, Traditions" all of which "must be excluded from...history" (1944: 2). As for India in Hegel's thought, he finds that "Hindoos...are incapable of writing History....All that happens is dissipated in their minds into confused dreams....What we call historical truth and veracity—intelligent, thoughtful comprehension of events, and fidelity in representing them—nothing of this sort can be looked for among the Hindoos" (1944: 162). One can read throughout Hegel's work the word "dream" as a synonym for "memory" used to characterize the non-Western, nonmodern practices of recollection (see, for example, 1944: 139, 140, 141, 148, 155, 162, 166, 167).

By the time we arrive at the work of such figures as Benedetto Croce, Wilhelm Dilthey, and R. G. Collingwood in the first half of the twentieth century, memory is clearly understood to be history's opposite in the field of recollection (see, for example, Collingwood 1994: 56, 221–25, 293–94). As Collingwood said in his lectures on the philosophy of history in 1926, "History and memory are wholly different things.…Memory [is] *subjective* [and] *immediate*.…History on the other hand is *objective* [and] *mediate*," by which he meant that memory stands regardless of proof or rationale, whereas history must always rest on some ground of evidence, proof, and rationality (1994: 365–67; emphasis in original). The shape of this dialectic would largely remain intact, but the key characters would switch positions in the postmodern mode, wherein subjectivity and reflexivity would be lauded as method and wherein memory would become the protagonist of a story that opposed the meta-theories of "objective, mediate" history.

In the emergent study of memory, challenges to history were less common. Halbwachs does not directly oppose memory and history, and his sociological concerns tend more toward social reasons for organizing memory in particular contexts, a kind of sociological historicism. Aby Warburg's work on art, archetypes, and social memory was well within the nascent field of cultural history in the first quarter of the twentieth century. These two streams—of an uncomplicated relationship between memory and history in the philosophy of history and an emerging field of memory studies both from sociology and within the history of art and culture—did not merge until the "linguistic turn" of the 1980s, when together they came to embody a critique of modern historiography and modernity itself. This critique takes the forms we have already discussed, of a challenge to modernity on several grounds: (1) the valorization of the individual through an appraisal of memory as a person-centered psychological effect; (2) the teleology of superior development, humanistic principles, and democratic freedoms, countermanded by the horrors of the Holocaust in Europe; (3) the defeat of religious life worlds by rational modern systems (the state, science, and so on); (4) the supremacy of literacy, and hence of history, as a technology of communication, rationality, and recollection; and (5) the superiority of history over memory in the faithful recall and adjudication of the past.

Memory Studies and Hinduism

The study of memory in Hinduism is much older than the study of memory in Western contexts, but it is also less concerned with issues of social theory, modernity, and individual-collective questions. Instead, the study of memory in Hinduism has tended to explore particular applications of memory in religion, performance studies, literature, philosophy, and traditional education. Recently, scholars have been more interested in memory as it relates to the anthropology of recollection and narrative but also, equally important, to communal violence, such as the Partition of the subcontinent in August of 1947, the Bangladesh war of independence in 1971, and the anti-minority violence of 1984, 1993, 2002, and at other times.

In Sanskritic literatures, especially philosophical literature, the study of memory surrounds the key verbal root, *smṛ*, which demonstrates all the manifold complexity that has bedeviled Western memory studies. The verbal root can indicate a wide variety of things: to remember, of course, but also to feel nostalgia, sorrow, or regret and to teach or pass on. Memory is one of the five activities of the mind (*citta*) in Yoga.[8] The several nominative forms of *smṛ* can mean memory of many kinds and, as important, love, including sexual intercourse itself. In compounds with the noun *smara*, one finds a plethora of expression of sexual and romantic love. This intimate association suggests several alliances with Western memory theory, at least superficially, in its emphasis on social contexts, in this case, a context of only two lovers but a social one nonetheless.

Quite distant from this amorous genealogy, one key association with memory is *smṛti*, which literally means "memory" but comes to indicate that enormous body of religious, mythical, historical, and legal literature that has been "recalled" or rather theorized or produced by scholars over centuries. Materials in this genre include traditional treatises on law within the scope of Dharmaśāstra, such as the *Manusmṛti*, the *Śrauta* and *Gṛhya Sūtra*s, and the *śāstra*s generally, including the *āgamas* and the six traditional schools of Hindu philosophy or *darśana*s, but also the vast collections of materials under the rubrics of Itihāsa and Purāṇa, two genres often glossed as "history" and "myth," respectively. As Sheldon Pollock (1985) has argued, the creation of śāstric literature was understood to be a process of remembrance, of recalling past knowledge that had not been communicated directly, such as the Vedas. This includes the two massive and diversely imagined epics, the *Rāmāyaṇa* and the *Mahābhārata*. This heterogeneous genre of work is differentiated from *śruti*, "heard" literature, a record of the cosmic sound-discourse "heard" by ancient seers or *ṛṣi*s. The Vedas comprise the quintessential instance of *śruti* literature and are theoretically, or rhetorically, the basis of *smṛti*. Yet the traditional preservation of the Vedas was not written but oral or rather through memory (through repetition and recollection or anamnesis), whereby expounders of the Vedas were expected to memorize portions, and certain castes/individuals would serve as human archives for the untampered text. However, this was not memory as philosophical category but memory as rote action, tied to the idea that writing was a debasing practice and would consign the cosmic word to mundane plant material or parchment.

In Hinduism broadly speaking, *smṛti* does not differentiate between "memory" and "history," and this unity in Hindu thought of what have become two very different theoretical categories of knowledge in Western thought has aided the Orientalist conceit that India has no "history," by which is meant neither a historical literature or science nor a predisposition of mind to think historically. Hegel made this idea abundantly clear, and many scholars of India from James Mill to the present have concurred, more recently on the basis of understanding inherent qualities of Indian epistemology rather than Orientalist prejudice.[9] The debate over the presence, or absence, of history in India is too broad to engage here. But it is important to point out that in *smṛti* one finds a social impetus similar to that which characterizes memory studies in Western contexts: *Smṛti*, as law or discursive text, is clearly meant as a social injunction, and *smṛti* as myth or legend assumes audiences to whom moral tales are imparted. In the case of legal applications of *smṛti*, one even finds a broad caste designation, Smārta, indicating an orthodox Brāhmaṇical sect devoted to recalling and theorizing about legal religious texts.

Memory became a subject of debate in early Indian philosophical traditions, particularly around the question of "proof," or *pramāṇa*, which is to say, of legitimate forms of knowledge. Early philosophers argued that ultimate textual authority rested with the Vedas or *śruti*, of which *smṛti* was a "recollection" and hence a discursive expansion thereof. Likewise, human memory was a second-order recollection of the received information of direct experience (*anubhava*) and could not stand as any sort of reliable proof. The objects of knowledge in the case of memory were gone; they were in the past, and hence memory could not be correlated with its object (see Bhandare 1993; Carr 2000; Larson 1993). The knowledge of memory is recycled knowledge, made unreliable because of the distance it reveals from its source of information. But it is nonetheless important even if it cannot stand as first-order knowledge. Particularly in Yoga, *smṛti* is an important part of understanding the cycle of rebirth, or *saṃsāra*, and how our past experiences are imprinted on our beings, carried with us from birth to birth. Yoga offers ways of undoing these imprints but also of recalling them, and the dialectic of remembering and forgetting in this life and in multiple lives is a recurring theme, not just in Yoga but in myth, literature, and religious texts (Eliade 1963; Goldman 1985).

Though memory might have suffered some pummeling in philosophical circles, it was a favorite trope in Sanskrit literature, in plays, epic, myth, and so on. A survey of examples of memory, forgetfulness, and its consequences would be too long to be contained in this chapter, so a few examples should suffice. Perhaps the most famous case of an excellent memory is Vyāsa, the sage who recalls the epic story of the Bharat dynasty, the *Mahābhārata*, to his sacred scribe, the deity Gaṇeśa. Whatever the mythic nature of this story, it suggests that the predominant site for the transference, preservation, and alteration over time for the epics was through the channels of oral memory; what written records we have are but a fractional trace of a vast world of epic in the collective memory of centuries of South Asians. The "oral theory" of epic, first proposed in the context of Homeric compositions by A. B. Lord (1960) and Milman Parry (1971) in the first half of the twentieth century, contained within it an emphasis on the twin processes of memory or mnemonics (understood as formulas) and spontaneous composition during performance. Subsequent work in epic literature and its purported oral origins specific to South Asia has been studied, in part, as a site of memory (see Smith 1977). Indeed, the epics are a quintessential form of public memory in India.

Memory and one of its principle associations, love, fuse in many stories from South Asia, not just in Hinduism but throughout Indo-Persian tales of longing, from Ṣūfī romances to the famous Lailā and Majnūn story. Within the cultural field of early Hinduism, Sanskrit theater used memory effectively, as we see in many plays from the Sanskrit master dramaturge of the early first millennium CE, Kālidāsa, such as *Abhijñānaśakuntalā* (The Recognition of Śakuntalā), where a ring, as a kind of *lieu de mémoire*, triggers in a king the memory of his forgotten beloved (see Stoler-Miller 1984). The entanglement of love and memory in Sanskrit continues in multiple works, perhaps most famously in the composition of the twelfth-century poet Jayadeva's *Gītagovinda*, a song that supposes between Kṛṣṇa and his beloved, Rādhā, a dialogue in which the language of yearning and separation is filled with the memory of the missing beloved (Stoler-Miller 1977).

Gītagovinda is a key text in the broad, heterogeneous, millennia-old tradition in Hinduism (and in Buddhism, Jainism, and Sikhism) in India called *bhakti*, a practice of expressing a direct relationship between devotee and god and creating diverse communities of mutual companionship centered on the worship of a deity. From South India as early as the fifth century; throughout central, western, and northern India from the twelfth to eighteenth centuries; and even in the contemporary period, *bhakti* continues to create vast publics of remembrance that leave rich records of their devotion both to god and to their coreligionists. Memory is a key component of these multiple performances—lyrical, theatrical, textual, visual, and so on—that express the sentiment of *bhakti*. Indeed, memory is so ubiquitous that it is one of the few elements central to the two divergent thematic rubrics that characterize most *bhakti* in South Asia: *nirguṇa*, the ineffable, and *saguṇa*, the describable. In either case, memory serves the important purpose of invoking remembered characteristics of a beloved deity who is often absent (*saguṇa*), as in the *Gītagovinda*, or keeping in mind the Name, the signifier of the ineffable deity, a locus of meditation and devotion (*nirguṇa*). Furthermore, *bhakti*—particularly in its *saguṇa* aspect—is highly performative, engendering public displays of devotion, and both aspects of *bhakti* often espouse (though not always practice) ethics of broad inclusion across lines of caste, class, and gender. These moments of inclusion, as in performances of all sorts, are also acts of collective memory and are often undertaken at memorable times (births and deaths of deities or famous devotees), in memorable places, and in ritualistic ways that recall the memory of an important event. Given the deeply performative, and hence, oral nature of *bhakti* memory, even studies of the literary traces of *bhakti* traditions in South Asia often must contend with—and sometimes embrace—the "remembered" *bhakti* composer (*sant, bhakta,* and so on) and the texts attributed to that composer that remain extant (see Hawley 1984, 2005; Hess 1987; Lutgendorf 1991). I would argue that one finds in *bhakti* the longest, most sustained, most heterogeneous collective exploration of memory in South Asia.

Not only the memory of *bhakti* but the public memory of many other social, political, and cultural spheres have created in South Asia a "sacred geography" of sites associated with memory. In Islam, such sites are Ṣūfī *dargāh*s, the burial locations of famous "saints," or *pīr*s, and mosques that hold relics of memory (such as the Qadam Rasul and the Hazrat Bal); masoleums (such as the Taj Mahal); and other structures (such as the Qutab Minar complex in Delhi; see, for example, Ansari 1992). Likewise, in Hinduism, sites of memory are illimitable. They can take the form of *smṛtisthala*s ("places of memory") dedicated to famous religious figures and *samādhi*s that mark the final resting places of important individuals. Vital sites of memory through the centuries have been temples, where often religious and royal-state memory would converge (see Appadurai 1981; Dirks 1987; Orr 2000; Talbott 2001). One often finds texts that treat or record the memory of these places, and many times the places themselves bear the literary inscriptions of memory. However, the flux of collective memory in such places is strong, and these Indian *lieux de mémoire* often serve as focal points of countermemory vis-à-vis the state, chauvinistic ethnic groups, and other parties with vested interests.[10] The recently reignited century-old contention over the cultural memory surrounding the supposed birth-place of the Hindu deity Rāma, in the northern city of Ayodhya, is one among many examples of the volatility, and hence importance, of cultural memory coerced into forms of political action (see van der Veer 1988).

There is perhaps no more important location for the imbrication of state history, collective memory, and religious community formation than the events surrounding the Partition of the subcontinent in 1947. Like the passing of the living memory of the Holocaust, the last several years have seen a resurgence of scholarly interest in documenting the eye-witness accounts of the atrocities and genocides of the days surrounding the Partition before the living memory of those events vanishes (see Alam and Sharma 1998; Butalia 2000; Chakrabarty 1996; Kaul 2001; Moon 1998). This is a living memory, as the recent communal violence in Gujarat in 2002, sparked by a fire aboard a train car occupied by Hindu Right activists, shows. Media images of the burning car elicited comparisons to the iconic site of the Partition violence, the massacres of trainloads of people fleeing the two new nations of Pakistan and India. This collective memory around suffering and trauma is a key element in the rhetoric of communal difference between Hindus and Muslims on the subcontinent. Of the studies of this collective memory, several works have now explicitly engaged Western memory theory (see Mayaram 1996; Pandey 1999, 2001). Indeed, the greatest degree of dénouement between Western memory theory and empirical subjects pertaining to Hinduism seems to revolve around narratives of suffering, one of the key locations of memory studies, as noted above (Amin 1995; Gold and Gujar 2002; Dube 1998; Mayaram 1997; Prakash 1990; Skaria 1999). Yet the investigation of memory surrounding the Partition, like the memory surrounding the Holocaust, is also richly detailed in nonacademic venues, particularly in film and literature.[11] Like memory itself, reflection on the past refuses disciplinary, formal, or literary boundaries.

The challenge posed by memory to formal historiographic modes of recalling the past, and particularly those tied to the nation, is exemplified not only in Partition studies but in those investigations of nonelite, or subaltern, areas of experience. Much of the work of the Subaltern Studies Collective, for example, has explored religion as a site of "subaltern consciousness" (see Novetzke 2006), and one can find some brilliant uses of memory within the general context of Hinduism, deployed to unseat both the dominance of state historiography and the elitism of professional historiography in general (Amin 1984, 1997; Bhadra 1985; Chatterjee 1992; Devi 1987; Dube 1992; Guha 1987; Guha and Spivak 1988; Hardiman 1997; Kaali 1999; Kaviraj 1992; Pandey 1997; Ranger 1992; Sarkar 1989; Skaria 1996). For example, Partha Chatterjee (2002) weaves a fascinating story of a trial in 1930s Bengal regarding the identity of a Hindu holy man who some claimed was a prince of the region and, assumed to have died, had returned. Chatterjee observes how public memory met judicial historiography in the legal determination of the holy man's identity. As Chatterjee does here, many postcolonial historians find that memory—but not necessarily religious memory—offers an inherent challenge to state historiography.

One of the most recent and compelling studies of memory and Hinduism in India is the study of oral narratives of change and loss in Rajasthan written by Ann Gold and Bhoju Gujar (2002). Their book, *In the Time of Trees and*

Sorrows, brings together many of the features of Western memory studies outlined in this chapter. Their access to memories is ethnographic, through oral interviews, and this reinforces the close alliance between oral history and memory. Gold has sustained a deep ethnographic engagement with memory, orality, gender, and history over the course of several monographs and articles (see Gold 1988, 1992; Gold and Raheja 1994). Gold and Gujar manage to produce a lucid anthropology of memory that involves gender, orality, and history in recalling the pasts of kings and ecology, of landscapes of all sorts. Their subjects seem entirely aware of the interrelationship of power and nature in their memories, giving them a kind of "historical consciousness" that elides the necessity of literacy, professional historiography, or the influence of (colonial or postcolonial) modernity.[12]

The nuanced work of Gold and Gujar finds several points of connection to Western memory studies. The recollections coded as "memory" often involve tales of sorrow and suffering. Though Gold and Gujar depart from many studies of memory in Western contexts when they note that memory testimony was not solely of suffering but of happiness—the good and the bad (2002: 90)—they did find that women more than men expressed memories of sorrow or memories not considered "history" (92–93) and that the overall character of the interviews and the ethnographic history Gold and Gujar composed, Gold lyrically characterizes as "the articulated deterioration of love and landscape" (314).

One also finds in Gold and Gujar's work here a distinct difference between memory and history, which they share with Western memory theory. Yet the difference they recognize is not adjudicating between modernity and its antinomies but takes the form of a gendered differentiation. Gold and Gujar find that men never intervened in their discussions of memory or "women's things—rituals, stories, songs, and so forth"—but when they inaugurated a conversation on "history" or *itihāsa* in Rajasthani, men would interject their voices as exclusively authoritative (2002: 34, 41). The dialectical association of orality and memory with femininity on the one hand and literacy and history with masculinity on the other seems to play out here, in a South Asian context, more so than in a modern European one. Yet we also find a parallel to narratives of sorrow and suffering embodying "memory," whereas stories of victory, nation, and kingship are categorized as "history." In Gold's earlier work, women seemed specifically to embody the power of memory rather than history. This most recent monograph perhaps bears a greater investiture in men's memories because it also involves questions of bygone kingship—a subject stereotypically germane to male-gendered history. In general, the interviews Gold transcribes with women center on household labor and emotion. The dialectic of memory and history here moves from critiques of modernity to concerns of gendered difference in localized collective systems of memory.

The broad spectrum of studies that can be generally considered to touch on the cultural fields of Hinduism resists distillation into neat categories, but I have tried here to outline those areas of study that engage with memory in the most explicit and profitable ways. We have seen a broad alignment between Western memory studies and the study of memory in Hinduism in terms of a shared concern with social, cultural, public, and collective modes of memory's maintenance. We have noted that orality is intimately associated with memory as a device of recollection, but literacy, at least in the South Asian context, has not implied a more sophisticated mode of recollection, associated with "history," for example, as we find in Western historiography. However, we have seen a division between history and memory along several axes: one, in classical philosophical circles, excluded what we might call "history" for what would more precisely be called memory, even as memory was relegated to a second-order way of knowing; two, memory and history in public culture might be distinguished in ways both gendered and conditioned by its relationship to kingship, as Gold and Gujar have shown. So memory and history are different, but we do not see the same difference as we do in Western memory theory. However, one aspect of both sorts of memory study—within Hinduism and within Western contexts—is a preoccupation with suffering and trauma. The reasons for this are no doubt connected in the context of the Partition that, like the Holocaust, is a challenge to the teleology of the nation-state, whether that of Germany and other European nations or that of Pakistan and India. However, Gold and Gujar have also shown that memory and suffering do not rely on modern state-centered historiography for their association. Suffering and memory are, after all, universal traits of humanity, and, perhaps here, memory and the concerns of humanist study dovetail.

Notes

1 Freud and memory should be well understood but for the latter, see Carruthers (1992); Yates (2001).

2 Halbwachs was a Catholic who married a Jewish woman; politically, Halbwachs was a communist. His personal sentiments about religion are not speculated on here.

3 For a finer study in the tradition of this line of investigation, see Castelli (2004).

4 Nora wrote the entry for "collective memory" for an historical encyclopedia, *La nouvelle histoire* (1978: 398).

5 For the fountainhead of debates about orality and literacy and their impact on history and memory, see the work of Goody and Watt (Goody 1969, 1986; Goody and Watt 1963).
6 In particular see the work of Jan Assmann.
7 For a lucid survey of history, orality, and memory through the works of James Clifford, Claude Lévi-Strauss, and Jean-François Lyotard, see Kline (1995).
8 The other four are: knowing (*pramāṇa*), wakefulness/misapprehension (*viparyaya*), sleep (*nidrā*), and speech (*vikalpa*).
9 For exemplary treatments of this issue in classical India, see Aktor (1999); Perrett (1999); Pollock (1989, 1990); Sharma (2003); cf. Inden, Walters, and Ali (2000, especially Chapter 4); Rao, Shulman, and Subrahmanyam (2003).
10 For a brilliant ethnography of memory, see Kumar (2002).
11 Though nothing of the magnitude of Claude Lanzmann's documentary, *Shoah* (1985), exists to record the oral testimonies of the Partition in audio-visual form, there have been a good number of films, documentaries, and other media that investigate the Partition. See, for example, the documentaries *Beyond Partition* (2006, Lalit Mohan Joshi, director) and *Stories of the Broken Self* (forthcoming, Furrukh Khan, director); such films as *Garam Hawa* (1973, M. S. Sathyu director), *Earth* (1998, Deepa Mehta, director), *Hey Ram* (2000, Kamal Hassan, director), and *Pinjar* (2003, C. P. Dwivedi, director); and such non-Indian films as *Partition* (2006, Vic Sarin, director). For literary treatments, see Lahiri (1999); Manto (1987); Mistry (2001); Rushdie (1980); Sahni (2001); Sidhwa (1989); Singh (1990); see also the recent dissertation, Bhaskar (2005).
12 See also the excellent work of Feldhaus (1995, 2003), for example, who combines text, oral history, ethnography, folklore, gender, and regional studies in her scholarship.

References Cited

Aktor, Mikael. 1999. "Smritis and Jatis: The Ritualisation of Time and the Continuity of the Past." *In* Daud Ali, ed., *Invoking the Past: The Uses of History in South Asia*, 259–79. Delhi: Oxford University Press.

Alam, Javeed. and Suresh Sharma. 1998. "Remembering Partition." *Seminar* 461: 71–74.

Amin, Shahid. 1984. "Gandhi as Mahatma: Gorakhpur District, Eastern UP, 1921–2." *In* Ranajit Guha, ed., *Subaltern Studies III: Writings on South Asian History and Society*, 1–71. Delhi: Oxford University Press.

Amin, Shahid. 1995. *Event, Metaphor, Memory: Chauri Chaura, 1922–1992*. Berkeley: University of California Press.

Amin, Shahid. 1997. "Remembering Chauri Chaura: Notes from Historical Fieldwork." *In* Ranajit Guha, ed., *A Subaltern Studies Reader, 1986–1995*, 179–239. Minneapolis: University of Minnesota Press.

Anderson, Benedict. 1991 [1983]. *Imagined Communities: Reflections on the Origin and Spread of Nationalism*. London: Verso.

Ansari, Sarah F. D. 1992. *Sufi Saints and State Power: The Pirs of Sind, 1843–1947.* Cambridge: Cambridge University Press.

Appadurai, Arjun. 1981. *Worship and Conflict Under Colonial Rule: A South Indian Case.* Cambridge: Cambridge University Press.

Assmann, Jan. 2006 [2000]. *Religion and Cultural Memory: Ten Studies* (trans. Rodney Livingstone). Palo Alto: Stanford University Press.

Bellah, Robert N., Richard Madsen, William Sullivan, Ann Swidler, and Steven M. Tipton. 1985. *Habits of the Heart: Individualism and Commitment in American Life.* Berkeley: University of California Press.

Bhadra, Gautam. 1985. "Four Rebels of Eighteen-Fifty-Seven." *In* Ranajit Guha, ed., *Subaltern Studies IV: Writings on South Asian History and Society*, 229–75. Delhi: Oxford University Press.

Bhandare, Shaila. 1993. *Memory in Indian Epistemology: Its Nature and Status.* Delhi: India Books-Sri Satguru Publications.

Bhaskar, Ira. 2005. "'The Persistence of Memory': Historical Trauma and Imagining the Community in Hindi Cinema." Ph.D. dissertation. New York: New York University Library.

Butalia, Urvashi. 2000. *The Other Side of Silence: Voices from the Partition of India.* Durham: Duke University Press.

Butler, Thomas, ed. 1989. *Memory: History, Culture and the Mind.* Oxford: Blackwell.

Carr, Brian. 2000. "Śaṅkara on Memory and the Continuity of the Self." *Religious Studies* 36, 4: 419–34.

Carruthers, Mary J. 1992. *The Book of Memory: A Study of Memory in Medieval Culture.* Cambridge: Cambridge University Press.

Caruth, Cathy. 1991. "Unclaimed Experience: Trauma and the Possibility of History." *Yale French Studies* 79: 181–92.

Caruth, Cathy. 1996. *Unclaimed Experience: Trauma Narrative and History.* Baltimore: Johns Hopkins University Press.

Castelli, Elizabeth A. 2004. *Martyrdom and Memory: Early Christian Culture Making.* New York: Columbia University Press.

Chakrabarty, Dipesh. 1996. "Remembered Villages: Representation of Hindu-Bengali Memories in the Aftermath of Partition." *Economic and Political Weekly* 31, 32: 2143–251.

Chatterjee, Partha. 1992. "A Religion of Urban Domesticity: Sri Ramakrishna and the Calcutta Middle Class." *In* Partha Chatterjee and Gyanendra Pandey, eds, *Subaltern Studies VII: Writings on South Asian History and Society*, 40–68. Delhi: Oxford University Press.

Chatterjee, Partha. 2002. *A Princely Impostor? The Strange and Universal History of the Kumar of Bhawal.* Princeton: Princeton University Press.

Coleman Janet. 1992. *Ancient and Medieval Memories: Studies in the Reconstruction of the Past.* Cambridge: Cambridge University Press.

Collingwood, R. G. 1994 [1946]. *The Idea of History: With Lectures 1926–1928* (ed. Jan van der Dussen). New York: Oxford University Press.

Connerton, P. 1989. *How Societies Remember*. Cambridge: Cambridge University Press.

Davis, Natalie Zemon and Randolf Starn. 1989. "Introduction." *Representations* 26: 1–6.

de Certeau, Michel. 1988 [1975]. *The Writing of History* (trans. Tom Conley). New York: Columbia University Press.

Derrida, Jacques. 1998 [1967]. *Of Grammatology* (trans. Gayatri Chakravorty Spivak). Baltimore: The Johns Hopkins University Press.

Devi, Mahasweta. 1987. "'Breath-Giver'" (trans. Gayatri Chakravorty Spivak). *In* Ranajit Guha, ed., *Subaltern Studies V: Writings on South Asian History and Society*, 252–76. Delhi: Oxford University Press.

Dirks, Nicholas B. 1987. *The Hollow Crown: Ethnohistory of an Indian Kingdom*. Cambridge: Cambridge University Press.

Duara, Prasenjit. 1995. *Rescuing History from the Nation: Questioning Narratives of Modern China*. Chicago: University of Chicago Press.

Dube, Saurabh. 1992. "Myths, Symbols and Community: Satnampanth of Chattisgarh." *In* Partha Chatterjee and Gyanendra Pandey, eds, *Subaltern Studies VII: Writings on South Asian History and Society*, 121–58. Delhi: Oxford University Press.

Dube, Saurabh. 1998. *Untouchable Pasts: Religion, Identity, and Power among a Central Indian Community, 1780–1950*. Albany: State University of New York Press.

Eliade, Mircea. 1963. "Mythologies of Memory and Forgetting" (trans. Willard R. Trask). *History of Religions* 2, 2: 329–44.

Feldhaus, Anne. 1995. *Water and Womanhood: Religious Meanings of Rivers in Maharashtra*. New York: Oxford University Press.

Feldhaus, Anne. 2003. *Connected Places: Religion, Pilgrimage, and Geographical Imagination in India*. New York: Palgrave Macmillan.

Fentress, James and Chris Wickham. 1992. *Social Memory*. Oxford: Blackwell.

Foucault M. 1977. *Language, Counter-Memory, Practice: Selected Essays and Interviews* (ed. Donald F. Bouchard; trans. Donald F. Bouchard and Sherry Simon). Ithaca: Cornell University.

Friedlander, Saul. 1993. *Memory, History and the Extermination of the Jews of Europe*. Bloomington: Indiana University Press.

Gold, Ann Grodzins. 1988. *Fruitful Journeys: The Ways of Rajasthani Pilgrims*. Berkeley: University of California Press.

Gold, Ann Grodzins, trans. 1992. *A Carnival of Parting: The Tales of King Bharthari and King Gopi Chand as Sung and Told by Madhu Natisar Nath of Ghatiyali, Rajasthan*. Berkeley: University of California Press.

Gold, Ann Grodzins and Bhoju Ram Gujar. 2002. *In the Time of Trees and Sorrows: Nature, Power, and Memory in Rajasthan*. Durham: Duke University Press.

Gold, Ann Grodzins and Gloria Goodwin Reheja. 1994. *Listen to the Heron's Words: Reimagining Gender and Kinship in North India*. Berkeley: University of California Press.

Goldman, Robert P. 1985. "Karma, Guilt, and Buried Memories: Public Fantasy and Private Reality in Traditional India." *Journal of the American Oriental Society* 105, 3: 413–25.

Goody, Jack, ed. 1969. *Literacy in Traditional Societies.* Cambridge: Cambridge University Press.

Goody, Jack. 1986. *The Logic of Writing and the Organization of Society.* Cambridge: Cambridge University Press.

Goody, Jack and Ian Watt. 1963. "The Consequences of Literacy." *Comparative Studies in Society and History* 5, 3: 304–45.

Guha, Ranajit. 1987. "Chandra's Death." *In* Ranajit Guha, ed., *Subaltern Studies V: Writings on South Asian History and Society*, 135–65. Delhi: Oxford University Press.

Guha, Ranajit and Gayatri Chakravorty Spivak, eds. 1988. *Selected Subaltern Studies.* Delhi: Oxford University Press.

Halbwachs, Maurice. 1992 [1925]. *On Collective Memory* (ed. and trans. Lewis A. Coser). Chicago: The University of Chicago Press.

Hardiman, David. 1997. "Origins and Transformations of the Devi." *In* Ranajit Guha, ed., *A Subaltern Studies Reader, 1986–1995*, 100–39. Minneapolis: University of Minnesota Press.

Hawley, John Stratton. 1984. *Sūr Dās: Poet, Singer, Saint.* Seattle: University of Washington Press.

Hawley, John Stratton. 2005. *Three Bhakti Voices: Mirabai, Surdas, and Kabir in Their Times and Ours.* New York: Oxford University Press.

Hayes, Carlton J. H. 1960. *Nationalism: A Religion.* New York: Macmillan.

Hegel, G. W. F. 1944 [1830]. *The Philosophy of History* (trans. J. Sibree). New York: Willey.

Hervieu-Léger, Danièle. 2000 [1993]. *Religion as a Chain of Memory* (trans. Simon Lee). New Brunswick: Rutgers University Press.

Hess, Linda. 1987. "Three Kabir Collections: A Comparative Study." *In* Karine Schomer and W. H. McLeod, eds, *The Sants: Studies in a Devotional Tradition of India*, 111–142. Berkeley: University of California Press.

History and Anthropology 1986 (2.2), special issue on "Between Memory and History."

Hobsbawm Eric and Terence Ranger, eds. 1983. *The Invention of Tradition.* Cambridge: Cambridge University Press.

Hutton Patrick H. 1993. *History as an Art of Memory.* Hanover: University Press of New England, for the University of Vermont.

Inden, Ronald, Jonathan Walters, Daud Ali. 2000. *Querying the Medieval: Texts and the History of Practices in South Asia.* New York: Oxford University Press.

Johnson Richard, Gregor McLennan, Bill Schwarz, David Sutton, eds. 1982. *Making Histories: Studies in History-Writing and Politics.* London: Hutchinson.

Kaali, Sundar. 1999. "Spatializing History: Subaltern Carnivalizations of Space in Tiruppuvanam, Tamil Nadu." *In* Gautam Bhadra, Gyan Prakash, and Susie Tharu, eds, *Subaltern Studies X: Writings on South Asian History and Society*, 126–69. Delhi: Oxford University Press.

Kaul, Suvir, ed. 2001. *The Partitions of Memory: The Afterlife of the Division of India*. Delhi: Permanent Black.
Kaviraj, Sudipta. 1992. "The Imaginary Institution of India." *In* Partha Chatterjee and Gyanendra Pandey, eds, *Subaltern Studies VII: Writings on South Asian History and Society*, 1–39. Delhi: Oxford University Press.
Kline, Kerwin Lee. 1995. "In Search of Narrative Mastery: Postmodernism and the People Without History." *History and Theory* 34, 4: 275–98.
Kumar, Sunil. 2002. *The Present in Delhi's Pasts*. Delhi: Three Essays Press.
LaCapra, Dominick. 1998. *History and Memory after Auschwitz*. Ithaca: Cornell University Press.
Lahiri, Jhumpa. 1999. *Interpreter of Maladies*. Mariner Books/Houghton Mifflin.
Larson, Gerald James. 1993. "The *Trimūrti* of *Smṛti* in Classical Indian Thought." *Philosophy East and West* 43, 3: 373–88.
Le Goff, Jacques. 1992. *History and Memory* (trans. Steven Rendall and Elizabeth Claman). New York: Columbia University Press.
Lord, Albert B. 1960. *The Singer of Tales*. Cambridge: Harvard University Press.
Lutgendorf, Philip. 1991. *The Life of a Text: Performing the Rāmcaritmānas of Tulsidas*. Berkeley: University of California Press.
Manto, Saadat Hasan. 1987. *Kingdom's End and Other Stories* (trans. Khalid Hasan). Delhi: Penguin.
Matsuda Matt K. 1996. *The Memory of the Modern*. New York: Oxford University Press.
Mayaram, Shail. 1996. "Speech, Silence and the Making of Partition Violence in Mewat." *In* Shahid Amin and Dipesh Chakrabarty, eds, *Subaltern Studies IX: Writings on South Asian History and Society*, 126–64. Delhi: Oxford University Press.
Mayaram, Shail. 1997. *Resisting Regimes: Myth, Memory and the Shaping of a Muslim Identity*. New York: Oxford University Press.
Mistry, Rohinton. 2001 [1975]. *A Fine Balance*. New York: Random House.
Moon, Penderel. 1998 [1961]. *Divide and Quit: An Eyewitness Account of the Partition of India*. Delhi: Oxford University Press.
Nora, Pierre. 1978. "Mémoire collective." *In* Jacques Le Goff, Roger Chartier, and Jacques Revel, eds, *La Nouvelle histoire*, 398–401. Paris: Retz.
Nora, Pierre. 1989. "Between Memory and History: *Les lieux de mémoire*." *Representations* 26: 7–24.
Nora, Pierre, ed. 1984–1993. *Les lieux de mémoire*. 7 volumes. Paris: Gallimard.
Nora, Pierre. 1996. "Preface to the English Language Edition." *In* Pierre Nora, ed., *Realms of Memory: Rethinking the French Past*. Volume 1: *Conflicts and Divisions* (trans. Arthur Goldhammer), xv–xxiv. New York: Columbia University Press.
Novetzke, Christian Lee. 2006. "The Subaltern Numen: Making History in the Name of God." *History of Religions* 6, 2: 99–126.
Orr, Leslie C. 2000. *Donors, Devotees, and Daughters of God: Temple Women in Medieval Tamilnadu*. New York: Oxford University Press.
Pandey, G. 1997. "In Defense of the Fragment: Writing about Hindu-Muslim Riots in India Today." *In* Ranajit Guha, ed., *A Subaltern Studies Reader, 1986–1995*, 1–33. Minneapolis: University of Minnesota Press.

Pandey, Gyanendra. 1999. *Memory, History and the Question of Violence: Reflections on the Reconstruction of Partition*. Calcutta: K. P. Bagchi.

Pandey, Gyanendra. 2001. *Remembering Partition: Violence, Nationalism and History in India*. Cambridge: Cambridge University Press.

Parry, Milman. 1971. *The Making of Homeric Verse: The Collected Papers of Milman Parry* (ed. Adam Parry). Oxford: Clarendon Press.

Perrett, Roy W. 1999. "History, Time, and Knowledge in Ancient India." *History and Theory* 38, 3: 307–21.

Pollock, Sheldon. 1985. "The Theory of Practice and the Practice of Theory in Indian Intellectual History." *Journal of the American Oriental Society* 105, 3: 499–519.

Pollock, Sheldon. 1989. "Mīmāṃsā and the Problem of History in Traditional India." *Journal of the American Oriental Society* 109, 4: 603–10.

Pollock, Sheldon. 1990. "From Discourse of Ritual to Discourse of Power in Sanskrit Culture." *Journal of Ritual Studies* 4, 2: 315–45.

Prakash, Gyan. 1990. *Bonded Histories: Genealogies of Labor Servitude in Colonial India*. Cambridge: Cambridge University Press.

Rampley, Matthew. 2000. *The Remembrance of Things Past: On Aby M. Warburg and Walter Benjamin*. Weisbaden: Harrassowitz Verlag

Ranger, T. 1992. "Power, Religion and Community: The Matobo Case." *In* Partha Chatterjee and Gyanendra Pandey, eds, *Subaltern Studies VII: Writings on South Asian History and Society*, 221–46. Delhi: Oxford University Press.

Rao, Velcheru Narayana, David Shulman, and Sanjay Subrahmanyam. 2003. *Textures of Time: Writing History in South India, 1600–1800*. New York: Other Press.

Rushdie, S. 1980. *Midnight's Children*. New York: Knopf.

Sahni, B. 2001 [1975]. *Tamas*. Delhi: Penguin.

Sarkar, Sumit. 1989. "The Kalki-Avatar of Bikrampur: A Village Scandal in Early Twentieth Century Bengal." *In* Ranajit Guha, ed., *Subaltern Studies VI: Writings on South Asian History and Society*, 1–53. Delhi: Oxford University Press.

Sharma, Arvind. 2003. *Hinduism and Its Sense of History*. Delhi: Oxford University Press.

Sharma, Arvind. 2003. "Did the Hindus Lack a Sense of History?" *Numen: International Review for the History of Religions* 50, 2: 190–227.

Sidhwa, Bapsi. 1989 [1988]. *Ice-Candy Man*. Delhi: South Asia Books.

Singh, Khushwant. 1990 [1956]. *Train to Pakistan*. New York: Grove Press.

Skaria, Ajay. 1996. "Writing, Orality and Power in the Dangs, Western India." *In* S. Amin and D. Chakrabarty, ed., *Subaltern Studies IX: Writings on South Asian History and Society*, 13–58. Delhi: Oxford University Press.

Skaria, Ajay. 1999. *Hybrid Histories: Forests, Frontiers and Wildness in Western India*. Delhi: Oxford University Press.

Smith, Anthony D. 1986. *The Ethnic Origins of Nations*. Oxford: Blackwell.

Smith, John D. 1977. "*The Singer or the Song?* A Reassessment of Lord's 'Oral Theory'." *Man (ns)* 12, 1:141–53.

Spiegel, Gabrielle M. 2002. "Memory and History: Liturgical Time and Historical Time." *History and Theory* 41, 2: 149–62.

Stoler Miller, Barbara, ed. and trans. 1977. *Love Song of the Dark Lord: Jayadeva's Gitagovinda*. New York: Columbia University Press.

Stoler Miller, Barbara, ed. 1984. *The Theater of Memory: The Plays of Kālidāsa*. New York: Columbia University Press.

Sturkin, Marita. 1997. *Tangled Memories: The Vietnam War, the AIDS Epidemic, and the Politics of Remembering*. Berkeley: University of California Press.

Talbott, Cynthia. 2001. *Precolonial India in Practice: Society, Religion, and Identity in Medieval Andhra*. New York: Oxford University Press.

Terdiman, Richard. 1993. *Present Past: Modernity and the Memory Crisis*. Ithaca: Cornell University Press.

Thapar, Romila. 1990 [1966]. *A History of India*. Volume 1. Delhi: Penguin.

van der Veer, Peter. 1988. *Gods on Earth: The Management of Religious Experience and Identity in a North Indian Pilgrimage Centre*. London: Athlone.

Yates, Frances A. 2001 [1966]. *The Art of Memory*. Chicago: University of Chicago Press.

Yerushalmi, Yosef Hayim. 1982. *Zakhor: Jewish History and Jewish Memory*. Seattle: University of Washington Press.

18

Myth

Herman Tull

History
German Romanticism and the Study of Myth
F. Max Müller
Late Nineteenth-Century Developments
The Study of Vedic Mythology
The Study of Post-Vedic Mythology: Epic and Purāṇa
Concluding Reflections

Modern studies of myth invariably begin by pointing out that, for scholars studying culture, history, and religion, the term "myth" does not mean what it is commonly understood to mean, namely, something false or unfounded (Cohen 1969: 337; Doniger 1998: 1; Dundes 1984: 1; Eliade 1963: 1; Middleton 1967: x). As Percy Cohen points out, this usage is "almost always intended pejoratively: here my beliefs are a strong conviction, yours a dogma, his a myth" (1969: 337). Looking beyond (or beneath) the modern sense of myth as falsehood, scholars point to the primary role of myth in traditional societies, in which it appears as a *sacred narrative*, one that frequently speaks of origins and, in particular, is "shared by a group of people who find their most important meanings in it" (Doniger 1998: 2; cf. Cohen 1969: 337; Dundes 1984: 1; Eliade 1963: 5). Yet, despite the scholarly distaste for the notion of myth as falsehood, it is not a bad place to begin delving into myth, for it reflects the fact that myths open windows into unreachable realms and that they therefore do not reflect and are not subject to everyday notions of truth. But, of course, not being true in an ordinary sense does not mean that myths are falsehoods (if they are not subject to ordinary notions of truth, then, too, they are not subject to ordinary notions of falsehood). The difficulty of locating myth is apparent in an observation made by Mircea Eliade, one of the premier historians of religion of the latter half of the twentieth century, that myth is a "true history" describing the acts of "Supernatural Beings" who existed in the long-ago of the "transcendent times of the 'beginnings' " (1963: 6; cf. Pettazzoni 1984: 99). Yet, this "true history" describes something that has no empirical existence and hence, is neither "true" nor "history" in the ordinary sense of these words. Cohen, in presenting a survey and general assessment of modern theories of myth, avoids these notions of truth and falsehood by noting that myths narrate events that often belong to their own world; Cohen's definition is a comprehensive one and largely agrees with the characterizations of myth proposed by other modern scholars: "A myth is a narrative of events; the narrative has a sacred quality; the sacred communication is made in symbolic form; at least some of the events and objects which occur in the myth neither occur nor exist in the world other than that of myth itself; and the myth refers in dramatic form to origins of transformations" (1969: 337; cf. Honko 1984: 48–51).

History

Notwithstanding Cohen's definition, the notion of myth as falsehood is deeply embedded in the word's history. The English word "myth" descends directly from the Greek *mythos*, a word widely used for a tale or a speech that, particularly as used in epic language, denoted a powerfully *persuasive* type of speech (Kirk 1970: 8; Lincoln 1999: 12–17). By Plato's time, however, and in his usage, *mythos* primarily indicates the stories told by the poets about the gods, stories that taken as a whole are seen as largely false (*Republic* 377a, d). Along with their falsity, Plato rues what he sees as the deplorable values represented in the Greek myths, citing both the wars, plots, and family intrigues between the gods and the gods' deceptive natures (*Republic* 377–80; see also Lincoln 1999: 37–42), and concludes that the old myths must be abandoned. Plato, however, also follows earlier Greek usage in acknowledging the persuasive power of *mythos*; accordingly, in the *Republic*, he suggests that myths—when chosen judiciously—be employed to educate the young; indeed, insofar as myths promote uplifting values, Plato states that the false may be treated as true (*Republic* 382d). Within a few centuries, along with the growth and establishment of Christianity, even this slightly positive assessment of myth is lost. For the Christian church, myth stood in opposition to biblical narrative, the one true and authoritative source of sacred history; accordingly, at least up to Renaissance times, myth remained relegated to the shadowy realm of the false story (Lincoln 1999: 47).

German Romanticism and the Study of Myth

The modern rehabilitation of myth—and the modern study of the mythology of India—coincided with, and was to a great degree impelled by, the emergence of the German nationalist and romantic movements in the late eighteenth and early nineteenth centuries. A key element in this coordinate development was the idea of the *Volk*—literally, "folk"—but more extensively referring to a people as defined by certain shared cultural and racial characteristics, people whose ancestral heritage was preserved in their tales ("folktales") and myths. In an odd confluence of historical factors, just as German intellectuals were developing their ideas about the *Volk*—and seeking out their own ancestral *Volk*—translations from Sanskrit texts (e.g., William Jones' *Śakuntalā* and Horace H. Wilson's *Hitopadeśa*) became available for the first time in Europe. The results of this confluence are clearly visible in the work of Johann Herder (1744–1803), a seminal figure in the early German romantic movement. He, like so many of the later German romantics, extracted a glorified image of India from his reading of the Hindu texts. Depicting the ancient Indians as "pure" and "childlike"—particularly in their conception of the divine—Herder saw ancient India as the first stage in mankind's cultural development, a development from which Greek, Roman, and eventually European cultures emerged; in other words, for Herder, ancient India represented Europe's own "childhood" (Halbfass 1988: 69–71; Lincoln 1999: 52–54).[1]

Herder's idiosyncratic ideas—which over time undoubtedly would have disappeared on their own—received unexpected support from the nascent study of Indic languages. William Jones, famed eighteenth-century British Orientalist, jurist, and linguist, in his oft-celebrated third address to the Asiatic Society, declared that Sanskrit, Persian, Greek, and Latin (and so too by extension the modern Romance languages) had a common origin:

> The *Sanscrit* language, whatever be its antiquity, is of a wonderful structure; more perfect than the *Greek*, more copious than the *Latin*...yet bearing to both of them a stronger affinity, both in the roots of verbs and in the forms of grammar, than could possibly have been produced by accident; so strong, indeed that no philologer could examine all three, without believing them to have sprung from some common source.
>
> (Jones 1993a: 173)

Although Jones' assessment was absolutely correct—indeed, its prescience is still celebrated to this day—as Bruce Lincoln has recently shown, its basis was more tenuous and slightly less original than is generally supposed (1999: 81–93), for it appears that Jones' ideas about language were driven in part by his romantic notion that ancient man lived in a single *ur*-culture, the existence of which he had already attempted to prove in a groundbreaking comparative study of Greek, Roman, and Indian mythology, in which he showed a number of spurious connections between the ancient gods (1993b: 179).

F. Max Müller

These several streams—the nascent field of comparative philology, the romantic notion of and yearning for a common childlike past, and a deep, though often unrealistic fascination with ancient India—culminate in the second half of the nineteenth century in the work of F. Max Müller, who was a Sanskrit scholar and an astute student of religion and produced a copious body of scholarly and popular publications. Although Müller's work was paradigmatic in establishing the value of studying mythology as a means of understanding religion, Müller is often remembered for his unfortunate theory that myths result from a "disease of language" (see Dorson 1955: 25; Stone 2002: 3–5). In brief, according to this theory, myths originate from the misunderstanding or perversion of mankind's aboriginal language, a language Müller believed to be pure, simple, and childlike:

> There was a tendency to change the original conception of divine powers, to misunderstand the many names given to these powers, and to misinterpret the praises addressed to them. In this manner, some of the divine names were changed into half-divine, half-human heroes, and at least the mythes which were true and intelligible as told originally of the sun, or the dawn, or the storms, were turned into legends or fables too marvelous to be believed of common mortals.
>
> (Müller 1867b: 259–60)[2]

In Müller's schematization, myths emerged directly from mankind's *ur*-period and thus contained not only a great deal of man's aboriginal yearnings and thoughts, but also the earliest forms of the human religious imagination. Unfortunately, once formed into myths, these noble thoughts became "absurd and irrational"—evidenced, Müller noted even among the ancient Greeks and "honest Brahmans," who were shocked by the immoral elements contained in the stories told of their gods (1867a: 11, 14); however, Müller also believed that through the comparative study of ancient language this largely meaningless mythical veneer could be penetrated.

Continuing in the tradition of the German romantics and bolstered by the evidence he saw in the comparison of languages, Müller proposed that the earliest glimmerings of man's "childhood" could be seen nowhere more clearly than in the ancient Indian Vedic texts (*ca.* 1600 BCE), the authors of which Müller argued were the direct ancestors of the Germanic and European people: "An unbroken chain connects our own generation with the ancestors of the Aryan race...and the Veda is the oldest book we have in which we have to study the first beginnings of our language and all that is embedded in language" (Müller 1873: 4). Müller imagined that the Vedic texts preserved a mythology that was not yet tainted by misunderstanding and misinterpretation; it was, in his words "a whole world of primitive, natural, and intelligible mythology" that reflected the simple expression of the "human mind endowed with the natural consciousness of a divine power." This divine power was that of the natural world, particularly that found in solar phenomena, as evidenced by the "original" names of the Vedic gods—Sūrya, "sun"; Dyaus, "sky"—before they became mired in mythologies of marriages, offspring, and human and divine relations (Müller 1867a: 75–77).

Late Nineteenth-Century Developments

Although many of Müller's ideas were short-lived, his influence on the study of Hindu mythology was profound.[3] In particular, Müller changed the way in which scholars viewed myths; though he saw myths themselves as the perversions of some original, nobler aspirations, he strongly affirmed that underlying myths were layers of deep meaning—if not profound truth—awaiting interpretation, a principle that remains standard for modern historians of religion (although vastly different interpretive tools—among them the insights of psychoanalysis and structuralism [see O'Flaherty 1980: 5–7]—have taken the place of Müller's generally flawed linguistic approach). During the latter part of the nineteenth century, however, anthropologists and folklorists, following the lead of E. B. Tylor and Andrew Lang (who was a fierce opponent of Müller's theories of mythology [see Dorson 1968: 208–12]), moved sharply away from the romantic approach that depicted myths as the preserve of early man's noble aspirations. In its place, they asserted that early man lived largely in a state of savagery and that myths and folklore were "survivals" from the "lower" stages of human culture, the flotsam and jetsam of a rude past that remained irrationally preserved in modern thought. As Richard Dorson has observed of this position: "While the main march of mankind is upward, from savagery through barbarism to ascending levels of civilization, relics of savagery, such as witchcraft, still survive among civilized peoples, and occasionally burst into revivals, as in the fad of spiritualism, a revival of primitive sorcery" (1968: 193). Though the implicit social evolutionary stance in this theory of survivals was later seen as deeply flawed—particularly in the study of religion (see Bellah 1972: 37)—Tylor's and Lang's work gave a tremendous boost to the general study of folklore and mythology, especially among ethnologists who were concerned with studying myth *in situ* and who placed great emphasis on how myths *functioned* as an element of a larger societal system. Among the most influential theories to emerge from this school were those of the anthropologist Bronislaw Malinowski, whose central theory of myth asserted that myths function in a particular society as support and justification for all types of social mores, cultural values, and even religious beliefs. Here, myths are seen as statements of social and cultural reality and not symbolic statements possibly masking some deeper underlying truth (Malinowski 1954: 146, 1984: 199).

At least initially, however, Tylor's and Lang's theories had little effect on the study of Hindu mythology. Following Müller's lead, it continued to focus on Vedic religion and mythology—that is on textual rather than ethnological materials[4]—and continued to reflect at least in muted tones Müller's idea that underlying the myth was the direct celebration of the powers of the natural world and that the myths themselves were symbolic expressions (flawed or not) of those natural powers (see, for example, Hillebrandt 1980: 5; Keith 1925: 45; Oldenberg 1988: 25; Winternitz 1981: 60, 67). As these studies advanced, however, greater recognition was given to the notion that the obscure nature of the Vedic mythology was not due to the directness of man's early language (or its later diminution in malapropisms) but to the fact that the Vedic texts were overwhelmingly oriented to the Vedic sacrificial rituals, whether in the form of praises to the gods (as, for example, in the *Ṛg Veda Saṃhitā*) or in the form of symbolic explications and dialogic discussions of the higher meaning of the Vedic sacrifices (as in the Brāhmaṇas and Upaniṣads).[5] Indeed, the enigmatic quality of the Vedic myths itself stands as an important element of the cosmic mystery that underlies the Vedic rites (Bonnefoy 1991: 27). As Wendy Doniger, the doyenne of scholars of Hindu mythology, observes of the *Ṛg Veda Saṃhitā*: Although "one does sense a mythological corpus behind the [Ṛg Vedic] hymns," the fact is that "the *Rig Veda* has no true mythology; it is written out of a mythology that we can only try to reconstruct from the Rig Vedic jumble of paradoxes heaped on paradoxes, tropes heaped on tropes" (1981: 18).

The Study of Vedic Mythology

Despite the obscure nature of Vedic mythology, its general parameters are well known and have been described repeatedly by scholars (Bergaigne 1969–73; Bhattacharji 1970; Doniger 1981; Hillebrandt 1980; Jamison and Witzel 2003; Keith 1925; Macdonell 1897; O'Flaherty 1975; Oldenberg 1988). Best known are Indra, the warrior god, and personification of the Āryan warrior *par excellence*, who is known for his feat of conquering the cosmic serpent Vṛtra and for the prodigious draughts of *soma* he imbibes; Agni, the god of fire, the priest of the sacrifice, whose mysterious birth is clearly connected to the enactment of the sacrificial ritual; and Soma, the personification (or deification) of the pressed plant and its juice that was imbibed as part of the Vedic ritual. The Vedic mythology knows several classes of divine beings, such as the Ādityas (of whom Varuṇa and Mitra are best known), the Maruts, the Asuras, and the Devas (the term that eventually became the generic one for the highest divine beings), and there are references to enmity between some of these classes of beings. There are slight references to the names of two gods who later dominate Hindu mythology—Viṣṇu and Rudra (the latter is an older name of the god more often called Śiva). In addition to these bits and pieces of mythology about the Vedic gods, the texts enumerate several creation stories, cite certain details regarding the nature of the afterlife, and contain a small but significant stock of tales that have a "folkloristic" quality (O'Flaherty 1985).

The Study of Post-Vedic Mythology: Epic and Purāṇa

Given the difficulty of elucidating the Vedic myths, the late nineteenth- and early twentieth-century scholarly tendency to focus on the Vedic texts alone had a retarding effect on the general study of Hindu mythology. It was not until scholars turned their attention to the post-Vedic texts, the Epics (*Mahābhārata* and *Rāmāyaṇa*, *ca.*, 400 BCE to 400 CE) and, most especially, the Purāṇas (completed sometime between 400 and 600 CE)—texts that chiefly hold the riches of Hindu India's mythological traditions—that progress in the study of Hindu mythology resumed. Ironically, some of the earliest studies of Hindu texts undertaken by Europeans focused on the Purāṇas (Burnouf 1840; Kennedy 1831; Ward 1817–20; Wilson 1840); however, the mid-nineteenth-century "discovery" of the Veda and the general romantic bias toward exploring India's "original" Āryan culture doomed these studies to second-class status (Rocher 1986: 5). Additionally, scholars inclined to study the Purāṇas confronted a number of discouraging factors, among them the vast size and somewhat unfixed nature of the textual corpus (the total of the eighteen major Purāṇic texts is estimated at 400,000 verses; there are also eighteen minor Purāṇas, though the list of texts varies [see Rocher 1986: 5, 30–34, 53, 67]); uncertainty about whether the texts were original or were adulterated forms of an as-yet unfound *ur*text (Wilson 1980: iv); and, perhaps most important of all, the overtly sexual nature of a number of the myths found in these texts—as one reviewer noted: "Many of them are highly extravagant; and even, viewed as allegories, they are degrading, and, in some respects, immoral" (Freer 1844: 391; cf. Winternitz 1981: 384).

Whereas the Vedic texts have a piecemeal mythology woven through them, the Epics and the Purāṇas contain extensive narrative tales that revolve around the deeds of gods, men, and heroes who lived in the long-ago. And, unlike the Vedic texts, which were recited in limited circumstances and only to a limited audience of religious cognoscenti (for they are represented as holy writ, or *śruti*), the Epics and the Purāṇas and the tales they originated from were the preserve of an ancient bardic tradition and were openly recounted as a means of upholding right action, whether in battle or in devotion to the gods (Rocher 1986: 54; Winternitz 1981: 499). Although the myths found in the Epics and the Purāṇas may derive from a narrative tradition that once stood parallel to the Vedic texts and certainly show a basis common to those referred to in the Vedic texts, they long ago lost their direct connection to the Vedic mythology.

The Epics and the Purāṇas share a great many similarities—"the Mahābhārata is to a great extent a Purāṇa and even the later books and chapters of the Rāmāyaṇa partake of the character of the Purāṇas" (Winternitz 1981: 495; cf. Hopkins 1915: 2)—and a great deal of common material, including extensive narratives recounting the deeds of divine beings and semidivine men, king-lists, descriptions of the duties of the castes, discussions of the afterlife, the nature of time, and the constitution of the cosmos. The Epics each center on a lengthy hero narrative. In the case of the *Mahābhārata*, the narrative frame is that of the war between two factions of the great Bharata clan; in the *Rāmāyaṇa*, it is the coming of age and exile of Prince Rāma and the abduction and rescue of his wife, Princess Sītā. A great mass of mythological material hangs, though sometimes only by a thread, on these hero narratives. (This material was described by Hopkins [1915], and substantial elements of the Mahābhārata material have been carefully and brilliantly analyzed in recent years by Hiltebeitel [1988–91, 1990, 1999, 2001].) Unlike the Epics, the Purāṇas do not have a central core; although they are ostensibly sectarian, the majority of them devoted to one or the other of the two great Hindu gods, Viṣṇu or Śiva, and the texts are loosely structured[6] with wide-ranging mythological materials that may be devoted to any of several gods (Rocher 1986: 21). The dominant religious force of the Purāṇic milieu is devotionalism (*bhakti*), and it clearly colors the mythology; related to this is the highly syncretistic nature of the stories recounted in these texts, as the feats of originally distinct gods are amalgamated into the feats of a single god, a process that is clearly visible in the myths of Viṣṇu's incarnations (*avatāra*s; Dimmit and van Buitenen 1978: 59), and the cycle of Śiva and his wife-consort Pārvatī (Devī) (O'Flaherty 1973: 30–32, 319–20). The effects of Hindu devotionalism are perhaps best exemplified in the mythology of Kṛṣṇa, who is depicted as an incarnation of Viṣṇu but is possibly rooted in the figure of an ancient king, whose life-story dominates one of the most popular Purāṇic texts, the *Bhāgavata Purāṇa* (Bryant 2003: xii). The authors of this text recount in detail Kṛṣṇa's life-story from his birth and infancy, through his boyhood and adolescence, to his kingship and death, employing alternating tones of intimacy and wonder and thereby providing his devotees with numerous models for his worship (e.g., the love of a mother for her infant, the infatuation between adolescents, or the respect of subjects for their king) and impressing on them a deep sense of the deity's divine majesty and mystery.

In recent decades, the study of Purāṇic mythology and the general study of Hindu mythology have been advanced considerably through the work of Wendy Doniger (who has also written under the surname O'Flaherty).[7] Doniger's studies of myth began with a groundbreaking exposition of the mythology of Śiva (1973), a deity whom she notes "is in many ways the most uniquely Indian god of all" (1)—but one whose mythology, with its deep erotic undertones, had been hardly touched by scholars—and in recent years has developed into a rich body of work that ranges freely through a great variety of mythologies while still remaining centered in Indic (particularly Sanskrit) materials. Doniger has long resisted defining myth, stating that her interest is not in what myth *is* but in what myth *does* (1998: 1); accordingly, her work, though textual in nature, also possesses a strong element of seeking out the meaning of myths *in situ*, "to use methods which reveal what the Hindus saw in them, to enjoy them as the exotic and delightful creations they are" (O'Flaherty 1973: 2). Doniger has referred to her general methodology as the "toolbox approach" (i.e., employing a range of interpretive tools—historical, linguistic, psychoanalytic, theological, and so forth—and often chosen intuitively, to tease out the widest range of meanings from the text; O'Flaherty 1980: 5). A central point in Doniger's interpretative methodology has been the stucturalist approach espoused by the French anthropologist, Claude Lévi-Strauss. Among the many important elements of this method (some of which, unfortunately, defy logical analysis—but then, as Doniger or Lévi-Strauss might say, myths are not logical), two have stood out in Doniger's work: first, that myths embody oppositions, sometimes overtly and sometimes under the cover of their resolution within the myth; and second, that "every version [of a myth] belongs to a myth" (Lévi-Strauss 1955: 94, 98). In application, the recognition of the oppositions contained within a myth effectively reveals the myth's own logic, expressed both in the mysterious terms of its own symbolism and in the terms of the cultural truths it upholds (recalling the functionalist approach to myth); the second methodological element, that all versions of a myth contribute to its meaning, opens up the text-historical dimensions of myth, for in each instance of a myth's telling what *is not* said in a myth is often as important as what *is* said.

Concluding Reflections

More than any other class of Hindu literature, the Purāṇic tales fulfill the criteria that modern scholars see as fundamental to myth: they have a narrative quality; they speak of the long ago of the world's origins and of the origins of various social institutions; they serve as a model for human behavior; and they interpenetrate—at least on a symbolic level—elements of the world of ritual performance (Honko 1984: 49–51; cf. Cohen 1969: 337). Yet, as Cornelia Dimmit and J. A. B. van Buitenen point out, "India, extraordinarily rich in myth, has no special word for it" (1978: 3). The Sanskrit word "*purāṇa*" means "belonging to the past," and the term itself is frequently associated with the word "*itihāsa*", "thus it was said" (Winternitz 1981: 496); taken together the terms indicate a "narrative of past events" and thus are more akin to the Western concept of history than they are to the concept of myth (Rao 1993). This notion of *purāṇa* questions the pervasive Western notion of myth as "falsehood," or at least as the representation of events that are empirically unverifiable and thus stand beyond the pale of ordinary belief, just as it does the idea that history is truth, narrating events that *actually* occurred. Indeed, within the last century, the interpenetration of "history" and "myth" in India has taken on a special significance as the so-called "Hindutva" movements have looked to "mythical" narratives of the ancient king Rāma as hard evidence of the nature of past Indian regimes (Tamminen 1996). Here, the idea of empirical verification—of "true history"—succumbs to the larger role of myth as the repository of a culture's most deeply held values and ideologies; from the perspective of myth, what is *believed* to have happened has a far greater hold on human minds than that which actually has happened.

Notes

1 At the same time, Herder, like other German romantics, took a harsh view of many of India's institutions, such as the caste system and the idea of *karma* (Halbfass 1988: 71); in a similar vein, Arthur Schopenhauer extolled the Upaniṣad texts, yet remarked that he found Indian poetry and sculpture to be "tasteless and monstrous" (cited in Müller 1879: lxi).

2 Müller's theory was not entirely original but appeared to extend a principle already enunciated by Jones, who attributed the rise of mythology to the perversion of "historical, or natural truth...by ignorance, imagination, flattery, or stupidity" (1993b: 179).

3 A number of studies, more broadly devoted to Müller's general theories of ancient Āryan mythology appeared throughout the late nineteenth century; see, for example, Cox (1870); Titcomb (1889); see also Dorson (1968: 174–76).

4 Ethnological studies of India did draw on the influential theories of Malinowski; see, for example, von Fürer-Haimendorf (1948: 99).

5 Within the general study of mythology, particularly as espoused by Raglan (1955), the theory arose that myths are in nearly all cases intimately connected to rituals, either as explanation or as part of their enactment. Although in certain

cases the Vedic myths do relate directly to the myths seen, for example, in the mythology of the cosmic man and the ritual building of the fire altar (see Tull 1989: 57–69), for the most part the myth-ritual theory throws little light on the interpretation of ancient Indian mythology and was not adopted by scholars studying these myths.

6 Purāṇas are said to be characterized by five marks, that is, five subjects that they describe: creation; recreation; genealogies of gods and sages; the ancient ages of man; and the genealogies of the kings. In fact, it has been estimated that less than three percent of the material in the Purāṇas is devoted to the topics specified under the five marks (Rao 1993: 87).

7 Although, following Doniger's lead, scholars have increasingly turned their attention to the Purāṇas, these texts still largely remain the specialist's domain. Dimmit's and van Buitenen's work (1978) remains the only translation of a broad range of Purāṇic mythology. Other recent works translating Purāṇic myths have either included Hindu myths from several periods and textual milieus (Bhattacharji 1970; O'Flaherty 1975) or from one specific Purāṇa (Bryant 2003) or have focused on a single deity (Courtright 1985). Two important general studies of the Purāṇas are Doniger (1993) and Rocher (1986).

References Cited

Bellah, Robert N. 1972 [1964]. "Religious Evolution." *In* William A Lessa and Evon Z. Vogt, eds, *Reader in Comparative Religion: An Anthropological Approach*, 36–50. New York: Harper and Row.

Bergaigne, Abel. 1969–73 [1878–97]. *Vedic Religion According to the Hymns of the Ṛgveda* (trans. V. G. Paranjpe). 4 volumes. Poona: Aryasamskrti Prakasana.

Bhattacharji, Sukumari. 1970. *The Indian Theogony: A Comparative Study of Indian Mythology from the Vedas to the Purāṇas*. London: Cambridge University Press.

Bonnefoy, Yves, ed. 1991 [1981]. *Asian Mythologies* (trans. Wendy Doniger). Chicago: University of Chicago Press.

Bryant, Edwin. 2003. *Krishna: The Beautiful Legend of God. Śrīmad Bhāgavata Purāṇa Book X*. London: Penguin Books.

Burnouf, Eugène. 1840. *Le Bhāgavata Purāṇa; ou, histoire poétique de Krichna*. Paris: Imprimerie Royale.

Cohen, Percy S. 1969. "Theories of Myth." *Man (n.s.)* 4, 3: 337–53.

Courtright, Paul. 1985. *Gaṇeśa: Lord of Obstacles, Lord of Beginnings*. Oxford: Oxford University Press.

Cox, George W. 1870. *Mythology of the Aryan Nations*. 2 volumes. London: Longmans, Green & Co.

Dimmitt, Cornelia and J. A. B. van Buitenen, eds. and trans. 1978. *Classical Hindu Mythology: A Reader in the Sanskrit Purāṇas*. Philadelphia: Temple University Press.

Doniger, Wendy, trans. 1981. *The Rig Veda*. New York: Penguin Books.

Doniger, Wendy, ed. 1993. *Purāṇa Perennis: Reciprocity and Transformation in Hindu and Jaina Texts*. Albany: State University of New York Press.

Doniger, Wendy. 1998. *The Implied Spider: Politics and Theology in Myth*. New York: Columbia University Press.

Dorson, Richard. 1955. "The Eclipse of Solar Mythology." *In* Thomas A. Sebeok, ed., *Myth: A Symposium*, 25–63. Bloomington: Indiana University Press.

Dorson, Richard. 1968. *The British Folklorists: A History*. Chicago: University of Chicago Press.

Dundes, Alan. 1984. "Introduction." *In* Alan Dundes, ed., *Sacred Narrative: Readings in the Theory of Myth*, 1–3. Berkeley: University of California Press.

Eliade, Mircea. 1963. *Myth and Reality* (trans. Willard R. Trask). New York: Harper & Row.

Freer, Allan. 1844. "The Vishnu Purána; A System of Hindu Mythology and Tradition." *The North British Review* 1, 2: 366–96.

von Fürer-Haimendorf, Christoph. 1948. *The Raj Gonds of Adilabad: A Peasant Culure of the Deccan*. London: Macmillan.

Halbfass, Wilhelm. 1988 [1981]. *India and Europe: An Essay in Understanding*. Albany: State University of New York Press.

Hillebrandt, Alfred. 1980 [1891]. *Vedic Mythology* (trans. Sreeramula Rajeswara Sarma). Volume 1. Delhi: Motilal Banasidass.

Hiltebeitel, Alf. 1988–91. *The Cult of Draupadī*. 2 volumes. Chicago: University of Chicago Press.

Hiltebeitel, Alf. 1990 [1976]. *The Ritual of Battle: Krishna in the Mahābhārata*. Albany: State University of New York Press.

Hiltebeitel, Alf. 1999. *Rethinking India's Oral and Classical Epics: Draupadī among Rajputs, Muslims, and Dalits*. Chicago: University of Chicago Press.

Hiltebeitel, Alf. 2001. *Rethinking the Mahābhārata: A Reader's Guide to the Education of the Dharma King*. Chicago: University of Chicago Press.

Honko, Lauri. 1984 [1972]. "The Problem of Defining Myth." *In* Alan Dundes, ed., *Sacred Narrative: Readings in the Theory of Myth*, 41–52. Berkeley: University of California Press.

Hopkins, Edward Washburn. 1915. *Epic Mythology*. Strassburg: Trubner.

Jamison, Stephanie W. and Michael Witzel. 2003. "Vedic Hinduism." *In* Arvind Sharma, ed., *The Study of Hindusim*, 65–113. Columbia: The University of South Carolina Press.

Jones, William. 1993a [1786]. "The Third Anniversary Discourse." *In* Satya Pachori, ed., *Sir William Jones: A Reader*, 172–78. Delhi: Oxford University Press.

Jones, William. 1993b [1784]. "On the Gods of Greece, Italy, and India." *In* Satya Pachori, ed., *Sir William Jones: A Reader*, 179–84. Delhi: Oxford University Press.

Keith, A. B. 1925. *The Religion and Philosophy of the Veda and Upanishads*. Harvard: Harvard University Press.

Kennedy, Vans. 1831. *Researches into the Nature and Affinity of Ancient and Hindu Mythology*. London: Longman, Rees, Orme, Brown, and Green.

Kirk, G. S. 1970. *Myth: Its Meaning and Functions in Ancient and Other Cultures*. Berkeley: University of California Press.

Lévi-Strauss, Claude. 1955. "The Structural Study of Myth." *In* Thomas A. Sebeok, ed., *Myth: A Symposium,* 81–106. Bloomington: Indiana University Press.
Lincoln, Bruce. 1999. *Theorizing Myth: Narrative, Ideology, and Scholarship.* Chicago: The University of Chicago Press.
Macdonell, A. A. 1897. *The Vedic Mythology*. Strassburg: Trubner.
Malinowski, Bronislaw. 1954 [1925]. *Magic, Science, and Religion and Other Essays.* New York: Doubleday.
Malinowski, Bronislaw. 1984 [1926]. "The Role of Myth in Life." *In* Alan Dundes, ed., *Sacred Narrative: Readings in the Theory of Myth,* 193–206. Berkeley: University of California Press.
Middleton, John. 1967. "Introduction." *In* John Middleton, ed., *Myth and Cosmos: Readings in Mythology and Symbolism,* ix–xi. Austin: University of Texas Press.
Müller, F. Max. 1867a [1856]. "Comparative Mythology." *In* Max Müller, *Chips from a German Workshop*, 2: 1–143. London: Longmans, Green & Co.
Müller, F. Max. 1867b [1865]. "On Manners and Customs." *In* Max Müller, *Chips from a German Workshop*, 2: 250–85. London: Longmans, Green & Co.
Müller, F. Max. 1873 [1865]. "Lecture on the Vedas." *In* Max Müller, ed., *Chips from a German Workshop*, 1: 1–48. New York: Scribner.
Müller, F. Max. 1879. "Introduction to the Upanishads." *In* F. Max Müller, trans., *The Upanishads*, lvii–ci. Oxford: Clarendon Press.
O'Flaherty, Wendy Doniger. 1973. *Śiva: The Erotic Ascetic.* Oxford: Oxford University Press.
O'Flaherty, Wendy Doniger, ed., and trans. 1975. *Hindu Myths.* London: Penguin Books.
O'Flaherty, Wendy Doniger. 1980. *Women, Androgynes, and Other Mythical Beasts.* Chicago: University of Chicago Press.
O'Flaherty, Wendy Doniger. 1985. *Tales of Sex and Violence: Folklore, Sacrifice, and Danger in the Jaiminīya Brāhmaṇa*. Chicago: University of Chicago Press.
Oldenberg, Herman. 1988 [1894]. *The Religion of the Veda* (trans. Shridhar Shrotri). Delhi: Motilal Banarsidass.
Pettazzonni, Raffaele. 1984 [1954]. "The Truth of Myth." *In* Alan Dundes, ed., *Sacred Narrative: Readings in the Theory of Myth,* 98–109. Berkeley: University of California Press.
Plato. 1961. *The Republic. In* Edith Hamilton and Huntington Cairns, eds, *Plato: The Collected Dialogues* (trans. Paul Shorey), 575–844. Princeton: Princeton University Press.
Raglan, Lord. 1955. "Myth and Ritual." *In* Thomas A. Sebeok, ed., *Myth: A Symposium,* 122–35. Bloomington: Indiana University Press.
Rao, V. Narayana. 1993. "Purāṇa as Brahminic Ideology." *In* Wendy Doniger, ed., *Purāṇa Perennis: Reciprocity and Transformation in Hindu and Jaina Texts*, 85–100. Albany: State University of New York Press.
Rocher, Ludo. 1986. *The Purāṇas.* Wiesbaden: Otto Harrassowitz.
Stone, Jon R. 2002. "Introduction." *In* Jon R. Stone, ed., *The Essential Max Müller: On Language, Mythology, and Religion,* 1–24. New York: Palgrave Macmillan.

Tamminen, Tapio. 1996. "Hindu Revivalism and the Hindutva Movement." *Temenos* 32: 221–38.

Titcomb, Sarah Elizabeth. 1889. *Aryan Sun Myths: The Origin of Religions*. London: Trübner.

Tull, Herman W. 1989. *The Vedic Origins of Karma: Cosmos as Man in Ancient Indian Myth and Ritual*. Albany: State University of New York Press.

Ward, William. 1817–20. *History, Literature and Mythology of the Hindus*. 4 volumes. Serampore: The Mission Press.

Wilson, Horace Hayman., trans. 1980 [1840]. *The Viṣṇu Purāṇa: A System of Hindu Mythology and Tradition*. Delhi: Nag Publishers.

Winternitz, Maurice. 1981 (1909). *A History of Indian Literature*, Volume 1 (trans. V. Srinivasa Sarma). Delhi: Motilal Banarsidass.

19

Nationalism

Peter Heehs

Ideas of Hinduism and India under Colonialism
Early Nationalism and Hinduism
Election-Based Separatism
Gandhi
Hindu Nationalism and Hindutva
Proliferation of Sectarian and Caste-Based Separatism
Sectarian Politics and Partition of India

Cultural nationalism first appeared in India during the latter half of the nineteenth century. The same period saw a consolidation of the idea of a Hindu religion and lively debates about what Hinduism was and ought to be. When thinking about the nation converged with thinking about religion, two themes emerged: definition and organization. Indian thinkers who had been exposed to Western religion and thought observed that Hinduism lacked the doctrinal and organizational unity that Christianity and Islam possessed. In response, some of them tried to isolate a common core of Hindu belief and to organize separate Hindu sects into a coherent Hindu *saṅghaṭan* or organization. As the national movement gained force and the British government was compelled to introduce elected assemblies, protonationalist organizations transformed themselves into political parties and pressure groups. In democracies, numbers mean power, so sectarian and caste groups configured themselves in such a way as to maximize their demographic strength. Patterns established along these lines during the anticolonial movement are still visible in the religious and caste identities of independent India.

Ideas of Hinduism and India under Colonialism

By around 1860, English-speaking people in Calcutta, Bombay, and Madras had a pretty good idea of what they meant when they said "India" and "Hinduism." The former term, in use in the West for many centuries, was given a defined body in 1858 when the Crown assumed sovereignty over the territories of the British East India Company. The latter term was a neologism, only about eighty years old (Sweetman 2005), but it was fairly well established by the middle of the century, and those who used it in speech or writing did not find it meaningless or misleading (Lorenzen 2006: 4; Pennington 2005: 172).

During the latter part of the century, the idea of India as a distinct country encompassing the various British provinces and princely states grew in tandem with the idea of Hinduism as a distinct religion encompassing its various sectarian and regional forms. There can be no doubt that British administrative, legal, scholarly, and other discourses had an enormous influence on the growth of these two ideas. Modern India as a political unit (as opposed to a geographical or cultural region) was clearly a creation of British imperialism; the modern idea of India took shape within the outlines of the British colonial state. Similarly, the concept "Hinduism," to a considerable extent, assumed its modern form in response to pressure from British missionaries, scholars, and government officials. However, the concept had a history that long preceded the British conquest, and its modern features were elaborated in a many-sided discussion involving Indian and British intellectuals (Lorenzen 2006: 14; Pennington 2005: 61). There is little empirical evidence to support the idea, fashionable during the 1990s, that "Hinduism" was nothing but a construction or invention of British colonial discourse.[1]

The nineteenth-century discussion was not about whether Hinduism existed—everyone took this for granted—but what Hinduism was or ought to be. The central problem was to find the essence or distinguishing characteristics of the diverse though related practices subsumed under the English term. The proposed solutions were themselves diverse. Rammohan Roy, the founder of the Brāhmo Samāj, affirmed that the central truth of Hinduism was to be found in such texts as the Upaniṣads, not in such practices as image-worship or customs such as *sahamaraṇa*. The Prārthanā Samāj of Bombay combined traditional Maharashtrian devotionalism with Western-style social reform. Svāmī Dayānanda Sarasvatī, the founder of the Ārya Samāj, saw the Vedas as the bedrock of religious belief but took innovative positions in regard to social questions, such as caste.

Wherever they emerged, these new denominations were opposed by the orthodox. Some of them organized religious associations (*dharma sabhā*) to push their traditionalist agendas. By the mid-1870s, a wide range of positions—reform-minded modernism, conservative innovation, moderate conservatism, and outright reaction—were competing for the attention of people in an emerging "public space" (Zavos 2002: 12).

These positions were by no means rigid. In 1872, Rajnarayan Bose, the head of the Ādi or "original" Brāhmo Samāj, delivered a speech in which he declared that Hinduism was superior to all other religions. For this he was praised by the orthodox, though he was not departing from the existing Brāhmo line that the purpose of the Samāj was to restore the primordial truth of Hinduism. The flux and diversity of opinion at the end of the nineteenth century makes it hard to apply the conventional label "Hindu revivalism" to all that was then going on. The distinguishing characteristic of Hinduism at this time was not a return to old beliefs but the tendency to establish organizations that were open to any qualified individual, had clearly defined missions, and practiced public persuasion (Jones 1990: 1–2; Zavos 2002: 34). Such organizations differed markedly from the comparatively closed and amorphous *sampradāya*s of the late classical, medieval, and early modern periods.

Early Nationalism and Hinduism

Public organizations played an important role in another contemporary development: the birth and growth of nationalist feeling. Often, people who were active in debates about the essential nature of Hinduism were involved in the activities of protonationalist organizations, such as the Jātīya Melā or "National Gathering" of Calcutta and the Poona Sarvajanik Sabhā. Those involved in such groups did not find any inconsistency between the impulse to discover the fundamental truth of their religion and the drive to create community networks. M. G. Ranade, an important member of the Prārthanā Samāj, was also a founder of the Sarvajanik Sabhā. The Jātīya Melā (later renamed the Hindū Melā) was created by Nabagopal Mitra and Rajnarayan Bose and supported by the family of Devendranath Tagore, all prominent Brāhmos. Such men did not feel they were jumbling the religious and civic spheres together when they "defended Hindu national identity" at the same time that they "supported constructive programs of self-help and development" (Kopf 1979: 185).

Nationalism emerged first in the cultural and religious fields and only later began to express itself in political action. Partha Chatterjee explains this phenomenon in Gramsian terms. Refusing the status of colonial subjects, the colonized were driven to "construct their national identities" by creating an "inner domain of culture," which was "declared the sovereign territory of the nation" (1993: 237). The interesting part of this analysis is the distinction it makes between the "outer" domain, wherein the colonized were not free, and the "inner" domain, wherein they enjoyed some measure of autonomy. Its flaw is to treat the inner, spiritual realm as a derivative of outward, socioeconomic realities. In the Medea's caldron of late nineteenth-century India, no single factor—cultural, spiritual, economic, social, or political—outweighed all the others.

Some of the most important literary figures of the last decades of the century combined an interest in Hinduism, as they conceived it, with some form of cultural nationalism. The last works of Bankimchandra Chatterji (1838–94), the preeminent Bengali writer of the period, were historical novels with a strong nationalist flavor and monographs on Hinduism. Bankim felt that a new approach to the old religion was needed because "past traditions of Hinduism had not generated any impulse for freedom and nationhood" (Sarkar 1996: 169). The hero of his *Kṛṣṇacarita* (The Life of Krishna, 1892) was an historical and martial figure; his Bengali commentary on the *Bhagavad Gītā* (1902) was a gospel of engaged action. At the end of his *Dharmatattva* (Principles of Religion, 1888), he has a *guru* tell a student: "Love of one's country (*svadeś-prīti*) is greater than all *dharma*s—let this never be forgotten" (Chattopadhyaya 1941–42: 151).

Bankim gave a new turn to old traditions and texts to demonstrate the resilience of Hinduism and the importance of patriotic action. Bharatendu Harishchandra, "the father of modern Hindi," was a traditionalist in religion and a loyalist vis-à-vis the Rāj, yet he too was dedicated to the uplift of India, seeking "the cleansing, reform, of tradition in the very name of tradition" (Dalmia 1997: 21–22). Svāmī Vivekānanda also saw national progress as a function of reform based on a recovery of the truths of the ancient tradition: "You must go down to the basis of the thing, to the very root of the matter. That is what I call radical reform. Put the fire there and let it burn upwards and make an Indian nation" (1989, 3: 216). A conservative innovator, Vivekānanda attacked Brāhmaṇical "priest-craft" but approved of the *varṇa* system. He was confident that Vedāntic Hinduism was the only possible basis for a universal religion; yet he insisted (when writing to a Muslim) that the universal religion would harmonize and surpass the Vedas, the Bible, and the Qurān (Vivekananda 1989, 3: 182; 6: 416).

At the same time that Hindu-flavored cultural nationalism was developing, secular organizations with protonationalist programs were being established in the major urban centers. Such groups as the Indian Association of Calcutta, the Madras Mahājana Sabhā, and the Bombay Presidency Association gave a voice to members of the middle and upper classes whose interests were affected by British administrative policy. The founding of the Indian National Congress in 1885 provided these classes with a yearly public forum where they could air their grievances. Though it did not concern itself with religion *per se*, the Congress was viewed by many participants as an ally or even an offspring of the movement of religious and social reform. Reformer and Congress *éminence grise* M. G. Ranade started a National Social Conference that met yearly after the Congress in the same venue. The socially conservative but politically radical Congressman Balgangadhar Tilak vehemently opposed this linkage and in 1895 forced the Congress to abandon it. Seeking a means to bring the nationalist movement to the masses, Tilak transformed the largely domestic Gaṇapati Pūjā into a public festival in 1894. This move is often cited as an early expression of "Hindu nationalism." It may also be taken as an expression of nationalistic Hinduism, in which religion enthusiasm was given a patriotic outlet.

During the first twenty years of its existence, the Congress passed dozens of resolutions that were routinely ignored by the government. The national movement did not really take off until August 1905, when the province of Bengal was partitioned. Mass protests were organized in Calcutta and other places, and a boycott of British products was declared. Some protestors made use of religious symbols and practices. The family rite of *rakṣā-bandhan* (in which girls tie a thread around their brothers' wrists) was given a nationalistic turn, people tying *rākhīs*, threads, around one another's wrists as a sign of Bengal's indivisibility. Patriotic songs combining religious and political language were sung in public processions. The most famous was "Vande Mātaram," written by Bankimchandra thirty years earlier and published in his novel *Ānandamaṭh* (1884). In it Bengal is personified as the Mother Goddess, described using conventional literary imagery, and at one point identified with Durgā, Lakṣmī, and Sarasvatī. The metaphor of Bengal as Mother-Motherland was taken up by physical culture groups who dreamed of revolutionary action. It was developed in speeches and newspaper writings by Bipin Chandra Pal, Aurobindo Ghose, and other radical politicians. These Extremists (as they were called) linked up with like-minded men in different parts of the country, notably Tilak in Maharashtra and Lālā Lajpat Rai in Punjab. The views of these leaders and their moderate opponents were discussed in distant provinces. The metaphor of the Mother-Motherland soon had all of India as its referent.

One result of the cult of the Mother-Motherland was the estrangement of Bengali Muslims. During the early months of the anti-Partition movement, many Muslims joined with Hindus in opposing the measure. By and large cooperation ceased after 1906. The charge that the administration used divide-and-rule tactics to split the opposition is not unfounded. British officials courted elite Muslims, promising them enhanced influence in the new order and, in 1906, encouraging them to found the All-India Muslim League as a counterweight to the Indian National Congress. But the causes of Hindu-Muslim discord were diverse and complexly interrelated: economic, social, cultural, and political factors all helped drive a wedge between the two communities. Hindu-Muslim riots broke out in 1907 in areas of East Bengal where the anti-Partition movement was active. Aggression and retaliation on both sides helped to polarize the national movement along religious lines and also changed the way that members of the two religions regarded their own and the "other" community.

Election-Based Separatism

The idea that Hindus and Muslims formed separate *political* constituencies was given official sanction by the Morley-Minto Reforms (which became law as the Indian Councils Act of 1909). This provided among other things for separate Muslim electorates, which would guarantee Muslims a certain number of seats in legislative assemblies. The Congress opposed the Reforms because they were undemocratic. Hindu religiopolitical groups, such as the Hindū Sabhā of Lahore, opposed them because they hurt Hindu interests. What is common to both positions is an awareness that both religious and political groups had to organize to be heard. In 1909, a meeting of the Punjab Hindū Sabhā attracted national attention. Among the main points on the agenda was to find and articulate the beliefs or principles that united all Hindus. Shared concerns in the face of a common adversary blurred the line between "revivalists" and "reformists," as orthodox or *sanātana* Hindus came together with members of the Ārya Samāj (Zavos 2000: 118–19). Hindu identity, formerly regarded as a religious and cultural question, became a subject of political debate. At the 1909 meeting, Lajpat Rai announced that Hindus were "a 'nation' in themselves, because they represent a type of civilisation all their own" (cited in Jaffrelot 1996: 19). Aurobindo Ghose, a radical nationalist and a champion of universalistic Hinduism, rebutted this early articulation of the "two-nation theory": "We do not understand Hindu nationalism as a possibility under modern conditions....Under modern conditions India can only exist as a whole" (Aurobindo 1997: 304). He saw the national movement as a sort of civic religion, in which Hindus and Muslims would be united in love of the motherland, their sense of separateness "drowned in fraternal feelings, in a common love and worship of the Mother" (Aurobindo 1999: 118). In the years that followed, relations between the two communities, far from being drowned in fraternal feelings, were convulsed by discord.

The Extremists were expelled from the Congress in 1907–8 and swept away by the government repression that followed an outbreak of revolutionary terrorism. The Congress lapsed into pseudo-parliamentary posturings that the government could easily ignore. Religious rhetoric fell out of favor, as moderate Hindus attempted to build bridges with the Muslims—without notable success. It was not until 1916 that nationalists of the two communities began to work together again. In the Lucknow Pact, formalized that December, Muslims agreed to endorse the Congress's demand for eventual "self-government," while Hindus accepted the principle of weighted representation, allowing Muslims one-third of the seats in the central legislature. Religious identity was now a political fact. No room was left for syncretic forms of practice. In the eyes of the census-taker and election official, one was either a Hindu or a Muslim.

Gandhi

During his formative years in South Africa, Mohandas K. Gandhi perfected a style of nonviolent noncooperation that he called *satyāgraha*. This was, in its origin, an amalgam of political, philosophical, and religious ideas from different quarters. From Vaiṣṇavism and Jainism, Gandhi learned the goal of liberation through detachment and the ideal of nonviolence or *ahiṃsā*. From John Ruskin and Leo Tolstoy, he picked up a distrust of mechanistic Western civilization. Such Bengali politicians as Bipin Chandra and Aurobindo helped him refine his ideas of passive resistance; Bengali revolutionaries were to him object lessons in the futility of political violence. After returning to India in 1915, Gandhi launched *satyāgraha* campaigns in Bihar and Gujarat. Emerging as the most prominent nationalist in the country, he took charge of the agitation against the Rowlatt Bills in April 1919. Later that year he found an issue that he hoped would draw Muslims into his campaign of nonviolent noncooperation. This was the break-up of the Ottoman Caliphate after the First World War. For about a year, Hindus and Muslims worked together to a greater extent than they ever had. But after Gandhi called off the *satyāgraha* campaign in 1922, the two communities went their separate ways, and there was a recrudescence of Hindu-Muslim violence.

Gandhi regarded himself as a *sanātanī* Hindu, but he was far from orthodox. Like Rammohan, Vivekānanda, and other religious innovators, he grounded a modern, eclectic understanding of Hinduism in ancient texts and beliefs. He was a Hindu, he once wrote, because he believed in the Vedas and other Hindu scriptures and in the doctrines of reincarnation and *avatāra*-hood, in the system of the four *varṇa*s (but not the caste system as currently practiced), and in cow-protection in a "much larger sense than the popular" and because he did "not disbelieve in idol-worship" (Gandhi 1958–84, 21: 246). Yet he was prepared to ignore scripture if it went against his inner convictions. When Hindu Mahāsabhā leader Balkrishna Shivram Moonje tried to prove to him that untouchability was an integral part of Hinduism, he replied: "Happily for me, my Hinduism does not bind me to every verse because it is written in Sanskrit....Yours is a distorted kind of Hinduism. I claim in all humility to have lived Hinduism all my life" (letter of 14 May 1927, cited in Nanda 2004: 15). For him, the greatness of Hinduism lay especially in its tolerance and nonviolence. These principles became the basis of his action. He claimed to have entered politics because "politics encircle us today like the coil of a snake from which one cannot get out." Obliged "to wrestle with the snake" to find inner peace, he experimented "with myself and my friends by introducing religion into politics." But the religion he spoke of was not Hinduism *per se* but "the religion which transcends Hinduism, which changes one's very nature, which binds one indissolubly to the truth within and which ever purifies" (Gandhi 1958–84, 17: 406). Here the universalism of Rammohan and Vivekānanda is combined with a secular activism that Gandhi, like Bankimchandra and Tilak, found in the *Bhagavad Gītā*.

Hindu Nationalism and Hindutva

The three or four years that followed the collapse of the noncooperation movement saw the rise of hard-line Hindu nationalism. Vinayak Damodar Savarkar provided an ideology for this movement with his 1923 book, *Hindutva*. Savarkar often is credited with the coinage of this term, but "Hindutva" had been employed, in various senses, for more than fifty years. The editor of a conservative Hindu journal used it in 1872 to refer to Hindus generally and Hindu institutions that were under attack by Brāhmoism (Bhattacharya 1998: 9). Fifteen years later, Brāhmo leader Rajnarayan Bose used it to signify the defining characteristics of his universalistic Hinduism (Bagal 1955–56: 94–95). Bankimchandra used it in the historical novel *Ānandamaṭh* (1884) to mean a feeling of Hindu identity that people sought after Hinduism (*hindū-dharma*) had been suppressed. In his Bengali book, *Hindutva*, published in 1892, Chandranath Basu defended traditional Hindu practices and affirmed the superiority of things Hindu to Western philosophy and religion (Sen 1993: 215–16). Tilak (1974–76, 6: 979), in a travel piece of 1900, spoke of Hindutva as the common factor that united Indian society and Hindu believers. In an essay of 1901–2 originally entitled *Hindutva* (later changed to *Bharatbarsher Samāj*), Rabindranath Tagore (1939–49, 3: 522, 525) wrote that Hindutva, in a broad inclusive sense, was what gave Indian society its coherence and upheld the unity of the Indian nation. When Savarkar took up the term more than two decades later, he used it in an exclusive rather than an inclusive sense, stripping it of its religious connotations except as a means to exclude Muslims and Christians. Hindutva was not, he wrote, reserved for "believers of the dogmas and religious practices that go by the name Hinduism." (If it were, Savarkar, an atheist, would have been excluded.) The markers of Hinduism were national, racial, and cultural. A Hindu was one who (1) lived in Hindustan, (2) shared "the bond of common blood," and (3) looked on India as the "Holyland" (Savarkar 1942: 64–67, 90–93). By this definition, indigenous Sikhs, Buddhists, and Jains were Hindus, whereas Muslims and Christians whose families had lived in the country for centuries were not. This had obvious demographic and electoral advantages.

Savarkar's *Hindutva* was published at a time when certain Hindus were growing afraid that their community would sooner or later cease to be a majority in India. Even before this demographic catastrophe took place, Hindus would find themselves dominated politically by Muslims, who had been granted separate electorates by the colonial government and who doubtless would insist that this arrangement be preserved in independent India. In the face of this challenge, it was necessary for all Hindus to stand together. This was the idea behind the Hindu *saṅghaṭan* ("organization" or "unity") movement. For a while, the Hindū Mahāsabhā (Great Hindu Council) was the principal promoter of this idea. Formed in Punjab in 1915 through the consolidation of earlier Hindu Sabhās, the Mahāsabhā was reorganized and extended during the 1920s by Madan Mohan Malaviya and others. Its goals were the protection and uplifting of the Hindu race, Hindu culture, and the Hindu Rāṣṭra (nation). Politically, it allied itself with other Hindu interest groups who were dissatisfied with the secular stance of the Congress. It championed such causes as cow-protection and the reconversion of Muslims and Christians. During the mid-1920s, Ārya Samāj leader Svāmī Śraddhānanda became the most visible champion of Hindu *saṅghaṭan* in general and of reconversion in particular. His proposals for halting the decline of the "dying race" of Hindus included the building of nondenominational Hindu Rāṣṭra Mandiras (temples of the Hindu nation) in every city and major town. The presiding deities would be Gau-mātā (the cow-mother), Sarasvatī (the goddess of learning), and Bhūmi-mātā (the motherland). The temples would be large enough to allow worship by enormous congregations: not a few hundred, as in the largest Hindu temples, but tens of thousands, as in such mosques as the Jama Masjid of Delhi (Jaffrelot 1996: 22).

The approach of Śraddhānanda and the Hindū Mahāsabhā to the organization and expansion of Hinduism was comparatively moderate. Those desiring a more aggressive approach were obliged to look elsewhere. In 1925, dissatisfied members of the Mahāsabhā formed the Rāṣṭrīya Svayamsevak Saṅgh. This National Volunteer Society became the standard-bearer of extreme Hindu nationalism. The Saṅgh accepted and developed Savarkar's Hindutva ideology and the aim of Hindu *saṅghaṭan*. Organization was the group's keyword. Local *śākhās*, or branches, became centers of physical and ideological education. Hindu unity was defined in terms of opposition to Muslims, Christians, and members of other "foreign" cultures.

During the late 1930s, the ideology of the Saṅgh took a frankly fascist turn. Saṅgh leader Madhav Sadashiv Golwalkar commended the Nazi's purging of German Jews as "race pride at its highest" and affirmed that non-Hindus in India would have to live "wholly subordinated to the Hindu nation, claiming nothing, deserving no privileges, far less any preferential treatment—not even citizen's rights" (1939: 43, 47–49). The book in which these observations were published was later withdrawn from circulation, but the racialism, xenophobia, and belief in Hindu supremacy that it put forward have remained central parts of the Saṅgh's ideology.

Proliferation of Sectarian and Caste-Based Separatism

Between 1924 and 1928, Gandhi took little active interest in the issues of mainstream nationalist politics. For the next four years, he was involved with religious, social, and economic problems: Hindu-Muslim relations, the uplift of the untouchables, hand-spinning, opposition to child marriage, cow-protection. Customary practices that had gone unchallenged for centuries now became matters of public debate.

In 1927, the British government announced the formation of a constitutional commission that included no Indian members. This was the signal for a renewal of mass political action. The years 1928 to 1932 were among the most eventful in the history of the freedom movement: the acceptance of independence as the goal of the Congress, the Salt March, and the Civil Disobedience Movement. While these events were capturing headlines around the world, politicians claiming to represent religious, caste, and other constituencies were formulating their demands and presenting them to the British government. At issue was the composition of legislative assemblies, in particular whether certain communities should be granted separate electorates. In the Nehru Report of 1928, the Congress and allied parties endorsed reserved seats for Muslims but rejected communal electorates. M. A. Jinnah of the Muslim League insisted on separate electorates, demanding again that one-third of the seats in the central legislative assembly must be reserved for Muslims. Meanwhile, Bhimrao Ramji Ambedkar persuaded the British government to grant separate electorates to the Depressed Classes (otherwise known as untouchables and now generally called Dalits). Gandhi, who had been working for many years for the uplift of those he called Harijans (children of God), was vehemently opposed to this division of the Hindu community. He undertook a "fast unto death" until the proposal was modified. Ambedkar, who disliked Hinduism and distrusted Gandhi, agreed eventually to accept an increased reservation of seats for Depressed Class legislators in the general electorate. This was a step toward political representation that eventually would lead to the election of Dalit chief ministers in some states of independent India. More broadly, the agreement acknowledged that even the lowest stratum of Hindu society was now a political and social force with views that had to be considered. Politics had begun to bring about a change in a socioreligious system that had endured for many centuries.

The movement for caste reform and depressed-class rights had begun in the late nineteenth century. In Poona, Jotirao Phule, a Śūdra, opened girls' schools, an orphanage, and other social institutions and started the Satya Śodhak Samāj (Society for Seekers of Truth) to promote the interests of Śūdras and agitate against Brāhmaṇa oppression. Phule condemned such organizations as the Prārthanā Samāj, the Sarvajanik Samāj, and the Indian National Congress as Brāhmaṇa-dominated groups that did nothing to help the masses. He repudiated the Vedas at a moment when many Hindus were holding them up as the central scripture of a unified Hindu religion. During the early twentieth century, the non-Brāhmaṇa movement was continued and extended in Maharashtra by Mahārājā Shahu Chhatrapati, a Marāṭhā; in Kerala by Svāmī Nārāyaṇa Guru, an Izhavar; and in Tamil Nadu by E. V. Ramaswami Naicker, a rationalist and atheist. Naicker's Justice Party was influential in Tamil Nadu during the 1920s and 1930s and laid the groundwork for the various Dravidian parties that have dominated Tamil politics since 1967.

Sectarian Politics and Partition of India

The Government of India Act of 1935 established provincial autonomy and a federally organized central government. The first provincial elections were held in 1937. Congress candidates won in most provinces and assumed office. Congress put itself forward as a secular party, but was regarded by the Muslim League as Hindu-dominated and by the Hindū Mahāsabhā, now led by Savarkar, as a betrayer of Hindu interests. Congress governments resigned in October 1939 over differences with the British about the conduct of the Second World War. The League, the Mahāsabhā, and other parties took control of provincial ministries to advance their interests. During and after the war, several conferences were held, and parties and pressure-groups representing Hindus, Muslims, Sikhs, Christians, caste organizations, the Depressed Classes, and so forth were all given a hearing. The clash of their demands made it impossible to work out a constitutional framework that satisfied everyone. In 1940, the Muslim League demanded a separate state for Indian Muslims. This became the most fractious issue in subsequent negotiations with the British. Attempts to find a compromise solution failed, and in 1947, the British granted independence to two separate states: India and Pakistan. The violence that accompanied the Partition of British India claimed hundreds of thousands of lives and left scars that have not yet healed.

Note

1 This theory, first put forward during the 1960s, was popularized by Frykenberg (1989), Stietencron (1989), King (1999), and others. It still has its supporters (e.g., Visvanathan 2003); but Lorenzen (2006), Pennington (2005), Sweetman (2005), Sharma (2002), and others have shown it to be empirically indefensible.

References Cited

Aurobindo, Sri [Aurobindo Ghose]. 1997. *Karmayogin: Political Writings and Speeches 1909–1910*. Pondicherry: Sri Aurobindo Ashram.

Aurobindo, Sri [Aurobindo Ghose]. 1999. *Bāṅlā Racanā*. Pondicherry: Sri Aurobindo Ashram.

Bagal, Jogeshchandra. 1955–56 (1362 Bengali era). *Rajnārāyaṇ Basu*. Calcutta: Bangiya Sahitya Parishad.

Bhattacharya, Abhijit. 1998. *A Guide to the Hitesranjan Sanyal Memorial Collection*. Calcutta: Centre for Studies in Social Sciences.

Chatterjee, Partha. 1993. *The Nation and Its Fragments: Colonial and Postcolonial Histories*. Princeton: Princeton University Press.

Chattopadhyaya, Bankimchandra. 1941–42 (1348 Bengali era) [1888]. *Dharmatattva*. Calcutta: Bangiya Sahitya Parishad.

Dalmia, Vasudha. 1997. *The Nationalization of Hindu Traditions: Bhāratendu Hariśchandra and Nineteenth-Century Banaras*. Delhi: Oxford University Press.

Frykenberg, Robert Eric. 1989. "The Emergence of Modern 'Hinduism' as a Concept and as an Institution: A Reappraisal with Special Reference to South India." *In* Günther D. Sontheimer and Hermann Kulke, eds, *Hinduism Reconsidered*, 29–49. New Delhi: Manohar.

Gandhi, Mohandas K. 1958–84. *The Collected Works of Mahatma Gandhi*. 90 volumes. Ahmedabad: Navajivan Trust.

Golwalkar, M. S. 1939. *We, or Our Nationhood Defined*. Nagpur: Bharat Publications.

Jaffrelot, Cristophe. 1996. *The Hindu Nationalist Movement in India*. New York: Columbia University Press.

Jones, Kenneth W. 1990. *Socio-Religious Reform Movements in British India*. Cambridge: Cambridge University Press.

King, Richard. 1999. *Orientalism and Religion: Postcolonial Theory, India, and "The Mystic East."* London: Routledge.

Kopf, David. 1979. *The Brahmo Samaj and the Shaping of the Modern Indian Mind*. Princeton: Princeton University Press.

Lorenzen, David N. 2006. *Who Invented Hinduism?: Essays on Religion in History*. Delhi: Yoda Press.

Nanda, B. R. 2004 [2002]. *In Search of Gandhi: Essays and Reflections*. Delhi: Oxford University Press.

Pennington, Brian K. 2005. *Was Hinduism Invented?: Britons, Indians, and the Colonial Construction of Religion*. New York: Oxford University Press.

Sarkar, Tanika. 1996. "Imagining Hindurashtra: The Hindu and the Muslim in Bankim Chandra's Writings." *In* David Ludden, ed., *Making India Hindu: Religion, Community, and the Politics of Democracy in India*, 162–84. Delhi: Oxford University Press.

Savarkar, V. D. 1942 [1923]. *Hindutva*. Nagpur: S. R. Date.

Sen, Amiya P. 1993. *Hindu Revivalism in Bengal c. 1872–1905: Some Essays in Interpretation*. Delhi: Oxford University Press.

Sharma, Arvind. 2002. "On Hindu, Hindustān, Hinduism and Hindutva." *Numen* 49, 1: 1–36.

Stietencron, Heinrich von. 1989. "Hinduism: On the Proper Use of a Deceptive Term." *In* Günther D. Sontheimer and Hermann Kulke, eds, *Hinduism Reconsidered*, 11–27. New Delhi: Manohar.

Sweetman, Will. 2005. "Hinduism." *In Keywords in South Asian Studies*. London: SOAS Centre of South Asian Studies <http://www.soas.ac.uk/centres/centreinfo.cfm?navid=912>.

Tagore, Rabindranath. 1939–49 (1346–55 Bengali era). *Rabīndra Racanābalī*. 26 volumes. Calcutta: Biswabharati.

Tilak, Balgangadhar. 1974–76. *Samagra Lokamānya Tīlaka*. 7 volumes. Pune: Kesari Prakashan.

Visvanathan, Gauri. 2003. "Colonialism and the Construction of Hinduism." *In* Gavin Flood, ed., *The Blackwell Companion to Hinduism*, 23–44. Oxford: Blackwell.

Vivekananda, Swami. 1989. *The Complete Works of Swami Vivekananda*. 8 volumes. Calcutta: Advaita Ashram.

Zavos, John. 2002. *The Emergence of Hindu Nationalism in India*. Delhi: Oxford University Press.

20

Orientalism

Carl Olson

Religious Constructions of the Hindu Other
Colonialist Constructions of the Hindu Other
Romantic Orientalism: East Enriches and Mystifies West
Hindu Responses to Oppressive Colonial Constructs
Assessments of Said's Concept of Orientalism
Concluding Reflections

Discussion of Orientalism in recent years has been heavily influenced by the work of Edward W. Said (1935–2003). He was a diaspora Palestinian who had been born in Jerusalem during the British Mandate in Palestine, lived for some years in Cairo, and immigrated to the United States as a teenager. His higher education was at Princeton University and then at Harvard University, where he received a doctorate in English literature in 1964. His active career as a university professor was in the department of English at Columbia University. Although an Episcopalian who married a Quaker, Said was a defender of Islamic civilization and the political cause of the Palestinians. His books, *Orientalism* (1978) and *Culture and Imperialism* (1993), can be interpreted as political tracts that are critical of the West and advocate a single binational state for Jews and Palestinians based on the conviction that separate states are not a viable option. In general, Said tended to interpret the Middle Eastern situation in terms of binary opposites: Zionist atrocity versus Palestinian victimhood. After contracting leukemia in 1991, he succumbed to the disease at the age of 67 in 2003.

Said transformed "Orientalism" from a relatively neutral term that referred to the study of non-Western cultures and their classical texts by Western scholars into a central term of critical analysis that has been taken up and widely applied in postmodern and postcolonial studies. Said used the term to characterize scholarship that is (or should be) associated with colonial domination and, according to his most prominent critic, he turned it into an instrument of polemical abuse and demonization (Lewis 1993: 100–101, 104) that nevertheless became a highly influential model of resistance to imperial pasts.

Said himself was influenced by Frantz Fanon, Antonio Gramsci, and Claude Lévi-Strauss. The greatest influence, however, almost certainly was Michel Foucault's understanding of the relationship between culture and power that supports Said's view (1978: 2–3) that Orientalism as an attitude and ideology became used as an authoritative instrument to subjugate peoples and cultures of the East.

Said's understanding of Orientalism is grounded in a fundamental presupposition: there has been no neutral, unbiased, objective scholarship on the Orient. All Western scholarship on the Middle East and Asia is embedded in cultural prejudices concerning the non-Western world that resulted in distortions, misconceptions, misunderstandings, and negative stereotypes. These reflect a Western racism and ethnocentrism, whether conscious or unconscious, that have produced hardly more than caricatures of the Orient. In short, Western accounts of the cultures and peoples of the East are products of imagination—with little or no basis in reality—that have supported imperial interests.

Said (1978: 15–16) starts from a point of view about representation as the displacement of the real that enables him to conclude that Orientalism is an invention of the Western scholarly mind that may have been stimulated by an empirical experience of the Orient but is not shaped by a real Orient. The so-called Orient found in Orientalist writings is constructed by the biased minds of Western scholars to serve political purposes, making the writers into partners with those who have imperial intentions to subjugate, denigrate, and dominate the peoples and cultures of a supposedly unchanging Orient (Said 1978: 22). The Orientalism that is identified by Said is a constructed body of theory and practice that functions as a tool of colonial hegemony.

Said (1978: 93) finds it significant that the results of Western scholarship describing the Orient appeared in books because books assume a greater authority and utility over time than the actual subject that they allegedly describe. Orientalism contributes to a crisis for the people and cultures being described in those books because readers accept as true what they read. They are shaped by a literary experience that functions to reinforce and determine what they regard as knowledge. A reader becomes what he or she reads, which in this case would be a member of a dominant colonial regime or an instance of the category of a subjugated native. Books by themselves create the knowledge and reality that they purportedly describe within their covers. A book has power to create a way of looking at foreign cultures that constrains thought and limits what can be examined in an unprejudiced way. Therefore, Orientalism is politically dangerous because it objectifies the cultural Other, overemphasizes differences among cultures, and encourages anti-human attitudes towards indigenous people living under colonial regimes.

When a reader accepts the image of the Orient embodied in a text, it constrains further attempts to interpret the subject more adequately. Like Nietzsche and Foucault (1977), Said maintains that texts are fundamentally instruments of power. In the context of colonial domination, Orientalist texts function as hegemonic instruments of Western political entities to confirm an unequal relationship between the oppressors and the dominated (Said 1983: 47).

Although a text typically functions as an instrument of power and can keep a person in bondage, Said was convinced that a text also can be used to free the oppressed. His writing against Orientalism was an attempt to produce texts that would be countervailing instruments of power against Western dominance and the means to free subjugated peoples. That was Said's agenda for emancipation or liberation. His work was hardly a disinterested use of history and hermeneutics because his intention as a writer was to turn the tables on the West and use books to exert power over the powerful on behalf of the powerless victims in the Orient. Even though he was mainly concerned with the Middle East, Said's notion of Orientalism applies to other parts of the Orient that experienced colonial oppression and were misrepresented to the extent of caricature by Western writers.

Religious Constructions of the Hindu Other

Evangelical Protestant Christians in early colonial India were convinced that their faith represented the highest form of religion and that Hindu religious institutions and practices "needed to be dismantled and replaced by Christian civilization" (van der Veer 2001: 42). Such terms as "pagan," "primitive," "barbarian," "ignorant," and "superstitious" were used by missionaries to describe Hindus. Evangelical missionaries were appalled by the use of consecrated images in Hindu worship and considered it to be equivalent to idolatry. The iconoclastic attitudes of Protestant Christian missionaries toward Hindus paralleled their anti-Catholicism at home in England in the same era (Pennington 2005: 59), a fact that may help our historical understanding but does not soften their effect in India.

Missionaries criticized Hinduism as a religion created by Brāhmaṇa priests for their own benefit to the detriment of a naïve and deluded populace. Reverend William Ward, a Baptist missionary who died of cholera in 1823, represented Hindus as effeminate, deceitful, lazy, and ignorant (van der Veer 2001: 95). He also identified social problems, such as infanticide, child marriage that led to early widowhood and prostitution, widow immolation, absence of education, and a pernicious hereditary caste system. Ward was an influence on the *History of India* (1817) by James Mill, a semi-official

"Anglicizing" text that perpetuated the kind of prejudicial view of Hindus that Ward had advocated.

Other Christian writers presented a more complex picture of Hindus. To contest reports by evangelical Christians, the French Catholic priest Abbé J. A. Dubois composed *Hindu Manners, Customs, and Ceremonies* (1806) for which the East India Company financed a translation and its publication in England (Pennington 2005: 70). His description was neither as polemical as those of the evangelicals nor was it simple advocacy of the superiority of Hindu society. He did argue, however, that Hindus would never convert to Christianity in substantial numbers and that Europeans should respond affirmatively to Hindu social and economic needs instead of trying to convert them. Dubois seems to represent a reaction to anti-Catholicism and to the anti-Hinduism that he encountered among evangelical Christians in India.

Colonialist Constructions of the Hindu Other

Sir William Jones (1746–94) anticipated there would be potential benefits for Indians if they were encouraged to learn deeply about their own culture, and he is probably the most important early Orientalist (in a pre-Saidian sense) in colonial India. He founded the Asiatic Society of Bengal in 1784, having arrived in India only a year earlier to work for the East India Company, and went on to a distinguished career. Eventually he mastered Sanskrit, Persian, and Arabic languages, and he helped to confirm a connection between Sanskrit and European languages that resulted in his being counted among the founders of comparative linguistics. The Asiatic Society of Bengal played a major role in supporting a renaissance of traditional learning in colonial India.

Jones was followed by such scholars as Charles Wilkins (1749–1836), who translated the *Bhagavad Gītā* into English; Thomas Colebrooke (1765–1837), whose work on Indian religion and philosophy introduced Indian thought to a Western audience; and Horace Hayman Wilson (1786–1860), who produced the first Sanskrit–English dictionary. These scholars and others employed in various capacities for the Company and the Asiatic Society are credited with the advent of an Orientalist scholarship in India that valued Hindu tradition. In retrospect, what may be problematic about their scholarship is that it assisted the imperial West to identify itself in contrast to the Orient, despite the openness and tolerance of many of these scholars to Hindu culture and customs (Halbfass 1988: 63). On the other hand, it valorized and idealized Hindu traditions and sought to encourage their retrieval, preservation, and distribution to the world at large.

These early Orientalists advocated the study of Indian languages and traditional texts, education for Indians in the indigenous vernaculars, and restoration of ancient religious sites and centers. Their opponents were evangelical missionaries and secular Anglicists who tended to denigrate Hindu culture and sought to introduce modern (i.e., contemporary Western) education, English language, and European styles in dress, diet, marriage arrangements, and social institutions in general (Kopf 1969: 7).

Added to the Christian impetus to convert Hindus and act as instruments in a divine plan for humanity, Darwin's theory of evolution also influenced the way in which Hindu society was understood within a framework of evolutionary stages by Anglicists and some Evangelicals. The assumption was that societies higher on the evolutionary ladder had a duty to educate societies on the lower. When joined to an activist optimism about social progress (evidenced in John Stuart Mill's 1859 essay *On Liberty*) and combined with Western scientific practice of classifying and comparing new data, the acceptance of an evolutionary model resulted by the mid-nineteenth century in the widespread presumption by British imperialists of European racial superiority (van der Veer 2001: 41). Early Orientalism in India had lost ground to an aggressive Anglicism that became less optimistic after the institution of Crown rule after the so-called 1857 Mutiny against the Company. The Hindu had become the Other of the imperialist.

By compiling data pertaining to caste, religion, and race within the context of collecting census data, British officials used the method of classification to rank various castes hierarchically and to create an official discourse of caste that influenced relations among Indians, resulted in more rigid social distinctions, and enhanced the acceptance of such distinctions throughout the subcontinent (van der Veer 1994: 19). Although some scholars claim that the British invented the caste system (Dirks 2001: 5), others find the claim exaggerated (Bayly 1999: 97; van der Veer 1994: 19). Gathering information is not itself a notable exercise of power, although it is a precondition for such an exercise.

Romantic Orientalism: East Enriches and Mystifies West

Increased knowledge of India in Europe attracted the attention of the German Romantics. The tendency to romanticize the Orient led to exotic forms of positive rather than negative stereotyping (Clarke 1997: 20; King 1999, 2005). The first German to use the Orient to promote the goals of Romanticism was Johann Gottfried Herder (1744–1803), who used an idealized image for Europeans to gauge their own moral failures. This was a form of Western self-criticism, an impetus for renewal, and a quest for the recovery of a lost paradise (Clarke 1997: 27; Halbfass 1988: 72). Goethe

(1749–1832) was attracted to the monistic idealism that he discovered in the Upaniṣad texts; Friedrich Schlegel (1772–1829) became convinced that human culture originated in India; and F. W. J. Schelling (1775–1854) was profoundly influenced by Eastern thought. Arthur Schopenhauer (1788–1860) thought that Eastern philosophy represented a universal wisdom and an opportunity for renewal of European culture, but G. W. F. Hegel (1770–1831) did not share this enthusiasm because of a conception of the irreversible course of history. Even though the East can function as a corrective and antidote for what afflicts the West from Hegel's perspective, the East has been historically superseded by the West, the ascendancy of which is characterized by consciousness of individual freedom and evolution of human autonomy (Halbfass 1988: 93).

The influence of a richly imagined Hindu India on German Romantics was part of a movement that Raymond Schwab identifies in his *The Oriental Renaissance* (1984, first published in French in 1950) as a further transformation of the European Renaissance into an Oriental Renaissance that extended it and perhaps completed it. The earlier European Renaissance found resources for cultural renewal in Western classical texts and ancient cultures, whereaas this later extension found it in Eastern sources. Schwab explains: "What the expression refers to is the revival of an atmosphere in the nineteenth century brought about by the arrival of Sanskrit texts in Europe, which produced an effect equal to that produced in the fifteenth century by the arrival of Greek manuscripts and Byzantine commentators after the fall of Constantinople" (1984: 11).

Hindu Responses to Oppressive Colonial Constructs

Said's version of Orientalism explicitly restricts the Orient to the Middle East but can be applied by extension to wherever and whomsoever is "other" than Europe and the New World. He represents victims of Orientalism as helpless and without recourse and having to endure their bondage to hegemonic colonial powers. One reason for this perspective is that Said was influenced by Gramsci's hierarchical understanding of power rather than by Foucault's view of power as something all-pervading, like oxygen, and it led him to stress the victimization of the inhabitants of the Orient. In any case, Said (1993: xii) acknowledged in his book, *Culture and Imperialism*, that he had failed to affirm the capacity for active resistance by non-Westerners. There is in fact ample evidence of robust responses by Hindus to colonial domination.

Hindus responded to British colonial domination and to cultural criticism leveled by missionaries. They did so by means of violence, nonviolent resistance, verbal protest, social reform, and revival movements. Rammohan

Roy (1771–1833), who is often called the father of modern India, was inspired by reading ancient Indian scriptures to hold regular meetings with friends to discuss religion and philosophy. These meetings evolved into the Brāhmo Samāj in 1829. Dayānanda Sarasvatī (1824–83) founded the Ārya Samāj to stimulate a Hindu revival by returning to the ancient Vedic scriptures. Madadev Govind Ranade (1842–1901) founded the All People's Association, and his disciple Gopal Krishna Gokhale (1866–1915) led more direct resistance to British hegemony. These men developed forms of nationalism that insisted that Indians must take responsibility for reforming their own society. Bal Gangadhar Tilak (1856–1920) was a major cultural revolutionary and nationalist who published a commentary on the *Bhagavad Gītā* in which he stressed working in the world for the benefit of others without desiring any rewards. Mohandas K. Gandhi (1869–1948) arguably did more than anyone to expose the evils of colonialism to the world. The activism of these individuals is ample historical evidence that Hindus should not be represented merely as passive victims.

It is also possible to find resistance evidenced in popular literature, for example, Bankimcandra Chatterji's novel *Ānandamaṭh* (The Sacred Brotherhood), which was published serially in 1881 and 1882 in the journal *Baṅgadarśan* and is available to readers of English in a scholarly translation (2005). The novel is set in the transitional era of 1770 when Mughal authority had declined and British influence was increasing. The novel criticizes the British for supporting the Muslims, although British rule is accepted until a time in the future when Hindus become more virtuous, stronger, and worthy of ruling themselves. Muslims, rather than the British, are represented as the main oppressors of Hindus, and this is a circumstance that complicates Said's concept of Orientalism.

Assessments of Said's Concept of Orientalism

It is possible to classify the responses to Said's work as theoretical and methodological. From a theoretical perspective, some scholars have questioned his notion of the Orient as too limited and too general because his Orient is explicitly limited to the Middle East and it is so abstract that it transcends time and history (Lewis 1993: 108; Sardar 1999: 70; Smith 2003: 46; Young 2001: 39–91). Others have suggested that it is impossible to free any culture being studied from all nonindigenous categories of understanding (Bhabha 1994: 72; Halbfass 1991: 12–13; Rocher 1993: 215–49). Said also has been criticized for ignoring the complex motivations for Orientalism and failing to recognize the agency of Oriental subjects (Clarke 1997: 27; Frykenberg 1993: 534; Inden 1990: 217; Urban 2003: 88). Scholars have also concentrated their criticism on Said's weak historical method and its replacement by political rhetoric (Casadio 2004: 124–25).

From the perspective of poststructural and postmodern thinkers, the basic problem with a representational way of thinking is that there is no reality behind the image. At the center of Said's political struggle is a battle against the representational mode of thinking, but Said was no more able to overcome it than were Foucault or Derrida (Mellor 2004: 99–112; Olson 2000, 2005). Said recognized that representations function as a form of human economy that is necessary for social life, and they are as fundamental to social life as language. What he wanted to accomplish was the elimination of representations that are essentially authoritative and repressive (Viswanathan 2001: 41–42). And yet Said creates his own form of representation in his hegemonic version of "the West." Said responds to such criticism by acknowledging that cultures make representations of foreign cultures with the intention of mastering and controlling them. He objects, however, to the actual mastery and control of others (Said 1993: 100). If there is an alternative to Said's approach to "the Other," it may be one found in the philosophy of Emmanuel Levinas.

Levinas conceives of the other as a positive moral and ethical force because the egoist tendencies of the self are reconditioned when the self is exposed to otherness (alterity). Although we recognize the other as external to us, we also become aware that the other resembles us (Levinas 1987: 76). When we encounter the other in an intercultural dialog, we become more concerned for that person, and we can substitute ourselves for the other, even though the other remains a mystery for us. Levinas stresses the absolute alterity of the other to protect it from representation and annulment of its alterity. What Levinas finds significant is that another reveals himself or herself as a face with an overflowing nature that cannot be adequately conceptualized. The face of the other visits me and identifies itself. When I see the face of the other, I am questioned and challenged to respond. The face of the other obliges me to become responsible for it, even though the face represents a trace that never fully arrives (Levinas 1990: 220).

Concluding Reflections

Within the context of cultural history, the operation of Orientalism is nothing innovative or unique. Inhabitants of the subcontinent of India have defined themselves against others throughout history, and such other cultures as the Greeks and Persians have done the same thing against the unknown and at times threatening other (Halbfass 1988: 175–81; Lorenzen 1999: 648). It is an over-simplification to view Orientalism as neither more nor less than imperialist ideology, because Orientalism—whether the Saidian or generic version—also has represented a subversive countermovement to imperial power that stimulates a reaction by those subjugated (Clarke 1997: 9). Said's limitations were related to the political agenda that shaped his work.

Said, however, is correct to recognize that no representation of the Orient perfectly corresponds to the real thing, which suggests that there is always some distortion or misrepresentation. When something is represented, it is also transformed into something new. Does this mean that "Orientals" are the best qualified to create representations of their cultures? If we consider the ways in which Europeans have misrepresented themselves and others, it is my conviction that the answer must be negative. I think that it is safer to recognize that all scholarship is imperfect. This is why the task of scholarship is an ongoing labor that should be infused by empathy for the other instead of feelings of superiority and a will to dominate. Anyone doing serious scholarly study of another culture needs to combine empathy with a search for the face of the other.

References Cited

Bayly, Susan. 1999. *Caste, Society, and Politics in India from the Eighteenth Century to the Modern Age*. Cambridge: Cambridge University Press.

Bhabha, Homi K. 2002 [1994]. *The Location of Culture*. London: Routledge.

Casadio, Giovanni. 2004. "Studying Religious Traditions between the Orient and the Occident: Modernism vs Post-modernism." *In* Christoph Kleine, Monika Schrimpf, and Katja Triplett, eds, *Unterwegs: Neue Pfade in der Religionswissenschaft. Festschrift für Michael Pye zum 65. Geburtstag*, 119–35. München: Biblion Verlag.

Chatterji, Bankimcandra. 2005. *Ānandamaṭh, or The Sacred Brotherhood* (trans. Julius J. Lipner). Oxford: Oxford University Press.

Clarke, J. J. 1997. *Oriental Enlightenment: The Encounter between Asian and Western Thought*. London: Routledge.

Dirks, Nicholas B. 2001. *Castes of Mind: Colonialism and the Making of Modern India*. Princeton: Princeton University Press.

Foucault, Michel. 1977 [1971]. "Nietzsche, Genealogy, History." *In* Donald F. Bouchard, ed., *Language, Counter-Memory, Practice: Selected Essays and Interviews* (trans. Donald F. Bouchard and Sherry Simon), 137–64. Ithaca: Cornell University Press.

Frykenberg, Robert Eric. 1993. "Constructions of Hinduism at the Nexus of History and Religion." *Journal of Interdisciplinary History* 23, 2: 523–50.

Halbfass, Wilhelm. 1988 [1981]. *India and Europe: An Essay in Understanding*. Albany: State University of New York Press.

Halbfass, Wilhelm. 1991. *Tradition and Reflection: Explorations in Indian Thought*. Albany: State University of New York Press.

Inden, Ronald B. 1990. *Imagining India*. Cambridge: Blackwell.
King, Richard. 1999. *Orientalism and Religion: Postcolonial Theory, India and "The Mystic East."* London: Routledge.
King, Richard. 2005. "Orientalism and the Study of Religions." *In* John R. Hinnells, ed., *The Routledge Companion to the Study of Religion*, 275–90. London: Routledge.
Kopf, David. 1969. *British Orientalism and the Bengal Renaissance: The Dynamics of Indian Modernization, 1773–1835*. Berkeley: University of California Press.
Levinas, Emmanuel. 1987 [1947]. *Time and the Other* (trans. Richard Cohen). Pittsburgh: Duquesne University Press.
Levinas, Emmanuel. 1990 [1961]. *Totality and Infinity: An Essay on Exteriority* (trans. Alphonso Lingis). Pittsburgh: Duquesne University Press.
Lewis, Bernard. 1993. *Islam and the West*. New York: Oxford University Press.
Lorenzen, David N. 1999. "Who Invented Hinduism?" *Comparative Studies in Society and History: An International Quarterly* 41, 4: 630–59.
Mellor, Philip A. 2004. "Orientalism, Representation, and Religion: The Reality Behind the Myth." *Religion* 34, 1: 99–112.
Olson, Carl. 2000. *Zen and the Art of Postmodern Philosophy: Two Paths of Liberation from the Representational Mode of Thinking*. Albany: State University of New York Press.
Olson, Carl. 2005. "Politics, Power, Discourse and Representation: A Critical Look at Said and Some of His Children." *Method and Theory in the Study of Religion* 17, 4: 317–36.
Pennington, Brian K. 2005. *Was Hinduism Invented?: Britons, Indians, and the Colonial Construction of Religion*. New York: Oxford University Press.
Rocher, Rosane. 1993. "British Orientalism in the Eighteenth Century: The Dialectics of Knowledge and Government." *In* Carol A. Breckenridge and Peter van der Veer, eds, *Orientalism and the Postcolonial Predicament*, 215–49. Philadelphia: University of Pennsylvania Press.
Said, Edward W. 1978. *Orientalism*. New York: Vintage Books.
Said, Edward W. 1983. *The World, the Text, and the Critic*. Cambridge: Harvard University Press.
Said, Edward W. 1993. *Culture and Imperialism*. New York: Vintage Books.
Sardar, Siauddin. 1999. *Orientalism*. Buckingham: Open University Press.
Schwab, Raymond. 1984 [1950]. *The Oriental Renaissance: Europe's Discovery of India and the East 1680–1880*. New York: Columbia University Press.
Smith, David 2003. "Orientalism and Hinduism." *In* Gavin Flood, ed., *The Blackwell Companion to Hinduism*, 45–63. Oxford: Blackwell.
Urban, Hugh B. 2003. *Tantra: Sex, Secrecy, Politics, and Power in the Study of Religion*. Berkeley: University of California Press.
van der Veer, Peter. 1994. *Religious Nationalism: Hindus and Muslims in India*. Berkeley: University of California Press.
van der Veer, Peter. 2001. *Imperial Encounters: Religion and Modernity in India and Britain*. Princeton: Princeton University Press.

Viswanathan, Gauri. 2001. *Power, Politics, and Culture: Interviews with Edward W. Said*. New York: Pantheon Books.

Young, Robert J. C. 2001. *Postcolonialism: An Historical Introduction*. Oxford: Blackwell.

21

Postcolonialism

Saurabh Dube

Critical Categories
Orientalism and After
Colonial Constructions
Community and History
Nation and Modernity

In this chapter, I discuss postcolonial perspectives—or, postcolonialism, the rubric under which the perspectives have come to be grouped and known—in relationship to understandings of Hinduism. First, I provide a brief understanding of my own use of postcolonialism and of Hinduism, recognizing exactly the notorious imprecision of these terms. Second, I attend to critical considerations of Orientalist knowledge that proved formative for postcolonial understandings. Third, building on this discussion, I explore debates surrounding the colonial construction of caste and the imperial invention of Hinduism. Fourth, I consider the manner in which such debates have been taken forward in newer understandings of community and history. Finally, I highlight some of the ways in which postcolonial perspectives have approached issues of nationalism, nation-state, and modernity in conversation with questions of caste and religion, especially Hinduism.

Critical Categories

When I write of Hinduism, the reference is to arrangements of lived religious meanings and practices, the everyday transactions of the different members and groups within the sacred universe of an Indic religion. Here, the social, ritual, and cosmic domains have been integrally bound to each other. Indeed, a crucial aspect of the quotidian transactions that I am referring to concerns the several elaborations and contestations of the intermeshing of divine, ritual, and social hierarchies, all of which have been central to Hinduism (Dube 1998).

My effort is to highlight two interconnected issues that are central to lived Hinduism. These are questions of, first, "hierarchical inequality," and second, the "partial continuity between humanity and divinity" (Fuller 1992: 3–4), which I emphasize are both inflected by power. It follows that my emphasis on practices, processes, and power in historical and ethnographic understandings of Hinduism makes it possible to approach its constitutive relationships as being variously constructed and contested through time, part of a wider dynamic between domination and subordination and, indeed, religion and power (for a wider discussion of such issues, see Dube 1998).

As a category, the problem with the postcolonial is not only that it has many meanings but that this multiplicity registers unproductive ambiguity. Of course, there have been distinct attempts at defining the term, and both the interested and the uninitiated reader should find useful works by Leela Gandhi (1998), Ania Loomba (1998), John McLeod (2000), Robert Young (2001, 2003), and Sharada Sugirtharajah (2003), the last providing a postcolonial understanding of Hinduism. At the same time, however, all too often appreciations, criticisms, and discussions of postcolonialism treat the term as ready shorthand. Here, postcolonialism pervasively if variously signifies: scholarship produced by ex-colonized subjects, usually of the Anglophone empire, including scholars who are now frequently based in the West; learning produced by such scholars that is decisively disposed toward high theory, especially of a literary bent and a philosophical persuasion; a distinct stage of history—with its attendant understandings based on critical ruptures—that follows the prior phase of colonialism; and, of course, a combination of two or more of these elements. As I have discussed elsewhere (Dube 2004a), all these different usages of the postcolonial as a shorthand reveal the tendency of the concept to homogenize history and to sanitize politics, resting on the divide between the colonial and the postcolonial, wherein one totalized terrain leads to another undifferentiated arena.

Yet, there is also much to be learned from postcolonialism. (This is apart from the fact that given its entrenched institutionalization within the academy, the term is unlikely to simply disappear.) My reference is especially to the ways in which abiding endeavors articulating postcolonial understandings (e.g., Chakrabarty 2000; Chatterjee 1993) have undertaken salient tasks. To begin with, they have pointed to the prior place and persistent presence of colonial schemes in contemporary worlds. Moreover, these efforts have questioned the place of an imaginary yet tangible West as history, modernity, and destiny for each society and every culture. Finally, they have unraveled the terms and limits of state, nation, and modernity in Western and non-Western worlds, further underscoring the significance of critical difference in such distinct yet entangled terrain.

How, then, do I approach and understand postcolonialism? Recognizing at once the limits and the possibilities of postcolonialism—and postcoloniality and the postcolonial—and registering that they bid no easy exorcism by being considered as analytical nightmares, I consider these terms as a critical rubric. As rubric, the postcolonial emerges intimately linked to other theoretical orientations, from cultural history to critical ethnography and from social theory to historical anthropology, including the understandings of religion that they offer. Here, I see postcolonial propositions as interlocutors in wider, ongoing debates rethinking the nation-state and the West, the colony and the postcolony, and history and modernity as concept and entity and process and destiny (Dube 2004a contains a broader discussion). This would be clarified by the arguments ahead. The point now is that in the emergence of such critical discussion, including postcolonial understandings of Hinduism, incisive interrogations of the modern West have played a crucial role.

Orientalism and After

Around three decades ago, Edward Said's seminal study, *Orientalism* (1978), critically underscored the mutual entailments of European colonialism and empire and Western knowledge and power. Of course, long before the appearance of this work, there existed several studies of European images of non-European peoples that identified various stereotypes. However, such work tended to be "documentary rather than critical or analytical," so that an intriguing array of European representations was presented, but their "discursive affiliations and underlying epistemologies" were frequently underplayed (Thomas 1994: 22–23). Intervening in this field, *Orientalism* made a persuasive case for the systematic textual fabrication of the Orient through the profound dynamic of European knowledge and Western power. Indeed, Said's work had shifted the terms of debate and discussion on metropolitan representations of non-European peoples from uncovering the singular biases of determinate depictions to unraveling the deeper domains of discursive domination. This also highlighted the connection and complicity between earlier imperial imaginings and contemporary academic renderings of the Orient.

Although Said's principal focus in the book was on Western representations of the Middle Eastern world and Islam, his arguments had a ripple effect on scholarship, including the study of India and Hinduism, an issue to which I will return. The point now is that a polemical and provocative work, such as *Orientalism*, was bound to have its intellectual silences and theoretical tensions. Principally, Said tended to homogenize both the terrain and the tenor of European representations of non-European worlds. Here, the limited place given to the practices of the colonized in the making of colonial projects was itself part of emphases that overplayed the efficacy of colonial power, under-enunciating thereby the contradictory and contingent historical dynamic of empire driven by class and gender, race and sexuality.

Together, the potentialities and problems of Said's study have entailed significant consequences. Since the 1980s, they have prompted critical theories of colonial discourse, leading to the emergence of a new field of postcolonial criticism not only in metropolitan but in provincial academic arenas. In this terrain, the implications and weaknesses of *Orientalism* have been elaborated, extended, and exceeded by studies bearing distinct orientations (e.g., Bhabha 1994; Spivak 1999). At the same time, in tune with the work of Said, colony and empire often continue to be rendered as somewhat monolithic endeavors in the domain of literary postcolonial theory. Conversely, important interventions by historians and anthropologists—and by postcolonial critics—have variously questioned the homogeneity and efficacy accorded to colonial projects. Such studies have further drawn on historical and ethnographic materials to trace the interplay between the construction and institutionalization of religious formations, caste boundaries, gender identities, and class divisions in explorations of imperial imaginings, colonial cultures, and postcolonial locations (Dube 2004b contains a wider discussion of the issues raised in this section; also see Breckenridge and van der Veer 1993; King 1999). As important, all of this has led to key consequence for understandings of Hinduism in, what might be called, the postcolonial ecumene.

Colonial Constructions

Hinduism and Hindu as categories have been variously debated by students of religion, history, and anthropology for a long time now. More recently, arguably in the wake of the challenges of *Orientalism* and postcolonialism, scholars of different persuasions have taken up matters of etymology and taxonomy to assert that the category of Hinduism is a nineteenth-century creation of colonial imaginings (Fuller 1992; Hawley 1991; Oberoi 1994). Similarly, before this period, it has been argued, the term "Hindu" seems to have been barely used by the people whose religious affiliation it purported to describe. This is because the very homogeneity of the category ran counter to the fabric of the "interpenetration and overlapping of communal identities," characteristic of the "highly localized" nature of religious formations in India, that continued well into the nineteenth century (Oberoi 1994: 1–17).

Thus, it was only in the nineteenth century that the categories of Hinduism and of the Hindu, in conjunction with each other and precisely under colonial rule, came to clearly specify religious affiliation. This circle stood fully drawn when the English educated, middle-class social reformers and nationalists of the period responded to such Western appraisals of Indian religions by undertaking a series of different steps toward constructing their vision and practice of Hinduism. Here were to be found blueprints that often tended to fashion homogeneous meanings and to reproduce the significance of colonial categories in their very articulation of difference from the West. Indeed, the blueprints came to be elaborated alongside the measures constructed by the imperial government with regard to religious communities (Dube 1998).

From the other side of the epistemic breach, historians, anthropologists, and religious studies scholars have explicitly and implicitly argued that philological and etymological issues apart (although see Lorenzen 1999), far too much is "currently [being] made of the colonial construction of caste and religious categories and too little of the precolonial basis for these categories, on which the colonial state had its impact" (van der Veer 1994: 20). In brief, precolonial India was not devoid of supralocal identities, and these historically construed identities, from the twelfth century onward, involved different renderings of a Hindu "self" and various constructions of a Muslim "other" as part of wider patterns on the subcontinent of processes of state formation; elaborations of a royal cult of the god-king Rāma as a political theology; and the fabrications of discursive, linguistic, and popular-devotional communities (Lorenzen 1999; Pollock 1993; Talbot 1995; van der Veer 1994: 12–24).

Similar debates have surrounded the nature of caste—its continuities and transformations—under the colonial regime. Several scholars have asserted that the British in India fundamentally reordered caste, re-inventing it in the image of their own predilections and policies. Here, an important role has been played by the work of Nicholas Dirks (1987, 2001) who argues that under empire, the institution of caste lost its fundamental moorings in kingship and politics (also see Quigley 1993; Raheja 1988) to become instead a "hollow crown." Indeed, after 1858, as measures and modalities of imperial rule, history stood replaced by ethnography, village community by caste, erasing protean precolonial forms. A new construction of caste now augmented colonial power, while undermining the colonized subject. As Dirks (2001) and others (e.g., Appadurai 1993) have argued, this novel imperial sociology and colonial politics severally entailed missionary and official determinations of caste and conversion; evangelical and secular fabrications of "tradition," "custom," and "barbarism"; and the work of anthropometry, the census, and the ethnographic survey. Here lie fictions of "martial races" and "criminal castes," the labors of race in the productions of caste, entailing the colonized body.

Conversely, arguing against an apparent a priori analytical prerogative accorded to the ruptures introduced by colonialism, various scholars have stressed the continuities in formations of caste between precolonial regimes and British rule. Though such salient writings (e.g., Bayly 1988; Peabody 2001) on the eighteenth and nineteenth centuries in India have revised our understanding of this period, they tend to accord something of an innate heuristic privilege to continuities in state and society between Indian and colonial regimes, also primarily predicating questions of caste transformations on issues of state formation and processes of political economy (Dube 2004a). At the same time, these emphases foreground the importance of attending to the particular attributes and limits of colonial processes to better probe the wider stipulations and effects of imperial power.

Together, these debates reveal that more than any easy insinuation of ideological or national identifications among their scholarly protagonists at stake in them is a wider questioning of apparently stable categories, which is underway in the postcolonial ecumene. Here are to be found both the need to carefully query a priori understandings of Hinduism and caste and the necessity to explore the ways in which the relationships ordered by these categories had a basis in precolonial India and were then transformed under colonial rule. This means further tracking the diversities and discontinuities in the production and articulation of the distinct meanings and practices of Hinduism and caste, their construal as ineluctably negotiated and inevitably contested resources, including by communities who stood on the margins of these categories.

Community and History

Such tasks have been imaginatively undertaken in reconsiderations of community as part of postcolonial perspectives. Here, the querying of pervasive projections of community as an ineluctably anachronistic, tightly bounded entity—one tending toward consensus in its expression, entailing allegiance to primordial tradition, and as broadly opposed to modernity—has had compelling consequences. Communities have come to be understood as active participants in wider processes of colonialism and empire, state-formation and modernity, and nation and nationalism, which imbue such processes—themselves made up of diverse relationships of meaning and power—with their own terms and textures (Dube forthcoming-a).

Ethnographic and historical studies in the postcolonial ecumene have explored the many meanings of community construed by its members, especially their symbolization and elaboration of boundaries as providing substance to their differences and identities. This has also involved examinations of the constitutive location of community within wide-ranging processes of power and of its internal divisions as expressed in terms of property, gender, law, and office (Das 1995; Dube 2004a; Gupta 2002; Kasturi 2002; Oberoi 1994; also see Banerjee-Dube 2001). These efforts have been further fortified by incisive accounts of communities as questioning and contesting dominant projects of meaning and power, including those turning on Hinduism and caste and empire and nation, unraveling their challenge to authority in a historically and ethnographically layered manner (Banerjee-Dube 2007; Dube 1998; Guha 1983; Hardiman 1987; Skaria 1999; also see Pandian 2005).

No less than community, the critical rethinking of history has been at the core of postcolonial perspectives. Three overlaying emphases have played a salient part here (for a wider discussion, see Dube forthcoming-a). To begin with, it has been diversely admitted that forms of historical consciousness vary in their degree of symbolic elaboration, their ability to pervade multiple contexts, and their capacity to capture people's imaginations. Second, it has been increasingly noted that history does not just refer to events and processes out there but that it exists as a negotiated resource at the core of shifting configurations of social worlds. Third, there has been an opening up of critical questions considering the coupling of history writing with the modern nation and concerning the haunting presence of a reified West in widespread beliefs in historical progress.

These emphases have not resorted to oppositions involving cyclical notions of the past as characteristic of the Hindu East and linear conceptions of history as constitutive of the Christian West. Rather, they have precisely probed such overwrought schemes by tracking expressions of history as made up of interleaving, conflict-ridden processes of meaning and authority (Banerjee-Dube 2007; Mayaram 2004; Saikia 2004; also see Rao, Shulman, and Subrahmanyam 2001). In this terrain, the explorations have extended from tracing the variability and mutability that can inhere in the perceptions and practices of the past of historical communities through to tracking the persistence of oppositions between myth and history in authoritative projections (Amin 1995; Dube 1998; Gold and Gujar 2002; Skaria 1999); and from unraveling the uses of the past and their contending validities in the making of worlds, especially the play of power in the production of history, through to the placing of question marks on pervasive projections of the West and the nation as history, modernity, and destiny (e.g., Chakrabarty 2000, 2002; Dube 2004a; Pandey 2005; also see Nandy 1995).

Nation and Modernity

The presumptions projecting India as a "never-never land" of endless tradition, recently rising from its slumber in the wake of globalization to truly embrace a Western modernity, share common ground with the pictures presenting the Indian subcontinent as having combined, for some time now, the traditional with the modern. Critical postcolonial perspectives suggest that both orientations rest on prior blueprints and hierarchical oppositions of an essentially Western modernity and an innately Indian tradition. Instead, processes of modernity, including their contentions, on the subcontinent over the last two centuries need to be understood as shaped by diverse subjects of modernity and by distinct modern subjects.

What do I mean by this? Influential discussions and commonplace conceptions of modernity have frequently proceeded by envisioning the phenomenon in the image of the European and Euro-American, also often male, modern subject. In contrast, in speaking of subjects of modernity, I am referring to historical actors who have been active participants in processes of modernity, both *subject to* these processes but also *subjects shaping* these processes (Dube 2004a). Over the last few centuries, the subjects of modernity have included, for example, indigenous communities across the world under colonial and national rule; peoples of African descent not only on that continent but in different diasporas; and, indeed, subaltern, marginal, and elite women and men in non-Western and Western theatres. In the Indian instance, the subjects of modernity have consisted not merely of the Westernized, progressive middle classes but of peasants, artisans, and workers who have diversely articulated processes of colony and postcolony, an issue to which I shall return.

The point is that, time after time, subjects of modernity have revealed that there are different ways of being modern. They have now accessed and now exceeded the determinations of the modern subject, suggesting the need to rethink exclusive concepts of the latter entity—as image and as practice. Yet, all too often, subjects of modernity have also betrayed scant regard for the niceties of the modern subject exactly while articulating the enduring terms of modernity. Here, it bears emphasis that there are other modern subjects besides Western ones. These various modern subjects in the West and the non-West are also subjects of modernity, but not all subjects of modernity are modern subjects, of course. Unsurprisingly, all these different subjects have registered within their measures and meanings the formative contradictions, contentions, and contingencies of modernity

Consider the case of anticolonial political nationalism on the subcontinent, which had its beginnings in the late nineteenth century. On the one hand, subaltern endeavors in the wider terrain of Indian nationalism were the work not of modern subjects but of subjects of modernity. The endeavors participated in procedures of the modern nation by articulating specifically subaltern visions of freedom and their own initiatives of independence, which could be closely bound to particular projections of caste practices and religious norms (see Dube 2004a, 2004b). Here are to be found frames of meaning and idioms of struggle that accessed and exceeded the aims and strategies of a generally middle-class nationalist leadership. It is not only that the supplementary nature of subaltern practices straddled their particular renderings of the nation and their distinct politics of nationalism, entailing often-discrete expressions of Hinduism and caste. It is also that subaltern nationalisms carried forward agendas of peasant insurgents in nineteenth-century India, insurgents who—precisely in their states of religious and caste consciousness—were not "pre-political" subjects but ones entirely coeval with, contemporaries and constituents of, politics under modern colonialism and colonial modernity (Guha 1983). In each case, Indian subalterns engaged and expressed modern processes as subjects of modernity.

On the other hand, middle-class nationalisms in India, the work of Indian modern subjects who were rather different from their Western counterparts, expressed their own distinctions. Drawing on Enlightenment principles and post-Enlightenment traditions of the West, these nationalisms did not simply replicate but reworked such protocols in distinct ways. Here were to be found translations and transformations of the ideals of the sovereign nation and the free citizen of Europe through grids of the subjugated homeland and the colonized subject in India, especially entailing mappings of (Hindu) "spiritual" and (Western) "political" domains of nationalism (Chatterjee 1993; on other distinctive dimensions of the Hindu-Indian modern, see, for example, Chakrabarty 2000, 2002; Prakash 1999). Such emphases received only a distinct twist in the religious politics of Mohandas K. Gandhi, who conjoined various strains of modern Romanticism, Western philosophies, and Hindu schemas to construe thereby his own "critical traditionalism" (the term comes from Nandy 1987). Gandhi's radical critique of liberal politics and modern civilization was in fact thoroughly expressive of modernity, particularly its contestations, enchantments, and disenchantments (Skaria forthcoming). In each instance, at stake were the fashioning and formation of the Indian modern subject, who drew on, yet went beyond, images and ideas, precepts and practices of the Western modern subject, telling us once more that there are different ways of being modern.

To argue for such disjunctions and distinctions of the modern and modernity at the core of Indian anticolonial nationalisms is not to posit that, whether in their subaltern or middle-class *avatār*s, such endeavors embodied innocent and immaculate alterity. The picture is muddier and murkier, which is forcefully brought home by feminist discussions of a postcolonial provenance that have focused on the gendered politics of Hindu reform and Indian nationalism in imperial India. Here, a variety of writings (e.g., Mani 1998; Rao forthcoming; Sarkar 2001) have shown the complex consequences of the emergence and intensification of the "woman's question" in nineteenth-century India. There was a tightening of control over the sexuality of lower-caste women, including new formations of Dalit masculinity that accompanied efforts to reform Dalit women's status; and there were elaborations of a reconstituted, modern Hindu domesticity that saw the construal of the "new woman," who at once embodied a resurrected "tradition" and symbolized a reorganized space of familial intimacy.

Concerning the presence of gender and the place of women in formations of nation and articulations of nationalism, the explorations have extended, for instance, from the mapping of the nation in terms of domesticity and the gendered construal of the homeland as a feminine figure through to the terms of participation of women in nationalism and the ambiguities attending their definition as citizen-subjects (e.g., Menon and Bhasin 1998; Roy 2005; Sarkar 2001). In these ways, the analytic of gender has incisively interrogated the attributes of authority and alterity at the heart of nation and nationalism (and Hinduism and caste) in their dominant and subaltern incarnations.

The foregoing discussion suggests that processes of modernity in India, as elsewhere, have been characterized not only by contrariety and contention but by ambiguity and ambivalence. This is as true of the present as it was of the past. In concluding, therefore, I briefly turn to the manner in which modernity is being articulated and debated in political fields in India today, as sieved through postcolonial perspectives.

On the one hand, the current politics of the Hindu nationalist Right, which is thoroughly modern, nonetheless embodies a profound ambivalence toward modernity. This is expressed, for example, in its articulation of an alternative Hindu universalism, which is not a mere critique of the West. As Thomas Hansen has argued, this alternative universalism forms "part of a strategy to invigorate and stabilize a modernizing national project through a disciplined and corporatist cultural nationalism that can earn India recognition and equality (with the West and other nations) through assertion of difference" (1999: 90, see also 231). Within Hindu nationalism, its fetish of the modern nation stands closely connected to such ambivalence, at once animating and using ideological control and disciplinary strategies. The assertion of the difference and purity of Hindu civilization and the salience of a strong and powerful modern nation go hand in hand.

On the other hand, in recent years, wide-ranging critical postcolonial perspectives have served to open up questions of modernity and religion in India (Dube forthcoming-b; also see Nigam 2006). They provide valuable lessons. First, these discussions suggest that to register the contingency and plurality of modernity across the world is not merely to harp on "alternative modernities" but to reconsider modalities of power, formations of difference, and their restless interplay at the heart of processes of modernity, including especially articulations of caste and Hinduism and religiosity and Dalits in India today. Second, this also means not turning way from but unraveling prudently the exclusive images of Western modernity as shaping the concatenations and contentions of diverse formations of modernity on the subcontinent and beyond, while further recognizing that such stipulations are differently worked on by social subjects to yield expected outcomes and unexpected consequences. Third, we are reminded that the very meanings of modernity, delineations of democracy, and purposes of pluralism cannot be separated from inherently different formations of social subjects in inescapably heterogeneous worlds, shaped by the past and emergent in the present. It is in the practices of these subjects that there inhere ethics and politics for realizing or rejecting the possibilities of modernity, plurality, and democracy.

Clearly, there is much to be learned from postcolonial perspectives, provided we are willing to unlearn our prior predilections toward considering the postcolonial as a settled stage of history or a prefigured form of knowledge (or both).

References Cited

Amin, Shahid. 1995. *Event, Metaphor, Memory: Chauri Chaura 1922–1992.* Berkeley: University of California Press.

Appadurai, Arjun. 1993. "Number in the Colonial Imagination." *In* Carol A. Breckenridge and Peter van der Veer, eds, *Orientalism and the Postcolonial Predicament: Perspectives on South Asia*, 314–39. Philadelphia: University of Pennsylvania Press.

Banerjee-Dube, Ishita. 2006. *Religion, Law and Power: Tales of Time in Eastern India, 1860–2000.* London: Anthem Press.

Banerjee-Dube, Ishita. 2007. *Divine Affairs: Pilgrimage, Law and the State in Colonial and Postcolonial India.* Shimla: Indian Institute of Advanced Study.

Bayly, C. A. 1988. *Indian Society and the Making of the British Empire.* Cambridge: Cambridge University Press.

Bhabha, Homi K. 1994. *The Location of Culture.* London: Routledge.

Breckenridge, Carol A. and Peter van der Veer, eds. 1993. *Orientalism and the Postcolonial Predicament: Perspectives on South Asia.* Philadelphia: University of Pennsylvania Press.

Chakrabarty, Dipesh. 2000. *Provincializing Europe: Postcolonial Thought and Historical Difference.* Princeton: Princeton University Press.

Chakrabarty, Dipesh. 2002. *Habitations of Modernity: Essays in the Wake of Subaltern Studies.* Chicago: University of Chicago Press.

Chatterjee, Partha. 1993. *The Nation and its Fragments: Colonial and Postcolonial Histories.* Princeton: Princeton University Press.

Das, Veena. 1995. *Critical Events: An Anthropological Perspective on Contemporary India.* Delhi: Oxford University Press.

Dirks, Nicholas B. 1987. *The Hollow Crown: Ethnohistory of an Indian Kingdom.* Cambridge: Cambridge University Press.

Dirks, Nicholas B. 2001. *Castes of Mind: Colonialism and the Making of Modern India.* Princeton: Princeton University Press.

Dube, Saurabh. 1998. *Untouchable Pasts: Religion, Identity, and Power among a Central Indian Community, 1780–1950*. Albany: State University of New York Press.

Dube, Saurabh. 2004a. *Stitches on Time: Colonial Textures and Postcolonial Tangles*. Durham: Duke University Press.

Dube, Saurabh. 2004b. "Terms that Bind: Colony, Nation, Modernity." *In* Saurabh Dube, ed., *Postcolonial Passages: Contemporary History-writing on India*, 1–37. Delhi: Oxford University Press.

Dube, Saurabh. Forthcoming-a. "Anthropology, History, Historical Anthropology." *In* Saurabh Dube, ed., *Historical Anthropology*. Delhi: Oxford University Press.

Dube, Saurabh. Forthcoming-b. *After Conversion: Cultural Histories of Modern India*. Delhi: Oxford University Press.

Fuller, C. J. 1992. *The Camphor Flame: Popular Hinduism and Society in India*. Princeton: Princeton University Press.

Gandhi, Leela. 1998. *Postcolonial Theory*. New York: Columbia University Press.

Gold, Ann Grodzins and Bhoju Ram Gujar. 2002. *In the Time of Trees and Sorrows: Nature, Power, and Memory in Rajasthan*. Durham: Duke University Press.

Guha, Ranajit. 1983. *Elementary Aspects of Peasant Insurgency in Colonial India*. Delhi: Oxford University Press.

Gupta, Charu. 2002. *Sexuality, Obscenity, and Community: Women, Muslims, and the Hindu Public in Colonial India*. Delhi: Permanent Black.

Hansen, Thomas Blom. 1999. *The Saffron Wave: Democracy and Hindu Nationalism in Modern India*. Princeton: Princeton University Press.

Hardiman, David. 1987. *The Coming of the Devi: Adivasi Assertion in Western India* .Delhi: Oxford University Press.

Hawley, John S. 1991. "Naming Hinduism." *Wilson Quarterly* 15, 3: 20–34.

Kasturi, Malavika. 2002. *Embattled Identities: Rajput Lineages and the Colonial State in Nineteenth-Century North India*. Delhi: Oxford University Press.

King, Richard. 1999. *Orientalism and Religion: Postcolonial Theory, India and "The Mystic East."* London: Routledge.

Loomba, Ania. 1998. *Colonialism/Postcolonialism*. London: Routledge.

Lorenzen, David N. 1999. "Who invented Hinduism?" *Comparative Studies in Society and History* 41, 4: 630–59.

Mani, Lata. 1998. *Contentious Traditions: The Debate on Sati in Colonial India*. Berkeley: University of California Press.

Mayaram, Shail. 2004. *Against History, Against State: Counterperspectives from the Margins*. New York: Columbia University Press.

McLeod, John. 2000. *Beginning Postcolonialism*. Manchester: Manchester University Press.

Menon, Ritu and Kamla Bhasin. 1998. *Borders and Boundaries: Women in India's Partition*. New Delhi: Kali for Women.

Nandy, Ashis. 1987. *Traditions, Tyranny, and Utopias: Essays in the Politics of Awareness*. Delhi: Oxford University Press.

Nandy, Ashis. 1995. "History's Forgotten Doubles." *History and Theory* 34, 1: 44–66.

Nigam, Aditya. 2006. *The Insurrection of Little Selves: The Crisis of Secular-Nationalism in India.* Delhi: Oxford University Press.

Oberoi, Harjot. 1994. *The Construction of Religious Boundaries: Culture, Identity, and Diversity in the Sikh Tradition.* Chicago: University of Chicago Press.

Pandey, Gyanendra. 2005. *Routine Violence: Nations, Fragments, Histories.* Stanford: Stanford University Press.

Pandian, Anand. 2005. "Securing the Rural Citizen: The Anti-Kallar Movement of 1896." *The Indian Economic and Social History Review*, 42, 1: 1–39.

Peabody, Norbert. 2001. "Cents, Sense, Census: Human Inventories in Late Precolonial and Early Colonial India." *Comparative Studies of History and Society* 43, 1: 819–50.

Pollock, Sheldon. 1993. "Rāmāyaṇa and Political Imagination in India." *The Journal of Asian Studies* 52, 2: 261–97.

Prakash, Gyan. 1999. *Another Reason: Science and the Imagination of Modern India.* Princeton: Princeton University Press.

Quigley, Declan. 1993. *The Interpretation of Caste.* Oxford: Clarendon Press.

Raheja, Gloria Goodwin. 1988. *The Poison in the Gift: Ritual, Prestation, and the Dominant Caste in a North Indian Village.* Chicago: University of Chicago Press.

Rao, Anupama. Forthcoming. *The Caste Question: Untouchable Struggles for Rights and Recognition.* Berkeley: University of California Press.

Rao, Velcheru Narayan, David Dean Shulman, and Sanjay Subrahmanyam. 2001. *Textures of Time: Writing History in South India.* Delhi: Permanent Black.

Roy, Anupama. 2005. *Gendered Citizenship: Historical and Conceptual Explorations.* Hyderabad: Orient Longman.

Said, Edward. 1978. *Orientalism.* New York: Pantheon.

Saikia, Yasmin. 2004. *Fragmented Memories: Struggling to Be Tai-Ahom in India.* Durham: Duke University Press.

Sarkar, Tanika. 2001. *Hindu Wife, Hindu Nation: Community, Religion, and Cultural Nationalism.* Delhi: Permanent Black.

Skaria, Ajay. 1999. *Hybrid Histories: Forest, Frontiers and Wildness in Western India.* Delhi: Oxford University Press.

Skaria, Ajay. Forthcoming. "Gandhi's Politics: Liberalism and the Question of the Ashram." *In* Saurabh Dube, ed., *Enchantments of Modernity: Empire, Nation, Globalization.* New Delhi: Routledge.

Spivak, Gayatri Chakravorty. 1999. *A Critique of Postcolonial Reason: Toward a History of the Vanishing Present.* Cambridge: Harvard University Press.

Sugirtharajah, Sharada. 2003. *Imagining Hinduism: A Postcolonial Perspective.* New York: Routledge.

Talbot, Cynthia. 1995. "Inscribing the Other, Inscribing the Self: Hindu-Muslim Identities in Pre-Colonial India." *Comparative Studies in Society and History* 37, 4: 692–722.

Thomas, Nicholas. 1994. *Colonialism's Culture: Anthropology, Travel, and Government.* Princeton: Princeton University Press.

van der Veer, Peter. 1994. *Religious Nationalism: Hindus and Muslims in India.* Berkeley: University of California Press.

Young, Robert J. C. 2001. *Postcolonialism: An Historical Introduction*. London: Blackwell.
Young, Robert J. C. 2003. *Postcolonialism: A Very Short Introduction*. New York: Oxford University Press.

22

Psychoanalysis

Paul B. Courtright

A Brief Overview
Interpretation of Hinduism

A Brief Overview

Psychoanalysis emerged in the early twentieth century, initially founded by Sigmund Freud (1856–1939) in Vienna, as a procedure for the investigation of mental processes and treatment of neurotic disorders. For Freud and the early psychoanalytic community, the procedure involved a sustained period of, ideally, four one-hour sessions per week with a patient, sometimes called the analysand, and the analyst, working one-to-one. Over the last century, psychoanalytic procedure and its underlying theories have evolved considerably into multiple strategies for the treatment of neurotic disorders: disabling anxiety, depression, compulsive behavioral disorders, and a range of nervous system diseases. In it, classical, Freudian pattern psychoanalysis has been largely eclipsed by behavioral and neuropharmacological approaches. Psychoanalysis as a therapeutic practice has been located primarily in Europe, the United States, and Latin America. In India, psychoanalysis has attracted a small but impressive group of practitioners, to which we turn shortly.

The area wherein psychoanalysis has made arguably its greatest impact is in the interpretation of culture. Many of the concepts and categories that Freud and the early generation of analysts developed have extended far beyond the practitioner's office and the patient's couch and have been applied with intriguing if sometimes controversial, results in the interpretation of culture, literature, film, myth, and religion. As advocates for a system of interpretation of culture and the human mind, the early practitioners, and Freud especially, understood their emerging project as a branch of science that had universal application. As the psychoanalytic procedure and ideas evolved, critics and practitioners alike have come to appreciate more fully the extent to which the basic assumptions and ideas of psychoanalysis reflect European cultural conditions at the apex of its imperial hegemony over non-Western cultures.

Psychoanalysis is based on a conflict model of the mind; that is, mental activity is the result of discharges of energy in which the individual organism seeks maximal pleasure and stability that is continuous with the initial formation within the body of the mother. Later formulations emphasized a deficit notion, a primordial lack within the emerging psyche that seeks compensation. As the individual comes into the world, it goes through a series of stages beginning with a primary pleasure-seeking oral stage focused on the mother's body, especially her breast as the source of nourishment and comfort. As the pressures and demands of the external world impinge on the individual, it moves through a process demanding increasing control over its body and social relations. From the initial stage of oral satisfaction, control over the body's excretory functions are next, what Freud called the anal stage. From there comes the child's awareness of its genital zone as a source of pleasure and differentiation from the mother, focusing on her as the initial object of desire. Finally, the fuller separation from the mother and entry into the larger world of the family and society bring on the phallic stage, where gender difference becomes conscious. Freud's own theorizing about these stages centered on male development; later psychoanalytic theories have focused on early female formation.

This pathway of early development, according to psychoanalytic theory, moves inexorably toward increasing levels of awareness and the need for discipline of primary desires to achieve acceptance into the social world. For man, this process is reasonably successful; for some, the collision of primary desires—what Freud called "narcissistic" impulses—collide with social constraints in ways that leave long-lasting psychological wounds. It is the work of psychoanalysis as a procedure to unravel the adult's initial formation to locate where the conflicts lie hidden, bring them to awareness, and enable the patient to redress them from the perspective of conscious understanding. This procedure, sometimes called "the talking cure," brought some measure of relief for patients.

As Freud developed his ideas over the length of his career he saw the emerging self as consisting of three parts: the *id* (Latin for "it"), the primary location of energy discharge seeking pleasure; the *super-ego*, or the external "I" that includes the expectations, models, and pressures from society bearing down on and disciplining the individual; and the *ego*, or "I" wherein the individual negotiates its own drives for pleasure and the demands of the "other" for socialization.

In seeking to map the terrain of the emerging self, psychoanalytic theory draws on metaphors and ideas from culture and literature. For example, the male passage through the genital and phallic stages involves coming to terms with letting go of the maternal attachment and encountering the father as the initial "other" and rival. Freud drew on the story of Oedipus, the king in ancient Greek drama who unknowingly killed his father and married his mother. When he came to know the identities of each of these primary objects of conflict and intimacy, he poked out his eyes in horror. This story gave Freud an initial narrative structure around which to interpret the initial confrontation of the young male in which he unconsciously longs for continued union with his mother and fears castration by his father. He must go through a process in which he surrenders his primary attachment, identifies with his father, and seeks a female love-object of his own. Along the way, he may also experience the mother as conspiring with the father and reexperience in a reverse way; instead of her being the source of food (the breast) she becomes devouring, a motif elaborated later by Melanie Klein (1984). Freud also theorized that for females, the Oedipal stage involved a sense of betrayal by the mother for her lacking a penis, a longing that she must fulfill elsewhere by seeking a love-object who possesses one.

Late in his career, Freud developed the idea of a "death-instinct" in which the individual longs for stasis or psychic repose. Here he saw a parallel with what he understood to be Buddhist notions of *nirvāṇa*.

Within this brief overview of early psychoanalytic theory and procedure, a vocabulary emerges that has been taken into modern Western culture in a more general way. The notion of "projection" involves a process in which internal experiences of pleasure or pain are externalized and associated with objects—called symbols—that allow the self to engage these experiences as coming from outside. For Freud, symbols usually had universal and unvarying meaning. "Repression" is the process in which external demands and wishes and memories that conflict with them are taken inside the self in ways that conceal their sources. "Splitting" is the process of dividing external objects into good and bad qualities while holding them within an ambivalent whole. "Transference" is where the patient's fantasies and unconscious wishes are projected onto the analyst.

Psychoanalytic theory is not a static ideology but an evolving and self-critical discourse about the dynamics of the unconscious. From Freud's own circle, the tradition has gathered many revisions, and the names of Erik H. Erikson, Karen Horney, Carl Gustav Jung, Heinz Kohut, Jacques Marie Émile Lacan, Abraham H. Maslow, and Donald Woods Winnecott have added important nuances and new directions. Freud himself saw religion as a culturally sanctioned "illusion" that served the pressures of the super-ego in largely destructive ways, and he looked toward a secular, scientifically shaped secularism as offering a more mature resolution of individual formation. However, later psychoanalytic theorists have taken a more complex and nuanced view of the roles that religion plays in providing reservoirs of symbols and narratives that can be drawn on fruitfully in the analytic process.

With this brief overview in mind, we now turn to India and the application of psychoanalysis to the interpretation of Hinduism.

Interpretation of Hinduism

Though Freud himself took little interest in India, India took interest in Freud early on. In Calcutta (Kolkata), a small but important circle of doctors led by Girindrasekher Bose in the 1920s formed the Indian Psychoanalytical Society. Bose wrote to Freud that he did not think psychoanalysis's emphasis on individuation as the goal of human development was universal but reflected more the circumstances of modern Western culture. Bose was skeptical of the isolation of the individual that the analytic procedure imposes. He also developed the idea of contrary wishes at the unconscious level that added greater complexity to Freud's emphasis on monolithic primal drives. Bose's pioneering work notwithstanding, psychoanalysis as a clinical practice in India remains small and confined largely to middle-class urban practitioners and patients. It is in the area of a broader interpretation of culture, religion, and notions of selfhood in the Indian context that applications of psychoanalytic theory have been most important.

The enormous repertoire of Hindu myth offers many examples of stories that, like Freud's reading of Oedipus, offer insights into unconscious developmental processes that have a more distinctly Indian resonance. Three stories that are universally known in Hindu India may serve as examples: Gaṇeśa, Satī, and Sītā.

Gaṇeśa is the widely revered elephant-headed deity, the son of Śiva and Pārvatī. According to the various tellings of the story from the ancient Purāṇas to the present, it is said that once, when Śiva was away on Mount Kailasa engaged in meditation, Pārvatī was feeling lonely. She rubbed the surface of her body, and from that substance she formed a boy whom she instructed to stand guard at her door and not allow anyone to enter. As the boy was protecting his mother's privacy, Śiva returned and sought entry, but the boy prevented him. Śiva became angry and cut off the boy's head. When Pārvatī heard the commotion outside and saw that Śiva had beheaded the boy she had made, she demanded that Śiva repair him. The original head would no longer fit, so Śiva found an elephant nearby and took its head and placed it on the boy. He also adopted the boy as his own "son," naming him Gaṇeśa—the lord (*īśa*) of Śiva's followers (*gaṇa*).

From a psychoanalytic perspective, taking this story as a narrative projection of the transitional genital-phallic stage, what is striking is that it offers a reverse of the Oedipus story. Whereas Oedipus kills his father and marries his mother, Gaṇeśa is formed by his mother alone and "killed" by his father and then restored, but altered. The result of this process in the Gaṇeśa story is not a tragic and alienating one, as with Oedipus, but one of rupture and reintegration. Gaṇeśa's father, Śiva, separates him from his mother, gathers him into his own world, and offers him a nonrivalrous proximity with his mother. The Gaṇeśa story, as a "reverse-Oedipal" process, charts a process of self-formation in the Hindu context that is distinctive. The outcome in the Hindu story is one of integration and continuity within the social fabric, a contrast to the "Western" case wherein individuation leads toward loss, guilt, and alienation.

The story of Satī's self-immolation addresses a different primary process. According to the story, again widely known as early as the *Mahābhārata* and the *Rāmāyaṇa*, Satī was the daughter of the king Dakṣa. The gods wanted Śiva to find a wife, but he was reluctant. They approached the Great Goddess, Devī, and she agreed to take birth as Satī and marry Śiva but warned that if she were mistreated, she would abandon that body. Dakṣa agreed, the marriage took place, and Satī and Śiva lived happily in the mountains. Later on, Dakṣa sponsored a great sacrifice and invited all the gods and other beings, except Śiva. Dakṣa said that Śiva was an ascetic and a heretic. Satī was angry at her father's exclusion and went to the sacrifice and confronted him. When he again abused Śiva, Satī told her father that she was shedding that body she had received from him. She entered the sacrificial fire through the power of her ascetic practice. Śiva learned of her self-immolation and destroyed the sacrifice, beheaded Dakṣa, and replaced his head with that of a goat, the sacrificial animal. With that head, Dakṣa came to see that Śiva was the greatest of gods, the embodiment of the sacrifice. According to some versions of the story, Śiva took Satī's smoldering body from the fire and went back into the mountains. The gods followed him and cut her body into pieces that fell to the ground and formed temples to Satī where Śiva, in the form of the *liṅga*, joined her in her dispersed presence.

When this story is given a psychoanalytic inflection, the triangular conflict of Dakṣa-Satī-Śiva, father-daughter, wife-husband, son-in-law, lays out unconscious ambivalences with the primary family system. Dakṣa's hatred of Śiva and consequent exclusion from the sacrifice seems excessive. Although Dakṣa alleges that it is Śiva's ascetic and heretical practices that he finds offensive, another dimension may be that his rage at Śiva betrays Dakṣa's own incestuous desire for Satī. The incest taboo is culture's way of demanding separation of primary relations, a separation that protects the community from destructive narcissism. When Satī confronts her father, she is placing marriage above the paternal bond. In casting off the body her father had given her, she is punishing him by removing that object of his inappropriate attachment. When Śiva beheads Dakṣa, the goat-head—from another species altogether—places Dakṣa where the super-ego function of culture requires him to be. He now defers to Śiva, as a father who has given his daughter to his son-in-law must so that the social order may prevail. With this story, a psychoanalytic interpretation foregrounds the issues of separation and attachment—again to a nontragic conclusion. Dakṣa becomes the proper devotee, Satī and Śiva are reunited, and the sacrifice is fulfilled.

The story of Sītā, the wife of Rāma, the heroic prince of the *Rāmāyaṇa*, offers another narrative of self-formation. From the moment of their marriage, Sītā devotes herself to Rāma, accompanying him in his exile in the forest. She is captured by the demon Rāvaṇa, and, during her captivity, she thinks only of Rāma, despite Rāvaṇa's many attempts to seduce her. When she is finally rescued, Rāma rejects her, suspicious that she has not remained faithful to him while she was Rāvaṇa's prisoner. She protests her innocence and enters the sacrificial fire to demonstrate her devotion. When the fire does not burn her, Rāma is persuaded that she has remained devoted to him alone. Later on, when Rāma and Sītā return victoriously to their kingdom of Ayodhyā, rumors persist regarding Sītā's chastity, and again Rāma rejects her. She again goes into exile, eventually returning to the earth from which she originally emerged.

Sītā's story has served and continues to serve as a culturally sanctioned paradigm for females: devoted wife, ever loyal despite the husband's rejection. The *Rāmāyaṇa* articulates this ideal when it has Sītā expound, "A noble woman should treat her husband as god even if he is of evil disposition. How much more so, if he is as godly as Rāma! Except for the service of her husband a woman has no other form of worship or asceticism" (2.118). Yet, Sītā also demonstrates a strength and self-assertion, as when she was accused of infidelity to Rāma, that has inspired women. Though Freud's own notions of female psychology could not account for such assertiveness, later theories, such as those of Carol Gilligan (1993) or Nancy Chodorow (1994), embrace it. Sītā, as both a story and an icon, offers an ideal self for Hindu women's inner worlds.

When read through the lens of psychoanalytic theory and as shared narratives of unconscious ambivalences or models for identity formation within a social matrix, these three stories offer an additional level of meaning that may supplement the explicit uses of the stories at the conscious levels of cultural practices, such as story-telling and ritual. Just as Freud's readers were offered a new reading of the familiar Oedipus story, these and other well-known Hindu stories may be opened to new interpretations that give additional resonance and meaning.

Psychoanalytic studies of Hindu culture have been undertaken by both Western and Indian scholars. Some studies from the earlier stages of psychoanalytic theorizing, mostly unwittingly, have tended to view Hindu culture as having excessively powerful super-ego function that has constrained the individuation process (e.g., Carstairs 1957; Spratt 1966).

More recent studies have been more successful at filtering out some of the Western cultural preoccupations with the autonomous individual as the model of mature selfhood and reflect a greater appreciation of ways in which psychoanalytic theorizing needs to attend to cultural differences (Kakar 1997; Nandy 1995). A number of recent studies in Hindu mythology demonstrate the interpretive potential of psychoanalytic perspectives (Courtright 1985; Doniger 1999; Goldman 1978; Ramanujan 1989). Ethnographic and biographical studies that have drawn on psychoanalytic theory likewise are adding important nuances to our understanding of Hindu culture (Daniel 1984; Erikson 1969; Kakar 1991; Kripal 1998; Nabakov 2000; Obeyesekere 1990; Trawick 1990).

In the Hindu cultural context, more emphasis tends to be placed on continuity and integration of the individual into the social matrix of family and community in ways that shape very early stages of development. Extended families and multiple caregivers provide a context different from the nuclear model that early psychoanalytic theorizing presupposed (Kurtz 1992). Anthropological studies of structures of social interaction emphasize ways in which Indian selfhood is "transactional," involving complex negotiations of self in relation to multiple and hierarchically arranged personae—human and divine. Identity, therefore, is more plural and multiple than early psychoanalytic theory presupposed. Moreover, culturally shared notions of rebirth and *karma* make possible different strategies of preconscious projections onto previous lives.

The most thorough and engaging psychoanalytic interpretation of Hindu and Indian culture in recent decades has been done by Sudhir Kakar. Kakar began his psychoanalytic career as a colleague of the noted European-American psychologist and biographer, Erik Erikson, received his analytic training in Vienna, and maintains a psychoanalytic practice in India, and frequently lectures in various international settings. He draws on psychoanalytic theory with a subtlety that is not only illuminating about Indian realities but offers important insights about the ways in which the theory has been inflected by modern Western cultural issues that may be less latent in India. Moreover, his work in the Indian context offers important reinterpretations of some of the psychoanalytic traditions' core concepts.

Kakar's early work, *The Inner World: A Psychoanalytic Study of Childhood and Society in India* (1978), explores the notion of a shared "inner world" that a child assembles through the developmental process surrounded by Indian stories, social relations, expectations, and sensory experience. His study of the robust pluralism of Hindu mythology connects with the social constructions of extended family and community that create the Hindu "self." Interpreting the extraordinary importance of the goddess tradition, both as nurturing mother and disciplining power, draws important attention to one of the distinctive characteristics of Indian society and in crisp contrast to Western culture, wherein the mother-goddess tradition has been largely eclipsed in the modern period, with the notable exception of Latin America, where veneration of Mary as mother of god (Christ) remains robust.

In writing about his clinical work with patients, Kakar develops the theme of "maternal enthrallment" which he describes as "the wish to get away from the mother together with the dread of separation, hate for the mother one longs for so much, incestuous desire (and near-incestuous experiences) coexisting with the terror inspired by assertive female sexuality." (Kakar 1997: 74). In the contexts of Hindu family life, child-rearing practices, and goddess traditions, Kakar's exploration of this psychoanalytically inflected paradox in the mother–son relationship is particularly illuminating.

In addition to the importance of the mother figure, Kakar's studies (1982) of the *guru* in Hindu culture show how the *guru* serves as a locus of embracing proximity in the Hindu's inner world. As one who remains outside the primary social structure and yet draws the devotion of vast numbers of devotees, the *guru* provides a kind of living icon of cultural and moral values while also offering the community of devotees additional opportunities for solidarity outside kinship and community traditions.

In his exploration of India's cultural distinctiveness and its similarities to what might be imagined as universal human challenges of psychological formation, Kakar has explored indigenous forms of healing in *Shamans, Mystics, and Doctors* (1982). He notes that Hindu culture's tendency to view the self as a network of relations within a world of multiple objects of attachment and resistance tends to generate healing situations populated not by internal and concealed repressions but by semi-external forces, such as demons and ghosts. The healing process involves a context in which the social fabric is involved, a marked contrast to the highly individualized matrix of Western psychoanalytic practice. Though "possession" may focus on an individual, the therapeutic work of the healer is to draw on the resources of the social community, mythic entities, and the textures of the cosmos as a whole to reposition the possessed person within a more nurturing setting. Kakar skillfully unravels any residual notions that possession is "primitive" or "backward"; rather, it is an alternative theory and practice that addresses issues of human suffering and well-being that are deeply embedded in the collective social experience of its practice.

Kakar also finds within traditional Hindu practices some parallels to psychoanalysis. The traditions of Yoga and Tantra are highly disciplined practices of self-transformation that provide progressive cues for gaining insight and control over destructive patterns within an individual's inner world. Tantra may have the greatest family resemblance to psychoanalysis in that it addresses issues of sexuality explicitly as part of its practices of self-transformation. Like its counterpart in Western culture, Tantra in India possesses a subversive and controversial character. Kakar notes:

> It is only through a consideration of the practice of both disciplines that one becomes aware of their emancipative core; in the case of psychoanalysis, an "enlightenment" which is not only individual but also societal in nature and, in the case of Tantra, a "liberation" not only in the mystical sense but one which is also relevant to the individual's concrete, historical condition. Finally, like psychoanalysis, Tantra too is based upon a recognition, even celebration, of man's sensuous nature.
>
> (1981: 87)

Kakar's psychoanalytically informed research into social and religious violence in India offers considerable insight into how aspects of negative self-feelings within a Hindu inner world become projected onto an "other." Mythic formations of gods and demons provide paradigms for viewing the social world as inhabited by a social self that is pure and valued and an "other" that is degraded and untrustworthy.

In exploring the usefulness of psychoanalytic theory for the interpretation of Hinduism and Indian culture, it is important to keep in mind what this approach makes visible and what its limits are. Psychoanalytic theory posits what Kakar terms an "inner world," akin to Lacan's notion of the imaginary, which is both individual and shared. Focusing on early identity formation within the context of Indian culture, the stories, ritual practices, family organizations, cosmological notions, attitudes toward food, body, sex, death—the thick texture of human life—the psychoanalytic gaze into the Hindu world provides an angle of vision. It has little to offer in terms of sociological, economic, or political life but does contribute a back-story that may be illuminating to the more empirically based forms of knowledge. It is also important to keep in mind that psychoanalysis, as a mode of inquiry, is subversive by its nature. It attempts to probe beneath the surface, to inquire into primary formation of identity at stages in which the constraints of what is proper or acceptable have not yet reached articulation. Just as Freud and the psychoanalytic tradition were received with considerable ambivalence in the early stages by a culture not comfortable with public examination of the private and shame-associated aspects of the body, sexuality, and family, some in India—and in its diasporic communities worldwide—continue to regard them with skepticism and hostility.

As psychoanalysis as a procedure of interpretation of Hindu culture has matured, it is no longer—if it ever was—a matter of putting Hinduism "on the couch" and finding it neurotic. What psychoanalysis offers to the larger project of the interpretation of Hinduism is an additional perspective, another point of reference, an exploration of possible subtexts of Hindu texts and practices. It also provides a kind of transformational grammar for moving from one cultural language to another. Increasingly, psychoanalytic theory is growing beyond the parochialism of the modern West and being rethought by scholars and practitioners in other cultures. From the perspective of psychoanalytically framed Hindu formations of self as self-in-integration, new insights about Western self-as-individual formations come into greater clarity. The longer-term prospect for psychoanalysis and the interpretation of Hinduism is that it enlarges the pool of experience, insight, and imagination in ways that will continue to serve the growth of this "procedure" in ways that will help it to fulfill its initial effort: relief from suffering. The relief from suffering is a goal as ancient as the Upaniṣads and the Yoga Sūtras. It is only in recent decades that some of the convergences and resemblances of goal and effort are becoming clearer.

References Cited

Carstairs, G. Morris. 1957. *The Twice-Born: A Study of a Community of High-Caste Hindus*. Bloomington: Indiana University Press.

Chodorow, Nancy. 1994. *Femininities, Masculinities, Sexuality: Freud and Beyond.* Lexington: University of Kentucky Press.

Courtright, Paul B. 1985. *Gaṇeśa: Lord of Obstacles, Lord of Beginnings.* New York: Oxford University Press.

Daniel, E. Valentine. 1984. *Fluid Signs: Being a Person the Tamil Way.* Berkeley: University of California Press.

Doniger, Wendy. 1999. *Splitting the Difference: Gender and Myth in Ancient Greece and India.* Chicago: University of Chicago Press.

Erikson, Erik H. 1969. *Gandhi's Truth: On the Origins of Militant Nonviolence.* New York: Norton.

Gilligan, Carol. 1993. *In a Different Voice: Psychological Theory and Women's Development.* Cambridge: Harvard University Press.

Goldman, Robert P. 1978. "Fathers, Sons, and Gurus: Oedipal Conflict in the Sanskrit Epics." *Journal of Indian Philosophy* 6, 4: 325–92.

Kakar, Sudhir. 1978. *The Inner World: A Psycho-Analytic Study of Childhood and Society in India.* New Delhi: Oxford University Press.

Kakar, Sudhir. 1981. "The Person in Tantra and Psycho-Analysis." *Samikṣā* 35, 4: 85–104.

Kakar, Sudhir. 1982. *Shamans, Mystics, and Doctors: A Psychological Inquiry into India and its Healing Traditions.* New York, Knopf.

Kakar, Sudhir. 1991. *The Analyst and the Mystic: Psychoanalytic Reflections of Religion and Mysticism.* Chicago: University of Chicago Press.

Kakar, Sudhir. 1997. *Culture and Psyche: Selected Essays.* New Delhi: Oxford University Press.

Klein, Melanie. 1984 [1975]. *The Psycho-Analysis of Children.* New York: Free Press.
Kripal, Jeffrey J. 1998 [1995]. Kālī's Child: *The Mystical and the Erotic in the Life and Teachings of Ramakrishna.* Chicago: University of Chicago Press.
Kurtz, Stanley N. 1992. *All the Mothers Are One: Hindu India and the Cultural Reshaping of Psychoanalysis.* New York: Colmbia University Press.
Nabakov, Isabelle. 2000. *Religion Against the Self: An Ethnography of Tamil Rituals.* New York: Oxford University Press.
Nandy, Ashis. 1995. *The Savage Freud and Other Essays on Possible and Retrievable Selves.* Princeton: Princeton University Press.
Obeyesekere, Gananath. 1990. *The Work of Culture: Symbolic Transformation in Psychoanalysis and Anthropology.* Chicago: University of Chicago Press.
Ramanujan, A. K. 1989. "Is There an Indian Way of Thinking?: An Informal Essay." *Contributions to Indian Sociology (ns)* 23, 1: 41–58.
Spratt, Philip. 1966. *Hindu Culture and Personality: A Pscyho-Analytic Study.* Bombay: Manaktala.
Trawick, Margaret. 1990. *Notes on Love in a Tamil Family.* Berkeley: University of California Press.

23

Ritual

Kathryn McClymond

Hindu Ritual's Contribution to the Study of Religion
Looking Ahead
Concluding Reflections

Hindu life centers on ritual activity. The activity may be simple or complex, and it may be directed toward otherworldly goals (*mokṣa*) or mundane concerns (health, wealth, a good marriage, etc.). The limited scope of this chapter does not allow for a detailed explanation of the full spectrum of Hindu ritual. Instead, I outline several general categories of ritual practice: life-cycle rituals, devotional rituals, and festival rituals.

Life-cycle rites (*saṃskāra*, from the Sanskrit meaning "preparation") vary by caste and gender, and the timing of each ritual performance is determined by the lunar calendar and by an individual's age and caste. Mary McGee notes that these rituals are meant to prepare the participant "spiritually, socially, and culturally to assume the dharmic duties and responsibilities of adulthood" (2004: 333). Certain elements are common to all the life-cycle rites: opening purifying rites; worship of various deities; elements of fire and water; food; and gifts. Although the number of *saṃskāra*s varies (McGee 2004: 333), there are sixteen commonly referenced classical *saṃskāra*s (Flood 1996: 202–3; Lipner 1994: 265–66), although it should be noted that many of these are not observed regularly (marriage and funeral rites are the most commonly observed). The first four rituals deal with pregnancy and childbirth, and the next six are performed during childhood (e.g., naming, tonsuring, ear-piercing).

One of the most well-known life-cycle events is the *upanayana* ("leading near") ceremony, which initiates a high-caste young man (ranging in age from eight to twenty-four years) into his second, spiritual birth. The young man is ritually bathed and shaved, and he has his nails cut. He also offers ritual oblations. His father or *guru* teaches him the Gāyatrī *mantra*, whispering it quietly into his ear. The young initiate should recite this *mantra* each morning throughout his life. The ritual culminates in his investiture with a sacred thread (*yajñopavīta*). This three-stranded cord is worn around his body, draped over the left shoulder, and it marks his movement into the adult male phase of his life. At the end of the ritual, the young man is symbolically sent off to pursue Vedic study. Traditionally, at this point the young man spends a period of time living with a teacher as he studies the Vedas. His entry into this student period is marked with a vow of celibacy, which continues until the ritual bath that marks the end of this student phase. From this time forward, the young man is considered *dvija* ("twice-born"), and he is considered qualified to recite the Vedas and establish the sacred fires.

The next major rite is marriage (*vivāha*). Traditionally, marriage is arranged by the couple's parents. The choice of a marriage partner is largely driven by caste status, and "love matches" are still very rare by Western standards. Marriage ceremonies follow a betrothal period, which can be somewhat lengthy if the parties are engaged when they are young or completing their education. In a traditional wedding, the groom processes (traditionally on horse) with his family to his bride's home. The groom is greeted by the bride (who is richly dressed), and she places a garland around his neck. The wedding ceremony, directed by a *purohita* (family priest), begins with the bride being given to the groom by her father. The ceremony involves fire offerings and requires the bride and groom to take seven steps around a ritual fire; most people view this circumambulation as the act that binds the couple to one another. *Mantra*s are recited to encourage fertility and prosperity in the newly established household, and the couple makes vows indicating their acceptance of the responsibilities that accompany householder status.

For most Hindus, marriage is the most important life transition. For most families, this is the most lavish ritual celebration they will ever provide. Traditionally, the bride's family gives gifts to the groom's family in addition to bearing the cost of the wedding itself, and the hosts are expected to serve an abundant feast to family and friends, who come from around the world to attend if possible. All of this effort marks the major change that both families experience in this ritual and the bride and groom's movement into householder status.

The final life-cycle ritual is the funeral rite (*antyeṣṭi*, "last sacrifice"). Though this ceremony may help to comfort grieving family members, its primary purpose is to purify the deceased soul and to facilitate its liberation (*mokṣa*). Soon after an individual dies, the body is ritually bathed, anointed, wrapped, and taken to a funeral pyre at a local cremation ground. Traditionally, the eldest son leads a procession to the funeral ground, where the body is placed on a funeral pyre, oriented toward the south (the direction of Yama, god of death). The funeral pyre is lit, and the eldest son cracks open the skull of the deceased to allow the soul to leave the body. Ultimately, the entire body is consumed by fire. After the cremation, there is a period of mourning, during which time the family is considered ritually impure. Three to ten days after the cremation, the deceased's ashes and bone fragments are buried or deposited in a local river; if possible, they are taken to a holy river, such as the Gaṅgā. Memorial rites (*śrāddha*) are performed on behalf of the deceased several days after and on the anniversary of the death. These rites include rice balls and water libations. Other memorial rites including similar offerings may continue for years afterward. If a deceased man leaves behind a widow, she traditionally dresses in plain white, removes her bangles, and omits the red *kumkum* powder from her hair from this time forward.

Gender and caste play crucial roles in all of these life-cycle rituals. As McGee notes, "In practice the actual performance of *saṃskāras* has been restricted by the orthodox tradition largely to those of higher classes and the male gender, groups viewed as having greater purity" (2004: 335). Gender and caste determine whether an individual can participate in a certain ceremony and how those ceremonies are conducted. For example, women do not submit to the *upanayana* rite. Gavin Flood notes Manu's assertion that "marriage is a woman's *upanayana*, serving her husband is equivalent to vedic study, and housework equivalent to the fire oblations" (1996: 204). Śūdras are traditionally forbidden from reciting or even hearing the Vedas, so they are prohibited from certain rites and from using Vedic *mantras* in others. Other elements of ritual celebration (gestures, dress) may also reflect caste distinctions. Alterations to various aspects of the ritual reflect the traditional view that life-cycle rites are centered on issues of purity. Ritual practice both generates ritual purity and isolates differing levels of purity-pollution from one another. The performance of certain rites—and the exclusion of lower-caste individuals and women from certain rites altogether—grows out of these concerns.

In addition to life-cycle rituals, individuals engage in many devotional rituals. These can occur in private homes and in public temples and shrines or through pilgrimages to holy sites, cities, rivers, or "crossings" (*tīrthas*). As any visitor to India soon realizes, natural and human-made objects of devotion are everywhere, encouraging worship at virtually any time or place. Devotional practices themselves can be very simple (such as the morning recitation of the Gāyatrī *mantra*) or very complex (as in extended festival celebrations). Individuals and families may worship in home shrines or at a local temple. Though worship has historical roots in sacrifice (*yajña*), what dominates contemporary practice is largely known as *pūjā*, offerings to a *mūrti* (an image of a deity). There are sixteen classic *upacaras* or "honor offerings" that one can offer to deities, including food, water, sandalwood, incense, betel nuts, and fabric. Numerous scholars have noted that *pūjā* is much like receiving an honored guest with generous hospitality. In private homes, images are installed in separate rooms or smaller designated areas, and *pūjā* is performed by family members. In temples, the regular care and feeding of the *mūrti*s—which occurs three or four times a day—is the responsibility of the temple priests (*pujārī*), although individuals present private offerings as well. Priests waken and dress the deity, present appropriate offerings, and circumambulate the image with an oil lamp (*ārati*). Food that has been offered to a deity is understood to be ritually consumed, and the "leavings" of the offering (*prasāda*) are made available for ritual consumption by devotees in order to convey the god's blessing. Julius Lipner explains, "These substances have been symbolically consumed by the deity in its image form. As a result, these substances have been ritually transmuted to become *prasada* imbued with divine power and grace" (1994: 351).

The most intimate act of worship, whether at home or in a temple, is *darśana* or "auspicious viewing." As Diana Eck explains, "The visual apprehension of the image is charged with religious meaning. Beholding the image is an act of worship, and through the eyes one gains the blessings of the divine" (1998: 3). *Darśana* is as intimate an act as touching—through this act, the devotee knows and is known by the deity manifest in the *mūrti*. The devotee encounters the sacred directly. During major festivals, a *mūrti* may be brought out from the temple to an open outdoor space to make this encounter possible for large numbers of worshippers.

Individuals may also commit themselves to private ritual activity on behalf of themselves or others. The classic examples of this are the daily recitation of the Gāyatrī *mantra* in the morning and a wife's performance of specific *vrata*s (vows) regularly undertaken on behalf of her husband or household. *Vrata*s traditionally involve ritual baths, fasting, and specific devotional rituals for the deity associated with the *vrata* day or season. Certain deities are associated with specific days of the week (e.g., Monday is associated with Śiva, whereas Hanumān is associated with Tuesday), phases of the moon, and the three seasons of the year (hot, rainy, and cool). As a result, virtually every day can be a minor or major holiday, and devotees can "target" specific deities with their prayers and fasts on appropriate days.

In addition, countless Hindus participate in pilgrimages each year, many of which are lengthy and physically demanding. Pilgrimage (*tīrthayātrā*) is one of the most common forms of devotion, and it is tied to specific cities, hills, rivers, and "crossings" that dot India's landscape. Countless sites in India are linked to the mythology of specific deities, and pilgrimages draw devotees to land that is said to be charged with the divine.

David Haberman's *Journey Through the Twelve Forests* (1994) is one of several detailed studies of Hindu pilgrimage (see also Entwistle 1987; Gold 1988; Sax 1991). In this work, Haberman provides a thoughtful account of his participation in the "Ban Yātrā," a cyclical pilgrimage of devotion to Kṛṣṇa that is widely practiced in Braj (northcentral India). Key to Haberman's discussion is the notion of "play" or *līlā*. Haberman notes that though some pilgrimages have specific goals, others (such as the Ban Yātrā) are intentionally purposeless: "It opens up a new perspective, namely, that all life is *lila*, or purposeless play. The subjective experience of this realization, the theologians of Braj tell us, is *ananda*, or limitless joy" (1994: viii). Thus, pilgrimage involves an internal experience as much as—or more so than—any external journey. William Sax muses, "Thus *līlā* appears to mark a delightful difference between European and South Asian traditions, embodying a ludic dimension in Indian religious life that is muted or even absent in the dominant religions of the West" (1995: 3).

Finally, the Hindu liturgical calendar includes countless festival holidays dedicated to various deities. This calendar is far more complex than most Western calendars. As Nancy Falk notes, "Every day is a holy day of sorts, although different people may choose different days for special observance" (2006: 128). Some annual festivals are pan-Hindu. For example, Dīvālī (also known as Dīpāvali, "a row of lights"), is the festival of lights. It is celebrated for three to five days throughout India at the transition from the months of Aśvina and Kārttika (in late fall). The focus of the celebration is Lakṣmī, the goddess of prosperity, and Hindus around the world celebrate with lights and fireworks.

Other celebrations have a more regional focus. For example, the Kumbha Melā is celebrated every three years in progressive festivals in Hardwar, Nasik, Ujjain, and Prayaga (Allahabad). The great celebration Pūrṇa Kumbha Melā, "full *kumbha* gathering," occurs at Allahabad every twelve years. Pilgrims from all castes and all regions of the world gather for this festival, stepping into the river waters to wash away their sins. Many view the journey to the celebration site, in and of itself, as a ritual act that generates merit. In another example, in the western state of Maharashtra, devotees celebrate Gaṇeśa Caturthī by sinking images of Gaṇeśa in the Arabian Sea. The Rāmlīlā, a celebration of Rāma, is performed in northern India, and in Bengal, Durgā Pūjā is celebrated each fall (see Lipner 1994: 299–303).

Historically, Western scholars who have observed life-cycle, devotional, and calendrical rituals have been struck by several elements of Hindu worship, and these elements have informed both the study of Hinduism in general and specific interpretations of Hindu ritual life. First, Hindu worship largely (but not entirely) focuses on devotion to a form of a deity, either in iconic form, such as a *mūrti*, or in aniconic form, such as a *liṅga* or a *maṇḍala*. Though in some streams of thought these images act as "pointers," directing the devotee's attention to a specific god, in other streams of Hinduism the deity is understood to inhabit consecrated icons. This has led to numerous difficulties as the West encountered and then attempted to interpret Hinduism. Visitors associated Hindu image-making with the "idolatry" proscribed by the Abrahamic traditions. As Eck notes, "The Western traditions, especially the religious traditions of the 'Book'—Judaism, Christianity, and Islam—have trusted the Word more than the Image as a mediator of divine truth" (1998: 20). Hindu ritual, by contrast, is unabashedly embodied, appealing to devotees with colorful and symbolic imagery, the sounds of chanting and song, purposeful gestures, varied food offerings, and complex scents. Scholarly work indicates that the sensory elements not only express the incarnational theology associated with the various deities, but also help direct the devotee's attention to the divine through the use of imagery.

In addition, early Western travelers rejected the henotheistic theology that undergirded these devotional practices. Hindu devotionalism tends to center on Śiva, Viṣṇu, and the Devī (Goddess). However, as any beginning student of Hinduism quickly learns, though individuals may identify one deity as their supreme deity, they often worship many deities in various ritual contexts. Historically, Western scholars often pointed to this to argue for the superiority of the Abrahamic (specifically Christian) religions.

Hindu Ritual's Contribution to the Study of Religion

Hinduism, of course, has provided rich data for scholars in the field of religious studies for generations. Only recently, however, have scholars of Hindu ritual begun to make significant contributions to the study of religion more broadly. No one has been more influential (or more controversial) in the recent past than Frits Staal. Staal attracted wide attention for his work on "meaninglessness" in ritual in *Rules Without Meaning* (1990). In this work, Staal examines the Vedic sacrificial tradition through the close study of texts and observation of live performances, particularly an elaborate *agnicayana* ("piling up of *agni*") sacrifice in Kerala, India. Staal argues that Vedic rituals, far from being arbitrary, have densely packed, complex internal structures that organize the movements of each ritual player. The rules that govern these movements are strict and make sense within the context of the ritual itself, but they have no referent in the "outside" world. In that sense, the ritual is meaningless; there is no correlation between elements within the ritual arena and elements within the mundane world. Staal has been taken to task by numerous scholars for his conclusions, but it is important to acknowledge that he was among the first to argue that Vedic ritual, which for a long time was characterized as "marked by shallow and insipid grandiloquence, by priestly conceit, and antiquarian pedantry" (by one of its foremost scholars, no less!), has its own sophisticated logic that has nothing to do with the dramatization of a myth.

Staal's work is also important because it reflects a growing trend among Indologists to move beyond narrowly circumscribed investigations of Hindu ritual to analysis that contributes to the study of ritual more broadly. Hindu data have forced scholars of religion to rethink the relationship between ritual and myth, rejecting the notion that myth has logical and chronological priority over ritual. In addition, Hindu data encourage scholars to think of religious self-identification in terms of "orthopraxy" rather than "orthodoxy." Though a strict dichotomy between these two categories is simplistic, it has been helpful to note the Western tendency to privilege belief and confession over action and tradition. From a common Western perspective, ritual is "empty"—and thus worthless—if it does not follow belief or informed intent; sustained study of Hindu ritual challenges this simplistic understanding of the relationship of ritual to other religious phenomena.

Scholars of Hindu ritual have drawn largely from two types of research: textual studies of ancient ritual guidelines and ethnographic research on specific local practices. Indologists from various disciplines have debated vigorously how scholars should weigh these two approaches, arguing for preferred balances between the "textual" and "contextual" approaches. These two streams of research have drawn attention to certain themes that dominate Hindu ritual practice and its interpretation. First, Hindu ritual has long been concerned with issues of purity and pollution (largely, but not exclusively, related to food) and ways in which these issues play out in social hierarchies. In addition, Hindu ritual is often subdivided into certain categories of practice: sacrifice, *pūjā*, pilgrimage, and festival. Each subcategory reflects specific concerns as well as formalized activity, concerns which influence the domestic or public, individual or corporate nature of the ritual activity. Moreover, the study of Hindu ritual has often betrayed a preference for Brāhmaṇical (priestly) or popular religion, with the Brāhmaṇical dimension tied more closely to the Vedic texts, whereas the popular religion draws more from Epic and devotional literature. Haberman notes that early scholars

> insisted that a proper understanding of Hinduism must be based on the right set of authoritative, written texts.... Medieval and modern texts, living traditions, and contemporary forms of Hinduism (such as pilgrimage) were often regarded with suspicion from the interpretive environment within which the true or 'essential' tradition was constructed.
>
> (1994: x)

Modern ritual studies, by contrast, revel in the wide range of popular ritual expression.

One of the dominant concerns that has persisted in the study of Hindu ritual is the connection between purity–pollution concerns and caste hierarchy. The key work in this area originates with Louis Dumont (1911–98), a French structuralist anthropologist. Dumont is best known for *Homo Hierarchicus: The Caste System and Its Implications* (1970), a landmark work in which he argues that the Hindu caste system is not arbitrary or primitive but rather the expression of a highly complex society in which relations between individuals are ordered by hierarchies that are maintained to benefit society overall. Dumont extrapolated from this analysis to argue that *every* society includes a tension between the person as an individual and the person as a member of a hierarchical society. This tension is expressed in ritual action. Ritual manipulation of food is controlled by concerns for purity, caste, and gender that generate an elaborate social hierarchy in Hindu culture. Subsequent studies of food, ritual practices, and social hierarchy offered a new configuration of these cultural elements that differed markedly from previous Western approaches.

In addition, Hindu ritual practice ranges across a wide spectrum of activity, from the highly formalized and complex Vedic sacrificial system, through the simpler, but closely regulated, *pūjā* system, to more open-ended pilgrimage and festival events. Though Hindu studies in the West originally were limited to textual research (for example, The Sacred Books of the East series), the emphasis was on Brāhmaṇical versions of Hinduism. As ethnographic, anthropological, and sociological research developed, scholars became increasingly aware of the diversity within Hindu practice. The recognition of the dynamics involved between localized, lay-people practices and Brāhmaṇical or pan-Indian versions of Hinduism has been made most explicit in the work of two key scholars, M. N. Srinivas and McKim Marriott. Social anthropologist Srinivas (1916–99) is best known for his concept of "Sanskritization," first introduced in his book *Religion and Society among the Coorgs of South India* (1952). Although narrowly the term may refer to Sanskrit language, in Srinivas's use it is better understood to refer to a cultural tradition, one that traces itself back to the Upaniṣads and the Epics. By "Sanskritization," Srinivas meant the deliberate appropriation of upper-caste practices by lower-caste groups as a means of elevating themselves in the caste hierarchy. Srinivas summarizes, "All-India Hinduism…[includes] the extension of Sanskritic deities and ritual forms to an outlying group, as well as by the greater Sanskritization of the ritual and beliefs of groups inside Hinduism" (1952: 214). Examples of Sanskritization include a shift to a vegetarian diet, *yoga* practice, and meditation. Axel Michaels explains, "Non-Brahmin population groups accept the customs of Brahmanic-Sanskritic Hinduism (vegetarianism, cow worship, etc.) to attain a higher status. But this process is not one-sided. If a previously non-Hindu divinity acquires a Sanskrit name and is worshipped according to a purely Brahmanic ritual, this can happen from 'below,' to enhance the status of the divinity in question" (2004: 26). Lipner notes, "The cult of Pābūjī is beginning to be Sanskritised, e.g. by associating the epic of Pābūjī with the Rāma story, and Pābūjī himself, in images of the *paṛ*, with established deities of the 'great tradition'" (1994: 144). From the perspective of ritual studies, this process is important because it forefronts the interplay of religion, economics, and political relationships between subgroups in Hindu culture, and the use of praxis rather than doctrine to signal a desired improvement in status. Behavioral imitation is at the heart of Sanskritization, and it is a two-way street: localized, lower-caste traditions act to elevate their own status by imitating elements of an upper-caste lifestyle, whereas pan-Indian Hinduism often spreads by absorbing localized traditions, specifically by absorbing or transforming local deities into Hindu deities and by shaping local dietary, worship, and lifestyle practices. Numerous scholars have used Srinivas's term to explain the behavior of lower-caste Hindu and non-Hindu communities, both in India and abroad. The term "Sanskritization" has become a shorthand for the self-elevation of one group via the imitation of another, socially superior group.

Scholarship on Hindu ritual has often suffered from the temptation for Western scholars to import Western or Christian (or both) categories into their analysis of non-Western traditions. Anthropologist McKim Marriott was one of the first scholars to address this problem by constructing an alternative interpretative approach to Hindu practices via what he viewed as indigenous categories: "Attending to what is perceived by Indians in Indian categories should at least promote a more perceptive Indian ethnography" (1989:1). In his work, Marriott self-consciously positioned himself in opposition to Dumont and Srinivas. In contrast to Dumont (of whom Marriott is especially critical), Marriott draws on local fieldwork that emphasizes the microlevel of Hindu lived experience over a pan-Hindu approach, which Marriott views as ideological and overly simplistic in its attempt to provide a falsely unified sociology. Marriott attempts to use indigenous Hindu categories to develop a template for interpreting Hindu communities that simultaneously provides room for variety while drawing attention to widely recognized Hindu categories for self-identification. He constructs a "cube" framework, "building from the culture's natural categories a general system of concepts that can be formally defined in relation to each other" (1989: 4). From Marriott's perspective, Hindu culture develops around personal "transactions," yielding individuals who are ranked in a variety of ways (e.g., gender, caste, purity). To make it even more complicated, one's "rank" is constantly in flux, depending on the company one keeps. As a result, there is no essential, static sense of identity; rather, there is constant fluidity—

a hallmark of Hindu culture and identity in Marriott's mind. In response to Srinivas's concept of Sanskritization, Marriott argued that "little" groups need not shed their localized practices; instead, communities often identified their local deity with a pan-Hindu deity rather than shedding the local deity. In this scenario, Sanskritized elements were added to—rather than replacing—local elements. Thus, local communities did not lose their particular flavor, but they established bridges between themselves and the developing pan-Indian "Hinduism" by adding Hindu elements to their own distinctive deities and ritual traditions.

Looking Ahead

There are at least three specific ways in which focusing on Hindu ritual contributes to a better understanding of religion in general. First, ritual underscores the interdisciplinary nature of religious studies. To develop a thorough and sophisticated understanding of Hindu ritual, one must draw from history, anthropology, performance studies, even linguistic theory. In addition, the study of ritual is incomplete without attention to its relationship to other religious phenomena: myth, doctrine, sacred space, and so on. No category of religious experience exists independently; rather, each expression of individual and communal religious identity shapes and is shaped by others. Finally, the study of ritual draws attention to a sense of the "other" in various ways: I do this action rather than another action; I speak these words rather than others; I act in specific times and places rather than in others. Most important, I use ritual to position myself in relation to an "other": another individual, another transcendent reality, another culture, or even another version of myself. Ritual is about us and them, then and now, here and there, the construction or transgression (or both) of boundaries.

Just as ritual has enjoyed a revival as a lens through which to study religion in general, ritual is also enjoying renewed appreciation as a lens through which to study Hinduism. Hindu ritual activity reflects the broader Hindu assumption that there are certain correspondences between elements in the natural, human, divine, and cosmic realms. Ritual "works" because ritual activities align elements in the various realms, tapping elements and energies in one realm by manipulating corresponding elements in another realm. Ritual, then, is efficacious, not merely commemorative or dramatic. And ritual works because of a sophisticated understanding of a certain kind of metonymic structure that underlies the universe. Ritual in Hinduism is not simply the dramatization of Hindu mythology. Rather, it provides a means for direct contact or communion with the divine, the devotee, the natural world, and the cosmos; it reinforces and generates socially approved divisions according to purity–pollution codes; and it prompts experiences of *ānanda* or bliss. The ritual realm is the arena in which the mundane world expresses and experiences the divine. This understanding of ritual has enriched scholars' research on the relationship between ritual and other analytic categories, particularly work on ritual and myth.

Second, events in the last twenty-five years or so have forced scholars to recognize the political face of ritual. The most well-known example of this is Lal Krishna Advani's ritual procession to Ayodhya. This procession culminated in the destruction of the unused Babari mosque in 1992. Conflict had surrounded this mosque since before British rule, exacerbated when the British built a railing separating Hindu and Muslim worshippers in the Babari compound. In December 1949, Hindus entered the mosque and installed an image of the legendary figure Rāma, arguing that the mosque occupied his birthplace. Their actions effectively converted the mosque to a temple. Despite the tensions that followed, the *mūrti* was not removed, and Hindu worship never completely stopped at this site. In 1984 the Visva Hindu Pariṣad (VHP, "World Hindu Council") began to wage a campaign for full control of the site, arguing again that the mosque was situated on Rāma's birthplace and that Muslims had destroyed an earlier temple to build that mosque. Tensions surrounding the proper use of this site were fueled in 1987, when a televised version of the *Rāmāyaṇa* epic was broadcast throughout India. Ayodhya became caught up in a nationalist conflict. A *rathayātrā* ("chariot journey") was conducted by Advani, beginning in Somnath. This procession was meant to remind viewers of the *aśvamedha yajña*, a Vedic ritual designed to demarcate the boundaries of ancient kings' lands. By framing his journey as a *rathayātrā* and invoking rituals that established political boundaries, Advani intended to instill Hindu control over India, suggesting that India is properly a Hindu nation, thereby setting aside years of Muslim rule. Advani's march culminated in the destruction of the Babari mosque in 1992 by thousands of militants. Members of the VHP tore down the mosque, and this sparked nationwide riots, leaving more than three thousand people dead across India. This was followed by riots in July 2005, when five militants attacked the site, and conflict over the site continues to this day.

In this instance, ritual and mythology were invoked to promote political goals, and the investigation of this by scholars revealed the "ugly" side of religion, the use of religious rite and rhetoric for political gain. There is, of course, nothing new about this strategy; religion and politics have always had an intimate relationship. However, given earlier romantic Orientalist characterizations of Indian religions by Western scholars, the Ayodhya event (and others like it) served as a reminder of the complexity of religious ritual and the need for hermeneutics of suspicion as well as hermeneutics of belief.

Third, as increasing numbers of Hindus have migrated and settled in Western countries, more and more Indians are living (and being raised in) diaspora settings. This has raised new questions about the role of ritual as a means for Hindus outside of India to transmit their heritage and cultural elements to succeeding generations. Rituals—particularly rituals tied to food practices and life-cycle events—construct ties to the mother country, to the mother tongue, and to family and regional cultural traditions. Ritual is increasingly being recognized as an important window onto diasporic community life and as a means for that community to transmit religiocultural identity to subsequent generations.

Concluding Reflections

The term "ritual," much like the terms "religion" and "Hinduism," has become increasingly problematic in recent years. Yet the term continues to be useful in spite of the difficulties involved in trying to pin down a definition. Within the study of religion, changes in the focus and methodology of ritual studies have reflected changes in the field of religious studies more broadly: expanded interest in and respect for non-Christian traditions; shifts from liturgical-theological emphases to historical and anthropological research; and an increased willingness to rethink seemingly fixed categories of analysis in light of non-Western, particularly non-Christian, traditions. Hinduism's rich ritual tradition offers data to ritual studies scholars that not only add to their data pool but forces them to rethink how to frame categories of religious and ritual experience. In so doing, Hindu ritual offers much to the study of religion more broadly.

References Cited

Dumont, Louis. 1970 [1966]. *Homo Hierarchicus: An Essay on the Caste System* (trans. Mark Sainsbury). Chicago: University of Chicago Press.

Eck, Diana L. 1998 [1981]. *Darśan: Seeing the Divine Image in India.* New York: Columbia University Press.

Entwistle, Alan W. 1987. *Braj: Centre of Krishna Pilgrimage.* Groningen: Egbert Forsten.

Falk, Nancy Auer. 2006. *Living Hinduisms: An Explorer's Guide.* Belmont: Thomson Wadsworth.

Flood, Gavin. 1996. *An Introduction to Hinduism.* Cambridge: Cambridge University Press.

Gold, Ann Grodzins. 1988. *Fruitful Journeys: The Ways of Rajasthani Pilgrims.* Berkeley: University of California Press.

Haberman, David L. 1994. *Journey Through the Twelve Forests: An Encounter with Krishna.* New York: Oxford University Press.

Lipner, Julius J. 1994. *Hindus: Their Religious Beliefs and Practices.* London: Routledge.
Marriott, McKim. 1989. "Constructing an Indian Ethnosociology." *Contributions to Indian Sociology (ns)* 23, 1: 1–39.
McGee, Mary. 2004. "Saṃskāra." *In* Sushil Mittal and Gene Thursby, eds, *The Hindu World*, 332–56. London: Routledge.
Michaels, Axel. 2004. *Hinduism: Past and Present.* Princeton: Princeton University Press.
Sax, William S. 1991. *Mountain Goddess: Gender and Politics in a Himalayan Pilgrimage.* New York: Oxford University Press.
Sax, William S. 1995. *The Gods at Play.* New York: Oxford University Press.
Srinivas, M. N. 1952. *Religion and Society among the Coorgs of South India.* Oxford: Clarendon.
Staal, Frits. 1990. *Rules Without Meaning: Ritual, Mantras and the Human Sciences.* New York: Peter Lang.

24

Romanticism

Dorothy Figueira

Romantic Myth Theory
Romantic Literature
Romantic Indology
Concluding Reflections

The European Enlightenment gave the Romantics a sense of individual self-identity, freedom from the constraints of social confines, and the promise of progress among all peoples. Its promotion of social self-consciousness made possible the development of linguistics in the second half of the eighteenth century. This chapter gives particular attention to the contributions of German Romantics because they were instrumental in creating images of India and of Hinduism that have continued to be influential in popular consciousness and in academic scholarship down to the present time.

The study of language played a significant role in the Enlightenment's quest for human origins. Gottfried Wilhelm Leibniz and Étienne Bonnot de Condillac believed that the understanding of language held the key to understanding the origins and character of nations. Johann Gottfried Herder diverted his focus on the arbitrariness of the sign to the reciprocal relationship between language and thought, and he shared the assumption that language provided the medium through which the thoughts of a given people could best be understood. Language certainly was not divine but instead was the result of conscious human efforts acted on by climatic conditions and geographical surroundings.

Herder's focus on semiotic representation paved the way for philological-historical hermeneutics. Between 1770 and 1790, traditional philology was transformed from mere analysis of the text to interpretive philology. At the beginning of the Romantic era, when the forces of European nationalism were about to become dominant, Herder's view of language found a ready audience. Then, with the claims of William Jones in his Third Anniversary Discourse, delivered February 2, 1786 at the Asiatick Society of Bengal, regarding Sanskrit's affinity to classical and European languages, speculation regarding Sanskrit figured prominently into European attempts to discover a universal language.

German Romantics viewed both myth and language as a key contributor to the creation and interpretation of national character. In 1796, Herder called for the revitalization of national mythology on the assumption that myths are intentional and invented by individuals out of an arbitrary freedom of consciousness. Herder (at least in his *Sturm und Drang* [Storm and Stress] period) challenged traditional conceptions of his fellow countrymen and encouraged them to seek new inspirational models for Germans and to question the influence of Greek classical norms. Study of the songs, fables, and myths of other nationalities, including India, could contribute toward the development of one's own national culture and in turn contribute to the development of *Humanität* at large (Herder 1877–1913, 13: 256; 14: 230). Herder defined *Humanität* as the sum of the virtue and talents peculiar to human beings and that aspect of the divine that existed in all mankind (1877–1913, 13: 350). Herder's understanding of myth focused on the democratic potentials in its revealed truths. India, with its rich myth tradition, figured significantly in his speculations.

Beginning with Friedrich Wilhelm Joseph Schelling and culminating with Johann Jacob Bachofen, German Romantics shifted the origin of myth from the individual sphere into the collective and from the conscious into the unconscious. They proposed that it was through myth that the great nations of the world defined themselves and put their stamp on all history. Under the influence of the historical school and its founding leader, Friedrich Karl Savigny, myth was thought to emanate from unconscious necessity and the regulation of natural instinct, out of a general human need as shaped within specific national *Volksgeister*. Historically real and concrete myth traditions, such as that of India, needed to be collected, deciphered, and categorized, as they held the power to mediate the unconscious nature of humanity. By placing the source of myth in the collective unconscious, German Romantic myth theorists, such as Bachofen, Johann Joseph Görres, and Johann Arnold Kanne, presupposed a unified mythical *Weltanschauung* among all peoples, epochs, and generations that evidenced objectively knowable and legitimate Truth. This mythological *sensus communis* developed unmistakably from the Enlightenment construction of natural religion and Herder's cosmopolitanism. Görres, in particular, affirmed the underlying unity of existence in myth by which he meant the collective unconsciousness as expressed through particular mythologies.

These Romantics viewed myth as a language of nature, a hieroglyph of creation, and the innocent human response to the world. The genre of myth expanded to include within the term "national" any indigenous or popular forms of expression. Thus, the Grimm brothers saw folk literature as an heir to myth and related to divine revelation. The assumption was that the further one moves from the mythical and paradisiacal past, the greater the devolution and deterioration of consciousness and culture. The obvious corollary is that the closer one approaches one's origins, the better. This led the Grimm brothers (Jakob Ludwig Carl Grimm and Wilhelm Karl Grimm) to collect legends and folktales as part of their contribution to Ludwig Achim von Arnim and Clemens Brantano's *Des Knaben Wunderhorn* (The Youth's Magic Horn, 1805–8). They interpreted the myth of a nation or group as a product of the collective imagination of humanity as a whole. This supra-personal function of myth mediated the God–nature complex and its primitive content, namely, secularization of the image of a paradise in a presumed Golden Age. In this context, myth in German Romanticism no longer was limited to the symbolic stories of gods and supernatural beings. Achim von Arnim, Friedrich de LaMotte-Fouqué, and the Grimm brothers enlarged the category to include all traditional lore, including popular customs and beliefs, songs, tales, and legends. These genres were seen as remnants of an archaic German mythology that had been shattered and invited restoration.

Just as Romantic *Naturphilosophie* valued nature as the emanation and objectification of the Divine, so too did myth function as *Naturpoesie*, developing out of nature and returning to the Divine. In every time and place, myth variously expressed the repetition of divine revelation that had potential for cultural renewal. The German Romantics were inspired by India in their speculations regarding religion, poetry, philosophy of language, myth theory, and *Naturphilosophie*. India, in turn, exemplified Romantic assumptions about the decline of peoples and religions from an original purity and unity toward multiplicity and polytheism. Speculation about Brāhmaṇical Hinduism was used to interpret the origins of European society and to foster nineteenth-century nationalism. German Romantic concepts informed early academic study of Hinduism in the West, gave highest priority and prestige to early Vedic tradition, and continue to influence our images of India and Hinduism even now.

Romantic Myth Theory

In *Philosophie der Kunst* (Philosophy of Art, 1802–3), Schelling (1985, 2: 245–47) defined myth as a system of signs and symbols. He believed that the finite and earthbound reality of history united with the infinite unconditional Truth of the Absolute through symbols. He shared this belief with Karl Wilhelm Friedrich Schlegel, a pioneer in the study of Sanskrit and the author of the first direct translation from Sanskrit into German. Schlegel idealized India and its culture as a source for the aesthetic and spiritual Absolute. It was Schlegel who directed fellow Romantics to India. For Schlegel

(1846, 4: 179), mythology was an untapped reservoir for poetic inspiration, but he claimed that the West itself lacked a mythology and that one would have to be invented by taking inspiration from the East. The highest ideal of the Romantic (*das hochste Romantische*) was to be found in the Orient, by which Schlegel meant India. This translator of "Oriental" myth was also a prophet who lamented the intellectual and cultural state into which his country had fallen (Schlegel 1906, 2: 362).

Schlegel's admiration for Indian mythology was so great that it subsumed even German mythology. In *Gespräch über die Poesie* (Dialogue on Poetry, 1800), he claimed that what properly ought to be termed Germanic mythology included material from India, and his argument for the "Rede über die Mythologie" (in *Gespräch über die Poesie,* 1800) was for the renewal of German poetry by taking help from the Indian muse. Myth signified for Schlegel a literary or historical theme in which an ancient power (*alte Kraft*) could be revealed and awakened to liberate philosophical and moral energy to animate a literary work. One evident influence on Schlegel's enlargement of the notion of Germanic mythology was his brother, August Wilhelm, who held the first professorship of Sanskrit in Bonn and produced the first Latin translation of the *Bhagavad Gītā* in 1823.

August Wilhelm von Schlegel understood Germanic mythology as anything pervaded by what he called the "Geist des göthischen Ritterthums" (1884, 3: 17), and nearly everything fit into this category. He preferred a shift from classical models to the chivalric tradition that would acknowledge the role played by Germans in Europe after the fall of the Roman Empire. Europe at its best was essentially German, after all, because Germans gave medieval Europe its political unity (A. Schlegel 1884, 3: 15–16). F. Schlegel took this argument one step further: Germany was essentially Indian. In *Über die Sprache und die Weisheit der Indier* (On the Language and Wisdom of the Indians, 1808), F. Schlegel sought to make the case, on mythological and linguistic grounds, for the filiation of India with Germany. According to F. Schlegel, all that Romantics regarded as religion, myth, and poetry had originated in India, so one must go to India to learn about God and Poetry. *Über die Sprache* was his attempt to realize this goal of making explicit the filiation of India with Germany, but in the event it only charted the failure of his quest, his disillusionment with Indian thought, and his rejection of the Indian model.

In his Cologne lectures of 1805, F. Schlegel claimed that Indian thought represented the union between the finite and the infinite, matter and spirit, man and God. In his *Über die Sprache*, however, Schlegel expressed misgivings about Hindu astrology, superstitions, and worship of Śiva. He could not accept the worship of God in the form of a *liṅgam*. His access to a wide variety of Sanskrit texts while preparing *Über die Sprache* led Schlegel to discover a Hinduism that was radically different from the one he had dreamed of finding in India. In the 1805 lectures, his Hindu India centered in a spiritual tradition with some faults that could be corrected in an "Oriental-Occidental synthesis." By the time he had completed *Über die Sprache* in 1808, he realized that the synthesis was impossible because the traces of divine truth that continued to exist in India had become inextricably mixed with error.

Even though Hinduism became a problematic locus of the divine for F. Schlegel, India remained for him the cradle of humanity and Sanskrit the mother tongue of the Indo-European languages. Schlegel focused on Sanskrit and affirmed its perfection and divine origin. He projected onto Sanskrit in particular the perfection that he no longer hoped to find at large in Hindu religion. In the linguistic chapters to *Über die Sprache*, Schlegel went beyond the analysis of the superficial similarities among Greek, Latin, German, Persian, and Sanskrit that had dominated earlier discussions regarding the nature of Sanskrit (Filippo Sassetti, Thomas Stevenson, Andreas Jäger, Father Coeurdoux, and, most notably, William Jones). He sought to analyze grammatical structure, declensions, and conjugations. He labeled Sanskrit an inflected language and, as such, superior to agglutinative languages, such as Hebrew and Chinese, but he went on to repudiate that formulation in 1828.

F. Schlegel ultimately overreached with his Indic studies, but he remained a long-term influence on the reception of Hinduism in Europe and in North America. His metaphorical journey to India involved a conscious search for a unifying principle and a belief that Hindu mythological formulations could be appropriated to enrich the biblical catechumen. Finally, F. Schlegel's India supported the possibility that there exists an *Urvolk*, *Ursprache*, and *Urreligion* for which the Romantics were so ardently yearning.

Romantic Literature

In an effort to reveal creative connections, Romantic authors often reached beyond themselves to express something they could neither fully comprehend nor adequately communicate. The new mythology they sought seemed to demand a hieroglyphic system of correspondences (F. Schlegel 1958–, 2: 318) because Romantic symbolism appeared to be vague and yet pregnant with meaning as writers sought to negotiate the tensions between a quest for an infinite idea and the reality of finite phenomena. Romantic literature in all its permutations confronts us with this conundrum. In *Heinrich von Ofterdingen* (1802), Novalis offers what may be its most exemplary expression in the blue flower as a symbol of longing that appears as a goal in a dream. The Romantic concept of nature, combined with a symbolism that cultivated the imprecise, became indistinguishable from mysticism. Nature mysticism of the German Romantics could be Christian or Oriental, or both. Often it was vaguely Hindu as, for instance, in Klingsor's poetry and Zulima's songs in *Heinrich von Ofterdingen*.

In some European Romantic literature, the connection to India was tangential to the plot structure. One finds in Novalis's *Die Lehrlinge zu Sais* (The Novices at Sais, 1798) a spiritual teacher who reveals to his disciples the mystical bonds between humans and the stars, stones, animals, clouds, and plants. The disciples live in an atmosphere of magic wherein both master and disciple aspire after hidden truths and live in direct contact with the experience of nature, as in the lost Golden Age. This vision of nature owes much to Johann Gottlieb Fichte's notion of the fusion of Self with nature and to Schelling's speculation on natural history as inspired by the holy world of nature and spirit.

Again in Jean Paul's *Hesperus* (1795), Victor and Clotilde are brought to a realization of their eternal love through the intercession of an Indian philosopher and discover a transfigured world wherein nature becomes an expression of their interior joy. The lovers do not so much plunge themselves into nature as the sun, stars, and flowers appear to reflect the movements of their spirit.

In other works by Romantics, the connection to Hindu themes and imagery was more direct and evoked the perceived fatalism in Hinduism that attracted Romantic poets to India. Jules Laforgue, in the "Complainte d'une convalescence en mai" (1885), speaks of deliverance from suffering in *nirvāṇa*. In "La lune est stérile" (1885), we learn that *māyā* leads the poet to embrace "nothingness" (*le néant*). Alfred de Vigny presented Indian thought as based on absorption in which the only hope was *nirvāṇa*. Vigny claimed that to reach that ideal state of inertia, Indians tended to distance themselves from moral constraints. Charles Marie René Leconte de Lisle composed a series of poems that were based on information culled from the *Bhāgavata Purāṇa* and were published in *Poèmes antiques* (1852), which presented a Romantic panoply of then standard Hindu tropes. He paid homage to and absolutized the experience of *māyā* in poems titled "Bhagavat" (1852), "Vision de Brahma" (1857), "La mort de Valmiki" (1881), and "La Maya" (1884). He described the Indian desire for immobility and presented Hinduism as a religion the goal of which consisted of absorption into the void of *nirvāṇa*. In Leconte de Lisle, who culled from Hinduism neither more nor less than a vision of apathy, French *ennui* involves embracing the abyss of *nirvāṇa* as an aesthetic and religious ideal. Such appropriations, however, posed a dilemma for Romantic poets. How could one reconcile the Hindu quest for self-recognition with the self-conscious disenchantment patterned after that of Jean-Jacques Rousseau and François-Auguste-René

Chateaubriand? Rather than following Hinduism's call to close one's eyes to sensual seduction, Romantic would-be Indian poems encourage readers to revel in it.

Herder was impressed by Sanskrit poetry and felt that it illustrated the Romantic conception that primitive and natural worlds were interchangeable and that poetry and nature were synonymous. One of Bhartṛhari's maxims that he translated from the Dutch into German was subsequently reworked as a suicide poem by the poet Karoline von Günderrode. She wrote other poems inspired by Indian themes, and virtually all of them focus on an understanding of *nirvāṇa* as nothingness, exemplifying how India became for the Romantics the prime site for the expression of their own *Weltschmerz*. Günderrode was initiated into Indian thought by her lover, the mythographer Georg Friedrich Creuzer, with whom she read the *Bhagavad Gītā*. She was also influenced by Schelling's *Vom Ich als Prinzip der Philosophie oder über das Unbedingte im menschlichen Wissen* (Of the I as the Principle of Philosophy or on the Unconditional in Human Knowledge, 1795). In that work, Schelling presented a vision of the union of the individual "I" with the Absolute, perhaps indicating that he too had been influenced by the *Bhagavad Gītā*.

For many years, Johann Wolfgang Goethe contemplated India's contribution to religion and the arts. He was introduced to Sanskrit poetry by Herder, with whom he shared an appreciation for Kālidāsa's *Śakuntalā*. Goethe and Johann Christoph Friedrich Schiller corresponded frequently regarding Sanskrit drama as an inspirational model for the formation of an indigenous German theater tradition. Goethe also composed poetry based on Indian imagery and imitated the *ghazal* form in his *Westöstlicher Diwan* (West-Eastern Divān, 1819). In "Der Gott und die Bajadere" (The God and the [Temple] Dancer, 1797), Goethe presents a Christ-like Indian god who descends to earth to test the quality of human love. This poem inspired several subsequent operas and ballets featuring the bayadera character, which was based on the Hindu temple dancer or *devadāsī* (Charles Simon Catel, *Les Bayadères,* 1810; Daniel François Esprit Auber, *Le dieu et la bayadère, ou La courtisane amoureuse,* 1830). The Parnassian poet Pierre Jules Théophile Gautier appropriated the bayadera type to represent the Hindu woman as a poetic fantasy come to life. An actual troupe of *devadāsīs* who performed in Paris inspired Gérard de Nerval to equate the bayadera's devotion to God with the Romantic cult of the prostitute with the heart of gold. This equation became quite popular; indeed, Gustave Flaubert's Emma Bovary is compared to a bayadera (*Madame Bovary*, 1857).

India was not simply the favored locale of the divine for Romantic authors; it also provided a sexualized geography of social depravity. The opium, perfume, hashish, and sexual excess of the Romantic bayadera character foregrounded a Romantic-Orientalist critique of Indian religious and social structures. Romantics who deflect their social critiques to a distant land could imagine a Hinduism that was both older and other than Catholicism but with superstitions inviting condemnation. Marginal figures, such as the *satī* and the pariah, are prominent in Jacques-Henri Bernardin de Saint-Pierre's *La chaumière indienne* (1790); Michael Beer's *Der Paria* (1823); and Jean-François Casimir Delavigne's *Le Paria* (1821). In Romantic literature, these become self-sacrificing and spiritually enlightened figures, the equivalents of idealized primitives who possess qualities esteemed by the Romantics, such as deep sentiment and love unto death. Goethe's second Indian work, the "Paria" trilogy (1824), developed these themes on a more sophisticated level. Goethe's pariah represents the split between the body and the mind, the spiritual and the physical. For Goethe, the *satī* and the pariah allowed him to pursue a larger intellectual concern with the ramifications of death and the transmigration of the soul. Authors as disparate as Friedrich Gottlieb Klopstock, Edward Young, Thomas Gray, and Ossian also epitomize Romanticism's fascination with death and its optimistic expectation of an afterlife.

Some Romantics were as concerned with social reform as with depravity and death. A critique of the caste system communicated hopes for a more egalitarian social order but displaced to a safe distance. Pariahs depicted in Romantic literature provided the opportunity for authors to critique locally relevant topics, such as class and victimization in the Europe of their time. An India peopled by male fanatics and despots incarnating superstitious fatalism and arbitrary power provided a cover for Europeans to question their own cultural deficiencies. That male India they supposed must coexist with a female India of sexual license tinged with suicidal disgust for life. The bayadera types in their own cafés and concert halls supplied actual erotic diversion, and the imagined India similarly supplied the Romantics with a source of colorful sexualized imagery and an inspiration for social reform.

Romantic Indology

Romantic mythography and linguistics set the stage for readers to believe that through the study of Sanskrit and Indian myth, modern Europeans could gain knowledge regarding their own archaic past and cultural origins. Friedrich Max Müller's compilation of the *editio princeps* of the *Ṛg Veda* (1849–74) and his voluminous commentaries on the Vedic Āryans confirmed many Romantic fantasies regarding India. According to Müller, the Āryans were the nearest intellectual relatives of the Europeans, hence the Āryan past was our own past. Their literature and art informed our science, art, and philosophy. Moreover, unlike modern Indians, Europeans had direct access to the knowledge imparted by ancient India. The implications of this line of reasoning were quite radical. Contemporary Hinduism was an unfortunately distorted version of the religion, myths, and philosophy of Vedic India. In modern India, the wisdom of the Āryans persisted only in vestigial form, whereas in Europe, and particularly in Germany, the cultural heritage of the Āryans somehow had survived intact. The Veda spoke to Europe and a "conscientious Anglo-Saxon" could understand it better than even India's great Vedic scholar Sāyaṇa. Müller's pronouncements were significant on an ideological and political level. He claimed that the culture of the West came from India and acknowledged the Vedic Āryans as spiritual kith and kin, thereby explicitly distancing Europeans from the Semitic dimensions of their heritage.

William Dwight Whitney, an American Sanskritist, correctly understood Müller's point of reference. He described Müller's vision of the Vedic Āryans in terms of Romantic landscape paintings hanging in Berlin museums. He recognized that Müller's multi-volume commentary on the Vedas, and the image of the Vedic Āryans that it codified, elaborated Romantic aesthetic and philosophical concerns. Romantics subscribed to a model of cultural evolution that supposed that simplicity of religious dogmas defined an original state of religion, that primitive revelation had progressively degenerated, and that monotheism was a recent emergent. Such a vision of religion was at the heart of Romantic mythography and animated the spiritual quest of a would-be devotee such as F. Schlegel. From a Romantic viewpoint, when a people have unfolded their spirituality to its fullest expression, they have fulfilled their role in history, and only repetition (revivals), stagnation, and decay could follow. Georg W. F. Hegel, otherwise a critic of Romanticism and its infatuation with India, adhered to this Romantic vision of India's role in history when he ascribed to Hinduism a theology of immobility, inaction, and quietism. The critique that Hegel leveled against the Romantic reception of Hinduism—that it represented a theology of origins—would apply to Müller's Vedic India. Hegel accused F. Schlegel of projecting onto India a decay of revelation, of primitive peoples, and of the original unified state of mankind. This seems quite similar to the paradigm that Müller created for the discipline of Indology. Hegel also saw Romantic Indomania as a sentimental nostalgia for origins and a blatant disregard for the present. He disliked how the Romantics read Indian thought to support notions of an *Urvolk*, Asian origins of European mythology, and a nonrationalist yet ego-centered concept of faith.

Müller's interpretation of the Veda corresponded to the very Romantic theses that Hegel condemned. On an aesthetic level, Müller's Veda replicated F. Schlegel's requirements for Romantic poetry, as he claimed that it preserved unconscious poetry and primitive thought that elsewhere had been washed away or decayed. Müller consistently presented the *Ṛg Veda* as simple and natural. With his model of henotheism or one God at a time, he even found in it a primitive sort of monotheism. Müller maintained that the Veda brought us back to the origins of religious thought and language. He idealized the Vedic Āryans. Modern Indians had degenerated from the Āryans, and Hinduism offered only a decayed form of Vedic revelation. Müller's prioritization of Vedic India continues to haunt modern academic scholarship and popular fundamentalist restorationist projects. Friedrich Max Müller's reception of the Veda must be viewed in light of his adherence to Romantic theses and Romantic emplotment of India. One should not forget that Müller's father was the renowned Romantic poet, Wilhelm Müller, and the case can be made that Max Müller was the final avatar of Romanticism in service to linguistics. Moreover, his Romantic reading of the Āryan world later had serious political repercussions in late nineteenth- and early twentieth-century race theory.

Concluding Reflections

For the German Romantics, myth was viewed in the ethical sense as an internal embodiment of the *summum bonum*: uncontrived, original, and natural. Myth was thought to reveal the inner nature of the universe by articulating the infinite in the finite terms of symbol. The Romantic sacralization of the world sought to fulfill a compensatory function in connection with a crisis in the worldview brought on by the Enlightenment. In those instances in which something else was found to replace the need for the mythic, such as the militant Catholicism of F. Schlegel or the rabid nationalism of Fichte, it invariably led to the abandonment of Romantic mythological paradigms. Myth faded away, and revealed religion, the sacred nation, or some other equivalent supplanted it.

F. Schlegel is an exemplary case of Romantic Indology. Schlegel's search for a new mythology led him first to history and increasingly to the history of religion. His translations from Sanskrit and epoch-making studies in Indian thought led him to think of mythology more exclusively in terms of religion, whether it be the spiritual idea of the Church itself (Schlegel 1958–, 4: 166) as manifested in medieval Europe or the ideals he projected onto India. With his formal conversion to Catholicism in 1808, he shifted from his earlier quest for salvation in literature to salvation through language. Ardent hope transformed itself into ultimate hope; the quest for poetic divination became the desire for revelation and cultural goals transformed into the workings of salvation.

Myth, and particularly myths concerning India, functioned as an index of internal and external life, a medium whereby modern European society and culture could be analyzed. The childlike, pure, and innocent virtues imagined in the myths of ancient India appeared as a positive *Gegenbild* to the rotten and degenerative affectedness of modern civilization. The Āryan past was better than the European present; it could be viewed as a model for an ideal form of present and future society. Romantic fascination with India was in effect a flight from worldly, artistic, and political difficulties and duties of the modern world into a sentimental and idealized past. Mythology of an ideal past, promulgated by Romantic mythographers, was developed by Romantic linguistic theory and informed the experiments undertaken within the literature of Romanticism. The discipline of Indology had its origin in Romanticism, especially in the quest in Romantic mythography and linguistics for the oldest forms of religion and languages. Indology emerges out of Romantic theories of language through the initial development of philology as a discursive institution with a specific historical organization of knowledge and textual strategies.

Romantic concepts of myth, language, and the Absolute were fundamental to the development of German nationalism in the later half of the nineteenth and early years of the twentieth centuries. In the work of such figures as F. Schlegel and Max Müller, we find so clearly the Romantic theses of the degeneration of original and primitive religion and the view of history as an unfolding expression of the spirit of a people, followed by decay and stagnation. These themes were crucial to the European intellectual climate late into the nineteenth century. Stagnation would become a keyword in discussions of national identity and would eventually find its way into the general writings of such philosophers as Hegel, Karl Marx, and Oswald Spengler.

Romantic myth theory and linguistics set the stage for the subsequent emplotments of myth that were to derail much of German late nineteenth- and early twentieth-century history. The Romantics bequeathed to the Fascists the celebration of myth as the most majestic form of expression and action. For both, myth supplied a poetic realization of truths pertaining to natural and supernatural realities. Myths, however histrionic or sentimental they might be, revealed sublime truths. For a future generation, Romantic literature valorized notions of a fictive past, and it glorified presumed ancient native virtues. It conditioned nineteenth- and twentieth-century Germans to view themselves as bearers of culture and custodians of truth. In Romantic literary praxis, mythic India remained fragmented and obscure, but in subsequent social manifestation as the Āryan myth, it became an effective agent of terror. The hieroglyph of the world now became clearly deciphered, and those outside the structure of the new myth suffered the consequences.

References Cited

Herder, Johann Gottfried. 1877–1913. *Sämtliche Werke* (ed. Bernhard Suphan). 33 volumes. Berlin: Weidmannsche Buchhandlung.

Schelling, Friedrich W. J. 1985. *Ausgewählte Schriften* (ed. Manfred Frank). 6 volumes. Frankfurt: Suhrkamp.

Schlegel, August Wilhelm von. 1884. *Vorlesungen über schöne Literatur und Kunst* (ed. Jakob Minor). 3 volumes. Heilbronn: Henniger.

Schlegel, Friedrich. 1846 [1822–25]. *Sämmtliche Werke.* 15 volumes [1st edition, 10 volumes]. Wien: Klang.

Schlegel, Friedrich. 1906 [1882]. *Friedrich Schlegel, 1794–1802: seine prosaischen Jugendschriften* (ed. Jakob Minor). 2 volumes. Wien: C. Konegen.

Schlegel, Friedrich. 1958–. *Kritische Friedrich Schlegel Ausgabe* (eds Ernst Behler, with collaboration of Jean-Jacques Anstett and Hans Eichner). 35 volumes. Paderborn: Schöningh.

25

Sacred

Ramdas Lamb

Defining Sacred in the Abrahamic Religious Traditions
Defining the Hindu Concept of Sacred
Pavitra as Sacred
Purification and the Creation of Sacred
Nature as Sacred
Space as Sacred
Symbols and Objects as Sacred
Actions as Sacred
Beings as Sacred
Concluding Reflections

The concept of "sacred" can be found in nearly every religious tradition, although the way it is understood and employed varies greatly. Though it can be easily argued that no other major religious tradition uses the concept as comprehensibly and at the same time contextually as does Hinduism, there is no equivalent Hindu term. Thus, to understand the sacred in Hinduism, a valuable first step is to look at the manner in which the Abrahamic religious traditions have constructed it and then use this as a point of juxtaposition in considering its diverse Hindu manifestations. This chapter, then, begins with a Western religious understanding of the term, turns to various Hindu words that have connotative intersections with it, and ends with an overview of the Hindu perception and use of what is referred to in English as "sacred."

Defining Sacred in the Abrahamic Religious Traditions

Latin roots of the term "sacred" include *sacer* (holy), *sacrare* (to devote), and *sancire* (to make holy). The early Greeks believed that many things could be *hieros* (holy or sacred) owing to their relationship or connection to one of the gods. Although it has been and continues to be employed as a noun, denoting the divine, the term "sacred" has come to be used primarily as an adjective, expressing a particular quality or characteristic. In the Abrahamic traditions, then, sacred typically refers to that which is "set apart for a god," "dedicated or set apart for the service or worship of a deity," "worthy of devotion," "worthy of religious veneration," "entitled to reverence," "not secular or profane," and so forth. At the same time, it comprises half of a duality in juxtaposition with "profane." In his *The Sacred and the Profane* (1959), Mircea Eliade expresses the common Western religious understanding of the term: "The first possible definition of the *sacred* is that it is *the opposite of the profane*....Man becomes aware of the sacred because it manifests itself, shows itself, as something wholly different from the profane" (10–11; emphasis in original). He adds that the sacred is "something of a wholly different order, a reality that does not belong to our world" (Eliade 1959: 11). In the Western traditions, then, that which is sacred, either through its nature or through some form of sanctification or consecration, tends to ever remain "set apart" and reserved for that which is holy and also to be permanently distinguished as such. In essence, the sacred and the profane remain ever distinct. Examples of the sacred include scriptures, places of worship, beliefs and, for some segments of each tradition, objects as well. All the Abrahamic traditions treat their respective texts as sacred, regardless of whether they identify them with that term. Such books exist strictly for the purpose of relating to the divine. They are typically not only viewed as sources of knowledge, but the actual physical presence of the text is believed by many to be sacred. Thus, they are often kept in elevated or special places, wrapped in special cloth, and treated with great reverence and respect. All three traditions have holy sites, too, such as Jerusalem, and in the form of temples, churches, and mosques. With respect to sacred objects, it is primarily Roman and Orthodox Catholic denominations that recognize these, and such objects include images, relics, ritual items, and so forth. Protestants, Jews, and Muslims typically reject the concept of sacred objects, although in everyday actuality many members of these traditions do hold material things in reverence. For example, many Jews treat the Wailing Wall as if it were sacred, and most Muslims revere the *al-ḥajar al-aswad*, a black stone embedded in one of the corners of the Kabah in Mecca. In such cases, the sanctity of the place or object sets it apart from the mundane and makes it a source of sacredness and even blessings.

The segments of the Abrahamic traditions that come closest to sharing aspects of the Hindu concept of sacred include ancient Judaism and Catholicism, where an open acceptance of sacred places, objects, images and, to some extent, people is most apparent. In early Judaism, the concept of sacred had a much more inclusive nature than did the current understanding. The term "*qadosh*" ("holy, set apart") can be found in earlier portions of the Bible in connection with a variety of objects. Additionally, such places as the Temple and Mount Sinai, such days as the Sabbath, and even categories of people, the Hebrews themselves, all were referred to as *qadosh*. However, influenced by the interpretation of the rules and restrictions embedded in the Holiness Code of the Torah (Leviticus 17–26) in developing Judaism, the term came to be interpreted almost exclusively as the preserve of the Creator and no longer connected with material things. With respect to Catholic Christianity, sacred has traditionally had a wide use and acceptance. Holy water, the Eucharist, the tabernacle and altar, and images in a church are all examples of objects that are sacred. Rituals, especially the tradition of sacraments, from baptism to last rites, are all seen to have a sanctifying effect. Additionally, the tradition of saints elevates individuals and even their relics to the status of holy and sacred. On the other hand, most Protestant Christian and Muslim religious denominations do not openly recognize sacred objects, places, or individuals, with the exception of their own sacred texts. Clearly, the Muslim concept of *shirk* (literally, association) specifically prohibits its followers from identifying anything created with the transcendental glory of Allāh.

Defining the Hindu Concept of Sacred

In seeking to comprehend the concept of sacred in Hinduism, the narrow definitional parameters that confine it in the Western traditions must be dropped. Though these traditions envision the sacred as separate, static, specific, dualistic, and under the interpretative domain of religious authorities, most Hindus view it as ubiquitous, amorphic, contextual, existing on a graded continuum, and not under the exclusive authority of anyone. Thus, the Hindu understanding is far more expansive, with a much different frame of reference. Therefore, one must look at the breadth of what is conceived or perceived by Hindus as sacred, the reasons for such identity, and the processes through which something is or can become so identified. Several key Hindu concepts facilitate this, including the belief in the omnipresence and essential nature of the divine and the connection between purity, sanctity, and divinity. Together, they play an integral role in the way sacred is both understood and actualized.

Because of the vast differences between Western and Hindu conceptualizations of sacred, there is in any Indian language no exact translation of the term that parallels the meaning of the English-language word. Instead, there are a diversity of Hindu terms that can, in one context or another, be translated as sacred, the most common being *pavitra*.[1] At the same time, there are more than a dozen additional terms that can, depending on context, be translated as sacred. Among the more popular of these are *brahmaṇya* (pious, relating to Brahman), *divya* (holy), *maṅgala* (auspicious), *puṇya* (virtue), *pūjya* (worthy of worship), and *śuddha* (clean, pure).[2] There are also several words that are more specifically used to designate a sacred state or status of a thought, word, deed, object, individual, and so forth. Thus, one must add to this list such terms as *ādhyātmika*, *ādhidaivika*, *atiśuddha*, *dhārmika*, and so forth. Some of these have very defined uses, whereas such others as *divya* tend to have a much broader application. In elaborating on the Hindu concept of sacred, then, the primary focus of this chapter is on *pavitra* in its relationship to the Western understanding of the concept and on the roles it plays in Hindu beliefs and practices.

Pavitra as Sacred

Pavitra is the term used by early Christian missionaries to translate "sacred" and is an adjective typically rendered in English as "pure" or "clean." Although the type of purity referenced is religious or spiritual, as opposed to physical, it is viewed as a bridge that connects physical cleanliness and sanctity and as residing in both. This is because Hinduism posits two different yet connected dimensions of the purity–pollution dynamic, the physical and the spiritual.

Pavitra actually has a variety of meanings and connotations depending on its usage and context (see below). The orthodox application of the term tends to be more limited and is traditionally used to justify restrictions and prohibition with regard to caste, gender, and ritual. At the same time, however, regional folk, devotional, and ascetic traditions tend to have a much broader, less defined, and more contextual application of the concept. In its stricter usage, it has only limited parallels with the Western concept of sacred, whereas the broader usage overlaps the Western view in many relevant and useful areas.

The concept of purity in a juxtaposition to pollution as a criterion for caste justification has been discussed in academic works dating back to the nineteenth century, and it has been the subject of extensive scholarly research during the last half-century or so. Most of these works express the Brāhmaṇical view that purity exists as a relatively static state, and, for the most part, it applies only to the higher castes and things associated with them and their religious practices. Though orthodox belief acknowledges that those born "pure" can become temporarily polluted and thus provides ritual means of repurification, it essentially disallows the possibility of anyone born impure of becoming pure. In his various writings, M. N. Srinivas (see, for example, 1952, 1962, 1966) tends to present this orthodox view of purity as the dominant one. Though allowing for some amelioration and modifications, he does not acknowledge the great diversity of understanding and application of the concept. Nevertheless, his work established in the eyes of many the direction they would take in studying the issue. Some other earlier scholars have discussed aspects of the broader usage of the theory of purity as well. In their 1968 *Village Christians and Hindu Culture*, coauthors P. Y. Luke and John Carman mention the elevated level of purity that ascetics are believed to possess. The authors suggest that this view exists primarily because ascetics "have placed themselves outside the ordinary structure of society" (Luke and Carman 1968: 32). They do not seem to acknowledge what R. S. Khare (1976: 176) does in the following decade, which is that religious practice is clearly believed to affect the level of purity of the individual. The importance of this in understanding the relationship between purity and sanctity is elaborated on below.

In 1970, Louis Dumont's highly influential *Homo Hierarchicus* was first published in English. The focus of the author is on the caste system, and he explains the concept of purity almost exclusively from the dualistic orthodox perspective, contrasting it with pollution. Though he elaborates on the pivotal role it plays in the justification for the caste system and all its prohibitions, except for a brief mention he ignores the multiple forms and contexts in which it can be and is applied. Later in that same decade, Veena Das' *Structure and Cognition* (1977) does a better job of problematizing the issue of purity with respect to caste, allows for greater contextualization, and includes the role of the renunciant, and by inference personal effort, in her writings. The work of McKim Marriott also questions the approaches of Srinivas and Dumont. His edited volume, *India Through Hindu Categories* (1990), furthers this process by suggesting alternate ways of understanding theories of purity. Last, two additional volumes are worthy of note here, for each contains several articles that move beyond the limited understanding of purity. These are *Purity and Auspiciousness in Indian Society* (1985), edited by John B. Carman and Frédérique A. Marglin, and Lance Nelson's more recent *Purifying the Earthly Body of God* (1998a). However, so influential were the writings of Srinivas and Dumont that they have set the tenor for most subsequent scholarly works addressing the concept of purity, and many newer works continue to reflect this. As a consequence, the broader use of *pavitra* has been paid relatively scant attention. It is this expanded understanding that aligns *pavitra* with the Western concept of sacred that this chapter hopes to bring to light. For clarification, though the terms "pure" and "purity" throughout this chapter are used to express the various Hindu understandings of *pavitra,* "sacred" will be used in reference to those aspects that more closely equate with the Western sense of the term.

For most Hindus, purity and sanctity begin with physical cleanliness. Thus, for something to be *pavitra*, it usually must first be *śuddha* or physically clean. One basis of the Hindu connection between *pavitra* and sacred is the belief that the divine is the source, essence, and substance of all existence. Therefore, the closer anything is to its natural, inherent, or pure state, the closer it is to expressing or revealing its divinity and thus to being sacred. Unlike the dualistic Western understanding, then, there is no wall of separation between the sacred and the profane. Instead, all existence is believed to reside on a continuum that runs from the profane and the polluted to the pure and the sacred. As the essence of all existence is sacred, any entity that is in a non-sacred state, which can occur for various reasons, is simply in a temporary perversion of its inherent nature, which is pure and sacred. Therefore, almost anything and anyone can exist almost anywhere on that continuum. The degree of purity (*pavitratā*) is what determines where on that continuum an entity resides, and this concept can be applied very broadly and can refer to places, objects, thoughts, events, time periods, and individuals. This concept is the primary basis for the hierarchical categorization of all the physical, social, and religious aspects of reality. In its breadth, *pavitra* subsumes, for the most part, that which is considered sacred in the Western sense, while not being limited by its parameters. Thus, though purity does not equal sanctity in all situations, the two share commonalities, whereas that which is sacred is always *pavitra*, that which is *pavitra* is either sacred or "ready" or "qualified" to become sacred (see below).

Purification and the Creation of Sacred

Though the Abrahamic traditions tend to have strict limits on what can be or become sacred and who can make these determinations, indigenous religious cultures are not so restricted. Moreover, the ability to make sacred, to sanctify or purify is an important aspect to the religious life of the latter, and this is integral to the Hindu tradition as well. Not only is the conceptualization of sacred diverse, so is the process of purification and sanctification. Because of the continuum approach to sanctity, the process of purification and sanctification is integral in the life of most Hindus. Both occur on a daily basis, in every temple, at nearly every home altar, and in many other "secular" aspects of life. How these occur depends on what is being purified and who is doing it. In the following sections, we discuss various categories of what is pure or sacred (or both) and how they are understood or realized in each. Because of the degree of regional differences that exist in India with respect to the sacred, the discussion focuses primarily on general beliefs and practices found in Hinduism, with some reference to regional examples. A significant difference between Western and Hindu approaches to the sacred that is to be noted is that the latter places the sacred much more in the hands of the commoner and thus less in the control of specific authority figures. The implications of this will become apparent.

The act of consecrating a place or object is both an act of spiritual cleansing and an attempt to bring out its inherent purity, its inherent sanctity. Purification and sanctification, then, do not entail the adding of a sacred element as much as the removal of the elements that block the inherent sanctity or purity from becoming apparent or manifest. The tools for accomplishing this include prayers, *mantras*, rituals, water, and other purifying articles. The latter can include such items as sandalwood paste, turmeric powder, Ganges water, *tulasī* (sacred basil) leaves, and even cow dung and cow urine. Once something has been purified, it will typically remain so for the duration of the ritual in which it is involved. After this, the site or object may "revert" to its prepurified state, although it could remain pure, depending on the surrounding context.

Nature as Sacred

Although the Hindu concept of omnipresence posits the essential nature of everything as divine or sacred, not all philosophical schools support this notion. According to Lance Nelson, Advaita Vedānta, for example, promotes a "wholesale objectification and radical ontological devaluation" of nature (1998b: 68). Sāṃkhya also postulates a dualistic understanding of reality but sees nature, or *prakṛti*, as the female half of the duality of nature and spirit. *Prakṛti* is the eternal animate aspect of reality. Although philosophically nature and creation may be seen either as spiritless matter or as spirit-filled matter, most Hindus tend toward the latter. For the most part, then, they see the Earth and nature as closely connected with the Divine and are, in essence, sacred. Such epithets as Pṛthvī Mā (Mother Earth), Bhārat Mātā (Mother India), or Pavitra Bhūmi (Sacred Land) express reverence to the land as a manifestation of the feminine aspect of the Divine. Additionally, every Indian river has a deity connected to it, usually a *devī* (a feminine form of the Divine); nearly every mountain has a deity associated with it; and valleys, forests, caves, and almost every unusual outcropping can be seen as special and even specially *pavitra*. Here, again, there are many regional variations. For example, because of the religious significance of Gaṅgā Mā (the Ganges River), many regional cultures associate a local river with her. Thus, in the Chitrakut area of Madhya Pradesh, the main river there is called Mandākinī Gaṅgā, and the residents relate a story to show that it is a manifestation of the Gaṅgā, making her purity and sanctity ever-present and available to them.

As previously mentioned, because of the essential purity and sanctity of reality, the more nearly that something is in its primal state, the more potential it has to express or exhibit the sacred. Consequently, natural things, such as fruits, flowers, leaves, grains, nuts, most river waters, and so forth, are inherently pure and can be offered at a temple by almost anyone. They require no ritual purification. Though they are not necessarily sacred in the Western sense of the term, they are clearly *pavitra* and thus capable of serving as a ritual offering, after which they become sacred and are then called *praśāda*.

Although all of nature possesses sanctity, there are specific natural phenomena that are inherently more expressive of the divine. These can be particular earthly formations and features (e.g., rivers, mountains, volcanoes), certain forms of plant life (*tulasī,* lotus flowers, *pīpala* tree, *rudrākṣa* seeds), or specific types of stones (*śālagrāma* or any natural *liṅgam*-shaped stone). All these are seen to have an elevated level of inherent purity and thus have a special presence and sanctity and are higher on the continuum between worldly and divine. For example, although water is one of the most purifying of natural elements, the water from one of the more sacred rivers, such as the Gaṅgā, Jamunā, and Narmadā, is believed to be especially pure and purifying. Bathing in them, then, is seen as an extremely spiritually cleansing ritual, even when the water itself is not necessarily believed to be physically clean or *śuddha*.[3]

Particularly *pavitra* items (like those mentioned above) are commonly found as offerings at a temple or on a home altar. It is common for Hindu pilgrims to return home with soil from a sacred place, mud from a sacred river, or a *liṅgam*-shaped stone to bless and sanctify their homes. The purifying leaves of the *tulasī* plant can also be found on most altars. Depending on the region, other types of soil, leaves, or items from nature may be used as well, such as a coconut or a conch shell. The latter are especially common in Central and South India. Additionally, certain creatures, such as cows, monkeys, elephants, cobras, and eagles, are traditionally believed to exist higher on the purity continuum than other animals, although there tends to be more of a regional aspect to this view.

However, once the natural state of something is altered, its inherent purity may become obscured. With respect to foodstuffs, for example, cooking them can destroy their natural state of purity. Thus, though a Brāhmaṇa priest will typically accept uncooked items from almost anyone, he will traditionally accept cooked food only from certain individuals, usually either other Brāhmaṇas or members of the upper castes. This is because the inherent purity of the foodstuffs may be believed by him to have been lost, depending on who cooked the food, in what utensils, and how. The food may be viewed as permanently impure or specific prayers or rituals may be deemed necessary to repurify it. Such rituals are typically done by Brāhmaṇa priests but can also be done by commoners in their homes. At the same time, some aspects of nature remain pure, irrespective of alteration or loss of physical cleanliness. Here, the Hindu concept resembles the Western tradition in the sense that something can be sacred but not clean. A good example of this is the polluted water of the Ganges River, a soiled copy of a sacred text, the leftover food of a person considered holy, or physical uncleanliness of a sacred place, such as a temple or pilgrimage site. In all these cases, the state of uncleanliness does not prevent those who hold these as sacred from continuing to believe in their sanctity.

Space as Sacred

In nearly every religious tradition and culture, there are spaces set aside for rites, rituals, religious practices, or other forms of communication with the divine. Indigenous religious cultures have a broad definition of such spaces, and this may include the entire geographic region in which the people of a particular culture live. Although prophetic religious traditions, such as Christianity and Islam, are far more limited in their interpretation and acceptance of sacred space, all the Abrahamic traditions acknowledge such spaces. For example, all three revere Jerusalem and environs as being sacred. Although Muslims do not commonly refer to it in that way, they do refer to Mecca and Medina, and to many mosques, as holy sites. Additionally, there are Quranic references to various places as sacred, such as the land of Israel and a valley in the Sinai known as Tuwa. Again, although Muslims treat such sites as sacred, they do not define them as such, for this would go counter to the Muslim concept of *shirk*, as mentioned above. In all three traditions, designated sacred spaces—such as temples, churches, mosques, and other pilgrimage places—tend to be permanently so until some unforeseen circumstance leads to a change, such as an earthquake or other natural disaster that renders the space unsuitable for designated religious activities. This is because such spaces are "set apart" in these traditions for specific religious uses. An exception to this general rule can be found in more contemporary situations where other than permanently reserved spaces and structures are used as temporary sites, such as a Christian religious group holding its services in a school cafeteria, rented building, and so on.

For Hindus, almost all spaces can be sacred, pure, or potentially so. Besides the naturally occurring sacred places mentioned above, temples, shrines, and pilgrimages sites are all viewed as sacred spaces. Though the sanctity of such sites is viewed as essentially permanent, there are other sites that can be temporarily sacred, such as the place where a particular ritual is to be performed. Home altars and shrines are also viewed by most Hindus as sacred space. They believe that by following ritual rules of purity with respect to one's home, the entire abode becomes a more purified and thus sanctified space. This is one reason for not wearing shoes inside a temple or a home. The "filth" of the outside world should not be brought into a sacred space. Even in urban India, where an increasing number of people wear shoes inside their homes, they will almost always remove them before entering the *pūjā* room, the place where the home altar is typically found and where daily or periodic rituals are performed. The space is sacred because of the presence of an altar or the fact that rituals are performed there. The significance of this is that having such a space in one's home often provides comfort and security, for it helps validate the proximity of the divine in one's daily life. Though Brāhmaṇas typically are called on to purify or sanctify a home or a site for a ritual, many Hindus have given to them by their *guru* or other respected religious figure a *mantra* that they themselves can use for purification. This is one reason why some priests resent ascetics acting as *gurus* for householders. The latter provide for free that for which the former usually collect a fee.

Symbols and Objects as Sacred

From an academic perspective, there are several approaches to the understanding of symbols and objects. Symbols that are seen to simply represent something can be referred to as representative symbols. They generally have no special status or power and are thus strictly symbolic. However, the vast majority of religious symbols, especially for Hindus, are presentative, that is, they are believed to have a direct link to that which they represent. They are viewed as hierophanies or theophanies because they manifest sacred presence. Such objects and symbols are found in the Roman Catholic tradition as well and include images, crucifixes, rosaries, blessed items, and so forth. For Hindus, sacred symbols are ever-present in nature as well as in human-created items such as images in temples, home altars, roadside shrines, the picture of a divinity, a *svastika*, the written name of a deity, yellow and red thread tied on the right wrist during a ritual, the ashes from a renunciant's fire, and so forth. Almost anything in nature can be viewed as a sacred symbol: a rock, soil, a leaf, a flower, a piece of bark; a river, mountain, valley, or outcropping; the wind, the sun, the moon, a star, the planets. There is no shortage. Moreover, the list of items that cannot typically be considered sacred is far shorter than that of items that can be. The most common examples here include anything associated with disease, death, or human or animal bodily excretions. However, even here there is an exception. The dung and urine of a cow are seen as *pavitra* and are used in rituals of purification. So great is the purifying power believed to be in the products of the cow that most Hindus believe their power to purify is equal to that of a purification *mantra*.

Human-created items are not believed to be inherently *pavitra* but can become so through a variety of ritual methods. Additionally, the intent of the maker, what is made, the substance from which it is made, and what its use will be are all factors in making something *pavitra* and qualified to be sacred.

For example, things made from gold and silver are believed to maintain their purity; things made from other metals, clay, or wood need to be purified; whereas items made from aluminum or plastic are typically seen as being incapable of becoming pure. Purification rituals and the articles involved in the process are similar to those used to purify spaces. Once *pavitra*, the sanctification of an object or symbol may be for a specific period, such as the length of a particular ritual, for a day or two, or permanently. It all depends on the use and intent of the person doing the ritual. Because the ability to purify an object is not confined to priests, almost anyone who knows a ritual or prayer to use and who has the desire can do so, for fundamental to purification and sanctification is intent of the performer.

Almost any image or any shaped rock, once cleansed and made *pavitra* through ritual and then empowered through other rituals can become the presentational aspect of a deity. This is obvious with respect to nonanthropomorphic images of Hanumān, which can be almost any uncarved stone. Here again, almost any object can be or become sacred in Hinduism, depending on region, reason, and context.

Actions as Sacred

The concept of *karma*, the belief that actions have consequences that affect one's spiritual growth and progress, is fundamental to the major religious traditions that have arisen in the Indian subcontinent. Like every other aspect of reality, Hinduism places actions on a continuum from profane to divine. At one end are those actions that pollute body and soul, such as the consumption of flesh products and intoxicants, violence, stealing, lying, and so forth. At the other end are those that purify, such as religious practices (collectively referred to as *sādhana*), moral behavior, truth, nonviolence, compassion, humility, and honesty. Additionally, there are specific forms of *sādhana* and a variety of chants and rituals that are done exclusively for purification purposes.

Rituals are the most common form of religious practice. Like symbols, rituals can generally be two types, representative and presentative. Social rituals tend to be of the former, whereas religious rituals are typically believed to be of the latter, for they help to make manifest the divine presence or power (or both). Within the class of religious rituals are those done in conjunction with *mantra*s specifically for the purpose of purification and sanctification, such as to purify a spot where a subsequent ritual is to be performed, to purify an object to be used in a ritual, or to purify an individual about to participate in a ritual. In actuality, all rituals are seen to indirectly purify participants and observers by granting blessings or by enhancing their awareness of or proximity to the Divine.

Sādhana is a general term that refers to all forms of practice done to enhance one's spiritual growth or understanding, usually with some form of regularity. It is a process by means of which one can work to both "purify" and "sanctify" oneself, and the forms of *sādhana* undertaken can be diverse. For most householders, these may include rituals, prayers, or food offerings to a deity on a home altar or at a temple. They may involve *mantra* recitation (*jāpa*), the reading or study of scriptures or religious texts, or the performance of selfless charity work. Key features include intention and regularity. Actions done on a regular basis as a part of one's religious discipline are generally said to be one's *sādhana*. Thus, whereas regular fasting to lose weight would not be considered *sādhana*, fasting to overcome attachment to food or to strengthen one's will power for spiritual growth would be. Moreover, the regular practice of *sādhana* is believed to be one of the most powerful forms of purification and sanctification.

Even with respect to *sādhana*, there is a continuum, with some forms more purifying than others. Though the daily practices of most householders are seen to be purifying, they are usually lower on the continuum. Those forms that are viewed as more powerfully purifying include austerity practices, such as silence, fasting, celibacy, not sleeping, and so forth. These are the forms generally undertaken by ascetics or *sādhu*s. For them, *sādhana* is ideally the foundation of their lives. Of the four goals of life in Hinduism, the first three (material gain, virtuous achievements, and sensual pleasures) are for householders, whereas the last one, *mokṣa*, or liberation, is for the ascetic, and the primary vehicle for achieving this for most ascetics involves the more austere forms of *sādhana*, known as *tapasyā*. *Sādhu*s' lives are defined and framed by the forms and degree of *sādhana* they undertake. Though any practice of *tapasyā* is believed to be both empowering and purifying, its effects can be enhanced by preceding it with a vow or set of vows, usually directed to a specific form of the Divine for a specific religious purpose. The commitment and promise to fulfill the undertaking is believed to enhance the purifying power of the activity.

Beings as Sacred

As one progresses in the performance of *sādhana* and other purifying practices, one moves higher on the spiritual continuum and thus becomes increasingly sanctified. This is true of both householders and ascetics. However, because of their focus on *tapasyā* and other such practices, the latter are traditionally viewed as higher on the purity scale than even Brāhmaṇa priests. Although renunciation of family life is seen as a form of *tapasyā*, it is not in itself considered to be necessarily sanctifying if it is not coupled with some sort of regular *sādhana* practice. Consequently, renunciants who do not integrate regular forms of *tapasyā* in their lives but whose *sādhana* may consist of little more than renouncing the householder life and living in an *āśrama* with other renunciants are not typically viewed as particularly pure or powerful. There is a common saying in North India that can be loosely translated, "Only one who does *sādhana* is considered a [genuine] *sādhu*" (*sādhu nāma sādhana*).[4]

Following ritual rules of personal purity in the form of a moral life, vegetarian diet, and physical cleanliness are all believed to work in conjunction with the practice of *sādhana* to make one's body made both physically and spiritually pure and sacred. Additionally, purity functions not only as empowerment but as protection. It is commonly held that when one follows all rules of purity, one is also largely protected from the dangers of evil spirits, curses, and so forth. There is a popular belief in India that ascetics who live in the jungle are not bothered by wild animals because the power of their *tapasyā* protects them.

Traditionally, it is believed that a highly elevated state of purity and sanctity is best exemplified in the being of *dharma guru*s or religious teachers. They are the ones who are believed to have made great advancements on the path and have, through the practice of *sādhana,* cleansed away the "pollution" of worldly existence and involvement from their bodies, minds, and hearts and have become pure expressions of the inherent divinity within. For most Hindus, the *guru* both defines and reveals to them sacredness and purity, and they express these through goodness, wisdom, devotion, and compassion, and sometimes spiritual power as well. Hindus will typically seek out such individuals to receive blessings, for purity and sanctity are believed to radiate and can be gained even by being in proximity to such individuals.

Concluding Reflections

The formulation and elaboration of the concept of the "sacred" are fundamental constructions of all religious traditions, for they set parameters regarding the ultimate and suggest the relationship between that ultimate and human beings. For both, there is a clear distinction between Western religious approaches and Hindu approaches. Although the omnipresence of the divine is a belief integral in the Western traditions, sanctity is defined by and integral with separateness. God, then, is presented as being most sacred in His remoteness. Humans can never know Him, much less become one with Him. In the Hindu tradition, on the other hand, the sanctity of the divine comes from its integral presence in all reality and its availability to the individual to be perceived and experienced. Just as the more a place or object becomes pure, the more it comes into proximity with the sacred, so is the case with humans. Physical, mental, and emotional purity are all believed to elevate one toward the sacred, toward the divine, and the greater the ability one has to have direct divine experience. In Hinduism, this is possible because of the manner in which the tradition understands and interprets omnipresence.

When individuals do *sādhana* or any other religious practice in seeking to purify themselves and progress on the spiritual path, nothing is being added from without. No thing is being gained. Instead, *sādhana* is the process or the vehicle by which one returns to one's original state of purity that is inherent in the individual spirit. As one's body becomes cleansed of toxins and disease, the natural state of health is attained. In the same way, when the mind becomes cleansed of ego, desires, attachments, fears, and so on, and the veil of ignorance is slowed wiped away, the inner light of wisdom becomes manifest, and the practitioner is able to both see the divine more clearly and also to express it in his or her life. Purity leads to sanctity, and it reveals sanctity. Ultimately, that which is truly pure is truly sacred.

Notes

1 In an informal poll of more than one hundred Western and Indian scholars and Hindi-speaking Indian university students conducted by me during 2006, more than 80 percent said that sacred is best translated *pavitra*.

2 These terms have been put in alphabetical order, not in the order of popularity. The definition given for each is the one most commonly used.

3 Numerous studies of the Ganges River and its current state of extreme pollution do not prevent countless Hindus from bathing in it and drinking its water, as it is, in their eyes, sacred irrespective of its physical state or properties.

4 I address the importance of *sādhana* in the life of a renunciant in Lamb (2006).

References Cited

Carman, John B. and Frédérique A. Marglin, eds. 1985. *Purity and Auspiciousness in Indian Society*. Leiden: E.J. Brill.

Das, Veena. 1977. *Structure and Cognition: Aspects of Hindu Caste and Ritual*. Delhi: Oxford University Press.

Dumont, Louis. 1970 [1966]. *Homo Hierarchicus: An Essay on the Caste System* (trans. Mark Sainsbury). Chicago: University of Chicago Press.

Eliade, Mircea. 1959 [1957]. *The Sacred and the Profane: The Nature of Religion* (trans. Willard R. Trask). New York: Harcourt, Brace.

Khare, R. S. 1976. *The Hindu Hearth and Home: Culinary Systems Old and New in North India*. New Delhi: Vikas.

Lamb, Ramdas. 2006. "Monastic Vows and the Ramananda Sampraday." *In* Selva J. Raj and William P. Harman, eds, *Dealing with Deities: The Ritual Vow in South Asia*, 165–85. Albany: State University of New York Press.

Luke, P. Y. and John Carman. 1968. *Village Christians and Hindu Culture: Study of a Rural Church in Andhra Pradesh, South India.* London: Lutterworth Press.

Marriott, McKim, ed. 1990. *India Through Hindu Categories.* New Delhi: Sage.

Nelson, Lance E., ed. 1998a. *Purifying the Earthly Body of God: Religion and Ecology in Hindu India.* Albany: State University of New York Press.

Nelson, Lance E. 1998b. "The Dualism of Nondualism: Advaita Vedānta and the Irrelevance of Nature." *In* Lance E. Nelson, ed., *Purifying the Earthly Body of God: Religion and Ecology in Hindu India*, 61–88. Albany: State University of New York Press.

Srinivas, M. N. 1952. *Religion and Society among the Coorgs of South India.* Oxford: Clarendon.

Srinivas, M. N. 1962. *Caste in Modern India and Other Essays.* Bombay: Asia Publishing

Srinivas, M. N. 1966. *Social Change in Modern India.* Berkeley: University of California Press.

26

Stratification

Joseph W. Elder

Models of Stratification in India's Classical Texts
British Administrative Decisions Regarding India's Stratification
Addressing Stratification in Independent India
India's Stratification Viewed Through
Different Conceptual Frameworks

Models of Stratification in India's Classical Texts

The ninetieth hymn of the tenth book of the *Ṛg Veda*, recited orally from at least the second millennium BCE, described how Puruṣa, the original cosmic being, sacrificed himself on a funeral pyre. From his consumed body emanated all components of the universe—sun and moon, earth and sky, hymns and chants, meters and spells, horses and cattle, and four varieties of humans. From Puruṣa's mouth came the Brāhmaṇa, from his arms the Rājanya (ruler), from his thighs the Vaiśya, and from his feet the Śūdra. By implication, these four categories (referred to as *varṇa*s, a term meaning category, color, and so on) of humans were stratified, inasmuch as Puruṣa's mouth was higher than his arms, thighs, and feet, and Brāhmaṇas were higher than the other three *varṇa*s. Subsequent Vedas described reciprocal relationships between the Brāhmaṇas (performing fire sacrifices and other priestly functions) and the ruling Rājanya (later referred to as Kṣatriya).

By the middle of the first millennium BCE the Brāhmaṇa authors of sacred texts agreed that the four-*varṇa* stratification of society with the Brāhmaṇas at the top was cosmically ordained, at least for the Āryan ("noble") people. Their Brāhmaṇaical view did not go unchallenged. Such teachers as Siddhārtha Gautama, founder of Buddhism, and Mahāvīra, founder of Jainism, (both of them Kṣatriyas) taught paths to enlightenment that bypassed Brāhmaṇa priests and challenged the legitimacy of the four-*varṇa* stratification system.

Brāhmaṇa-composed texts, such as the *Dharmaśāstra* attributed to the sage Manu, assigned specific occupations to each *varṇa* living north of the Vindhya Hills and south of the Himālaya mountains. Brāhmaṇas were to study and teach the Vedas and other sacred texts, perform fire sacrifices for individual sacrificers, and have little to do with temple priests. Kṣatriyas were to wage war, rule, sponsor sacrifices, and study. Vaiśyas were to trade, lend money, farm, breed cattle, sponsor sacrifices, and study. Śūdras were to serve the three higher *varṇa*s. They were prohibited from studying the sacred texts or sponsoring sacrifices. Women were also prohibited from studying the sacred texts, reflecting another dimension of stratification—based on gender—in the classical texts.

According to Manu's *Dharmaśāstra*, men of each *varṇa* were to marry women of the same *varṇa*—thereby making *varṇa* hereditary. Under certain conditions, such as times of distress, higher *varṇa* men could marry lower *varṇa* women. Lower *varṇa* men were never to marry higher *varṇa* women. According to Manu, the mixing or confusion of *varṇa*s seriously jeopardized society. Disapproved sexual activities between *varṇa*s produced new birth groups ("*jāti*s") with their own names and occupations. These *jāti*s were to marry among themselves. According to Manu, one of the most offensive mixing of *varṇa*s occurred when a Śūdra male impregnated a Brāhmaṇa female. Manu labeled the offspring of such miscegenation a "*caṇḍāla*." According to Manu, *caṇḍāla*s were to live apart and never enter villages or towns after dark. They were to execute criminals, carry out the corpses of unclaimed dead, wear the clothes of the executed and dead, and eat from broken dishes.

According to Manu, the *varṇa* and gender into which one was born were direct consequences of one's moral behavior in previous lives. The concept of reincarnation and the doctrine of *karma* (the cosmic order whereby every virtuous act is rewarded and every evil act is punished) provided legitimation for the four-*varṇa* stratification system and its permutations. Those in the higher strata deserved their privileges, and those in the lower strata deserved their disadvantages because of their moral conduct in previous lives. Brāhmaṇa-composed texts described stratified forms of marriages, gifts, foods, sacrifices, rebirths, sins, and penances. According to Brāhmaṇas, the natural order of the world incorporated legitimate inequalities and hierarchies.

The four-*varṇa* stratification system was frequently referred to in Sanskrit and folk narratives. In Buddha's previous-birth stories, the sight of a *caṇḍāla* was described as polluting to high-status people. In Sanskrit poems and plays and in the *Mahābhārata* and *Rāmāyaṇa* epics, the four *varṇa*s with their assigned duties, privileges, and disabilities were accepted as morally legitimate. The *Bhagavad Gītā* described the origins and different duties of Brāhmaṇas, Kṣatriyas, Vaiśyas, and Śūdras and declared that it was better to do one's own duty imperfectly than do another's duty perfectly. Although only a small Sanskrit-literate minority of India's population read the classical texts, through oral transmission the concepts of the four stratified *varṇa*s, their duties, and their levels of pollution were widely recognized in much of North India.

North India also saw continuing challenges to the four-*varṇa* system. If all components of the universe originally emanated from the cosmic sacrifice of Puruṣa, were not all beings ultimately one? The Upaniṣads presented the concept of the absolute, or world spirit, or "Brahman," existing in the "*ātman*," or soul, of every individual. Every person's *ātman* was part of the same ultimate Brahman. Differences between people were illusory. The seeker's philosophical task was to comprehend the Brahman-*ātman* mystery and the full implications of the spiritual unity of all beings. A major task of each individual now was to reduce the separation between one's individual *ātman* and the universal Brahman so that when one's body died, one's released *ātman* could blend into the Brahman the way that a drop of rain water blends into the ocean, never to be reborn as a separate *ātman* again. This was the way humans obtained "*mokṣa*"—liberation from the cycle of rebirths.

Manu's *Dharmaśāstra* fitted the concept of *mokṣa* into the four-*varṇa* stratification system. Only Brāhmaṇa males could achieve *mokṣa*. Men and women in other *varṇa*s, by performing their assigned duties in this life, could hope to be reborn into a higher *varṇa* in their next life—but not to achieve *mokṣa*. When they were finally reborn as Brāhmaṇa males, it was necessary for them to go through four stages of life: celibate student, married householder, forest dweller, and wandering mendicant. Only men in the final wandering-mendicant stage of life could sufficiently reduce the gap between their *ātman* and the ultimate Brahman so that at the moment of their death, their *ātman* could be released from their bodies and the cycle of rebirths and achieve *mokṣa* by uniting with the universal Brahman. Each time this occurred, it completed part of a cosmic process moving from undifferentiated unity to differentiated multiplicity back to undifferentiated unity.

The paradox of ultimate sameness existing within Hinduism's elaborately differentiated hierarchies continued to generate challenges to those hierarchies. The six schools of Hindu philosophy addressed this paradox in a variety of ways. As centuries passed, new pathways to *mokṣa* were identified. One of the most popular was the pathway of devotion or "*bhakti*." If each person's *ātman* were part of the universal Brahman, why could not each person approach the Brahman directly? What need was there for priests, sacred texts, fire sacrifices, or formal ceremonies? A person of any rank, age, or gender could hope to achieve *mokṣa* through devotion. *Bhakti* devotees generated rich oral and written texts adoring the divine in formless or formed manifestations (such as Kṛṣṇa, Rāma, Śiva, and Śakti). Again and again, their sung or recited texts challenged the *varṇa* system, its Brāhmaṇaa priests, and its notions of ritual pollution.

In South India, Tamil classical texts described both Brāhmaṇas and kings and ministers, warriors, merchants, artisans, musicians, and plowmen, but they largely ignored the four-*varṇa* system. Non-Brāhmaṇa Buddhist and Jain teachers in the Tamil narratives sometimes overshadowed the spiritual stature and leadership of Brāhmaṇas. The non-Brāhmaṇa authors of some of the Tamil devotional literature described their lowly births as, if anything, enhancing their closeness to the divine. Anti-*varṇa* devotional movements were popular in South India. One of them, the Śiva-worshipping Liṅgāyats in twelfth century CE Mysore, evolved in time into their own intra-marrying group or *jāti*.

Small communities of Christians and Jews were living in southern India during the early years of the first millennium CE. Within a few decades of the Prophet Muḥammad's death in 632 CE, Arab-speaking Muslim traders were settling on the southwestern coast of India. Intramarrying lineages and hierarchies evolved within these Jewish, Christian, and Muslim communities. A few centuries later, more Muslims began arriving in India through the northwestern mountains. Migration and conversion enabled Muslim and Christian communities to spread to other parts of India, extending and sometimes enhancing their own internal divisions and hierarchies. In sixteenth-century Punjab, Guru Nānak initiated Sikhism with egalitarian teachings drawn from both Hinduism and Islam. Within a few generations, the Sikh community included higher and lower castes paralleling those of their Hindu neighbors. Castes and stratification appeared almost everywhere.

British Administrative Decisions Regarding India's Stratification

In the sixteenth century CE, Portuguese traders interacting with Hindu and Muslim merchants on the southwestern coast of India used the term "casta," as they had in Brazil, to label people according to the proportions of Portuguese and other (indigenous, black, mulatto, and so on) "blood" in their veins. The British and French in India modified the Portuguese term "casta" to "caste" and applied it to India's many different intramarrying lineages. After the British East India Company acquired control of Bengal in 1757, India's caste system became an object of administrative concern. The Company courts in Calcutta, Madras, and Bombay presidencies found themselves dealing with civil cases involving such issues as inheritance, ownership, marriage, divorce, and adoption. Unfamiliar with local customs, the Company courts hired Muslim advisors to help British judges to apply *sharī'ah* laws to Muslims. It was unclear, however, what laws the Company courts should apply to Hindus. Initially the Company courts hired Brāhmaṇaa scholars of the *śāstra*s to give their opinions, but often their opinions seemed to have little to do with the cases at hand. Finally, for lack of better alternatives, the

Company courts based their decisions on precedents, that is, evidence of established patterned practices. Whatever hierarchies or patterns of privilege and discrimination existed prior to British rule were now enforced by British courts. In 1794, William Jones published his English version of Manu's *Dharmaśāstra* (in which he translated "*varṇa*" as "caste" and "Dharmaśāstra" as "laws"). Thus, through a series of cultural misunderstandings, Manu's *Dharmaśāstra*—presenting an idealized Brāhmaṇaical view of semi-mythical *varṇa*s' duties—became the "Laws of Manu" and a basis for legal decision rendered in British-Indian courts.

The British government recorded its first all-India census in 1871. The census required people to identify their castes or tribes. Individuals, most of whom had multiple complex kinship relationships, reported their castes or tribes with considerable variations. The British authorities, continuing their misunderstandings of Manu's *Dharmaśāstra*, tried to place each tribe and caste within Manu's four stratified *varṇa*s. When the 1871 census results were released, British government offices were flooded with memorials and petitions from caste leaders claiming higher status for their caste than that ascribed to them in the census.

Each subsequent ten-year census wrestled with problems of castes' identities and rankings. The 1891 census abandoned *varṇa*s and described subgroups and broad occupational categories. The 1901 census reintroduced castes and fitted them into a British-constructed eleven-rank *varṇa* system based on Manu but including four subdivisions of Śūdras, three subdivisions of polluting castes, and ending with castes that denied the priestly authority of Brāhmaṇas. The 1911 census commissioner noted that Brāhmaṇas did not perform ritual services for the lowest castes; the lowest castes had their own low-caste priests, and therefore perhaps the census should not record the lowest castes as Hindus. This suggestion aroused considerable alarm. After the 1921 census, increasing dissatisfaction with the changing caste figures, the dubious accuracy of the census returns, and the many troublesome appeals for higher status by disgruntled caste representatives led the census commissioner to announce that the 1931 census would no longer, in most cases, record castes.

By 1931, a new factor had entered caste record keeping. Mohandas K. Gandhi, B. R. Ambedkar, Ramaswamy Naicker, and other reformers had drawn the wider public's attention to the fact that nearly one-fifth of India's population (variously called by such terms as untouchables, outcastes, backward castes, exterior castes, and *ādivāsī*s) were being systematically discriminated against because of Hindu restrictions. Reformers called on the British government to identify these disadvantaged groups to attempt compensation for centuries of historical disabilities. In 1931, the census commissioner instructed provincial superintendents to draw up lists of those castes and tribes in their regions who were handicapped by their "degraded position in the Hindu social scheme." Handicaps generally included such disabilities as denial of admission into Hindu temples, prohibitions against drawing water from certain wells or walking on certain roads, and perceptions by higher castes that members of these castes and tribes caused ritual pollution. Higher castes imposing these disabilities sometimes justified their behavior because of the polluting nature of the lower castes' occupations (e.g., sweeping streets and cleaning latrines). Nevertheless, in accord with the census commissioner's instructions, groups meeting local "degraded" criteria were listed (i.e., "scheduled") in 1936 to enable them to receive special electoral representation according to the 1935 Government of India Act. Their official designation now became "scheduled castes" (about 15 percent of the population) and "scheduled tribes" (about 7.5 percent of the population).

Addressing Stratification in Independent India

On August 15, 1947, India became independent. Various national leaders expressed the hope that India could move toward a classless, casteless society. Subsequently, India's constitution, drafted under the guidance of B. R. Ambedkar, a member of the Māhār scheduled caste, declared that untouchability was abolished and any disability arising out of untouchability was an offense "punishable in accordance with law." Through its constitution, the Government of India initiated a policy of affirmative action sometimes described as "compensatory discrimination." Articles 330 and 332 of the constitution reserved seats in the national parliament and state assemblies so that the proportions of elected scheduled caste and tribe representatives reflected their proportions in the electorate (labeled "proportional representation"). Article 335 reserved posts (i.e., jobs) in the central and state governments for members of the scheduled castes and tribes—again proportionally representing the scheduled castes and tribes in the total population. The drafters of the constitution recognized that giving preference to the scheduled castes and tribes disadvantaged India's remaining population and thus violated Article 16 guaranteeing equal rights for all Indian citizens. To address this contradiction, the drafters of the constitution stipulated that the compensatory provisions of reserved seats and reserved posts for scheduled castes and tribes would expire after ten years. Historically, in every subsequent decade, as the constitutional provision has been about to expire, India's parliament has extended the life of the compensatory-discrimination provisions for another ten years through a constitutional amendment.

In 1960, the Government of India published an all-India list of 405 scheduled castes and 225 scheduled tribes. According to this list, some castes occupied degraded positions in the Hindu social scheme in one locale but not in a neighboring one. So in the first locale, they received scheduled-caste benefits but not in the neighboring one. Some scheduled castes were called by two or more names in the same location. Some scheduled castes were called by different names in different linguistic regions of India, suggesting that these castes were administrative constructs rather than intramarrying lineages. In 1976, the Government of India published an amended state-by-state list of 841 scheduled castes and 510 scheduled tribes. Muslim, Christian, and Sikh castes that experienced discrimination in a variety of ways were ruled ineligible for classification as scheduled castes because—as non-Hindus—they should not be affected by their "degraded position in the Hindu social scheme."

In response to the relative slowness with which their situations improved, members of scheduled castes and tribes and members of Muslim, Christian, and Sikh deprived castes began labeling themselves collectively as "Dalits," a Marathi term for "oppressed" used by Ambedkar. Just as higher castes had formed their own caste associations to build schools, raise scholarship funds, set up business associations, and provide welfare assistance, similarly Dalits formed their Dalit associations. Soon references were being made to Dalit leaders, electorates, agendas, agitations, and activism and to Dalit art, poetry, literature, drama, and film. A frequent feature of Dalit public protests was burning a copy of Manu's *Dharmaśāstra*. Evidence accumulated that the introduction of constitutional provisions for scheduled castes and tribes—even supplemented by Dalit activism—did not end violence against the lowest castes. In a 1990 constitutional amendment, parliament gave additional powers to the National Commission for Scheduled Castes and Tribes to pursue atrocities against scheduled castes and tribes.

As described, provisions in India's constitution addressed the scheduled-caste and scheduled-tribe disadvantages inherent in the Hindu caste system. India's constitution also addressed the disadvantages of its poorest but not ritually disadvantaged and hence not "scheduled" citizens. Article 15(4) authorized the state to make special provisions "for the advancement of any socially and educationally backward classes of citizens." Article 16(4) authorized the state to provide equal opportunities of public employment for "any backward class of citizens" under-represented in state services. The term "other backward classes" was already in official use to identify in different parts of India groups that were entitled to educational concessions. Neither article 15(4) nor 16(4), however, provided formal criteria for how to identify and therefore provide benefits for members of the "backward classes."

In 1978, the ruling Janata Party appointed ex-member of parliament B. P. Mandal to head a Backward Classes Commission. The Mandal

Commission's task was to determine the criteria for identifying India's "socially and educationally backward classes" and to recommend steps for their advancement. Between 1978 and 1980, the Commission generated an "Other Backward Class" (OBC) list of 3,743 castes and a more underprivileged "Depressed Backward Class" list of 2,108 castes. On December 31, 1980, the Mandal Commission submitted its report recommending that 27 percent of Central and State government jobs be reserved for members of the other backward classes and that the 27 percent figure be applied to other benefits including those provided by universities and affiliated colleges.

The V. P. Singh government's announcement in 1990 that it would implement the Mandal Commission Report's recommendations generated violent objections—especially among North India's higher castes. The V. P. Singh government fell, partly as a result of the agitation. Features of the Mandal Commission's recommendations were appealed to the Supreme Court. In 1992, the Supreme Court ruled that "caste" could be used to identify "backward classes," that "backward classes" could include non-Hindus, such as Muslims, Christians, and Sikhs, and that the "creamy layer" (i.e., the wealthiest members) of the backward classes could not receive backward-class benefits. The Supreme Court also ruled that the combined total of scheduled castes and tribes plus backward classes should not exceed 50 percent of India's population. As the scheduled castes and tribes already comprised 22.5 percent of India's population, the backward classes could not exceed an additional 27 percent. Therefore, the Mandal Commission lists of backward classes had to be pared back so that they did not exceed the 27 percent quota. In 1993, the Congress Party government, under Prime Minister Narasimha Rao, announced the implementation of the Mandal Commission recommendations. This time there was little public outcry.

India used its constitution to try to offset the inequalities of another historic stratification system—its stratification system advantaging men and disadvantaging women. After decades of elections in independent India, women were consistently under-represented on elected bodies. So in 1992, India adopted the 73rd and 74th constitutional amendments. These amendments required that one-third of the seats in village *pañcāyat*s, and intermediate-, municipal-, and district-level elected bodies be reserved for women. It was hoped that the resulting increase of women on these bodies would introduce more women's concerns onto their agendas and would affect the outcomes of their decisions. Unsuccessful efforts were made to introduce a similar constitutional amendment reserving seats for women in state assemblies and the national parliament. Resistance arose over how reserved seats for women could be incorporated with reserved seats for scheduled castes and tribes.

Beginning in India's first election in the 1950s, stratification and castes played important parts in voting behavior. At the local level, elections have been fought on straightforward caste bases. On the next higher level, caste leaders have frequently bargained with political parties and candidates, offering to deliver their caste's votes in return for benefits to them and their castes. The years after the implementation of the Mandal Commission recommendations saw the emergence of candidates and political parties on the state level specifically representing the scheduled castes and the backward classes, especially in India's heavily populated northern states of Uttar Pradesh and Bihar. For those who thought caste would fade away as India acquired higher levels of urbanization, education, and mobility, the new roles of castes in India came as a surprise.

India's Stratification Viewed Through Different Conceptual Frameworks

For centuries, outside observers were curious about India's religions and castes. Megasthenes, a Greek ambassador to North India about 300 BCE, returned to Europe and wrote descriptions of India's ranked occupations. Two Chinese Buddhist monks, one from 399 to 414 CE and the other from 629 to 645 CE, traveled through much of India and left detailed accounts of their observations of Buddhist monks, other religious figures, and pariahs. Marco Polo, who journeyed across southern and western India on his way back to Venice after leaving China in 1292, recounted his observations on aspects of Indian life. After Marco Polo came more travelers from Italy, Portugal, the Netherlands, France, Britain, and other parts of Europe. The term "caste" was incorporated into the English language. In 1853, Karl Marx, inferring that India's caste system was based on a stagnant low-technology division of labor, wrote that the modern industry and railroads Britain was introducing would "dissolve" India's caste system. American sociologists in the first half of the twentieth century described inherited group status extending along a continuum from a highly rigid caste system (as in India) to a flexible, loosely organized open-class system (as in the United States). Widespread misconceptions arose in the West regarding India's castes: that they determined one's lifetime occupation, that they never changed, that they related to each other in mutually accepted hierarchies, that everyone with the same caste name was a member of the same caste, that caste was based on race or skin color, that castes were uniquely Hindu, and that the legitimacy of the caste system rested on beliefs in rebirth and the law of *karma*.

Western intellectuals provided various explanations for the origins and uniqueness of the Hindu system of stratification. In 1896, the French scholar Émile Senart challenged the theory that caste was based on race and that caste resulted from specialization of arts and crafts. According to Senart, one of the defining characteristics of a caste was its ability to impose its authority on its members and to expel—temporarily or permanently—members who defied its authority. In 1939 another French scholar, Arthur Maurice Hocart, wrote in his *Caste: A Comparative Study* that the Indian caste system was one species of a genus of societies based on the principle that those who ruled must be pure. To that extent, the Hindu caste system was not very different from similar systems of hierarchy Hocart had observed in Egypt, Sri Lanka, and Fiji.

In 1946, J. H. Hutton, who worked on the 1931 India census before joining Cambridge University, published *Caste in India: Its Nature, Function, and Origins*. His book included such currently suggested theories for the emergence of the caste system as occupational and class distinctions; exclusivity of family worship accompanied by fear of outside pollution; racial, guild, and tribal intermarriage and hypergamy; and geographical and political divisions. Hutton stated that the Indian caste system probably resulted from "geographical, social, political, religious, and economic factors not elsewhere found in conjunction." However, he concluded that the unique sources for India's caste system were the "Rigvedic invaders with their definitely graded social classes" and their impact on a society "already divided into groups isolated by taboos" (189).

In 1950, G. S. Ghurye, in his *Caste and Class in India*, suggested that caste in India was being transformed "somewhat on the lines of the British social classes" (286). In 1952, M. N. Srinivas used the term "Sanskritization" to describe a process whereby castes tried to raise their status by imitating Brāhmaṇas' ways of life and adopting the "customs, rites, and beliefs" of Brāhmaṇas. In 1954, an English anthropologist, H. N. C. Stevenson, claimed that the Hindu Pollution Concept lay at the heart of the caste system. His argument was supported by Thomas Beidelman's (1959) and William Wiser's (1958) field reports from North Indian villages describing the "Hindu *jajmānī* system." Castes in the Hindu *jajmānī* system participated in fixed exchanges of services and grain. They also observed elaborate intercaste patterns of accepting and rejecting water, uncooked foods, fried or boiled foods, foods prepared in different types of pots, and so on. The patterns of acceptance and rejection identified the relative ranks of different castes.

In 1968, Irawati Karve, in her *Hindu Society—An Interpretation*, provided evidence that eight Brāhmaṇa castes in Maharashtra could not have come from a common genetic origin. She reported that a similar study in Maharashtra by R. K. Gulati provided evidence that nine potter castes could not have come from a common genetic origin.

In 1966, the French scholar Louis Dumont published *Homo Hierarchicus: An Essay on the Caste System*. In it he cautioned Western readers that their deeply embedded prejudices favoring egalitarianism interfered with their ability to comprehend the true dimensions of India's caste system. According to Dumont, hierarchies advantaging the high and disadvantaging the low were widely accepted as morally justified in India. Dumont, as a structuralist, assumed that whatever structures existed in a society were there because of deliberately-arrived-at but not-always-apparent underlying ideological historical design.

Furthermore, binary opposites (such as pure/impure or power/status) would always be empirically separated. Dumont identified two "absolutely distinguished" hierarchies in India—one based on power and headed by royal Kṣatriyas, the other based on status and headed by priestly Brāhmaṇas. Dumont maintained that the supremacy of the status hierarchy headed by Brāhmaṇas remained "unexportable" from India.

In 1974, University of Chicago professors McKim Marriott and Ronald Inden agreed with Dumont that Western scholars' egalitarian biases could prevent their correct understanding of India's caste system. They also endorsed Dumont's view that, because of India's uniqueness, Western scholars needed to develop an "Indian sociology" with premises differing from those of "Western sociology." Drawing on ancient Hindu philosophical and medical texts, Marriott and Inden concluded that every caste shared a unique corporate property embodying its code of conduct. Each caste's coded substance required that caste to follow a particular occupation and engage in correct exchanges with other castes. Each caste's borders were permeable, allowing for the transmission of pollution and the changing of a caste's coded substance. In the final analysis, India did not contain two separate hierarchies (as Dumont stated). Instead, India contained a single overarching ranked system composed of many profoundly particularized units, each with its permeable coded substances.

In 1977, Maurice Godelier, drawing on Marxist principles, concluded that India's caste system was embedded in the infrastructure or base rather than in the superstructure. Therefore, to attack the caste system, one should engage in caste action rather than class action, as classes were not embedded in the infrastructure or base of caste societies.

In 1999, Susan Bayly drew attention to caste consciousness and caste wars. A frequently cited instance of a caste war occurred in Tamil Nadu in 1968, when rural Dalit laborers who tried to assert their constitutional rights were massacred—purportedly by agents of higher-caste Hindu landlords. Similar incidents occurred in many parts of India. One telling feature of caste wars was that higher castes would rally their members of all social backgrounds to respond violently to challenges by lower castes and Dalits on the grounds that the lower castes were depriving the upper castes of privileges to which the upper castes were historically entitled.

In Bhopal, India in 2002 and Vancouver, Canada in 2003, Dalits from India and elsewhere in the diaspora convened, analyzed their situations, and issued declarations. These declarations denounced the continuing hurdles of caste-Hindu society, calling on the Indian state to protect Dalits from atrocities, demanding job reservations for Dalits in the private sector, and appealing to the United Nations to equate caste discrimination with race discrimination and to declare caste discrimination to be a violation of universal human rights. Were the United Nations to do so, this would be an instance of the world body taking principles of stratification unique to Hindu society and applying them to the worldwide community.

References Cited

Bayly, Susan. 1999. *Caste, Society, and Politics in India from the Eighteenth Century to the Modern Age*. Cambridge: Cambridge University Press.

Beidelman, Thomas O. 1959. *A Comparative Analysis of the Jajmani System*. Locust Valley: J.J. Augustin.

Dumont, Louis. 1980 [1966]. *Homo Hierarchicus: The Caste System and Its Implications* (trans. Mark Sainsbury, Louis Dumont, and Basia Gulati). Chicago: University of Chicago Press.

Godelier, Maurice. 1977 [1973]. *Perspectives in Marxist Anthropology* (trans. Robert Brain). Cambridge: Cambridge University Press.

Ghurye, G. S. 1950. *Caste and Class in India*. Bombay: Popular Book Depot.

Hocart, Arthur M. 1950. *Caste: A Comparative Study*. London: Methuen.

Hutton, John H. 1961 [1946]. *Caste in India: Its Nature, Function, and Origins*. Oxford: Oxford University Press.

Karve, Irawati. 1968 [1961]. *Hindu Society—An Interpretation*. Poona: Deshmukh Prakashan.

Marriott, McKim and Ronald B. Inden. 1974. "Caste Systems." *In Encyclopaedia Britannica*, 3: 982–91. Chicago: Encyclopaedia Britannica.

Marx, Karl. 1950 [1853]. "The Future Results of British Rule in India." *In* Karl Marx and Frederick Engels, *Selected Works in Two Volumes*, 1: 319–24. Moscow: Foreign Languages Publishing House.

Senart, Émile C.M. 1930 [1896]. *Caste in India: The Facts and the System*. London: Methuen.

Srinivas, M. N. 1952. *Religion and Society among the Coorgs of South India*. Oxford: Clarendon.

Stevenson, Henry N.C. 1954. "Status Evaluation in the Hindu Caste System." *Journal of the Royal Anthropological Society of Great Britain* 84: 45–65.

Wiser, William H. 1958. *The Hindu Jajmani System*. Lucknow: Lucknow Publishing House.

27

Structuralism

Carl Olson

Lévi-Strauss
Structuralism and Hinduism
Postmodernism and Deconstruction
Derrida
Hinduism and Deconstruction
Structuralism and Deconstruction

An important development in structural linguistics occurred with the theory by Ferdinand de Saussure (1857–1913), the author of *Mémoire sur le système primitive des voyelles dans les languages Indo-européennes* (1878). His students reconstructed from their class notes his *Course de linquistique générale* (1906–11). In these works, de Saussure argued that a word such as "cat" not only produces an inscription for a four-legged animal, but it creates a concept or mental image of such an animal. The initial inscription is called the signifier, whereas the concept is the signified. The relationship between the former and the latter is completely arbitrary, which implies that the system of language does not embody a natural meaning; however, it does mark distinctions within a system of identities and differences.

A science of linguistics, according to de Saussure, requires dual perspectives: the diachronic studies the historical development of a particular language, and the synchronic studies a language at a particular moment in time. He also distinguishes between *langue* as a system of rules and conventions that organize a given language and *parole* or a specific utterance that reflects the use of language. If we consider the category of games, it is only in the playing that their rules are manifest. The rules of a game are its *langue*, and the performance is its *parole*. A structural linguist explicates rules and conventions (i.e., language structure) that govern the production of meaning in the acts of parole.

As a result of a process of combination and selection, meaning arises with a language system and becomes complete after the final word is spoken or inscribed, a process that de Saussure calls the syntagmatic axis of language. Along this axis, meaning accumulates and can be changed by substituting new parts for aspects of the sentence. Because the relationship between sign and referent is always arbitrary, the meaning of a sentence is created through a process of selection and combination. Consequently, our spoken language does not reflect worldly reality but does provide us with a conceptual map that imposes an order on perceptions and experiences. Thus, spoken language plays a key role in constructing and organizing our notion of reality, and different languages produce different versions of reality. In short, human meanings result from the ways in which words are selected and combined.

Lévi-Strauss

Claude Lévi-Strauss (born 1908 in Brussels) was inspired by de Saussaure and by Roman Jakobson (1896–1982), who authored *Slavic Languages* (1955) and *Phonological Studies* (1962). A third influence was Nikolai Trubetzkoy, another important figure in the Prague school of linguists. The structural approach enabled Lévi-Strauss to identify rules of binary opposition in cultural artifacts, such as myths and kinship patterns, and to put forward the claim that binary oppositions (e.g., male and female, raw and cooked, nature and culture) reflect both the workings of the human mind and the internal logic of social systems.

Even though he called himself a disciple of sociologist Émile Durkheim (1858–1917), Lévi-Strauss sought to unite psychology with ethnology to identify the basic structures of the mind. He was convinced that mental structures are immanent within cultural data, such as myths and symbols. On the basis of his fieldwork in Amazonian Brazil, he concluded that an underlying unity exists among different societies owing to unconscious functions of the human mind that reveal themselves in mythical narratives (Lévi-Strauss 1966).

Myths operate like language in the sense that they comprise individual mythemes that are analogous to language such units as morphemes and phonemes, and the task of the anthropologist is to discover the rules or underlying grammar that enable myths to become meaningful. All myths are structured by binary oppositions (e.g., black–white, good–bad, rational–irrational, us–them) in which meaning emerges as a result of the interplay between similarity and difference. Myths help a culture to overcome inherent contradictions, empower its members to comprehend the world in a particular way, and make the world an orderly and habitable place. Moreover, myths are repetitive, and the function of repetition is to reinforce the structure of the myth (Lévi-Strauss 1963: 229). For the scholar, myths can make it possible to discover operational modes of the human mind that remain constant over long periods of time.

The method used by Lévi-Strauss to study a myth reduces it to its smallest narrative units and through its variants produces a two-dimensional time referent: synchronic and diachronic. The synchronic is nonreversible whereas diachronic is reversible, paradigmatic, and presumably the deep structure that repetitively manifests in variations over time (Lévi-Strauss 1963: 210). Thus, although the growth of myth is continuous, its structure remains constant.

The type of thinking associated with myth is binary and functions to resolve human problems framed as logical contradiction. Lévi-Strauss (1963: 230) argues that the logic of mythical thought is as rigorous as science and differs not in quality of intellectual processes but in the things to which it is applied. In Lévi-Strauss, we have a holistic approach to the study of society that is rationalistic and reflects the influence of the structuralism of de Saussure.

His work has not avoided criticism. Clifford Geertz has observed that Lévi-Strauss proposes a rationalist, antirelativistic position by evoking the universality of cognitive processes. What Geertz (1984: 274) objects to is the danger that it undermines cultural diversity. Another scholar critiques the method of Lévi-Strauss in favor of a more fully embodied rationalism, such as that espoused by the phenomenologist Alfred Schutz (Stoller 1998: 252).

Structuralism and Hinduism

Several scholars have applied the structural method to the study of Hinduism. Among the most prominent are anthropologist Louis Dumont, particularly in his classic work *Homo Hierarchicus*, and Indologist Madeleine Biardeau. Their approach is holistic rather than atomistic. Each challenges strictly empiricist and evolutionist approaches to Indology, and both find rational structures that support the patterns of Indian culture.

Dumont notes that the category of castes instructs us about a basic social principle: hierarchy. This principle ranks social groups as relatively superior or inferior to each other. In India, the chief basis for ranking is the hierarchical coexistence of two opposites: pure and impure. Hindu society is a structural whole with Brāhmaṇas at the top of the system and untouchables at the bottom.

Dumont also contrasts the type of the person in the world with the type of the world-renouncer who stands outside the social world, even though the renouncer remains dependent on society for daily support in the form of alms. By leaving the world to adopt an antisocial role, the renouncer becomes both a universal and personal individual in comparison to the role-determined person who remains within the social fabric and lacks individuality (Dumont 1970: 185).

Dumont's work rejects any dichotomy between thought and behavior, and he insists that an explanatory model cannot simply be limited to a replication of observed reality. If the anthropologist relies on what people say in response to questions raised and observed patterns of action, he or she would have a limited perspective; it is necessary to get beyond the merely objective perspective and into the hidden depths of the unconscious of the subjects because social actors remain unaware of the structural patterns buried in their unconscious minds. Anthropologist Veena Das (1987: 5) has followed Dumont's example in proposing that fieldwork data be complemented by Indological textual material, but she has recognized the need to introduce a historical perspective to structuralism. Dumont's neglect of history is a problem repeatedly cited by other scholars (Inden 1990: 151), and several also challenge his assumption that the caste system can be reduced to a hierarchical principle (Raheja 1988: 31).

Biardeau (1989: 4) uses organizing principles of binary opposites, as is typical of a structural method. Similar to Lévi-Strauss, she finds unity not with the mental constructs of the scholar but at a deeper level in the unconscious mind of the Hindu. She also admits to using the structural method in a modest way with Hindu cosmogonic myths from the Purāṇas (Biardeau 1981b: 6). In a more recent work entitled *Stories about Posts* (2004), she combines ethnology and textual study and weaves together elements from ancient Vedic literature and its sacrificial cult with Epic literature, goddess devotion, and village ethnography in an attempt to discern the significance of a type of pillar that can be found throughout India. Tracing narratives about these objects in texts from different regions, she becomes convinced that behind the existing variety of posts stands a prototypical Vedic sacrificial post. Biardeau's structural approach is, however, more evident in her earlier work on the goddess, depicted as the mediator between the opposites of pure–impure and divine–human. Not only is the goddess a fundamental category of Hindu consciousness and a complement to Viṣṇu and Śiva, but her association with the buffalo sacrifice is indicative of her oppositional relation to impurity (Biardeau 1981a: 9–16).

Inden objects to Biardeau's replacement of disparate ancient cultures in India with a unified Hindu culture and her view of Viṣṇu and Śiva as complementary figures rather than as sectarian rivals. He contends that she turns Hinduism into a unitary system of symbols and meanings that is devoid of history and sealed off from other religions, and she makes Hindus into static agents or mere instruments of their actions by privileging the unconscious (Inden 1990: 126).

Wendy Doniger (previously O'Flaherty) also was influenced by structuralism for many years and, in her more recent work, continues to comment favorably on Lévi-Strauss. In her book on the mythology of Śiva, she argues that variations of a myth are important because each version of a myth adds an essential element to the whole. In agreement with Lévi-Strauss, Doniger regards myth as significant in relation to the total mythical structure of a culture. That does not reduce the importance of context because universal elements of myths are less important than the points at which a myth diverges from the general pattern (O'Flaherty 1973: 15). In her later scholarship, Doniger moves away toward a more nuanced comparative approach to myth but has continued to defend Lévi-Strauss against his postmodern critics (Doniger 1998: 151–52).

Postmodernism and Deconstruction

Postmodernism is a disputed and nebulous term, although numerous writers have offered opinions about its characteristics and origins. Certain philosophical attitudes have shaped postmodernism, and Martin Heidegger (1889–1976) anticipated the term: "Western history has now begun to enter into the completion of that period we call the modern, and which is defined by the fact that man becomes the measure and the center of beings" (1982: 28). He articulated a vision of the end of metaphysics in a lecture at Halle in 1957 on "Identity and Difference" (Heidegger 1969). The emphasis on difference is a thread that runs throughout postmodern thought.

Jean-François Lyotard thinks that the "post" of postmodernity suggests more a matter of tone, style, experimentation, and multiplicity. In fact, he thinks that the term "postmodern" is always implied in the term "modern"—"because of the fact that modernity, modern temporality, comprises in itself an impulsion to exceed itself into a state other than itself" (Lyotard 1991: 25). Lyotard provides an example of an experiment with the notion of rewriting, which represents a new beginning that is exempt from any prejudice.

There is also an additional sense of rewriting that reflects Sigmund Freud's notion of "Durcharbeitung" (working through), which suggests working with a hidden thought obscured by past prejudice and future dimensions. This suggests that postmodernity is thus not a new epoch but is rather a rewriting of aspects of modernity and a type of experiment that reduces the importance of grand theories. In brief, the grammar of postmodernism seems to be in the future perfect rather than the present tense.

In *The Postmodern Condition* (1984), first published in 1979 in France, Lyotard views postmodernism as a crisis of narratives, which he claims are the quintessential forms of knowledge that refine our sensitivity to differences. The crisis can be traced to making knowledge into a commodity to be produced for consumers to buy it. Therefore, knowledge ceases to be an end in itself and loses it useful value. This suggests that postmodernism heralds the collapse of all universal metanarratives, such as Christianity, Marxism, liberalism, or any other overarching framework. We are left with a plurality of voices from the margins of various cultures with their insistence on difference, cultural diversity, and the privileging of heterogeneity over homogeneity.

Postmodernism represents the negation of structuralism in the sense of calling for the end of grand schemes or narratives, a search for essences or structures, or a quest for meaning. Postmodern thinkers find hidden within the theory of Lévi-Strauss a metaphysical position that they cannot accept. They also reject his conviction that meaning, certainty, and truth can be discovered. From the postmodern perspective, structuralism is a rotting dinosaur whose flesh and bones call to be picked apart and placed in a museum dedicated to the preservation of modern artifacts to be observed but no longer used. The picking apart can be executed by the nonmethod of deconstruction espoused by Jacques Derrida.

Derrida

The method—or more precisely the nonmethod—of deconstruction is identified with the French postmodern philosopher Jacques Derrida (1930–2004), whose influence extends beyond philosophy to literary criticism and even postcolonial studies. Derrida is a very playful and ironical philosopher because he claims that his writings are meaningless. In fact, there is a strong element of risk in his philosophy because his thought takes the gamble of meaning nothing. Moreover, his philosophy offers no thesis or position, and that reflects his tendency to make distinctions and simultaneously undermine them. This type of approach to philosophy contributes to the elusive nature of deconstruction. By advocating uncontrollable, free play, Derrida stresses that deconstruction is not a method.

The origin of deconstruction extends back to the phenomenological philosophies of Edmund Husserl and his student Heidegger. Husserl used the term "*abbau*"(dismantling) to suggest a nonreflective procedure that made it possible to regress to something that cannot in principle be given by the pregiven world. In his work *Being and Time* (1962), Heidegger discusses his notion of *Destruktion* within the context of arguing for the necessity of destroying older philosophical traditions to allow Being to become concrete. By assuming a nonreflective and nonobjective mode of thinking, Heidegger envisions a calm surrender to Being, which would constitute a nonrepresentational mode of thinking in contrast to ordinary consciousness and its ontotheology or metaphysics. Embracing these philosophical threads from Husserl and Heidegger, Derrida's use of deconstruction promises to continue the work of undoing ontotheology, or what he calls logocentrism (a subordination of writing to the spoken word), to which Western philosophy has been captive for centuries as the metaphysics of presence. The archenemy of deconstruction is presence or the logocentric error connected to the illusion that reality and its categories are directly present to the human mind. In general, the impetus of Derrida's philosophical work (1976, 1981, 1987, 1988) is to deconstruct the presence of the present moment.

Rather than producing anything for Derrida, deconstruction reveals something that is already present. If every philosophical position possesses both its pro and anti aspects and if every assumed position can be negated, deconstruction can be understood as a simultaneous smashing down and building up. If we take, for instance, a sentence, deconstruction disarranges the sequence of terms in a sentence and disassembles the parts of the whole. In other words, deconstruction uses the individual parts of a whole sentence or document to turn it against itself by indicating its self-contradictory aspects. By following this procedure, the deconstructionist attempts to locate an instance of difference or otherness within a text to expose metaphysical conceptuality from the viewpoint of difference. The otherness or alterity of a text represents a form of writing that one finds at the margins of a text.

Deconstruction is also exorbitant, which suggests that it goes outside the normal track, even though it is assumed that one was within the orbit at one time. Exceeding the track of the orbit involves crossing it by passing through the line that it traces. This passage is a crossing out of the track of the orbit accomplished in the act of crossing it. Derrida is using a twofold sense of crossing: a breaking through and a violation, a double-cross. By stressing the exorbitant nature of deconstruction, Derrida wants to emphasize its ability to exceed what is reasonable, just, or proper. This suggests that deconstruction undermines the propriety of reason.

Derrida imagines deconstruction to be like an inscription on the face of a coin or the title page of a book, which suggests rendering it evident, displaying it, or bringing it forth. In its inscription-like character, deconstruction possesses value only within a context or in a series of possible substitutions or inscriptions. By turning a text against itself, deconstruction discovers concepts that are, for instance, cracked and fissured by differences and contradictions. Once these cracks and fissures are exposed, deconstruction does not attempt to overcome any internal difference; it rather works to maintain any differences. This aspect of deconstruction is indicative of its parasitic nature because it continually preys on the text, other readings, or interpretations.

Deconstruction is also a kind of double reading in the sense of retracing a text to its limits and marking the limits of the text. The portion that exceeds the text is the trace of *différance*, an exposing of the blank spaces of the written text. The process of deconstruction leaves a track in the text that is similar to memory. It is important to grasp that the track is already within the text; it is only revealed by deconstruction. When a person reads a text, spaces are made in the text by raising certain questions and producing certain remarks. This process leaves a track in the original text that renders it neither dissimilar from its state prior to beginning to deconstruct it nor the same. The remarks represent cuts in the text that perform the work of castration or a simultaneous double reading of a text. What gets castrated, or clipped, is the logos (concept) of the text. Deconstruction is also repetitive and parasitic in the sense that one can continually return to the text and deconstruct it again and again. By deconstructing the language of a text, a person is engaged in a process of becoming more self-aware. Overall, the aim of deconstruction is to return to metaphoric, poetic language where the power for signification has not been exhausted.

Hinduism and Deconstruction

Few scholars of Hinduism have availed themselves of the nonmethod of deconstruction. Among the exceptions are Homi K. Bhabha and Gayatri Chakravorty Spivak. In addition to deconstruction, Bhabha uses psychoanalysis, literary criticism, and history, whereas Spivak uses feminism and Marxism to supplement her use of deconstruction. Both writers embrace the political cause of the neglected, abused, and abject subaltern people of South Asia. There is a strong political emphasis in the writings of both authors to redress the ways in which subalterns have been victimized by historical forces and the Western colonial powers.

Bhabha thinks that we need to formulate critical revisions within the context of "cultural difference, social authority, and political discrimination in order to reveal the antagonistic and ambivalent moments within the 'rationalizations of modernity'" (1994: 171). To the loss of meaning and hope, Bhabha thinks that we should respond with a radical revision of social temporality, to confront the concept of culture beyond its limits, and to engage the uneven, incomplete production of cultural meaning and value. If culture is to be a strategy for survival, it must be transnational owing to the displacement of people (e.g., migrations, diaspora, or relocation) and translational because of a need to discern what it signifies.

Bhabha provides a vision of what a transnational and translational type of culture might resemble with his notions of a "vernacular cosmopolitanism" and a subaltern secularism. As a continuation of the anticolonial struggle, "vernacular cosmopolitanism" unifies local concerns with international political relevance within the context of a dialogical relationship between colonial and neocolonial discourses (Bhabha 2001: 39). This would enable the postcolonial subject to gain genuine political power, to become a historical person, and to be a contemporary of others with international influence. Subaltern secularism retains contact with the traditionally neglected people.

The freedom associated with such a liberal secularism is, for instance, a testing of boundaries and limits that is a communal process that can become a collective demand.

Bhabha also calls for the need of dialectical thinking that does not sublate the other. At the same time, he wants to extricate the West from its central place in theoretical knowledge by radically substituting the representational mode of thinking about and writing history. It is questionable whether it is possible to achieve a dialectical type of thinking that would also be a non-representational mode of thinking.

In contrast to Bhabha, Spivak (1999) is more faithful to the spirit of Derrida's notion of deconstruction because she does not adopt a particular philosophical position, and she does not thereby have to defend her position from critics. Addressing postcolonial intellectuals, she instructs them to lose their biases, prejudices, and preunderstandings in part because she wants to do away with all privileged positions.

When she looks at history, she sees epistemic violence by which she means the construction of a particular object of study. This does not mean that there is any reality behind the representation. This is especially true of Western constructs of colonial people. Joining political allegiance with the subaltern, she wants to compose a new narrative that will counter the West and do justice to the subaltern. Spivak claims that the subaltern, especially its women, do not have a voice that can be heard, and she appoints herself to become such a spokesperson for the abject members of the Third World.

Overall, Spivak faces methodological conundrums similar to those of Bhabha because feminism and Marxism that tend to acknowledge essentials and universals do not easily coalesce with deconstruction with its radical skepticism and distrust of ever successfully finding essences. Moreover, Marxism is a dialectical philosophy that stands in opposition to the anti-dialectical nature of deconstruction. Bhabha and Spivak do share a strong political agenda with the intention of overthrowing the hegemony of prior historiography.

Structuralism and Deconstruction

Structuralism and deconstruction are far apart when it comes to the search for truth and meaning. From Derrida's perspective, deconstruction is not intended to disclose the truth, which is plural. And if meaning represents the space among terms, relations, and interrelations, meaning is not something that can be discovered, and the search for it involves a risk. Moreover, there is nothing that can be termed real because everything is a combination of presence and absence within the matrix of *différance*, which for Derrida represents a play of traces without sense.

For Derrida, the impossibility of finding truth, meaning, or reality by using deconstruction gives rise to questions about the possibility of nihilism. Whether deconstruction leads to nihilism is debatable with respect to Derrida, but deconstruction embraces a pernicious relativism and leads to a radical skepticism that dangerously moves into the direction of solitary solipsism. The playful nature of Derrida's philosophy enables him, however, to avoid nihilism, allows differences to unfold, and hold binary oppositions—which are so dear to structuralists—in tension. Moreover, play can become as problematic as the hierarchical structure that it opposes (Olson 2002: 288–89).

The rationality characteristic of structuralism is replaced with spontaneity by deconstruction. The goal of deconstruction is to subvert methods, such as structuralism, from within it and to break down its binary opposites and hierarchical structure, because Derrida wants to investigate what is prior to reason or even thinking. Derrida is convinced that there is an opacity embodied within the system of rationality. As reason possesses a supplementary nature for Derrida, the origin of reason must be nonrational. Moreover, Derrida thinks that the Enlightenment conception of reason tends to be self-legitimizing because it takes a single and universal standard for all forms of reason. This tendency is also something against which Lévi-Strauss argued for his subjects.

From the perspective of Derrida and deconstruction, structuralism is a perfect example of and captive to the representational mode of thinking with which a person assumes a correspondence between appearance and reality, which is supported by a metaphysical edifice. Deconstruction is intended to overcome captivity to any metaphysical position and a coherence theory of truth within the context of a search for new paradigms. From one perspective, structuralism is a product of Enlightenment thinking that clings to the possibility of precision and certitude in thinking and faith in the ability to identify fundamental principles that are implicit in valid knowledge. Derrida and his notion of deconstruction call all of this into question with its emphasis on difference, constant change, and simulation. Nevertheless, in the quest to overcome the representational mode of thinking, Derrida and other postmodern thinkers are unsuccessful (Olson 2000).

References Cited

Bhabha, Homi K. 2001. "Unsatisfied: Notes on Vernacular Cosmopolitianism." *In* Gregory Castle, ed., *Postcolonial Discourses: An Anthology*, 39–52. Oxford: Blackwell.

Bhabha, Homi K. 2002 [1994]. *The Location of Culture*. London: Routledge.

Biardeau, Madeleine, ed. 1981a. *Autour de la déesse hindoue*. Paris: École des Hautes Études en Sciences Sociales.

Biardeau, Madeleine. 1981b. [1954–58]. *Études de mythologie hindoue*. Volume 1: *Cosmogonies purāṇiques*. Paris: École française d'Extrēme-Orient.

Biardeau, Madeleine. 1989 [1981]. *Hinduism: The Anthropology of a Civilization* (trans. Richard Nice). Delhi: Oxford University Press.

Biardeau, Madeleine. 2004 [1989]. *Stories about Posts: Vedic Variations around the Hindu Goddess* (trans. Alf Hiltebeitel, Marie-Louise Reiniche, and James Walker; eds Alf Hiltebeitel and Marie-Louise Reiniche). Chicago: University of Chicago Press.

Das, Veena. 1987 [1977]. *Structure and Cognition: Aspects of Hindu Caste and Ritual*. Delhi: Oxford University Press.

Derrida, Jacques. 1976 [1967]. *Of Grammatology* (trans. Gayatri Chakravarty Spivak). Baltimore: Johns Hopkins University Press.

Derrida, Jacques. 1981 [1972]. *Dissemination* (trans. Barbara Johnson). Chicago: University of Chicago Press.

Derrida, Jacques. 1987. *Psyché: Inventions de l'autre*. Paris: Galilée.

Derrida, Jacques. 1988 [1972]. *Limited Inc* (trans. Samuel Weber, ed. Gerald Graff). Evanston: Northwestern University Press.

Doniger, Wendy. 1998. *The Implied Spider: Politics & Theology in Myth*. New York: Columbia University Press.

Dumont, Louis. 1970 [1966]. *Homo Hierarchicus: An Essay on the Caste System* (trans. Mark Sainsbury). Chicago: University of Chicago Press.

Geertz, Clifford. 1984. "Anti-anti Relativism." *American Anthropologist* 86, 2: 267–78.

Heidegger, Martin. 1962 [1927]. *Being and Time* (trans. John Macquarrie and Edward Robinson). New York: Harper & Row.

Heidegger, Martin. 1969 [1955–57]. *Identity and Difference* (trans. Joan Stambaugh). New York: Harper & Row.

Heidegger, Martin. 1982 [1961]. *Nietzsche*. Volume 4: *Nihilism* (trans. Frank A. Capuzzi, ed. David Farrel Krell). San Francisco: Harper & Row.

Inden, Ronald B. 1990. *Imagining India*. Cambridge: Blackwell.

Lévi-Strauss, Claude. 1963 [1958]. *Structural Anthropology* (trans. Claire Jacobson and Brooke Grundfest Schoepf). New York: Basic Books.

Lévi-Strauss, Claude. 1966 [1962]. *The Savage Mind* (trans. George Weidenfeld). Chicago: University of Chicago Press.

Lyotard, Jean-François. 1984 [1979]. *The Postmodern Condition: A Report on Knowledge* (trans. Geoffrey Bennington and Brian Massumi). Minneapolis: University of Minnesota.

Lyotard, Jean-François. 1991 [1988]. *The Inhuman: Reflections on Time* (trans. Geoffrey Bennington and Rachel Bowlby). Cambridge: Polity Press.

O'Flaherty, Wendy Doniger. 1973. *Asceticism and Eroticism in the Mythology of Śiva*. London: Oxford University Press.

Olson, Carl. 2000. *Zen and the Art of Postmodern Philosophy: Two Paths of Liberation from the Representational Mode of Thinking*. Albany: State University of New York Press.

Olson, Carl. 2002. *Indian Philosophers and Postmodern Thinkers: Dialogues on the Margins of Culture*. New Delhi: Oxford University Press.

Raheja, Gloria Goodwin. 1988. *The Poison in the Gift: Ritual, Prestation, and the Dominant Caste in a North Indian Village*. Chicago: University of Chicago Press.

Spivak, Gayatri Chakravorty. 1999. *A Critique of Postcolonial Reason: Toward a History of the Vanishing Present*. Cambridge: Harvard University Press.

Stoller, Paul. 1998. "Rationality." *In* Mark C. Taylor, ed., *Critical Terms for Religious Studies*, 239–55. Chicago: University of Chicago Press.

28

Subaltern

Christian Lee Novetzke and Laurie Patton

What is "the Subaltern"?
The Literature
Hinduism in Subaltern Studies
Hinduism Assessed
Ambivalence Assessed
The Subaltern in Hindu Studies
The Literature
The Subaltern and Hinduism:
Recent Work and Unresolved Questions

What is "the Subaltern"?

In 2006, almost sixty years after the Italian social theorist Antonio Gramsci began using the term "subaltern" to signify those made subordinate by hegemonies of power (of state, class, patriarchy, gender, and race, for example), one can find that "subaltern" has proliferated as a noun and adjective in contemporary discourse, indicating everything from the position of the average contemporary artist in Chicago (see www.subaltern.org) to a description of street food in Calcutta (Mukhopadhyay 2004). Gramsci originally used the term in some of the key, brief essays that he wrote during his eleven years in prison, beginning in 1926 under Benito Mussolini's fascist regime. Though Gramsci's choice of terms was perhaps meant to evade the attention of Italian state censorship, which a word such as "proletariat" would certainly have attracted, the term "subaltern" came to have other advantages. The term could encompass spheres outside capital and labor (which was Gramsci's primary concern) to have a broader descriptive power that might point toward other kinds of subjection to hegemonic force, to envelop the critical social theory pointed by E. P. Thompson at the "working classes" of England (1963), or by Simone de Beauvoir at the gendered subjectivity of the "second sex" (1949), or by Frantz Fanon toward the people he called "les damnés de la terre" (1961).

Gramsci's concern with the state and culture is important in understanding how the term "subaltern" can indicate a person or community in a position "inferior" to others in some fundamental way (i.e., by class, caste, gender, or location). However, it also can be used as a term to designate the relationship of two entities to each other vis-à-vis their access to power or capital (of the material and social varieties). Therefore, one might speak of a "subaltern" person but also of subalternity as a condition of being for everything from a community to a nation to a particular discourse (a set of texts, of practices, of histories, and so on).

The Literature

The elasticity of the idea of "the subaltern" has been most fully and systematically expressed by the core group of scholars who created the Subaltern Studies Collective and the series of edited volumes the Collective, and its later members, have created.[1] Inspired by Gramsci, on the one hand, and Michel Foucault, on the other, the Collective applied the idea of the subaltern to Indian historiography (and later culture, more broadly) and hence to a colonial and postcolonial context. The Collective's agenda in the first several volumes was summarized by its founder, Ranajit Guha, who suggested that nationalist historiography, produced by European, American, and Indian elites, could not represent the historical realities of nonelites. Guha (1983: 43) described this situation as the "failure of the [Indian] nation to come into its own," to expand beyond explorations of the past centered on the activities and concerns of elites. Guha has defined the regular use of the term "subaltern" by the Collective as "a name for the general attribute of subordination in South Asian society whether this is expressed in terms of class, caste, age, gender, and office or in any other way" (1988: 35). Over two decades, and twelve volumes, the Collective has published essays that engage the site of the subaltern in many ways but with particular emphasis on history, politics, and culture and, in later volumes, gender as well. Critics have noted a shift from the work of the early decade (epitomized in the work of such figures as Shahid Amin, David Arnold, Partha Chatterjee, Ranajit Guha, and Gyan Pandey), wherein one found a greater emphasis on documenting the historical condition of the subaltern as a class in South Asia and marking moments of "peasant insurgency," to a later engagement with cultural and social theory (Dipesh Chakrabarty, Gyan Prakash, and Gayatri Chakravorty Spivak are representative) filtered through the lens of subaltern subjectivity more generally and applied to transglobal issues of theorizing culture and historiography.[2]

The deployment of the critical term "subaltern" has grown outside the bounds of the edited series, expanding into numerous monographs by authors published within the series and by authors outside this group. Subaltern, as a category of investigation, is present in East Asian Studies (Gladney 2004), African Studies (Kandeh 2004), and Education Studies (Apple and Kristen 2006). Most notably outside South Asia, one finds the study of the subaltern has flourished in Latin American Studies, with the founding of the Latin America Subaltern Studies Group in 1993 (see Latin America Subaltern Studies Group 1993; Rabasa, Sanjinés, and Carr 1996; Rodríguez 2001). These contexts increasingly expand the definition of the "subaltern" outside the confines of "peasant insurgency" and postcolonial studies, as do the various theoretical investments made with the term as interventions into literary studies, historiography, anthropology, sociology, and other fields.

A commonality woven throughout this body of literature is the way in which religion (primarily as an anthropological and epistemological category) appears conjoined to the subaltern, and here we see a significant departure from both traditional Marxism and Gramscian Marxism (see Novetzke 2006; see also Patton 2005). For Marx, religion is ambiguous: infamously the "opiate of the masses" yet, at least in German intellectual history, "the criticism of religion is the premise of all criticism" (1986: 301), which is to say, the central problematic of the bourgeoisie and the public sphere. For Gramsci (1995: 1–137), writing in Italy in the interwar years, religion is synonymous with the Roman Catholic Church, a participant in the hegemony of "common sense" that suppresses the subaltern. Yet from the earliest work of the Collective to the numerous important monographs produced by its principal members (especially Dipesh Chakrabarty, Partha Chatterjee, and Gyan Prakash), religion has been a central feature of "subaltern consciousness" and often in a way that expresses "insurgency" rather than acquiescence to hegemonies of power. In the next section of this chapter, we discuss the ways in which members of the Collective have engaged this relationship between religion and the condition of subalternity in the context of South Asia and especially of Hinduism. The third section investigates how some studies of Hinduism not situated within the field of Subaltern Studies have nonetheless explored some of the same concerns of how the subaltern condition is expressed, engaged, and mitigated.

Hinduism in Subaltern Studies

How do Subaltern Studies scholars approach their material when a peasant resistance movement and a Hindu religious movement are one and the same phenomenon? The key founding member of the Subaltern Studies Collective, Ranajit Guha, has displayed an intriguing combination of Marxist materialist historiography and an abiding interest in religion, and in particular Hinduism, as it is practiced among India's subaltern communities and among India's

Hindu elite. In an essay in the second volume of Subaltern Studies, Guha (1983) discussed a *hūl*, or "uprising," in 1855–56 undertaken by the Santals, a tribal group well represented in northeastern India, in the modern-day regions of Bihar, Orissa, and West Bengal. The economic explanation for the uprising is simple: the Santal believed that land they cleared for agriculture was their property, whereas the colonial authority laid claim to the land through the land-tenure system in place in the early nineteenth century. Discussing this uprising, Guha studies the testimonials of Santals who stood trial in Calcutta for the uprising. Rather than cite the economic reasons for their action, they attributed their activities to the divine call of their Ṭhākur, their chief deity, as well as to various miracles the deity engendered, and not to any materialist reason. Guha states,

> Religiosity was, by all accounts, central to the [Santal] *hool*. The notion of power which inspired it...[was] explicitly religious in character. It was not that power was a content wrapped up in a form external to it called religion....It is not possible to speak of insurgency in this case except as religious consciousness.
>
> (1983: 34)

Guha uses this particular historical moment to challenge the way in which historians dismiss explanations given by historical agents when those explanations fall outside the paradigms of historical explicability. In this case, religion stands outside the rational explanatory power of normative historiography. Guha, who composed only six essays within the twelve volumes published to date, also returned to the subject of religion in his famous essay, "Dominance Without Hegemony and Its Historiography" (1989), especially when discussing the elite uses of Hinduism (both the invocations of *dharma* and of *bhakti*) (especially pages 244–70), and in discussions of an abortion and the death of a low-caste Bagḍi Vaiṣṇava woman, Chandra, in Bengal in 1849 (1987) and of caste as a mode of discipline and the *svadeśī* movement before independence (1992). In these last examples, religion as "Hinduism" is exploitative and coercive rather than defiant: an expression of elite hegemony rather than subaltern agency.

An even greater concern with religion, and in particular with Hinduism, is evident in the contributions of Partha Chatterjee, another of the principal members of the Collective. In the first volume of the series, Chatterjee (1982) demonstrates how Hinduism deeply influenced communal identification in agrarian contexts, appearing as a weapon of dominance (wielded by a Hindu majority under a secularist banner) and a foil for resistance, uniting Muslim peasants. In "Caste and Subaltern Consciousness" (1989) in the sixth volume of the series, Chatterjee juxtaposes "Brahminical religion" with "the beliefs and practices of subordinate caste groups" (169). Chatterjee (1989: 172) understands religion in this essay to be a common fabric shared by elite and subaltern alike but which is restructured, even inverted, by the subaltern as a means of marking the intention of insurgency. In doing so, he aligns Hinduism as "Brahminical religion" with caste as an anthropological practice, while tapping "popular religions" for modes of resistance.

Chatterjee reads religious history along the lines of a dialectic between elite religious force and a subaltern inversion of that force, and this dialectic is evident from a later essay (1993a) that examines the life and recorded discourses of the Bengali mystic, Rāmakṛṣṇa (1836–86) in relation to the construction of a middle-class cultural identity in Bengal. Here we have Chatterjee's (1993a: 68) influential equation of the "private" and "inner" with the "secret history" of India, a history in which religion, and particularly Hinduism, deeply influenced resistance to "the most universalist justificatory resources produced by post-Enlightenment rationalist discourse," which is to say, the discourse of European colonialism.[3]

Studies by two other key members of the Collective—Dipesh Chakrabarty and Gyan Prakash—are also indicative of the way in which religion, and particularly Hinduism, is central to the study of subaltern agency in colonial and postcolonial contexts. However, departing from Guha and Chatterjee, these two authors use examples of religion as subaltern consciousness to think through large issues of postcolonial epistemology, particularly in the context of historiography. Prakash's widely read essay on the "Impossibility of Subaltern History" (2000) provides a cogent treatment of how religion is a site for the management of a culture's relationship to modernity and "Western reason" (293) while at the same time constituting a locus of resistance against hegemony. The genealogy for this idea is generated within a postcolonial understanding of the ways in which "indigenous" religious practices can challenge, subvert, and emend the hegemony of colonial modernity; in other words, this is not a study of religion in the service of the colonial (or other) state but as a mode of resistance to the state's hegemonic coercion, a position similar to that given to Rāmakṛṣṇa by Chatterjee (1993a). Prakash's (2000: 293) discussion involves the ways in which the reformist agenda of late colonialism in India, the Ārya Samāj, sought to excise "superstition," of which *purāṇa* or "mythic" literature was exemplary, from "a rational religion of the nation," epitomized by Vedic Hinduism in reformist thought. Prakash finds in the failure of this project "the possibility of overcoming the imperative to arrange culture and power according to the demands of Hinduism as a rational religion of the nation and to construe religion according to the demands of western reason" (2000: 293). He argues astutely that Western reason seeks a certain kind of religion, one conforming to a rational understanding of this anthropological category as it has grown within Western academic fields of knowledge. However, religion, in its multiple and sometimes nonrational formulations, resists a single character, in Prakash's view. While discussing the work of Chatterjee, Prakash (1999: 202) notes that Chatterjee delineates the "imagination of the nation" as a space constituting an "inner sphere, a 'spiritual' domain," and this space, in both authors' estimation, is one conditioned by new forms of Hinduism that resist what we might consider new forms of "Christianity" in the guise of colonial humanism.

Chakrabarty recalls Guha's study of the "Prose of Counter-Insurgency" in *Provincializing Europe* (2000). Chakrabarty notes that Guha, in the work of making "the subaltern the sovereign subject of history, to take their experiences and thought seriously," found "a phenomenon common in the lives of the peasants: the agency of supernatural beings" (2000: 102–3). Following Guha's critique of Erik Hobsbawm's designation of peasants as "pre-political," Chakrabarty (2000: 12–13) reiterates from Guha that the "peasant-but-modern" sphere is one that integrates the supernatural with the machinations of politics, a field of power available to subalterns that reflects the access to networks and worldviews through which they operate. This alignment of subaltern consciousness with the material of religion intrudes on the authorized space of elite historiography. Chakrabarty disapprovingly writes: "Historians will grant the supernatural a place in somebody's belief system or ritual practices, but to ascribe to it any real agency in historical events will be [to] go against the rules of evidence that gives historical discourse procedures for settling disputes about the past" (2000: 104).

For Chakrabarty, histories written through the logic of religious sentiment constitute "subaltern pasts, pasts that cannot ever enter academic history as belonging to the historian's own position," because a modern historian, "unlike the Santal, cannot invoke the supernatural in explaining/describing an event" (2000: 105–6). Chakrabarty, here and elsewhere, wishes to argue for ways in which the political and the religious are articulated simultaneously and, in India, this articulation is very frequently within the sphere of "Hinduism" (2002: 22–28). Thus, the problem of "religion" in the work of the Collective is engaged on several levels simultaneously: the politics, the social, and the historical at once.

Hinduism Assessed

The majority of invocations of Hinduism in the work of the Collective can be grouped under three rubrics: (1) religion as definitive of subaltern consciousness and thus a vehicle of insurgency and resistance among nonelites; (2) religion as the "private" or "secret" sphere of the middle class under colonial rule, which is often also construed as antithetical to hallmarks of modernity, science, and reason in the service of colonialism, thus a means of resistance for urban elites against colonial dominance; and (3) religion as a sociopolitical form of dominance itself, usually in relation to nationalist or independence movements in the colonial period or postcolonial nationalisms, urban civil social forms, or other coercive forms—thus, here, religion is a form of oppression rather than resistance. Let us look at these three forms in turn. It should be noted at this point that these forms are heuristic categories only, and there is a great deal of overlap and "gray areas" between them.

In the first category, we have the hallmark essay of Guha on the Santals noted above, though this is not strictly about Hinduism. We can cite the work of David Arnold (1982: 96–101) in the first Subaltern publication; he noticed the way in which religion (a syncretism of Hinduism and "tribal" religion) motivated subaltern "hillmen" in Andhra, linking them to their neighbors and also distinguishing their beliefs. In the third volume, Arnold (1984) investigated Hindu cosmologies of responsibility (*dharma*) during a time of famine in Madras in the late nineteenth century. In the same volume, David Hardiman (1984) observed how religious practice provided a position in the religioeconomic sphere for *ādivāsī*s ("original inhabitants") in South Gujarat as part of the Devī or "Goddess" movement in a way reminiscent of the Santal movements of the century before. Saurabh Dube (1992) traced religion as "myth" and "symbol" in the Satnāmpanth of northern India, a Hindu religious community of Camārs, or "Untouchables," founded in the nineteenth century.[4] Tanika Sarkar (1985) wrote about the charismatic tribal leader Jitu Santal, returning to the group studied by Guha in 1983 but highlighting the efforts by Jitu in the early twentieth century to transform Santals into normative Hindus. We also have the investigation of religion, history, and place in Tamil Nadu by Sundar Kaali (1999), which uses oral history—often the "archive" for the recovery of subaltern voices—and a study of "spatial politics" to uncover the history of Tiruppuvanam's urban mode of Śaivism among subaltern communities, both urban and rural. Consider also Shahid Amin's (1984) study of how Mohandas K. Gandhi became a divine, miraculous figure in Gorakhpur, where Amin teases out the implications of Gandhi's hagiographical, Hindu character. In Amin's view, Gorakhpur villagers did not simplistically respond to the "holy man" Mahātmā Gandhi but rather developed a kind of millennialism whereby *svarāj* figured directly as a form of local political agency.

Surprisingly, perhaps, the particular way of engaging religion, and specifically Hinduism, by the Collective that sees religion as the vehicle for subaltern agency and articulation is the least presented category of the three we have outlined. Though we return to this issue below, it is worth noting that, though Gramsci himself understood religion, this more complex view of Hinduism as agency would require a larger view of Hinduism than is usually embraced by Subaltern Studies authors.

What is more common is the second category, the use of religion as a mode of resisting "colonial hegemony" or "modernity" by elites in India. In the second category, we can consider most of the work of Chatterjee that engages religion, and especially Rāmakṛṣṇa, and essays by Sumit Sarkar, such as his reading of the "Kalki Avatar" scandal in early twentieth-century Bengal and its reception in the Bengali public sphere (1989, see also 1984: especially 308–17). Sarkar, who has subsequently left the Collective, has a somewhat ambivalent view of Hinduism. At times, S. Sarkar suggests that Hinduism appears crucial to understanding "subaltern militancy," as in an essay in the third Subaltern Studies volume wherein he (1984: 309) discusses Gandhian civil protest in Bengal. Yet his understanding of religion seems pejorative at times. He qualifies religion as "magico-religious" and invokes Marx's comments on religion—where we find the infamous "opium" metaphor (S. Sarkar 1984: 308, 310). S. Sarkar (1984: 308) understands subaltern militancy that invokes religion to be uninformed by a "disenchantment with the world" that is the product of Western Enlightenment. Thus, S. Sarkar also appears to suggest a previous "enchanted" vision, one lacking a rational sense of the real, which is replaced by the magical.

On the contrary, Prakash (1996) situates religion in a counterpoise to science, as we saw above, and, as such, in a dialectic of resistance not subordination (see also his 1999). We might also include the work of Chakrabarty, both in the pages of the series (1994) and in separate monographs (2000, 2002), wherein he grapples with the possibilities and limitations of "religion" as an epistemological category in the context of historiography.

In general, urban and "modern" forms of Hinduism are the most likely candidates for sites of "resistance" of elite Indians against the dominance of European thought-forms. Yet these same sites of resistance easily transform into sites of internalized oppression, what Sheldon Pollock (1993a) has called "deep Orientalism."

The oppressive use of Hinduism as a political or social force—our third category—might include Gyan Pandey's essay, "Rallying Round the Cow" (1983), in the second Subaltern Studies volume, wherein he reads the discourse of communalist violence between Hindus and Muslims in the Bhojpuri area of northern India in the 1890s and 1910s as a product of the skillful manipulation of Hindu sentiment. Pandey further argues that peasant movements, such as the Eka and the Kisān Sabhā in 1921, were not Congress-inspired and therefore "top-down" but rather motivated by the structure of land ownership that led to land shortages and high rents. Likewise, his essay, "The Prose of Otherness" (1994), observes the description, often in Hindu religious terms, of the "fanatics" who are the antithesis of the modern, rational citizen.

In addition, we might consider Ishita Banerjee Dube's (1999) compelling study of religious reification and jurisprudence in Orissa and Shail Mayaram's (1996) study of partition violence in Mewat.[5] Satish Deshpande (2000) and, to a lesser extent, Qadri Ismail (2000) directly engage religion and nationalism in India and Sri Lanka, respectively. In a publication outside the scope of the Collective's series, S. Sarkar (1985), who at this point had left the Collective, finds that Hinduism provides a means of expression and social organization but also quells action with a narrative of subordination, particularly in relation to *bhakti*, a thought system, he contends, that presents subalterns with a logic for bearing their oppressive conditions. Here he is in agreement with Guha, who in his essay "Discipline and Mobilize" (1992), refers to the *svadeśī* use of Hinduism as "soul control" (112).

Ambivalence Assessed

Overall, we can see a consistent concern with religion, and in particular with Hinduism, in the work of the Collective generally, but this concern oscillates between two positions: (1) a positive assessment of Hindu expression and belief as part of the "prose of counterinsurgency" or of the "secret history" of the Indian nation under the radar of colonialism and modernity, and (2) the negative assessment of Hinduism (often Brāhmaṇical Hinduism set in equation with caste) as a coercive force in nationalist and postcolonial contexts.

It is worth exploring here in a little more depth the nature of the ambivalence about Hinduism (or indeed any religion) as a form of agency. Early attempts to deal with religious aspects of peasant consciousness led to the problem of the Subaltern Studies' relationship to conventional Marxist theory. Chatterjee (1993b: 58–65) argued that peasant modes of being cannot be called simply class consciousness but are more complex types of consciousness and practice. Rosalind O'Hanlon (1988, 2000) also put forward the view that changes in religion, as well as such other essentialized categories as caste or nation, present the scholar with "the problem of mapping what on the surface look like fundamental transformations of mentality" (2000: 92–93). She also noted that Subaltern Studies must trace the origins of such transformations in their relationship to the state or to organized religions, without slipping into a rigid teleology or a denial of historical specificity.

This concern grew even stronger as Subaltern Studies became deeply inflected with postmodern cultural studies, especially in the United States. Many assessments of this trend trace its beginnings to the publication of

Edward Said's *Orientalism*, a hugely influential work concerned with Western intellectual tradition's representation of its colonial subjects, particularly those in the Middle East. Said's post–Orientalist perspectives then combined with contemporary postmodern concerns with textual and discourse analysis; through this confluence postcolonial studies became the reigning episteme through which much of the subaltern was then studied. Later, Said himself had misgivings about the ways in which "Post-orientalism" became an academic field in its own right. However, leading writers in the new field of postcolonial studies took up the questions of philosophy, historiography, and cultural representation. From this postcolonial perspective, they have argued forcefully for several basic changes in the study of Third World histories: (1) explorations of cultural difference (inspired in part by Jacques Derrida's idea of *différance*); (2) nonessentialized cultural categories; and (3) the writing of a postfoundationalist and a postnationalist historiography (Bhabha 1994; Chakrabarty 1992, 2000; Prakash 1992, 1994, 1996; Spivak 1985a, b). Among many other priorities, these writers state the need for writing a history that is influenced neither philosophically by an idea of a single cultural "mind" that applies to all members of a society nor anachronistically by a false idea of a unifying nation or set of origins set somewhere in a hoary past.

Given these views, many subaltern writers are overtly suspicious of disciplines and fields, such as religious studies, and particularly the study of Hinduism, in the Western academy. Such a field is, in their view, prone to hegemonic and essentializing constructions of the other under a dominant institutionalized gaze. However, subaltern theorists are also concerned among themselves about the reification of religion in their own writings. Some later postmodern writers, such as Dipankar Gupta (1985), have criticized the tendency in subaltern writers to attribute primordiality to the masses or to assume a traditional consciousness or even primordial loyalties of religion, community, kinship, and language. Many subaltern writers have wondered aloud whether subaltern ideas of a moral community, albeit in the guise of "folk" Hindu values of peasant community, are nonetheless well on their way to yet another essentializing category. If peasant or worker consciousness can be reified and severed from history in this way, why not caste, nation, or most importantly for our purposes, Hindu religious community? Thus the problem remains. As one Subaltern Studies critic put it, although many subaltern writers accept the autonomy of peasants, their accounts are ultimately not that different from the processes of Sanskritization, Islamicization, or popularization—ideas that have all come under fire for essentializing and reifying historical processes of change (Bayly 1988: 120). How can subaltern writing avoid the problem of making the community an "it" with firm boundaries and, as Marxist secularists increasingly suspect, "expressing a sympathy for the Hindu religious as a way of defining that community?" (Spivak 2000: 326).

The Subaltern in Hindu Studies

The reaction of the religious studies scholarly community to the idea of subalternity has been somewhat less ambivalent than the reaction of Subaltern Studies to the phenomenon of religion. Although the Subaltern school, even in its more marked "cultural studies" form of later years, is mostly ambivalent (and occasionally hostile) to the idea of religion as a category of analysis, many students of Hinduism have welcomed the category of the subaltern. Though not all scholars of Hinduism are convinced by the Subaltern Studies methods and commitments (see, for instance, Smith and Caldwell 2000),[6] some have embraced much of the Gramscian tradition in two significant ways: (1) Subalternist writing can further define and criticize religious studies' own Orientalist perspectives, both colonial and postcolonial, and (2) more postcolonial writing in Subaltern Studies can help religious studies scholars to nuance their descriptions of the cultural identity of the religious groups with whom they concern themselves.

Many scholars of religion, such as those mentioned above and their numerous area studies counterparts, would not fundamentally disagree with the premises of later Subaltern school works on religion, such as those essays found in the 1993 volume of Subaltern Studies: Chatterjee's study of the Rāmakṛṣṇa movement as a religion of urban domesticity, and S. Dube's study of the construction of mythic communities in Chhattisgarh. More generally, Richard King addresses Subaltern Studies' later, more postmodern incarnations: his *Orientalism and Religion* (1999) outlines some of the issues in the relationship between religious and postcolonial studies.

To be sure, early works in social movements and religion may have engaged many of the same issues that Subaltern Studies scholars have engaged, only without explicit use of the term. One might say that Owen M. Lynch's 1969 treatment of the religion of untouchables in his now classic *Politics of Untouchability* is one of the best, and earliest, explorations of the relationship between religion and oppression. Part of Lynch's contribution is that he sees a long tradition of saints, both from within the category of Hinduism and without, that have abjured the caste system (1969: 139–40). Thus, there might be not only *moments* of agency in religious movements on which social resisters might call, but long-standing *traditions*. This idea of a tradition of religious resistance as such, based on religious experience, is a controversial one on which Subalternists and Religionists may not agree.

The Literature

The earlier works of Eleanor Zelliot and David N. Lorenzen also come immediately to mind as excellent early examples of ways in which late medieval and early modern *bhakti*, or devotional, movements also focus on modes of empowerment and social change. Lorenzen's earlier (1987) work on Kabīr argues that Kabīr's poetry can and should be read as a form of social protest—perhaps even more persuasively than as a form of "religious devotion" per se. Zelliot (1980) takes a similar view on Eknāth in her article published about the same time (see also Israel and Wagle 1987). John Stratton Hawley's anthology of *bhakti* writings (including Sūrdās, Mīrābāī, Ravīdās, and Kabīr) coedited with Mark Jurgensmeyer (1988) also raises this question of the role of *bhakti* in social resistance, as do his slightly later writings on Mīrā (1995) and *bhakti* and social democracy (1996).

About a decade later, as more Subaltern Studies work was read in departments of religion and anthropology in India, Europe, and the United States, work in the history and anthropology of religion explicitly using the ideas of Subaltern Studies began to appear. Norbert Peabody (1997) thinks through the questions of hegemony and resistance in the performance of the *Rāmāyaṇa* in North India—arguing that certain "mainstream" modes of expression, such as the Hindu *Rāmāyaṇa*, can also be an effective fulcrum for expressions of dissent, precisely because they are seen as mainstream. So, too, Peter Gaeffke (1998) focuses on *bhakti* tradition in North India as a mode of forming community identity which can in turn be a basis for political action.

Even the idea of religious experience per se became open to examination with a subaltern lens: Felix Wilfred, anticipating Christian Novetzke's recent, more theoretical article on religious experience and the subaltern (2006), writes about untouchables in Tamil Nadu in his work "Subaltern Religious Experience," in a 1998 *Journal of Dharma* issue that takes up some of these important themes. A later issue of that same journal, edited by Thomas Kadankavil (2001), takes up the subaltern theme more comprehensively and includes work on apocalypticism and nationalism in subaltern perspectives, as well as the interaction between Christian and Hindu subaltern identities (see in particular Forsthoefl's [2001] piece on apocalypticism as a creative form of agency). The larger question that has been opened in these pieces, and will continue to be debated, is whether the idea of an authentic religious experience can be combined with a commitment to analyzing historical agency in a Hindu religious movement.

In the mid-late 1990s and continuing into the present, studies of specific saints and their traditions also began to involve a discussion of subalternity. Ira Bhaskar's "Allegory, Nationalism, and Cultural Change in Indian

Cinema" (1998) studies the emergence of nationalism in the film treatment of Tukārām, a sixteenth-century untouchable Maharashtrian saint. Recent dissertations, such as that of Shandip Saha "Creating a Community of Grace: A History of the Puṣṭi Mārga in Northern and Western India (1470–1905)" (2004), also use some Subaltern Studies methods to write new histories of the various *bhakti* movements (see also his 2005). Hawley's later *Three Bhakti Voices* (2005) develops some of the basic insights in *Songs of the Saints* to discuss the modes of protest and resistance within both the poetry and hagiography of individual saints.

The Subaltern and Hinduism: Recent Work and Unresolved Questions

One of the most important pieces of basic work is that of recovery of lesser-known Hindu saints who may well have contributed to forms of social resistance. Eleanor Zelliot and Rohini Mokashi-Punekar's recent edited volume, *Untouchable Saints* (2005), practices a basic hermeneutics of recovery to bring to light the low-caste saints who have been treated less thoroughly than their mainstream counterparts, such as Mīrā and Sūr. Tīrupan Āḻvār and Nandanar in South India have a quite small corpus of songs attributed to them but are remembered in legend and still held as models of piety. In Maharashtra, the saint Cokhāmela, his wife Soyrabāī and son Karmamela, and Cokhāmela's sister Nirmalā and Baṇka, her husband, constitute an entire family of devotion, now near-forgotten by the contemporary Dalit movement. In North India, the more well-known Ravidās/Raidās, is also known as Rohidās in the Maharashtra Camarkar population. The volume features previously untranslated songs and poems of each of these saints, analyses of the dynamics of the saints' lives and movement, and assessments of how and why they "survived" or were "forgotten" in subsequent *bhakti* movements.

Increasingly larger, more general studies of South Asian history, anthropology, and sociology of religions have incorporated ideas friendly to, if not identical with, the ideas of Subaltern Studies.[7] Recently, for example, Lorenzen's *Religious Movements in South Asia 600–1800* (2004) makes a plea for studying religious movements not only as systems of symbols and metaphysics but as social structures and organizations with particular relationships to power—whether that be the empire or the state. R. Champakalashmi's essay, "From Devotion and Dissent to Dominance: The Bhakti of the Tamil Āḻvār s and Nāyanārs" (1996), and Burton Stein's "Social Mobility and Medieval South Indian Hindu Sects" (1968), both chronicle the gradual process of decline of dissent within these movements. In his "Rāmāyaṇa and Political Imagination in India" (1993b), Sheldon Pollock argues that the emergence of *Rāmāyaṇa* images and tales in the period of the twelfth to the fourteenth centuries CE is an imaginative attempt to construct a way of representing the strife between Hindus and Muslims during the period. Richard Burghart (1978) argues that the rise of the Rāmānandī tradition had as much to do with competition between traditions for scarce resources (devotees, pilgrimage routes, and political patronage) as it did with the actual saint himself. P. D. Barthwal (1978) argues that the Kabīr and similar movements arose from a double and not a single oppression: in his view, both the punitive policies of Mughul rulers and the discriminatory practices of high-caste Hindus led to the formation of the Kabīr movement. Though many of these authors do not use explicitly subaltern terms in their work, their concerns with the political contexts and social agency of the various groups falling under the Hindu religion is very much consonant with the Gramscian views of the subalternists.

The discussion of subalternity in Hinduism is not truly complete, however, without a brief discussion of the relationship between Hindus and Dalit theology. Much of the concern with Dalit theology has to do with its double rejection of both high-caste Hindu oppression, such as that articulated as early as B. R. Ambedkar and studied by Zelliot and many others, and high-caste Indian Christian theology, which they viewed as a legacy of missionary Christian theology. Both modes are irrelevant to the needs of Dalits, as James Massey writes:

> Many felt that the theological task of India need not be the preserve of the "Brahmanic Tradition" within the Indian Church, which had always used "intuition, inferiority oriented approach" to theologising. Dalit theologians were of the opinion that the theological and cultural domination of Brahmanic traditions within Indian Christianity, ignoring the rich cultural and religious experience of the Dalits had to be ignored, if not rejected completely.
>
> (1995, cited in Oommen 2000: 22)[8]

As a result, many tribal and scheduled caste writers and thinkers are interacting both with and very much against Hindu (and mainstream Christian) ideas and practices as they develop their own liberational ways of thinking. Oddly enough, this explicitly religious usage is somewhat consonant with Spivak's recent, and rather remarkable, statement that subaltern theology (religious thought as a form of political resistance) cannot be ignored, for if it is then Subaltern Studies becomes a matter of law enforcement rather than "agency in the active voice" (1985b: 358–60; see also 2000: 326–27).

There is, however, much more to be done. With the exception of Pollock (1993, 2005),[9] whose work on precolonial Orientalism is sympathetic to subaltern concerns, there are very few studies of culture in ancient or even premodern India that look at questions of subalternity as such. A fresh analysis of the śūdra in ancient India and the relationship between *sudras* and women could be a real contribution from a Subalternist perspective. Aloka Parasher-Sen's *Subordinate and Marginal Groups in Early India* (2004) is an excellent beginning toward this massive project.

Pandey[10] more generally and Wakankar[11] among others have opened up the overall question of how the precolonial has been framed by the "postcolonial" worldview, including Subaltern Studies, and this is an excellent beginning. Wakankar's work, as well as that of Zelliot and Mokashi-Punekar (2005), on untouchable saints raises the issue of why some untouchable religious movements are remembered and some are not, and these kinds of questions deserve full analysis as we juxtapose the precolonial, colonial, and postcolonial movements. Indeed, the saints are in a certain sense figures that could push subalternists beyond their traditionally colonial and postcolonial emphases.

As mentioned above, the thorny question of the authenticity of religious experience raised by Christian Novetzke (2006) has yet to be fully engaged by theorists on both sides of the issue. As mentioned above, Subaltern Studies writers have acknowledged the possibility of religious language and rhetoric as a kind of historical agency of resistance. However, whether they would acknowledge the basic validity of an inner experience that moves beyond historical agency, as many religionists do, is another issue. Zelliot and Mokashi-Punekar's volume (2005) and the essays by Prentiss, Lochtefeld, and others in that volume assume the validity of religious worlds of the saints. Many scholars of Hinduism do not feel the need to use categories of subalternity precisely because they want to assert the validity of such religious worlds. Subaltern scholars might argue that they are unwilling to trouble their own assumptions about the "givenness" of these worlds.

In addition, the idea of the subaltern as it might move across Hindu diasporic boundaries is another fresh venue for research and theoretical engagement. How might we rethink the questions of relative subalternity in complex situations wherein Hindus are a "minority" in one country and a majority in another? Though this issue has been raised in recent shorter works (see, for instance, Patton and Ram-Prasad 2006), it has not been fully treated in a full-length historical study.

Real theoretical and historical engagement between the ideas of the subaltern citizen and the ideas of Hindu thought and practice has just begun. These two intellectual traditions are still very rarely discussed in the same classrooms of academe. It is our hope that, in the narrow meeting place where "agency" and "religious identity" are one and the same, the two traditions be discussed together more frequently but without tiresome repetition of the centuries-old opposition between Gramscian-Marxist and religious perspectives. The next generation of scholars of South Asia would greatly benefit from the mutual critique and enlightenment that would be sure to ensue.

Notes

1 The key members include (in alphabetical order) Shahid Amin, David Arnold, Gautam Bhadra, Dipesh Chakrabarty, Partha Chatterjee, Ranajit Guha, and Gyan Pandey.

2 For "strategic essentialism," see Spivak (1988). For critiques of the Collective's work, see Ludden 2001; Masselos 1992; O'Hanlon (1988).

3 The idea of the "secret history" of India is much evident one year later in Chatterjee 1993b, especially in the final chapter. See also Chatterjee's other essays in the series volumes (1984, 1994). On Rāmakṛṣṇa, see S. Sarkar (1985, 1993).

4 Dube is not studying the earlier Satnāmī tradition, founded in the sixteenth century, which is a more syncretic mix of Hinduism and Islam.

5 Religion is more fully explored in Mayaram's monograph, *Against History, Against State* (2003).

6 Smith and Caldwell (2000: 708–9) argue that though subaltern views claim to speak for the other and reject Western scholarship, they are still using Western modes of argumentation to make their points. See also Illaih (1996); Omvedt (1995), where she discusses the Dalit rejection of Sanskrit Hinduism and colonial curriculum of John Milton and the Bible.

7 For a larger scope anthropological study that engages the issue of subalternity and the nation, see Narayan (2005); Shah (2006).

8 For an overview and a list of important thinkers in this field, see Oommen (2000). See also Omvedt (1995), wherein the same critique is made; Das and Massey (1995); Massey (1995); Nirmal (1989, 1991). More "insider" Christian perspectives might include Clarke (1998: 40); see also Nirmal (1994).

9 However, "religion" as such is not Pollock's concern nor a category he wishes to engage.

10 Pandey's compelling recent paper, "Subaltern Citizens and Their Histories" (2006) is an excellent suggestion that, to move away from an essentialized view of the "peasant" consciousness as discussed earlier in this chapter, we open up the idea of the subaltern and look at relative questions of power in any given relationship within the state. Re-presenting the subaltern as subaltern citizen gives us new lens on the possibilities of agency and belonging.

11 Wakankar (2006a, 2006b) looks at early modern *bhakti* movements as a kind of anti-state sensibility that gets written out of the nationalist movements of the nineteenth century.

References Cited

Amin, Shahid. 1984. "Gandhi as Mahatma: Gorakhpur District, Eastern UP, 1921–2." *In* Ranajit Guha, ed., *Subaltern Studies III: Writings on South Asian History and Society*, 1–71. Delhi: Oxford University Press.

Apple, Michael W. and Kristen L. Buras, eds. 2006. *The Subaltern Speak: Curriculum, Power, and Educational Struggles.* New York: Routledge.

Arnold, David. 1982. "Rebellious Hillmen: The Gudem-Rampa Risings, 1939–1924." *In* Ranajit Guha, ed., *Subaltern Studies I: Writings on South Asian History and Society*, 88–142. Delhi: Oxford University Press.

Arnold, David. 1984. "Famine in Peasant Consciousness and Peasant Action: Madras, 1976–8." *In* Ranajit Guha, ed., *Subaltern Studies III: Writings on South Asian History and Society*, 62–115. Delhi: Oxford University Press.

Barthwal, P. D. 1978. *Traditions in Indian Mysticism based upon Nirguna School of Hindi Poetry*. New Delhi: Heritage Publishers.

Bayly, C. A. 1988. "Rallying around the Subaltern." *Journal of Peasant Studies* 16, 1: 110–20.

Bhabha, Homi. 1994. *The Location of Culture.* New York: Routledge.

Bhaskar, Ira. 1998. "Allegory, Nationalism and Cultural Change in Indian Cinema: *Sant Tukaram*." *Literature and Theology* 12, 1: 50–69.

Burghart, Richard. 1978. "The Founding of the Ramanandi Sect." *Ethnohistory* 25, 2: 121–39.

Chakrabarty, Dipesh. 1992. "Postcoloniality and the Artifice of History: Who Speaks for 'Indian' Pasts?" *Representations* 37: 1–26.

Chakrabarty, Dipesh. 1994. "The Difference-Deferral of a Colonial Modernity: Public Debates on Domesticity in British India." *In* David Arnold and David Hardiman, eds, *Subaltern Studies VIII: Essays in Honour of Ranajit Guha*, 50–88. Delhi: Oxford University Press.

Chakrabarty, Dipesh. 2000. *Provincializing Europe: Postcolonial Thought and Historical Difference*. Princeton: Princeton University Press.

Chakrabarty, Dipesh. 2002. *Habitations of Modernity: Essays in the Wake of Subaltern Studies*. Chicago: University of Chicago Press.

Champakalakshmi, R. 1996. "From Devotion and Dissent to Dominance: The Bhakti of the Tamil Āḻvār s and Nāyanārs." *In* R. Champakalakshmi and S. Gopal, eds, *Tradition, Dissent, and Ideology: Essays in Honour of Romila Thapar,* 135–63. Delhi: Oxford University Press.

Chatterjee, Partha. 1982. "Agrarian Relations and Communialism in Bengal, 1926–1935." *In* Ranajit Guha, ed., *Subaltern Studies I: Writings on South Asian History and Society*, 9–38. Delhi: Oxford University Press.

Chatterjee, Partha. 1984. "Gandhi and the Critique of Civil Society." *In* Ranajit Guha, ed., *Subaltern Studies III: Writings on South Asian History and Society*, 153–95. Delhi: Oxford University Press.

Chatterjee, Partha. 1989. "Caste and Subaltern Consciousness." *In* Ranajit Guha, ed., *Subaltern Studies VI: Writings on South Asian History and Society*, 169–209. Delhi: Oxford University Press.

Chatterjee, Partha. 1993a. "A Religion of Urban Domesticity: Sri Ramakrishna and the Calcutta Middle Class." *In* Partha Chatterjee and Gyanendra Pandey, eds, *Subaltern Studies VII: Writings on South Asian History and Society*, 40–68. Delhi: Oxford University Press.

Chatterjee, Partha. 1993b. *The Nation and Its Fragments: Colonial and Postcolonial*. Princeton: Princeton University Press.

Chatterjee, Partha. 1994. "Claims on the Past: The Genealogy of Modern Historiography in Bengal." *In* David Arnold and David Hardiman, eds, *Subaltern Studies VIII: Essays in Honour of Ranajit Guha*, 1–49. Delhi: Oxford University Press.

Clarke, Sathianathan. 1998. *Dalits and Christianity: Subaltern Religion and Liberation Theology in India*. Delhi: Oxford University Press.

Das, Bhagwan and James Massey, eds. 1995. *Dalit Solidarity*. Delhi: ISPCK.

Deshpande, Satish. 2000. "Hegemonic Spatial Strategies: The Nation-Space and Hindu Communalism in Twentieth-Century India." *In* Partha Chatterjee and Pradeep Jeganathan, eds, *Subaltern Studies XI: Community, Gender and Violence*, 167–211. New York: Columbia University Press.

Dube, Ishitia Banerjee. 1999. "Taming Traditions: Legalities and Histories in Twentieth-Century Orissa." *In* Gautam Bhadra, Gyan Prakash, and Susie Tharu, eds, *Subaltern Studies X: Writings on South Asian History and Society*, 98–125. Delhi: Oxford University Press.

Dube, Saurabh. 1992. "Myths, Symbols and Community: Satnampanth of Chattisgarh." *In* Partha Chatterjee and Gyanendra Pandey, eds, *Subaltern Studies VII: Writings on South Asian History and Society*, 121–58. Delhi: Oxford University Press.

Forsthoefl, Tom. 2001. "Uses and Abuses of Apocalypticism in South Asia: A Creative Human Device." *Journal of Dharma* 26, 3: 417–30.

Gaeffke, Peter. 1998. Review of David N. Lorenzen's *Bhakti Religion in North India: Community Identity and Political Action*. *The Journal of the American Oriental Society* 118, 2: 308–9.

Gladney, Dru C. 2004. *Dislocating China: Muslims, Minorities, and Other Subaltern Subjects*. Chicago: University of Chicago Press.

Gramsci, Antonio. 1995. *Further Selections from the Prison Notebooks* (ed. and trans. Derek Boothman). Minneapolis: University of Minnesota Press.

Guha, Ranajit. 1982. "On Some Aspects of the Historiography of Colonial India." *In* Ranajit Guha, ed., *Subaltern Studies I: Writings on South Asian History and Society*, 1–8. Delhi: Oxford University Press.

Guha, Ranajit. 1983. "The Prose of Counter-Insurgency." *In* Ranajit Guha, ed., *Subaltern Studies II: Writings on South Asian History and Society*, 1–43. Delhi: Oxford University Press.

Guha, Ranajit. 1987. "Chandra's Death." *In* Ranajit Guha, ed., *Subaltern Studies V: Writings on South Asian History and Society*, 135–65. Delhi: Oxford University Press.

Guha, Ranajit. 1988. "Preface (I. Methodology)." *In* Ranajit Guha and Gayatri Chakravorty Spivak, eds, *Selected Subaltern Studies*, 35–36. Delhi: Oxford University Press.

Guha, Ranajit. 1989. "Dominance Without Hegemony and Its Historiography." *In* Ranajit Guha, ed., *Subaltern Studies VI: Writings on South Asian History and Society*, 210–309. Delhi: Oxford University Press.

Guha, Ranajit. 1992. "Discipline and Mobilize." *In* Partha Chatterjee and Gyanendra Pandey, eds, *Subaltern Studies VII: Writings on South Asian History and Society*, 69–120. Delhi: Oxford University Press.

Gupta, Dipankar. 1985."On Altering the Ego in Peasant History: Paradoxes of the Ethnic Option." *Peasant Studies* 13, 1: 9–20.

Hardiman, David. 1984. "Adivasi Assertion in South Gujarat: The Devi Movement of 1922–3." *In* Ranajit Guha, ed., *Subaltern Studies III: Writings on South Asian History and Society*, 196–230. Delhi: Oxford University Press.

Hawley, John Stratton. 1995. "Mirabai as Wife and Yogi." *In* Vincent L. Wimbush and Richard Valantasis, eds, *Asceticism*, 301–19. New York: Oxford University Press.

Hawley, John Stratton. 1996. "Bhakti, Democracy, and the Study of Religion." *In* K. Satchidananda Murty and Amit Dasgupta, eds, *The Perennial Tree*, 213–36. New Delhi: Indian Council for Cultural Relations.

Hawley, John Stratton. 2005. *Three Bhakti Voices: Mirabai, Surdas, and Kabir in Their Time and Ours*. New Delhi: Oxford University Press.

Hawley, John Stratton. N.d. "Introduction." *The Bhakti Movement: Says Who? International Journal of Hindu Studies*, Forthcoming.

Hawley, John Stratton and Mark Juergensmeyer, trans. 1988. *Songs of the Saints of India*. New York: Oxford University Press.

Illaih, Kancha. 1996. "Productive Consciousness Labor and History: The Dalitbahujan Alternative." *In* Shahid Amin and Dipesh Chakrabarty, eds, *Subaltern Studies IX: Writings on South Asian History and Society*, 165–200. Delhi: Oxford University Press.

Ismail, Qadri. 2000. "Constituting Nation, Contesting Nationalism: The Southern Tamil (Woman) and Separatist Tamil Nationalism in Sri Lanka." *In* Partha Chatterjee and Pradeep Jeganathan, eds, *Subaltern Studies XI: Community, Gender and Violence*, 212–82. New York: Columbia University Press.

Israel, Milton and N. K. Wagle. 1987. *Religion and Society in Maharashtra*. Toronto: Centre for South Asian Studies, University of Toronto.

Kaali, Sundar. 1999. "Spatializing History: Subaltern Carnivalizations of Space in Tiruppuvanam, Tamil Nadu." *In* Gautam Bhadra, Gyan Prakash and Susie Tharu, eds, *Subaltern Studies X: Writings on South Asian History and Society*, 126–69. Delhi: Oxford University Press.

Kadankavil, Thomas. 2001. *Special Issue: Subaltern Traditions and National Culture. Journal of Dharma* 26, 3: 282–430.

Kandeh, Jimmy D. 2004. *Coups from Below: Armed Subalterns and State Power in West Africa*. New York: Palgrave.

King, Richard. 1999. *Orientalism and Religion: Postcolonial Theory, India and "The Mystic East."* London: Routledge.

Latin America Subaltern Studies Group. 1993. "Founding Statement." *Boundary* 2 20, 3: 110–21.

Lorenzen, David N. 1987. "The Kabir Panth and Social Protest." *In* Karine Schomer and W. H. Mcleod, ed., *The Sants: Studies in a Devotional Tradition of India*, 281–303. Delhi: Motilal Banarsidass.

Lorenzen, David N., ed. 2004. *Religious Movements in South Asia 600–1800*. Delhi: Oxford University Press.

Ludden, David, ed. 2001. *Reading Subaltern Studies*. New Delhi: Permanent Black.

Lynch, Owen M. 1969. *The Politics of Untouchability: Social Mobility and Social Change in a City of India*. New York: Columbia University Press.

Marx, Karl. 1986. "Introduction to *Contribution to the Critique of Hegel's Philosophy of Right* (1844)." *In* John Elster, ed., *Karl Marx: A Reader*, 301–2. Cambridge: Cambridge University Press.

Masselos, Jim. 1992. "The Disappearance of Subalterns: A Reading of a Decade of Subaltern Studies." *South Asia* 15, 1: 105–25.

Massey, James. 1995. *Dalits in India: Religion as a Source of Bondage or Liberation with Special Reference to Christians*. Delhi: Manohar.

Mayaram, Shail. 1996. "Speech, Silence and the Making of Partition Violence in Mewat." *In* Shahid Amin and Dipesh Chakrabarty, eds, *Subaltern Studies IX: Writings on South Asian History and Society*, 126–64. Delhi: Oxford University Press.

Mayaram, Shail. 2003. *Against History, Against State: Counterperspectives from the Margins*. New York: Columbia University Press.

Mukhopadhyay, Bhaskar. 2004. "Between Elite Hysteria and Subaltern Carnivalesque: The Politics of Street-Food in the City of Calcutta." *South Asia Research* 24, 1: 37–50.

Narayan, B. 2005. "DomiNation: How the Fragments Imagine the Nation: Perspectives from Some North Indian Villages." *Dialectical Anthropology* 29, 1: 123–40.

Nirmal, Arvind P., ed. 1989. *Towards a Common Dalit Ideology*. Madras: Gurukul.

Nirmal, Arvind P., ed. 1991. *A Reader in Dalit Theology*. Madras: Gurukul.

Nirmal, Arvind P. 1994. "Toward a Christian Dalit Theology." *In* R. S. Sugirtharajah, ed., *Frontiers in Asian Christian Theology: Emerging Trends*, 27–41. Maryknoll: Orbis.

Novetzke, Christian Lee. 2006. "The Subaltern Numen: Making History in the Name of God." *History of Religions* 46, 2: 99–126.

O'Hanlon, Rosalind. 1988. "Recovering the Subject: *Subaltern Studies* and Histories of Resistance in Colonial South Asia." *Modern Asian Studies* 22, 1: 189–222.

Omvedt, Gail. 1995. *Dalit Visions: The Anti-Caste Movement and the Construction of an Indian Identity*. New Delhi: Orient Longman.

Oommen, George. 2000. "Emerging Dalit Theology: A Historical Appraisal." *Indian Church History Review* 34, 1: 19–37.

Pandey, Gyan. 1983. "Rallying Round the Cow: Sectarian Strife in the Bhojpuri Region, c. 1888–1917." *In* Ranajit Guha, ed., *Subaltern Studies II: Writings on South Asian History and Society*, 60–129. Delhi: Oxford University Press.

Pandey, Gyan. 1994. "The Prose of Otherness." *In* David Arnold and David Hardiman, eds, *Subaltern Studies VIII: Essays in Honour of Ranajit Guha*, 188–221. Delhi: Oxford University Press.

Pandey, Gyan. 2006. "Subaltern Citizens and Their Histories." Keynote paper presented at the conference, "Subaltern Citizens and Their Histories: India and the U.S.," Emory University, Atlanta, Georgia, October 13–15.

Parasher-Sen, Aloka. 2004. *Subordinate and Marginal Groups in Early India*. New Delhi: Oxford University Press.

Patton, Laurie. 2005. "Religion and Subaltern Studies." *In* Lindsay Jones, ed., *Encyclopedia of Religion*, Vol 13: 8800–803. New York: Macmillan/Thompson Gale.

Patton, Laurie and Chakravarthi Ram-Prasad, with Kala Acharya. 2006. "Hinduism with Others: Interlogue." *In* John Stratton Hawley and Vasudha Narayanan, eds, *The Life of Hinduism*, 288–99. Berkeley: University of California Press.

Peabody, Norbert. 1997. "Inchoate in Kota?: Contesting Authority Through a North Indian Pageant-Play." *American Ethnologist* 24, 3: 559–84.

Pollock, Sheldon. 1993a. "Deep Orientalism?: Notes on Sanskrit and Power Beyond the Raj." *In* Carol A. Breckenridge and Peter van der Veer, eds, *Orientalism and the Postcolonial Predicament: Perspectives on South Asia*, 76–133. Philadelphia: University of Pennsylvania Press.

Pollock, Sheldon. 1993b. "Rāmāyaṇa and Political Imagination in India." *The Journal of Asian Studies* 52, 2: 261–97; also in Lorenzen, 2004: 153–208.

Pollock, Sheldon. 2005. *Literary Cultures in History: Reconstructions from South Asia*. California: University of California Press.

Prakash, Gyan. 1992. "Postcolonial Criticism and Indian Historiography." *Social Text* 31–32: 8–19.

Prakash, Gyan. 1994. "Subaltern Studies as Postcolonial Criticism." *American Historical Review* 99, 5: 1474–90.

Prakash, Gyan. 1996. "Who's Afraid of Postcoloniality?" *Social Text* 49: 187–203.

Prakash, Gyan. 1996. "Science Between the Lines." *In* Shahid Amin and Dipesh Chakrabarty, eds, *Subaltern Studies IX: Writings on South Asian History and Society*, 59–82. Delhi: Oxford University Press.

Prakash, Gyan. 1999. *Another Reason: Science and the Imagination of Modern India*. Princeton: Princeton University Press.

Prakash, Gyan. 2000. "Impossibility of Subaltern History." *Nepantla: Views from South* 1, 2: 287–94.

Rabasa, José, Javier Sanjinés, and Robert Carr, eds. 1996. Special Issue: Subaltern Studies in the Americas. *Dispositio/n* 46.

Rodríguez, Ileana. 2001. *The Latin American Subaltern Studies Reader*. Durham: Duke University Press.

Saha, Shandip. 2004. "Creating a Community of Grace: A History of the Puṣṭi Mārga in Northern and Western India (1470–1905)." Ph.D. dissertation. Ottawa: University of Ottawa Library.

Saha, Shandip. 2005. "Multiple Emplotments of the Puṣṭimārga in 'Bhakti Movement' Thinking." Paper presented at American Academy of Religion Annual Meeting, Philadelphia, Pennsylvania, November 18–20.

Sarkar, Sumit. 1984. "The Conditions and Nature of Subaltern Militancy: Bengal from Swadeshi to Non-Co-operation, c. 1905–22." *In* Ranajit Guha, ed., *Subaltern*

Studies III: Writings on South Asian History and Society, 271–320. Delhi: Oxford University Press.

Sarkar, Sumit. 1985. "Social History: Predicaments and Possibilities." *Economic and Political Weekly* 20, 25–26: 1081–86.

Sarkar, Sumit. 1989. "The Kalki-Avatar of Bikrampur: A Village Scandal in Early Twentieth Century Bengal." *In* Ranajit Guha, ed., *Subaltern Studies VI: Writings on South Asian History and Society*, 1–53. Delhi: Oxford University Press.

Sarkar, Sumit. 1993. *An Exploration of the Ramakrishna Vivekananda Tradition*. Shimla: Indian Institute of Advanced Study.

Sarkar, Tanika. 1985. "Jitu Santal's Movement in Malda, 1924–1932: A Study in Tribal Protest." *In* Ranajit Guha, ed., *Subaltern Studies IV: Writings on South Asian History and Society*, 1–53. Delhi: Oxford University Press.

Shah, A. M. 2006. "Sects and Hindu Social Structure." *Contributions to Indian Sociology (n.s.)* 40, 2: 209–48.

Smith, Brian K. and Sara Caldwell. 2000. "Introduction." *Journal of the American Academy of Religion* 68, 4: 705–10.

Spivak, Gayatri Chakravorty. 1985a. "Can the Subaltern Speak: Speculations on Widow Sacrifice." *Wedge* 7–8: 120–30.

Spivak, Gayatri Chakravorty. 1985b. "Discussion: Subaltern Studies: Deconstructing Historiography." *In* Ranajit Guha, ed., *Subaltern Studies IV: Writings on South Asian History and Society*, 330–63. Delhi: Oxford University Press.

Spivak, Gayatri Chakravorty. 1988. "Can the Subaltern Speak?" *In* Cary Nelson and Lawrence Grossberg, eds, *Marxism and the Interpretation of Culture*, 271–313. Urbana: University of Illinois Press.

Spivak, Gayatri Chakravorty. 2000. "The New Subaltern: A Silent Interview." *In* Vinayak Chaturvedi, ed., *Mapping Subaltern Studies and the Postcolonial*, 324–40. London: Verso.

Stein, Burton. 1968. "Social Mobility and Medieval South Indian Hindu Sects." *In* James Silverberg, ed., *Social Mobility in the Caste System in India*, 78–94. The Hague: Mouton; also in Lorezen, 2004: 81–102.

Wakankar, Milind. 2006. "The Allegory of the Anti-State in Medieval Western India." Paper presented at the conference, "Subaltern Citizens and Their Histories: India and the U.S.," Emory University, Atlanta, Georgia, October 13–15, 2006.

Wakankar, Milind. 2006. "The Anomaly of Kabir: Caste and Canonicity in Indian Modernity." *In* Shail Mayaram, M. S. S. Pandian, and Ajay Skaria, eds, *Muslims, Dalits, and the Fabrications of History*, 99–139. London: Seagull.

Wilfred, Felix. 1998. "Subaltern Religious Experience." *Journal of Dharma* 23, 1: 57–75.

Zelliot, Eleanor. 1980. "Chokhamela and Eknath: Two Bhakti Modes of Legitimacy for Modern Change." *Journal of Asian and African Studies* 15, 1–2: 136–56.

Zelliot, Eleanor and Rohini Mokashi-Punekar. 2005. *Untouchable Sants: An Indian Phenomenon*. New Delhi: Manohar.

Index

ābhāsa (reflection) 202
abhijñatā (experience, knowledge, wisdom) 155
abhimāna (introspection) 195
Abhinavagupta 68
Abrahamic monotheism 78, 98, 183, 319, 344, 347
Ādityas 257
ādivāsīs ("original inhabitants") 358, 384
Advaita 66, 77, 98, 104, 117, 159, 201–04, 345
Advani, L. K. 144, 324
āgamas 237
agnicayana (piling up of *agni* ritual) 65, 319
ahaṃkāra (ego-generation) 195, 199, 202, 204
ahaṃpratyaya (conceit of identity) 202
ahiṃsā (non-violence) 105, 106, 271
ākāra (form) 197
Ālhā-Ūdal 52
All People's Association 284
Alley, Kelly 102
All-India Muslim League 269
Alter, Joseph S. 67, 119
Āḻvār, Tīrupan 390
Amar Chitra Katha (book series) 91, 173
Ambedkar, Bhimrao Ramji 274, 358, 391
Amin, Shahid 379, 384
Anand, Mulk Raj 170, 172, 173
ānanda (bliss) 31, 158, 318
Ānandamaṭh 169, 269, 272, 284
Andresen, Jensine 63
antaḥkaraṇa (inner agent or sense) 195–9
antaḥkaraṇavṛtti (intellection) 197
antar-ātman (inner Self) 24
anubhava (direct experience) 156, 238
anuvyavasāya (apperception) 199
Apasmura 8
Appadurai, Arjun 143
apūrva (transcendent effect) 223
"Arampur: A Virtual Village on the Worldwide Web" (Gottschalk and Schmalz) 119–20
ardhanārīśvara (half-woman lord) 181
Arnim, Ludwig Achim von 329
Arnold, David 379, 384
ārṣajñāna (intuition) 164
art: affinities 11–12; Hinduism through study of 15–16; icons in worship 6–11; as material embodiment of divine 13–15; problems defining 3–6; *see also* iconography 3–16
Ārya Samāj 266, 270, 284, 382
Āryans 28, 79, 334, 335, 337, 354
asamprajñāta (spontaneous *samādhi*) 159
Ashbrook, James 68
Asiatic Society of Bengal 75, 253, 281, 327
āśramas (stages of life) 26, 132, 186, 223, 351
Atharva Veda 98
atiśuddha (pure, error-free) 342

ātman (self) 23, 24, 104–5, 158, 198, 201, 204, 356
ātmavidyā (self-knowledge) 67
ātmika (inner essence) 33
Auyung, Sunny 63, 67
avatāra (divine descent) 100, 161, 180, 271
avidyā (ignorance) 204
Ayodhya 108, 143–4, 324

Babb, Lawrence A. 118
Bachofen, Johann Jacob 328
Backward Classes Commission (Mandal) 360–62
Baden-Powell, Robert 146
bahirmukha (outward facing) 202
Bahuguna, Sunderlal 107, 108
Ballard, Roger 90, 94
Ban Yātrā (cyclical pilgrimage) 317–18
Bandyopadhyay, Bhabanicharan 168
Bangladesh war of independence 237
Banker, Ashok K. 167, 173
Barrett, Justin 64
Barthwal, P. D. 391
Basava (Basavaṇṇa) 82, 117, 176
Basu, Chandranath 272
Bate, Bernard 143
Baumann, Martin 94
Bayly, Susan 364
Beauvoir, Simone de 378
Beer, Michael 334
Beidelman, Thomas 363
Bengali kinship 128–9
Bernardin de Saint-Pierre, Jacques-Henri 334
Bhabha, Homi K. 373
Bhagavad Gītā 12, 75, 77, 78, 99, 106–8, 163, 221, 268, 281, 355
Bhagavan 30, 31
Bhāgavata Purāṇa 30, 31, 32, 33, 161, 258, 332
Bhairu 208
bhajānanda (bliss of love) 162
bhakti 22, 29–30, 161–63, 221–22, 239, 356, 389; as devotion to divinity 212; as discourse of devotion 21, 28, 29
Bhakti Sūtra (Narada) 161
Bhaktirasāmṛtasindhu 162
Bhārat Mātā (Mother India) 180, 345
Bhashkar, Ira 389–90
Bhatt, Chandi Prasad 107
Bhāṭṭa, Kumārila (school of Mīmāṃsā) 200
bhāva 33, 155
Bhave, Vinoba 107
bheda (physically distinct) 203
bhedābeda (same and different) 204
bhodakatva (productions of the intellect) 200
Bhū Devī (Goddess Earth) 100, 103
Bhūmi-mātā (Motherland) 273
bhūyodarśana (direct perceptions) 155
Biardeau, Madeleine 130, 368, 369
Blackburn, Stuart 52
Blakeslee, Sandra 65
body 19–34; ascetic bodies 24–6; devotional body 28–30; divine body 27–30; purity body 27–9; ritual body 21–3, 26; Tantric body 20
Bombay Presidency Association 268
Booth, Gregory 51
Bose, Girindrasekher 306
Bose, Mandakranta 185
Bose, Rajnarayan 266, 267, 272
Boyer, Pascal 64
Brahmā Kumārīs 118–19
Brahman (ultimate reality) 24, 30, 158, 201; Brahman-Ātman 24, 25, 356
Brāhmaṇa-king relationship 142–5
Brāhmaṇas (priests) 7, 14, 21, 23, 28, 132, 144, 354
Brāhmaṇical customs and laws 76, 114
brahmaṇya (pious, relating to Brahman) 341
brahmapadārtha (life-substance) 13
Brāhmo Samāj 170, 266, 284
Brantano, Clemens 329
Bṛhatsaṃhitā 13
Buchanan, Francis 113, 115
buddhi (intellect, mind) 165, 195, 202
Buddhism 4, 8, 10, 11, 66, 98, 133, 194, 205, 272, 354

buddhyārūḍha (faculty of awareness) 199
Bulkeley, Kelly 68
Burghart, Richard 391
Butalia, Urvashi 188

Caitanya 30, 162
Caldwell, Sarah 122
calendar, Hindu 214, 318
Camār 117
caṇḍāla (child of intercaste marriage) 355
Carey, William 78, 80
Carman, John 343
Cārvāka 194, 205
caste system 115, 116, 129–30; associations 91, 275; British reordering of 293; and caste reform 274; characteristics of 362–3; and "disabilities" 359; as division of labor 145; as effect of collapse of kingships 134; hierarchy in 109, 130, 132, 147; *jāti*s 29, 114, 145, 355; legitimatization of 27–8; as organizing factor for society's benefit 321; scheduled 359; strategies to maintain varied natures 148–9; theology and 141, 391; untouchables or Dalits in 117, 120, 134, 227, 271, 274, 297, 358, 359, 360, 364; *varṇa*s (social class) 23, 29, 26, 27, 131, 268, 271, 354, 355
ceremonies and rituals 11, 26, 64–5; ancestor worship 213–14; *antyeṣṭi* (last rites) 315–16; *aśvamedha yajña* 324; birth and pregnancy 211, 215; *darśapūrṇamāseṣṭi* (new and full moon sacrifices) 64; domestic rituals 184–5; Kerala ritual-drama (Muṭiyēṯṯu) 122; life-cycle rituals 209–11; marriage *(vivāha)* rites 315; *pūjā* ceremonies 22; sacrifice and healing 214; *śrāddha* (memorial rites) 316; thread ceremony *(upanayana)* 210, 269, 314; *tīrtha*s (crossings) and pilgrimages 316
Chakrabarty, Dipesh 379, 380, 382, 383, 384
Chalmers, David 68
Champakalashmi, R. 390
Chandra, Bipin 271
Chateaubriand, François-Auguste-René 332–33
Chatterjee, Partha 241, 267, 379, 380, 381, 383, 386, 388
Chatterji, Bankimcandra ("Bankim") 169, 268, 284
Chaudhuri, Nirad 172
Chhatrapati, Mahārājā Shahu 275
Chipko movement 107
Chodorow, Nancy 308
Chomsky, Noam 60
Christianity 113, 272, 273, 275, 280–2, 341; and colonialism 80; high-caste Indian Christian theology 391; and Hindu customs 81; and memory 233; and missionaries 79, 80, 113, 280; myth and Biblical narrative in 168, 252; and postmodernism 370; spiritual discernment and 164
cinema: and hearing 48–9; and seeing 45–7; and tasting 49–50; and telling 51–2
cit (consciousness) 31, 158
citta (mind) 67, 69, 237
citta-vṛtti-nirodha (silencing activities of consciousness) 159
Civil Disobedience Movement 274
cognitive science 59–68; cognitive theories of religion 63–8; Indic cognitive style 131
Cohen, Lawrence 187
Cohen, Percy 251
Cohn, Bernard 74, 76, 134
Colas, Gérard 15
Colebrooke, Thomas 281
Collingwood, R. G. 236
colonialism 74–83; colonial and missionary perceptions of Hinduism 80–3; hermeneutical presuppositions about 76–80; Hinduism as problematic category 83; as justification for intervention

in politics 141; and law 226; textual knowledge and 74–6
Condillac, Étienne Bonnot de 327
Constitution of India 226, 359
Coomaraswamy, Ananda K. 6
cow protection 271, 273, 274, 321
Coward, Harold 93
Creuzer, Georg Friedrich 333
Crick, Francis 62
Croce, Benedetto 236
Crooke, William 113, 115

Daitas (ex-tribals) 13
Dakṣiṇā Gaṅgā (Ganges of the South) 102–3
Dalits *see* caste system
Dalmia, Vasudha 83
dāna (gift) 144, 145, 147
Daniel, E. Valentine 121
D'Aquili, Eugene 65
darśana (as viewing) 14, 45, 114, 120, 140, 155, 237, 317; as scholastic system 194
Darwin, Charles 79, 282
Das, Veena 343, 369
Dasgupta, Manasi 185
Dāsimayya 187
Dasoli Gram Svarajya Sangh 107
Dawkins, Richard 65
Dayānanda Sarasvatī, Svāmī 82, 266, 284
De Nobili, Roberto 113, 116, 120
Delavigne, Jean-François Casimir 334
Derrett, J. Duncan 76
Derrida, Jacques 235, 285, 371–3, 374, 375, 387
Desai, Narayan 107
Desani, G. V. 174, 175
Deshpande, Satish 386
devadāsī (temple dancer) 333
devī (goddess) 180, 207, 345
Devī Māhātmya (Greatness of the Goddess) 181, 183
Devi, Lalla 159–60
dharma 21, 26, 27, 128; as coherence 118; and *karma* as cosmic fair play 117; as sacred duty 100, 201, 218; as *sanātana* (eternal) *dharma* or Hinduism 120, 270, 271–72
Dharmarāja 203
Dharmaśāstras (Hindu law books) 20, 21, 27, 29, 76, 100, 130, 223, 225, 354, 355, 356
dhyāna (meditation) 66, 67
diaspora 86–94; Hindu attitudes toward 89–90; Hindu identity in 91–3; patterns of 87–9; transmission of culture in 90–1; trends in different parts of world 92–3
Dilthey, Wilhelm 236
Dimmit, Cornelia 260
Dirks, Nicholas 134, 142, 293
Dissanayake, Wimal 51
Doniger, Wendy 83, 256, 259, 369
Dorson, Richard 255
Dube, Ishita Banerjee 386
Dube, Leela 184
Dube, Saurabh 147, 149, 384, 388
Dubois, Jean-Antoine (Abbé) 113, 116, 120, 281
Duff, Alexander 78, 80
Dumont, Louis 27, 130–1, 133, 141, 321–2, 343, 363, 368
Durkheim, Émile 60, 230, 233
Dvaita (Dualist school of Vedānta) 201, 204–05
dvija (twice-born) 315

East India Company 74, 80, 115, 266, 281, 357
Eck, Diana 3, 155, 317
ecology 97–109; ecofeminism 104–5; Gandhi and 105–8; possibilities and resources for 98–101; problematic issues in 101–5
Eliade, Mircea 251, 340
Erikson, Erik H. 305, 309
ethnography 112–23; encounters with Hinduism 113–16; experiencing Hinduism 120–3; religious vs. social customs 113–14; representations of Hindusim 116–20; Western knower vs. Eastern known 134–5

ethnosociology 118, 125–35, 148; construction of 127–33; critics of 133–5; ethnic- and ethno-disciplines 125–7; etic vs. emic 127–8; and study of Hinduism 135
evolution 61–2, 78, 282
exchange 139–50; intercaste 145–7; money and 149–50; reciprocity of 140–1, 144; redistribution of honor and power through 141–4; transaction worldview of 148–9
experience 155–65; critiques of 161–5; in Tantric tradition 160–1; in Vedas and Upanisads 156–9; in Yoga tradition 159–60

Falk, Nancy 179
Fanon, Frantz 279, 378
Farquhar, J. N. 77, 78
Fauconnier, Gilles 68
feminism 119, 168, 178, 297, 373, 374
Fenton, John Y. 91
Fichte, Johann Gottlieb 332
fiction 167–77; Hinduism in early Indian fiction (1855–1955) 168–73; narrative experiments in contemporary literature 173–8
Flueckiger, Joyce 52
food practices 26, 29, 119, 147, 325, 346; vegetarianism 105, 116, 321, 351
Forster, E. M. 172
Foucault, Michel 280, 283, 285, 379
Freud, Sigmund 230, 233, 303, 306, 370
Frykenberg, Robert 83
Fuller, C. J. 140, 147, 207

Gadamer, Hans-Georg 14
Gaeffke, Peter 389
Gandhi, Indira 107
Gandhi, Leela 290
Gandhi, Mohandas K. 99, 105–8, 171, 271, 274, 284, 297, 358, 384
Gaṅgā Devī (Goddess Ganges) 99, 102
garbagrāha (deity's chamber) 139
Gauḍīya Vaiṣṇavism 20, 21, 104, 162
Gāyatrī-*mantra* 98, 314, 317
Geertz, Clifford 60, 368
Gell, Alfred 5, 14
gender 178–88; beyond male and female 186–7; Devi, multiforms, and singularity of 182–4; domestic rituals 184–5; gender and ritual authority in kinship 210–12; gendered politics 188; gendered power 167–77, 181–3; gendered practice 184–8; outside domesticity, saints, *sannyāsinī*s, and *guru*s 185–6; *śakti, prakṛti,and māyā* 181–2; third gender and 184–7; *varna* and 355
Ghose, Aurobindo 269, 270, 271
Ghosh, Amitav 176
Ghurye, G. S. 363
Gilligan, Carol 308
Gītagovinda (Jayadeva) 239
goddesses 180–3, 208, 211, 369
Godelier, Maurice 364
Goethe, Johann Wolfgang 282–3, 333
Gokhale, Gopal Krishna 284
Gold, Ann Grodzins 101, 121, 211, 241
Golwalkar, Madhav Sadashiv 273
Gonda, Jan 14
Görres, Johann Joseph 328
Gosvāmī,Rūpa 162
Gottschalk, Peter 119
Government of India Act of 1935 275, 359
Gramsci, Antonio 279, 283, 378–80, 384, 392
Grant, Charles 80
Gray, Thomas 334
Gṛhya Sūtras 237
Grimm brothers 328–9
Gross, Rita 179, 183
Guatier, Pierre Jules Théophile 333
Guha, Ramchandra 105
Guha, Ranajit 379, 380, 381
Gujar, Bhoju 241
Gulati, R. K. 363
Günderrode, Karoline von 333
Gupta, Dipankar 387
guru 91, 164, 175, 188
Guthrie, Stewart 64

Haberman, David 317–18, 320
Halbwachs, Maurice 230, 232–3, 236
Halhed, Nathanial 75, 78
Hallman, Ralph 5
Hallstrom, Lisa 186
Hardiman, David 384
Hardy, Friedhelm 161
Hariharan, Githa 168, 176
Harijans (children of God) 274
Harishchandra, Bharatendu 268
Hastings, Warren 74, 75
Haṭhayoga-pradīpikā (Svātmarāma) 159
Hausner, Sondra 186
Hawley, John Stratton 389, 390
Hayes, Glen Alexander 68
Hegel, Georg W. F. 235, 238, 283, 335, 337
Heidegger, Martin 370, 371
Herder, Johann 253, 282, 327, 332, 333
hijrās (males as females) 187
Himalayan Academy (Hawaii) 91
Hindu Code Bills 226
Hindū Mahāsabhā 271, 273, 275
Hindu *saṅghaṭan* (organization or unity) 265, 273
Hinduism (definitions) 3–4, 76–83, 113, 118, 265–6, 271, 383–84
Hindutva (Hindu essentials) 108, 260, 272
Hinnels, John 93
Hocart, Arthur Maurice 147, 215, 363
Holdrege, Barbara 66
Horney, Karen 305
Horton, Robin 64
Hosbawm, Erik 383
Houben, Jan 65
Humes, Cynthia 182
Husserl, Edmund 371
Hutton, J. H 363

iconography 6–11; in *bhakti* tradition 22; codification of Brahmanical tradition 9–10; of Hindu goddesses 183; male and female deities in 210
Inden, Ronald 125, 128–9, 132, 133, 148, 364, 369
Indian Councils Act of 1909 270
Indian National Congress 268, 275
indriya (sense organ) 202
intellect 194–205; Mīmāṃsā 200–1; Sāṃkhya and Yoga 195–8; Vaiśeṣika and Nyāya 198–200; Vedānta 201–5
Islam (and Muslims) 53, 74, 83, 119–20, 137, 169, 240–1, 272, 273, 275, 357
Ismail, Qadri 386
itihāsa ("history" genre) 237, 242, 260

Jacobsen, Knut 93
jaḍa (unconscious matter) 104
Jai Santoshi Maa 47
Jainism 132, 133, 194, 271, 272, 354; imagery in 4, 8, 10
jajmani system 145–47, 363
Jakobson, Roman 367
Jama Masjid (mosque in Delhi) 273
James, William 63
"Jana Gana Mana" (Tagore) 169
Janata Party 360
jāpa (*mantra* recitation) 350
jātis *see* caste system
Jayadeva 239
Jayakar, Pulpul 182
Jeyalalitha 143
Jinnah, M. A. 274
jīva (individual soul) 32, 104, 202, 204
jīvanmukti (liberation while living) 160
jīvātman (soul) 156, 159, 161
jñāna (knowledge, cognition) 24, 30, 155, 210, 221
Jones, William 75, 76, 77, 253, 281, 327, 358
Judaism 341
Jung, Carl Gustav 305
Jurgensmeyer, Mark 389
Jyotir Liṅga shrines 100

Kaali, Sundar 384
Kabīr 49, 82, 389, 391
Kadankavil, Thomas 389
kaivalya (liberation as isolation) 159, 196

Kakar, Sudhir 42, 309–11
Kālidāsa 231, 239, 333
kāma (attachment) 118
Kanne, Johann Arnold 328
Kant, Immanuel 77
kanyādān (gift of the daughter) 209
Kapadia, Karin 212
Kapur, Manju 168
karaṇa (instrumental cause) 198–99, 202
karma (action and consequences) 24, 117, 159, 165, 196, 218, 221, 349, 355
kartā (agent, agency) 198, 202
Karve, Irawati 211–12, 363
Kathāsaritsāgara (Ocean of Story) 53
Kāverī River 102–3
Kazmi, Fareed 43
kesins (ascetics) 156
Khandelwal, Meena 186
Khanna, Madhu 183
Khare, Ravindra S. 117, 118, 343
King, Richard 113, 388
kingship 134, 141–2, 147
kinship 207–15; American 128; ancestor worship 213–14; caste and 208, 209; death and social regeneration 213–14; divine and human reproduction and sexuality 210–12; divine beings and human beings 207–8, 212; and first all-India census 358; group nurturing 212–13; hypergamous, hypogamous, and isogamous marriage 209; landownership, clans, lower-caste and tribal communities 215; marriage and 209, 210; relationship between husbands and wives 210–11; renunciation, devotion, and attachment 212–13; ritual purity and pollution 208–9; worship and ritual 210, 214
kīrtana (hymns) 163
Kishwar, Madhu 182, 188
Klein, Melanie 305
Klopstock, Friedrick Gottlieb 333
Knott, Kim 87
knowledge: as commodity 370; oral vs. textual 77
Koch, Christof 62
Kohut, Heinz 305
kōlam (or *rangoli*) designs 4, 103, 184
Kolenda, Pauline 146
kṣaṇa samādhi (momentary ecstasies) 160
Kṣatriyas (royalty and warriors) 21, 131, 133, 354, 355
Kulārṇava Tantra 160–61
Kumar, Pratap 93
Kumbha Melā 318
Kurtz, Stanley 212–13
Kuvalayānanda, Svāmī 67

Lacan, Jacques Marie Emile 305
Laforgue, Jules 332
Lamb, Sarah 182
LaMotte-Fouqué, Friedrick de 329
Lang, Andrew 114, 255
Lashley, Karl 62
law 218–27; advancing and arresting acts 220, 221; as command in Hindu religious imagination 220–3; commensality 29; *dharma* and 220–1; Hindu Code Bills 226; Hindu law as system 225; householder traditions and 223–25; as instrument of ethical formation 218–20; legal treatises and *śāstra*s 220; modern notion of law 222, 226; and renunciation 221–2
Laws of Manu see *Manusmṛti*
Lawson, E. Thomas 61, 64, 65, 66
layayoga 67, 159
Leconte de Lisle, Charles Marie René 332
Leibniz, Gottfried Wilhelm 327
Levinas, Emmanuel 285
Lévi-Strauss, Claude 259, 279, 367–68
līlā (play) 31, 32, 33, 318
Lincoln, Bruce 253
liṅga (Śiva emblem, subtle body) 4, 196, 199, 307
Lipner, Julius 3–4, 113
Locke, John 60

loka-saṃgraha (world-maintenance) 99
Loomba, Ania 290
Lord, A. B. 239
Lorenzen, David 83, 266, 389
Lucknow Pact (1916) 270
Luke, P.Y. 343
Lynch, Owen M. 388
Lyotard, Jean-François 370

Macaulay, Thomas 80
Madhva 104, 162, 204
Madras Mahājana Sabhā 268
Mahābhārata 12, 41, 51, 133, 163, 237, 238, 257, 307, 355
mahābhāva (highest state) 162
mahat (intellect in Sāṃkhya) 196
Mahatma Gandhi *see* Gandhi, Mohandas K.
Mahāvīra 354
Maine, Henry 146
Malaviya, Madan Mohan 273
Malinowski, Bronislaw 255–56
manas (mind) 195, 202
Mandal Commission 360–2
Mani, Lata 82
mantra 11, 12, 14, 65, 159, 163
Manu 130, 221, 316, 354
Manushi 188
Manusmṛti 27–29, 76, 78, 144, 179, 218, 223, 237
Marglin, Frédérique A. 343
Mārkaṇḍeya Purāṇa 181
marriage and sexuality 26, 29, 128, 208, 209, 357; arranged marriage 315; and *varṇa* 355
Marriott, McKim 118, 120, 125, 127, 128, 129, 130–3, 134, 135, 148, 215, 321–2, 343, 364
Marx, Karl 60, 146, 337, 362, 385
Marxism 146, 370, 373, 374, 380, 386, 392
Massey, James 391
Mathew, Biju 90
Mathura 7–8, 10–11
Maturana, Humberto 62
Mauss, Marcel 139, 144
Mawdsley, Emma 108
māyā (illusory) 97, 104, 180, 181, 182, 332
McCauley, Robert 61, 64, 65, 66
McGee, Mary 101, 314
McLeon, Johan 290
Megasthenes 362
Meister, Michael 4
memory 230–43; and *bhakti* 239–40; and cycle of rebirth 238; and gender 242; and history 231, 234, 236, 238; memory studies and Hinduism 236–43; modern theories of 231–6, 242; orality and literacy 231, 235, 239; and sacred geography 233–4, 240; and social environment 230, 233
Menon, Ritu 188
Metz, Christian 47
Michaels, Axel 321
Mill, James 80–81, 238
Mill, John Stuart 282
Mīmāṃsā 199, 200–01, 204
Mīrābāī 82, 389, 390
Miśra, Vācaspati 197
Mitra, Peary Chand 168
Mokashi-Punekar, Rohini 390, 392
mokṣa (liberation) 24, 105, 314, 350, 356
Monier-Williams, M. 77
Moonje, Balkrishna Shivram 271
Morley-Minto Reforms 270
mothers 90, 103, 182, 210, 212
mūlāvidyā (fundamental ignorance) 203
Müller, F. Max 59, 73, 75, 77, 79, 114, 254–5, 334–6, 337
Müller, Wilhelm 335
Murthy, U. R. Anantha 171
mūrti (image or icon) 4, 13–15, 32, 33, 317
Muslim League 274, 275
myth 251–60; and Aryan race 254, 256–7; in Epics and Purāṇas 257–9; German Romanticism and study of myth 252–3; late nineteenth century developments and 255–6; and structuralism 367; and the study

of post-Vedic mythology 257–60; Vedic texts and 254–5

Nagarajan, Vijaya 103, 184
Naicker, E. V. Ramaswami 275, 358
Nānak, Guru 357
Nanda, Meera 108
Nārada 161
Narayan, Jayaprakash 107
Narayan, R. K. 172–3
Narayanan, Vasudha 102, 179, 187
Nasreen, Taslima 176
National Commission for Scheduled Castes and Tribes 360
National Social Conference 268
nationalism 265–75; early nationalism and Hinduism 267–9; election-based separatism 270–2; Hinduism and India under colonialism 265–7; Hindu nationalism and Hindutva 272–3; and sectarian and caste-based separatism 274–5; sectarian politics and Partition 275
Nāṭya Śāstra 48–50
Nehru Report (1928) 274
Nelson, Lance 343, 345
Nerval, Gérard de 333
Neumann, John von 61
Newberg, Anthony 65
Nicholas, Ralph 128–9
Nietzsche, Friedrich 280
Nimbārka 104
Niranjana, Seemanthini 184
nirguṇa (ineffable) 239
nirvāṇa 305, 332
niṣkāma (desire-free, nonattachment) 106, 118
Nora, Pierre 233
Novetzke, Christian 389, 392
Nyāya (Logic) 66, 198–200

O'Flaherty, Wendy Doniger *see* Doniger, Wendy
O'Hanlon, Rosalind 386
Olivelle, Patrick 26
Oriental Renaissance 75, 283
Orientalism 73, 75, 76, 78, 278–86; assessments of Said's concept of 284–5; constructions of the Hindu other 280–2; "deep orientalism" 385; Hindu responses to oppressive colonial constructs 283–4; romantic orientalism 282–3
Ortner, Sherry 188
Other Backward Class (OBC) 361

Pal, Bipin Chandra 269
Pande, Mrinal 179
Pandey, Gyan 379, 385, 392
paṇḍitas (learned men) 169, 226
parama prema (highest love that brings a person to perfection) 161
paramātman (highest self) 30, 159, 161
Parasher-Sen, Aloka 392
Parekh, Bhikhu 87, 89, 93
Parry, Jonathan 144, 149
Parry, Milman 239
Parsons, Talcott 127
Partition, the 108, 237, 240, 275
Patañjali 196, 197
Patton, Laurie 65
Paul, Jean 332
pavitra (sacred) 341, 342, 343, 345
Peabody, Norbert 142, 389
Pechilis, Karen 186
Pennington, Brian 83
Peritore, N. Patrick 109
Persinger, Michael 65
phala (fruit or outcome) 213
Phalke, D. G. 47, 54
Phule, Jotirao 274
Pierce, Charles 121
Pinker, Steven 62
Pintchman, Tracy 185
pitṛ (ancestors) 214
Plato 194, 252
Pollock, Sheldon 237, 385, 390, 391
Polo, Marco 362
Poona Sarvajanik Sabhā 267
postcolonialism 289–99; and colonial constructions 292–4; community and history 294–5; critical categories of 289–1; nationalism

and 168; nation and modernity 295–9; orientalism and after 291–2
Prabhākara (school of Mīmāṃsā) 200
Prakash, Gyan 379, 380, 382, 383, 384
prakṛti 32, 68, 104, 180, 181, 196, 345
pramāṇa (proof) 66, 238
prāṇa pratiṣṭhā (to endow an image with divine power) 14
prāṇāyāma (breathing techniques) 66, 67
prapatti (self-surrender) 162
Prārthanā Samāj 266, 267, 275
Prasad, M. Madhava 43–4
prasāda (mercy, grace) 120, 140, 317, 346
Prashad, Vijay 90
pratibhājñāna (flash of intuition) 164
prema bhakti (selfless devotional love) 33
premānanda (bliss of selfless love) 161
Price, Pamela 142, 143
Pṛthvī Sūkta ("Hymn to the Earth") 98
psychoanalysis 303–12; and interpretation of Hinduism 306–12; overview of 303–6
pūjā (devotional worship) 14, 114, 140, 316
Punjab Hindū Sabhā (1909) 270
puṇya (merit) 209, 213, 341
Purāṇas 78, 237, 257, 261n
purity and pollution 89, 115, 130, 147, 209, 316, 320, 368
purohita (family priest) 315
Puruṣa 21, 22, 24, 25, 98; as consciousness 68, 104, 159, 181; as primordial person 196, 354
Puruṣa-Sūkta 21–3, 25, 27, 354
Pūrva-Mīmāṃsā 66, 200, 221
Pyysiäinen, Ilkka 64

Rādhā 162, 163
Rādhāsoāmī 118
Raheja, Gloria 142, 145, 146, 147, 148, 211, 215
Rai, Lālā Lajpat 269, 270
rājadharma (work of the king) 142
rākhī (celebration of bonds between sister and brother) 214, 269
Ramachandran, V. S. 65
Ramaṇa Maharṣi 67
Rāmānandī tradition 391
Rāmānuja 104, 162, 204
Ramanujan, A. K. 180, 187
Ramaswamy, Sumathi 180, 188
Rāmāyaṇa 42, 51, 87, 163, 167, 173, 175, 237, 257, 307, 355, 389
Rāmlīlā 318
Ranade, M. G. 267, 268, 284
Rao, Narasimha 361
Rao, Raja 172, 174
rasa (flavor, essence of experience) 163
Rāṣṭrīya Svayamsevak Saṅgh 120, 273
Rauschenberg, Robert 165
Ravidās (aka Raidās, Rohidās) 390
Ray, Himanshu 7
Ray, Satyajit 41, 51
Reddy, Gayatri 186–7
Redfield, Robert 129
reincarnation (rebirth) 105, 196, 238, 271, 355
religious experience 155; critiques of 163–5; false or illusory experience 164; as "magico-religious" 385; practice and goals of contemplation 157; religious practice in past lives 155; in *Ṛg Veda* and Upaniṣads 156–9; scholarship of erasure 165; similarities between Hinduism and the West 163–4; as site of subaltern consciousness 241; Tantric traditions 160–1
Ṛg Veda 12, 45, 75, 98, 156, 256, 354
Richman, Paula 175
ritual 314–25; calendrical 318; devotional 316–17; in diaspora settings 324; elements common to life-cycle rites 314; funeral rites 315–16; Hindu contribution to study of religion 319–23; and politics 324; private ritual activity 317; relationship with myth 320
romanticism 327–7; and Indology 334–6; and literature 331–4; and

"Oriental-Occidental synthesis" 331; and the origins of myth 328; and romantic myth theory 329–31; Romantic-Orientalist critique 334; and social reform 334
Rowlatt Bills (1919) 271
Roy, Rammohan 82, 266, 284
ṛṣi (seers) 45, 156, 237
Ruether, Rosemary 97
Rukmani, T. S. 93
Rushdie, Salman 167, 173–4, 176
Ruskin, John 271

śābdībhāvanā (word-force) 221
sacred 339–52; in Abrahamic traditions 339–41; actions as 349–51; beings as 350–1; Hindu understanding of 341; purification and the creation of 344–5; purity and pollution dynamic 342; sacralization of nature 103, 104; space as 347–8; symbols and objects as 348–9
Sacred Books of the East series (Müller) 74, 79
sacred geography 86, 89, 240
sacred spaces 102, 184
sādhana (religious practices) 33, 67, 349–50
*sādhu*s (ascetics) 350
saguṇa (describable) 239
Saha, Shandip 390
Sahai, Malti 51
sahaja samādhi (spontaneous realization) 160
sahasrāra (topmost energy center) 68
Said, Edward 76, 134, 278, 283–4, 291
śākṣin (ultimate witness in Sāṃkhya) 196, 202
*śākta-pīṭha*s (sacred Goddess sites) 100
śakti (power) 68, 140, 180, 181, 210
Śakuntalā (Kālidāsa) 231, 239, 333
śālagrāma 346
samādhi (absorption) 159–60; sacred tomb or shrine 240
Sāṃkhya 104, 133, 148, 194–6, 345
*sampradāya*s (lineages, schools) 161, 267
samprajnāta (*samādhi* achieved by yogic effort) 159
saṃsāra (world made of cycles of embodiment) 24, 26, 29, 105, 238
saṃskāra (life-cycle rites) 148, 224, 314–6
Śaṅkara (or Śaṅkarācarya) 202–3
Sannyāsī Rebellion (1773) 169
Sanskritization (M. N. Srinivas) 116–17, 321, 322, 363, 387
Sarasvatī (goddess of learning) 269, 273
Sarkar, Sumit 385, 386
Sarkar, Tanika 169, 384
Sarvajanik Sabhā 267, 275
Sarvodaya movement 107
śāstra 33, 219, 237; *śāstric* (according to *śāstra*)76, 175
Satī (spouse of Śiva) 100; *satī* ("good woman") 81, 184
*sāttvika bhāva*s (ecstatic emotions) 156, 162
Satya Sāī Bābā 119
Satya Śodhak Samāj 274
satyāgraha (nonviolent social action) 105, 271
Saussure, Ferdinand de 366–7
Savarkar, Vinayak Damodar 272, 275
Savigny, Friedrick Karl 328
Sax, William 318
Schechner, Richard 50
Schelling, F. W. J. 283, 328
Schiller, Johann Cristoph Friedrich 333
Schlegel, August Wilhelm 330
Schlegel, Friedrich 283, 329, 335
Schmalz, Mathew 119
Schneider, David 128–9
Schopen, Gregory 8
Schopenhauer, Arthur 283
Schumacher, E. F. 106
Schutz, Alfred 368
Schwab, Raymond 283
Searle, John 68
Sen, Sukumar 168
Senart, Émile 362
Seth, Vikram 176
Shannon, Claude 61
Sherma, Rita DasGupta 183

Shils, Edward 127
Shiva, Vandana 104, 181
Showalter, Elaine 178
siddha (saint) 162, 164
Siddhāntamuktāvalī (Vallabha) 99
siddhis (supernatural experiences) 159
Sikhs 272, 275, 357
Śilpaśāstras 5, 12
Singer, Milton 129
Skinner, B. F. 60
Skora, Kerry Martin 68
Slavery Abolition Act (1833) 87
smṛti (remembered) 77, 231, 237, 238
soma 6, 156
Spengler, Oswald 337
Sperber, Dan 64
Spivak, Gayatri Chakravorty 373, 374, 379, 391
śrāddha (memorial rites) 316
Śraddhānanda, Svāmī 273
Śrī Vidyā tradition 160
Śrīharṣa 203
Srinivas, M. N. 116, 117, 118, 321, 322, 342, 343, 363
Srinivasan, Doris 4, 7
śruti (revealed) 156, 231, 237, 257
Staal, Frits 65, 319
Stein, Burton 390
Stevenson, H. N. C. 363
Stietencron, Heinrich von 83
stratification 354–65; British administrative decisions and 357–9; and different conceptual frameworks 362; in independent India 359–61; in India's classical texts 354–7
structuralism 366–75; and deconstruction 374–5; and Derrida 371–3; and Hinduism 368–79; Hinduism and deconstruction 373–4; and Lévi-Strauss 366; postmodernism and deconstruction 370–1
subaltern 374, 378–93; and ambivalence 386–8; definitions 378; Hinduism in subaltern studies 380–8; in Hindu Studies 388–93; and subalternity 379
Subaltern Studies Collective 241, 379
śuddha (clean, pure) 341, 343, 346
Śūdra 21, 132, 355
Sugirtharajah, Sharada 290
Sūrdās 389, 390
Svaccha Nārāyaṇī (Cleanliness Lady) 188
svadeśī movement 381
svarga (heaven) 23, 156, 201
svarūpa (essential nature) 31, 32, 203
Svātmarāma 159
svayaṃprakāśa (self-luminous) 200

Tagore, Devendranath 267
Tagore, Rabindranath 169, 272
Tantric traditions 67, 160, 183, 221–2
tapas (heat, ascetic practices) 26, 117, 159, 350
Tarabout, Gilles 8, 10, 11
Thapar, Romila 83
Thomas, Rosie 44
Thompson, E. P. 378
Tilak, Balgangadhar 99, 268, 284
Timalsina, Staneshware 68
Tinker, Hugh 87
tīrthas (pilgrimage sites) 121–2, 316, 317
Tomalin, Emma 109
Toqueville, Alexis de 130
transmigration 13, 114, 196
Trawick, Margaret 122, 212
Tremlin, Todd 59
trimūrti 114
Trubetskoy, Nikolai 367
Tukārām 82, 390
tulasī (sacred basil) 345, 346
Turner, Mark 68
Turner, Victor 65
Tylor, E. B. 255

Upadhyaya, Ajay 120
Upaniṣads 20, 21, 24–5, 78, 98, 157–9, 266, 356
ur-text 79, 257
Utilitarians 80

Vaiśeṣika ("Particularist" metaphysics) 198

Vaiśeṣikasūtra (Kaṇāda) 198
Vaiṣṇavism 99, 161, 163, 271
Vaiśya (merchants, agriculturalists, artisans) 21, 132, 355
Vallabha 99, 162
van Buitenen, J. A. B. 260
"Vande Mātaram" 169, 269
varṇas see caste system
varṇāśrama-dharma 26, 27, 29, 131–2, 314–16
vāsanā (psychic traces) 197
Vātsyāyana 198
Vedānta 77, 159, 199, 201–5
Vedas 20–6, 98, 219, 237, 257, 275, 284
Vertovec, Steven 91, 92, 93
Vigny, Alfred de 332
Vijayanagar 143
Vijnānabhikṣu 197
village life 116–18, 146–7
viraha bhakti 231
Vīraśaiva tradition 176
Viśiṣṭādvaita 159, 201, 204
Viṣṇu Purāṇa 99
Viṣṇudharmottara Purāṇa 5, 13
Visva Hindu Pariṣad 108, 144, 324
vivāha (marriage) 315
viveka (discrimination) 104, 196
Vivekānanda, Svāmī 268, 271
vrata (vow) 10, 184, 317
vṛtti (modifications) 197, 202, 203
Vyāsa 197, 238

Wadley, Susan 181
Ward, William 78, 280
Whitney, William Dwight 335
Wilberforce, William 80
Wilfred, Felix 389
Wilkins, Charles 75, 281
Williams, Raymond 90, 93
Wilson, Horace Hayman 77, 281
Winnecott, Donald Woods 305
Wiser, William 145, 146, 363
Witzel, Michael 66
Wolf, Eric 126
women's concerns 10, 181–4, 210–13, 374; prohibitions against studying sacred texts 355; *vrata* (personal vows) 184, 317; widowhood 169, 184

yajamāna (patron of the sacrifice) 23
yajña (sacrifice) 20, 21, 23, 66, 316
yantras 14
yoga 65, 67, 68, 112, 159
Yoga Sūtra (Patañjali) 159, 196
yogīs and *yoginīs* 67, 159, 165
Young, Edward 334
Young, Robert 290
yuga 174; Kali Yuga (Dark Age) 52, 105, 174

Zelliot, Eleanor 389, 390, 391